WRITING SITUATIONS

SIDNEY I. DOBRIN
University of Florida

PEARSON

Boston   Columbus   Indianapolis   New York   San Francisco   Upper Saddle River
Amsterdam   Cape Town   Dubai   London   Madrid   Milan   Munich   Paris   Montréal   Toronto
Delhi   Mexico City   São Paulo   Sydney   Hong Kong   Seoul   Singapore   Taipei   Tokyo

This one is for Asher and Shaia.

Senior Acquisitions Editor: Lauren A. Finn
Senior Development Editor: Michael Greer
Editor in Chief: Joseph Terry
Market Development Manager: Necco McKinley
Executive Marketing Manager: Aimee E. Berger
Head of Marketing: Roxanne McCarley
Digital Content Specialist: Erin Jenkins
Digital Editor: Sara Gordus
Executive Digital Producer: Stefanie A. Snajder
Production Manager: Ellen MacElree

Editorial Assistant: Celeste Kmiotek
Project Coordination, Text Design, and Electronic Page Makeup: PreMediaGlobal
Interior Design Manager: Wendy Ann Fredericks
Cover Designer/Manager: Wendy Ann Fredericks
Cover Art: © Shutterstock
Senior Manufacturing Buyer: Dennis J. Para
Printer/Binder: R. R. Donnelley & Sons at Crawfordsville
Cover Printer: Lehigh-Phoenix Color/Hagerstown

Credits and asknowledgments borrowed from other sources and reproduced, with permission, in this textbook, appear on page 713.

Library of Congress Cataloging-in-Publication Data

Dobrin, Sidney I., 1967-
    Writing situations / Sidney I. Dobrin.—First edition.
        pages cm ISBN 978-0-205-73543-3 (alk. paper)—ISBN 0-205-73543-6 (alk. paper)
    1. English language—Rhetoric—Study and teaching (Higher)   2. English language—Composition and exercises—Study and teaching.   3. Report writing—Study and teaching.   I. Title.
    PE1404.D638 2013
    808'.0420711—dc23
                                                                                                    2013030458

10 9 8 7 6 5 4 3 2 1—DOC—17 16 15 14

Student ISBN-13:   978-0-205-73543-3
Student ISBN-10:   0-205-73543-6
Exam copy ISBN-13:   978-0-205-73546-4
Exam copy ISBN-10:   0-205-73546-0

PEARSON

www.pearsonhighered.com

Detailed Contents

Part Two   Thinking, Reading, and Viewing 75

Part Four   Writing Visuals 351

16 Finding, Adapting, and Making Visuals 352

17 Designing Documents 377

Part Five   Writing Research 403

18 Planning and Conducting Research 404

Part Seven   Editing Writing 673

28 Correcting Errors 674

29 Writing Sentences 682

30 Punctuation and Mechanics 694

Preface

College students are frequently in situations that require writing in new and unfamiliar ways. Although new to the college setting, students need to respond to academic writing projects and conventions. Students taking first-year writing classes, for example, have told me about being required to write in genres new to them or to use research in ways they previously had not. "I've never written a research paper," many have said. Students complete writing assignments for courses in other disciplines, often with little or no instruction about how to write for those assignments or fields. I recently spoke with a student taking a course in visual anthropology in which the majority of the grade was based on five essays. Yet, as the student related, expectations for those essays were not clearly defined.

Equally as often, students write outside college in contexts that require adapting what they have learned in classes, whether through direct or indirect instruction, to other situations that affect their lives. Most teachers have heard stories from students about application letters for employment or professional school, blogs on personal and important issues, articles and editorials written to express themselves about an issue, and so on. Students write about things that matter to them; they write about things they have little or no choice in writing. They write to communicate with friends, family, and professional contacts. They text, blog, post status updates, comment, respond, write wikis, make videos. They write with digital technologies and with analog technologies. They write with words and with images.

Writing Situations teaches students how to analyze, navigate, and respond in many writing situations. Students learn to move fluidly among various contemporary writing situations like shifting from writing an essay in response to an assigned reading to writing a music review for a personal blog. Central to this agenda, *Writing Situations* focuses on helping students in becoming successful writers in their college settings and maneuvering into other writing situations.

Grounded in understanding writing situations as rhetorical (based in choices writers and readers make), political (based in the exchange and power of each situation), and ecological (based in the relationships and connections of each situation), *Writing Situations* aims to help students understand and effectively participate in academic, personal, and professional writing situations. *Writing Situations* expands the possibilities of students' experiences by providing rigorous instruction made accessible through visual pedagogy that illustrates the process of thinking through ideas. Questions for writers to ask themselves about their writing situation foster invention and transform guidance into practical action steps. Provocative readings create opportunities for analysis, discussion, and writing. Challenging and detailed writing assignments encourage print-based writing, visual analysis, researched writing, digital composition, and radical revision. Contextualized and integrated next generation instructor support include videos, PowerPoints, and print tools such as customizable rubrics and heuristics that support each project chapter.

Writing Situations is part of a complex network: the project works best when considered part of an ecosystem that includes the student writer, classmates, the instructor, the college's writing program, library resources, *Writing Situations'* digital and media resources, and many other available resources. Taken together, all parts of the *Writing Situations'* ecosystem contribute to students' ability to learn to write effectively for situations they encounter throughout college and beyond.

Organizational Overview

Part One **Writing Processes** teaches students how to write for any situation by introducing the rhetorical situation, placing purpose and audience at the center, encouraging deliberate discovery, showing how drafting and organizing are inseparable, and emphasizing revision as an integrated activity that saturates all phases of writing.

Part Two **Thinking, Reading, and Viewing** focuses on strategies for questioning and analyzing writing situations, understanding academic standards and traits, and problem solving. Different methods for decision-making as well as for active, independent, and networked thinking encourage students to look for factors that define and influence situations.

Part Three **Writing Projects** offers detailed instruction in writing for different purposes, including to Narrate, Describe, Inform, Respond, Analyze, Evaluate, Argue, and Propose. Writers determine which approach will be most effective in achieving their goals by considering all aspects of their writing situation, including their purpose but also their audience, context, medium, stakeholders, distribution method, and circulation networks.

Each chapter includes three readings, a diagram that illustrates how an author arrived at her thesis, a chart comparing the rhetorical situation of each reading, two invention diagrams, five writing projects, writing process guidelines, and end-of-chapter activities.

Part Four **Writing Visuals** helps students develop awareness that as text-based writing increasingly blends with visual communication, their own writing must adapt in ways appropriate to academic writing situations. A toolkit of strategies includes how to read visual information; how to use visuals effectively to convey information; practical guidelines for finding, adapting, and making visuals; and guidelines for designing documents.

Part Five **Writing Research** frames research as a form of investigation vital to how we learn, participate, and express ourselves. We research not only to answer questions but also to uncover further questions, allowing writers to better position themselves within a situation. Instruction includes developing research plans, finding and evaluating pertinent source material, writing research papers, and writing essay exams.

Part Six **Readings** organizes readings thematically (unique among purposes-organized writing guides) to facilitate synthesis assignments, but alternate tables of contents cluster readings by rhetorical purpose, rhetorical strategy, and genre. Readings invite challenging and thought-provoking conversations about Technology, Image/Culture, Sustainability, Education, Food, and Millennials. Conscientious apparatus fosters analysis, collaboration, discussion, and writing.

Part Seven **Editing Writing** provides strategies for editing; addresses the connection among correctness, style, and authority (ethos); and includes extensive and relevant examples of sentence level grammar, mechanics, and punctuation.

Key Features

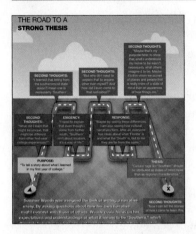

Road to a Strong Thesis fosters analytic thinking by making visible a writer's interior monologue about purpose, audience, and rhetorical situation when developing a strong thesis.

Next Generation Instructor Support is contextualized and integrated. Videos, screencasts, PowerPoints, and print tools support each project chapter—and are organized by chapter to create a one-stop-shop for course preparation.

Side by Side develops analytic reading skills by comparing three student and professional readings in each project chapter and spotlighting decisions each writer made when solving rhetorical problems in distinct but related situations.

Contemporary readings anthologized thematically rather than by genre better facilitate synthesis assignments. Engaging and relevant topics include technology, image and culture, sustainability, education, food, and the millennial generation.

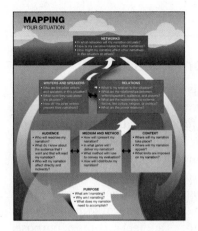

Mapping Your Situation helps students navigate any writing situation by suggesting questions to ask ranging from purpose, audience, medium, and context to networks, providing a starting point for planning and invention.

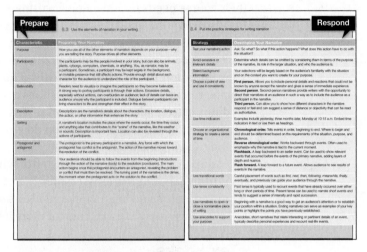

Prepare and Respond identifies characteristics of different kinds of writing and walks writers through steps for developing content of their own.

Writing Process Guidelines ensures students respond effectively to their writing situation: concrete action steps guide writers through their writing process from invention and research to drafting, revision, evaluation, and distribution.

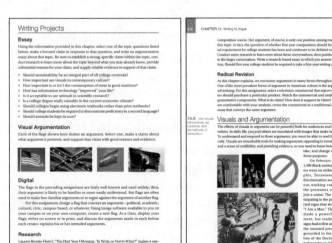

Formal assignments in each project chapter facilitate flexible and ranging teaching approaches by including a traditional academic essay, a project focused on using visuals, an online or digital variation, a research-based option, and a "radical revision/ translation" project to turn a print-based essay into a multimodal project.

Supplements

MyWritingLab **Now Available for Composition**

Integrated solutions for writing. MyWritingLab is an online homework, tutorial, and assessment program that provides engaging experiences for today's instructors and students. New features designed specifically for composition instructors and their course needs include a new writing space for students, customizable rubrics for assessing and grading student writing, multimedia instruction on all aspects of composition, and advanced reporting to improve the ability to analyze class performance. New for students and their course needs is an idea generator: the **Map Your Situation tool within MyWritingLab** allows students to work through a key chapter resource by answering questions about a paper's audience, context, purpose, medium, stakeholders, and networks. This "prewriting" about their specific writing situation is captured in an invention document and can serve as a starting point for drafting and organizing ideas.

Adaptive learning. For students who enter the course underprepared, MyWritingLab offers pre-assessments and personalized remediation so they see improved results and instructors spend less time in class reviewing the basics.

Visit www.mywritinglab.com for more information.

eTextbooks

Pearson eText

An online version of *Writing Situations* brings together the many resources of My-WritingLab with the instructional content of this successful book to create an enhanced learning experience for students.

CourseSmart eTextbook

Students can subscribe to *Writing Situations* at CourseSmart.com. The format of the eText allows students to search the text, bookmark passages, save their own notes, and print reading assignments that incorporate lecture notes.

Android and iPad eTextbooks

Android and iPad versions of the eText provide the complete text and the electronic resources described above.

Next Generation Instructor Support

Traditionally, instructor support materials for a course text are housed under separate covers—one booklet for an instructor's manual, another for a test bank, with a presentation solution available elsewhere—and instructors preparing lesson plans are left to their own devices to make these resources work together. By contrast, instructor support and professional development material for *Writing Situations* is contextualized and integrated.

Videos, screencasts, PowerPoints, and print tools support each project chapter. Videos suggest ideas for teaching the assignment and criteria to look for when responding to student work. Tools referenced in the videos (such as grading rubrics or heuristics), along with classroom-ready, customizable PowerPoints and handouts, are available as downloads and can be modified to suit your teaching style and the needs of your course. Time-stamped transcripts accompany each video and make it easy to follow along, skip ahead, or reference quickly and as needed. Resources are organized by chapter to create a one-stop-shop and facilitate course preparation.

Acknowledgments

As you can see from the expansive list of acknowledgments on these pages, this book came to fruition through the efforts, influence, and collaboration of many people. While I cannot express the depth of my gratitude to each in these pages, I do wish to acknowledge and thank those who have offered support and guidance throughout the process of writing and producing this book.

First and foremost, I would like to thank all of the wonderful folks at Pearson that I've had the opportunity to work with on this project and others over the years. I am deeply grateful for what each of you has taught me and for your support and encouragement. In particular, I would like to thank Gary Bauer, Leigh Ann Schmitz, Alicia Wozniak, Vernon Anthony, Thomas Hayward, David Gesell, Tonianne Tari, Eric Severson, Stacey Martinez, Yasminka Nemet McAllan, Dickson Musslewhite, Craig Campanella, Eric Krassow, Kevin Stone, Erica Teichman Clemons, Robin Baliszewski, Stephanie Freas, Ben Weber, Jodi McPherson, Leah Jewell, and Kevin Clarke.

In particular, I want to acknowledge and thank Brian Kibby, who has been a great mentor and friend, and Cindy Sullivan Davis, whose energy, enthusiasm, and wisdom are endless.

I would also like to acknowledge and express my gratitude to Brad Pothoff and Kevin Molloy, who initiated this project and whose influence and guidance can be felt on every page. I can never thank the two of you enough.

For their daily editorial guidance and friendship, I am deeply grateful to Lauren Finn and Michael Greer. In a more egalitarian world, their names would appear above mine on the cover, for this is as much their book as it is mine.

Likewise, I wish to offer my sincere gratitude to Joe Opiela, who is a master at handling the reins.

I am, of course, also grateful to Dr. Aimee Berger for her amazing vision in marketing this book and to Necco McKinley for her dedication to developing sales strategies for the book.

I would also like to thank the many reviewers who have provided feedback and revision suggestions that have been invaluable. I am grateful for the time and professional advice that each of you dedicated to this project. With the utmost respect, I acknowledge the following reviewers:

Deborah Allan, *Northern Kentucky University*

James Allen, *College of DuPage*

Jeffrey Andelora, *Mesa Community College*

Lauryn Angel, *Collin College*

Judy Arzt, *University of Saint Joseph*

Lillie Bailey, *Virginia State University*

Edward Baldwin, *College of Southern Nevada*

Bryan Bardine, *University of Dayton*

Nancy Barendse, *Charleston Southern University*

Deborah Barnard, *Middle Tennessee State University*

Sydney Bartman, *Mt. San Antonio College*

Subrata Kumar Bhowmik, *Arizona State University*

Tamara Ponzo Brattoli, *Joliet Junior College*

Ron Brooks, *Oklahoma State University*

Jo Ann Buck, *Guilford Technical Community College*

Jeffrey Carman, *California State Polytechnic University, Pomona*

Jennifer Chunn, *Harrisburg Area Community College*

Billy Clem, Jr., *Waubonsee Community College*

Regina Clemens Fox, *Oklahoma City University*

Tracy Darr, *Owens Community College*

Mark DelMaramo, *Thiel College*

Jason DePolo, *North Carolina A&T State University*

Michael Donnelly, *Ball State University*

Doug Downs, *Montana State University*

Dan Driscoll, *Drexel University*

Robin Ebert Mays, *The University of Southern Mississippi*

Margaret Ehlen, *Ivy Tech Community College*

Christopher Ervin, *Western Kentucky University*

Casie Fedukovich, *North Carolina State University*

Jean S. Filetti, *Christopher Newport University*

Christina Fisanick, *California University of Pennsylvania*

Elizabeth Fitzgerald, *Cecil College*

Patrice Fleck, *Northern Virginia Community College*

Michael Franco, *Oklahoma City Community College*

William Gahan, *Rockford University*

LeAnne Garner, *Middle Tennessee State University*

Val Gerstle, *University of Cincinnati*

Jennifer Pooler Gray, *College of Coastal Georgia*

John Hagaman, *Western Kentucky University*

Gregory Dennis Hagan, *Madisonville Community College*

Cynthia Hall, *Abraham Baldwin Agricultural College*

Joe Hardin, *University of Arkansas–Fort Smith*

Matthew Heard, *University of North Texas*

Richard Henry, *The State University of New York at Potsdam*

Kathleen M. Herndon, *Weber State University*

Geraldine Jacobs, *Jackson Community College*

Jay Johnson, *Gateway Technical College*

Peggy Jolly, *The University of Alabama at Birmingham*

Melvin Richard Jones, *South Suburban College*

Erin Karper, *Niagara University*

Julie Kratt, *Cowley College*

Kim Lacey, *Saginaw Valley State University*

Jeffrey Larsen, *Grand Rapids Community College*

Sharon G. Levy, *Northampton Community College*

Rossana Lhota, *Arizona State University*

Alfred Litton, *Texas Woman's University*

Robert Lively, *Mesa Community College*

Wanda Lloyd, *North Carolina State University*

Amy Lee Locklear, *Auburn University at Montgomery*

Glenda Lowery, *Rappahannock Community College*

Rosemary Mack, *Baton Rouge Community College*

Shannon Madden, *The University of Oklahoma*

Susan Matheny, *Pasco-Hernando Community College*

Christopher McBride, *Solano Community College*

Victoria McLure, *South Plains College*

James McWard, *Johnson County Community College*

L. Adam Mekler, *Morgan State University*

Brett Mertins, *Metropolitan Community College*

David Miller, *Mississippi College*

Susan Miller-Cochran, *North Carolina State University*

Bryan Moore, *Arkansas State University*

Stephen Moore, *Arizona Western College*

Roxanne Munch, *Joliet Junior College*

David Norman, *Savannah Technical College*

Mitchell Ogden, *University of Wisconsin–Stout*

Kathy Olson, *Lees-McRae College*

Shelley Harper Palmer, *Central Piedmont Community College*

Heather Pavletic, *Auburn University at Montgomery*

Scott Payne, *University of Central Arkansas*

Lydia Pearson, *California State University, San Bernardino*

Monique Perry, *York Technical College*

Michelle Pichon, *Northwestern State University of Louisiana*

Dan Portincaso, *Waubonsee Community College*

Sayanti Ganguly Puckett, *Johnson County Community College*

Katie Reichert, *Oklahoma City University*

Thomas Reynolds, Jr., *Northwestern State University of Louisiana*

Martine Courant Rife, *Lansing Community College*

Rochelle Rodrigo, *Old Dominion University*

Alison Russell, *Xavier University*

Bernd Sauermann, *Hopkinsville Community College*

Kelli Sellers, *The University of Southern Mississippi*

Tracey Sherard, *College of the Canyons*

Michelle Sidler, *Auburn University*

Melissa Smith, *University of South Alabama*

Lorelei Stenseth, *Cisco College*

Charles Tryon, *Fayatteville State University*

Rex Veeder, *St. Cloud State University*

Allison Walker, *High Point University*

Scott Warnock, *Drexel University*

Jaclyn Wells, *The University of Alabama at Birmingham*

Gayle Williamson, *Cuyahoga Community College*

Melvin Wininger, *Indiana University–Purdue University Indianapolis*

Mari York, *Northern Kentucky University*

Outside of the Pearson family, others have also influenced my approach to writing this book, including Rene Deljon and Nancy Perry, both of whom have been more than generous in sharing their wisdom and experience with me over the years. There is no question that I would not be able to do what I do without what they each have taught me. For this, I am forever grateful.

I am also fortunate to work with a remarkable group of faculty and graduate students at the University of Florida. I am indebted to my colleagues for their support and encouragement. In particular, I wish to acknowledge and thank the faculty of the Department of English: Kenneth Kidd, Pamela Gilbert, John Leavey, Phil Wegner, Susan Hegeman, Gregory Ulmer, Raul Sanchez, Laurie Gries, Kim Emery, Judith Page, Marsha Bryant, Robert Ray, Terry Harpold, Stephanie Smith, Bob Thomson, Jack Perlette, Leah Rosenberg, Barbara Mennel, Scott Nygren, Maureen Turim, Mark Reid, Anja Ulanowicz, Chris Snodgrass, Apollo Amoko, Malini Scheuller, Amy Ongiri, Padgett Powell, Tace Hedrick, Don Ault, Roger Beebe, John Cech, Jill Ciment, Michael Hofmann, Sid Homan, Brandy Kershner, Richard Burt, Debra King, David Leavitt, Sidney wade, William Logan, Ron Carpenter, Peter Rudnytsky, Jodi Schorb, and Al Shoaf. Likewise, my sincere gratitude to the amazing graduate students I have the opportunity to work with; their energy pushes me to be a better scholar and teacher: Linda Howell, Christopher Garland, Caroline Stone, Jacob Riley, Andrew Wilson, Joe Weakland, Scott Sunduval, Sean Printz, NaToya Faughnder, Kyle Bohunicky, Melissa Bianchi, Emily Sneeden, Aaron Beveridge, Shannon Butts, Jacob Greene, Kendra Holmes, Anastasia Kozak, and Rebecca McNulty.

I am grateful to my mentor and friend Gary A. Olson, President of Daemon College, for teaching me to love this profession.

Most of all, though, I want to thank those who most readily influence my work, those who have been there for me and with me through so much. Each of these people is more than dear to me; each has changed how I think about things and how I do things. With the most humble of gratitude, I acknowledge Joe Marshall Hardin, Raul Sanchez, Julianne Drew, Sean Morey, Christopher J. Keller, Anis S. Bawarshi, Christian Weisser, Todd W. Taylor, Andrea Greenbaum, Bonnie Kyburz, and Edward Braun.

Finally, I want to offer my never-ending gratitude and love to my family without whose support none of this would matter. To my parents Professor Leonard E. Dobrin and Professor Dora H. Dobrin; my brother Professor Adam Dobrin, his wife Lory, and their magnificent sons Jakob and Max; my brother Professor Ben Dobrin, his wife Laura, and their amazing son Luke; and my in-laws Nick and Laura Cocks: there are no words worthy of what you have given me. I love you all. And, of course, to my wife Teresa and my boys Asher and Shaia, this book and all I do is for you. My days rise and set with you, and all I can do is hope to make you proud. I love you three with all I have and am. Thank you for your patience, your support, and your love. Always.

About the Author

Sid Dobrin is University of Florida Research Foundation Professor and Graduate Coordinator in the Department of English at the University of Florida, where he previously served as Director of Writing Programs in the English Department for ten years. He is the author and editor of nineteen books, most of which are about writing, ecology, and technology. If you'd like to contact him about *Writing Situations*, feel free to email him at writing_situations@yahoo.com.

Writing Processes

1 Understanding Rhetorical Situations

Learning Objectives

1.1 Describe three primary reasons for writing in college

1.2 Describe the ten key elements in rhetorical situations

1.3 Recognize writing situations as part of an ecology of multiple situations

1.4 Identify the four categories of possible responses available to you in any given rhetorical situation

Before you read this chapter

Why do we write in college? What makes writing in college different from other kinds of writing? In your journal or blog, write about what distinguishes "college writing" from other writing, how you anticipate learning about college writing, and how writing might contribute to your college learning.

One of the most rewarding and satisfying parts of your college experience will be the writing you do. The writing you will produce will challenge you, it will affect how and what you learn, and it will affect how you engage the world around you. Ultimately, we write in college for three reasons:

1.1 Describe three primary reasons for writing in college

- *Learning*— We learn *how* to write in new and different situations and we *learn* from our writing.
- *Participating* —We write to participate in the world and in situations that affect our lives, both in college and beyond.
- *Expressing* —We write to make our voices heard, and to say what we have to say.

None of these reasons for writing in college can happen without the others, and they all require thinking.

Learning

Writing is an indispensable part of learning. Learning to write in college is important not only because it strengthens your ability to produce successful writing in your courses but also because the very act of writing enhances your learning. Writing is used in college as a method to get you to show what you know, but in the process, writing also helps you to figure out what you know.

Writing can stimulate your learning by helping you generate ideas, work through problems, develop solutions, formulate approaches, synthesize information, grasp difficult concepts, analyze complex ideas, and understand complicated material. The process of writing also helps you to remember details about a subject and, when combined with thinking and learning, encourages memory.

Writing to learn also provides a way for you to make connections with the material you study, with places, and especially with other people—one of your greatest resources for learning. Writing, that is, enhances the situations in which you find yourself.

Participating

Part of the goal of learning is being able to engage your world, being able to better participate. The idea of participating is to be an active contributor in your life. It is a form of citizenship—being a part of a community and having some say in how that community functions. A big part of participation centers on making decisions as well as considering the situations in which those decisions are made and how decisions affect you and others. Participation is about taking responsibility for your role in a situation.

College is an invitation to participate in academic conversations. When you study a particular subject—like accounting or medicine or literature—you decide to engage the situations of that community. And participating as a citizen means that you take an active role in larger communities, societies, and cultures. This kind of participation is crucial to the world in which we live.

Expressing

We write to express, to articulate our ideas and thoughts. Expression is a form of making meaning, of participating, and of contributing. When you express yourself, you stake a place in a situation as an individual who has something to say. Think about writing to express as a way of proclaiming identity—who we are in a given situation and where we stand. In addition, we want our audiences to remember what we wrote. We want what we express to strike a chord with our audience, to connect with them, to be memorable, to encourage others to remember.

Thinking

Each of the reasons you write in college—to learn, to participate, and to express— requires thinking. Through writing, you learn to think more clearly about situations and to better understand the situations you encounter. Both the degree and substance of your participation depend on your thoughts about where you want to be in the situation. You can also learn to think about your expression in a situation, that is, what you say and how you say it. Writing promotes thinking, and good writing requires thinking.

You are probably familiar with the term *critical thinking,* a kind of thinking used for analyzing and understanding. Critical thinking strategies are important for how you approach the kinds of writing assignments this class and other college classes ask of you.

Critical thinking enables you to better understand situations, create new ideas, and accept or question old ideas. It can lead to action and change by helping you to judge a situation and to adjust your own positions based on those informed judgments. Critical thinking is a process to assess authenticity, value, and accuracy. Consequently, it helps you clarify ambiguity and is the root of problem solving.

1.2 Describe the ten key elements in rhetorical situations

Rhetorical Situations

Rhetoric, quite simply, is how we use language to communicate—to persuade, to inform, to narrate, to remember, or to do any number of the things we use language to do. As writers and speakers, we make decisions, what we call *rhetorical choices,* about how to use language every day. *Writing Situations* is designed to help you learn to make effective rhetorical choices. The first thing you should understand about any rhetorical choice is that it is made in a particular context, a situation, and that the rhetorical choice you make in one situation may or may not work in another. Thus, understanding how rhetorical situations function helps you understand how to make good rhetorical choices in any situation.

In your lifetime, you will need to understand how to move into and between many writing situations, or rhetorical situations. Rhetorical situations can be thought of as the circumstances in which you write or speak. Traditionally, rhetorical situations have been characterized as occurring when four fundamental elements converge:

- *the writer or speaker*
- *the audience*
- *the purpose* of what is being written or spoken
- *the topic* of what is being written or spoken

All of these parts of a rhetorical situation take place in a given context. Likewise, all of these parameters operate within a cultural paradigm, which influences how writers write and how audiences respond. In addition, all of these elements influence a writer's choices about what genres (types or kinds of writing) are efficient or even acceptable in the situation.

You can get a clearer picture of how rhetorical situations work by examining ten of their key elements. These ten elements are part of rhetorician Lloyd Bitzer's definition of the rhetorical situation. They are introduced here in a convenient order for the sake of explanation, but that should not suggest an order of importance. All of these elements are critical to any writing situation, and depending on the given situation, any one may be of greater importance than the others. Each will be addressed in detail throughout *Writing Situations*.

Ten Elements of Rhetorical Situations

Element	Comments
Exigency	Exigency is the reason for writing—the incentive, the investment, and the motivation a writer has for writing. Exigency might be considered a situational need: why a writer needs to write. Exigency suggests change; it suggests that something should, and can, be done. Exigency influences purpose; the reason you respond to a situation is reflected in the purpose of your response to the situation.
Players	The players are all the people involved in the situation, including a speaker, a writer, someone implicated or named in the situation, or an audience. Keep in mind that players can also include people who may be affected by the situation but who are not part of the intended audience. For instance, a legislator may write a proposed trade law that affects a group of people outside his or her legislative jurisdiction by imposing import regulations on products that group of people produces. The legislator's writing is not intended for those people to read, yet they will be affected by the situation and the document, even if unknowingly.
Relations	Relations can refer to any relation of the situation, including relations between individuals, between speakers and audience, between writers and readers, between players and policies, between players and power, between degrees of power of different players, between writers and places, and even between power and external elements like culture, industry, or government. Understanding the dynamics of the situation's relations is crucial to understanding the situation, how to position oneself in the situation, and how to effectively respond to it.
Constraints	Constraints restrict what decisions can be made and what actions can be taken. Constraints may include beliefs, traditions, interests, motives, ideas, attitudes, and facts about either the situation or the kind of situation. For example, your instructor may impose constraints regarding what topics you can and cannot write about for class assignments, and the culture of college may impose constraints regarding what is and isn't appropriate to write about. Constraints may also be material, like the space in which you can respond. Twitter, for instance, limits tweets (posts) to 140 characters. Understanding under what constraints one must write—philosophically, ethically, politically, or even materially—will help you better understand the situation in which you participate and the options you have for participating.

(Continued)

Element	Comments
Location	Writing in a situation requires that the writing be available in some location: a web page, a newspaper, a book, a syllabus, etc. To participate in or respond to a situation, writers need to know not only where they are located but also where all other facets of the situation are located. Location is deeply connected to access. For instance, by posting your writing on the Web, you provide access to that writing for those who can access the Internet. But that location also denies access to some. That location, then, makes an assumption about what audience can reach your writing in that situation.
Speakers/Writers	Most often, you write because someone else has said, written, or done something that compels you to write—because a situation has arisen. Your position as a participant, a writer, is developed in relation to the positions of other participants, speakers, or writers. One of the most important parts of navigating writing situations is being able to figure out where you fit as a speaker.
Audience	Once you know who the writers/speakers in a situation are, you need to understand who *their* audiences are; that is, you must first understand who in the given situation is being spoken to, written to—and why. Once you understand the audience of the situation, you can then begin to analyze and understand who your audience is going to be and how that audience is attached to the situation.
Genre, Medium, and Method	Genre is the kind or type of writing, for example, short stories, novels, essays, poems, reports, e-mails, blogs, letters, manuals, and so on. Medium can be thought of as the material presentation of the writing, for example, a web page, a print document, a speech, a blog, a text message. The method is how the writer uses language to accomplish the task at hand: argumentative, assertive, cunning, elusive, subtle, and so on.
Institution/Power	All of the elements of any rhetorical situation are bound by conditions of the situation beyond just the constraints. These conditions are the politics of the situation—what can and can't be said or done—and power mechanisms such as race, class, culture, gender, or religion. Although you may not always be able to see or understand all of the institutional or power mechanisms that affect a situation, it is important to consider as many of them as possible. If the point of entering a writing situation is to bring about some form of change, then the writer must always recognize that doing so is an act of power. Convincing someone of something, explaining something, describing something, or any other possible response to a situation—including not participating in the situation—is an act of power.
Timing/*Kairos*	Every rhetorical situation is affected by timing. The point when something is said and written affects the situation and is affected by when other things have been said and written. Rhetoricians refer to the timing of a rhetorical situation as *kairos*, which literally means "the opportune occasion for speech." Chances are you have made a comment in a conversation that ends up confusing others because they had stopped talking about that subject much earlier. That's bad timing. Knowing when to enter a conversation so your writing or comments have the most impact is important.

Even though these ten elements are presented here as separate parts of rhetorical situations, it is more accurate to think of them as interactive and inseparable than as independent. Each part influences and affects all other parts. In addition, a rhetorical situation is already in place before you enter into it and will continue when you leave it. It might be most accurate to understand your participation in a rhetorical situation as playing a role in that situation's continual evolution rather than as making an isolated entry into a pre-established, fixed situation. Situations are never stagnant. For example, a situation's audience is likely to change as the situation evolves; thus, understanding audience requires that a writer/speaker be flexible and adaptable to changes in the situation and not wed to one concept of who the audience is. The dynamic nature of these ten elements within rhetorical situations creates a "rhetorical ecology."

Rhetorical Ecology

1.3 Recognize writing situations as part of an ecology of multiple situations

The term *rhetorical ecology* suggests a complex sense of connection, an intricate and evolving network that not only connects a speaker or writer and a situation but also connects that situation to a host of other factors, including its place and its historical context. In this way, then, a writer or speaker enters into a situation already connected with countless other situations that then affect how that writer engages the new situation. Writers engage those networks through a series of "encounters"; these encounters are becoming more complex as the current state of digital technologies encourages rapid, mass distribution and circulation of writing.

One way to understand how rhetorical ecologies work is to think about the kinds of connections various digital networks and documents make. For example, you might post an entry to your blog in which you embed a video from YouTube or another video sharing site. When you post your blog and video, your Twitter account can automatically send a message to people who follow your tweets that the blog has been posted and provide a link to the blog page. Likewise, your MySpace and Facebook venues may announce the same update and link. You may also decide to post the link to aggregate sites like Digg, Buzzflash, or Fark, all of which categorize and make available links to millions of readers. Within the blog post, you may include links to other blogs, articles, web pages, videos, applications, and so on that contribute to the rhetorical situation. And your blog page may now appear in search engine results when someone searches the Web for terms you have identified as key terms. Of course, your blog also encourages your readers to respond either in comment sections or in their own documents. Comment sections in blogs, newspapers, zines, and other digital media are one of the most common forms of writing and sustained interaction available today. And, unlike newspapers, books, or other print materials, this interaction allows readers to affect your document by altering the context in which others read it; by making suggestions for revisions, which you can make immediately; and by correcting inconsistencies and inaccuracies in your writing. Thus, your original blog post becomes part of an ecology of texts, not necessarily an autonomous artifact.

Mapping Your Situation is a visual that shows this dynamic relationship. Embedded in the graphic are questions that a writer should be asking during the writing process to map connections among key elements. Later chapters will present similar questions tailored to particular writing projects.

MAPPING
YOUR SITUATION

NETWORKS
- What networks can be identified?
- What other exigencies might exist?
- How does the audience change within this situation?

WRITER AND SPEAKER
- Who are the other writers and speakers in this situation?
- Who are the primary writers?
- Who are the secondary writers?

RELATIONS
- What is my relation to the situation?
- What are the relationships between writers/speakers, audience, and players?
- What are the relationships to external forces, like culture, religion, or politics?
- What are the power relations?

AUDIENCE
- Who is the audience in the situation?
- What do I know about my audience?
- Who does the situation affect?

MEDIUM AND METHOD
- What genres are available to me in this situation?
- What media do writers and speakers in this situation use?
- What methods should I use in this situation?
- How do the methods I use affect the situation?

CONTEXT
- Where and when does this situation take place?
- Where and when will my writing be available to my audience?
- How does the situation itself limit what I can say or how I can say it?

PURPOSE
- What is the reason I need to write in this situation?
- What is my incentive, my motivation?
- What is it about this situation that compels me to write?

Mapping your situation will help you generate ideas you can use to compose. Start by answering these questions about each part of the situation. Begin with your purpose and work outward to relations and networks.

Responding to Situations

1.4 Identify the four categories of possible responses available to you in any given rhetorical situation

Once you have analyzed the situation and positioned yourself in relation to it, you will want to determine how to respond to and participate in that situation. Every situation presents limited ways in which you can respond. Some of those responses may be determined by the institution and power of the situation; some may be constrained or expanded by the medium and methods available. Some responses may be inhibited by the audience, by the other speakers, by the location of the situation. Some of those responses may be conventional; some may be unconventional. Some responses may resist the situation or the conventions of the situation. And some may be abnormal or even inappropriate to the situation. No matter how you—or any writer—chooses to respond, those choices are initiated and bound by the situation and boil down to four broad categories: direct response, indirect response, resistant response, and no response.

Direct Response

You may respond directly to a situation by speaking or writing to the initial speakers and/or audience, participating firsthand in the situation that sparked the exigency. Within a direct response, options for the content of your response may be numerous, but options for your approach will be limited to the following:

- Argue in support of the speaker/writer's message.
- Argue against the way the speaker/writer is handling or resolving the situation (different from arguing against the *situation*—discussed under "Resistant Response").
- Correct or provide a different perspective.
- Engage in dialogue.
- Persuade the audience/speaker.

Indirect Response

Indirect responses do not engage the situation exactly. Instead, indirect responses might be thought of as responses *about* the situation rather than *within* the situation. Some of the ways to respond indirectly include the following:

- Expand the situation with additional information.
- In a fashion parallel to the situation, tell a similar story to a similar audience or situation.
- Use the situation as an example in another situation.
- Compare/contrast the situation with other situations.
- Argue for or against the issue of the situation.
- Explain the causes/effects of the situation.
- Describe the situation.

- Show the process that leads to the situation.
- Define the context of the situation.
- Classify the situation among other situations.
- Persuade the writer and audience about the situation.

Resistant Responses

Resistant responses can take either direct or indirect approaches. Although they may be counter to a situation, they are valid—and often important—responses nonetheless. Among the countless ways to resist a situation are the following:

- Oppose the situation itself and find no satisfaction in direct response.
- Attempt to stop movement or progress within the situation.
- Declare immunity to the situation.
- Be unresponsive.
- Initiate an oppositional position.
- Deny the situation.
- Refuse to participate in the situation.
- Disrupt the situation.

No Response

Sometimes the best response is no response. Not responding could be read as a resistant response, but a no-response approach can also be used in the following ways:

- A response in and of itself, identifying that the situation is not worth a response (or sending a message that you see the situation as not worth responding to—a rhetorical move to devalue the situation)
- A strategy to observe how the situation will evolve before staking a claim in it
- A strategy for learning more before entering the situation ineffectively
- A result forced on the writer by the situation itself, denying the writer the opportunity to respond

The Dynamic Nature of Response

Ultimately, how you write in any given situation is influenced by that situation. The possibilities for reacting to a situation—direct, indirect, resistant, or no response—help determine the possible choices you have in any given situation. Figure 1.1 offers a visual approach to the kinds of responses available to you in situations. As you can see, movement through these various avenues of response is rarely linear or simple. Any response to any situation inherently changes that situation, creates a new situation, or brings multiple situations together. Thus, any reaction to a situation leads to the potential of further response to the situation. Exigencies most often open the doors to further exigencies.

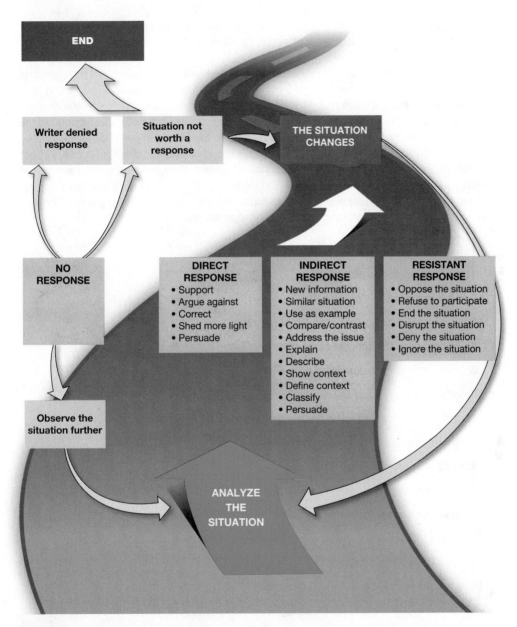

FIGURE 1.1 Responding to situations.

Summary

Writing—all writing—is situational. Rhetoric is the theory and practice of effective communication and persuasion. Rhetorical choices are the choices that you make when you write and speak; they are framed within and by the situation. A rhetorical situation provides the writer with the context or circumstances in which to write. Rhetorical situations can be broken down to ten key elements that interact in numerous ways: exigency; players; relations; constraints; location; speakers/writers; audience; genre, medium, and method; institution/power; and timing/*kairos*.

Rhetorical ecology suggests that situations do not exist independently of their relations to other situations and networks and that the parts of a rhetorical situation are not, in fact, independent parts, but more closely related, even inseparable. In every situation, the configurations of the rhetorical ecology limit the number of ways in which a writer can respond to the situation. No matter how you—or any writer—chooses to respond, those choices are initiated and bound by the situation and boil down to four broad categories: direct response, indirect response, resistant response, and no response. Movement through these various avenues of response is rarely linear or simple. Any response to any situation inherently changes that situation, creates a new situation, or brings multiple situations together. Thus, any reaction to a situation leads to the potential of further response to the situation.

Chapter Review

1. What is a rhetorical situation?

2. What is a situation's exigency?

3. In any given situation, who are the players?

4. To what does the concept of relations refer within a rhetorical situation?

5. What effect do constraints have on a rhetorical situation?

6. Why does a rhetorical situation require a location?

7. Why is it important to know the speakers and writers in a given situation?

8. Why do we need to understand audiences in a given situation?

9. What is a genre?

10. How might we think of medium?

11. To what does a writer's method refer?

12. How do institutions and power impose rules on a situation?

13. What is rhetorical ecology?

14. What are four possible kinds of responses to a situation?

A Situation of Writing

On Sunday, October 21, 2007, the Boston Red Sox beat the Cleveland Indians 11–2 to win the seventh game of the American League Championship Series and the right to play the Colorado Rockies in the 2007 World Series. The Red Sox would go on to sweep the Rockies and win the Series four games to none. On the night of the Red Sox win over the Indians, Boston fans celebrated—some a little too much. Twenty-six fans were arrested for disorderly conduct. Of those twenty-six, seven were sentenced by a judge to write essays about what they learned from being arrested.

Below, you will find the Associated Press article that reported the case. Read the article and consider the role writing plays in this situation.

Rowdy fans cheer the Red Sox after the 2007 World Series.

Rowdy Red Sox Fans Punished with Essay

October 23, 2007
The Associated Press

BOSTON—Seven rowdy Red Sox fans have a homework assignment, and it has nothing to do with baseball.

A judge has ordered them to write a five-page essay explaining what they have learned from their experience of being arrested after the Red Sox won the American League Championship Series on Sunday night.

The defendants must also provide proof to the court that their parents are aware of their arrests.

The seven were among 26 people—many of them college students—charged with disorderly conduct charges. A spokesman for the Suffolk District Attorney's office says many were arrested for ignoring police orders to clear the area around Fenway Park after the game.

Some in the crowd allegedly threw rocks and bottles at police.

Analyzing the Situation

1. In what ways are institution and power a part of this situation? How do they also contribute to the exigency of the situation?

2. Who do you imagine was the intended audience of the essays that the seven students wrote? Do you think they directed their essays to the judge? To the Red Sox? To themselves? Who do you think actually read the essays? In what ways does it even matter for the essay writers who the audience was?

3. What does this situation suggest about writing? In what ways might the situation itself be read as a lesson about writing more than a lesson about behavior?

Analyzing the Rhetoric

1. Why do you suppose the author of the AP article points out in the fourth paragraph that many of those charged were college students? Does saying this have a particular effect on how we read the article or on how we understand the situation? Does it contribute to a particular impression of college students?

2. The AP article is pretty brief. What information do you wish it had provided? How might that information have altered your understanding of the situation?

3. The short paragraphs of this article are characteristic of journalistic writing. In what ways does this journalistic style contribute to the authority of the article? In what ways does it contribute to our understanding of it as an "article" rather than another form of writing?

Discussing

1. Why do you suppose the judge sentenced the seven fans with writing an essay? What do you think the purpose of the essay was? Do you think this was a legitimate purpose? That is, what was the point to the imposed sentence?

2. Writing essays like the one described in the AP article is most often associated with school work, with the kinds of essays students traditionally write in college composition courses. Why do you suppose the judge chose this kind of writing?

3. Is writing a good punishment? What are the benefits of sentencing people to writing as punishment? What are the drawbacks—both for the purpose of the sentence and for the perception of what writing does?

4. Is this kind of writing what you anticipate having to do beyond college? In what ways might the college writing situation prepare you for unusual situations like this?

Collaborating

1. The assignment of writing as legal punishment is not unique to this situation. In small groups, conduct some research to locate three or four other cases in which judges have sentenced people to write as their punishment. Then compare the situations of the cases. What are the similarities and differences? Are there trends among the situations? Is there an identifiable relationship between the different contexts? Once you have gathered your information, collaboratively write an assessment of the situations, explaining what you have found in your comparison.

2. In a group of three or four students, consider what the benefits of sentencing someone to writing might be and what the negative effects might be. Collaboratively, create a chart that identifies what the positive and negative aspects of using writing as a legal sentence might be. Then use the chart to come to a group decision as to whether courts should continue using writing in this way. Write a brief explanation about what you decide and explain how you came to the decision based on the chart you created.

3. Consider the opening sentence of this article and think about situational ecology. Does the "homework" assignment really have nothing to do with baseball? As a class, discuss how the ecology of the situation is tied to baseball and other situations.

Writing

1. Imagine that, like these students, you had been sentenced to write an essay after being charged with

disorderly conduct, but imagine that the judge who sentenced you had also asked you to write not just the essay about what you learned from being arrested, but another, shorter essay, about using writing as a judicial sentence. Write an essay to the judge about what you see as the purpose of writing and the role that writing would play in such a situation.

2. Often, we think about judicial sentences both as a punishment for a crime committed and as a deterrent to those who might commit a crime. Do you think that writing essays like the one demanded in the Red Sox case serves as a deterrent? Write a short essay that considers how writing might serve in each of these capacities.

3. Throughout this chapter, you have considered what is involved in understanding writing situations. Using what you have learned from this chapter and the limited information found in the AP article, write an analysis of the situation, explaining what you see as the crucial issues in the situation.

Thinking and Writing about the Chapter

Reflection

Now that you have had the chance to read and think about rhetorical situations, and the college writing situation in particular, how would you explain to others why we write in college? Look back at your journal entry or blog post that you wrote in response to the Initial Thoughts prompt at the beginning of this chapter. Now, how would you characterize college writing? How will college help you learn about writing and how will your writing help you learn?

Discussion Threads

1. If the ten elements of writing situations are issues that we need to consider when writing, how might we use them in reading? As a class or in smaller groups, discuss the ways that we might become better readers by considering the ten elements of rhetorical situations. Which of those ten elements might be difficult to identify in reading a text? Which might provide insight into what we read?

2. If part of the reason we write in college is to learn, and part of learning requires that we adhere to particular standards—like the standards of academic writing—then can resistance be considered a legitimate response in college? As a class or in smaller groups, discuss the ways that resistance might be an important response to some writing situations and whether such situations might occur in college learning.

3. Why is it important to think about rhetorical ecology? Discuss how understanding rhetorical ecology might help you better understand not just a rhetorical situation, but how you would write in particular rhetorical situations.

Collaboration

Sometimes offering no response to a situation can be a difficult thing to do because we often feel a need to respond. But, at the same time, sometimes no response can be an effective response, or even the smartest choice we can make in a rhetorical situation. Talk with some of your classmates about situations that might be best served with no response. Discuss your own experiences, times you did respond and might have been better off not responding, and times you decided not to respond. Why was no response a useful response in these situations? After your discussions, collectively write a series of guidelines that might be used to help others decide when no response is the best response.

Writing

1. What have you written recently? What was the situation that led to you writing? Using the ten elements of writing situations described in this chapter, write an analysis of the situation in which you wrote.

2. Think about the situation of your writing class in terms of rhetorical ecology. In what ways does it participate in a rhetorical ecology with other classes on your campus? With other classes at colleges and universities around the country? With the discipline of composition studies? With writing situations you are likely to engage when you leave college? Write a document that addresses the rhetorical ecology of your writing classroom.

Local Situation

What do you consider to be the most pressing issue your college or university is currently facing or addressing? How would you define that situation? How would you describe the ten elements of that situation? What is the ecology of that situation? That is, what are the connections among the ten elements and how is the situation related to other situations in such a way that makes it a part of a larger whole?

Purpose and Audience 2

Learning Objectives

2.1 Explain the connection between purpose and audience

2.2 Develop methods for determining your purpose in writing

2.3 Analyze the audiences of your documents so you can write more directly to them

2.4 Practice recommended guidelines for writing to transnational and transcultural audiences

2.5 Explain the role that purpose and audience play in determining how you use visuals

Before you read this chapter

When you write for an audience other than yourself, how do you account for that audience in your writing? What do you do to your writing to make sure that what you write best reaches your audience? In your journal or blog, write about how you adjust your writing for different kinds of audiences.

Everything we write—for college or for any reason—has a purpose and an audience. In fact, most everything we write probably serves multiple purposes and is likely to have multiple audiences, even audiences we never anticipate. As you develop and use your college writing processes, it is useful to ask two questions at all stages of your process:

> What is my purpose?
>
> Who is my audience?

2.1 Explain the connection between purpose and audience

The answers to these two questions should surround everything you do when you write, including generating ideas, conducting research, taking notes, drafting, organizing, revising, and editing, as well as delivering and circulating. In some cases, keeping your audience and purpose in mind will require conscious, rigorous response to these questions; in others, a tacit understanding of them will be fine.

Writing Processes

Traditionally, students have been taught a linear, step-by-step process for writing. The details of that process may have varied, but the idea was that writing was a series of discrete tasks: prewriting, drafting, revising, proofreading, publishing.

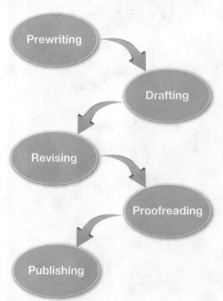

Most writers know that writing is more dynamic than such a picture can account for. Writing processes are recursive (the steps loop back on themselves) and not somehow independent of the situation they occupy. Writing requires critical thinking, detailed reading, and thoughtful analysis of situations at various points in the process. For this reason, *Writing Situations* teaches a situational approach to writing processes that considers the shifting conditions of any given writing scenario. Writing processes should be thought of as fluid, nonlinear processes that writers adjust and change with each situation to solve rhetorical and functional problems.

That said, however, we can recognize that most writers do some similar things: they have reasons for writing, they generate ideas, they plan what they will write, and they write. In many situations, they also revise and edit their writing. These activities are the foundation of all writing processes. *Writing Situations* guides you to look in detail at how these activities function by dividing writing processes into eight active phases: situate, plan, research, draft, review and revise, edit, evaluate, and distribute and circulate.

Writing Process
GUIDELINES

Use the guidelines in this chart to plan, review, and evaluate your process for writing. Each step in the process should support the overall purpose of your project.

SITUATE

- Understand your reasons for entering the situation **(exigencies)**
- Consider who the **players** in the situation are likely to be
- Understand how **relations** affect the situation
- Identify how the situation is limited by **constraints**
- Distinguish the role of **location** in the situation
- Recongnize the **speakers or writers** in the situation
- Identify and analyze the **audience** involved in the situation
- Consider what **genres, media, and methods** are used in the situation and which might be of use to you
- Acknowledge how various **institutions and power** affect the situation
- Consider the **ecological relationships** between this situation and others

PLAN

- Confirm your reason for entering this situation **(exigency)**
- Clarify your **purpose** in writing or by speaking to the situation
- Consider your form of **response** to the situation
- Understand the **purpose** of any document you wish to contribute to the situation
- Consider what might be the best **genre, media, and method** for you to use to enter into the situation
- Analyze what you know about the situation and what you need to discover before entering the situation
- Begin to take **notes**

RESEARCH

- Determine what kind of **information** you will need and the best ways to locate that information
- Conduct **research** to gather the information you need
- Confirm that your research will be **valid** within the situation
- Identify any **visuals** you may need
- **Organize** your information
- **Evaluate** your information in light of the situation and your purpose to determine whether you need to conduct further research

DRAFT

- Confirm your **purpose**
- Confirm that your choices in **genre, media, and method** will be effective within the situation
- **Draft and organize** the content of your document
- Use the **visual process** to develop any visuals you will need
- **Design** your document

REVIEW AND REVISE

- Review your document for **clarity and** concision
- Review your document for **accuracy**
- Review your document for **degree of detail** appropriate to the situation and purpose
- Review your document for **extraneous information**
- Review your document for **organizational approach**
- Review your document for explanations of **key terms** necessary within the situation
- Review your document for **style** appropriate to the situation
- Confirm your **research and citations**
- Review your document for **visual effectiveness and readabillity**
- Consider revising the **title** to most accurately reflect the document's purpose

EDIT

- **Proofread** carefully
- Correct all **mechanical and grammatical** errors

EVALUATE

- Seek **feedback** from peers (take advantage of **peer editing** opportunities)
- Self-evaluate
- Ask for feedback from a representative member of the **target audience**
- Ask for feedback from an **editor** in whom you are confident
- **Evaluate** the usefulness of any feedback you receive and revise accordingly

DISTRIBUTE/CIRCULATE

- Consider technologies of **circulation**
- Publish in a **form** that will be visible within the situation
- Identify methods for **increasing ciruclation** (like search engine optimization) within and beyond the specific situation
- Consider audience **access**
- Identify possible sources of **audience response**

2.2 Develop
methods for
determining your
purpose in writing

Rhetorical Purpose

Your rhetorical purpose can be thought of as the reasons for why and how you write in any situation. It is the rationale for the choices you make. Knowing your purpose can help you decide what method, genre, and medium to use in producing and delivering your writing. Writing with little or no awareness of your purpose will usually lead to unfocused, unsuccessful writing. Purpose is influenced by four primary facets: situations, exigency, rhetorical goals, and audience.

Situations, as you will see throughout *Writing Situations*, are what drive all components of any writing task. Thus, understanding as much as you can about a situation—like a college writing assignment—helps clarify what your purpose for writing in that situation is. Exigency is the reason for writing. Exigency is the writer's incentive, what motivates a writer. Part of understanding your purpose is understanding how your exigency is tied to a specific audience.

Rhetorical goals are what a writer hopes to achieve through writing. *Writing Situations* addresses eight primary rhetorical goals of writing: narrating, describing, informing, responding, analyzing, evaluating, arguing, and proposing. Part of what makes up your purpose in any writing situation is understanding what your goals in writing are: Do you want to describe? Do you want to evaluate? Do you want to propose? Understanding your rhetorical goal is part of understanding your rhetorical purpose, but you also have to understand your audience and your audience's need.

Audience is an indispensable part of determining what your purpose is. By determining whether your audience needs to be informed or persuaded, for example, you shape the purpose of your writing. Likewise, by recognizing what genre or medium best reaches your audience, you can more purposefully use that media. Your rhetorical purpose is ultimately to affect your audience, so you have to know who that audience is.

It is important to learn to focus your writing on specific purposes attuned to the particular needs of the situation. In a college writing assignment, you will want to focus your purpose so your writing accurately responds to the requirements of the assignment. To fine-tune your purposes, you should begin by developing a series of questions about the situation that helps you identify and focus your purpose. In many writing situations, your focused sense of purpose can help you make and support a clear claim.

You may want to consider using these kinds of questions to identify and focus your purpose:

- Why does the situation make you want to respond?
- Who would you respond to? (Who is your audience?)
- Who besides your primary audience might read your writing?
- What do you gain or what does the situation gain from your participation?
- What information do you want to convey?

- How do you want your audience to react and respond?
- What do you want your audience to understand about you as the writer?
- What tone do you want to take with your audience?
- What genre do you think you should write in, and how will that genre affect what you convey?

Many situations require that you write with more than one purpose. Often, to fulfill one purpose, you may have to embrace another. For example, your purpose may be to persuade, but to do so, you may also have to define. Also, keep in mind that your writing may be "repurposed" by your audience. That is, your audience may recirculate what you have written in ways that also serve their purposes. Because digital technologies allow for the rapid re-circulation of writing to numerous and varied audiences, you should always be aware that your writing may be repurposed, particularly in business and professional settings. For example, information used in a report may be repurposed in a marketing letter or a technical manual, even though the writer had not anticipated writing for those genres or media.

Audience

2.3 Analyze the audiences of your documents so you can write more directly to them

Knowing your audience drives your writing. Knowing your audience is inseparable from knowing your purpose, and it affects the content you provide; your word choice; and your choice of genre, method, and medium. Nearly all of your rhetorical choices in any given situation should be guided by what you know about your audience.

Sometimes writers enter writing situations knowing much about their audience. Writing an e-mail to a family member or close friend doesn't necessarily require any elaborate or formal audience analysis. You enter those situations already aware of how that audience affects your writing choices. These audiences can be categorized as *familiar audiences*. In other situations, however, you may not have direct knowledge about the audience, so you conduct a more formal analysis of the audience. These audiences are *unfamiliar audiences*. Often, too, you write for *multiple audiences*. In a classroom assignment, you may write for your classmates and your teacher; in a workplace environment you may write for a supervisor and your coworkers.

These three divisions of audience can be more specifically characterized as real or imagined. *Real audiences* are audiences you can specifically identify. Real audiences may be individuals such as "the people in my English class," or they may be groups of people like "college students." Real audiences are made up of primary audiences and secondary audiences. Primary audiences are ones you write to directly, the ones who most immediately receive and interpret your writing. Secondary audiences are those who read your writing secondhand. You may not have written to them directly, but they end up as an audience, nonetheless.

Imagined audiences are whom you picture in your mind as you write. These audiences don't actually read your writing, but imagining them guides your writing toward real audiences. Imagined audiences include self-audiences and ideal audiences. As it implies, a self-audience is yourself. If you are writing an argumentative essay, for example, you may imagine how you would respond to your own argument. An ideal audience is your target audience—how you imagine your real audience.

In college writing, your primary audience will often be your instructor. But your primary audience will often also include an assigned audience. In many instances, the audience for an assignment may not be explicitly defined, but the details of the assignment reveal information about how you should think of the audience. For example, if you have been assigned to keep a blog about your experiences as a college student, you can assume that because of the medium, your audience will extend beyond your instructor to a broader audience of college students who might access your blog.

To better understand any audience, you can develop analytical questions to ask when you enter a writing situation. The answers you discover to these kinds of questions can also help you better understand the purpose of your writing:

- How do I know who my audience is?
- How did I identify my audience?
- What is my relationship to the audience?
- What do I want the audience to know about me?
- What tone do I want to take with the audience and why?
- What is the audience's position in the situation?
- What are the audience's interests, and why might they be interested in what I have to say?
- Is there a secondary audience?
- Are there players in the situation who are not a primary or secondary audience?
- How might the audience be constrained within the situation?
- Where is the audience located?
- In what location is the audience most likely to engage my writing?
- How have other writers/speakers in the situation identified and accounted for audiences in this situation?
- Are there institutional powers that affect the audience in this situation? In particular, how do politics affect my audience: are my readers conservative, liberal, moderate?
- What does the audience already know about the situation?
- What does my audience believe about this situation?
- Why might the audience be interested in reading (or hearing) what I have to say?
- What do I want the audience to gain or do?
- What does my audience expect?
- How do I anticipate my audience responding to me? In what ways?

Transnational Audiences

When you write in college or beyond, your audiences are likely to have diverse cultural and international backgrounds. The possibility of worldwide circulation through digital technologies increases this likelihood. In addition, English may not be your native or first language, which adds to the challenge of writing to native English speakers. Audiences with different cultural, linguistic, or national backgrounds can be thought of as transnational or transcultural audiences—audiences that cross national, cultural, or linguistic borders. Why is it important to consider transnational and transcultural audiences when learning to write in a college English class? Because you should not rely on the idea that whoever reads your writing will be either a native English speaker or share your own cultural background and assumptions.

Consider the situation in which Richard Paez, a student in a first-year writing class, asked his classmate Ingrid Kalfus to read and evaluate an essay he had written. In her comments, Ingrid suggested that Richard put some of his information comparing MP3 players into a table to help clarify that information for readers. Richard was confused by the use of the word *table* because of his linguistic and cultural understandings of that word. Look carefully at the visuals in Figure 2.1, which represent ways different audiences might interpret the term *table*. The first shows how workplace writers in North America might understand the term; the second, how many European and North American general audiences are likely to understand the term; and the third, how many South American audiences understand the term, as happened in Richard and Ingrid's situation.

What may seem a common understanding—like the definition of the word *table*—may in fact be interpreted and understood in different ways among varied cultures and nationalities. All writing requires careful consideration of audiences, but accounting for transnational and transcultural audiences presents particular challenges for all writers.

FIGURE 2.1 Various interpretations of *table*.

Writing Directed at Transnational and Transcultural Audiences

The following chart recommends guidelines that you can follow when writing for any transnational and transcultural audience.

Guidelines for Writing Directed at Transnational and Transcultural Audiences

Guideline	Comments
Avoid stereotypes.	Stereotyping occurs when you reduce differences to simple formulas and don't acknowledge the complexity of difference, even within seemingly similar groups. Becoming more culturally aware requires dedicated research to understand another culture beyond shallow, often erroneous, assumptions.
Avoid assumptions.	A common mistake in learning about other cultures, languages, and nations is to make assumptions about them. For instance, people may assume that an entire cultural group can be addressed in the same way, but such a culture-specific stereotype does not allow for differences within that culture. Assumptions don't lead to accurate understandings.
Ask questions.	The best way to learn about differences is to ask questions. Whenever possible, you should find answers to your questions about an audience before writing for it. In the process, be careful that the phrasing or context of a question is not offensive. If you are asking for one person's perspective, you should not assume his response to be representative of the entire country or culture.
Collaborate.	Most people who speak another language are not only proficient in that language but also well versed in the culture. Consider collaborating with someone who is familiar with the language and culture of your target audience.
Write clearly.	Nonnative readers of English are more likely to understand clearly written documents. Be alert to issues of clarity and concision.
Use correct punctuation.	Ensure that your documents are punctuated correctly. Misuse or lack of punctuation can confuse nonnative readers and, more important, might lead to misinterpretation of information.
Include definitive articles.	Leaving definite articles out of sentences can confuse nonnative readers. For instance, although it may sound appropriate to say, "Class will meet in the library," it is more complete to write, "The class will meet in the library."
Use terminology consistently.	Consistency helps nonnative speakers contextualize information. Use of a single term throughout a document helps convey consistent meaning. Even though English may interchange multiple synonyms for a concept, other languages may not accommodate such word shifts.
Avoid idiomatic language.	Idioms are phrases (such as "down to earth") that do not translate literally but are understood figuratively through a culture's common use of the phrase. To understand an idiom, a reader must understand its cultural use; therefore, it is best to avoid idiomatic expressions. The same is true for acronyms, abbreviations, jargon, and slang. If you must use specialized language, provide definitions of the terms early in the body of your writing. Depending on the kind of document you are writing, glossaries or other forms of reference (like footnotes) can also clarify language use.
Avoid comparatives.	Comparing things makes sense only if the two things are culturally understood as similar. For example saying, "the fish was as big as a toaster oven" only works if the audience knows what a toaster oven is and has a general idea as to how big one is. Therefore, it's a good idea to avoid using comparatives because you cannot be certain that transnational and transcultural audiences are familiar with the things being compared.
Avoid cultural references.	Many things that you know well—like eating or cooking utensils, sports equipment, clothing styles, makes and models of cars, or holidays—are probably not common reference points for most of the people in the world. Similarly, references to celebrities, movies, books, music, or pop-culture details should be avoided because they do not always cross borders.
Avoid humor.	For the most part, humor doesn't translate universally. Using humor can possibly insult, offend, or alienate your audience. In addition, do not try to use another culture's humor unless you are well versed in the target language, culture, and humor; the result could be even more offensive than a poorly translated joke.

Visuals, Audience, and Purpose

2.5 Explain the role that purpose and audience play in determining how you use visuals

Although some visuals such as international icons are designed to convey universal information and are used worldwide, more often than not, visuals need to be used with a specific audience and purpose in mind. To insure that the visuals you choose to use will convey information to your audience in the ways that you intend, you may need to conduct further audience analysis to determine their visual literacy. For example, if you were to use the symbol of the red cross to signify medical aid or first aid, then your audience would have to already be familiar with the red cross as indicating such a meaning. Paying particular attention to an audience's demographics can help you ascertain what visuals might work best because visual literacies—like any literacy—are usually culturally, geographically, and nationally based.

Keep in mind, too, that visuals like graphics and typographical choices can help you clarify information and guide your readers. Depending on your audience, various use of graphics and headings can help them better access and understand your writing. Consider, for instance how typographical choices affect the purpose of the two e-mails shown in Figure 2.2 that contain the same content.

Visuals and Transnational Audiences

When your writing reaches culturally diverse or multinational audiences, the meaning conveyed through visuals is likely to be understood differently by different readers. The following chart suggests some guidelines to consider.

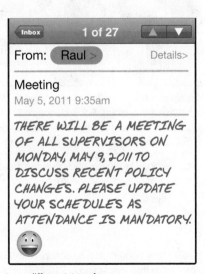

FIGURE 2.2 The same e-mail message shown in two different typefaces.

Using Visuals Effectively for Transnational Audiences

Approach	Comments
Use familiar images.	Large numbers of visuals, particularly icons, have been proven successful in reaching transnational audiences. For instance, the symbol for accessibility is already understood in many countries and cultures.
Direct readers.	Not all languages are read left to right, and not all individuals read. A visual was placed in South African mines to explain to miners unable to read that they should remove fallen rocks from the tracks. However, because the miners were not used to reading, they were not familiar with a left-to-right reading logic. As a result, many miners read the visuals from right to left and understood that they should place rocks on the track. Whenever possible, sequence visuals from top to bottom, and consider using arrows to direct readers through a sequence. Sign from South African mine.
Provide multiple examples.	Sometimes multiple visuals can clarify information for multiple audiences better than just one visual. Multiple examples of a grounded plug used to relate to multiple audiences.
Check for unintended visual interpretations, including symbols.	Visuals can convey different meanings to different people, and symbols can magnify often unintended meanings. For instance, in the United States, an image of an owl might symbolize wisdom; however, in parts of Central and South America, an owl might represent the blackness of night, implying death, black magic, or witchcraft.
Avoid using images of people and hand gestures.	Because body language and gestures are culturally defined, it is best to avoid using images of people or gestures; those images may not be interpreted as you intend. For example, you might use the icon to indicate a correct step or action. In the United States, that hand sign communicates correctness or that everything is OK. In France that same icon would likely be interpreted to mean zero or that something is worthless.

Summary

Everything we write has a purpose and an audience. At all stages of your writing, you should ask, What is my purpose? and Who is my audience? Your rhetorical purpose comprises the reasons for why and how you write in any situation. Your purpose is influenced by four factors: the situation, your exigency, your rhetorical goals, and most important, your audience. At some point, you will write for familiar audiences, unfamiliar audiences, and multiple audiences. Identify and account for your audience by asking analytical questions. Be sure to account for transnational and transcultural audiences. Writers can no longer rely on the idea that whoever reads their writing will be either a native English speaker or share the writers' own cultural backgrounds. When writing for transnational audiences, carefully consider seven points of difference that can help you account for what those audiences might need: language, technology, education, politics and law, economics, society, and religion. In addition to following guidelines that help you to write effectively for transnational and transcultural audiences, you should consider guidelines for using visuals in your writing for those audiences. Visuals can help you achieve your purposes in writing, but you should account for the visual literacy of your audience and consider how people in different cultures interpret and use visuals.

Chapter Review

1. How are purpose and audience related?

2. What are some strategies for determining what your purpose in writing is in any situation?

3. What kinds of analytical questions can you ask about an unfamiliar audience that will help you to write more directly to them?

4. Why is it crucial to be alert to the possibility of transnational audiences?

5. This chapter provides guidelines to take into consideration when writing for transnational/transcultural audiences. List ten of these recommendations.

6. How do purpose and audience affect how you use visuals in your writing?

7. What five guidelines might be useful when designing or integrating visuals into writing intended for a transnational audience?

Thinking and Writing about the Chapter

Reflection

At the beginning of this chapter, you were asked to write about how you account for different audiences when you write. Now that you have read this chapter and have had the chance to learn about directing your writing to specific audiences, including transnational audiences, post a follow-up entry in your blog or journal addressing how you will now account for audience when you write.

Discussion Threads

1. When you are given a writing assignment in school—in any class—how do you think about your primary audience—your instructor—for that assignment? How do you direct your writing to your instructor? How do you also account for any secondary audiences?

As a class, discuss how you write academic assignments for audiences of your teachers. Do you write differently for teachers? In what ways?

2. In the years surrounding the turn of the twentieth century, a tremendous number of people immigrated to the United States. Cities such as New York were populated with linguistically diverse populations. To answer the needs of these audiences—and to reach them as potential customers and clients—many newspapers, product packages, and other documents were published in a variety of languages, including Yiddish, German, Swedish, and Italian. Similarly, you now see documentation such as multi-language instruction manuals translated into many languages. It is already common to see products on U.S. store shelves in English, French, and Spanish, and it is becoming more common to also see packages written in Chinese, Hmong, Somali, and even Navajo. Why do you suppose it has become increasingly important to reach transnational and transcultural audiences in their native languages, and in what ways does this trend affect English as a global language?

Collaboration

1. Listed below are idioms commonly used by U.S. English speakers. Select five of these terms and work in groups to learn their origins/etymologies. What do they mean? How did these idiomatic expressions come to mean what they do? When did they start being used? Are they used in one region more predominantly than others? You should be able to find this information through research on the Web and through an idiom dictionary. Then, with your group, create a glossary for the expressions you have chosen, explaining what each one means. Assume that the glossary will be used to help non-U.S. speakers better understand U.S. English.

bite the dust	get off my back
play it by ear	tie the knot
spill the beans	jump the gun
all the bells and whistles	take the bull by the horns
water under the bridge	out on a limb
don't push my buttons	something smells fishy
when pigs fly	let the cat out of the bag
get your wires crossed	make ends meet
on the same wavelength	out of the blue
on the same page	drive me up a wall
the last straw	head over heels
wine and dine	over the top
the whole nine yards	cut it out
push the envelope	high five
three sheets to the wind	drop someone a line
saved by the bell	make no bones about it
neck of the woods	get the ball rolling
under the weather	drop in the bucket
the acid test	a piece of cake
out of steam	at the drop of a hat
a flash in the pan	learn the ropes
the ball is in your court	bite your tongue
wet blanket	go the extra mile
all thumbs	chew someone out

2. Although there is really no way to get an accurate number, it has been said that 80 percent of the content available on the Internet is presented in English; however, the fastest growing population of Internet users are non-English speakers. Consider this information provided by Internet World Stats in the table below.

   Increases in Internet access in countries like China have called into question the ubiquity of English on the Web and the need for more non-English-based web pages. In groups, first discuss the situation of the overwhelming presence of English on the Internet. In what ways does it limit information sharing? What are the ramifications of English's Internet dominance? Are there benefits? Does the presence of English on the Internet serve to promote the use of English? What power and institutions might be involved in the situation of English and the Internet?

   Once you have discussed the situation of English and the Internet, work together to locate a few web pages that are presented in languages you don't speak. Native English speakers may want to look for pages in Chinese, Korean, Spanish, and French, for instance. Then, as a group, try to navigate these sites and locate pertinent information. As you proceed, consider what it might be like for non-English speakers to navigate the Web and whether the richness of the Internet is really accessible to non-English speakers. Then, as a group, report what you have learned to your class.

Top 10 Languages in the Internet
2010 – in millions of users

Language	Millions of Users
English	536.6
Chinese	444.9
Spanish	153.3
Japanese	99.1
Portuguese	82.5
German	75.2
Arabic	65.4
French	59.8
Russia	59.7
Korean	39.4
All the rest	350.6

Source: Internet World Stats - www.internerworldstats.com/stats7.htm
Estimated Internet users are 1,966,514,816 for June 30, 2010
Copyright © 2000–2010, Miniwatts Marketing Group

Writing

1. Voice of America (VOA) is the official radio and television broadcasting service of the U.S. government. VOA broadcasts radio programming in 46 languages other than English and television programming in 25 languages other than English. In 1959, VOA began broadcasting in a form of English known as "VOA Special English." According to the VOA Special English website, Special English was designed to "communicate by radio in clear simple English with people whose native language was not English." VOA's Special English broadcasts have been popular around the world since they were introduced. Special English broadcasts are designed not only to share news with people around the world but also to help listeners learn "American English" and learn about American culture. VOA uses a limited core vocabulary of 1,500 words. Its writers use only short, simple sentences and never use idioms. They use only active verbs.

   Familiarize yourself with VOA's Special English broadcasts and the history of VOA (go to the VOA Special English website, which provides useful information, and search online for other discussions of VOA and Special English). Then write an assessment of how you see the role of VOA's Simple English in transnational communication. What factors affect the situation of Simple English?

2. The Modern Language Association's language map is designed to track the languages used in the United States. Interact with the map to learn a little about the languages that are most commonly used in your state and your county. If you are from a country other than the United States, use the map to learn more about the languages used in the state and county where your college is located. Once you have a better idea of what languages are commonly spoken in your area, write an assessment of what this information might mean for you as a writer. What kinds of language and cultural characteristics might you need to take into consideration now that you know this information? How might you learn about those linguistic and cultural characteristics?

Local Situation

It is common for writing teachers to ask you to write for a "group of your peers." Using the audience analysis questions found in this chapter, describe the students on your campus as an imagined audience of your peers. Assume that you have been asked to write a document that will be distributed to all of the students on your campus. What characteristics about that general audience would affect how you write your document?

Generating Ideas | 3

Learning Objectives

3.1 Explain the concept of invention as it applies to writing

3.2 Put into practice strategies and approaches to help get you started in your writing

Before you read this chapter

Where do your ideas come from? When you are given a writing assignment for a class, how do you decide what to write about? How do you select a topic? In your journal or blog, write about how you usually discover your ideas.

3.1 Explain the concept of invention as it applies to writing

The word *invention* typically means the creation of something new, whether it is the creation of a new object or a new idea, and in many ways, this meaning can also apply to invention in terms of writing. However, as it applies to rhetoric and writing, invention can mean more than just making up something new. The idea of invention comes from the rhetorical concept of *inventio*, which pertains to how a speaker or writer discovers the appropriate argument for a situation. In a rhetorical framework, invention is the process a writer uses to figure out what the best response to a situation is. Invention can be thought of as an act of discovery. But in this process of invention, one does not discover by chance or luck. Instead, one examines the situation critically and in detail to determine the best way to engage that situation. In that sense, invention is akin to problem solving.

In his book *Where Good Ideas Come From: The Natural History of Innovation*, Steven Johnson reminds his readers of a scene in the movie *Apollo 13* that depicts an immediate problem for the astronauts onboard the lunar module. They risk poisoning the air with the carbon dioxide they exhale. The "scrubbers" they have that are used to clean the carbon dioxide fit the damaged spacecraft from which they have just escaped, not the lunar module in which they have taken refuge. The engineers back at mission control assemble to solve the problem. In the film, the head of Flight Crew Operations dumps a pile of gear onto the conference table where they are meeting; in the pile are tubes, hoses, canisters, bags, duct tape and other assorted items. In one hand he holds up a scrubber like the ones the astronauts have in the lunar module; with the other he points to the pile of gear and says "We gotta find a way to make this fit into a hole for this using nothing but *that*."

The *Apollo 13* example clearly illustrates how you might think about invention: in a given situation, you have access to a limited set of rhetorical gear, and using that gear, you devise ways to express new or different ways of positioning ourselves in the situation. Invention is not a process of pulling something new from thin air. It is a process of thinking about what the situation provides and allows for, and how to use those resources as best you can. When writing, a writer identifies rhetorical and functional problems that must be solved. Invention, then, is always directed by a situation, but it is also always constrained by that situation. Unlike the *Apollo 13* engineers, writers can and do rely on strategies they bring from other rhetorical situations; however, the original situation will prescribe what can and cannot be brought to the table.

3.2 Put into practice strategies and approaches to help get you started in your writing

Invention Strategies for Getting Started

Sometimes, getting started can be the hardest part of writing. Many college writers put off responding to assignments until an impending deadline leaves them no choice but to start writing. This strategy of self-imposed pressure may force writers to write, but it doesn't always result in finding the best way to respond to an assignment.

Strategies for Invention

Strategy	What You Can Do
Reading	Read to learn about a topic or issue, and read to see other writers' rhetorical choices.
Thinking	Use active, generative thinking tools to generate ideas.
Questioning	Ask questions about your subject or situation, and consider using an established questioning approach to guide you.
Writing	Use various writing invention strategies to generate and organize ideas.
Remembering	Explore your memories, of your own lived experiences and of what you have read and learned.
Wandering	Take time to explore physical and digital places and spaces.
Discussing	Talk with someone about your ideas and your writing situation.
Viewing	Look at various visual texts as a way to spark ideas about a subject or situation.
Dramatizing	Apply the five questions of the dramatic pentad to your writing situation.
Experimenting	Try new approaches and methods you haven't used before to explore your subject and situation.

You can use numerous methods to invent—to stimulate your thinking to locate the best way to respond to a situation. The strategies found in this chapter are designed to help you generate ideas applicable to the situation, hone your ideas, and focus your approaches. They are provided to help you get past the difficulty of starting and get to the act of writing. But these invention strategies go beyond helping to get started; invention should saturate all aspects of your writing and thinking.

Reading

Reading and writing are closely related; learning to be a better writer includes learning to be a better reader. Reading can teach you about subjects, and it can show you the results of other writers' rhetorical choices. Both of these benefits of reading can contribute to invention because they provide avenues for thinking about and developing your own ideas and approaches.

In many ways, digital technologies contribute to the ways that reading assists in invention because how one reads changes in digital environments. Web surfing, for instance, allows for rapid movement between linked texts. Web surfing can provide organic connections between texts that you might not recognize in print reading, leading you to think in new ways about subjects and make connections between subjects that might not have come about through print reading. As an invention strategy, reading is one of the most useful, particularly when you read in dynamic, networked, free-flowing ways about wide ranges of subjects as well as multiple positions regarding any subject.

Invention Strategy 2: Thinking

Thinking is perhaps the most important part of invention, particularly active, generative thinking. When using thinking as an invention strategy, you will often want to start by asking a series of questions. Likewise, you can use a heuristic—a tool designed to systematically help you discover or find ideas—to direct your thinking. A number of writers and educators, like Benjamin Bloom, have developed effective heuristics and approaches to help student writers think about subjects and situations about which they have to write. The heuristic listed here is based on Bloom's but also includes other elements.

A Heuristic to Help Launch Your Thinking

Thinking Approach	What You Can Do
Situate	Think about where your subject or situation fits. What relationships are involved? Who is involved? Where are things located?
Analyze	Look at your subject or situation carefully, as though you were disassembling it to determine how all of the parts work as a whole. Think about where the parts fit and how they work. Think about the details. Think about what the obvious parts are, and then think about what isn't so evident. This kind of analyzing can be useful, in particular, when starting to write classifications, analyses, comparisons and contrasts, definitions, and cause-and-effect documents.
Evaluate	Similar to analyzing, consider the details and parts of a subject or situation, but include a degree of judgment. You can evaluate simply: do I like this? Or you can evaluate with more complexity and detail: why do I like this? No matter the degree of evaluation, the key to evaluative thinking is determining your evaluation criteria and sticking to them. Criteria are the standards you use to measure something. Be certain to apply the criteria in the same way to comparable things you evaluate. Evaluative thinking often works well when you are comparing and contrasting similar or different things and when developing arguments.
Synthesize	To synthesize, you will make connections, bringing ideas together to form more complex ideas. In the invention process, synthesize by thinking about how you can connect your subject or situation to what you already know, to experiences you've had, and to other familiar subjects and situations. Synthesis can also be useful in making connections between ideas, texts, subjects, and situations that are new to you.
Apply	Think about where and how you can apply your ideas to accomplish your purpose. Actively thinking about how you can use your ideas in your writing helps you to formulate approaches and methods.
Comprehend	Carefully review what you understand about the situation or subject, which can help you identify either things you need to explore further or ideas and avenues of inquiry that interest you. This review process can also help you see how what you already understand might lead to new ways of looking at the subject or situation.
Recall	Think about what you remember to recall important details. Recollections can be useful in identifying details that might be useful when writing descriptions, summaries, narrations, or processes. Recalling details requires that you think specifically about what you have observed, and it often helps you develop stronger observation skills.

Invention Strategy 3: Questioning

Asking questions can reveal information, can guide the trajectory of your invention, and can help you establish your invention within a specific situation. For example, you might begin by simply asking, What is my purpose in writing? Once you have a sense of what your purpose might be, consider asking, How can I fulfill that purpose? There are many possible answers to these questions, and you may find that your responses will lead you to new questions. In fact, to get the most out of questioning, you should expect that your questions will lead to more questions.

When you begin asking questions about a subject or situation, you may be uncertain of either where to begin questioning or what direction to follow in questioning. Your questions might be scattered, unconnected, and difficult to follow. You may not yet be certain of what questions you need to ask, which to ask first, or where to locate

Two Useful Approaches to Questioning

Approach	Questions to Ask
Classical rhetoric focuses on three kinds of question: questions regarding purpose, questions regarding topoi (topic categories), and questions regarding stasis.	
Questions of Purpose:	<ul><li>What is my purpose in writing?</li><li>How can I achieve that purpose?</li><li>Do I have multiple purposes?</li><li>What is the relationship between my purpose and my audience?</li><li>How does the situation influence my purpose?</li></ul>
Questions of Topoi (topic categories):	<ul><li>What categories are relevant to this situation (legal, cultural, historical, definitions, comparisons)?</li><li>How can I learn about or research those categories?</li><li>Are there definitions that need to be identified?</li><li>Can the situation and/or subject be divided into parts?</li><li>Are the subject and/or situation comparable to other subjects and situations?</li><li>What relationships should I be aware of (cause and effect, contradictions, consequences)?</li><li>Are there specific circumstances I should account for (possibilities and impossibilities, historic significance, unique moments)?</li><li>Do testimonies contribute to the situation (witnesses, rumors, official statements, documents)?</li></ul>
Questions of Stasis:	<ul><li>Confirmation of facts: Can I confirm and cite what I want to say (e.g., Did he do it?)?</li><li>Establishment of definitions: What terms do I need to understand and what terms do I need to clarify for my audience (e.g., What did he do, and how do I define it?)?</li><li>Qualification of information: Do I need to explain or qualify the condition in which what I want to say is relevant or accurate (e.g., Was what he did justified?)?</li><li>Location of jurisdiction: Is my position a legal position or a cultural position (e.g., Am I making my claim about what he did in the right venue?)?</li></ul>

(Continued)

Approach	Questions to Ask
Rhetorical situation analysis can help you begin by better understanding the situation before you respond to it. Your questioning process should unpack as much as possible about the situation so you can best respond to it. You can develop initiating questions using the ten key aspects of a rhetorical situation.	• What is my *exigency*? • Are there *players* in this situation, and if so, who are they? • What situational *relations* might affect my purpose and approach? • Are there situational *constraints* that might limit my writing? • Where is the situation *located* and where might I locate my response? • Who are the *speakers/writers* who already contribute to the situation? • Who is my *audience* and what do I know about them? • What *genres, media, and methods* are already used in the situation and which might be effective for me to use? • Are there any *institutional or power structures* evident in the situation that I need to account for? • How might my response fit within the situation's *ecology*?

the answers. Consider using any of these series of questions as a starting point, or consider combining parts of these approaches.

Invention Strategy 4: Writing

Writing facilitates thinking by helping you recall, develop, and retain ideas. Writing as invention also allows you to flesh out ideas, to articulate approaches that you might use in your writing, and to generate elements that may contribute to your draft document. Some writing invention strategies involve writing full sentences or complete thoughts, which can help you develop and retain ideas. Some strategies require only that you write single words or short phrases, which can help you generate topics for further exploration and identify key terms or vocabulary that might spark inventive thought.

Invention Strategies that Use Writing

Strategy	What You Can Do
Freewrite	To freewrite, just start writing about a subject to get your ideas out. Write for a set period of time (five or ten minutes, for example) without regard for spelling, grammar, or mechanics. Write about whatever comes to mind regarding the topic. This kind of subject-focused, free-form writing can help you find what you already know and assume about your subject, what you still need to discover, and even what subjects are applicable to the situation in which you write. Freewriting can help you make connections and generate ideas.
Cluster	The clustering technique uses diagrams—most frequently simple circle drawings—to show relationships among pieces of information. To create a cluster, first write the primary subject or purpose of your writing in the middle of a sheet of paper or in the middle of your screen and draw a circle around it. Then add secondary circles around the primary circle that include words or phrases describing what you see as the main issues of the subject. Connect those circles to the primary

The relationship between visuals and writing

The first step of clustering.

Strategy	What You Can Do
	circle by drawing lines between them. Next add more circles around the secondary circles, identifying facts, ideas, examples, and other pertinent information that support or explain the secondary circle to which they are attached. Repeat as often as needed. 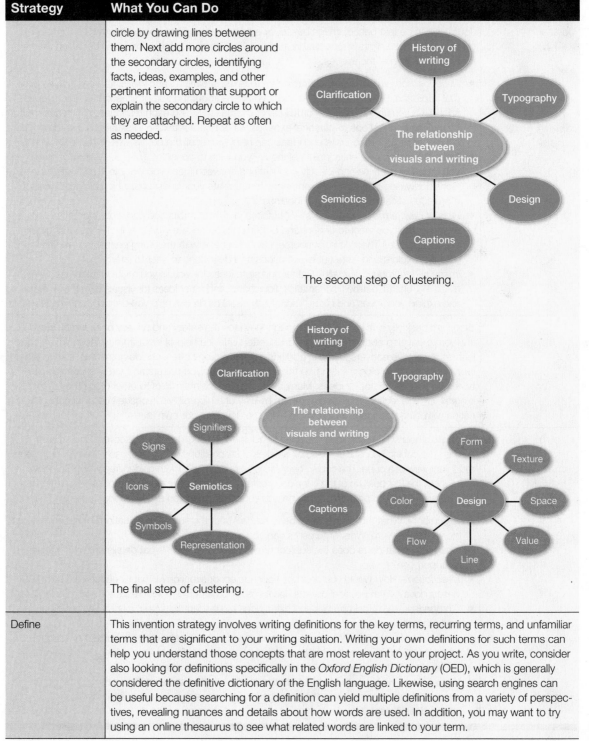 The second step of clustering. The final step of clustering.
Define	This invention strategy involves writing definitions for the key terms, recurring terms, and unfamiliar terms that are significant to your writing situation. Writing your own definitions for such terms can help you understand those concepts that are most relevant to your project. As you write, consider also looking for definitions specifically in the *Oxford English Dictionary* (OED), which is generally considered the definitive dictionary of the English language. Likewise, using search engines can be useful because searching for a definition can yield multiple definitions from a variety of perspectives, revealing nuances and details about how words are used. In addition, you may want to try using an online thesaurus to see what related words are linked to your term.

(Continued)

Strategy	What You Can Do
Journal	Journals can be text based, image based, or a combination. They can be handwritten, written on-screen, or even digitally recorded in audio or video form. For invention, consider using the following four journal techniques: • *Response journals*—Record your reaction to texts, situations, and ideas. You can use an informal approach, writing down any thought you have about the text or situation to which you respond. Or you can establish a formal set of criteria for writing each response. You can respond by making connections to personal experiences or to other texts and situations. Having a journal record of your responses and ideas can help you recall the details when you begin writing. • *Lists of questions*—Identify points of inquiry you wish to consider. These questions can help you organize inquiries and identify connections between ideas you want to investigate further. Consider writing out complete sentences to articulate your questions, which can lead you to more sophisticated analyses and inquiries. • *Lists of new terms and concepts*—Maintain a journal of terms and concepts that are unfamiliar to you or that you want to understand better. (This technique works well with the writing definitions technique.) These lists, of course, should not end with the listing phase; for everything in your list, explore and write out explanations and definitions to refer to later. • *Image and thumbnail journals*—Gather and store ideas for visuals you might want to use. Sketch diagrams, charts, outlines, schematics, flowcharts, and other ideas for visuals to help you recall and explain your ideas and plans. These early visual drafts can help you develop final images later.
Blog	Blogs are basically public journals. Although they lack the safety and privacy of a journal, blogs allow you to develop and work through ideas, often with the help of input from readers, which can lead to generative conversations. In addition, effective blogs often include numerous links to other web pages or other blogs; setting up these links can help you understand the relationships between your ideas and other ideas. Many bloggers also maintain links to other blogs they read—a blogroll. By connecting your blog to others by way of a blogroll, you engage in an indirect conversation with other bloggers, which might help you develop your own ideas.
Cubing	Cubing is a heuristic, a technique designed to guide you through learning, discovery, and problem solving. The cubing heuristic is based on a series of six positions or inquiries, each of which represents a different view of a cube. The cubing heuristic is commonly used with guided freewriting. To begin, write about the first position of the cube and continue to do so until you run out of ideas to write about. Then move to the next position, and so on until you have exhausted all six positions described here. • *Argument*—What arguments have been made about the subject or situation? What arguments do you agree with? What arguments can you make? • *Analysis*—What parts does the subject or situation comprise? What details are most relevant to your purpose? • *Description*—How would you describe your subject or situation? What language best suits your descriptions? What physical objects, locations, or other things might require specific description? • *Comparison*—What similarities and differences are evident between your subject or situation and others? • *Association/Synthesis*—What connections can you make between your subject or situation and others? What particular experiences of yours might relate to your subject or situation? What other texts can help you understand your subject or situation? • *Application*—How can the subject or situation be used to serve your purpose? What other resources can you use within the situation? Where does the subject or situation fit; that is, where does it apply?

Invention Strategy 5: Remembering

Often, your own experiences can help you find ways of inventing. For example, the award-winning Japanese industrial designer Naoto Fukasawa recounts that his memory of peeling potatoes as a child and the edges of a peeled potato influenced how he designed the unique angular shape of the Kyocera W11K cell phone (Figure 3.1).

Contemporary digital technologies have created what can be described as "prosthetic memory." Think for instance about the importance of memory size on your cell phone, your MP3 player, your computer, or your DVR. The more memory a device has, the more it can retain for you. This kind of digital memory allows you to store nearly endless forms of information that you can return to as often as you want. Digital databases and digital morgue files allow you to gather arrays of texts and artifacts that might spark your interest and help you find new ideas.

FIGURE 3.1 Cut potatoes as inspiration for the Kyocera W11K cell phone.

Invention Strategy 6: Wandering

It may surprise you, but just wandering around can spark useful ideas. In fact, some innovation theorists suggest that one of the best ways to get ideas flowing is simply to go for a walk because walking removes you from the task-based activities that can clutter your thinking. Often visiting someplace like a museum, a historical site, or some other location, whether relevant or irrelevant to your writing situation, can help you invent.

Wandering can be physical or digital—such as wandering through your neighborhood, your college campus, cyber environments, or other media environments. Think of wandering as you would exploring, seeking out places that are new to you, sometimes following a path or plan and sometimes bushwhacking and wandering off the trail into the thick of it. College campuses often provide environments rich with opportunities to wander intellectually—and often physically. No matter where you choose to wander, do so with open eyes and curiosity.

Invention Strategy 7: Discussing

Sometimes just talking with someone about your ideas or about a situation can help you begin to develop approaches to take in your writing. Sometimes discussing situations and ideas with someone else invested in the situation can help provide other information, and sometimes discussing the situation or idea with someone unfamiliar with the situation may provide unique perspectives or insight into how to think about and address issues you hadn't considered. Of course, face-to-face conversation isn't always possible. Online discussion boards, chat sessions, and forums can let you engage in conversation with a diverse audience, both familiar and unfamiliar, expert and novice. Familiar communities like those you establish on Facebook, MySpace, or other social media can offer great opportunities for discussing your ideas and learning new ideas.

Invention Strategy 8: Viewing

Often done hand in hand with wandering, just looking at other stuff is one of the best ways to spark ideas about a subject or situation. Watch movies or documentaries; surf through YouTube, Vimeo, or Hulu. You can search the sites for relevant or related subjects. Browse image databases. Commercial image databases like Corbis, Getty, or istock can help you develop ideas about visuals. Getty and Corbis store images of current and historical events, so viewing those images can help you think about specific situations. Visiting exhibits at visual display sites such as museums, galleries, zoological parks, historic sites, or local sites of interest might fuel your thinking and invention.

Invention Strategy 9: Dramatizing

Kenneth Burke, a philosopher, developed a five-phase method for analyzing, which he claimed helps generate ideas. He called his pentad (a group of five things) approach "Dramatizing" because it was inspired by how critics analyze drama. The parts of the pentad are act, scene, agent, agency, and purpose.

- The *act* names what happened, what is happening, or what will happen—in other words, the action.
- The *scene* identifies where the action takes place and refers to the situation and location, including the background and the setting.
- The *agent* identifies the person or type of person who commits the action. Agents perform acts.
- The *agency* names how the agent performs the act. How did the agent act? What were the methods of the agent's action?
- The *purpose* identifies why an agent acts and what the agent expects from the act.

The questions the pentad poses can be summarized with the familiar journalistic questions: What? Where and when? Who? How? Why? But Burke's dramatizing approach is more dynamic than journalistic questions because it is designed to show how these parts function together as a whole (see Figure 3.2). By answering these questions, you can identify what information you have about the situation, where your information is weak, and how the information is connected.

For example, let's imagine that you have been assigned to write an essay about the influence of Nelson Mandela's 1964 speech "An Ideal for Which I Am Prepared to Die" on the fight against apartheid in South Africa. Chances are you will need to conduct research and read the speech and read about the speech. Reading may provide some direction for you to respond to the assignment; however, you will also likely need more ideas for the assignment.

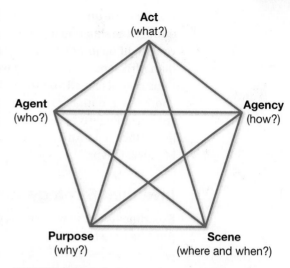

FIGURE 3.2 Burke's pentad approach to invention.

By using Burke's Pentad as a guide, you should be able to start asking questions about the speech, the situation of the speech, and the effects of the speech on the fight against apartheid. Start simply, making certain you have the basic information:

• What is the **act** in this situation?	The speech
• Who is the **agent** delivering the speech?	Nelson Mandela
• What is the **purpose** of the speech?	To take a stand in his trial for sabotage
• What is the **scene** of the speech?	The courtroom of his trial on April 20, 1964
• What is the agent's **agency** in the situation?	He delivers it in English to the court.

Once you have this basic information, you can begin to examine the connections between the various points of the pentad:

- How might the fact that the speech was part of a legal trial affect how Mandela delivered it?
- How did the speech influence people at the time it was given?
- How did it influence those who heard it firsthand, and how did it influence those who heard a recording of it or read it later after the trial?
- How does who Mandela is affect how he gave the speech?
- How does the outcome of the trial affect how the speech was received?
- How does the moment in history affect how the speech was received?
- Why did he give the speech in English rather than Afrikaans?

Each of these questions, based on relationships within the pentad, can help you think through the situation in order to develop your ideas about the situation. For instance, you might be interested in arguing that Mandela gave the speech in English rather than Afrikaans so the speech would influence a larger, global audience. Your questions may also lead you to ask further questions and develop more dynamic ideas about the situation. For example, you might contend that Mandela had to give his speech in English because English was the language of the court and that use of English in the South African court signified the very structure of apartheid against which Mandela fought.

Invention Strategy 10: Experimenting

Experiments test new ideas. As you work to generate ideas or to begin writing, try approaches you haven't tried before. Take chances. The result may not be spectacular, or even successful, but see what happens and then determine its value. Experimentation often works best when you try several new ideas at once, then select the best facets of each experiment and combine them.

Keep in mind that experimenting may involve trying new research approaches, using unfamiliar resources, selecting nontraditional media, writing in genres or forms you usually wouldn't write in, or even using an approach not traditionally used in the situation in which you are participating. That is, experimentation can happen during any phase of your writing.

For example, assume that you have been assigned to write a document about the Great Pacific Garbage Patch, an area in the North Pacific Subtropical Gyre. After you have identified basic information, you might decide that, rather than search your library or the Internet for standard texts about the Garbage Patch, you will read historical narratives from sailors who navigate the North Pacific Subtropical Gyre. You may also opt to watch YouTube videos taken recently by activists and ship captains who traverse the Garbage Patch. You may decide to write to one of the captains you encounter online, asking for further firsthand information. You may decide to construct a working model of the North Pacific Subtropical Gyre to show how the garbage gathers in the gyre. You may try learning more about plastics and floatation, or you may decide to learn more about current and water temperature.

Don't be afraid to fail; instead, learn from your failures and failed experiments. Of course, experimenting with course writing assignments can lead to a different kind of failure that can have real ramifications in your life, so experiment in your generative, inventive phases about new ideas and directions, but be careful about experimenting with your final written projects that are graded unless your instructor encourages you to do so.

Summary

Invention can be thought of as an act of discovery. Invention is always guided and limited by the situation. Sometimes getting started can be the hardest part of writing, and invention strategies, especially the ten kinds of strategies described in this chapter, can help. These strategies can be used alone or in combination with other strategies to generate ideas, make connections, and get to the act of writing.

Chapter Review

1. What is invention?

2. When and where does invention occur?

3. What are some inventive strategies to help you write about a subject within a college course?

Thinking and Writing about the Chapter

Reflection

Now that you have read this chapter about invention, how do you suppose you will work to generate ideas when your teachers give you writing assignments? In your journal or blog, write a follow-up entry to your response to the Initial Thoughts prompt at the beginning of this chapter. Identify how your ideas about invention might now affect your invention practices.

Discussion Threads

In the past, what methods have you used to generate ideas and start writing in response to classroom assignments? What has worked and what hasn't? Does the way you approach writing assignments differ from how you approach starting other writing tasks? Discuss the ways you have gotten started writing in writing situations that you have encountered previously.

Writing

When you hear the word *invention*, what does it most often suggest to you? Do you think of particular inventions or inventors? Often, learning how an invention came to be not only can provide historical insight about that invention but also can show how methods of invention are used by others. Identify an invention that fascinates you: the airplane, the telephone, the flush toilet, or the home computer, for example. Conduct some research about how the invention came to be, paying particular attention to how the process of invention is addre sed in the materials you read. Then write a document that explains what writers can learn from the process of invention attributed to the invention you study.

Local Situation

A number of the invention strategies in this chapter either imply or directly identify invention as being connected to location: places you can wander, places you can view, places where you can have discussions, places where you can read, and so on. Likewise, many campuses around the country now have spaces dedicated to invention and innovation: places like hacker spaces, maker labs, collaboration studios, and other similar locations. Sometimes the locations are just for a campus community, and sometimes they are open to people from local industry or organizations to encourage collaboration between local and campus communities toward invention and innovation. How does your campus encourage invention through its spaces? What locations of your campus do you think of as spaces that encourage invention?

Drafting and Organizing

CHAPTER 4

Learning Objectives

4.1 Analyze the role of drafting in your writing

4.2 Develop strategies for initiating your drafts

4.3 Develop strategies for composing your drafts

4.4 Develop strategies for organizing your writing

Before you read this chapter

What strategies do you use to draft your papers? Do you just start writing at the beginning and end up at the end? In your journal or blog, describe your drafting process; explain how you get to the point of completing a draft you can then revise.

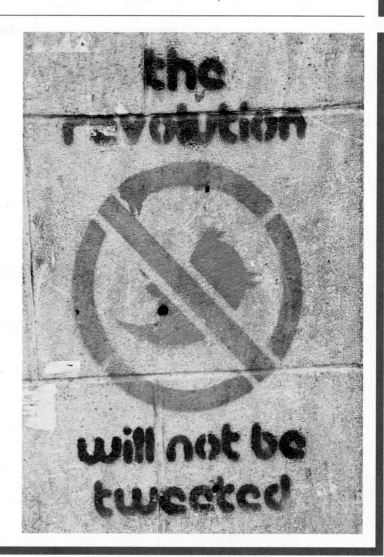

4.1 Analyze the role of drafting in your writing

Drafting is the process of writing the first version (or versions) of your document. For many writers, drafting is a specific, formal part of their writing processes. However, it is often difficult to identify a specific starting point to drafting because writers begin drafting when they first start developing responses and ideas, when they take notes, when they conduct research, and so on. For the purpose of this chapter, though, we will consider drafting as the activities you engage in to develop the first version of the complete document you write.

Organization is the way a writer arranges information within a document to present information coherently. Drafting and organizing are inseparable activities. Often drafting will help you discover more efficient ways to organize your document, and sometimes, organizing your content before you start writing a draft will help you plan how to write it. This chapter looks first at strategies for drafting and then at strategies for organizing, but remember that you'll likely be doing both these composing activities simultaneously.

4.2 Develop strategies for initiating your drafts

Strategies for Drafting

In most writing situations, writers don't sit down to write a draft without having first identified—even tacitly—their reason for participating in the rhetorical situation. Writers have an identifiable exigency and a purpose for writing. That is, they have thought about what it is they want to write and why they want to write. In many ways, then, writers have thought about their drafts before they begin a formal process of drafting. Likewise, drafting is an ongoing process that occurs throughout various stages of writing. So, the strategies found in this section are not intended to provide a linear formula for writing drafts; rather, they are strategies to incorporate throughout your writing process and to adapt to each writing situation.

Getting Started

In those instances where your exigencies are evident and your investment is strong, you may not have any trouble diving into your writing tasks. But in other cases, when you're not as enthused about the task of writing, you may find it difficult to begin writing. Sometimes writing tasks may not excite you. Other times writing tasks can seem daunting, as when you are asked to write five-, ten-, or even twenty-page papers. Fortunately, you can take advantage of the useful strategies in this chapter to work through these feelings and begin to write.

Strategies for Getting Started

Strategy	What You Can Do
Confirm your purpose.	Whether or not you are having trouble beginning, you can better see the task ahead of you by clarifying your purpose. One useful way to begin is to write a single sentence: "My purpose in writing this document is to _____." This sentence can also serve as the basis for your thesis statement or primary claim in your writing. You may not want to use this kind of evident language in your document, but identifying your purpose in a simple, specific statement can help you craft a readable claim.
Analyze your audience.	Your audience strongly determines how and what you will write. So analyze your audience to develop ideas about how you should write to your readers. For example, consider what your audience knows about your topic (or doesn't know), and then think about whether you have to include particular kinds of background information.
Don't wait.	Writers often put off writing until the pressure of deadlines forces them to respond to the assignment. No matter your writing task, begin your drafts early so you will have more time to devote to revising and editing your final drafts. Starting early can also reduce a good deal of the pressure associated with college writing assignments, including dealing with unexpected illness, power outages, corrupt flash drives, Internet crashes, empty printer cartridges, closed computer labs, delays obtaining library resources, and other obstacles. To start, tell yourself that you will begin to do one task for 15 minutes. Usually, you will be drawn into the writing process and will want to continue.
Think small.	If your writing task seems overwhelming, think of it as several smaller tasks instead of one big task. A writing task might seem more manageable if you think of it as five short four-page papers rather than one big twenty-page paper. Thinking in terms of subsections can also aid in organizing your information. Similarly, research might seem less intimidating if you set a goal to locate four resources to begin instead of twenty-five.
Gather information.	Whether through academic research or other means, you should gather all of the information you will need to complete your writing task. If you have started early and broken down your efforts into smaller tasks, then gathering information doesn't have to be a marathon effort. However, don't limit your writing by limiting your research in scope or form; you should look to numerous and different kinds of relevant sources, not just the first ones you locate.
Read.	Read about the subject of your writing so you can begin to focus on the subject and sift through your ideas. Be sure to take thorough notes in a clear, careful manner so you will be able to recall the details when it is time to begin your draft. If your notes are complete enough, you may also be able to transfer your notes directly into the draft.
Discuss.	As part of your efforts to become familiar with your subject, collaborate and discuss with others to help you focus your ideas, spark new ideas, clarify unclear information, and identify gaps in your information. Talking with others, both in person and in online forums, encourages an exchange of questions about the writing situation; answers to these kinds of questions can help you better understand how to construct your document.
List.	List as many ideas about your subject as you can. Don't worry about developing an order of importance; you can organize your ideas later.

(Continued)

Strategy	What You Can Do
Freewrite.	Sometimes just getting writing on paper or onscreen can help you think through the task at hand. Freewriting is an activity in which you begin writing about your subject and continue writing for a designated amount of time—like ten minutes. Write what you know, what you don't know, what you wish you knew, and anything else that comes to mind, just don't stop writing until your allotted time is up. The results of freewriting won't produce a draft, but if you carefully analyze your writing you can identify key ideas and themes that you may want to focus on.
Focus on your interests.	Even if there is just one point you have already decided you want to make in your paper, start there. Get it in writing, and then begin to develop the rest of the document around that point.

Getting It Down

Formal writing, especially college writing, is rarely written linearly, starting at an introduction and ending with a conclusion. Typically, you will draft the body of your text first, then turn to the conclusion and introduction. In fact, it is almost impossible to write your introduction first, because it is difficult to anticipate what you are introducing before you write it. Similarly, as you write, your ideas for what you wish to say in your conclusion may change several times. The exception to this is that for some digital forms of writing used in college—like academic blog posts, e-mails, or research wikis—writers do often write from beginning to end.

4.3 Develop strategies for composing your drafts

Although each kind of document you write will be unique, differing in length, content, form, approach, rhetorical aim, tone, and organization, the general guidelines provided in the following chart can help you write drafts of any document.

Guidelines for Drafting

Guideline	What You Can Do
Draft the body first.	When you draft a document, write the body first, even though it may not be the first part your audience reads. Introductions and conclusions are dependent on what is presented in the body, which is the primary part of your document. It is where you present your research, prove your claim, convince your audience, solve the problem, express yourself, and respond to the situation.
Draft the conclusion.	Surprisingly, after drafting and organizing the body of your document, good practice is to draft the conclusion next before you work on the introduction. Conclusions are influenced by the information provided in the body of a document. A good conclusion accurately supports the document's purpose. The challenge is to carefully select the most effective approach for your conclusion in any particular writing situation: • A summary of the information in the document • Analytical statements about the information in the document • Recommendations about how the audience should respond • A judgment or statement about the information • A restatement of the claim of the document A well-written conclusion both ends the document and draws something from the information in the document. Many effective conclusions end, not by offering closure, but by calling an audience to action.

Guideline	What You Can Do
Draft the introduction.	Write your introduction last. You will not be able to introduce readers to the main points and conclusions of your document until you have written them, so by necessity, the introduction is crafted at the end of the process. The introduction is important because readers usually pay attention to whatever they read first. Strong introductions provide substantial details that clarify the topic as well as excite and entice readers; they can also put your writing in context and give reasons why an audience should be invested in what you have to say. To begin, consider three popular strategies for drafting an introduction: • Start by directly stating your claim or thesis. • Start with a story or anecdote relevant to the document. • Start by asking a question. Your introduction will always depend on the kind of document you are writing and the needs of your audience. The introduction to a psychology research paper will be different from the introduction to a cover letter for a job search, and some genres may not include any formal introductory section. For example, web pages commonly use visual introductions that include only images, bulleted lists, and linked phrases. Despite these differences, most introductions provide similar kinds of information, listed here: • *Objective and Purpose*—Why a document was written and what the document will do. Many introductions include a specific statement of purpose (thesis), for example, "The purpose of this essay is to consider the value of images in contemporary news media." Sometimes a purpose statement may require more than one sentence. Regardless, you'll want to clearly state your main claim or thesis. • *Relevant Information and Background*—Details that help readers understand the context of a document. Relevant background information brings audiences up to speed with the topic and with your document's relevance to the situation. It can also spark readers' interest and point out their own investment in the situation. Further, by providing good background information, you can establish your voice and your ethos, showing that you have a grasp of the situation. • *Key Terms*—Clarification of terms that are pertinent to the situation and that an audience needs to be familiar with to better understand your writing. • *Overview of Organization*—Particularly in longer, more detailed documents, a synopsis of what follows in the document. Consider including an explanation as to why the document is organized as it is, and a summary of key points.
Adjust.	Just because you write something doesn't mean it has to remain permanent. You can rewrite, reword, change your mind, and even delete your writing. Remember: a draft is a process tool; it is neither permanent nor final.

Strategies for Organizing

4.4 Develop strategies for organizing your writing

Organizing your information well can help your readers not only better understand and follow your writing but also easily access the contents of your document. Before you decide on an organization, you should consider these four factors:

- *Purpose*—Your purpose in writing helps guide your organization. For example, you would organize a report for your engineering class about waste disposal differently from an article for the college newspaper about waste disposal because your purposes in writing each document differ.

- *Audience*—An audience's needs might change how you organize a document. When writing for an audience familiar with a situation, for example, you might include basic information only as supplemental information, perhaps in an appendix, or even leave it out altogether. Yet, for an audience not familiar with the situation, you may need to include basic information early in the document.
- *Logic*—You should organize the information in your document along a logical path to lead the audience to your intended conclusion. For example, if you were to take up the position that all undergraduate college students in the United States should be required to take a course that focuses on environmental stewardship, you would need to show readers how such a course would be useful for all majors, how the course would fit into college curricula, and how such a course would affect students' lives after college—and you would need to show the connection between all of these.
- *Ethics*—How you organize your writing can emphasize or deemphasize particular information and, consequently, your organization choices are of ethical significance. For example, if you were writing an essay that compares and contrasts documentaries about fast food consumption, you would need to consider the ethical implications of how you organize the attributes of one film that you like in relation to one you do not.

In addition to these four factors, you will need to consider which organizational strategy best serves the purpose of your document. But try to be flexible since you may need to change strategies as you continue to draft and revise. Keep in mind, too, that sometimes the organizational strategies available to you are constrained by the situation. For example, when assigning a lab report for a biology class, your instructor may dictate how to organize the information in the report. No matter what organizational strategy you use, be sure to make it explicit to your audience. Explained in the following section are organizational strategies that writers commonly use either independently or in hybrid forms that blend several strategies to create the most effective organizational patterns for their documents.

Tips for Thinking about Organization

1. Make your organizational approach explicit.
2. Be consistent in your organization within a given document.
3. Consider how readers will access your document.
4. Organize information in ways that present it ethically.

Organize by Sequence

Arrange information in the order in which it progresses or should progress, moving through information from beginning to end in a linear fashion. For example, in a set of instructions or in a description of a lab experiment, the body of the document would comprise a set of ordered steps for the reader to follow in sequence, one after the other. You can guide readers through sequentially organized information by using numbered lists or transitional markers like *first, second, next, then, followed by, after,* or *finally.*

Follow these tips for using a sequential strategy:

- Use numbered lists to guide readers through a sequence.
- Use transitional words to identify movement through a sequence.
- Use sequence guide words (such as *step, part, phase,* or *segment*) accompanied by an identifier such as a number or a descriptor to guide readers through a sequence—Step One: Telling the Story.
- Use visuals to help clarify a sequence by showing a process or procedure. Use visuals such as bullets and typography shifts to distinguish between parts of a sequence.

Organize by Time

Move your readers through a sequential process that is specifically related to time and the unfolding of events from beginning to end. You can use this strategy for many kinds of reports such as lab reports or accident reports and for narratives. Deciding where to begin and end is important and should be determined based on the requirements of the situation, purpose, and audience.

Also consider using reverse chronological ordering, which works backward through events, beginning with the last thing that happened, and shows how the events unfolded to get to that point. You can often use reverse chronological order to establish exactly why something is tied to the current moment or to emphasize the outcome and pertinence of events to the situation.

Follow these tips for using a chronological or reverse chronological strategy:

- Create a time line to identify the order of events.
- Use transitional words like *next, after, then, following, before, prior, earlier,* and *preceded.*
- Develop a flowchart to map out the events before you write about them.
- Combine chronological ordering with elements of sequential ordering.

Use a Flashback or Flash Forward Organization

Modify a chronological or reverse chronological strategy with either a flashback or a flash forward.

Flashback: Use a flashback to transition back to earlier events, particularly to show relevant events that occur before the events of the main organizational sequence. Flashbacks also allow you to make considerable leaps of time without having to explain all that occurred between events. As a result, flashbacks can add layers of depth that make especially narrative texts (including television and film) unpredictable or exciting; however, they can be distracting or confusing if the reason for the flashback is not clear or if the flashback overtakes the document as the primary focus. Because flashbacks can disrupt the flow of events, limit their use to writing that does not rely on strict chronological sequencing.

Flash forward: Use a flash forward just like a flashback, but instead of transitioning back in time, make a leap into the future to let audiences see results of events yet to come. Flash forwards have the same rhetorical benefits and disadvantages as flashbacks.

Follow these tips to insert flashbacks or flash forwards:

- Include only information readers will need; extraneous information can be distracting.
- Insert flashbacks and flash forwards in places that disrupt the organization least and provide information when and where readers need it.
- Avoid long flashbacks or flash forwards; readers may lose track of the primary organization if the flashback/flash forward is too long.

Organize by Type of Content

Use an approach that organizes content by types of information. This strategy allows readers to access and navigate the document in order to locate information as they need to. For example, the Wikipedia entry about surfing is organized by related concepts that are identified by subtitles that can be easily located and accessed independently, depending upon the type of information a reader requires: *Origins and history*, *Surf waves*, *Surfers and surf culture*, *Maneuvers*, *Common terms*, *Learning to Surf*, *Equipment*, *Famous locations*, and *Dangers*. In this way, the informative approach simply provides objective information instead of leading point by point to a conclusion. Keep in mind that the informative approach is best used when your purpose is not to emphasize, but to provide general information, as you might find in an encyclopedic or data-based type of writing.

Follow these tips for using an informative organizational strategy:

- Insert headings and subheadings as organizational markers.
- When using transition words, be careful not to suggest hierarchical or sequential ranking.
- Focus on providing objective information.

Use an Order-of-Importance Organization

Present information in either increasing or decreasing order of importance, which allows you to emphasize or deemphasize particular points. In an increasing order of importance, for instance, you would begin with the least important pieces of information and move to increasingly important items, ending with the most important item—like building to a crescendo. Placing the most important piece of information last keeps it fresh in your audience's minds when they reach the conclusion.

Use a decreasing order of importance for reports, letters, and many kinds of academic essays. With this strategy, you provide the most important information up front, followed by progressively less important details. This strategy is useful when you want to convey your primary information right away.

Follow these tips for using order-of-importance strategies:

- Use a decreasing-order-of-importance approach when making presentations to ensure that your audience gets the important information up front.
- Use an increasing-order-of-importance strategy if your document has many points; that way, the audience reads the most important information just before the conclusion.

- Consider alerting your audience at the beginning of your document to the order-of-importance strategy you use, for example, "In the following essay, I will first discuss the most critical aspects of water use on campus, followed by other contributing factors."
- Consider, too, explaining to your audience why you present some information as more important than other information.

Use a General/Specific Organization

In this approach, progress either from general to specific information or from specific to general information. Both ways can provide a balance of abstract ideas and concrete details.

Particularly in argumentative or persuasive writing, you may need to present general information before providing specific details so you can provide background and context for the more specific information to come. This approach is derived from deductive reasoning. For example, you might begin a document claiming that despite increased awareness about e-waste, the amount of e-waste is actually increasing. After making this general claim, you would need to provide specific reasons as to why you make the claim: economic development, technological development, and population growth. For each of these, you may need to provide even more specific information:

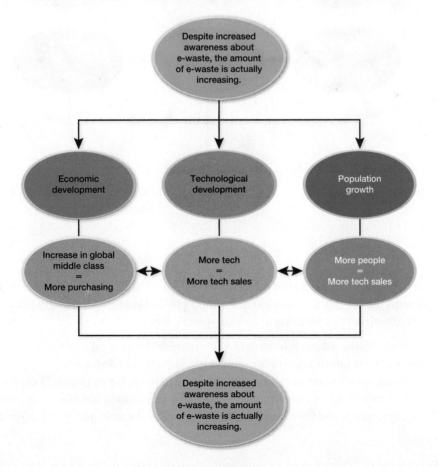

In other situations, such as journalistic writing and blogging, your audience will likely need specific information first, followed by general discussions after they have read the specifics. This strategy derives from inductive reasoning. For example, you could write a similar document about e-waste beginning with specific information and ending with more general information:

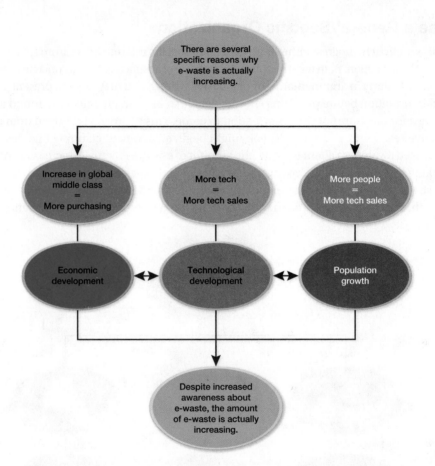

To choose which of these strategies to use, consider this question: do your readers need a general background before they can understand specific information, or do they need the specific information or examples before engaging the larger principles?

Follow these tips for using a general/specific strategy:

- Consider using a flowchart to help you organize the general and specific components of your information before you begin to draft your document.
- Early on, direct your audience through your pattern, for example, "I explain the general principles of water quality, followed by an examination of local water quality approaches, and then describe nine cases of local water quality management."

Organize by Trait

Present your information by dividing—and subdividing—a whole idea, object, or phenomenon into its various components. Division strategies are based on the idea that some things can best be understood by treating them as a collection of smaller parts. This approach is particularly useful in many analytical forms of writing in which writers break a thing—like a text—into its parts. In addition, if you are describing physical things, you can use a division approach to focus on various parts of the whole.

Follow these tips for using division strategies:

- Make sure you understand the relationships among the parts and the ways they come together to make the whole, and be specific and clear in describing, defining, and explaining those relationships to your audience.
- Consider using visuals to show how parts of physical objects come together to make the whole. You can also use visuals to depict relationships between conceptual or abstract parts and wholes.
- Use lists to identify parts.

Use a Classification Organization

Structure your information by grouping or classifying items, ideas, phenomena, or events according to their similarities. Classification strategies often use carefully defined categories to group various items, such as in the way the scientific taxonomy system classifies organisms into kingdom, phylum, class, order, family, genus, and species. You can effectively use classification strategies in documents that present multiple solutions or reach multiple conclusions. For example, in your writing class, you might be asked to write a text that would have a particular effect within a particular rhetorical situation. To do so, you might need to classify types of texts by rhetorical modes in order to determine the best solution to the assignment: should the text be informative, narrative, descriptive, argumentative, or analytical?

Follow these tips for using classification strategies:

- Be sure your classifications are clear and well defined.
- Be sure to explain the rationale for using the classifications you create.
- Present your classifications in a logical order.
- Create parallel structures among your classifications; that is, label each category in the same way, perhaps all nouns or maybe all action statements, for example.
- Be sure to cover everything in a classification; don't leave anything out.
- Use keywords or key phrases to identify the classifications.

Use a Cause-and-Effect Organization

Organizing your information in terms of cause and effect will focus on the relationships between events or the reasons that something has happened or will happen. In a history class, you might be asked to explain the cause and effect of a historical moment. In a science class, you might be asked to describe the cause and effect of a reaction. In your civic or work lives, you might need to explain the cause and effect of a new policy.

The tricky part about this strategy is that it can be difficult to prove that certain causes do or did indeed lead to certain effects. More often than not, then, your reporting of causes is really a reporting of possible causes.

There are two primary ways to organize using a cause-and-effect strategy. In the first, you report all of the information about the cause or causes followed by all of the information about the effects—or the reverse, explaining effects and then their causes. In the second way, you address causes and effects in tandem, working through one particular cause and effect, then another, and so on.

Follow these tips for using cause-and-effect strategies:

- Be sure that your readers do not have to make leaps of faith to accept the causal relationship.
- Be sure to use evidence of cause and effect that serves your purpose and supports your conclusion. Extraneous cause-and-effect explanations may distract your audience from the point you wish to make. However, do not omit key evidence just to strengthen your point.
- Particularly when you cannot address all causes and effects related to the situation, use evidence that represents more general data or an overview of the causes and effects.
- Use only plausible data that your readers will accept.
- Don't try to force or stretch relationships between causes and effects.
- Consider using visuals like charts or diagrams to aid in organizing your information and to *show* relations between causes and effects.

Use a Comparison-and-Contrast Organization

You can use a comparison-and-contrast approach to show readers how items, ideas, texts, and phenomena relate to one another, particularly in terms of similarities and/or differences. Comparison/contrast strategies are particularly useful when presenting multiple solutions to a problem or when analyzing multiple items. To effectively use comparison-and-contrast strategies, you will need to develop criteria by which to assess each item, idea, event, or phenomenon.

There are two primary ways to use the comparison-and-contrast strategy. The first is a comparison or contrast of wholes, in which all of the criteria of the first item are provided and then all of the criteria of the second (and so on). In this approach, for example, if you were writing a movie review that compares two action movies, you might evaluate the first based upon the criteria of realism, visual effects, acting, and story. Then you would evaluate the second film based on these same criteria in the same order in which you presented them for the first movie. The second approach is to compare/contrast each part of a whole, point by point, assessing one criterion, then another, and so on. In this second approach, you may want to examine all of the parts of one item and then all of the parts of another, or you may want to compare and contrast one point from one group with a similar point from the other, switching back and forth between items. Using this strategy for your movie review, you would first evaluate the realism of the first film, followed by the realism of the second film. Then you would follow suit with each of the other criteria, moving between the films, focusing on the criteria as the guiding thread in the review.

The order in which you present criteria and assessments in comparison/contrast has ethical implications because it can influence how your readers assess your presentation, so be aware of the choices that you're making as a writer, in terms of their effectiveness and ethical implications.

Follow these tips for using comparison-and-contrast strategies:

- Consider using visuals like charts and tables to depict comparisons.
- Consider using evaluative language to help guide your audience. For example, instead of saying "the first option has ten advantages," you may want to say "the first option has significantly more advantages."
- Be sure to compare and contrast only relevant elements using only relevant criteria.
- Don't force comparisons or contrasts; make sure they are plausible.

Spatial Organization

Strategies that use spatial organization help readers navigate texts about physical spaces or objects, for example, when describing a place. Spatial organizational strategies work well in conjunction with visuals, but they don't always require them. Written descriptions of a place and related visual representations can characterize large areas—a continent, for example—or can focus on much smaller spaces such as a room. But spatial organization can do more than merely help describe spaces; it can show readers how spaces either affect or are affected by information. For example, a county commission report might be organized by geographic locations, explaining how zoning policies will affect each region. In another example, brochures, web pages, and maps that convey information about your campus may do so by organizing various spaces according to their uses: classroom buildings, dormitories, libraries, laboratories, and so on. You can even use spatial organization to guide readers through a space, emphasizing the space in relation to an event, for instance, describing how two people entered a room, how they moved through the room, and where they ended up, explaining what they did as they moved through the space. In addition, you can use a spatial strategy to guide an audience through a process that uses a particular object or piece of equipment. For instance, a user's manual that instructs someone how to start a lawnmower is likely to show the reader where various controls are located within the space of the mower in order to show the user the process of starting and operating the mower.

Follow these tips for using spatial organizational strategies:

- Clearly show how the space you use to organize your document is relevant to the information you provide.
- Describe only the details of the space that are pertinent to the information you convey.
- In your organization, explicitly indicate connections between the various parts of the space.
- Consider using visuals to indicate subdivisions within larger, more detailed spaces.
- When using visuals, avoid cramming large amounts of spatial data into small visual spaces.
- Clearly label visual representations of space.

Summary

Drafting is the process of writing the first version (or versions) of your document. If you find it difficult to begin writing, use any of the proven strategies that help writers get started. Once you have begun to write, follow the guidelines for drafting a document, which efficiently direct you through what to write, in the appropriate order. As you draft, keep in mind that each document you write will respond to a different situation, and how you organize your information in each situation plays a critical role in how successful and coherent your document will be. Whatever the situation, good organization requires that you be alert to four factors: purpose, audience, logic, and ethics. In addition, you will need to decide which organizational strategy best serves the purpose of your document: sequential, chronological, flashback or flash forward, informative, order of importance, general/specific, division, classification, cause and effect, comparison and contrast, or spatial.

Chapter Review

1. What role does drafting play in your writing?

2. What are three strategies for getting started when writing a draft?

3. What are four strategies for writing drafts?

4. What are six organizational strategies, and for which situations is each useful?

Thinking and Writing about the Chapter

Reflection

The prompt at the beginning of this chapter asks you to describe how you get from a writing assignment to a draft of your response. Reflecting on your response to that prompt, how would you now describe the role of organizational strategies in your drafting process? Write a new entry in the journal or blog that describes how you determine the organizational strategies you use when you write.

Discussion Threads

How do you draft? Discuss the various methods you and your classmates have used in the past to draft documents. Does your drafting process in response to school assignments differ from your drafting policies when you write things outside of class?

Collaboration

In what ways do digital technologies make collaborating on writing drafts more efficient? Working in groups, identify two or three digital technologies that can be used to facilitate collaborative drafting. Then, as a group, write an explanation as to how collaborative drafting works using the technologies you have identified and describe how and why such collaborations might be useful. Include some discussion of how the drafting process may be affected by more than one person contributing to the document.

Writing

1. How has this chapter changed how you plan to approach responding to the next written assignment in your class? Write an explanation to your teacher describing how you now plan to write drafts and organize your writing.

2. Locate an article from an online news source. Analyze the manner in which the article is organized rhetorically, and then write an analytical paper describing the form and function of that organization in the article.

Local Situation

Locate your institution's home page on the World Wide Web. Then write an assessment as to how the web page is organized. Is the organization effective? Could the information be organized any other way?

5 | Revising

Before you read this chapter

How important is revision to your writing process? How do you revise? In your journal or blog, describe how you revise and what role revision plays in your writing.

Learning Objectives

5.1 Explain the importance of revision

5.2 Practice revision as a three-part process that involves identifying, analyzing, and adjusting

5.3 Use effective guidelines in your revision approaches

5.4 Practice specific strategies for revising

Revision is probably the most important part of any writing process. Revising, quite literally, means *re-seeing* or looking at your writing in a new way. All writers revise in one way or another. Take a look at the photograph on the facing page, taken by White House photographer Pete Souza.

President Obama is holding a copy of a speech he made in 2009, which addressed health-care reform. Notice how many changes the president and his speechwriter have made. Sure, the president needs to be exact in his wording, but the attention to revision depicted in this photograph suggests an important point: experienced writers know that revising improves quality and effectiveness.

5.1 Explain the importance of revision

Stages of Revising

No matter when or how you revise, revision is what ultimately shapes your writing into the form that will be read. Your goal when revising is to improve the content, style, organization, and design of documents. You might revise to better fulfill your purpose and reach your audience. You might revise because you have changed how you think about a subject or have learned more about your topic as you researched and drafted. You might revise to improve the readability of your document, to make it clearer and easier for your audience to understand. Revision is in fact a writer's ethical obligation because, by revising, writers confirm accuracy, access, and accountability of their work.

Whatever your goal, when reviewing your work, you will want to look at it as a whole, and you will also want to consider the smaller parts (the paragraphs, sentences, and words). You will want to pay particular attention to what we call the four Cs of revision—clarity, concision, cohesion, and coherence.

5.2 Practice revision as a three-part process that involves identifying, analyzing, and adjusting

- Clarity—Is the work clear, uncomplicated, and easy to understand?
- Concision—Is information presented in as few words as possible without compromising its meaning?
- Cohesion—How well does one sentence stick to the next sentence and how well does one paragraph stick to the next paragraph?
- Coherence—How effectively do the parts of a document work together in order to create a whole text that makes sense to an audience?

You will also want to consider revising for style, tone, accuracy, organizational approaches, clarification of key terms, confirmation of your research, correctness, and visual effectiveness. To simplify things, you can also think of revision as a three-stage process to **identify, analyze,** and **adjust.**

Stages for Revising

Stage	What You Can Do
Identify	Identify what needs to be revised, including inaccuracies and mechanical, grammatical, or structural problems. To identify these kinds of revision points, you will need to be familiar with the rules and conventions of the situation in which you write.
Analyze	Analyze those points of writing you've targeted for revision to determine the best ways to make the revisions.
Adjust	Adjust your writing to reflect the changes you wish to make. You might think of this adjustment as the actual rewriting.

5.3 Use effective guidelines in your revision approaches

Revising Globally

Start revising by looking at your document as a whole, getting an overview of it, and asking yourself revision questions such as these:

- Does the document serve its purpose and its audience?
- Does the document make sense?
- Does the organization of the document efficiently present the information contained in the document?
- Does the style of the document suit the kind of document it is?
- Does the document clearly provide the information it must convey?

Strategies for Re-seeing

You will be able to revise more effectively if you can learn to re-see your own work. It is often easier to recognize problems in the writing of others because you are not as intimately familiar with that work, so every inconsistency or difficulty appears evident to you. In contrast, as you read your own writing, your brain will often perceive what you think the writing should say as opposed to what it actually says. Part of revising effectively requires learning to distance yourself from your own writing so you can read it as your audience might.

Strategies for Re-seeing

Strategy	What You Can Do
Allow time.	Write your draft as early as possible, then set the draft aside for a day or so, or even a week, if you can. The longer you can wait between drafting and revising, the more likely it is you will be able to detect problems and errors.
Read backward.	Reading backward removes the familiarity of the writing's flow, logic, and coherence. For the best results, you should read your writing backward three times. First, read your writing backward going word by word. Words that seem unusual to you, words you typically wouldn't use, or words that seem to repeat often can signal places to examine word choice, repetition, and meaning. Second, read backward sentence by sentence, beginning with the last sentence. Ask yourself about the construction of the sentence: Does it make sense? Is the verb strong? What is the subject of the sentence? Pay careful attention to how that sentence functions as a sentence. Third, read the last paragraph, asking questions about the coherence of the paragraph. Does the paragraph address one theme or does it seem to address multiple themes? Is there a sentence or part of a sentence that states what the theme of the paragraph is? Look for flow between paragraphs and consistency in how you present information.
Change how you see your writing.	If you compose on screen, consider either printing your document to read for revision or changing the font size and color before reading for revision. Another useful approach is to revise the document in an environment different from where you composed it. If you have drafted in your room, consider revising in the library.
Read out loud.	Reading out loud allows you to hear what your sentences say. As you read out loud, you will sense the flow of your writing, and you will naturally focus on clarity, concision, cohesion, and coherence. You can read out loud to yourself, or you can read to someone else, which brings the benefit of another's ears and suggestions.
Use available writing technologies.	Your word processor offers many features, such as track changes and comment, that can help you, but other forms of writing technologies can also aid in your revision process. Online collaborative tools allow you to solicit and receive feedback from multiple readers. Consider posting your writing to a wiki to allow readers to make revision suggestions directly to the document. Wikis encourage a community-based approach to writing and revision.

Revise for Style

When revising, you'll want to look at the style of your writing, that is, the way your writing sounds to your readers. Style can refer to what gives your writing a unique voice and personality, but it can also refer to how your writing fits a particular situation. The style of your blog, for example, will be different from the style of a research paper because each situation makes different kinds of stylistic demands on your writing. Your writing style reflects the choices you make about words, organization, syntactical structure, logic, and complexity of thought.

Before thinking about style revision, you should identify the stylistic choices you have already made. Ask yourself the following questions:

- *Sentence length:* Do you tend to write short or long sentences?
- *Word choice:* Do you tend to use short or long words? Do you use many words where one will do? Do you repeat certain words? Do you tend to use a particular word or phrase a lot?
- *Paragraph length:* Are your paragraphs long and wandering or short and to the point? Are your paragraphs dominated by a single long sentence, or are they composed of numerous shorter sentences?
- *Location of emphasis:* Where in your sentences do you emphasize points? Are your sentences front-loaded with information, or do they hold information until the very end? Where in your paragraphs do you emphasize information?
- *Sentence consistency:* Are your sentences all written in a similar pattern: subject, verb, object? Or do you vary sentence construction?
- *Use of transitions:* Are your transitions smooth and announced, or are they rough, requiring readers to make leaps between blocks of information?

Looking Beyond

An interesting way to learn about how you use words in your writing is to use Wordle, a free web page that generates "word clouds." You cut and paste text into a window and then Wordle creates a word cloud based on the entered text. Words that appear often in the text appear larger in the word cloud, so you get a sense of what kinds of words you tend to rely on in your writing. When you generate a word cloud from your writing, analyze the word cloud for information about your writing. Are the biggest words the main subjects of your writing? If not, consider revising. Do weak or "to be" verbs appear large in the cloud? If so, revise for stronger verbs. Do important concepts appear lost in the cloud? If so, revise to make them more prominent in your writing. Below is a word cloud made from this paragraph that provides you with a visual way to consider the word choice of the paragraph.

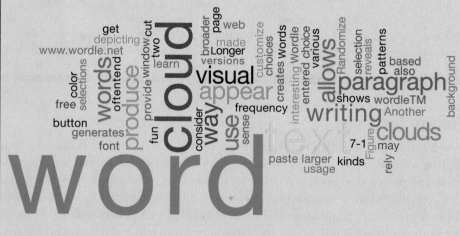

Revise for Tone

Think of tone as the attitude you project in your writing and the level of formality you adopt. A letter of complaint might project anger; a research proposal might project confidence and enthusiasm; a lab report might project neutrality and objectivity. All documents have a tone, and that tone affects how readers react to the documents.

Guidelines for Revising for Tone

Guideline	What You Can Do
Evaluate whether the level of formality is appropriate.	Consider the situation. Is the situation already formal, professional, casual, friendly, or intimate? Match your tone to the situation.
Check for the appropriate emotional connection to readers.	The tone you take with an emotionally invested reader will affect how that reader interprets your writing. For example, if your purpose is to rouse an already angry audience to action, then an aggressive or combative tone may work, but if your purpose is to problem solve or to introduce a new perspective to an angry, frustrated audience, then using a tolerant, calm tone might be a more productive approach.
Determine whether the level of bias is appropriate.	Different situations require different degrees of bias. Situations that require a writer to express a position or opinion—like a book review—are likely to be more tolerant of a writer's bias than a situation that anticipates more objective delivery of information—like a lab report.
Identify whether your piece comes across as positive or negative.	Readers react differently to positive and negative tone. Read your documents carefully to assess whether you are conveying a positive or negative tone, even if subtly. Consider, for example, the difference between word choices like: "you must attend the meeting" and "you should attend the meeting."
Evaluate the sense of confidence you project and what confidence you promote in your readers.	Remember that tone and ethos are connected. A confident tone implies a knowledgeable writer; readers have a difficult time finding confidence in a writer if the writing conveys a nonconfident tone. **Confident:** "The results are, indeed, accurate." **Nonconfident:** "I think the results are accurate."

Revising Locally

After you've reviewed your work for global issues, you'll want to look at it again for possible problems on the local level of paragraphs, sentences, and words.

5.4 Practice specific strategies for revising

Revise for Clarity

Clarity ensures that your writing is not ambiguous and that audiences understand your message as you intend them to. Writers tend to write more clearly when they are comfortable with the situation, understand the conventions of the context, and are familiar with the subject.

Guidelines for Revising for Clarity

Guideline	Comments
Make the subjects of your sentences specific and concrete.	**Unclear:** There was a worry that the instructor would assign an extra reading. **Revision question:** Who worries? **Revision:** The students worried that the instructor would assign an extra reading.
Use pronouns clearly.	**Unclear:** The engineers provided models as long as they were available. **Revision question:** Does *they* refer to the engineers or to the models? **Explanation:** The antecedent of *they* could be either the models or the engineers, giving the sentence different meanings. **Revision:** *They* was probably intended to refer to the models, so the revision could take one of two forms: (Option 1) The engineers provided models as long as the models were available. (Option 2) As long as the models were available, the engineers provided them.
Use modifiers clearly.	**Unclear:** The lab equipment was returned to the factory where it had been developed three years earlier by parcel post. **Revision question:** Does "by parcel post" tell about the manner in which the equipment was shipped or developed? **Explanation:** Because "by parcel post" is not close to what it modifies, the sentence is unclear, and readers may incorrectly interpret it. **Revision:** The lab equipment was returned by parcel post to the factory where it had been developed three years earlier.
Unpack sentences that contain too much information.	**Unclear:** This report provides a critical analysis and summary of all relevant literatures included in the course's extensive research agenda addressing the relationship between images and text throughout history, including specific analysis of various conventions of different periods such as the use of light in Renaissance painting, the use of photography in twentieth-century advertisement, and the use of video in twenty-first-century media. **Revised**: This report analyzes and summarizes the course's relevant literatures. The course addresses the relationship between images and text throughout history. It examines various conventions of different periods such as the use of light in Renaissance painting, the use of photography in twentieth-century advertisement, and the use of video in twenty-first-century media.
Clarify ambiguous statements.	**Unclear:** Recent inaccurate research has created product failures. This problem must be remedied. **Revision question:** Which problem must be remedied: inaccurate research or product failures? **Revision:** (Option 1) Recent inaccurate research has created product failures, which must be remedied. (Option 2) Recent inaccurate research has created product failures and must be remedied.
Change punctuation that causes confusion.	**Unclear:** The office manager files, reports and letters. **Revision:** The office manager files reports and letters.
Compress sentences carefully.	**Unclear:** Meeting at 12:00. **Revision question:** What is the meeting about? Who needs to be there? Where will it be? Why are we having the meeting? **Revision:** There will be a meeting at 12:00 on Wednesday in the conference room to discuss the latest budget prediction. I would like all senior administrators to be there.

Guideline	Comments
Use active and passive voice appropriately.	Active voice is usually clearer and more dynamic than passive voice. Consider the following two sentences: **Passive:** Word processors are used by most writers. **Active:** Most writers use word processors. However, the passive voice is useful in three ways: 1. When the action is stressed above the subject: Four buildings were demolished yesterday. 2. When the subject is unknown or unimportant: A new species of millipede has been discovered. 3. When the writer does not want to name the subject: Innacurate information was reported.
Eliminate numerous modifying nouns.	Often, writers get carried away and use strings of nouns, for example, *annual laboratory committee budget report*, which can become unwieldy and unclear. Try to avoid using too many modifying nouns.

Revise for Concision

The key to concision is cutting out unnecessary words. There are two primary objectives in revising for concision:

- To eliminate unnecessary words—wordiness
- To eliminate unnecessary information—excessiveness

Fortunately, revising for concision works hand in hand with revising for clarity; therefore, much of your revising accomplishes both at the same time.

Guidelines for Revising for Concision

Guideline	What You Can Do
Shrink wordy phrases.	Some inexperienced writers try to make their writing sound more professional by using phrases that they think sound elevated, sophisticated, or experienced. Table 5.1 lists commonly used wordy phrases and ways to revise them for clarity and concision.
Avoid modifiers that don't add meaning.	The following words are often unnecessary: actually really certain various generally very particular virtually practically **With meaningless modifiers:** *Virtually* all students take *certain* courses to meet the requirements of a *particular* major. **Revised:** All students take courses to meet the requirements of a major.
Avoid dummy subjects.	**Wordy:** It was the decision of the instructor that the assignment be revised. **Revision question:** To what does *it* refer? **Revised:** The instructor decided to revise the assignment.

(Continued)

Guideline	What You Can Do
Avoid using words that repeat the meaning of other words.	Here are examples of common redundant word pairs: any and all full and complete basic and fundamental hope and desire each and every various and sundry first and foremost **Wordy:** Each and every student should concentrate first and foremost on the basic and fundamental tasks of the assignment. **Revised:** Each student should concentrate first on the basic tasks of the assignment.
Avoid strings of prepositional phrases.	**Wordy:** The condition *of* the patient was documented *in* the patient profile written *by* the nurse *on* duty *during* the after-hours shift. **Revision:** The after-hours nurse documented the patient's condition in the patient profile.
Avoid nominalizations.	Nominalizations are verbs or other words that have been changed into nouns. **Nominalization:** The student conducted an investigation of peer writing practices. **Revision:** The student investigated peer writing practices.
Avoid too much information at the beginning of sentences.	**Unnecessary information:** In response to your letter of February 28, 2011, that details your complaint, your financial aid forms have been reprocessed. **Revision:** Your financial aid forms have been reprocessed.

Wordy Phrases and Concise Revisions

Wordy Phrase	Concise Revision
at the present time	now
aware of the fact	know
for all intents and purposes	actually
the reason, for the reason that, owing or due to the fact that, in light of the fact, considering the fact that, on the grounds that, this is why	because, since, or why
on the occasion of, in a situation in which, under circumstances in which	when
as regards, in reference to, with regard to, concerning the matter of, where _____ is concerned	about
it is crucial that, it is necessary that, there is a need or necessity for, it is important that, cannot be avoided	must or should
is able to, has the opportunity to, has the capacity for, has the ability to	can
it is possible that, there is a chance that, it could happen that, the possibility exists for	may, might, or could
the majority of	most
prior to	before
readily apparent	obviously or obvious

Revise for Cohesion

Cohesion is how your sentences stick together so a reader moves from one sentence to the next in such a way as to see the connection between the two sentences. The same principle can be applied to the connections between paragraphs. The word *cohesive* is similar to the word *adhesive*, which means a substance that bonds things together. When writing is cohesive, it fits or grows together in a way that helps readers move from one part of the writing to another.

Guidelines for Creating Cohesion

Guideline	Comments
Begin sentences and paragraphs with familiar information.	Readers can ease into a sentence or paragraph if it begins by connecting them to information provided in the preceding sentence or paragraph. Similarly, helping readers connect your information to what they already know can help them follow your points.
End sentences and paragraphs with new information.	Once you have brought readers into sentences and paragraphs with familiar information, introduce them to the new information you need to convey.
Carefully craft the transitions between old and new information.	The trick to cohesion is creating smooth and meaningful transitions between old and new information without becoming repetitive. For example: "I registered for three English classes next semester. I am looking forward to studying more about rhetoric."

Revise for Coherence

Coherence might be thought of in terms of how readers respond to the writing as a whole. Coherence is what makes a piece of writing meaningful—how the parts relate to form the whole in a way that makes sense. That meaning becomes evident when readers see a correspondence among ideas and a sense of continuity. When revising, pay particular attention to the coherence within and among your paragraphs.

Guidelines for Creating Coherence

Guideline	Comments
Confirm that the subjects of each sentence within a paragraph are related.	A subject that does not relate to others in the paragraph is likely to indicate a sentence that is not related to the paragraph's topic. All sentences within a given paragraph should address a common idea or theme.
Confirm that the subjects of beginning and ending sentences in a paragraph focus on the same topic.	By checking that the first and last sentences of the paragraph connect, you ensure focus. Eventually, each of the paragraphs should connect and flow to unify all the ideas into a larger, organized discussion.
Confirm that each paragraph has a topic sentence.	Your audience should be able to locate one sentence in each paragraph that states the general claim of the entire paragraph. On some level, the audience will be relying on these topic sentences to connect ideas and build coherence.

Revise for Correctness

Correctness involves following the rules of a situation so your writing fits that situation in the best way possible. Rules may cover grammar, punctuation, mechanics, language, word choice, and so on. Every situation has its own rules. No single set of rules applies to all situations, and what is deemed correct in one situation may be considered incorrect in another. For example, the various rules of writing you will encounter within academic writing and writing within various professions have been developed to make writing in particular fields more consistent, readable, and efficient.

Revise Your Visuals

First drafts of visuals can be as unclear and inaccurate as first drafts of words, and as you make changes to your text, you may also need to change the visuals to match.

Guidelines for Revising for Visuals

Guideline	Comments
Review your selection of visuals.	During revision you should ask these kinds of questions: • Did I use the right kind of visual? • Would a chart convey the information better than a graph? • Would a photograph be clearer than a line drawing? • Would a line drawing be more dynamic than clip art?
Include final versions of visuals.	When writing longer documents, writers often insert thumbnails or placeholders to identify where a visual will go and what kind of visual will be used. If you choose to use a placeholder for a visual, or even simply leave a gap in the document for one, be certain that the final version of the visual actually appears in the revised document.
Confirm that visuals and text correspond.	Review the discussion of each visual in the running text. Ideally, visuals should be mentioned in the text before they appear in the document. Check to be sure that visuals appear where they are supposed to in the document. Also make sure that any textual references to the visual and any caption accurately describe the final version included in the document.
Check visuals for accuracy and readability.	You should review charts, tables, and figures to confirm that the information they convey is accurate and compatible with the information and data provided in your writing. In addition, make sure that all visuals can be easily read and understood. Include labels and/or legends to explain components of the visual. If your document will be printed in black and white and you have included color visuals, make sure that readers will still be able to distinguish the various colored components in the black-and-white version. Resize, recolor, realign, and redraw visuals as necessary.

Revise for Completeness, Accuracy, and Timeliness

Be on the lookout for missing or deleted text. For example, look for things like references to appendixes that are not included or paragraphs that were accidentally deleted. In addition, you should verify that multiple references to the same concepts, data, or events are all consistent.

Finally, be sure to check for timeliness, that is, how up-to-date the content is, by asking these questions:

• Has the situation changed in any way that might affect your writing?
• Since you began writing your document, have other documents been created that might affect the information you are presenting?

- Have recent events affected your information?
- Are your data still relevant?

Use Peer Evaluation to Revise

Getting audience feedback during your revision process can anticipate and improve audience response to your finished document. Of course, not all readers read the same way, and some readers will likely provide you with more substantial and more useful feedback than others. You can gather useful feedback by guiding the peer review process:

- Ask someone who is qualified to review your writing.
- Don't just seek praise for your writing. Remember that the point of peer review is to help you revise the document; praise points out what you don't need to change, not what you do.
- Provide your reviewer with a final draft. Asking a reviewer to read an early draft can provide useful feedback early in your process, but chances are you are going to make revisions anyway, so you are best served by asking reviewers to provide feedback on the most polished version you have.
- Provide your reviewer with specific questions you'd like for her to answer about your writing.
- Ask your reader to provide her responses in writing and to talk with you about those responses. Having the reader's comments in writing will help you recall the details of the evaluation.
- Provide your peer reviewer with a copy of the document on which she can write. You are likely to find feedback more manageable if the reviewer has a copy of the document into which she can directly embed comments and corrections.
- Be a good reviewer. You should provide the same caliber of attention and professionalism you hope to receive about your writing.

One of the most effective methods for encouraging substantial response from reviewers is to provide your reader with a list of questions to respond to, both general questions and questions that are specific to the situation and to your document. You may also want to ask specific questions about the clarity, concision, coherence, and cohesion of your writing. Peer review questions include asking about:

Initial Reaction

- What are your initial reactions to this document?
- What do you see as the purpose of the document?
- What are the strengths of the document?
- What are the weaknesses of the document?
- Does the writing hold your interest?
- Generally speaking, what is the primary thing the writer must do to improve the document?

Situation

- Who do you understand this document to be written for?
- Does the document fulfill its purpose effectively?
- Has the writer accounted for the audience by explaining all that needs to be explained?

Readability

- Does the title provide an accurate, clear representation of the document?
- Did you understand the document?
- Are there parts that are difficult to follow or understand?
- Does the document provide the information you need to understand?
- Is the document focused?
- Is the organizational strategy sound?

Content

- Does the document make sense?
- Is the document's agenda clear?
- Does the writer provide the necessary information to support the agenda?
- Does the writer present anything particularly interesting?
- Is there unnecessary or extraneous information in the document?

Visuals

- Does the writer use visuals in the document?
- If so, are the visuals appropriate to the purpose?
- Are the visuals clear and easy to read?
- Does the document design distract from or support the document's purpose and/or readability?
- What recommendations regarding visuals do you have for the writer?

Mechanics

- Are there evident mechanical distractions in the document?
- Are there sentences that are unclear?
- Are there sentences or paragraphs that are particularly well written?
- Are all references cited appropriately?

Keep in mind that these are just some general questions that can be asked; you will want to devise questions for your peer editors that are specific to the situation and to the document you ask to be evaluated, and you may have specific questions about the clarity, concision, coherence, and cohesion of your writing.

Another way to strengthen your own revision skills is to offer revision suggestions for others' writing. As you read and respond to someone else's writing, helping them to develop revision strategies, you can also apply what you learn from their rhetorical choices to your own writing. Learning to articulate what should be revised in others' documents will strengthen how you think about, articulate, and adjust your own.

Summary

Revision is probably the most important part of any writing process. Revising refers to *re-seeing* and then modifying your writing to improve the content, style, organization, and design of documents. You might think of revision as a three-stage process in which you identify, analyze, and adjust your writing. The guidelines for revising, especially those that deal with revising for clarity, concision, cohesion, and coherence, are highly integrated; that is, revising for one aspect will improve the others. You should carefully review and revise visuals in your document, as well as the words. You can strengthen your revising skills by soliciting feedback about your writing and by providing feedback to other writers.

Chapter Review

1. Why is revision important?

2. What are the three parts of the revision process?

3. Identify five guidelines to follow when revising.

4. Why is it often difficult for you to revise your own writing?

5. What are three specific strategies you can use to improve your revision?

Thinking and Writing about the Chapter

Reflection

This chapter identifies that revision may be the most important part of one's writing process. With this emphasis on revisions in mind, and given what you have read in this chapter about revision, look back at the blog post or journal entry you wrote in response to the Before you read this chapter prompt at the beginning of this chapter and write a critique of your own process as you described it in that response.

Discussion Threads

Realistically, how much time do you devote to revision? When in your writing processes do you revise? What strategies do you use to revise? In small groups or as a whole class, discuss how you really revise when you have a writing assignment.

Collaboration

As a class, establish working, collaborative groups, possibly using a wiki or other online collaborative software, to help one another in revising your assignments.

Writing

1. How has this chapter affected how you think about revising? Do you plan to adjust how you revise? Write an explanation of what you plan to do differently to revise your response to your next writing assignment.

2. Various digital media have altered how many writers revise. Word processors allow writers to move, mark, and convert large pieces of texts. Collaborative software allows you work with others to revise a single document. Document-sharing mechanisms like Google Docs and Dropbox make it easier to involve others in your revision processes by seeking out feedback from others. Select one or two digital technologies that contribute to revision processes, and write a explanation as to how they work and what they contribute to a writer's ability to revise.

Local Situation

Chances are that in your local community you have seen writing that needs to be revised: advertisements, signs, restaurant menus, brochures, newspapers, and so on. Perhaps the tone is not appropriate for the intended audience/purpose, the word choice is confusing, visuals are not clear, or there is some other problem. Using your digital camera, photograph ten different examples of documents that should be edited. Then use the pictures to write an image essay about the importance of revising.

Thinking, Reading, and Viewing

6 | Thinking

Learning Objectives

6.1 Analyze how you think

6.2 Apply different problem-solving strategies

6.3 Engage in active thinking processes

6.4 Use networked thinking strategies

6.5 Use visual thinking strategies

Before you read this chapter

Do you think differently in different situations? What influences your thinking? In your journal or blog, write about what it means to generate initial thoughts and why initial thoughts might be different from other kinds of thoughts or ways of thinking.

In his best-selling book *Where Good Ideas Come From: The Natural History of Innovation*, Steven Johnson traces the processes and patterns

of innovation that have led to some of the most influential ideas in human history and emphasizes that effective thinking is a dynamic, complex, and interconnected activity.

As an example, Johnson explains how the myth of Charles Darwin "discovering" evolution is far from accurate. Johnson explains that Darwin's "discovery" was in fact based on years of study, teachers' influence, ideas published in other books, years of observation, and being in a location that allowed him to synthesize all of the information he had acquired over years. In fact, Darwin reveals in his own journals that he endured a "mental riot" of information and thought before recognizing the connections that would lead to his theory.

All people have their own kinds of mental riots as they try to make sense of the seemingly chaotic array of information, experiences, and encounters they each grapple with to come up with good ideas. Thinking can be a turbulent activity, but just as writing helps to generate questions and analytical thinking, writing can also help you organize and sharpen your thinking. With ordered approaches, a mental riot can lead to change, connection, clarity, discovery, and innovation. This chapter is about harnessing the power of the mental riot to develop strategies for complex thinking and strong writing in a complex world.

Looking Beyond

Steven Johnson talks about his ideas in *Where Good Ideas Come From* in his 2010 TED talk, which can be found at ted.com. You may also want to watch the RSA Animate version of his talk, which can be found on YouTube.

Traditionally, thinking strategies have been taught in terms of either creative thinking or critical thinking and are often explained as leading from the creative to the critical. For example, when brainstorming, thinkers first think creatively, often in collaborative groups, and write down as many ideas related to the subject as they can. Next, they apply critical thinking to their list, analyzing and evaluating the ideas to filter out those that do not have value for the situation. Figure 6.1 shows how you might visualize this process.

FIGURE 6.1 The process of brainstorming.

FIGURE 6.2 Dynamics of the thinking process.

Of course, this linear model oversimplifies how people actually think. Creative thinking and critical thinking aren't really separable like this model suggests. Thinking is creative and critical at the same time; it is dynamic and complex and rarely a step-by-step process (see Figure 6.2).

One of the reasons that the mental riot seems so chaotic is the abundance of "noise," or unwanted signals. In your daily life, you are bombarded with all kinds of noise: for example, when you conduct an online search, much of the information that appears is useless to you—just information noise. Learning to think in the chaos of the mental riot requires learning to filter out the noise, identifying what information is pertinent within a situation. Filtering noise is a kind of information literacy, which the National Forum on Information Literacy defines as "the ability to know when there is a need for information, to be able to identify, locate, evaluate, and effectively use that information for the issue or problem at hand."

You can learn to shut out the information noise—yours and that of others—by learning particular strategies to guide your thinking. That is, in navigating the mental riot, you can focus your thinking to function logically, solve problems, attain goals, make discoveries, formulate ideas, analyze information, respond to situations, and so on. *Writing Situations* recommends thinking strategies that are most effective within the context of college-level thinking and writing. Within such situations, successful and effective thinkers often rely on five characteristics that help them situate their thinking.

Characteristics of College-Level Thinkers and Writers

Characteristic	Definition	What You Can Do
Modesty	Awareness of what you know and what you don't know	Be willing to acknowledge when you need to learn more—and then take the time to learn.
Wonder	Desire to know and understand	Pursue your intellectual curiosities.
Courage	Willingness to try new things, even if they put at risk what you already know and believe	Let your curiosities take you places you haven't been before. You don't have to embrace what you learn, but fearing change can stagnate your thinking.
Compassion	Awareness of how your thinking affects others	Be sensitive to how concepts, theories, and information can affect the lives of others. Be willing to admit when you are wrong, even if what you are admitting to is rooted in tradition.
Integrity	Conviction and ability to adhere to your principles	Acknowledge and apply intellectual standards and be consistent in your methods. Give ideas fair consideration. Stand in support of ideas you value. Be willing to acknowledge when you are wrong.

For example, let's say you are researching mining practices in the west Amazon and as you do more research, you realize that you are more interested in economic and community pressures that lead to mining rather than the practices themselves. Have the courage to shift your research focus even if it means you need to discard some of your previous work. Be willing to admit you need to find and read different kinds of research sources as you pursue a shifted line of inquiry. Have compassion for the people whose lives and stories inform the statistics and data you uncover. Try to understand pressures on communities even if the decisions they make for their economic well-being seem at odds with your own biases and opinions. Let your research inform your opinions, and then stand behind your argument's central claim by presenting accurate and reasoned evidence.

Intellectual Standards

Writing in college requires that you also write within the expectations of institutional standards. Like any organization or institution, colleges have their own standards for achieving quality, appropriateness, and validity. Because it is difficult to assess someone's thinking directly, colleges examine instead how individuals express their thinking through their research, most often through their writing. Thus, in varying ways, colleges enforce expectations and intellectual standards for academic writers.

Intellectual Standards for College-Level Thinking and Writing

Standard	Definition	What You Can Do
Clarity	Concepts, theories, and information should be expressed in a manner others can understand.	The writer must first understand the idea and its complexities, then decide how to articulate the idea to the audience, and finally execute it in writing.
Accuracy	Concepts, theories, and information should be valid.	Because colleges make, evaluate, and circulate knowledge, every discipline has methods for assuring value and authenticity. Writers should confirm that what they communicate is accurate.
Relevance	Concepts, theories, and information should be pertinent to matters at hand.	Thinking and writing should always explicitly reveal a connection to a specific situation.
Complexity	Concepts, theories, and information should be considered in terms of all parts, intricacies, arrangements, and relationships. Complex does not mean complicated.	Thinkers should ask questions and explore to reveal connections and complexities within concepts, theories, and information.
Range	Concepts, theories, and information should be investigated extensively and from multiple perspectives.	Ask whether you've learned all you can about what you are considering. Examine the issue from all possible directions and weigh other points of view.
Logic	Reasoning should be well-grounded and valid.	Use systematic problem-solving methods. Move from one idea to the next in a consequent or coherent way. Explain theories or information rationally so your audience can follow your thinking.
Ethics	Concepts, theories, and information should be considered thoroughly without influence of personal gain, preference, or objectives.	Recognize and admit your bias when thinking about theories or information. Avoid limiting what you are willing to consider or advance.

In many academic fields researchers may violate intellectual standards for a number of reasons, including pressure to provide results in return for funding, career pressure to meet institutional research requirements, or pressure to reach results quickly and easily. Student writers face similar kinds of pressures in the academic atmosphere: pressure caused by limited time, the fear of failure, and the ease of cheating. However, most students and faculty adhere to these standards as an ethical imperative. A researcher, for example, who studies Near Earth Objects (NEOs), strives to uncover detailed, relevant, and accurate information that she can present to her peers and others in the field clearly. She is likely to provide many perspectives explaining her methods and findings, and she is likely to show the connections between those perspectives and her information. She will deliver her information to the academic community in a sequence that makes sense and that her readers will follow easily. And she does all of this without compromising her work through the influence of her institution, the corporation that funds her research grants, or her desire to succeed in the field.

Logic and Logical Fallacies

Simply put, logic refers to using well-grounded and valid reasoning. Logic and reasoning help you think through and articulate connections. Effective reasoning requires three significant parts to function: a claim, evidence, and a conclusion. A claim is the thinker's position on an issue, and a claim requires evidence to support it. Without evidence, a claim is merely an assertion that is unfounded or unproven. Conclusions summarize not only the connections between a claim and its evidence but also the validation of the claim. Figure 6.3 shows this relationship.

Logical fallacies are flaws in reasoning that lead to inaccurate and illogical conclusions. Logical fallacies can be deceptive because they seem to follow a logical order of thinking and, thus, can be used convincingly to persuade and argue. However, fallacies are generally considered to be incorrect thinking that misleads the audience. A partial list of common fallacies, with examples, is below.

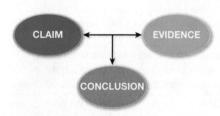

FIGURE 6.3 The interaction of claim, evidence, and conclusion in reasoning.

Common Logical Fallacies

Fallacy	Explanation	Example
Ad hominem	Literally means "against the man"—argues against the character of a person rather than the substance of the situation and the topic of the argument	We should discount what Steve Forbes says about the economy because he's already rich.
Ad populum	Literally means "appeal to the people"—appeals to an audience's general sense of grand positives—like patriotism or a religion—or to grand negatives—like terrorism—instead of to the specific subject of the argument	If you really wanted to end terrorism, you'd support our efforts to allow only Made in the USA products to be sold at the fund raiser.

Fallacy	Explanation	Example
Circular reasoning	Attempts to support the claim by restating the claim in a different way or assuming that the reason for the claim is implicit in the claim	Henrik Ibsen uses the duck in his play *The Wild Duck* as symbolism by using the duck to symbolize traits of the various characters in the play.
Either/or reasoning	Oversimplifies and reduces a claim by implying that there can be only two positions in the argument	We either continue drilling for oil in the Gulf of Mexico and in Alaska or we increase our reliance on foreign oil.
False analogy	Assumes because a comparison of two things results in a conclusion, that the conclusion can also be applied to other things	Restaurant A and Restaurant B have great food. Restaurant A is expensive. Restaurant B, therefore, will be expensive, too.
Fallacy of origin (or genetic fallacy)	Assumes that where something is from—like a person, an idea, or a thing—allows one to infer things about its characteristics	That toy was made in China; it must be defective.
Hasty generalization	Presents inadequate evidence and an unsupported, generalized conclusion, a typical component of prejudice.	My sister is a lousy driver, so all women are bad drivers.
Misleading authority	Relies on evidence from one or few authorities, despite authoritative evidence to the contrary	Dr. Alan Stanwyk of the Morton Salt Institute shows us that regular ingestion of substantial amounts of sodium chloride is beneficial to human development.
Oversimplification	Provides easy answers to complex problems and little evidence; usually relies on appeals to emotion to counter the lack of substantial evidence	Taxation is theft.
Post hoc ergo propter hoc	Literally means "after this, therefore because of this"—assumes something is the cause of something else because it happened first	A student purchases a new laptop at the beginning of the school year. Mid-semester, the student installs a software application borrowed from her roommate. The laptop crashes. The student blames the software for the crash.
Red herring	Tries to distract and divert an audience away from the real issue at hand by introducing an irrelevant point	I know I forgot to stop by the store, but nothing I do pleases you.
Slippery slope	Shows how a small event leads to a series of events that are then identified as an inevitable cause	The college should stop adding to the required student fees; soon they will be asking for us to pay thousands of dollars in fees beyond our tuition.
Straw man	Makes claims against an easy target so as to appear strong and convincing	Hippies want the country to fall apart.

Problem Solving

Problem solving is a way of thinking that uses discovery, analysis, and evaluation to arrive at solutions. Thinking, reasoning, and logic are all part of problem solving, and problem solving is always tied to a specific situation. Most problem-solving strategies comprise multiple steps for thinking through a problem that typically include the following parts:

Steps for Thinking Through a Problem

1	**Identify the problem.**	To solve a problem, one must know what the problem is. In many instances, people react only to the *result* of a problem, but any solution will depend on identifying the *source* of the problem.
2	**Analyze, evaluate, and define the problem.**	Once a problem is identified, it needs to be understood through careful analysis and evaluation to define precisely what must be solved.
3	**Organize information.**	Before locating or implementing any solution, you have to organize all you know about the problem.
4	**Form a strategy.**	The organized information obtained from analyzing, evaluating, and defining a problem is then used to develop a strategy to solve the problem.
5	**Account for and distribute resources.**	As you consider viable strategies, consider what resources you have available to solve the problem and how you will distribute those resources in the most effective way.
6	**Evaluate the results.**	Review what you found out in the above steps and determine whether it will solve the problem.

All writing solves problems, and all writers must consider two different kinds of problems when they write. First, writers must understand their document's purpose or the problem their document should solve. Second, writers must make decisions about how to organize their document and what evidence to include—as well as how to solve other rhetorical problems. Writers solve all writing problems by making choices and by determining what best solves each specific problem.

The following chart explains ten of the most common strategies for carefully thinking through and solving different kinds of problems.

Strategies for Problem Solving

Strategy	What You Can Do	Example
Abstraction	Test solutions on a model of the problem before applying the solution to the actual situation.	Students in the coastal and oceanographic engineering program tested their offshore oil recovery strategies several times in the simulation lab to refine their processes before implementing their process in the local reservoir.
Analogy	Apply a solution to the problem that worked on an equivalent problem.	When Abby's computer stopped working last year, the people at the help desk told her to turn off and restart her computer. The process worked, so this year when her phone stopped working she tried the same thing to see if it would fix the phone.
Brainstorming	First, think creatively and generate as many ideas as you can; then think critically about the list to filter out ideas that do not have value.	As co-treasurers of their dance club, Adrian and Jonathan were responsible for organizing two fundraising events during the semester. Together they made a list of 25 events that other clubs on campus had used to raise money and ten that had not been used before. Then they eliminated those ideas that had not generated very much money.
Division	Dissect complex problems into smaller, more manageable parts to identify a solution to the whole problem.	The professor in Reina's digital architecture course made an assignment asking students to use a computer-aided design program to develop three feasible yet distinct designs for a single, limited space. Reina approached the problem by dividing the problem into several parts: the current use of the space, the possibility for altering the current design of the space, the possibility of what the space could be used for, and the possibility of how to use the software to design the space.
Hypotheses	Test possible solutions, disproving them or proving them effective until the preferred solution is found.	Bao Yu's quantitative analysis project in her cellular engineering laboratory did not match the results of her lab partner. She considered five points in her analysis process that might have led to her error. She repeated the analysis five times, altering the process at those five points, until she identified that flaw and successfully completed her project.

(Continued)

Strategy	What You Can Do	Example
Means to ends	Use different strategies at different stages of the process, solving smaller, embedded problems first and using those solutions to then help solve the larger problem.	Dalia was working at the university computing help desk when she and her coworkers started receiving calls about the university web mail system not working. Because the web mail system works with several other embedded systems, Dalia decided to check each of the subsystems for any errors that might be responsible for the larger system flaw.
Synthesis	Develop new approaches to finding solutions by bringing together parts from different wholes or locations that were originally not connected.	For his project in an augmented-reality programming course, Sean hoped to design an application that could use a mobile phone's camera to capture images of birds and then identify what kind of bird was in the picture. In order to do so, he used visual-recognition designs he had developed in a cognitive engineering course, lens functions he learned about in a course about optics, and programming skills he had developed in his computer science major.
Proof	Find evidence that either confirms that the problem cannot be solved or that supports potential solutions.	For his final research paper, Jakob decided to write about natural language processing in artificial intelligence. Because the subject is often considered an "unsolvable problem," Jakob chose to prove why the problem would remain unsolvable and provided evidence that supported his claim.
Research	Use the research that is already available from solving similar or previous problems.	Emi is an art and art history major. Her favorite class is Digital Media in Art Education. Emi plans to be an art teacher when she graduates and she is interested in using digital tools to teach art. For her final paper in the digital media course, Emi wanted to learn more about how digital media could be used to teach not only art appreciation, art criticism, and histories of art but also production methods for nondigital forms, as well. Emi located four books and seven scholarly journal articles that supported her position and offered methods for such teaching approaches.
Trial and error	Keep trying different solutions until you find the one that works.	Luke was attempting his first digital animation for his course in digital animation. He was frustrated because after several weeks of work, he still could not get the sound and the mouth movements of his characters to align. Luke watched six different online tutorials, each offering a different solution to his problem and read several blog and chatroom posts about the alignment issue. He then began trying different recommended solutions until he found the one that solved his alignment problem.

Active Thinking

Active thinkers analyze, organize, interpret, and challenge information that they take in. They embrace their uncertainty and acknowledge that they can always learn more about something. Active thinkers are humble thinkers; they crave further explanation and aren't presumptuous about what they do know. They don't take things at face value, and they use specific methods to understand more thoroughly.

This form of thinking is grounded in ideas of problem solving and decision making. Writing that also has the aim of proposing solutions to problems includes editorials, political- or social justice–themed blogs, memos, proposals, white papers, or presentations. Active thinking seeks solutions, which requires the thinker to get involved. Active thinking strategies involve the writer asking lots of questions to gather information that can lead to potential solutions to problems or to innovative ideas. The following chart includes several strategies to stimulate active thinking.

Strategies to Stimulate Active Thinking

Strategy	Questions to Ask About the Situation, Problem, or Idea	Example
Consider prior knowledge.	What do I already know? Have I already encountered something similar? What assumptions or value judgments have I already made? What do others already know?	Max's second film course included a semester-long assignment in which he had to write an analysis of three films using a social perspective. Max began thinking about the project by considering what he had previously studied about the economic implications of cinema.
Ask questions and avoid settling for easy answers.	What kinds of questions should I ask to better understand the problem? What do we understand as the causes or consequences? Who has been defining the problem? What investment does each stakeholder have?	Lydia's ecology professor assigned the class the task of evaluating water quality standards as they relate to both human and nonhuman species. Lydia began thinking about the assignment by asking "who has the power to establish water quality standards?" Learning that there are numerous water quality standards imposed by a range of organizations, Lydia began inquiring as to why standards vary and how each organization determines its own standards.
Don't plan your response while you are listening; instead, concentrate on what is being said.	What is the main idea of what is being said? What points does the speaker seem to want me to take away? What points seem most important to me?	Mia was listening to her professor explain details of the class' next assignment. The professor explained not only the requirements of the assignment, but many of the possible avenues of research students should consider. Mia noticed that many of her classmates were writing notes about how they would answer the research questions the professor posed. Mia, though, thought it would be more useful to hear all of the details the professor was providing rather than try to begin answering the questions before understanding the details.

(Continued)

Strategy	Questions to Ask About the Situation, Problem, or Idea	Example
Anticipate outcomes and results.	What will this information explain? What could happen next if the problem is solved in a particular way? What could happen next if the problem is not solved? Who will benefit from this information?	In his business course, Dmitri was assigned to write a business plan for opening a retail store in a small suburban strip mall. Dmitri's plan anticipated what might happen if he opened a sports memorabilia store. He accounted for licensing, space rental, overhead, personnel, inventory, taxes, and advertising. However, he did not anticipate the effect of placing the store in the particular location the professor had denoted and overlooked the fact that a sports memorabilia store might be seen as selling luxury items beyond the economic means of the local community.
Evaluate information.	What is the most significant idea here? What information is extraneous or less important? What events contribute to the situation, problem, or idea? What is new in this situation—and what is familiar?	An assignment in Laura's marine biology class asked each student to monitor government agencies for updates about new policies that might affect local marine environments and people who use those environments. Laura found a proposed law in New Hampshire that would ban recreational fishermen from using lead jigs because fisheries management officials had determined that lead jigs had been responsible for the death of a number of loons in the state. Laura needed to figure out exactly how this proposed law would affect saltwater anglers in that state. She needed to know what the law actually said, whether it was being supported or not, and what effects the law would have on saltwater fishermen rather than freshwater fishermen.
Synthesize by connecting what you learn with what you already know, as well as with other ideas.	Have I heard similar discussions or seen similar ideas before? What have others said about this? What connections does this idea reveal? What other situations are connected to this one?	Santiago saw that Dennis Hong, the world-renowned robotics engineer, would be speaking about robotics during a conference at Santiago's school. Santiago listened to Hong's talk and was interested in Hong's concept of "passive dynamic locomotion." Santiago's own robotics professor had talked about the difficulties of locomotion and passive dynamics. Santiago thought about what his professor had said and what Hong at said about the subject and what he had read about locomotion and began to better understand how he might write about passive dynamic locomotion by bringing all of these perspectives together.
Identify new ideas that emerge from situations or problems, looking for unexplored avenues of inquiry.	How might I restate the problem or idea to gain a different perspective? What will I reveal if I think about the problem in a different context? What can I learn if I reverse engineer the idea to identify how it emerged and what parts it is made of?	Travis's environmental policy professor had been talking about declining fish populations in the Northern Atlantic and the restrictions that had been imposed upon New England commercial fishermen in an attempt to release some of the pressure placed on the fisheries, particularly cod and swordfish populations. Travis thought a lot about the situation and began to think about the boats the fishermen used and the cost of running such a boat, the government-funded loans like house mortgages people took out to buy the boats, and the policies surrounding boat loans. Travis began to think that discussing environmental policy required thinking about a lot of other kinds of policies that weren't being talked about in environmental policy situations.

Strategy	Questions to Ask About the Situation, Problem, or Idea	Example
Draw conclusions, and don't stop looking for solutions or give up until you find them.	Is my solution feasible? Can I justify my solution? Is my conclusion really a conclusion or just a stopgap? Will this information or approach suffice, or is there a better solution?	Cassie's research assignment required that she conduct a survey of patients at a local medical clinic about the way the patients used the clinic's medical history form to explain their current medical issues. Cassie also surveyed the doctors at the clinic to see how they interpreted the forms. Cassie's initial surveys showed that the doctors and the patients tended to think about the medical history forms differently, and Cassie began to conclude that the forms served little purpose because of these differences, but she could not reach such a conclusion until she identified the specific differences between patient use of the form and doctor use of the form and until she could clearly show the result of this discrepancy.

Networked Thinking

6.4 Use networked thinking strategies

Writers participate in rhetorical ecosystems; that is, they make complex connections within a situation and across other situations, just as biological ecosystems are complex networks of plant, animal, mineral, and climate relationships. Rhetorical ecology takes into account the complex relationships between a writer or speaker and a situation, including the intricate and endless networks in which they connect. Writers think in a networked way that acknowledges the potential of connection and relationship.

Traditional thinking methods and problem-solving techniques have used linear approaches, moving directly from problem to solution. But networked thinking acknowledges that networks do not support such straight lines. Networks don't have starting and stopping points; they don't remain still long enough to develop such characteristics. Rather, networks are dynamic and complex.

Through networked thinking, then, writers and thinkers embrace the complexity and emergence of networks as pathways to answers. Six primary characteristics of networked thinking stand out.

Characteristics of Networked Thinking

Characteristic	Definition	What You Can Do
Adaptability	The ability to adjust as the situation adjusts.	Adapt your ideas and solutions to changing situations and expanding knowledge. As you learn more, your ideas and solutions to problems should also change.
Emergence	The identification of information new to a situation and the ability to recognize its role in the situation and relationship to previous information in the situation.	Be open to and recognize new ideas that emerge as theories and information within the network change. Draw connections between old and new information.

(Continued)

Characteristic	Definition	What You Can Do
Circulation	Networks need their parts to flow; information, ideas, images, concepts need to be shared. Information that does not circulate dies; when none of a network circulates, the network dies.	Share and circulate new ideas, solutions, approaches, and so on.
Resilience	Networks can handle the stress of many approaches to a single outcome.	Understand there is more than one pathway to achieving a goal. As a result, if an obstacle severs your pathway, look for other pathways within the network.
Contribution	Where you are situated within a network is of less importance than what you contribute within it.	What you bring to the situation is new; what you contribute to the situation helps invigorate the situation and the ecologies in which the situation participates.
Diversity	Networked thinking requires openness to different kinds of thinking.	Welcome a diverse spectrum of ideas and experiences when working toward a solution.

Networked thinking contributes directly to participation, to seeing oneself as part of a network rather than as independent of a network. In terms of writing, this dynamic is particularly important because networked thinking helps writers connect their expressions within a situation rather than state them as removed from that situation. For example, when Travis spoke with his environmental policy professor about his ideas regarding other policies, like federal loan policies, affecting the situation of the New England commercial fishermen and declining fish stocks, his professor was intrigued by Travis's ideas and approved the subject for Travis's final paper in the class. Travis knew that to begin making his case, he would first have to learn about the boating industry, the boat loan industry, and the federal regulations surrounding both. He had not planned on learning about money lending when he enrolled in the course, but now he had to adjust to the needs of his project. As he adapted his research to this change, Travis began to learn that many of the captains that fish the area of the North Atlantic in question don't actually own the boats but either lease them from larger companies or work for companies who own the boats. As part of his research, Travis emailed and called a number of captains, boat owners, and loan officers to learn more from them. As he discussed his ideas with them, they provided different insights and thoughts about the situation. Many of the people he spoke with suggested other people he should speak with, too, and soon a number of captains and boat owners were talking amongst themselves about Travis's project, often then contacting Travis to share what they had learned. Despite their interest, though, few of the captains or boat owners were willing to provide Travis with actual numbers regarding boat costs and interest rates they were paying; many saw this as private information. So Travis began looking at bank lending rates and advertised boat prices to establish general figures. By the time Travis submitted his final report to his professor he had concluded that rising interest rates and other increasing costs to boat owners forced the captains to search larger areas of the North Atlantic for more fish in order to meet the economic demands placed on owners by federal loan policy.

Strategies to Stimulate Networked Thinking

Strategy	What You Can Do
Embrace complexity.	Innovative ideas emerge in a rich and diverse environments and networked thinking requires engagement with complex ideas. To embrace complexity, stop looking for a specific answer to a problem. Instead, recognize that every question leads to an array of other possible questions.
Understand the network.	Any network has some degree of organization and structure. Learn all you can about the relationships within the situation in which you work. Learn which paths are most likely to lead you to the most useful connections.
Develop network literacy.	Network literacy refers to more than just learning how to use the tools of a network (e.g., a computer or smartphone). Instead, network literacy refers to learning how people read, write, communicate, participate, and think within a network. Strive to use the information within a network—not just learn how to locate it.
Collaborate.	No degree of individual exploration, mapping, or analysis can reveal all that a given network has to offer; collaboration is critical to networked thinking. Network with others about ideas, information, and solutions to connect others' views of the network with your own—and provide all collaborators with expanded and diverse views.

Visual Thinking

6.5 Use visual thinking strategies

The approaches to developing more complex critical thinking skills addressed thus far in the chapter focus on verbal thinking. However, other extremely effective forms of thinking such as visual thinking rely on nonverbal thinking strategies. There is some debate about whether some people think predominantly in visuals and some think mostly in language; most likely, people think in a combination of ways.

Visual thinking is an approach that uses images and visuals to think through complex issues, solve problems, and communicate. Visual thinkers are not necessarily artists who draw, paint, or otherwise create works of art to communicate visually. Instead, visual thinking is a way of letting you take information out of your head so you can look at it, analyze it, and alter it. Visualizing can make complex ideas manageable. Given that we now live in a visual culture in which information is transmitted and circulated through images, learning to think visually is an important skill.

When you think visually, you create three kinds of representations—metaphors, models, and mindmaps.

Three Kinds of Visual Representations

Type	Definition	Example
Metaphors	Visual metaphors represent something by associating a concept with the thing. For example, a map is not an exact visual representation of a place; it is a visual metaphor that represents that place.	
Models	A visual model shows how something works or what it might look like. Visual models can take many forms ranging from sketches to three-dimensional structures to working simulations. Visual models represent conceptual information, not quantitative data.	
Mindmaps	A mindmap is a type of diagram that outlines and organizes information. Mindmaps usually map information radiating out from a central word or concept written on a page and identify connections between ideas.	

The following chart shows strategies you can use to stimulate visual thinking.

Strategies to Stimulate Visual Thinking

Strategy	What You Can Do	Example
Create a sketch.	Sketching is a method for getting ideas on paper quickly, generating variations, identifying connections, and exploring possibilities. Sketch in a notebook, on a scrap of paper, on a napkin, or in digital applications on smartphones or tablets.	
Take a photo excursion.	A photo excursion involves photographing examples of how others have addressed a problem or an idea. Take notes in conjunction with your photos to help you to recall what related thoughts you had at the time. This is a good strategy when you can find physical examples of your subject, but not when you are trying to conceptualize abstract information. The excursion should stimulate your thinking about a problem as you examine how others addressed it.	
Create a model through object simulation.	Object simulation makes a model of a thing as a way to study it more closely, and it is most often used with things you can't easily examine in their physical form. Space exploration, architecture, anthropology, and archaeology often use object simulation. Three-dimensional printing and software applications that create virtual-reality environments have enhanced the capacity for object simulation.	
Create a visual map.	Start at the middle of a page and write the primary problem you wish to explore. Around the main subject, write categories of subtopics that contribute to how you think about the primary topic. Connect subtopics with the main topic using arrows. Repeat the process for the subtopics. Visual maps are effective because they do not rely on linear thinking but can move in many directions.	
Make an evidence board.	Detectives in TV dramas often use evidence boards to help them think through complex cases. They stay focused on the problem, see pieces of information, and imagine connections. Place anything you need to represent various pieces of evidence—such as pictures or note cards—on a large surface like a bulletin board or a wall, using string to connect pieces of evidence. Or use a digital application.	

Summary

Thinking is critical and creative at the same time, and it is rarely a step-by-step process. Effective thinking is a dynamic, complex, and interconnected activity that can lead to change, connection, clarity, discovery, and innovation. One challenge in thinking is to filter out the inevitable "noise," or distractions that are not pertinent within a situation. Within the context of college-level thinking and writing, successful and effective thinkers display five characteristics that help them situate their thinking: modesty, wonder, courage, compassion, and integrity. Universities and colleges enforce a set of intellectual standards for writing, and indirectly for thinking, that all college writers should understand and adhere to. These standards address expectations for clarity, accuracy, relevance, complexity, range, logic, and ethics. Logic and problem solving are integral parts of all thinking. Logic refers to using sound and valid reasoning. Logical fallacies are flaws in reasoning. Problem solving is the component of thinking that refers to activities of discovery, analysis, and evaluation to find relevant answers.

Specific ways of thinking play dynamic roles that are inextricably linked to writing—active thinking, networked thinking, and visual thinking—all of which help thinkers to arrive at ideas, innovation, and solutions.

Chapter Review

1. What is the relationship between critical and creative thinking?

2. What are intellectual standards, why do we have them, and what are some examples of them?

3. What is logic?

4. What are logical fallacies? Why can they be detrimental?

5. Describe three problem-solving strategies.

6. What is active thinking?

7. What is networked thinking?

8. What is visual thinking?

Thinking and Writing about the Chapter

Reflection

Now that you have had the opportunity to think more about thinking, look back at the journal or blog entry you wrote in response to the prompt at the beginning of this chapter. Given what you now know about thinking strategies, what else would you add to your journal or blog entry? How has your thinking about thinking changed? Revise and expand your initial journal or blog entry.

Discussion Threads

1. Kirby Ferguson, who created the video series "Everything Is a Remix," has argued that the concept of remix is at the center of creative thinking, that ideas are founded on ideas

that came before. Watch Ferguson's brief TED Talk, "Embrace the Remix" at ted.com. Then, as a class, discuss the implications of Ferguson's argument and how what he says about innovation relates to the information about thinking strategies in this chapter.

2. Thinking, just like writing, requires you to adjust your habits, consciously pay attention to how you think, and make your thinking habits more rigorous. This approach can help you improve your writing, but can you really learn to change your thinking processes? As a class, discuss whether or not a person can adjust her thinking processes and what might be the best way for doing so.

Collaboration

1. Listed below are ten topics. Working in groups of two or three, select one of the topics and make a list of ten things you and your group agree that you all already know about that topic. Think about this list as being a list of ten "facts" about the subject, not ten opinions about the subject. Once you have your list written, locate at least three different sources that address the same topic. Using the sources, create a new list of twelve things at least one member of the group did not know about the topic before conducting the research—things that were not on your first list. Again, make this list of "facts." Once you have this list written, use the facts you have to write a single explanation of the topic you have chosen. Synthesize your information into a single, cohesive explanation. Be sure to cite the sources you used to locate the information when you use that information.

   • jobs robots really do in the United States
   • nutritional value of fast food
   • homelessness in the United States
   • the food industry's use of genetically modified organisms
   • the bombing of Pearl Harbor
   • management of the United States' National Parks
   • the most recent federal tax code
   • the history of computer technology
   • conflict minerals
   • the printing press

2. Like many things, over the years the cost of a college education has increased substantially. We may want to place the blame for this increase on one or two specific sources, but the causes are actually complex and diverse. To better understand why your college costs are what they are, you should begin to examine the complex relationships that contribute to the amount you pay. Working with a partner, write an essay that explains why college costs what it costs. Be sure to look well beyond the obvious. Look at how state and federal policies affect your tuition. Examine factors like institutional endowments. Consider loan regulations and availability. Consider how each of these factors came to be and the factors that contribute to their establishment, and on to how those factors came to be. Explore ideas that arise as you conduct research, tracing little details and new concepts. Work together to develop deeper levels of questions that reveal more about tuition than the obvious.

Writing

1. "Wicked problems" are complex problems that are difficult to solve and are resistant to resolution or conclusion. Many "big" problems, like environmental issues or political

issues, can be seen as wicked. Despite their inherent "insolvability," wicked problems provide the opportunity to think through wide ranges of possible solutions. Wicked problems have a no stopping rule; that is, because the problem is difficult to define, there can be no definitive ultimate solutions. For this assignment, create a mindmap, visual map, or evidence board of the following five wicked problems:

- the possible spread of a pandemic disease
- global ownership of marine food species
- regulation of scientific and technological research
- shaping an organization's internal culture
- monitoring social media

2. Based on what you know and think, write a paragraph answering the question "What does it mean to be human?" Once you have written your response, conduct some research and answer the same question from five of the disciplinary perspectives below (one or two sentences each):

Literature
Art
Psychology
Political science
Biology
Chemistry
Business
Law
Social work

3. Clive Thompson is a blogger and freelance writer who specializes in writing about intersections between science, technology, and culture. His writing regularly appears in *The New York Times* magazine, *Wired*, *New York* magazine, and *Slate*. Read Thompson's 2010 article titled "The Power of Visual Thinking" on Wired.com and write a brief response using what you've learned from this chapter.

Local Situation

Colleges actively teach different kinds of thinking. Take some time to search your college's website for key terms like "thinking" or "critical thinking." How does your institution teach thinking? Do some disciplines appear to focus on specific thinking strategies more than other disciplines? Write a summary of what you learn about your institution's approach to teaching thinking.

Reading and Viewing

7

Learning Objectives

7.1   Explain active reading and its relationship to rhetorical situations

7.2   Apply different reading strategies in different situations as needed

7.3   Evaluate the content of a visual

7.4   Analyze a visual's context

Before you read this chapter

How are thinking, reading, and viewing related? Why is viewing, in particular, addressed in a textbook about writing? In your blog or journal, consider why viewing might be an important part of learning about writing and reading.

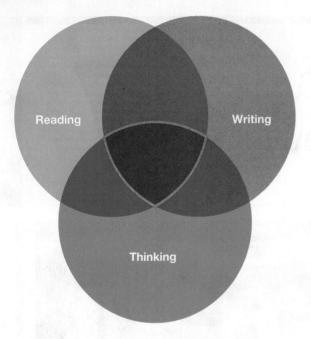

FIGURE 7.1 The core of the college learning experience unites reading, writing, and thinking.

7.1 Explain active reading and its relationship to rhetorical situations

Reading is more than just absorbing information from a page or screen. Reading requires meticulous thinking; readers learn to change how they read in different contexts and amid changing cultures and ecologies. In the academic world, reading is inseparable from writing and thinking. In college writing, this relationship is particularly important, not simply because teachers often assign and assess reading and writing, but because reading, writing, and thinking stand at the core of the college learning experience (see Figure 7.1). Research shows that reading loads for first-year students can range from 160 to 300 pages per week. Rather than feel overwhelmed by that amount of reading, focus on learning strategies for making your reading valuable. The reading you do should be an active, engaged process. Active readers look not only for an understanding of what the text says but also for the underlying situation, including the assumptions, histories, criticisms, conversations, politics, language, and structures of what they read.

Active readers consider not just what the page, screen, or artifacts provide in content but also where and how that content is situated. In addition, active reading requires analysis, evaluation, and synthesis. Active readers make connections among other texts they have read, other information, other ideas, their own ideas, and their own experiences. Questions of value are central to reading and the contexts in which it is done: what kind of reading do you value? What kinds of texts do you value? How does the kind of reading through which you engage a text alter its value?

Strategies for Active Reading

The strategies presented in this chapter are particularly useful for unfamiliar readings like difficult academic texts that you may think you don't understand or that you struggle to work through. First, recognize that you probably do understand some of the text, though perhaps not all of it. Through careful reading, thinking, and research, you will learn to improve your understanding. Second, use various strategies, depending on what meets the needs of your situation.

7.2 Apply different reading strategies in different situations as needed

---

Overview of Strategies for Active Reading

Reading for Value
Skeptical Reading
Skimming
Scanning
Surface or Horizontal Reading
Structural Reading
Reading for Information

Reading for Ideas
Reading Ecologically
Reading to Engage
Rereading
Reading to Synthesize
Reading for Pleasure

Reading for Value

Reading to determine value is a crucial part of active reading. Reading for value involves evaluating what you read for criteria important within a given situation. A number of intellectual criteria can be applied to college-level reading to help determine the value of that reading.

Reading for Value

Criterion	Questions to Ask About a Reading
Author's ethos	Who is the author? What are the author's credentials? What is the author's reputation?
Publication ethos	Where was the text published? Does a parent organization or company support or own the publication venue? Does the publication peer review what it circulates? Is the publication respected within the situation?
Reliability	Is there evidence that the text is reliable?
Relevance	Is the text relevant to the situation? Does the text provide information that you find relevant as a reader?
Timeliness	Is the text relevant now? Has the conversation or the situation changed since the text was written? Does the text provide a historical perspective?
Ecology	What relationships does the text establish? If the text has a bibliography, what does the bibliography reveal about the text's relationships with other texts or the situation? Is the text cited by others in other works? If so, what do those citations reveal about how the situation accepts or rejects the text?

Skeptical Reading

Skepticism is basically an approach of doubt. Skeptical reading is a method of obtaining knowledge through doubting, questioning, and refusing to accept information until it has been proven valuable within a given situation. A skeptical reader doubts the information, opinions, and experiences she encounters when reading.

Given the proliferation of texts through digital media such as the World Wide Web and the Internet, skeptical reading is a particularly necessary strategy. Skeptics do not accept what they see on web pages, blogs, wikis, news sites, and other online media (or any media) until they are satisfied with the evidence to support what they have encountered. Skeptical reading adopts a familiar mantra: "don't believe everything you read."

Skimming

Skimming is an activity that occurs at the surface level; it can provide a general overview of the text. Readers often skim texts to determine whether the text warrants closer, more-attentive reading. In particular, skimming can be useful for readers who need to determine whether a text might be useful in their research. For example, if you have located fifty sources that appear to be relevant to your research, you likely won't be able to read or use all fifty. Skimming the sources can provide enough of an overview for you to gain an idea as to what each text is about and whether or not it is of value to your project. In many instances, this level of understanding may suit your needs within the situation. If you determine a text to be valuable, then you would read it more in depth.

Beware, however, that readers who skim risk missing details and do not get the benefit of the breadth or depth of a text. Skimming should never replace careful, active reading, but it can be a useful tool for determining what texts to selectively neglect and which to be attentive to.

Techniques for Effective Skimming

- Read the first and last paragraphs of the text.
- Scan the index for terms relevant to the situation and then locate those terms within the identified pages.
- Read titles, headings, and subheadings.
- Read captions on any visuals in the text.
- Read the first and last sentence of every paragraph.

Scanning

Like skimming, scanning is a quick-read strategy. Readers scan to identify specific information they require within a text. Scanning does not provide the kind of overview of a text that skimming does, but scanning allows readers to move through a text quickly with an eye attuned to locating specific information. Readers who scan have a general idea as to what they are looking for within a text. By moving rapidly through a text looking for key terms or other cues, readers can locate what they need without slowing to follow the flow of the content. In some instances, scanning precedes skimming in that a reader may scan a text looking for a specific term or other piece of information to determine whether she should get a better idea as to what the text is about.

Techniques for Effective Scanning

- Identify the terms you want to locate.
- Move your eyes quickly across and down the page looking for the key term.
- Use organizing markers like numbered steps, transitional words, or numbers to direct your scanning.
- Consider scanning the text backward so you do not get distracted by the flow of the content.
- Use typographical features like bold or highlighted words or phrases as guides to where important information might be located.
- Look for visual cues like page breaks, titles and subtitles, margin notes, or captions.
- Use organizational tools like tables of contents and indices to locate specific information.

Surface and Horizontal Reading

Surface reading is a single, deliberate, complete reading of a text from beginning to end. Surface reading allows readers to receive and understand the information, the ideas, and the argument in a text. The process is a linear beginning-to-end reading that does not extend into analysis or evaluation of the text beyond initial response.

When readers surface read a number of texts, they engage in horizontal reading. Horizontal reading is beginning-to-end reading of multiple texts of either similar or disparate content. Horizontal reading can provide a cursory understanding of one or many subjects. With the proliferation and rapid circulation of countless texts in the digital age, horizontal reading can be an efficient strategy for covering a lot of territory and for learning general information about one or more subjects.

Structural Reading

Structural reading is a close reading that focuses on examining the structure of the work, the logic of the argument, and the organization of the content. Structural reading not only identifies structure but also analyzes and evaluates it. This strategy is best done in a second or third reading of a text. Before one can read for structure, a reader must first have a general understanding of the entire text. It is difficult to identify and evaluate structure when first encountering a book.

By reading to examine the structure of an argument, for example, readers can better evaluate the logic and evidence of the argument. By reading to understand the structure of a text, readers can see why a writer built the text as she did. Knowing the structure of the book, then, allows readers to better understand the book and to see its ecological connections to other texts, other narratives, and other traditions.

Reading for Information

Reading for information is a more expressly detailed reading than surface reading, and its purpose is to gather and retain information. Reading for information is a kind of close reading that is best conducted after an initial reading of a text. As you read for information, you recognize, record, and recall specific details provided within the text.

Reading for information requires careful, attentive reading and note taking to promote retention and accuracy. When reading for information, readers want to leave a text with an in-depth understanding of the information and details conveyed in it. One of the most efficient ways of achieving that goal is to blend reading and writing in ways that help you identify and retain needed information. Marking and note taking are two approaches that enhance reading for information.

Marking

Marking the text itself can help you read for information in two ways. First, marking requires that you slow your reading and deliberately pay attention so you can mark it. Second, marking functions is a memory apparatus, allowing you to return to the text and quickly identify and remember key points of information.

Most e-readers, pdf readers, and other digital reading applications and software include useful mechanisms for marking texts. Print text, of course, can easily be marked with pens, pencils, highlighters, and so on. Remember, though, don't mark print texts you do not own—like library books—and don't save your digital marks on a primary, sharable file; save a copy of the file.

You may mark the text when you first read it to identify things that immediately come to your attention, but you will mark more deliberately if you do so after having read the text once without marking. As you mark a text, underline or highlight information such as

- primary claims
- main subjects
- key facts
- supporting data
- explanatory examples
- relevant citations
- important names
- unfamiliar vocabulary

In the margins, record information such as

- ideas the reading sparks for you
- paraphrasing of passages
- questions you may have
- connections you make
- reminders to yourself about why you marked something in the text

Taking Notes

In addition to marking, expect to take the majority of your notes in a space other than within the text you are reading. Writing directly on a text can be useful, but the limits of margins and other textual spaces can restrict your ability to expand your note taking to explore and explain. Note taking can be an important part of invention,

Techniques for Effective Note Taking

- Write down all main ideas you encounter.
- Write down any thoughts you have about those ideas, including their value to your project, how you might want to address them in your writing, connections they make you think about with other information, questions you have about them, ideas you want to pursue about them, and any interpretation or critique you may have of them.
- Write down any direct quotation you may want to refer to, including detailed citation information in case you choose to include it in your writing.
- Write down any reference the text uses that you think you might need to look up to better understand the context of the text you are reading.
- Write down all key terms that appear central to the text's objective within the situation. Having the right terminology can help you more accurately write about the text.
- Write down any word or concept you don't understand. Then look those up in a dictionary or other resource. Write the definitions into your notes.
- After you have finished taking notes about the text, review your notes. Elaborate and clarify any notes that do not fully explain what you wanted to write down.
- Fill in gaps that you left while taking notes, including spelling out abbreviations or other shorthand versions you used.
- Consider transferring handwritten notes to an electronic file. Typing the handwritten notes will give you yet another opportunity to review and recall what you wanted to explain in your notes, and the digital form will be easier to incorporate into your writing.

allowing you to tease out ideas as you think through them while reading. It can also contribute to identifying and retaining information within a text. Effective note taking is important for remembering what you were thinking while you were reading.

The proliferation of mobile devices has generated a number of convenient note-taking applications such as Evernote, Springpad, OneNote, Simplenote, Google Docs, and Fetchnotes. These applications offer users the ability to take and retain/store dynamic, multimedia notes and to use those notes toward all phases of their writing. Likewise, any of these note-taking applications include not only collaboration features, making it easy to share your notes with others, but also cloud storage, making it easy to retrieve your notes from any digital device.

Reading for Ideas

When reading for ideas, readers focus on understanding larger conceptual content instead of specific details. Reading for ideas enables a reader to understand ideas the writer conveys and to develop his own ideas. Reading for ideas, then, can be a powerful invention strategy. For example, if you needed to write about innovative reading strategies, you might want to read others' ideas about reading strategies to focus your thinking on the subject and react to what others have said, which can lead to new ideas. Reading for ideas, then, is acutely linked to strategies for thinking. Keep in mind, though, that reading for ideas does not mean simply identifying others' ideas and then repeating them in your own writing. Rather, when you read for ideas, others' ideas should inspire your own ideas, including your critiques of others' ideas.

Techniques for Effectively Reading for Ideas

- Identify the main concepts a text conveys.
- Identify the reason the text presents those ideas.
- Take notes about the concept, summarizing and paraphrasing the ideas in ways that clarify them for yourself. Revised versions of these notes may also be useful summaries when you explain the ideas in your writing.
- Speculate about the ideas. Let your thinking take you to your ideas and to other ideas beyond those. Consider the implications of those ideas and the possibilities of where they might lead you.

Reading for ideas can also help you find footing within a situation. By reading for ideas, you can gain a sense of how others have addressed ideas, problems, situations, theories, and so on. This kind of reading can then help you not only develop ideas but also develop them within the frame of the situation.

Reading Ecologically

Reading ecologically involves reading to identify relationships. The purpose of reading ecologically is to understand how the primary text participates within the web of its relationships to other texts. Ultimately, this approach can be a never-ending process as each text you connect to reveals connections to many other texts. Reading ecologically might be thought of as reading hypertextually: every idea, piece of information, or word you encounter can be associated with other texts, other reading. The trick to ecological reading is to follow paths or links to related readings based on your purpose in reading the primary text in the first place.

Techniques for Reading Ecologically

- Read the works cited or bibliographies of a text first to see the evident relationships with other texts.
- As you read, consider reading texts that are cited frequently within the primary text, particularly if those cited texts are identified as prominent in the situation.
- Identify information and ideas within the primary text and then research and learn about the origins and histories of those ideas and information.
- Look up key terms that you don't understand; but even if you do understand them, consider researching their histories and uses.

Reading to Engage

Especially in an academic setting, you will often read to engage texts, that is, respond to them or use them to support your own writing. Reading to engage requires reading for information and reading for ideas, but it also requires reading to respond. In this form of reading, think carefully about how you respond to main points, claims, and ideas. The process of reading to engage takes place over the course of multiple readings of a text. Initial responses during a first reading can be useful, but they serve as points of departure. Subsequent, detailed readings will allow you to consider the details of the text, not just in terms of ideas and information but also in terms of explicit word choice and nuances within the text. When reading to engage, you may also need to read beyond the text to better understand the context of the initial text. Reading to this degree of detail is often considered the norm within an academic, intellectual context. Ideally, reading to engage is an approach that combines all of the approaches to reading discussed here.

Rereading

Rarely do readers recognize, record, or recall all that a text offers in a single reading, nor do they typically retrieve all they need from the text by reading it only once. The essence of active reading—particularly academic reading—requires multiple engagements with a text to develop detailed, nuanced understandings and responses. However, simply reading a text over and over will not necessarily result in such an understanding. Instead, active readers use particular strategies for each reading of a text.

- First reading—Identify the general meaning and purpose of the text. Identify points that you don't fully understand. Form an initial response and initial questions you may have.
- Second reading—Analyze for rhetorical information by identifying a text's exigency, players, relations, constraints, location, speakers/writers, audience, genre, medium, method, institutional relations, power, and kairos. Revisit and answer questions that arose in the first reading either through the text itself or through other sources.
- Subsequent readings—Read for information, ideas, and ecologies; read to engage.

Reading to Synthesize

When you read ecologically, you read to identify relationships in which a text participates; when you read to synthesize, you read to actively place a text in conversation or in relationships with other texts, ideas, and situations. To synthesize is to bring different parts together to create a new whole. Reading to synthesize is an effort to understand a text in such a way that, either in part or in whole, you can place it in relationship with other texts to forge a new intellectual whole. You will read to synthesize, in particular, when you conduct research. Reading in this way allows you to bring other texts to bear on your own writing and ideas.

Reading for Pleasure

When people read for pleasure, they read texts they want to read rather than texts they feel they have to read. You can read any text for pleasure; believe it or not, some people may even read *Writing Situations* for fun. Reading for pleasure can be a valuable activity because it lets you relax and focus on thoughts more casually. Reading for pleasure can be such an important mental release that many people—including students and faculty alike—promise themselves a certain amount of pleasure reading each day to help them relax. Given the amount of reading you will have to engage in while in college, much of it requiring the hard work of active reading, you should set aside some time to read for pleasure. Just like any activity, if you engage it only as work, chances are you will learn to resent it. Read for pleasure; read for escape. Enjoy the act of reading.

Viewing

Many writing and communications experts have suggested that visuals are now the primary form of public communication and that people receive most of their information through visuals. Consequently, you will need to develop refined and rigorous methods for viewing visuals as a form of information delivery. Viewing is much like reading: it requires that you analyze, evaluate, and question what you see and observe (see Figure 7.2). Serious engagement requires viewing, reading, and thinking.

Each situation will demand that you view in different ways. How you view is a kind of interpretive process. Viewing connects discursive response, emotional response, and intellectual response. Viewing requires determining what mix of these responses best suits each particular situation in which you view. You can never be certain that you see or understand a visual in the same way others do, but that uncertainty does not reduce viewing to a purely subjective form of interpretation. Rather, critical viewers learn the conventions, codes, methods, and grammars of visuals and learn how to apply them in varying situations.

Visual Filtering

Let's face it: there's a lot to see. The volume of visual information can be overwhelming, so viewers must find a way to filter the enormous volume of all there is to see.

Generally speaking, the term *noise* refers to unwanted sound. As a listener, you learn to filter noise, to listen for what you want or need to hear. Of course, sometimes noise overwhelms and you can't hear what you need to. A similar phenomenon occurs in how you see: often there is a lot of unwanted or unneeded visual information that distracts or overwhelms. Part of learning to critically view—as opposed to simply seeing—is learning to filter out visual noise.

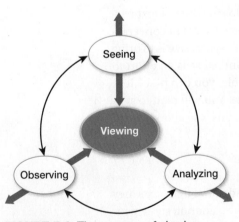

FIGURE 7.2 The process of viewing.

There are many ways to filter visually, all of which require practice and careful attention:

- By category: Focus your view on the particular kind of thing you need to see.
- By action: Focus on a particular kind of action.
- By style: Focus on a particular characteristic.
- By object: Focus on a particular thing.

For many visual specialists, the abundance of advertising, for example, constitutes visual pollution because it distracts viewers, fighting for their attention. Viewing requires focusing on task-relevant information and recognizing what is visual noise within the viewing situation. For example, Figure 7.3 shows a scene containing dramatic visual noise. To avoid being overwhelmed and to make sense of the scenes, a viewer would want to filter the scenes, perhaps focusing on category, action, style, or object elements.

FIGURE 7.3 A scene with an array of visual stimuli. How might you filter what you see?

Visual Content

7.3 Evaluate the content of a visual

The content of a visual is what is contained within its limits. Medium and genre may constrain or enable what content may be included. You interpret meaning in what you view, in part, based on what you see (and don't see) in a visual, so any alteration in content will affect interpretation. A commonly accepted way to alter content is to crop, or trim, visuals to help guide viewers to the point of interest. However, cropping can also change the meaning of a visual, so you will need to make careful rhetorical and ethical choices. You can't always tell whether a visual has been cropped, so it is a good idea to ask yourself what you don't see outside of the visual's frame.

FIGURE 7.4 Original and cropped image.

Elements of Visual Content

Element	Comments
Subject	The subject of a visual is the matter that the visual presents and that you view and interpret. Just as in a written text, the subject is the concept, idea, person, place, or thing that the visual is about.
Culture, symbols, background	Within the content and subject of a visual, you readily interpret what you view by way of what you already know because of your culture, including related symbols and icons associated with that background. Certain styles, genres, media, or methods may also evoke a cultural association. The depth of your interpretations will depend on how much you know of a particular culture. For example, on one level, you may recognize the image on the left, below, as Mexican because of the style and some of the symbols. However, you may not fully understand the deeper meanings that the symbols associated with the Day of the Dead convey to those more engrained in the culture.

Element	Comments
Body language	When you look at visuals of people, you will interpret the body language of those depicted. You "read" body language not only in photographs of people but also in paintings, films, illustrations, and sculptures. The body language depicted in the images below conveys dramatic messages that may differ depending on the cultural filter. For example, the third image depicts a woman raising her fist. In some cultures, this gesture might be read as rebellious or militant; in others it might be read as a sign of victory; and in others still it might be interpreted as vulgar or rude.    
Intertextuality	Intertextuality is when a text gains part of its meaning through its relationship with and reference to another text. Intertextuality may manifest through a direct and obvious reference, through replication of features, through allusion, or through parody. The images below use the cultural familiarity with the first photo in the series, which was taken by Joe Rosenthal during World War II on February 3, 1945, on Mount Suribachi during the Battle of Iwo Jima.   
Visual metaphor	Metaphors describe by using or considering one thing to represent another thing. Visual metaphors use an image of one thing to link meaning or information with another unrelated thing. Advertising frequently uses visual metaphor to convey meaning. For example, PETA uses a visual metaphor of a woman portrayed as a tiger in an advocacy campaign on behalf of zoo animals. 

7.4 Analyze a visual's context

Visual Context

Every visual appears within a set of circumstances that contribute to how you understand that visual. The situation in which a visual appears dictates the context of that visual, and how you view and understand that visual is dependent on that context. You may view a visual out of its original or intended context, but what you view always has some sort of context. Change in the context changes what you view. Being alert to the context and viewing with the context in mind can help viewers better understand the meaning and relevant aspects of a visual.

Elements of Visual Context

Element	Comments
Exigency	Exigency is the factor, or reason, within a situation that drives a writer to write or make a visual. A writer may have multiple reasons for making a visual within a situation, and writers within a situation may make visuals for different reasons, even within the same context.
Purpose and audience	Every visual has a purpose. A visual may be informative, argumentative, evaluative, or narrative. Similarly, visuals have to reach audiences, just like writing. When you view a visual, you can critically assess the audience for which the visual was intended. For example, a visual's style, composition, and content might suggest that it was designed for an audience of children, an adult audience, or a general audience.
Genre and medium	Genre is the kind or type of visual; visual genres include photographs, paintings, sculptures, films, animation, illustrations, graphics, designed objects, charts, graphs, typography, architecture, screen captures, video recordings, and so on. Medium refers to the material presentation, or media form, of the visual: a digital image, a printed visual, a painting, a sculpture, a television show, a film, an animation. Visual genres and visual media may often merge. For example, a painting embodies both the genre and the medium used to make it; you would want to distinguish which categorization is useful in a situation.

Element	Comments
Selection	In many media forms, including your own writing, the writer makes careful rhetorical choices about what he or she wants people to see. Consider, for example, the photographs below, each of which depicts Olympic swimmer Ryan Lochte swimming in a backstroke event. Although different photographs of someone swimming backstroke may appear to be extremely similar, their differences do change how the reader can interpret the moment captured in the photograph.   
Location	Where a person sees a visual affects how she sees that visual. The space in which a visual is situated contributes to its context along with genre and medium and thus influences how viewers interpret the visual). A film, like Joss Whedon's *The Avengers*, for example, is viewed differently in a theater from how it is viewed on a mobile device—and even more differently as a still image on a wall in a museum or in a photograph. Similarly, when a single visual is used to represent a given event through different media sources (such as newspapers), the placement of that visual affects how a viewer will read it, particularly when the different media sources surround the visual with differing text.  

Summary

Reading is a dynamic process that changes over history and across situations. Especially in academic settings, reading is inseparable from writing and thinking; all three skills are integral to one's efforts to actively learn, engage, and participate. Active readers attempt not only to understand what a text says but also to discover how that content is situated. Active reading takes time and effort along with practice and concentration. Serious engagement with visual texts requires that you learn to view, observe, and analyze visuals within and through the situations in which you live. Part of learning to critically view is learning to filter out visual noise. Doing so helps you focus on a visual's content, what is contained within the limits of the visual. Altering the content of a visual, especially through cropping, may change how viewers interpret it, which raises rhetorical and ethical questions you must consider. Elements of content include the subject, the cultural symbols, body language, intertextuality, and metaphor. To more fully understand the content, you must also account for the visual's context, including exigency, purpose, audience, genre, medium, selection, and location.

Chapter Review

1. Why do we read to determine value? How do we read to determine value?

2. Why should we read skeptically?

3. How should a reader skim a text? What does skimming provide as a reading strategy?

4. How should a reader scan a text? What does scanning provide as a reading strategy?

5. What is reading to engage?

6. Why should you reread a text? Explain the three phases of actively reading a text.

7. What does one do when reading to synthesize?

8. What is visual noise?

9. What is defined as a visual's content?

10. What is intertextuality?

11. What is a visual metaphor?

12. What kinds of things contribute to a visual's context?

Thinking and Writing about the Chapter

Reflection

At the beginning of this chapter, you were asked to consider and write about why viewing might be considered in a writing textbook alongside reading and thinking. Now that you have worked through this chapter, write another entry in your journal or blog addressing which elements of viewing discussed in the chapter you see as contributing most to thinking and reading.

Discussion Threads

1. As a class, discuss what experiences different class members have had with reading assignments thus far in your college careers. How do your teachers assign reading? What role do assigned readings play in the structure of your classes? How are you assessed to confirm you do your reading? Do you do all of the reading you are assigned?

2. As a class, use the information found in this chapter to analyze and discuss the following two photographs. Consider what you understand each picture to convey and why you come to that interpretation.

Collaboration

1. For this assignment, work in pairs. Each person should locate a text that might be useful within an academic context. Exchange texts and explain your context to the other person. Each person should then read the other's text for value within the stated context. Write an assessment of the text as being valuable or not for an academic research project. Share and discuss the evaluations.

2. Photographer Lewis Hine (1874-1940) took over 5,000 photographs between 1908 and 1924 to document the lives of young children working in a variety of industries. Hine, working for the National Child Labor Committee (NCLC), sought to use the photos to raise awareness of what many children faced in an era before child labor laws. For example, the caption for the photograph here reads, "Manuel, the young shrimp-picker, five years old, and a mountain of child-labor oyster shells behind him. He worked last year. Understands not a word of English. Dunbar, Lopez, Dukate Company. Location: Biloxi, Mississippi." View the complete NCLC collection on the Library of Congress web site. Then, working in groups of three or four, write an evaluation of Hine's project and its effectiveness. How might a similar project function today?

Writing

1. Locate today's newspaper or an online news source. Read the headline article. After you have read the article once, read it again from a skeptical position. What is not being reported? What seems unbelievable or in need of further explanation? What evidence is reported? Write a list of all of the questions you think you would like to have answered before accepting the article's claims. Once you have developed the list of questions, conduct research to see whether you can locate the answers or corroborate what the article conveys.

2. Conduct an online search to locate an image of a "zebra frog." Look for other examples of "animal mashups" that, like the zebra frog, include fabricated images of striking and sometimes disturbing animal hybrids. Then, write an analytical essay describing what the visual conveys, both intentionally and unintentionally. How do you come to your interpretation? What is in the content and context of the visual that leads you to such an understanding?

Local Situation

Open the home page for your college or university. What is the visual that is presented? Using the information found in this chapter, analyze and evaluate your school's web page.

Writing Projects

PART 3

8 | Writing to Narrate

Learning Objectives

8.1 Describe the objectives of narration

8.2 Apply narrative strategies in nearly every rhetorical situation

8.3 Use the elements of narration in your writing

8.4 Put into practice strategies for writing narration

8.5 Write a literacy narrative

8.6 Use visuals in narratives and as narratives

Before you read this chapter

Chances are that you are already familiar with narration, with telling stories, whether fictional or nonfictional. Before reading this chapter, write a short narration in your journal or blog. Narrate an event, a memory, or a fantasy.

Colby Buzzell enlisted in the United States Army in 2002 at the age of 26 to break a personal trend of drug use and dead-end jobs. In November 2003, he deployed to Iraq to serve as an infantryman machine gunner. While there, Buzzell started writing an anonymous blog about his experiences as an infantryman. The blog attracted attention because his narrations were frank and provided an "insider's" firsthand account of the war in Iraq, often with more details than what the news was reporting.

On August 4, 2004, one of the worst battles of the war erupted at Mosul, and Buzzell found himself right in the middle of it, his platoon under heavy attack. In his blog for that week, "Men in Black," he wrote: "I observed a man, dressed all in black with a terrorist beard, jump out all of sudden from the side of a building, he pointed his AK-47 barrel right at my ... pupils, I froze and then a split second later, I saw the fire from his muzzle flash leaving the end of his barrel and brass shell casings exiting the side of his AK as he was shooting directly at me. I heard and felt the bullets whiz literally inches from my head."[1]

Buzzell's "Men in Black" post garnered worldwide attention. Soon his superiors began monitoring his blogs, and after he posted antiwar statements by Jello Biafra, a Green Party leader and lead singer of the Dead Kennedys, they ordered him to stop blogging. Though Buzzell's blog was active for only ten weeks, it provided a view of the war that few outside of Iraq would ever have, one not crafted, censored, or tempered by either the military or the press. It established precedent for other military personnel to share their stories through blogs. In fact, the military now encourages personnel to write blogs about their experiences, though it imposes stringent restrictions regarding publication of sensitive or classified information.

Narration

To narrate is to give an account of an event or events—to tell a story. The resulting narrative, the rhetorical object, can be a piece of writing, speech, discussion, image, film, or any other medium through which one tells that story. Narration is closely related to description because narratives describe how things happened, and many of the strategies for writing descriptions can be used when writing narratives.

Narratives can be presented in the first person ("I heard the crowd cheer when the president made his declaration.") or in the third person ("The crowd cheered when the president made his declaration."). Some narratives, like the one in this chapter by Diane Metzger, may even be written in the second person, though they are rare. Narratives can be fictional or nonfictional, long (like an autobiography or novel) or brief (like an accident report statement, a blog post, or a testimonial). Narratives can work independently or in conjunction with other rhetorical objectives, for example, as examples to support the purpose, claim, thesis, or central ideas of a description, argument, or comparison. Part of participation is to bear witness, to share with others what we have seen or experienced, to testify, and to place our stories in relation to others and to connect them. Narration participates in that process.

8.1 Describe the objectives of narration

8.2 Apply narrative strategies in nearly every rhetorical situation

---

[1]Griggs, Brandon. "Soldier Finds His Voice Blogging from Iraq." CNN.com. 23 Jan. 2009. Web. 29 Oct. 2012.

annotated example

David P. Bardeen grew up in Seattle, Washington. He graduated in 1996 from Harvard University and went to work for J.P. Morgan & Co. as an investment banking analyst. He graduated from New York University School of Law in 2002; while there, he worked as managing editor of the *Law Review*. As a lawyer, Bardeen has specialized in working with international businesses and Latin American clients. He is also active with Immigration Equality, an organization that fights "for equality under U.S. immigration law for lesbian, gay, bisexual, transgender, and HIV-positive individuals."

Bardeen's narrative was first published in *The New York Times Magazine* on February 29, 2004. As you read it, consider what Bardeen's exigency might have been in writing this piece. Pay particular attention to how he uses dialogue to express the difficulty of the conversation he recounts and how he uses short sentences, even sentence fragments, to strike a particular tone.

Lives; Not Close Enough for Comfort

David Bardeen

I had wanted to tell Will I was gay since I was 12. As twins, we shared everything back then: clothes, gadgets, thoughts, secrets. Everything except this. So when we met for lunch more than a year ago, I thought that finally coming out to him would close the distance that had grown between us. When we were kids, we created our own language, whispering to each other as our bewildered parents looked on. Now, at 28, we had never been further apart.

> Notice the amount of information David Bardeen provides in this opening paragraph: he introduces characters, relationships, conflict, context, chronology, and purpose.

I asked him about his recent trip. He asked me about work. Short questions. One-word answers. Then an awkward pause.

Will was one of the last to know. Partly it was his fault. He is hard to pin down for brunch or a drink, and this was not the sort of conversation I wanted to have over the phone. I had actually been trying to tell him for more than a month, but he kept canceling at the last minute—a friend was in town, he'd met a girl.

> Notice these previous two paragraphs: Bardeen uses short sentences, short fragments, and short paragraphs. What does he accomplish in his narrative by doing so?

But part of me was relieved. This was the talk I had feared the most. Coming out is, in an unforgiving sense, an admission of fraud. Fraud against yourself primarily, but also fraud against your family and friends. So, once I resolved to tell my secret, I confessed to my most recent "victims" first. I told my friends from law school—those I had met just a few years earlier and deceived the least—then I worked back through college to the handful of high-school friends I still keep in touch with.

> Notice Bardeen's use of time in this paragraph and how his chronology of events affects how we anticipate the tension of the impending conversation between him and his brother.

Keeping my sexuality from my parents had always seemed permissible, so our sit-down chat did not stress me out as much as it might have. We all mislead our parents. "I'm too sick for school today." "No, I wasn't drinking." "Yes, Mom, I'm fine. Don't worry about me." That deception is understood and, in some sense, expected. But twins expect complete transparency, however romantic the notion.

Although our lives unfolded along parallel tracks—we went to college together, both moved to New York and had many of the same friends—Will and I quietly drifted apart. When he moved abroad for a year, we lost touch almost entirely. Our mother and father didn't think this was strange, because like many parents of twins, they wanted us to follow divergent paths. But friends were baffled when we began to rely on third parties for updates on each other's lives. "How's Will?" someone would ask. "You tell me," I would respond. One mutual friend, sick of playing the intermediary, once sent me an e-mail message with a carbon copy to Will. "Dave, meet Will, your twin," it said. "Will, let me introduce you to Dave."

> The previous two paragraphs help solidify the importance of Bardeen's relationship with his brother in the narrative. Notice, too, that in these two paragraphs, Bardeen introduces dialogue as a method for delivering parts of the narrative.

Now, here we were, at lunch, just the two of us. "There's something I've been meaning to tell you," I said. "I'm gay." I looked at him closely, at the edges of his mouth, the wrinkles around his eyes, for some hint of what he was thinking.

"O.K.," he said evenly.

"I've been meaning to tell you for a while," I said.

"Uh-huh." He asked me a few questions but seemed slightly uneasy, as if he wasn't sure he wanted to hear the answers. Do Mom and Dad know? Are you seeing anyone? How long have you known you were gay? I hesitated.

> Consider the way in which Bardeen conveys this moment of anticipation. There are very few details. The description of the event is direct, almost bland; yet its brevity and directness are effective in bringing us to that moment.

> Bardeen returns to using dialogue to show us how the conversation unfolded. He uses direct quotations and indirect quotes to give the details of the conversation.

I've known since I was young, and to some degree, I thought Will had always known. How else to explain my adolescent melancholy, my withdrawal, the silence when the subject changed to girls, sex and who was hot. As a teenager I watched, as if from a distance, as my demeanor went from outspoken to sullen. I had assumed, in the self-centered way kids often do, that everyone noticed this change— and that my brother had guessed the reason. To be fair, he asked me once in our 20's, after I had ended yet another brief relationship with a woman. "Of course I'm not gay," I told him, as if the notion were absurd.

"How long have you known?" he asked again.

"About 15 years," I said. Will looked away.

> Notice the shift in Bardeen's narration from reporting the dialogue with his brother to directly addressing the audience, providing us as readers the answers he might otherwise provide his brother through the dialogue. In this way, Will's questions become our questions, and Bardeen's answers are directed at our curiosities.

annotated example

Food arrived. We ate and talked about other things. Mom, Dad, the mayor and the weather. We asked for the check and agreed to get together again soon. No big questions, no heart to heart. Just disclosure, explanation, follow-up, conclusion. But what could I expect? I had shut him out for so long that I suppose ultimately he gave up. Telling my brother I was gay hadn't made us close, as I had naively hoped it would; instead it underscored just how much we had strayed apart.

> In this paragraph, Bardeen starts to draw the narrative to a close, not only in his recount of the events but also in terms of providing his audience with suggestions for what they should learn from the narrative. This isn't just a narrative told for the sake of telling; it has an agenda, a purpose.

As we left the restaurant, I felt the urge to apologize, not for being gay, of course, but for the years I'd kept him in the dark, for his being among the last to know. He hailed a cab. It stopped. He stepped inside, the door still open.

"I'm sorry," I said.

He smiled. "No, I think it's great."

A nice gesture. Supportive. But I think he misunderstood.

A year later, we are still only creeping toward the intimacy everyone expects us to have. Although we live three blocks away from each other, I can't say we see each other every week or even every two weeks. But with any luck, next year, I'll be the one updating our mutual friends on Will's life.

> Bardeen's conclusion ends the narrative, but it does so without a sense of closure. Instead, it concludes with a sense that the ending to the story should still unfold, that we do not yet know what will happen with Will and David.

Summer Woods is majoring in English and history on a pre-law track and plays on her school's Division I soccer team. When she graduates, she plans to tour the world, taking photographs and writing about the different kinds of people and places she encounters. After traveling, she hopes to attend law school and become an international human rights lawyer, working with places like the United Nations to ensure all people are given the basic freedoms they deserve. Summer loves reading anything from novels to newspapers. Her favorite author is Kurt Vonnegut, and her favorite book is *To Kill a Mockingbird*. She also writes short fiction stories and poetry. In addition, Summer is a longboarder and a wakeboarder, and she loves classic rock greats such as Bob Dylan, the Beatles, Tom Petty, and the Rolling Stones.

When Woods went away to college, she left her home state of Florida for a school in South Carolina, a fair distance north. There, she learned about what "The South" really is. In her narrative, Woods describes her experiences as she learns what it means to be a Southerner.

A Southern State of Mind

Summer Woods

Sweat and adrenaline plague the air as the two sides get tangled up in a mix of pride and hunger for victory. The crowd around them reminds them of whom they're fighting for, and every scream pushes them harder and harder.

But this isn't an ancient Roman gladiator fight; it's Saturday, and this is just another southern football game.

The air is filled with the screams of thousands of girls in pretty dresses and the calls of boys in bow ties. The opening whistle may have just blown, but the games started long ago underneath canvas tents stained with Greek letters and beer. The crowd cheers just as loudly for their school's team as they did earlier when their favorite Luke Bryan song blared through the speakers. But they're dancing for touchdowns now, instead of for a swing dance in cowboy boots.

People might assume that, growing up in Florida, I would feel right at home in this scene of Southern hospitality. But those people would fail to realize that Florida isn't the South; it's something more akin to a Yankee state that accidentally floated all the way down the Atlantic and got stuck below the Mason-Dixon line. In most parts of Florida, our sweet tea tastes more like plastic than Aunt Mabel's kitchen, and "Southern Tide" refers to what brings the waves crashing onto our coast in a torrent of blue majesty.

So, I ironically began to realize when I left for college in my red Mustang packed tight with memories and new beginnings that, even though I was headed north, I was really going south. My rearview mirror was filled with Democratic voting, religious ambiguity, and orange juice as I began instead to cruise past roadside stands selling conservative morals and stories of the "good old days." I had always thought that the country's reunification after the Civil War meant simply that: a unified country. I didn't realize that the South still stands apart, and holds its own strong culture that mentally you have to belong to in order to ever completely understand. They are proud to be Americans, let me tell you, but they are also proud to be Virginians, South Carolinians, Tennesseans, Mississippians and Texans. The area is connected to the North by politics and geographic lines, but also tied together by a loyalty that transcends patriotism; the southern states are unified by habitats and a history.

They may have fraternities in the North, but they're nothing like the organizations in the South. They juggle everything on a balance as precarious as the relationship between John C. Calhoun and Andrew Jackson. They enjoy top shelf bourbon and the cheapest light beer, wear the North while they represent the South, and pride themselves on the number of women they sleep with while being the first to jump up to defend a girl's reputation. They create strong bonds by torturing each other, as hazing is the foundation of every fraternity, and instead of gaining empathy from their experience, thrive on doing it to the next set of fresh faced banker's sons. I still vividly remember the night three of my best friends got initiated. One of them called me at 2 in the morning and met me outside my room. He collapsed in a heap in the hallway, and we just sat there in silence for over an hour. He didn't seem to want to speak, just wanted to sit there, and his eyes were the size of saucers. But they eventually survived pledging, and plan to continue on the tradition in the spring.

Conservative politics are also a huge component of the Southern culture, as I learned quickly. After being at school for just over two months, one of my new close friends invited a few of us out to dinner with his grandparents who lived in the area. We went to a very high-end country club, and I felt as if I had been transported back into the Antebellum South. All of the waiters were black and answered every question with a "yes ma'm," while I attempted to stumble around in heels and act as if I frequented the place often. The lights were almost as dim as the sound of the piano being played softly by the tuxedoed man in the fancily draped corner, and the round tables were arranged perfectly around the room. I finally made the treacherous journey to my chair, after almost starting a fire when I had a surprising encounter with the side of a candle laid table. The waiter winked at me after seeing my eyes explode by the sight of the number of utensils beneath me. As he came by to push my chair in and drape my napkin across my lap, he subtly whispered in my ear.

"Just start from the outside and work your way in."

I stifled a grateful laugh and began to prepare myself for the task in front of me. The first part of the meal went perfectly smoothly. His grandparents were the perfect representation of the South: his grandfather had been a hunter, his grandmother the perfect quiet spoken housewife, and they were regular patrons of the church as well as model citizens. Her delicate hands handled the food with perfect grace, allowing nothing to tumble off her spoon and into the folds of her lap as I often did. My friend and his grandfather talked business, and discussed the potential of our football team this year. I didn't contribute much to the conversation; I was busy concentrating on the refrain of "elbows off the table" that I had running on a steady stream in my head. So I was taken completely off guard by the turn in conversation.

I took a slight elbow in my ribs from my friend to the left, and realized I had been zoning out completely. When I finally snapped to, I found myself surrounded by a normal lull in the conversation as everyone stared at the decadent meals beneath them. My friend, who had invited me to dinner, looked around awkwardly as if he was searching for something to say. Then, out of nowhere, he pointed across the table at me and burst out,

"She's a liberal!"

I sat stunned in a state of shock. Then, as if he had turrets, my other friend chimed in his slight southern drawl,

"Yeah, a flaming liberal!"

One of the fifteen thousand forks I had been using dropped out of my hand into my plate in unison with my jaw. Everyone looked around, like spectators of the Super Bowl who were unsure whether or not Justin Timberlake really had just pulled down Janet Jackson's shirt.

Surprisingly, it was his grandmother who finally broke the silence. She patted my hand softly and whispered,

"That's okay dear. We love all kinds of people."

I've somewhat adjusted to the "Southern State of Mind." I've gained a few country albums on my iPod along with a new perspective about morals and lifestyle different than my own. I still don't own cowboy boots, but if you dig deep enough, you might be able to find a Lily Pulitzer dress in my closet.

Thinking about Summer's Essay

1. Summer Woods's narrative isn't a story about a single event but, instead, is a personal narrative about growth and awareness that uses glimpses of smaller stories to create the overarching narrative. In it, we see Woods recognize the limits of what she knew about the South and learn more about it. How does she bring together the different parts of this essay to construct the narrative she provides?

2. How does description play into Woods's narrative? What details stand out for you? How do those details contribute to how you relate to her narrative?

3. What role does dialogue play in Woods's narrative? How does the dialogue contribute to the overall tone of the narrative?

THE ROAD TO A
STRONG THESIS

SECOND THOUGHTS:
"Maybe that's my purpose here: to show that what I understood my home to be wasn't necessarily what others imagine it to be. Maybe it's this vision we accept of places and people that is really more of a state of mind than an awareness of how things are."

SECOND THOUGHTS:
"I learned that being from the southernmost state doesn't mean one is necessarily 'Southern'"

SECOND THOUGHTS:
"But why do I need to explain that to anyone other than myself? And how did I even come to that realization?"

SECOND THOUGHTS:
"What did I learn that might be unique, that might be different from other first-year college experiences?"

EXIGENCY:
"I need to explain that even though I come from further south, 'Southern' isn't about location; it's a way of life."

RESPONSE:
"Maybe by seeing these differences, I am also seeing how cultural narratives form. After all, everyone has ideas about what 'Florida' is and what the 'South' is, but to me they are far from the same."

PURPOSE:
"To tell a story about what I learned in my first year of college."

THESIS:
"Cultural tags like "Southern" should be attributed as states of mind more than as regional characteristics."

Summer Woods was assigned the task of writing a narrative essay. By asking questions about how her own narrative might connect with those of others, Woods could focus on her expectations and understandings of what it means to be "Southern," which ultimately helps her readers arrive at similar insights about their own stories.

SECOND THOUGHTS:
"Now I can tell the stories of how I came to learn this."

professional example

After finishing high school near Philadelphia, Diane Hamill Metzger planned to go to college but got married instead. Her husband, involved in a custody battle with a previous spouse, killed his ex-wife while Metzger and her baby son waited in a car outside. Metzger admitted to aiding her husband in hiding from police for over a year before she was arrested in Boise, Idaho. In 1975 she was sentenced to life in prison for providing intentional assistance—a sentence with no chance for parole under Pennsylvania law. Metzger has earned four college degrees since entering prison. In fact, the Pennsylvania House of Representatives and Senate have recognized her for being the first woman to earn a college degree while incarcerated.

Metzger's narrative is unusual because it is written in the second person. The effect is strategic, hefting the weight of the narrative onto you, the reader, even though we "know" the narrative is about the narrator. The narrative blends the present tense, creating a sense of urgency, with past-tense verbs, establishing a sense of prolonged time. As you read this narrative, consider how Metzger's unconventional approach makes her narrative effective.

The Manipulation Game: Doing Life in Pennsylvania

Diane Hamill Metzger

If you are serving a life sentence in Pennsylvania's prison system, you should be well acquainted with the game I'm about to describe. If not, it's not hard to learn. The only rules are to have enough hope in happy endings to be gullible and want something so badly that you'll grasp at any straw. The game is called the Manipulation Game, and this is how it goes.

You're arrested for the crime of murder in the first or second degree. It really doesn't matter if you did it or not, or what your degree of involvement was, because when you go to court, chances are good that you'll be convicted. Let's face it: Any self-respecting jury member *knows* that if the cops *say* you did it, you *did* it. So, the verdict comes in and, with it, a sentence of life in prison, mandatory in Pennsylvania. (Either that or death—are the two any different?) And now, my friend, you are a *statistic*. You can never have work-release. You can never have a furlough, not even at Christmas, even though your buddy with ten to twenty for third-degree murder ("plea-bargain murder") just won one. You are the best player on the prison softball team, but don't expect to go to any away games (though those not doing life are going). You have earned your college degree, but don't expect to go to graduation (although the baby-killer with ten to twenty went to hers). Your mate may be doing time in another prison, but don't ever expect visits. Your whole family may die, but don't expect to go to the funerals. *But,* if you've got to go to court to get more time, they'll sure let you off the prison grounds for that! Or, if you're breaking your back at eighteen cents an hour on the prison farm crew, that's *different*! After all, you are a LIFER! That label makes you more "dangerous," more of a risk than any other kind of prisoner—no matter what the others are here for, or plea-bargained their sentences down to. None of the good you've ever done, are doing, or will do will change that. If you are innocent of the crime, in the eyes of the state and society you are guilty. If you are guilty, the remorse you may feel, the desire to change your life around—they don't matter, either. You owe time to the state. An infinite time. In Pennsylvania, that time amounts to an average of twenty-three years, usually more. The average is going up, and the slogan "Life means life" is becoming a chilling reality. As a Pennsylvania lifer, you are now four times more likely to die in prison than to ever be released. After all, by taking your life and turning it into a living death, the state and society will give meaning to the life of your alleged victim: an eye for an eye, a tragedy for a tragedy … right? You begin to consider taking drastic measures—maybe suicide, maybe escape, maybe a descent into madness …

But wait! They tell you that you have hope. Your lawyer can put in an appeal with the Pennsylvania Superior Court. So you wait …

You've been in prison seven years now. Your appeal has been denied. But wait! They tell you that your appeal can go to the Pennsylvania Supreme Court, and you can win a new trial. So you wait … You really want to do the right thing now. You have patience.

You've been in prison for nine years now. They say the wheels of justice grind slowly. You heard from your lawyer today: Your appeal was denied. It's time to look at alternatives, drastic alternatives. But wait! They tell you not to be a fool. You have nine years in, nine "good" years. File a P.C.R.A. [Post Conviction Relief Act]! Get back into court. So you do; you have a hearing and you wait …

You've been in prison for twelve years now. Oh yeah, your P.C.R.A. was denied some time back. Thoughts of *taking* your future back enter your mind … But wait! They tell you to file for commutation of sentence with the Pennsylvania Board of Pardons. So you begin the long, soul-killing process of applying for clemency.

Your case was heard by the Board of Pardons for the second time. You were denied again. You look back on your fourteen years you've wasted, years you can never get back … But wait! Don't be a fool, they tell you. You've put in fourteen years now, and it would be crazy to throw them all away. You're always turned down for commutation the first couple of times. Try again in another couple of years. So you wait …

You've been in prison eighteen years now. You've been denied by the Board of Pardons for the third and fourth times. This has gone far enough; it's time to do things *your* way now. But wait. They ask you how you could even consider throwing away eighteen years. Try commutation again in a couple of years. When you have twenty years in, you'll have a real *good* shot. So you wait …

You've been in prison twenty years now. The Board of Pardons denied you again. They want more time out of you. After all, you're asking for *mercy*. When you first came to prison, the average time done on a life sentence was between eleven and fifteen years; it's almost double that now. You've done all that was expected of you, and more, but they've kept changing the rules on you. Maybe you're too tired to think of alternatives now ... but *no*, damn it, you've had *enough*. But wait! *Twenty years!* You're almost there, they tell you. Don't throw it all away! So you wait ...

How long *do* you wait? When should the waiting end? At seven years, fifteen years, twenty years? Your children are grown now. Your parents have passed away. Everything out there has changed, and you're just too damned tired and empty to start all over again, and maybe too old ...

The manipulation game is an insidious game. Its perpetrators are those in power, maybe even your own family and friends play their parts, and the object of the game is to dangle the carrot, that hope of freedom, endlessly, until with each passing year it seems more and more foolish to risk blowing the time you have accumulated, the time you have *wasted* ...

Hope is a beautiful thing, *if* you are one of the very few lucky ones in this game of political roulette and you make it out. But if hope turns out to be fruitless, then it becomes destructive— a tool used by the vicious to control the helpless.

Tell me, where do you draw the line?

1994, State Correctional Institute Muncy

Muncy, Pennsylvania

Analyzing the Situation

1. Who is the "they" to whom Metzger refers? What role do "they" play in the narrative? In what ways do "they" take on the role of antagonist?

2. Who is Metzger's audience? What is her purpose in addressing this audience? How do you know?

Analyzing the Rhetoric

1. In the opening paragraph, Metzger acknowledges that she is the narrator, but at the same time, she creates a hypothetical situation: "If you are serving a life sentence." How does Metzger use point of view to bring the audience into the narrative?

2. What role does location play in this narrative? As you think about location, notice that Metzger does not locate herself in prison or as a participant in the game. In fact, if you had not read that information in the headnote, the narrative would not have revealed those details about the narrator.

3. Metzger strategically uses the retort "But wait!" throughout the narrative. What function does it serve? Notice that in the retort of "But wait!" the exclamation point is replaced with a period later in the narrative. How does this small change in punctuation alter the tone of the retort?

professional example

Discussing

1. In the second paragraph, Metzger writes, "Either that or death—are the two any different?" What effect does this statement elicit? Why do you suppose Metzger made this statement so early in the narrative and why is it made in parentheses? In groups, discuss the role of this parenthetical in the overall narrative.

2. The first-person pronoun is absent from the narrative after the first paragraph, replaced by the rhetorical deflection of "you," shifting the point of view from the narrator to the audience. As that audience, how do you respond to this strategy?

3. Metzger concludes the narrative with a single question. What is the effect of this conclusion? What is her final appeal? As a class, discuss Metzger's concluding statement.

Writing

1. Metzger interjects statistical information into the narrative at a point of high emotional frustration. Think about how that information works to provide ethos. Think, too, about how that ethos is strategically provided at a moment of strong appeal to pathos. Write an analysis of Metzger's use of logos and pathos.

2. Notice how often Metzger uses ellipses in her writing. In some ways, we might read the sentences that end with ellipses as indicative of the objective of the narrative. Are these sentences like Metzger's prison sentence? Does writing a sentence like this aid in the narrative's purpose? Write a response to Metzger's essay addressing her repetitive use of ellipses.

3. How does Metzger's narrative make you feel? Write a response to Metzger explaining how her narrative affected you.

SIDE BY SIDE

Each of the three examples narrates differently: Bardeen narrates a personal and difficult event, Woods recounts experiences of personal identity, and Metzger tells a frustrating story of power. Each takes a different approach, but each successfully draws readers into the narration. Consider how each writer uses narration toward an overall agenda.

	annotated example	student example	professional example
	David P. Bardeen, "Lives; Not Close Enough for Comfort"	Summer Woods, "A Southern State of Mind"	Diane Hamill Metzger, "The Manipulation Game: Doing Life in Pennsylvania"
PURPOSE	To share a personal story through which readers might connect to their own situations.	To tell a story of personal growth and to use that story to connect with readers and their situations.	To express frustration, to inform readers about a difficult situation, and to invite readers to share those feelings of frustration.
AUDIENCE	Readers of *The New York Times Magazine.*	Other college students.	A general audience.
PARTICIPANTS	The writer, the writer's twin brother, and the writer's friends.	The writer, "Southerners," the writer's friends, and the grandparents of the writer's friend.	The writer, the prison institution, and the reader.
DIALOGUE	Dialogue is central to this narrative. The narrative itself is about a dialogue, and the writer uses direct dialogue to detail a specific situation.	The writer uses some dialogue at the end of the narrative to describe a particular situation within the narrative.	The writer does not use any direct dialogue, though the narrative is constructed so the writer appears to be speaking to the reader.
LOCATION	An unnamed restaurant in an unnamed city; specific location is irrelevant to the narrative.	The South, specifically Florida and South Carolina; location is central to the narrative.	Prison in Pennsylvania; location is central to the narrative.
PLOT/ACTION/ CONFLICT	The narrative is about a personal conflict within the writer as well as the tension between the writer and his twin brother.	The narrative relates an individual's active learning about distinctions of perception.	The narrative centers on a conflict between an individual and an institution.
POINT OF VIEW	The narrative is written from the writer's perspective.	The narrative is written from the writer's perspective.	The narrative is written from the writer's perspective but is written in the second person to force the perspective onto the reader.
DETAIL	The writer provides details about the difficulties of the situation and about conversations that contribute to that situation.	The writer provides details about different perceptions, behaviors, and conversations.	The writer provides details about the passing of time and the institutional processes that occupy that time. These details contribute to the overall sense of frustration the writer expresses.

8.3 Use the elements of narration in your writing

Characteristic	Preparing Your Narrative
Purpose	How you use all of the other elements of narration depends on your purpose—why you are telling the story. Purpose drives all other elements.
Participants	The participants may be the people involved in your story, but can also be animals, plants, cyborgs, computers, chemicals, or anything. You, as narrator, may be a participant. Sometimes, a participant may be kept largely in the background, an invisible presence that still affects actions. Provide enough detail about each character for the audience to understand the role of the participant.
Believability	Readers need to visualize or imagine the participants so they become believable. A strong way to portray participants is through their actions. Excessive details, especially without actions, can overburden an audience; lack of details can leave an audience unsure why the participant is included. Dialogue between participants can bring characters to life and strengthen their effect in the story.
Description	Descriptions are the narrative's details about the characters, the location, dialogue, the action, or other information that enhances the story.
Setting	A narrative's location includes the place where the events occur, the time they occur, and anything else that contributes to the "scene" of the narrative, like the weather or sounds. Description is important here. Location can also be revealed through the actions of participants.
Protagonist and *antagonist*	The *protagonist* is the primary participant in a narrative. Any force with which the protagonist has conflict is the *antagonist*. The action of the narrative moves toward the resolution of the conflict.
Action	Your audience should be able to follow the events from the beginning (introduction) through the action of the narrative (body) to the resolution (conclusion). The main action begins once the protagonist encounters an antagonist, revealing the problem or conflict that must then be resolved. The turning point of the narrative is the climax, the moment when the protagonist acts on the solution to the conflict.

8.4 Put into practice strategies for writing narration

Strategy	Developing Your Narrative
Test your narrative's action	Ask: So what? So what if this action happens? What does this action have to do with the situation?
Avoid excessive or irrelevant details	Determine which details can be omitted by considering them in terms of the purpose of the narrative, its role in the larger situation, and who the audience is.
Select background information	Your selections will be largely based on the audience's familiarity with the situation and on the context you want to create for your purpose.
Choose a point of view and use it consistently	**First person.** Allows you to include personal details and reactions that could not be known by anyone except the narrator and gives a sense of immediate experience. **Second person**. Second-person narratives provide writers with the opportunity to direct their narratives at an audience in such a way as to include the audience as a participant in the narrative. **Third person.** Can allow you to show how different characters in the narrative respond or feel and can suggest a sense of distance or objectivity that can be read as authoritative.
Use time indicators	Examples include *yesterday, three months later, Monday at 10:15 a.m.* Embed time indicators in text or use them as headings.
Choose an organizational strategy to create a sense of time	**Chronological order.** Tells events in order, beginning to end. Where to begin and end should be determined based on the requirements of the situation, purpose, and audience. **Reverse chronological order**. Works backward through events. Often used to emphasize why the narrative is tied to the current moment. **Flashback.** A leap backward to an earlier event. Can be used to show relevant events that occurred before the events of the primary narrative, adding layers of depth and nuance. **Flash forward.** A leap forward to a future event. Allows audience to see results of events in the narrative.
Use transitional words	Careful placement of words such as *first, next, then, following, meanwhile, finally, eventually*, and *previously* can guide your audience through the narrative.
Use tense consistently	Past tense is typically used to recount events that have already occurred over either long or short periods of time. Present tense can be used to narrate short events and tends to suggest a sense of intensity and rapid succession.
Use narratives to open or close a nonnarrative piece of writing	Beginning with a narrative is a good way to get an audience's attention or to establish your position within a situation. Ending narratives can serve as examples of your key points or highlight the points you have previously established.
Use anecdotes to support your purpose	Anecdotes, short narratives that relate interesting or pertinent details of an event, typically describe personal experiences and recount real-life events.

professional example

Raymond Queneau's book *Exercises in Style* argues that a story can be told countless ways and still convey the same information. To prove this point, Queneau tells a single, two-paragraph story 99 different ways. Artist Matt Madden, intrigued by Queneau's project, attempts to show how a visual story can be told in different ways. His book *99 Ways to Tell a Story: Exercises in Style* offers 99 one-page comics, all telling the same story from different points of view. Two of Madden's 99 versions are shown here. Notice how the perspective shifts in the second version, "Subjective." After viewing them, take a moment to think of other ways the story could be drawn or told.

Version 1: "Template"

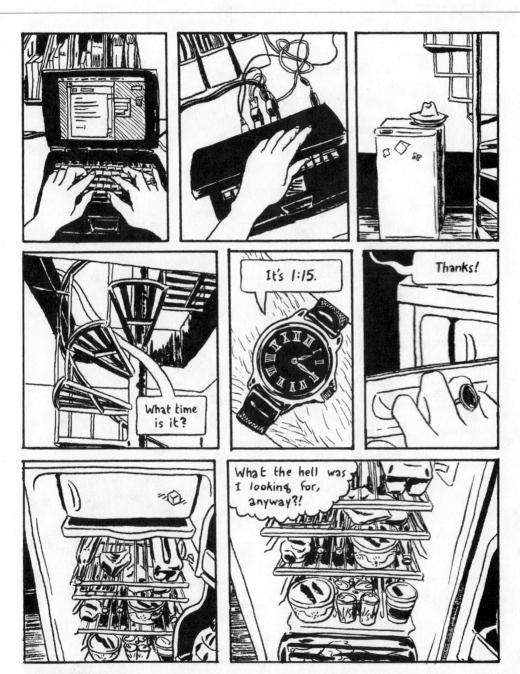

Version 2: "Subjective"

MAPPING
YOUR SITUATION

NETWORKS
- In what networks will my narrative circulate?
- How is my narrative related to other narratives?
- How might my narrative affect other narratives in this situation or others?

WRITERS AND SPEAKERS
- Who are the other writers and speakers in this situation?
- What have they said about the situation?
- How do the other writers present their narratives?

RELATIONS
- What is my relation to the situation?
- What are the relationships between writers/speakers, audience, and players?
- What are the relationships to external forces, like culture, religion, or politics?
- What are the power relations?

AUDIENCE
- Who will read/see my narration?
- What do I know about the audience that I want and that will read my narration?
- Who will my narration affect directly and indirectly?

MEDIUM AND METHOD
- How will I present my narration?
- In what genre will I deliver my narration?
- What method will I use to convey my evaluation?
- How will I distribute my narration?

CONTEXT
- Where will my narration take place?
- Where will my narration appear?
- What limits are imposed on my narration?

PURPOSE
- What am I narrating?
- Why am I narrating?
- What does my narration need to accomplish?

Mapping your situation will help you generate ideas you can use to compose. Start by answering these questions about each part of the situation. Begin with your purpose and work outward to relations and networks.

Literacy Narratives

A literacy narrative is a specialized type of personal narrative that tells a story about one's experiences with reading, writing, and other knowledge areas. Most often, a literacy narrative focuses on one or two significant events in a person's life that affect what he or she thinks about reading and writing. When writing a literacy narrative, consider the following guidelines.

Guideline	What You Can Do
Be honest with yourself and your audience.	You do not have to preach about the wonders of reading and writing. Sometimes reading and writing can be hard, tedious, boring, tiresome, or time consuming, and it's OK to say so. Remember, the literacy narrative is an analysis of why you might think of reading and writing as you do.
Set realistic expectations.	Don't feel trapped by the expectation that you should have had a literacy-based, life-changing experience; most of us haven't. Your literacy events may be common or familiar, for example, some routine thing that happened last week. They might be about educational experiences—like a teacher who had an effect on you—or about a nonschool-related event. Literacy narratives may also consider literacy in math, computers, art, and others.
Focus.	Don't try to write about all of your experiences. Focus on one or two specific events and describe them in detail, particularly when, where, why, and how they unfolded, explaining their relevancy.
Analyze.	Do more than tell the story. In addition, analyze how the event affected you and explain how such events shape our thinking about reading and writing (or other literacies). A good literacy narrative leaves the audience wanting to respond and engage, and it makes connections.
Be flexible.	There is no one right way to write a literacy narrative. Craft your narrative to fit the objectives of the story you plan to tell. Consider how your narrative might benefit from approaches other than the typical academic essay (but confirm your plans with your teacher first).

Writing Projects

Essay

Select a significant, funny, traumatic, terrifying, eye-opening, or pointless event in your life and write a narrative about it. Be sure to explain the details of the event and its relevance.

Literacy Narrative

Write a literacy narrative, a specialized personal narrative that tells a story about your experiences with reading, writing, and other knowledge areas. Focus on one or two events through which you learned about your own relationship with—and value of, perhaps even power of—reading, writing, and visuals. Be sure to provide details of those events, and explain to your readers what you learned from those events and what they might learn.

Visual

Write a narrative explaining what happened, is happening, or will happen next in the following image. Be sure to analyze the image carefully, especially in terms of situation, culture, identity, institution, and power. Pay particular attention to the point of view from which you write the narrative.

Digital

As digital technologies become increasingly more widespread and accessible, "digital storytelling" is evolving as a new form of narrative. Digital storytelling is like any other form of narrative, except that stories are recorded using various media and multimedia technologies and then posted on media sharing sites like Vimeo and YouTube. Some digital stories incorporate video; others use only audio (a podcast, for example). These narratives can be nonlinear, hypertextual, and even interactive. They often include video, animation, photographs, music, sounds, text, and voice-overs. For this assignment, write and produce a two- to three-minute digital narrative using any digital tools you choose. Make the completed project available publically by uploading it to a media sharing site.

Research

We come to know about many events and situations through narratives. In many cases, those narratives may conflict depending on point of view, speaker/writer, purpose, relations, and ecologies of the narrative, especially if they tell different stories about the same event. For this assignment, conduct some research to identify an event about which you could write more than one narrative. Write a short summary of at least two of the differing narratives. Then use both narratives to piece together a single, comprehensive narrative.

Radical Revision

For this assignment, first write a narrative about a particular recent situation in which you have found yourself. Pay particular attention to how you provide details about the situation and the events. Then, using a series of still visuals—photographs, drawings, cutouts, etc.—retell the narrative using only these images, no captions or text. Focus on maintaining the flow of the narrative and on keeping the style of the narrative consistent.

Visual Narratives

8.6 Use visuals in narratives and as narratives

Visual components can enhance a narrative, and visuals, themselves, can narrate. Narratives often have visual characteristics; for example, through description and action, you "show" your audience what happened, encouraging them to visualize the details. Writers also incorporate visuals such as graphics into their narrations or use visuals alone to narrate. Consider the following ways in which your narration could be visual.

- **Writing as visual.** Good narratives move readers to visualize what is being described. Narratives that *show* readers are likely to be more powerful than narratives that *tell* readers. Consider this brief passage from Willie North's 1967 memoir *North Toward Home:*

  > One afternoon in late August, as the summer's sun streamed into the car and made little jumping shadows on the windows, I sat gazing out at the tenement-dwellers, who were themselves looking out of their windows from the gray crumbling buildings along the tracks of upper Manhattan. As we crossed into the Bronx, the train unexpectedly slowed down for a few miles. Suddenly from out of my window I saw a large crowd near the tracks, held back by two policemen. Then, on the other side from my window, I saw a sight I would never be able to forget: a little boy almost severed in halves, lying at an incredible angle near the track. The ground was covered with blood, and the boy's eyes were opened wide, strained and disbelieving in his sudden oblivion. A policeman stood next to him, his arms folded, staring straight ahead at the windows of our train. In the orange glow of late afternoon the policemen, the crowd, the corpse of the boy were for a brief moment

immobile, motionless, a small tableau to violence and death in the city. Behind me, in the next row of seats, there was a game of bridge. I heard one of the four men say as he looked out at the sight, "God, that's horrible." Another said, in a whisper, "Terrible, terrible." There was a momentary silence, punctuated only by the clicking of wheels on the track. Then, after the pause, I heard the first man say: "Two hearts."

- **Text as visual.** Even written forms of narrative are intended to be seen, and their visual design and material delivery can affect the narrative itself. Consider, for instance, typographical choices, spacing, and paper.

- **Visuals used to clarify or enhance.** An image might clarify a difficult-to-explain moment or enhance its power. For example, when describing events, news media include images that not only convey details but also shape audiences' interpretations. But just because you can include a visual doesn't mean you should. Sometimes, not providing a visual might be more powerful than including one.

- **Visuals that narrate without writing.** A single image or a series of images can narrate events without words. Some forms of art such as cave paintings or medieval tapestries and paintings relied on narrative elements to tell visual stories.

- **Visuals combined with text to create a single narration.** This type of visual writing relies on both the words and the image. Comics are a great example because a worded comic relies on image and text to tell a story. The following example is taken from Phoebe Gloeckner's book *The Diary of a Teenage Girl: An Account in Words and Pictures.* The book uses a narrative comic format of text and images to tell a detailed story of Minnie Goetz, a 15-year-old girl living in San Francisco.

Writing Process
GUIDELINES

Use the guidelines in this chart to plan, review, and evaluate your process for writing. Each step in the process should support the overall purpose of your project.

SITUATE

- Understand your reasons for using narration.
- Consider how narration will account for players.
- Understand how **relations** affect what you can and can't narrate.
- Identify how your narrative will be limited by **constraints**.
- Distinguish the role of **location** in the narration.
- Recognize the **speakers or writers** and their use of narration.
- Identify and analyze how to use narration to reach your **audiences**.
- Consider what **genres, media, and methods** might best convey your narration.
- Acknowledge how various **institutions and power** affect your narration.
- Consider the **ecological relationships** your narration will create.

PLAN

- Confirm your reason for using narration.
- Clarify your **purpose** in narrating.
- Consider your form of narrative **response** to the situation.
- Understand the **purpose** of your narration.
- Consider what might be the best **genre, media, and method** to deliver the narration.
- Analyze what you know about the **situation** and what you need to discover before narrating.
- Begin to take **notes**.

RESEARCH

- Determine what kind of **information** you will need and the best ways to locate that information.
- Conduct **research** to gather the information you need.
- Confirm that your research will be **valid** within the situation.
- Identify any **visuals** you may need.
- **Organize** your information.
- **Evaluate** your information in light of the situation and your purpose to determine if you need to conduct further research.

DRAFT

- Confirm that narration will accomplish your **purpose**.
- **Draft and organize** the content of your narrative.
- Employ the **visual process** to develop any visuals your narrative requires.
- **Design** your narrative.

REVIEW AND REVISE

- Review your narrative for **clarity and concision**.
- Review your narrative for **accuracy**.
- Review your narrative for **degree of detail** appropriate to the situation and purpose.
- Review your narrative for **extraneous information**.
- Review your narrative for **organizational approach**.
- Review your narrative for explanations of **key terms**.
- Review your narrative for **style** appropriate to the situation.
- Confirm your **research and citations**.
- Review your narrative for **visual effectiveness and readability**.
- Consider revising the **title** to most accurately reflect your narrative's purpose.

EDIT

- **Proofread** carefully.
- Correct all **mechanical and grammatical** errors.

EVALUATE

- Seek **feedback** from peers (take advantage of **peer editing** opportunities).
- Self-evaluate.
- Ask for feedback from a representative member of the **target audience**.
- Ask for feedback from an **editor** with whom you are confident.
- **Evaluate** the usefulness of any feedback you receive and revise accordingly.

DISTRIBUTE/CIRCULATE

- Consider technologies of **circulation**.
- Publish in a **form** that will be visible within the situation.
- Identify methods for **increasing circulation** (like search engine optimization) within and beyond the specific situation.
- Consider audience **access**.
- Identify possible sources of **audience response**.

Seeking Feedback

Peers, target audiences, and editors can offer valuable observations that will strengthen your writing. You will encourage more constructive feedback from these people if you structure your questions for them carefully. Consider asking these kinds of questions to get feedback:

EVALUATION Guidelines

INITIAL REACTION

- What are your initial reactions to this narrative?
- What do you see as its purpose?
- What are the strengths of the narrative? The weaknesses?
- Does the narration hold your interest?
- What main thing could the writer do to improve the narrative?

SITUATION

- Who do you think this narrative is written for and why?
- Does the narrative fulfill its purpose effectively?
- Has the writer explained all that needs to be explained?

READABILITY

- Does the title represent the narrative?
- Did you understand the narrative? If not, why not?
- What organizational strategy does the writer use?
- Could you follow the organization and how the events unfold?

CONTENT

- Does the narrative make sense?
- Is the narrative's purpose clear?
- Does the writer provide necessary information to support the purpose?
- Does the piece contain unnecessary or extraneous information?
- What details stand out for you?
- How is dialogue used, and is it effective? Why or why not?

VISUALS

- Do the descriptions help you to visualize details?
- Does the writer use visuals in the narrative? Are they appropriate? Why or why not?
- Do the visuals work with the writing or independently?
- Are the visuals clear and easy to read?
- Does the document design distract from or support the narrative's purpose and/or readability?
- What recommendations regarding visuals can you offer?

MECHANICS

- Do mechanical errors or problems cause distractions?
- Which sentences are unclear, if any?
- Which sentences or paragraphs are especially well written?
- Are all the references cited appropriately?

Summary

To narrate is to recount, to give an account of an event or events, essentially, to tell a story. Narratives can be told from first-, second-, or third-person points of view. All narratives have participants, and all players have different narratives—even of the same event, though not all are given the opportunity to relate their narratives in all situations. Thus, a narrative may be altered based on the point of view, or who is telling it. Dialogue, conversation between characters, often enhances a story.

Like any other type of writing, narratives must fulfill a purpose. They also require a setting—a place somewhere in time and space in which they take place. In this setting, something has to happen and unfold in relation to a situation. How the author organizes what happens (through chronological, reverse chronological, flashback, or flash forward strategies) is crucial to accuracy, purpose, and how the audience perceives the story. Use of consistent verb tense is key to helping the audience avoid being confused. Good narration must consider genre, purpose, location, and audience.

Short narratives such as anecdotes are useful strategies for beginning or ending any rhetorical situation. A literacy narrative is a specialized type of personal narrative that tells a story about the writer's experiences with reading and writing (including visual and audio media). Visual components can enhance a narrative, and visuals, themselves, can be narrative.

Chapter Review

1. What are the objectives of narration?

2. Why is narration applicable to nearly every rhetorical situation?

3. Why is knowing the purpose of your narrative crucial?

4. Who are the characters in a narrative, and what function do they serve?

5. Why might you include dialogue in a narrative?

6. Why is location important in a narrative, and how does a narrative help establish location in a rhetorical situation?

7. In what ways are narration and description similar?

8. What is the role of conflict in writing narratives?

9. How should you determine what details to include and what details to leave out of your narrative?

10. What are some advantages and disadvantages of using the different forms of point of view when writing a narrative?

11. Explain four possible strategies for organizing narratives.

12. How can your choice of verb tense affect your narrative?

13. Why are your choices of transitions important when writing a narrative?

14. What is an anecdote? How can it be used in other genres of writing?

15. What is the purpose of a literacy narrative?

16. Identify four ways in which visuals can be important to narrative.

Thinking and Writing about the Chapter

Reflection

Now that you have learned more about writing narratives, look back at the narration you wrote for the prompt at the beginning of this chapter. Revise the narration based on what you have learned from the chapter and your class.

Discussion Thread

Why are narratives important? What role do they play in participation in a rhetorical situation? How do narratives work, specifically, as a form of participation? Take some time to discuss the function and role of narratives.

Collaboration

1. As a class, watch the 1989 Jim Jarmusch film *Mystery Train*. Then, in small groups, collaborate to write a summary of the movie, explaining how the various points of view and narrative threads support an overarching account of what happens.

2. Work in groups of two or three to write a collaborative narrative describing what happened in your class last week. As you work, you might want to consider how screenwriting teams or creators of advertising collaborate. Think about how the collaboration will affect the point of view, the consensus, and the tone of the narration. Once all groups in your class have completed these narratives, share them and discern how they describe moments of consensus and moments of disagreement regarding the classroom events. Compare how various groups describe the class and the events that took place.

Writing

1. Flash fiction—also known as *sudden fiction, microfiction, skinny fiction, furious fiction*, or *postcard fiction*—is a form of writing that challenges writers to compose narratives within a prescribed word limit. Although flash fiction is typically limited to fewer than a thousand words, many writers set limits of 100 words, 50 words, or even fewer. Ernest Hemingway once wrote a six-word short story: "For sale: baby shoes, never worn." In 2006, *Wired* magazine

challenged dozens of well-known writers to write six-word stories of their own. Write your own six-word narrative about what you did today and create a visual to depict it. Consider these examples of flash fiction from *Wired* to help you get started.

Failed SAT. Lost scholarship. Invented rocket. —*William Shatner*

Automobile warranty expires. So does engine. —*Stan Lee*

With bloody hands, I say good-bye. —*Frank Miller*

Gown removed carelessly. Head, less so. —*Joss Whedon*

Three to Iraq. One came back. —*Graeme Gibson*

2. Go back to the literacy narrative you wrote for this chapter's project and use either images (photographs, drawings) you have made yourself or images taken from other sources to create a visual literacy narrative. The medium for delivery (still or moving images) is central to this project.

3. Survival stories make popular narratives. Using a search engine, search for "survivors' stories" or search on a common theme such as survivor stories for Holocaust survivors, 9/11, cancer survivors, natural disaster survivors, military survivors, or school cafeteria survivors. After choosing three or four narratives, read and analyze them. Write an assessment of their similarities and differences.

Local Situation

What narratives about issues on your campus or in your community need to be told? Consider not only narratives about positive things that happen around your campus and community but also those that expose the negative. Consider the power of narrative to lead to change or acknowledgment. Select a local event or issue, and write the narrative that tells that story.

Writing to Describe

CHAPTER 9

Learning Objectives

9.1 Identify the multiple uses of description

9.2 Differentiate between sensory, spatial, chronological, and coding descriptions

9.3 Use numerous strategies for writing descriptions

9.4 Create and apply descriptive strategies for search engine optimization

9.5 Explain the role of visuals as description

Before you read this chapter

Description is part of our everyday communication. We describe our daily events to our friends and family. We listen to descriptions of incidents on the news; we watch and read descriptions of places, people, and ideas. What descriptions do you hear? What do you describe to others? In your journal or blog, write about the role description plays in your daily communication.

On December 21, 1968, three astronauts—Frank Borman,

James Lovell, and William Anders—piloted the first human space mission to leave Earth's gravitational pull, orbit another celestial body—the moon—and then return to Earth. The Apollo 8 mission paved the way for future missions, including those that landed on the moon, and drastically altered how humans viewed the universe, even Earth itself.

In 1969, *Life* magazine asked each of the Apollo 8 astronauts to write a short essay providing firsthand accounts of the mission and the astronauts' first views of the moon. Their descriptions and the pictures they took were some of the most influential in human history. James Lovell, the Apollo 8 command module pilot, used the *Life* essays as an opportunity to also describe the Earth as he saw it from the Apollo 8 module:

> Up there, it's a black-and-white world. There is no color in the whole universe, wherever we looked, the only bit of color was back on earth. There we could see the royal blue of the seas, the tans and brown of the land, and the white of the clouds. It was just another body, really, about four times bigger than the moon. But it held all the hope and all the life and all the things that the crew of Apollo 8 knew and loved. It was the most beautiful thing there was to see in all the heavens. People down here don't realize what they have. Maybe because not many of them have the opportunity to leave it and then come back as we did.[1]

William Anders, Apollo 8's lunar module pilot, explained, too, that "at the time, I tried to describe [the moon] to the ground, and the words I used have made a few poets angry. I said the back of the moon looked like a dirty beach. That isn't very poetic, but it's true. It looked grayish-white and churned up, like sand of a volleyball court on a beach."[2]

Looking Carefully

The Apollo 8 mission patch insignia, designed by James Lovell, describes the mission. It is designed in the cone shape of the Apollo command module. The red figure 8 signifies the mission number (Apollo 8) as well as the circumlunar objective of the mission, and it suggests that the figures of the moon and the earth are bound together.

---

[1]To the Moon and Back." *Life Magazine.* August 10, 1969. Special Issue
[2] Ibid. p. 30

Anders, who was in charge of the mission's photo plan, famously said about the mission: "We came all this way to explore the moon, and the most important thing is that we discovered the Earth." On December 24, 1968, mission commander Borman snapped a black-and-white photo of Earth "rising" over the moon's horizon. So amazed by the sight, Borman asked Lovell and Anders to take a color photo of the scene before them. The photo—NASA image AS8-14-2382—known as *Earthrise* became one of the most influential and well-known photographs in human history. As a visual, *Earthrise* described for the first time what Earth looked like from space and altered forever our perceptions.

What Borman, Lovell, and Anders described altered how humans saw themselves and their planet. Their efforts highlight the power of description to *show* audiences vivid details.

Description

9.1 Identify the multiple uses of description

To describe is to depict, to portray details. The purpose of describing is to encourage an audience to imagine whatever is described. The mantra of description is "show, don't tell." Your goal is to show or present to your audience whatever you are describing in interesting, vivid ways.

Description can be used to many ends, so it supports patterns such as narrating or informing. In fact, few documents are solely descriptive. Using description in conjunction with other purposes strengthens writing by showing readers details—information about the qualities, features, and characteristics of whatever is described.

Traditionally, descriptions have been organized into three categories: sensory, spatial, and chronological. These categories identify how description works in written text. However, electronic media and information circulation also rely on a fourth category, coding, which uses description to catalog, store, and locate information—a purpose that is central to how our writing now reaches audiences.

9.2 Differentiate between sensory, spatial, chronological, and coding descriptions

- **Sensory.** Sensory descriptions appeal to the five senses. Although description often relies on visual elements, effective descriptions "show" also through other sensory details of sound, smell, touch, or taste when applicable.
- **Spatial.** Spatial descriptions depict space and location, always relying on the perspective from which things are perceived. Spatial descriptions are often highly conceptual rather than tangible or concrete and often help illuminate relational characteristics.
- **Chronological.** Chronological descriptions describe events in time and depend on clear patterns of organization. Chronological descriptions are most often embedded within narration.
- **Coded.** Coded descriptions ensure that audiences can find the information you are posting online. Search engines—like Google and Yahoo—rely on mechanisms that "search" through indexed descriptors, called meta tags, to find information matching a user's search terms. In fact, search engine optimization (SEO) has become invaluable because these descriptors change how information is accessed and located.

annotated example

Rachel Carson was a marine biologist who is credited as being one of the central figures in the development of the environmental movement. Her 1962 book *Silent Spring* is considered one of the most influential texts in that movement, and it led directly to the ban of the pesticide DDT in the United States. A decade before writing *Silent Spring*, Carson published two books about the world's oceans: *The Sea Around Us* (1951), which won the National Book Award and the Burroughs Medal, and *The Edge of the Sea* (1955), from which the excerpt below is taken. Most of Carson's writing shows readers two sides of the environment: the scientific and the aesthetic. In the excerpt that follows, pay close attention to how Carson conveys her observations in rich, vibrant descriptions.

Excerpt from *The Edge of the Sea*

Rachel Carson

In my thoughts of the shore, one place stands apart for its revelation of exquisite beauty. It is a pool hidden within a cave that one can visit only rarely and briefly when the lowest of the year's low tides fall below it, and perhaps from that very fact it acquires some of its special beauty.... When I looked out into the early morning the sky was full of gray dawn light but the sun had not yet risen. Water and air were pallid. Across the bay the moon was luminous disc in the western sky, suspended above the dim line of distant shore—the full August

> Carson names the thing she is going to describe and gives a context for the description. Carson specifies that her description is to be visual by telling us about her "glimpse of the pool," but she also situates a chronology of the description by giving us clues about the time of the observation. Notice her use of color descriptors and the spatial details.

moon, drawing the tide to the low, low levels of the threshold of the alien sea world. As I watched, a gull flew by, above the spruces. Its breast was rosy with the light of the unrisen sun. The day was, after all, to be fair.

Later, as I stood above the tide near the entrance to the pool the promise of that rosy light was sustained. From the base of the steep wall of rock on which I stood, a moss-covered ledge jutted seaward into the deep water. In the surge at the rim of the ledge the dark fronds of oarweeds swayed, smooth and gleaming as leather. The projecting ledge was the path to the small hidden cave and its pool....

And so I knelt on the wet carpet of sea moss and looked back into the dark cavern that held the pool in a shallow basin. The floor of the cave was only a few inches below the roof, and a mirror had been created in which all that grew on the ceiling was reflected in the still water below.

Under water that was clear as glass the pool was carpeted with green sponge. Gray patches of sea squirts glistened on the ceiling and colonies of soft coral were a pale apricot color. In the moment when I looked into the cave a little elfin starfish hung down, suspended by the merest thread, perhaps by only a single tube foot. It reached down to touch its own reflection, so perfectly delineated that there might have been, not one starfish, but two. The beauty of the reflected images and of the limpid pool itself was the poignant beauty of things that are ephemeral, existing only until the sea should return to fill the little cave.

Carson establishes chronology, identifying that her description takes place over time, and she establishes her position in relation to the pool to describe her perspective. Pay particular attention to how Carson uses naming to ensure we know exactly what she is describing. At least one instance of naming—oarweeds—requires that we have specific geographical/cultural awareness of what that name indicates.

Carson combines her visual description with a spatial description.

Carson's simile "clear as glass" might be considered a cliché, but why do you suppose it works here?

Born in Nashville, Tennessee, Ndidi Madu is of Nigerian descent, but as she says it, "I am Nigerian. Igbo." The Igbo, one of the largest ethnic populations in Nigeria, maintain a strong sense of ethnic identity and culture worldwide.

While in college, Ndidi, a 6'1" power forward, has played basketball for an NCAA Division I team and in the NCAA Women's Basketball Tournament, an event that millions of viewers can only watch and imagine what it must be like. In the following essay, Ndidi describes that unique experience of making it to the tournament with her team and the feelings she and her team shared.

NCAA Tournament Experience

Ndidi Madu

On the evening of March 12, 2012, my teammates and I, along with our coaches, gathered together at our head coach's house to watch the women's basketball selection show. One word described everyone's mood: *anxious.* But, describing how we felt about the tournament experience can be challenging. To give a brief history, our team had fallen short the previous two years and not made it into the NCAA tournament. So, this year was an important time for me because this was my last time and also the other four seniors' last time to have the experience of going to the NCAA tournament. Having a season in which our record didn't really reflect how good we were, we knew that if we were given the opportunity to further our season by going to the NCAA tournament that it would be a huge accomplishment for us.

The ESPN announcers had filled in the brackets on three of the four regions. All I kept thinking was "come on, come on." They began to call the teams for the fourth region, "overall number one seed Baylor will play number sixteen University of California, Santa Barbara." Bracket predictions had us as a number eight seed; the next two teams that would be called were the eighth and ninth seeded teams. I held my breath. When we heard the announcer call the name of our team, everyone in the room started jumping up and hugging each other. All I could do was dance as a way to show how happy I was. This was a chance for me to go back to the NCAA tournament in my senior year. For the next fifteen to twenty minutes everyone just kept hugging each other and smiling, but we all knew the next day in practice would be the toughest practice that we had all season.

Day one of practice began with a lot of film. Preparing for an opponent does not just entail physical preparation; it also includes a lot of mental preparation, as well. We had to learn about our opponent's personnel and all of their play calls because each team we play has a different style of play.

When Coach walked in the film room that morning before practice, we were all completely focused on our opponent; we were ready to learn all we could about them and what our game plan would be. We were all watching film, taking notes about every player on the other team. Coach had given us each a written scouting report with each player's picture, tendencies, and weaknesses.

Two days later, after practice, we flew to Bowling Green, Ohio, where we would be playing both the first and second rounds of the NCAA tournament. When we got to the airport to leave, a crowd of Boosters were there cheering and wishing us good luck as we walked into the airport. After checking in and going through security, we boarded the plane and saw that the airline staff had decorated the boarding stairs with our team colors. That was really nice. As we entered the plane, we all got even more excited once we realized that we were all sitting in first class. Behind us in the rest of the plane were our coaches, administration, media staff, cheerleaders, dance team, and the band members. This was the first time that we were on the same plane with the cheerleaders, dancers, and band members. We knew then that they weren't just behind us on the plane; they were all behind us all the time. That really felt good.

Once we landed, we waited on the plane until the bus arrived. One great thing about flying to basketball games is that when we land the bus picks us up right next to the plane. After everyone got onto the bus we went straight to the hotel where we were staying. It was exciting to see that the hotel employees were wearing blue NCAA shirts and our room keys were decorated with NCAA pictures.

On game day our emotions were running high; I was particularly excited. Walking into the gym we were all focused on the task at hand. We knew that the national media was predicting our opponent to beat us. They were, after all, the home team. This just motivated us even more.

Walking on the court of a sold out arena as the away team was intimidating, but also motivating. All I saw were thousands of people staring and I heard a lot of boos from our opponents. We were used to playing in this type of environment, so we ignored the taunts and pressure. The only difference between this game and others we had played was that this game could potentially be the last game of the season—and of my college career.

We started the game off great, which increased our confidence. Since I came off the bench I knew my energy had to match the energy of the starters. We were doing a great job of rebounding and pressuring their best player. It was so exciting to be having a great game against the team that the national media picked to beat us. We had a fan base that had come to support us; they were very loud and the cheering us gave us even more energy. Our emotions were high because we did not want this to be the end of our season.

As the game progressed, we went on a run and then the other team would go on a run. The score was very close the whole game. After having such a great start, we wanted to finish out the game exactly how we started. And we did. We won the game 70 to 65.

When the buzzer sounded, we were all jumping around, cheering, smiling, and congratulating each other. It was a great feeling to be advancing to the second round of the NCAA tournament. All of our fans were standing up cheering for us as the opponents started making their way to the exits. The coaches were cheering, the cheerleaders were cheering, the band was cheering, and the dancers were cheering. They were all still right behind us as we celebrated. As we walked off of the court everyone was hugging and our coaches were high-fiving us as we made our way to the locker room. In the locker room, our associate athletic director danced with us in celebration; that was a real highlight for us.

We each have moments in our lives that we try to describe to others, but those descriptions can never really explain the experience. After that first game of the tournament, I realized what was happening was important to us and that no one else would ever feel it the way we did. That felt really good.

Thinking about Ndidi's Essay

1. Ndidi takes on a difficult task in her essay. She narrates a series of events, but in doing so she tries to describe those events in terms of how the moments made her and her team feel. At the end of her essay, Ndidi admits that describing feelings is tough because feelings are individual and personal, but do her descriptions convey the experience to us as readers successfully?

2. To understand the events and the related emotions in Ndidi's essay, readers have to understand their importance. Many readers, for example, may not know about the NCAA Tournament. Some readers may know but still not share Ndidi's investment in it. Considering that a description usually affects a reader only to the degree that the reader is invested in the situation, what besides women's basketball and the NCAA tournament might entice a reader to connect with Ndidi's essay?

3. At the end of her essay, Ndidi explains that it is difficult to describe emotions. Do you agree with her? If so, what makes describing emotions so difficult? If not, what makes describing emotions possible?

student example

THE ROAD TO A
STRONG THESIS

SECOND THOUGHTS:
"I've just finished playing in a tournament that only a few people ever experience."

SECOND THOUGHTS:
"But just describing the tournament won't really get at what it feels like to be there. Maybe I can't really describe what that feels like."

SECOND THOUGHTS:
"Maybe that's my objective here: to describe how hard it is to describe the emotions I felt or the emotions I shared with my team."

SECOND THOUGHTS:
"What experiences have I had recently that others might not have?"

EXIGENCY:
"I need to describe that experience so others will understand what my team and I experienced."

RESPONSE:
"No. It's not that I can't; it's just that it will be difficult."

PURPOSE:
"To describe a unique experience."

THESIS:
"Participating in the NCAA Women's Basketball Tournament is an incredible experience, but it is challenging to describe the emotions of that experience."

Ndidi certainly had a unique event to describe in her essay, but she didn't want to simply describe the event. Ndidi thought carefully about what made the events of the tournament important to her and challenged herself to describe emotions she attached to her experiences, focusing on what she wanted the essay to accomplish.

FINAL THOUGHTS:
"Now I can describe my experience while acknowledging the difficulties of describing the emotional aspects of that experience."

professional example

Jeffrey Tayler is a Moscow-based freelance travel writer whose writing regularly appears in high-profile magazines like *Atlantic Monthly, Spin, Harper's,* and *Condé Nast Traveler*. He also is a regular commentator on NPR's *All Things Considered*. Tayler's first book, *Siberian Dawn* (1999), recounts his travels across Russia and Ukraine in the early 1990s. Tayler explains his perspective on travel writing in this way:

> My writing derived from the conviction I conceived during my college years: one should lead one's life as if one were the protagonist of an epic novel, with the outcome predetermined and chapter after chapter of edifying, traumatic, and exhilarating events to be suffered through. Since the end is known in advance, one must try to experience as much as possible in the brief time allotted. Writing is a way of ensuring that you pay enough attention along the way to understand what you see.[3]

The essay reprinted here was first published in *The Atlantic Monthly* on May 26, 1999, and then online in the "Atlantic Abroad" section of the *Atlantic* website. As you read the essay, consider how Tayler's writing fulfills his vision of his writing conviction and how his descriptions contribute to those convictions. That is, how do Tayler's descriptions support the larger purpose of this essay?

The Sacred Grove of Oshogbo

Jeffrey Tayler

The driver steered his moped down the corrugated red mud road outside of the Nigerian town of Oshogbo, north of Lagos, with me bouncing along on the back seat. In front of a wooden gate he wobbled to a halt. The surrounding rain forest was dripping with humidity; wraiths of mist wandered between the big trees. I got off, paid him, and entered.

The Sacred Grove of Oshogbo was one place I had been looking forward to visiting in Nigeria. As prevalent as indigenous religions still are in West Africa, it is often hard to find public expressions of them in towns and cities; the Christianity brought by European slavers and colonialists has taken root and pushed most of these religions out of mainstream life. But in the Sacred Grove shrines honor all the local deities, including Obatala, the god of creation, Ogun, the god of iron, and Oshun, the goddess of water, whose aqueous essence is made manifest by the river running through the trees. The place is unique in the Yoruba religion, and that intrigued me.

As I passed through the gates I heard a squeaky voice. A diminutive middle-aged man came out from behind the trees—the caretaker. He worked a toothbrush-sized stick around in his mouth, digging into the crevices between algae'd stubs of teeth. He was barefoot; he wore a blue batik shirt known as a *buba*, baggy purple trousers, and an embroidered skullcap. I asked

---

[3]Tayler, Jeffrey. "Jeffrey Tayler." *Rolf Pott's Vagabonding Update*. n.d. web 9 May 2012.

him if he would show me around the shrine. Motioning me to follow, he spat out the results of his stick work and set off down the trail.

We stopped in front of a many-headed statue. "Ako Alumawewe," he blurted out, sucking on the stick. A deity? I asked. He nodded and spat, then headed down the trail to another stone effigy, that of Egbe. After kissing the ground at its base, he held forth at length in mellifluous Yoruba. Since I spoke no Yoruba and he, it turned out, no English, it became clear that my visit wasn't going to be as edifying as I had hoped.

"Hello!"

I looked back up the trail. A Nigerian man in penny loafers was making his way gingerly around the puddles and heading our way. He was young but a belly was already spreading under his white Izod shirt; he wore tight beige highwater trousers. It was clear that he was living a life of relative plenty. He introduced himself as Pastor Paul, from a church in Benue State.

"You come to look at the Grove?" he asked, shaking my hand. "Good. It's very touristic."

A young woman emerged from the trail. Her wardrobe, too, could have been bought on sale at JC Penney's, but unlike Pastor Paul, she was fit, with fresh eyes.

"My interpreter," Pastor Paul said, pointing to her. "Of course I can't understand these people. We have our own language in Benue State."

The little man talked up a storm in Yoruba, but the interpreter said nothing. Our guide then led us down to the river. The water ran bright green between the trees; monkeys jumped around the canopy above. Arising from a mess of roots was Oshun's statue, which occasioned a monologue from the little man.

"What is he saying?" I asked the translator.

"He says locals bring sacrifices to the gods here. Maize, moi-moi, cola nuts."

Father Paul shook his head, his brow wrinkling, his lips pursing. There were no locals about, I noticed. Where were they? Dodging oversized ferns, our guide hopped down the trail, and we followed him.

"Debel! Debel!" he said, pointing with disdain at a pug-nosed bust with an evil smirk standing amid a tangle of roots. The Devil.

The pastor's face retained its pinched expression. "Of course, this man is ignorant," he said to me, waving his arm in dismissal. I said nothing.

Up at a promontory above the river we found Olu Igbo — the lord of the forest. Placing his stick in his back pocket, the little man fell silent and bowed. It was indeed an awesome sight— a giant stone effigy standing among great trees, with huge eyes and long arms spread out like wings. Hoots and warbles percolated in from the foliage; rain began to fall but its drops, intercepted by the manifold layers of leaves above, hardly touched us.

The pastor harrumphed. "I tell my people in church to abandon these beliefs for God." His voice rang loud in the amphitheater of great trees. "Such ignorance. Our American pastors have a lot to say about how ignorant we are. We are trying to change, but these beliefs persist. Life is hard in our country. The people want to insure themselves, so they worship God and these idols. But it's ignorance. Don't you agree?"

professional example

"Why did you come here then?" I asked him as we walked back to the road.

"To see the skilled work of our artisans."

That was as good an answer as any. At the gate we tipped the guide and parted ways.

Analyzing the Situation

1. Why do you suppose readers of *The Atlantic* might be interested in an essay like this? That is, what is the purpose of this essay? What role does description play in achieving that purpose?

2. Does the fact that Tayler is labeled a "travel writer" have an effect on how you read this essay? In what ways is the label "travel writer" itself a descriptive term?

3. There's a lot more going on in this essay than just a trip to a sacred place. In this situation, there are suggestions of power and institution at play, undertones of conflict and resistance, and hints that this situation involves many more people than those described here. How does Tayler make these suggestions and use them toward his purpose?

Analyzing the Rhetoric

1. Make a list of the descriptive words in the essay that paint particularly vivid descriptions. Then, come up with synonyms that Tayler might have used instead. Insert those words in place of Tayler's original words and explain how those word choices alter what is described.

2. Identify where Tayler uses naming as a descriptive strategy and what effect it has on the overall description.

3. This essay suggests many things—institutions, power, culture, conflict, and players, for instance—which are never directly engaged. What role does the "unstated" play in this essay? How do Taylor's descriptions contribute to what is left unsaid?

Discussing

1. In groups, discuss which description you find most vivid and detailed—the description of the caretaker, Pastor Paul, or the forest—and what you see as the most descriptive part of the essay.

2. We know that Tayler is a travel writer and that travel writers not only describe places but also inform audiences and encourage them to travel themselves. Do the descriptions in "The Sacred Grove of Oshogbo" encourage you to want to see the Sacred Grove? As you respond, consider, too, how your own situation, beliefs, and knowledge interact with

Tayler's descriptions and affect your conclusion. Discuss why you would or would not want to travel to the Sacred Grove of Oshogbo in Nigeria.

3. There are number of ways to interpret what Tayler is describing in this essay. As a class, discuss not only his purpose in this essay but also what he is describing, both evidently and subtly.

Writing

1. Summarizing or paraphrasing might be thought of as a way of describing what someone or some text has already said. How would you describe "The Sacred Grove of Oshogbo" to a classmate who has not read the essay? Write a description of the essay for someone in your class (or another class) who has not read it.

2. In addition to his substantial, detailed visual and spatial descriptions, Tayler also includes a good deal of auditory description beyond the use of dialogue. Identify how many times sound is described, and write an analysis explaining how Tayler uses sound, particularly to support his overall purpose.

3. "The Sacred Grove of Oshogbo" was published online and, thus, was posted with a series of meta tag descriptors to enable online searching. Using the text as a guide, create a list of ten meta tags you feel best describe the indexing information for search engines and the terms readers would use to locate this essay.

SIDE BY SIDE

Each of the previous three descriptive essays takes a different approach to describing: Carson describes what she sees in the pools, relying on visual descriptions. Madu relies on an experiential description, showing us how she remembers the events she describes. Tayler uses a good deal of dialogue to convey his description, letting us hear his conversations. Each of these approaches successfully helps us grasp each description.

	annotated example Rachel Carson, From *The Edge of the Sea*	**student example** Ndidi Madu, "NCAA Tournament Experience"	**professional example** Jeffrey Tayler, "The Sacred Grove of Oshogbo"
PURPOSE	To describe a hard-to-reach tidal pool that few people will ever see	To describe a unique experience	To describe a Nigerian shrine that few Westerners will ever see
RHETORICAL MODE	Uses description with narration, though the primary purpose of description dominates	Uses description to help narrate a series of events within a more encompassing experience	Uses description in conjunction with narration to tell of a single experience that points to larger issues
AUDIENCE	Readers interested in coastal ecosystems and conservation	Readers interested in college sports	Readers of *The Atlantic Monthly*
PATHOS	Conveys the pleasures and wonder of wild places	Conveys a sense of excitement and pride	Conveys a sense of being solemn along with hints of conflict
DOMINANT IMPRESSION	A sense of beauty and wonder	Excitement, pride, and accomplishment	Adventure, exploration, wonder
SENSES	Primarily uses visual descriptions, with some description of the spatial and tactile as well as scent	Primarily uses visual and emotional descriptions	Strong use of visual description as well as some tactile and auditory description
NAMING	Naming is central to the description; Carson names the things she sees to provide context for the things she describes.	Naming is of less importance, except for naming the larger event and for identifying a few specific places.	Naming is of moderate importance, including naming the location where the narrative occurs and the various gods.

MAPPING
YOUR SITUATION

NETWORKS
- How will my description circulate?
- How is my description related to other descriptions in the situation?
- What effect will my description have on the situation?

WRITERS AND SPEAKERS
- Who are the other writers and speakers in this situation?
- How have others described the situation?
- How do the other writers present their descriptions?

RELATIONS
- What is my relation to the situation?
- What are the relationships between writers/speakers, audience, and players?
- What are the relationships between the audience and other players?
- What are the relationships to external forces, like culture, religion, or politics?
- How does my description account for or establish relationships?

AUDIENCE
- Who will read/see my description?
- What do I know about my intended audience?
- Who will my description affect directly and indirectly?

MEDIUM AND METHOD
- In what genre will I deliver my description?
- What senses will my description appeal to?
- What method will I use to convey my description?
- How will I distribute my description?

CONTEXT
- Where will my description take place? Where will it appear?
- Am I describing a specific space?
- What limits are imposed on my description?

PURPOSE
- What am I describing?
- Why am I describing?
- How should I approach my description to accomplish my purpose?

Mapping your situation will help you generate ideas you can use to compose. Start by answering these questions about each part of the situation. Begin with your purpose and work outward to relations and networks.

Characteristic	Preparing Your Description
Sight	Descriptions of color can be strengthened by linking them with other adjectives and nouns: the child's red shirt. The word *child's* changes how we see the shirt. Many other visual adjectives such as *thin, shiny, huge, glossy, foggy, pale, bright, round, flat, lacy, swollen*, and *angular* also contribute to description. In addition, visual verbs can make descriptions come alive with action, for example, *snake, plod, dance, glimmer*, or *pant*.
Sound	When describing sounds, try to link the sound something makes with what is making the sound: "the bird's chirp" describes something different from "the computer's chirp." Also consider the quality of the sound, for example, whether it is soft, loud, high, low, piercing, or calming. Onomatopoeia refers to words that imitate sounds, like *oink, hiccup, splash*, or *ding*. Comics often use onomatopoeia, for example, *splat, wham, biff*, or *thpbft*. Keep in mind that onomatopoeia differs widely transculturally or transnationally. For instance, in English, a rooster may say "cock-a-doodle-do," but in Spanish, a rooster says "qui-qui-ri-qui."
Smell	Smells can be powerful triggers for memory, association, and emotion. There are not a lot of English words to describe smells and the physical act of smelling, so it can be tough to describe this sense in original ways. Yet words like *aroma, stink, fragrant, putrid, odor*, and *scent* can provide a sense of smell to a description. Comparisons can be quite useful if they are recognized culturally by the audience: the room smelled like a wet sock.
Touch	Tactile sensations include qualities such as texture or temperature, even inner body sensations such as a pounding headache or bloated stomach. Words like *gritty, sticky, smooth, rough, hot, moist, damp, burning, itchy*, or *slick* can describe how things feel. Comparisons can be helpful: the shark's skin was rough like sandpaper.
Taste	Words like *salty, sweet, bitter, tart, fruity, smoky, meaty, gamey*, or *spicy* can help convey a sense of taste. Words that describe smells or tactile sensations—for example, *juicy, creamy*, or *acrid*—work well in conjunction with taste descriptions.

Strategy	Developing Your Description
Develop Pathos	Strong descriptions encourage readers to imagine what is being described, place themselves in relation to that description, and react emotionally.
Strengthen the Dominant Impression	Focus on a dominant impression, the overall thought or feeling you want your audience to come away with. Concentrate on providing the details needed to establish the dominant impression; then provide details that support it.
Observe	Begin by studying the macro-scene; then zoom in and scrutinize the micro-level details. In addition to sensory details, notice differences and similarities, locations and positions, perceptions and distortions.
Name	By naming or identifying things, writers offer a concrete context for a description. For instance, "red, juicy, and sweet" might describe a thing, but by naming it "a red, juicy, and sweet *apple*" readers can readily visualize the thing described.
Choose or Omit Details	Include relevant, vivid details to help an audience interpret your description. You might leave out details that either are contradictory or don't serve the purpose of the description, which can be helpful, but be sure to consider ethically what you leave out, and don't hide, distort, or obfuscate information through such omissions.
Control Word Choice	Descriptions primarily rely on well-chosen adjectives, adverbs, and verbs. Long strings of adjectives (the thin, hairlike, two-inch, black fragment) are usually less effective than one or two well-chosen words. Consider how verbs add to this description: The putrid slime oozed out of the rotting animal and snaked toward my bare foot.
Compare	Comparatives occur in two distinctive forms: similes and metaphors. Similes express direct similarities or resemblances, using the words *like* or *as*: eyes like pools of water. Similes also can combine sensory indicators with *like—smells like, sounds like, tastes like, feels like*, or *looks like* (for example, the salad looked like lawn trimmings). Metaphors compare things indirectly, as though one thing were the same as the other: "she was a rock" suggests that "she" was steady and unyielding, without using a comparing word.
Maintain Consistency	Make sure descriptions are consistent and don't contradict themselves. For instance, don't describe a body of water as calm at one point and rough at another (unless, of course, the purpose is to describe changing conditions).
Provide Objective or Subjective Descriptions	An objective description will come across as factual: "The backpack is teal and black. It has three zippered pockets on the front and a large mesh compartment on the back." A subjective description will include factual information along with personal observation from the writer/speaker: "The backpack is an attractive teal and black. It has three useful zippered pockets on the front that I find convenient and a large mesh compartment on the back that I use to store extra sandwiches."
Avoid Clichés	A description that is cliché is one that is trite and no longer elicits the desired response from an audience. Avoid clichés and offer original, dynamic descriptions. Clichés can ruin a good description.

Strategies for Writing to Describe

Evoking sensory details is central to vivid descriptions. Most people are aware of their visual perceptions, but they may not be as aware of perceptions from their other senses. Putting an audience in touch with these other perceptions can deepen the description.

1. Expand your visual vocabulary. Make a list of 50 words that could be used to describe by seeing, especially words that can be used to describe colors (*azure* for *blue*, for example).
2. Tune in to sounds. Write a paragraph describing the sounds in the room where you are now. What sounds give clues as to where you are?
3. Focus on smells. Describe how your home smells. Would you describe the smells you associate with home in positive or negative ways? What memories or associations do they trigger?
4. Experiment with touch. Write a paragraph describing how an item on your desk feels. Try comparing it to the way something else feels to strengthen your description.
5. Detail taste. Write a paragraph describing your favorite food. Focus on describing how the food tastes. Now, build in descriptions of that food using the other senses, too.

Writing Descriptors for Online Texts

Search engine optimization (SEO) is a process to improve the ranking a web page receives in a search engine. The goal of SEO is for documents to appear on the first page of search results. Thus, it is a way to increase the numbers of visitors your web page gets and improve the likelihood that your intended audience will see it. A document intended for the Web should include descriptors that will help readers find it. These descriptors will also affect how human audiences and search engines see your document. Consider these suggestions for writing descriptors.

- **Key words.** Don't assume that you know what the most effective key word descriptors will be. Research what specific key terms are most frequently used in the subject area your web writing addresses. You can test key words by searching on them and noting what they bring up.
- **Title tags.** Title tags are words embedded in your title that are designed to register with search engines. Titles are also what appear on the search engine result page, so they become descriptions of your document. Thus, your title needs to function as an indexing mechanism and to entice readers to click on it.
- **Key words as meta tags.** Search engines are more apt to identify terms that appear not only in the body of the document but also in the meta tags, so be sure the key words in your document also appear as meta tags.
- **Repetition.** Search engines are more likely to index your site based on descriptors that appear frequently in your document. Thus, you will want to repeat a key term

often, but be careful not to overuse the term, jeopardizing readability for the sake of SEO. Writers struggle with achieving this balance because they are often trying to maximize web attention through search engine hits.

- **Audience.** Search optimization relies heavily on understanding what kinds of descriptions your audience already associates with the information in your document. Anticipate the kinds of descriptions readers expect and include those descriptions in your meta tags.
- **Meta tags.** Don't limit your meta tags to single-word descriptors; phrases like "lightweight, waterproof digital camera" provide more detail than "camera," offering more to index and more possibilities for key word searches.

Guidelines for Observing

- Be patient, and don't rush your observation.
- Be curious and ask questions.
- Be ethical in your observation. Don't distort.
- Take notes to capture the details while you observe; don't rely on your memory.
- Record the dominant impression.
- Consider who, what, when, and where.
- Note what senses you are using and consider what other senses might be used.
- Note what details are obvious and which are more subtle.
- Notice the position from which you are observing.
- Consider your perspective.

Writing Projects

Essay

What is the most prominent feature of your campus? How would you describe it to a prospective student? Try to go beyond thinking of features as being physical, for example, a plaza or building or bell tower; other types of campus features could include the atmosphere, the academics, the social life, and the activities. Write a description of the most prominent feature you identified.

Visual Description

Write a description of the this image. Consider the level of detail you need to provide, including background information that might help establish the context of the description. Think, too, about how you will appeal to your audience's visual sense.

Digital

If we were to place this chapter on the Web for public access, what descriptors would be most effective in directing readers to it? Develop a list of 25 terms that appear within the chapter and could be used to describe it. Discuss which terms you anticipate readers first using to locate this chapter and which terms would involve specialized searches.

Research

Description is one of the primary rhetorical modes. Conduct some research to learn how description has been addressed by rhetoricians and scholars of rhetoric. How has description changed over history? What role has it played in rhetorical studies? Write a research paper of about 1,500 words that describes description as a rhetorical mode.

Radical Revision

Locate or take a photograph that is descriptive of a particular place. Then, using the photograph as a point of departure, write a description of the same place, but one that describes the place in terms of any senses except sight.

9.5 Explain the role of visuals as description

Visuals that Describe

The Apollo 8 image *Earthrise* described more about the Earth than words ever could. Visuals can be powerful tools in describing because they "show." In some instances, visuals may show the unspoken, that which cannot be effectively described through writing. Visuals most often appeal to emotion (pathos) or clarify data such as numeric information. Keep in mind, however, that visuals represent only a particular, fixed perspective. A camera's lens, for instance, cannot show the entire scene from all perspectives.

When using visuals to describe, pay particular attention to the relationship between the visual and the written text. Make sure the visual supports the written description either by clarifying or extending the description.

Writing Process
GUIDELINES

Use the guidelines in this chart to plan, review, and evaluate your process for writing. Each step in the process should support the overall purpose of your project.

SITUATE

- Understand your reasons for using description in this situation.
- Consider how your descriptions will account for the players in the situation.
- Understand how relations affect what you can and cannot describe.
- Identify how your descriptions might be limited by constraints.
- Distinguish the role of location in your descriptions.
- Recognize how other speakers or writers in the situation have described relevant things.
- Identify and analyze how to use description to reach your audience.
- Consider what genres, media, and methods might best convey your descriptions.
- Acknowledge how various institutions and power affect your description.
- Consider the ecological relationships your descriptions establish.

PLAN

- Confirm your reason for using description.
- Clarify your purpose in describing.
- Consider what might be the best genre, media, and method to deliver your description.
- Analyze what you know about the situation. and what you need to discover before writing descriptions.
- Begin to take notes.

RESEARCH

- Determine what kind of information you will need to accurately provide description.
- Conduct research to gather the information you will need.
- Confirm that your research will be valid within the situation.
- Identify any visuals you may need.
- Organize your information.
- Evaluate your information in light of the situation and purpose to determine whether you need to conduct further research.

DRAFT

- Confirm that description will accomplish your purpose.
- Draft and organize the content of your description.
- Include detailed sensory descriptions.
- Develop any visuals your description requires.
- Design your description.

REVIEW AND REVISE

- Review your description for clarity and concision.
- Review your description for accuracy.
- Review your description for degree of detail appropriate to the situation and purpose.
- Review your description for extraneous information.
- Review your description for organizational approach.
- Review your description for style appropriate to the situation.
- Confirm your research and citations.
- Review your description for visual effectiveness and readability.
- Consider revising the title to most accurately reflect the description's purpose.

EDIT

- Proofread carefully.
- Correct all mechanical and grammatical errors.

EVALUATE

- Seek feedback from peers.
- Ask for feedback from a representative member of the target audience.
- Ask for feedback from an editor in whom you are confident.
- Evaluate the usefulness of any feedback you receive and revise accordingly.

DISTRIBUTE/CIRCULATE

- Consider technologies of circulation and the way meta tags and coding will effect circulation.
- Publish in a form that will be visible within the situation.
- Identify methods for increasing circulation (like search engine optimization) within and beyond the specific situation.
- Consider audience access.
- Identify possible sources of audience response.

Seeking Feedback

Peers, target audiences, and editors can offer valuable observations that will strengthen your writing. You will encourage more constructive feedback from these people if you structure your questions for them carefully. Consider asking these kinds of questions to get feedback:

EVALUATION Guidelines

INITIAL REACTION

- What are your initial reactions to the descriptions in this document?
- What do you see as the purpose of the descriptions?
- What are the strengths of the descriptions?
- What are the weaknesses of the descriptions?
- Which descriptive moments, if any, do you find particularly memorable?
- Which descriptions, if any, are weak, clichéd, or generally flat?
- Overall, what is the primary thing the writer must do to improve the descriptions?

SITUATION

- Who do you think these descriptions are written for and why?
- Do the descriptions support the overall purpose of the document?
- Do the descriptions seem appropriately detailed for the situation?

READABILITY

- Did you understand the descriptions?
- Does the writer make use of multiple sensory descriptions?
- If the writer uses comparisons, are they clear and appropriate?

CONTENT

- Do the descriptions make sense in relation to the document's purpose?
- Is the reason for including the descriptions clear?
- Does the writer provide the necessary information to support the agenda?
- Is there anything particularly interesting that the writer presents?
- Is there unnecessary or extraneous description in the document?
- Does the writer provide extraneous or unnecessary details?
- Does the writer name the things described?

VISUALS

- Does the writer's writing encourage you to visualize the things described?
- Does the writer use visuals to describe?
- If so, are the visuals appropriate to the purpose?
- Do the visuals work in conjunction with the writing or independently?
- Are the visuals clear and easy to read?
- Does the document design distract from or support the document's purpose and/or readability?
- What recommendations regarding visuals do you have for the writer?

MECHANICS

- Do mechanical errors or problems cause distractions?
- Which sentences are unclear, if any?
- Which sentences or paragraphs are particularly well written?
- Are all references cited appropriately?

Summary

To describe is to portray details. Descriptions can be organized into sensory, spatial, chronological, and coded categories, with sensory being vital to most description. Descriptions usually do not function alone but play a supporting role in various rhetorical situations. Effective strategies for writing descriptions include developing pathos, strengthening the dominant impression, observing, naming, choosing or omitting details, controlling word choice, comparing, maintaining consistency, providing subjective or objective descriptions, and avoiding clichés. As codes, descriptors play a key role in search engine optimization (SEO), a form of describing web documents to enhance their access. Visuals can either support descriptions or serve as descriptions themselves.

Chapter Review

1. What is the purpose of description?

2. List the four ways that description can be categorized.

3. In what ways do specific rhetorical situations affect how you write descriptions?

4. What are five of the ten key strategies for writing descriptions?

5. What are five strategies for enhancing search engine optimization?

6. How do visuals function as descriptions?

Thinking and Writing about the Chapter

Reflection

1. At the beginning of this chapter, you wrote about the role description plays in your daily communication. Now that you have had the chance to learn more about description, look back at your "Before you read this chapter" response and revise and expand your discussion regarding the role of description in your daily communication.

Discussion Threads

1. In what ways does description serve other rhetorical objectives such as reporting, narrating, or persuading? Discuss with your class how integrating description into writing might enhance writing objectives.

2. It is likely that you have read, heard, or seen a description at some time that was powerful enough to leave a lasting impression. In groups or as a class, discuss those descriptions: where you encountered them, what you recall about them, what descriptive elements they used, and why they were so memorable.

Collaboration

1. With another student, follow this process for each of the ten images below:

- Examine the first image.
- Discuss what terms most obviously describe the image, and make a list of them.
- Independently, write a list of ten additional words that describe the image.
- Compare lists and discuss commonalities and differences in your descriptors.
- Do the same for each of the subsequent images.

2. One of the things not addressed in this chapter is that visual description assumes an audience has already seen some form of what is being described or what it is being compared to. But what about a visually impaired audience—individuals who have severely or entirely limited visual reference—or an audience whose visual references are different? As a class, consider and discuss how description can be effective for these audiences.

Writing

1. Write a description of any one of the following using at least two senses:

a paperclip	a corn flake	a key
a toothpick	a pencil	a penny
a peanut butter and jelly sandwich	a comb	a light bulb
	a glass of water	

2. Write a description of the last meal you ate. Include the perspective of your situation during that meal (eating in a rush, while sick, while on a diet, etc.).

3. Describe your home.

4. Write a description of the image below for someone who has not seen it.

Local Situation

How does your school describe itself? How do you describe your school? Consider the numerous ways in which your college or university gets described by those with various perspectives.

1. How does your university or college describe itself in official publications like web pages, press releases, and brochures? Do descriptive approaches vary depending on what's being described: academics, campus life, athletics, facilities, expectations? Do the descriptions vary depending on intended audiences: prospective students, current students, alumni? Write an analysis of those descriptions. Which descriptors are used most frequently? Which only occasionally? Which words do you consider to be good descriptions and which inaccurate? Where do you find official descriptions of your school?

2. Write a description of your school for prospective students. Describe the things you think would give them a student's perspective.

3. Open your school's official home page, use the "view source" function (in Microsoft Internet Explorer you can do this by clicking "View" in the toolbar and "Source" in the drop-down menu) and read the source codes to see what words are used in the meta tags. What words does your school use to describe itself in meta tags? What other descriptors do you think might be added to the tags to accurately direct search engines to your school's home page?

Writing to Inform

10

Learning Objectives

10.1 Describe differences between informative writing and other forms of expository writing

10.2 Make ethical choices when writing to inform

10.3 Identify situations that require the delivery of information

10.4 Apply strategies for writing to inform

10.5 Write to inform within other rhetorical purposes

10.6 Use visuals as a means of informing

Before you read this chapter

What kinds of information do you need every day? Where do you get your information? Do you get information from one source for all you need to know, or do you rely on many different kinds of sources? What kinds of information do you regularly provide? How do you provide it? In your journal or blog, write about how you receive and transmit information.

On January 9, 2007, Steve Jobs introduced three revolutionary products at MacWorld Expo, Apple's annual trade show and conference. Using a mix of images, written text, and oral presentation, Jobs introduced a wide-screen iPod with touch controls, a breakthrough Internet communication device, and a revolutionary cell phone. He then shocked the audience by informing everyone that these three new products were, in fact, a single device: the iPhone, which *Time* magazine named the Invention of the Year in 2007. There is little question that the iPhone has had a great impact on how people communicate and exchange information and that Steve Jobs's 2007 presentation had far-reaching consequences.

Jobs's purpose was to inform his audience about the iPhone, to show them what it was, how it worked, why it was different, who might use it, when it would be available, and where it might work. By the time Jobs completed his presentation, what people knew and understood about the possibilities of a "smart phone" changed. Jobs's audience, whether skeptical of his claims or eager to own one of the new phones, now possessed new information.

Informative Writing

10.1 Describe differences between informative writing and other forms of expository writing

Informative writing imparts knowledge and meaning. It can be thought of as a kind of reporting. Informative writing delivers information in a way that the audience can visualize or understand, giving it form and organizing it so it makes sense.

Informative writing is also a type of expository writing. The purpose of expository writing, generally, is to inform, explain, define, describe, or instruct. Expository writing is not intended to persuade, but the way you choose to convey facts and describe information will likely influence an audience's acceptance of those facts. Nearly all writing contains elements of informative writing. The degree to which writing informs is dependent, in part, on what the audience already knows and doesn't know.

Explaining, one element of expository writing, is actually an extension of informative writing. Explaining suggests evaluation, whereas informing suggests delivery of information without analysis. Informative writing directly and objectively *tells* the who, what, when, where, why, and how of a situation; explanatory writing more subjectively *analyzes* who, what, why, when, where, and how. Whether you are informing or explaining can drastically affect how your audience interprets the information you provide. Both are valuable depending on your rhetorical purpose.

10.2 Make ethical choices when writing to inform

Informing requires careful ethical consideration. How you inform, the degree of detail you include, and the accuracy of what you convey can have a real impact on how the information affects the situation. Writers should consider two central ethical concerns when informing:

- *Disclosure* means informing an audience of everything that is pertinent to the situation and not leaving out any essential information. Disclosure is closely linked to the degree of detail you provide.

- *Accuracy* refers to the degree of correctness or truthfulness a writer conveys when informing. Leaving out key information can affect accuracy. Stretching the truth—like exaggerating on a job résumé—is a form of inaccurate informing and is ethically objectionable.

Informative writing should be directed by audience needs. Audiences turn to informative writing for four reasons:

10.3 Identify situations that require the delivery of information

- *Immediate need.* Audiences may have a pressing need for information. For example, someone installing a new software application likely requires information about how to install the software at that moment. Audiences in immediate need situations require concise, clear, direct delivery of information.
- *Investigatory need.* Some audiences simply may seek information to satisfy their curiosities, whether personal or professional. These audiences might seek out sources that provide general levels of information, like *Wikipedia* or other encyclopedic, overview documents. Or they might need more extensive and detailed documents like formal reports or technical documents.
- *Direct need.* Some audiences seek information because they require specific information within a situation such as a briefing or a training event. For example, during an emergency situation, Red Cross administrators deliver briefings because workers and volunteers need information to perform their duties. Documents like procedure manuals and policy manuals function as direct-need informative writing.
- *Indirect need.* Some audiences may engage one subject and then realize they need information about a another subject. For example, someone reading about the usefulness of social media as marketing tools may encounter a reference to RSS feeds (Really Simple Syndication feeds). Unaware of how RSS functions, the reader may need information regarding RSS feeds to support learning about social media and marketing. In these kinds of situations, audiences are best served if the indirect information they need is already contained within the content and if the indirect information does not supersede the primary purpose of the document.

Perhaps more than any kind of writing, informative writing is likely to affect people not always identified as part of the audience. That is, when providing informative writing, it is important to consider all of the players that the information might affect. For instance, when Steve Jobs introduced the iPhone, the information he delivered certainly affected his immediate audience, the population who would most readily purchase the iPhone, the employees at Apple, investors and stockbrokers, and even Apple's competitors in the mobile phone business. But we must also consider that Jobs's announcement also affected others such as companies that make third-party applications for the iPhone and the labor forces that manufacture and assemble the iPhone. The information also affected people who cannot afford the iPhone or who don't have access to iPhone technologies, creating a split between those with particular information-access technologies and those without. None of these additional players appeared to be Jobs's direct audience, yet the information he delivered affected their lives to some degree.

annotated example

The informative text that follows is a biographical essay about singer Celia Cruz. The essay can also be considered an encyclopedic reference because it appeared originally in an online reference database published by Gale, a publishing group that publishes e-learning for schools, libraries, and businesses. Gale is best known for its accuracy in reporting information and prides itself on attentive organizational strategies in its reference materials. As you read this biographical essay, pay particular attention to how the Gale writers have used a general-approach organizational strategy as well as visual cues such as headings to organize information and guide readers through that information.

Celia Cruz

Hispanic Heritage Biographical Essay
Published by Gale

Although the Cuban-born music known as salsa, like other forms of Latin jazz and dance music, has been primarily male-dominated, its biggest vocal star is female. Celia Cruz has a powerful voice that transfers the rhythmic energy of salsa into the vocal medium, and she has been a prominent figure in the music since the beginnings of her career in Cuba in the 1950s. Leaving Cuba for the United States after the Castro takeover in 1959, Cruz has become a true legend of Latin American music and something of an emblem of Latin American identity.

> Notice how this introductory paragraph works to establish a context for the information the essay will provide. The paragraph situates Celia Cruz's career, her reputation, and her biography, but it does not overwhelm the reader with details.

The early facts of Cruz's life are somewhat obscure. Always reluctant to discuss her age, Cruz—according to some accounts—was born in Havana, Cuba, on October 21, 1924. Growing up in the city's poor Santo Suárez neighborhood in a household of 14 children (some were her cousins), she stood out because of her singing ability. Cruz won a singing contest called "La hora del té" and with her mother's encouragement began to enter other contests in various parts of Cuba.

> This paragraph begins to provide relevant details. Notice how the writer clarifies the uncertainty of Cruz's birth date and uses the parenthetical to clarify details about the 14 children living with Cruz.

Traveled on Streetcar to Contests

Sometimes Cruz would travel to the contests with a cousin named Nenita. "I was very skinny and tiny," she told *Billboard*. "And since the tram cost five cents each way and we didn't have enough money, I'd sit on Nenita's lap, because she was bigger. The drivers knew us and, sometimes, they'd let me sit on the seat beside her, if it was empty. One time, we had no money to return and we walked back. We arrived at 2 a.m."

> A heading starts this paragraph. Notice three things about the use of the heading: (a) as a function of general organizational strategy, the heading allows the writer to inform about specific information without having to use a more narrative-like transition; (b) the heading identifies specifically what kind of information can be found within the subsection; and (c) this heading becomes a visual cue that distinguishes a separate section. Also in this paragraph, notice the use of direct quotes as a way of establishing accuracy and authority.

Cruz's father, however, believed that she should become a teacher, an altogether more common profession for a Cuban woman at the time. She enrolled at the national teachers' college, but dropped out after finding more and more success with her music in live and radio performances. Something of a compromise was reached when she enrolled at Havana's National Conservatory of Music—but there a professor encouraged her to consider a full-time singing career.

Her breakthrough came in 1950 when she became the lead vocalist for a big band called La Sonora Matancera. Bandleader Rogelio Martínez showed faith in Cruz when he continued to feature her despite the protests of fans of the band's previous vocalist, and once again when an American record executive resisted the idea of making a Sonora Matancera disc that featured Cruz, believing that a rumba record with a female vocalist would not sell well. Martínez promised to pay Cruz himself if the recording flopped. It did well in both Cuba and the United States, and Cruz toured widely through Central and North America with La Sonora Matancera in the 1950s.

> Recognize that the writers do not editorialize in reporting these events. There is no evaluation, just a direct account of events.

Group Fled Cuba

At the time of the Communist takeover of Cuba in 1959, the group was slated to tour Mexico; from Mexico, rather than returning to Cuba, they entered the United States and remained there. Cruz herself became a U.S. citizen in 1961. Cuban Communist leader Fidel Castro was furious and barred Cruz from returning to Cuba, enforcing the ban even after Cruz's parents' deaths. Cruz for her part has vowed not to return to Cuba until such time as the Castro regime is deposed. In 1962 she married La Sonora Matancera trumpet player Pedro Knight.

Although Cruz had made numerous recordings with La Sonora Matancera, she experienced little success in the United States in the 1960s. Although she spoke English well she refused to record in the language. Younger Hispanic Americans at the time were gravitating away from big-band dance music and toward rock-and-roll, in both Latin and non-Latin inflections. Cruz's fortunes began to improve when she meshed her talents with those of the musicians and bandleaders who were creating the new music called salsa—chief among them Tito Puente, Johnny Pacheco, and Willie Colón.

Salsa was firmly rooted in Cuban dance traditions, but it was a high-energy new hybrid that incorporated elements of jazz, traditional Afro-Caribbean rhythms, and other forms. It was an ideal medium for the showcasing of Cruz's vocals, for she was both an exciting improviser (she

> Consider the organizational structure of this paragraph. The first four sentences all report information tied directly to Cruz's departure from Cuba and immigration to the United States. The final sentence, however, provides information about Cruz's marriage, which might seem out of place in the organization of the paragraph. However, because the essay is reporting chronological events within a general organizational structure and because Cruz's marriage took place chronologically relevant to her immigration, the sentence can function as a direct part of the information reported.

is known for her vocal imitations of instruments in the manner known as "scat" singing in the jazz world), and a singer with the power to stand up to an intense rhythm section. Cruz on stage was a commanding figure whose control over audiences resulted not only from her flamboyant, stage-filling attire, but also from her ability to engage them in call-and-response patterns that spring from salsa's Afro-Cuban roots.

> Notice that the first part of the preceding paragraph includes indirect need information—information that the audience may not have sought out but the writer provided as a means of clarification. Readers would likely seek out the biographical essay about Cruz to learn more about her life; indirectly, though, they may need to understand a bit about salsa to understand Cruz's biography. The writers have provided a general definition of salsa to satisfy that indirect need.

Recorded for Fania Label

In 1973 Cruz appeared in *Hommy*, a Spanish-language adaptation of The Who's rock opera *Tommy*. Her reputation spread both within and beyond the Hispanic community in the 1970s after she signed with the new salsa label Fania and recorded with a cream-of-the-crop lineup, the Fania All-Stars, drawn from its stable of artists. The Fania All-Stars album *Live at Yankee Stadium* (two vols., 1976) documented the power of her performances. Cruz has appeared in several films, including *The Mambo Kings Play Songs of Love* (1992) and *The Perez Family* (1995).

> Why do you suppose the writer decided to include the qualifying phrase "a Spanish-language adaptation of The Who's rock opera *Tommy*" in the first sentence? What need does this fulfill?

One of Cruz's performance trademarks is a full-throated shout of "Azucar!" (Sugar!); she explained its 1970s origins in a 2000 *Billboard* interview. "I was having dinner at a restaurant in Miami, and when the waiter offered me coffee, he asked me if I took it with or without sugar. I said, 'Chico, you're Cuban. How can you even ask that? With sugar!' And that evening during my show … I told the audience the story and they laughed. And one day, instead of telling the story, I simply walked down the stairs and shouted 'Azucar!'"

> Notice that the writer identifies the source of the Cruz anecdote to provide confirmation and validation of the quote.

Cruz might be compared with U.S. jazz vocalist Sarah Vaughan in her ability to bring vocal techniques to a primarily instrumental music, but she has a more essentially popular appeal than any jazz singer. Seemingly indestructible vocally, Cruz continued a full schedule of concerts and recordings throughout the 1980s and beyond. She received a Grammy award for the album *Ritmo en el corazón*, recorded with conga player Ray Barretto, in 1990, as well as an honorary doctorate from Yale University.

Still a major star in her own right, Cruz became an inspiration for numerous younger performers (such as Gloria Estefan) in the 1990s; her audience hardly aged along with her. "We've never had to attract these kids," she told *Time*. "They come by themselves. Rock is a strong influence on them, but they still want to know about their roots." For most Hispanic Americans, indeed, Celia Cruz has been and remains a much-loved figure, an icon of Latin culture.

> Notice that the *Time* quote identified in the previous paragraph, when considered with the earlier *Billboard* quote, reveals that the writer conducted research about Cruz before writing the biographical essay. Notice, too, that the writer provides a specific example to qualify "numerous younger performers."

student example

Bertrhude Albert was born in Cap-Haitian, Haiti. When she was nine, her family moved to the United States with the hope of providing Bertrhude and her five siblings greater educational opportunities. After graduation, Bertrhude plans to pursue a graduate degree in Latin American Studies, with a concentration on Haiti. Bertrhude invests a lot of time thinking about Haiti. As she says, "Haiti is my future. My heart beats for Haiti. During the day I think about my country, and at night it remains engraved on my eyelids. In the deepest compartments of my heart, my country lies."

On January 12, 2010, a magnitude 7.0 earthquake struck Haiti and killed an estimated 316,000 people and injured or displaced approximately a million others. Haiti's need for support far outweighed the relief provided by many countries. One month after the earthquake and only three semesters into college, Bertrhude Albert flew to Haiti to help in any way she could. While there, Bertrhude took video of the devastation and the earthquake's effect on Haiti's population. When she returned, using the footage she shot and her experiences in Haiti, Bertrhude produced an informative video and wrote a number of essays about the situation in Haiti. Within a year, enough people had responded to her writing and her video that Bertrhude was able to launch a nonprofit organization to provide aid and support for Haiti. Since that time, Projects for Haiti has provided some remarkable work in support of Haiti. In the essay that follows, Bertrhude writes about how and why she formed Projects for Haiti and some of what the organization has accomplished.

The Stand Against Social Injustice: Projects for Haiti, Inc.

Bertrhude Albert

Haiti stands alone as the poorest country in the Western Hemisphere. The majority of Haitians find themselves plagued by social injustice every day. According to the Children's Hunger Relief Fund, an estimated 44 children die hourly of hunger and starvation. Less than 50% of Haitians have access to clean drinking water and over 80% of Haitians live below the poverty line. Simply put, the quality of life in Haiti is at a bare minimum. The people of Haiti fight for daily survival in their economic, social and political lives.

The pains of Haitians have only heightened as time has progressed. On January 12, 2010, a catastrophic earthquake struck Haiti. By January 24, 2010, there were at least 52 aftershocks measuring 4.5 or greater. These quakes crippled the very core of Haiti's existence. Misery was the song of many Haitians as they found their troubles buried under pounds of rubble. The effects of this Earthquake were overwhelming. Over 200,000 Haitians lost their lives, over 300,000 Haitians were injured, and over 1 million Haitians became homeless as a result of this earthquake. The poorest country in the Western Hemisphere experienced a horrific natural disaster, which left them with a 14 billion dollar debt on top of their previous economic problems.

These words are more than just facts; they're my earthshattering reality. As a Haitian Native I found myself burdened by the trials of my people. A month after the earthquake I returned to my country only to find it abused and battered by the earthquake. I spent my time in Haiti aiding and supporting Haitians through relief programs and building relationships. After spending a week in my hometown, Cap-Haitian, I flew back to the United States without one of my vital organs, my heart. I found myself burdened by the trials of my people and I knew that I could no longer let the pangs of social injustice sting without a fight. My duty to humanity beckoned me to respond to the travesties in Haiti. I knew that my experience in Haiti left me with a destiny that is fastened to Haiti.

After returning to the United States, I knew that I couldn't keep silent about Haiti. I wanted everyone to experience what I had experienced. I knew that if people saw what I saw they would be drawn by compassion and compelled to support the Haiti cause. With that, I partnered with my roommate, Priscilla Zelaya, in order to form a group of students that would go back to Haiti. In less than a year we organized a group of 19 college students to go on a mission trip during our spring break. We stayed in Cap-Haitian, Haiti, for 7 days. During this time we held a mobile clinic, taught English classes, hosted a children's program and much more. Every member of the team was exposed to the deep sense of fortitude, resilience and joy that these Haitians had amidst their trials. Our hearts became tethered to the people of Haiti.

This was only the beginning of our partnership with Haitians. After our trip, Priscilla and I knew we would be working with Haiti for the long haul. We began to brainstorm sustainable ways to empower and partner with Haitians. We were confident that Haitians were not in need of another "foreign savior." Rather, we desired to go along side of Haitians and empower them with the practical tools needed for sustainable development. With that in mind, we returned to Haiti two months later in order to further survey the needs of Haitians in Cap-Haitian. We took surveys and spoke directly to the Haitians around us. Speaking with the locals one on one enabled us to gauge their needs by acknowledging their suffering and affirming their strengths. We returned with the confidence that we should and could start a nonprofit for Haiti.

On July 6th, 2011, Projects for Haiti, Inc. was officially birthed. After much research and unofficial surveys, Priscilla and I created and incorporated the nonprofit, Projects for Haiti, Inc. The heart behind this nonprofit was to create and support various projects in and for Haiti that would empower Haitians to develop sustainably. Within a matter of weeks, we were able to rally up a board of 5 and a staff of 7. We worked ceaselessly at formulating the structure of a nonprofit that would best equip and empower Haitians. Although there are hundreds of NGO's in Haiti, we felt a strong need to partner with Haitians through creating a new NGO. Through our months of research, we were able to take note of the various crippling effects of many NGO's in Haiti. We strategically aimed at working against those effects.

Just two months later, Projects for Haiti, Inc. began formulating a team of 19 college students that would travel to Cap-Haitian for their 2011 Spring Break. This fivefold team would include a medical team, an English language instructing team, an orphanage team, a construction team and a prayer team. Within the span of 7 days, these students were able to interact with over 1,000 Haitians. This trip employed Haitian nurses, construction workers and regular workers. Through this trip Projects for Haiti, Inc. was able to support Haitians but also gauge the extent of the needs and potential support needed to create a system of sustainable development. Since then, Projects for Haiti, Inc. has continued to grow and develop. This mission trip was followed by various other trips that have allowed over 35 college students to partner with Haitians.

Projects for Haiti, Inc. currently has several projects going on that all work towards empowering Haitians. One of the prime examples is The English Association. Over 40% of Haitians are unemployed. 80% find themselves under the poverty line. Many Haitians struggle to bring a meal to their table. Jobs aren't easily accessible. One of the few ways that Haitians are able to find work is if they know English. English has essentially become a profession. Haitians become prime candidates for jobs if they are able to communicate in the language of business, the language of foreigners. In August 2011, Projects for Haiti, Inc. began The English Association. Every Friday at 2:00 p.m., 16 Haitians meet in an attempt to strengthen their English. For two hours a week, they discuss various topics, write prompts, listen to English grammar and pronunciation CD's and give presentations. They are also assigned to tutor a Haitian (an hour a week) who knows no English. This Association attempts to create leaders, build community, and empower Haitians.

Another project that is currently in progress is the New Public Library in Cap-Haitian. In August 2011, Projects for Haiti received a donated facility. We decided to turn it into a free public library in Cap-Haitian. There are currently no public libraries in that region, and we are excited to form this one. Through partnerships with organizations, businesses, churches and individuals' support, we have been able to collect many books (in French, Spanish, Creole and English). We are continuously raising funds and materials for this project.

Projects for Haiti is also able to support a local Orphanage called The Hope Center. This orphanage was built in response to the high levels of homeless children in Cap-Haitian. On February 16, 2012, the house parents and the first 4 children moved in. There are now 15 children living in The Hope Center. Although this orphanage was made to house 30 children, financial burdens do not allow for more children to enter. Projects for Haiti has been able to partner with this organization through money donations that go directly towards supporting the education of the children.

As an organization, we continue to strive to partner with Haitians and Americans in order to bridge a line of connection. We would love to connect with everyone who is willing to stand against the prevailing sting of social injustice.

student example

Thinking about Bertrhude's Essay

1. Informative writing conveys information. What does Bertrhude convey in her essay? What do you now know that you didn't know before reading her essay?

2. Much of Bertrhude's credibility in this essay comes from her testimonial about her visit to Haiti. In what ways do that testimonial and the way she conveys information in the essay contribute to how readers respond to the information she delivers?

3. Who is Bertrhude's audience? How do you know who the audience is? Are there any evident players in this situation who are not part of Bertrhude's primary audience?

THE ROAD TO A
STRONG THESIS

SECOND THOUGHTS:
"Why do I want others to know about what's going on Haiti or why I worked to start Projects for Haiti?"

SECOND THOUGHTS:
"But it's not just that I want them to know; I want them to care and I want them to act."

SECOND THOUGHTS:
"So, really, I need to inform readers about two things: what happened there and what I'm doing to help."

PURPOSE:
"To inform people about Projects for Haiti and to convey why the situation in Haiti inspired me to start the organization."

EXIGENCY:
"Haiti will only get the help it needs if people know what happened there. I need to share that information."

RESPONSE:
"Maybe if I inform readers about why I care and have taken action, they will care and act as well."

RESPONSE:
"I suppose, then, I need to inform in order to persuade."

ASSIGNMENT
To write an informative essay.

THESIS:
"As a Haitian native, I want you to know what happened in my country and what I'm trying to do to help."

Bertrhude Albert recognized that she could not communicate all of the information she had obtained about Haiti in a single essay. She had to make a number of choices to determine what to report and what to leave out. To make these decisions, Bertrhude had to think carefully about what she wanted readers to take away from her essay. She likely followed a path like this one.

FINAL THOUGHTS:
"Now I know what I need my audience to know and how I'll let them know about it."

Lisa Hix is the associate editor of *Collectors Weekly*, an online resource for people who collect antiques and other vintage items. Her essay, reprinted here, was originally published by *Collectors Weekly*. Hix has served in editorial capacities for a number of newspapers and magazines, both print and online. Her articles and interviews, covering a wide range of subjects, address news issues, pop culture, fashion, the arts, and local interests for residents of San Francisco. Her writing has appeared in many publications, including *The SFist*, *Glamour*, *Elle Girl*, *Teen Vogue*, *Bust*, *Venus Zine*, *D.I.W.*, and *Yahoo! Year in Review*. She is also an avid roller skater. In the essay that follows, Hix informs readers about the fascinating history of fake barf, an important branch of the novelty industry.

The Inside Scoop on the Fake Barf Industry

Lisa Hix

Have you ever stopped to contemplate the existence of rubber barf? It opens up enough philosophical quandaries to make your head spin. Who would ever think of such a thing? Why would he feel the need to manufacture it?

Fortunately, Stan and Mardi Timm, the foremost experts on famed novelty company H. Fishlove & Co., have the answers to these vexing questions. The couple even got a personal tour of the factory where "Whoops," the original fake vomit, is still churned out.

Chicago gag kingpin Irving Fishlove, son of the company's founder, loved nothing more than a good prank—particularly when the prankster gets a laugh at the expense of his unwitting target. So when presented with the first prototype of latex puke in the late 1950s, he howled with laughter and declared that he loved it.

Not only did Irving Fishlove buy the idea to mass-produce and sell, he also took matters into his own hands. His son, Howard Fishlove, told the Timms about coming home as a school kid to find his kitchen counter covered in various types of fake barf. Turns out, Dad was so excited about this upchuck gag, he was experimenting with his own formulas of brown or yellow latex mixed with chunky bits of colored foam. "He told us it was the most disgusting thing he had ever seen," says Mardi Timm.

How this invention got tossed at Fishlove's feet, though, is a matter of debate. The Timms explained that there are two creation myths around fake throw-up.

First, you have to understand that Fishlove was a collaborator with Marvin Glass, the famed toy designer who, with his company, devised some of the most beloved toys and board games of the 20th century, including Mouse Trap, Operation, Rock 'Em Sock 'Em Robots, and Lite Brite, produced by major companies like Hasbro and Ideal. Another of Glass's claims to fame was the invention of Yakity-Yak talking teeth, an idea he sold to H. Fishlove & Co.

One story goes, "A fellow by the name of Ayala worked at Marvin Glass and Associates," Stan says. "He was walking down the street and saw somebody's vomit on the street, and he did a double-take. First, he said, 'Yuck!' And then, 'Oh, what a great gag item!' He went to work, made up one with some latex, and presented it to his boss. Glass didn't care for the idea. In fact, he was rather disgusted.

"One day, Glass was showing some jokes to Irving Fishlove, and Fishlove wasn't particularly interested in any of them. All of a sudden Ayala burst in, plopped down this latex fake barf, and Fishlove cracked up. Glass suddenly thought it was funny, and that's how it got started."

"The other story is that there was a fellow by the name of Ray Suggett, from Arkansas," Stan continues. "He made prosthetics, like false legs, et cetera, for people who were injured in the mines. He also made joke items for Fishlove. One day some latex plopped on the ground. It looked like barf, and he didn't particularly like it. He thought it was kind of ridiculous, but he didn't throw it away.

"Not long after that, Irving Fishlove stopped by. He asked Suggett if he had any new gags. Suggett opened up the drawer and took out this fake vomit. Fishlove was very impressed. And so goes the second story."

The Timms think the Glass story is the more likely of the two to have led to the scene young Howard encountered of Irving experimenting with his own blown-chunks mixtures in the family's home kitchen. Whichever story is true, rubbery puke was an immediate hit with jokesters all over the U.S. when it debuted in 1959.

"It was an instant success," Stan says. "It's not surprising, because it meets all the criteria of a good gag. It's very cheap to make, so you could make a decent profit on it. It sells for a very cheap price, so it's easy to sell. And people just went after it. The numbers we hear tend to vary, but the story is it initially sold about 100,000 units a year, which, at the time, was a lot. Fishlove did very well with it."

In fact, Irving Fishlove loved this joke so much, he used it himself all the time, even when he was dining at a posh, five-star restaurant.

"When Irving's daughter, Dianne Stone, visited our Fishlove museum, she told a story about the time when she was a teenager and the family went to this very exclusive restaurant. Everyone was dressed incredibly fancy," Stan explains.

"Of course, Irving decided to pull the gag. He started heaving and retching, and then he threw a 'Whoops' fake-barf patty down on the floor. Right away, the waiter was like, 'Oh my God, we're sorry, Mr. So-and-So!' They were thinking, 'This poor man!' Then, he told them what had happened. She said it was one of the most embarrassing moments in her life."

H. Fishlove & Co.—and now Fun Inc., which bought the company in the '80s—has kept a lid on the formula Irving came up with, the same way Coca-Cola guards its recipe and KFC protects its special herbs and spices.

"It is a secret recipe," Mardi says. "But I think we know what's in it. It's got foam pieces cut up, and it's got latex. But the actual recipe, nobody outside the company knows that."

The Timms have close ties to Fun Inc., who invited them to tour the Chicago factory where the fake upchuck is crafted by hand.

"We discovered this room on the upper floor that was filled with what looked like a bunch of chocolate-chip cookies," Mardi says, "But it wasn't cookies. It was just tray after tray after tray of this fake vomit."

These "cookies" were 500 pieces of fake barf, spread out as far as the Timms' eyes could see, "curing" under the skylights in the Chicago summer sun. The secret formula is mixed up in a big bucket, and the workers ladle it out, "like you make pancakes," Stan says. "Each one comes out a little different, of course, but that's okay."

The latex is initially white, but after a day or so, dries into the perfect puke-yellow. "Then, they attach it to a card that says 'Whoops' and sell it," Stan says.

Of course, now, the original "Whoops" has many gnarly competitors. "One of the better ones is called Glop, made by the famous S.S. Adams joke company. Others made across the Pacific include Fake Barf and "Oops."

Buckets of the "Whoops" fake barf mixture, seen on the Timms' tour of Fun Inc.'s Chicago warehouse.

Puke "cookies" curing in the sun at the Fun Inc. warehouse in Chicago during the Timms' tour.

"There are all sorts," Stan says, "In fact, I was looking on the Internet, and there's even fake barf that comes in a canister. Apparently, you can pour it out, so it looks very realistic.

"Speaking of realism, the 'Whoops!' card states—and I'll read this for you—'Instructions: sprinkle with water to make it look more realistic.' After all, it's barf, so it should be wet, right?"

Regardless of its myriad competitors, "Whoops" has remained more or less unchanged in 50-plus years.

"Why mess with a good thing?" Mardi says. "It's probably one of the greatest gags of all time because it just spanned all these decades and it's still going. It works well. It's easy to make, cheap to make, and nobody knows the formula because none of the others look like it. And there are lots of other companies that try to make the same thing, but they're not as good. The best one is really the original 'Whoops.'"

"Whoops," far right, with its competitors, "Oops," Glop, and Fake Barf!

Some of the many competing products novelty shoppers might find next to the original "Whoops"

Analyzing the Situation

1. Why do you suppose Lisa Hix decided to interview the Timms and write an article about fake barf? That is, what situation requires this information to be conveyed?

2. What do you suppose Hix's exigency was in writing this essay?

Analyzing the Rhetoric

1. Most of this essay is direct quotes from the Timms. In fact, it is the Timms who convey the bulk of the information to the audience. Lisa Hix primarily informs her audience through the Timms. Why do you suppose she chose to convey the information through their voices? What does she gain or lose by doing so?

2. What is the tone of Hix's essay? Why is tone so important in this essay?

3. What role does nostalgia play in Hix's essay?

4. Is Hix's essay funny or disgusting? Can an essay about fake barf be funny, and should it be? What role can humor play in informing?

Discussing

1. Did you want to know this much about fake barf? Are you glad that you did learn this much? Do you feel sufficiently informed about fake barf? As a class, discuss what aspects of this essay could be important.

2. Keep in mind, as Hix explains, fake barf has been a very successful product. As a class, discuss what we might learn from the success of such a seemingly unpleasant product.

Writing

1. All products have a history, whether in the joke industry or in any other industry. Products are thought of, invented, developed, tested, and sold. Take some time to learn about another product made, marketed, and sold by the joke industry. Write an informative essay about that product.

three examples

SIDE ᴮʸ SIDE

Each of the three previous examples informs differently: The "Celia Cruz": Hispanic Heritage Biographical Essay provides encyclopedic information, offering general information about Celia Cruz; Bertrhude Albert informs through a chronological narrative of her experiences in Haiti, and Lisa Hix relies on a combination of reporting and dialogue to inform about the fake barf industry. Each informs differently, but each provides readers with substantial information.

	annotated example	**student example**	**professional example**
	Hispanic Heritage Biographical Essay, "Celia Cruz"	Bertrhude Albert, "The Stand against Social Injustice: Projects for Haiti, Inc."	Lisa Hix, "The Inside Scoop on the Fake Barf Industry"
PURPOSE	To provide information about the life and career of Celia Cruz	To provide information about Haiti and the work Projects for Haiti is doing	To provide information about the fake barf industry
AUDIENCE	Readers conducting research about Hispanic heritage or specifically about Celia Cruz	Readers interested in Haiti or in how people can provide aid to Haiti	Collectors, joke enthusiasts, or readers interested in nostalgia
NEED	Readers would likely read this information for investigatory need.	Readers would likely read this essay for direct need.	Readers would likely read this article for indirect need.
TYPE OF INFORMATIVE WRITING	Web page/report	Essay	Article/web page
TYPES OF INFORMATION	Biographical, occupational, personal	Personal, testimonial, statistical	Testimonial, historical
TONE	Encyclopedic; strives to be objective, not necessarily flat in tone, but lacks a sense of emotion	Synthesizes both enthusiasm and concern	Tries to maintain a journalistic tone, but given the subject matter, also includes a subtle humorous tone
RHETORIC	Focuses on clarity and concision in its delivery; dependent primarily on logos and ethos	Blends the informative with the personal, using the personal to establish ethos	Relies primarily on the logos of informative writing, but can't avoid pathos because of the subject matter. Relies on dialogue to help establish ethos
ORGANIZATION	In its encyclopedic approach, uses a general to specific organizational scheme and uses subtitle divisions to classify information	Uses a chronological organizational scheme	Moves from general to more specific information
CIRCULATION	Circulates as a digital resource available to anyone with web access	Written initially as an essay for a class assignment, revised versions were repurposed and remixed in promotional materials that circulate on the Web	Written for an online news source for those interested in antiques and vintage items; circulation occurs globally within this audience base

10.4 Apply strategies for writing to inform

Type of Informative Writing	Preparing Your Writing
Essays	Focus on a primary subject, question, or premise. Clearly detail points of information. Develop a coherent discussion of the essay's subject. Provide evidence. Follow a logical pattern of organization.
Reports	Conduct research as needed. Use careful ethical considerations of disclosure and accuracy.
Instructions and Manuals	Provide readers with the following information: the *scope* of the document; *descriptions* of the item, policy, or procedure; *definitions* of key terms and concepts; *alerts* readers should be aware of; *equipment, tools,* or *systems requirements; parts lists; steps* in a process or procedure; and *troubleshooting* approaches.
Tweets and Status Updates	Not all of these networking posts are inherently informative, but they can be important ways to disseminate information.
Web Pages	Learn to critically analyze and evaluate information found on the Web. The vast amount of information provided throughout the Web makes it difficult to discern what information is reliable and what is erroneous or fallacious.
Blogs	Popular blogs such as Mashable, TechCrunch, and Boing Boing inform their readers about news in the world of technology, social networking, gadgets, and similar cultural information.
Articles	The value of academic, scholarly, or scientific articles is that their content is usually vetted by other professionals in the field who validate the content as authentic, accurate, and significant.
Press Releases	A central function of a press release is to establish a context for the information, including key dates. Because some press releases are issued to promote an organization's product or actions, they may also contain elements of persuasion, explanation, and/or editorializing.

10.5 Write to inform within other rhetorical purposes

Strategy	Developing Your Informative Writing
Conduct research	Begin your informative writing by gathering the information you need to report; then analyze, confirm, and interpret it to ensure you have it right. Be sure to document your sources.
Be clear; inform ethically	Present your information completely, clearly, and accurately, without confusing or distorting it. Relate the facts, and don't manipulate or editorialize the information. Some information might be difficult to understand or may contain numerous details that are challenging for an audience to connect. Pay close attention to how clearly you are presenting the information and how visuals, like charts and graphs, might help clarify content.
Focus	Stick to the topic at hand; don't confuse your audience by providing tangential, excessive, or extraneous information. Good informative writing sticks to its purpose. Good research and a good understanding of what you are informing can help you maintain focus.
Be direct	Get to the point. Opening paragraphs should serve as direct introductions, not as teasers, and should introduce subject, ideas, and key concepts without distractions.
Define key terms	Define key terms, particularly when writing for a general audience. Key terms might be defined in the body of the text or in a glossary, depending on your situation. Keep in mind that definitions themselves are a type of informative writing. Unclear definitions can lead to confusion. Many words can be interpreted differently or have subtle, nuanced meanings, so your word choice in a definition can critically affect understanding. Teachers will often expect you to define key terms in assigned writing to demonstrate your understanding of those terms.
Provide details	Disclose all relevant details. Avoid irrelevant or tangential details because they might distract from the purpose, focus, and directness of the information you provide.
Use descriptive adjectives	Use adjectives that accurately represent the information, but avoid editorial adjectives that imply value or judgment. Descriptive adjectives usually indicate characteristics of appearance, condition, shape, size, time, sound, touch, taste, and quantity—for example, *few, cold, curly, dirty, slippery, smooth, strong, hard, ripe, old, quick, loud, high-pitched, large, small, broad, narrow, green, and dark*.
Provide examples	Examples help readers visualize details. Be sure to include relevant examples, but avoid extraneous or distracting ones.
Organize effectively	Informative writing often relies on either chronological organizational strategies or a general-approach organization strategy.
Use visuals	Visuals, in particular graphics such as charts, tables, and graphs, are effective in clarifying detailed or difficult information. However, be certain that any visual you use clarifies information and does not end up causing confusion.

MAPPING
YOUR SITUATION

NETWORKS
- In what networks will my information circulate?
- How does my information compare with others' information in this situation?
- How does my information change this situation?

WRITERS AND SPEAKERS
- Who are the other writers and speakers in this situation?
- How do the other writers present their information?
- Why do readers accept or dismiss their information?

RELATIONS
- What is my relation to the situation?
- What are the relationships between writers/speakers, audience, and players?
- What are the relationships to external forces, like culture, religion, or politics?
- How does my information affect different relationships—like readers' relationships to the information?

AUDIENCE
- Who will read/see the information?
- What do I know about my intended audience?
- Who will the information affect directly and indirectly?

MEDIUM AND METHOD
- In what genre will I inform?
- What information must I convey?
- How will I present my information?
- How will I distribute my information?

CONTEXT
- Where will the information come from? Where will it appear?
- What limits the information I can convey?
- Who knows this information and who needs to know it?

PURPOSE
- Why am I informing?
- What does my information need to accomplish?
- Does the information I need to convey support a specific purpose?

Mapping your situation will help you generate ideas you can use to compose. Start by answering these questions about each part of the situation. Begin with your purpose and work outward to relations and networks.

Writing Projects

Essay

The U.S. Fish and Wildlife Service (USF&WS) keeps track of wildlife (both animals and plants) that it categorizes as either "threatened" or "endangered." According to the USF&WS, an "endangered" species is "one that is in danger of extinction throughout all or a significant portion of its range." Use online resources, including the USF&WS web pages, to learn more about how different species are categorized as threatened or endangered. Next, identify one species listed by the USF&WS as endangered and, after learning about that species and why it is endangered, write an essay that informs your audience about the species and its endangered status. As a class, plan to compile all work into a single volume, making sure that every student chooses a different species. Your class may also want to restrict the species selection to those that are regional or local to your campus.

Visual Information

Information graphics (also known as infographics) are visuals that combine graphics and written text to present information that would be difficult for an audience to understand in written form only. Create an infographic to answer one of the questions listed here and to inform readers about that topic. This assignment requires that you conduct research to locate information, interpret and analyze the information, and present the information using graphics and writing.

Questions:

- How does offshore drilling work?
- Who uses Facebook?
- What do people use social media for?
- How much energy per capita do countries use?
- What kinds of pets do Americans keep?

Digital

The "Information Age" usually refers to the period beginning in the 1970s, when personal computers first became available, and leading into the present. Digital technologies have played a tremendous role in the evolution of this period, which is also called "the Digital Age." Create a digital video that can be shared on the Internet and that informs a general audience about how Information Age technologies affect and interact with American cultures.

Research

This chapter discusses a number of genres that are particularly well suited for informative writing, but there are many other genres that also inform. Think, for instance, about how the copyright page of a book informs, or CD liner notes, or the dietary information panels on a box of cereal, or the credits in a movie. Select a type of document not discussed in the chapter (those mentioned in this exercise are fine) and research the history or conventions of that kind of document. Write an informative research paper about the history of that kind of document as an informative form. Go beyond simply listing the information that might be contained in that type of document so you also inform your audience about how the document functions, its rhetorical strategies, the situations in which that information might be needed, its audience, how it reaches that audience, and anything else that addresses the rhetorical situations of that type of document.

Radical Revision

The research assignment listed above asks you to write a research paper about a form of informative document not addressed in this chapter. Once you have written that paper, take the research you gathered and present it in the form of an infographic, particularly one that emphasizes the history of the chosen type of informative document. Your infographic should be more in depth than simply a series of examples of the form.

10.6 Use visuals as a means of informing

Visuals that Inform

Visuals can be useful in informing because they can convey information clearly, efficiently, and quickly and can assist an audience in understanding it. Information visualization becomes increasingly important as more readers rely on digital media to gather information. Visuals can improve informing in seven ways, discussed below.

Increase Comprehension

Visuals can present details in ways that help readers understand, retain, and recollect information.

Clarify

Visuals can clarify difficult concepts, abstract information, or detailed processes and procedures. In some documents, visuals provide examples that allow readers to see what is described and build a mental frame of reference. Consider the example in Figure 10.1, taken from the U.S. Geological Survey, a scientific agency of the U.S. government. The figure is part of an educational web page about the water cycle. Certainly, the writer of this web page could have described the water cycle through technical text; the visual, though, helps to readily clarify the information explained in the written text.

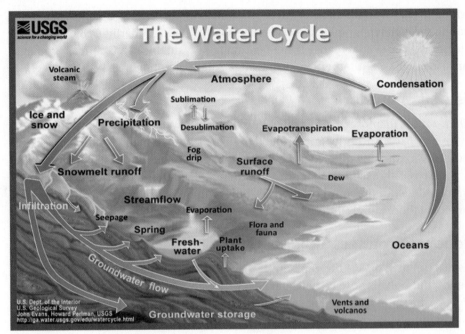

FIGURE 10.1 A visual used to clarify.

Illustrate

Visuals can illustrate key information. Illustrative visuals are generally linked directly to written or spoken text to reinforce what an audience reads or hears. People who make presentations—like Steve Jobs's iPhone introduction (see Figure 10.2)—often use visuals to illustrate points because audiences are more likely to remember information they see.

Organize

Visuals such as charts, tables, bullets, title fonts—even white space—can help organize information into clear, accessible forms. Consider, for instance, how informational web pages like Wikipedia (see Figure 10.3) use title fonts and white space to delineate pieces of information.

Emphasize

Visuals can effectively emphasize key information—a usage that carries ethical implications writers must not overlook. When including informative

FIGURE 10.2 Steve Jobs uses a visual to illustrate information.

writing as part of another rhetorical purpose such as persuading, emphasizing information through typographic effects (such as *italics*, **bold**, <u>underline</u>, color, and size alterations) can sway a reader either legitimately or unethically. Graphics or images can also emphasize information by drawing readers' attention to it.

Establish Authority

When writing to inform, writers often find that visuals such as graphs and charts can evoke a sense of authority and professionalism. Because such visuals are often associated with quantifiable, statistical information that experts and scholars generate, they are typically assumed to represent expert information. Visuals may help establish credibility in the minds of readers, but for that credibility to be authentic, the content of those visuals must be accurate and ethical.

Reach a Broader Audience

Visuals can help bridge the gap between the writer and a broader, more diverse audience, but only if those visuals make cultural sense to the audience. Not all visuals have the same meaning for readers in every culture. Consequently, writers must make culturally aware choices when using visuals.

FIGURE 10.3 This blog page uses visual elements like photos, type, white space, and color to clarify organization.

Writing Process
GUIDELINES

Use the guidelines in this chart to plan, review, and evaluate your process for writing. Each step in the process should support the overall purpose of your project.

SITUATE

- Understand your reasons for informing in this situation.
- Understand how relations affect what information you can and cannot present.
- Identify how the information you present will be limited by constraints.
- Ascertain the role of location in your information.
- Recognize the speakers or writers in the situation and what information they have or have not already provided.
- Identify and analyze the audiences involved and determine the best way to convey information.
- Consider what genres, media, and methods might be best to deliver information.
- Acknowledge how various institutions and power will affect the information you are presenting.
- Consider the ecological relationships of the information and how it connects with other situations.

PLAN

- Clarify your purpose in informing.
- Consider how the information you will convey responds to the situation.
- Consider what might be the best genre, media, and method to deliver your information in the situation.
- Analyze what you know about the situation and what you need to discover before writing to inform.
- Begin to take notes.

RESEARCH

- Determine what information you will need to provide.
- Conduct research to gather the information you need.
- Confirm that your research results will be valid within the situation.
- Identify any visuals you may need to support or clarify your information.
- Organize your information.
- Evaluate your information in light of the situation and your purpose to determine whether you need to conduct further research.
- Collect citation information as you research.

DRAFT

- Confirm that the information you wish to convey is appropriate to the situation and your purpose.
- Draft and organize the content of your informative writing.
- Develop or identify any visuals you may want to use to clarify or support your information.
- Design your document.

REVIEW AND REVISE

- Review your informative writing for clarity and concision.
- Examine it for accuracy.
- Review it for degree of detail appropriate to the situation and purpose.
- Inspect it for extraneous information.
- Review it for organizational approach.
- Examine it for explanations of key terms necessary within the situation.
- Consider whether your writing style is appropriate to the situation.
- Confirm your research and citations.
- Look over your informative writing for visual effectiveness and readability.
- Consider revising the title to most accurately reflect the informative writing's purpose.

EDIT

- Proofread carefull.y
- Correct all mechanical and grammatical errors.

EVALUATE

- Seek feedback from peers.
- Ask for feedback from a representative member of the target audience.
- Ask for feedback from an editor with whom you are confident.
- Evaluate the usefulness of any feedback you receive and revise accordingly.

DISTRIBUTE/CIRCULATE

- Consider technologies of circulation.
- Publish in a form that will be visible within the situation.
- Identify methods for increasing circulation (like search engine optimization) within and beyond the specific situation.
- Consider audience access.
- Identify possible sources of audience response.

Seeking Feedback

Peers, target audiences, and editors can offer valuable observations that will strengthen your writing. You will encourage more constructive feedback from these readers if you structure your questions for them carefully. Consider asking these kinds of questions to get feedback:

EVALUATION Guidelines

INITIAL REACTION

- What are your initial reactions to the information provided in this document?
- What do you see as the purpose of the information found in this document?
- What are the strengths of the document?
- What are the weaknesses of the document?
- Does the information hold your interest?
- Generally speaking, what is the primary thing the writer must do to improve this document?

SITUATION

- Who do you understand the intended audience to be? Why?
- Does the information fulfill its purpose effectively?
- Has the writer explained all that needs to be explained for the audience?

READABILITY

- Does the title provide an accurate, clear representation of the document?
- Did you understand the information?
- Are there parts that are difficult to follow or understand?
- What organizational strategy does the writer use to convey information?
- Are you able to follow the organization of the information?

CONTENT

- Does the information make sense?
- Does the writer provide the necessary information to support the agenda?
- What, if anything, does the writer present that is particularly interesting?
- Which information, if any, is unnecessary or extraneous?
- Does the writer present information objectively or with evaluation? How does that presentation affect how you understand the information?
- What details stand out for you?
- Does the writer provide enough details to make the information clear?

VISUALS

- Does the writer use visuals to clarify or explain written information?
- If so, are the visuals appropriate to the purpose?
- Do the visuals work in conjunction with the writing or independently?
- Are the visuals clear and easy to read?
- Does the document design distract from or support the document's purpose and/or readability?
- What recommendations regarding visuals do you have for the writer?

MECHANICS

- What mechanical distractions, if any, are evident in the writing?
- Which sentences, if any, are unclear?
- Which sentences or paragraphs are particularly well written, if any?
- Are all references cited appropriately?

Summary

Informative writing imparts knowledge and meaning. Yet how you inform depends on your purpose; nearly all writing includes some degree of the informative. In addition, informative writing requires careful ethical consideration, particularly of disclosure and accuracy. Audience need should direct informative writing, and audiences turn to informative writing for four primary reasons: immediate need, investigatory need, direct need, and indirect need. Authors writing to inform must first research to gather information that is accurate. Finally, visuals can be useful in informing because they can present complex information in a simple way that is more easily comprehended, retained, and remembered.

Chapter Review

1. How is informative writing different from other forms of expository writing?

2. What ethical considerations should you take into account when writing to inform?

3. What are four reasons audiences might need information?

4. How might informative writing affect players beyond the audience of a situation?

5. How are information and power related?

6. In what ways do microblogs and tweets encourage informative writing?

7. Why are essays a prominent genre of informative writing in college?

8. What role does research play in informative writing?

9. List four of the twelve strategies critical to informative writing.

10. How can informative writing integrate with other rhetorical purposes?

11. List five of the seven reasons why visuals might be useful in informative writing.

Thinking and Writing about the Chapter

Reflection

At the beginning of this chapter, you wrote about the role information plays in your daily life. Now that you have had the chance to learn more about informative writing, look back at your initial response and revise and expand your discussion regarding the role of information in your daily life and written communication.

Discussion Threads

1. One of the most difficult aspects of writing to inform is remaining attuned to the informative rather than venturing into the explanatory or editorial. As a class, discuss this difficulty and develop a list of strategies for writers that will help them stay focused on the purpose of informing.

2. Why do you suppose writing to inform is important in college? In what kinds of classes other than writing classes do you imagine it will be useful to know how to write to inform? As a class, or in groups, discuss what you see as the role of informative writing in college.

3. In the 2011 movie *Contagion*, the character Dr. Ian Sussman (played by Elliott Gould) tells blogger Alan Krumwiede (played by Jude Law) that "Blogging isn't writing; it's graffiti

with punctuation." As a class, discuss Sussman's assessment of blogging and why someone—even a movie character—might reach such a conclusion. Do you agree with the assessment? Why or why not?

Collaboration

1. Work in small groups to identify an issue on your campus that you believe more people should be aware of. Then collaboratively write a public service announcement (PSA) about that issue. Write a script for the PSA, including instructions for what visual components the PSA should include. If time allows and if you have the resources, make the PSA, post it to a public viewing space (like YouTube), and publicize the PSA so your information reaches its intended audience.

2. Often, we encounter places but are unaware of their histories or significance. For example, public buildings typically carry the names of people or groups—The Batten Center, Anderson Hall, The Graham Building—yet we don't know who those people are or why their names are on the buildings. For this assignment, work in small groups. Identify a named location on your campus. Then conduct some research to learn about the person or group for whom the location was named and why that name was given to that location. Next, together, write a report detailing the information you have gathered.

Writing

1. Select a historical figure—anyone, even a current political figure or celebrity—and write a short biographical essay about that person's life. Convey important facts about the person's life and accomplishments while avoiding subjective commentary (for example, why the person is important to you).

2. Definitions are often crucial to how information is conveyed. What we mean specifically by a term affects how a reader understands the information. Write an extended, informative definition of one of these terms, using research to fully develop your definition:

technology   information   culture   nature

Local Situation

1. Every university and college has a set of policies that affect students' lives; some policies address residential issues (such as dorm policies), some address academic issues (such as absentee or plagiarism policies), and some address social policies (such as conduct policies). Consider which of your school's policies you think is most important for new students to know and understand. Then write a policy statement for new students that informs them as to what the policy is, why the policy is in place, how the policy affects them, and what the ramifications are for violating the policy.

2. Every university or college shares a general understanding of what a student is; however, every college and university also has some specific definitions of how *student* should be understood in its local context. For instance, a person at one college might be required to be enrolled in four classes to be considered a full-time student, whereas, on another campus, a person might not be considered a student unless she lives on campus. Research how your institution specifically defines a student. Then write a detailed definition of what it means to be a student on your campus according to various university policies.

Writing to Respond

Learning Objectives

11.1 Describe how and why you respond to texts in college

11.2 Identify the characteristics of response

11.3 Develop strategies for writing responses

Before you read this chapter

Nearly all of the writing you produce is in response to some situation. You respond to something someone has said or written; you respond to an assignment. No matter how or why you respond, your response always participates in a situation that someone else has established. In your journal or blog, write about what it means to respond to what others have written and why you might feel obligated to respond in particular situations and not others.

 Katie Hatch · 10 months ago
Great post! At our NGO in Uganda, the aunties liked using Maggi as it showed they had the economic ability to purchase them, which gave them an elevated social standing. Seen as a Mzungu/foreigner item, it holds a specific meaning about culture, social circles and economic standing. It's taken lots of education to move the Aunties away from using them and onto a more natural, locally sourced path.
∧ · ∨ · Reply · Share ›

 Laura@EYW [EYW] → Katie Hatch · 24 days ago
Yes, showing economic ability is yet another reason for its popularity in some places, I am sure. I'd be curious to know what locally sourced ingredients the Ugandans are using now in place of Maggi...
∧ · ∨ · Reply · Share ›

 stefanieramsay · a year ago
Great post! The use of Maggi cubes fits in with the growing world trend of choosing convenience over health. As you pointed out, it comes at a cost. With all of the delicious local flavors you've both described from your trip, it seems like a shame to use anything else! Its interesting to think of this as a global issue and to promote utilizing one's native tastes to enhance their dishes. Thanks for the info!
∧ · ∨ · Reply · Share ›

 Laura@EYW [EYW] → stefanieramsay · a year ago
You're right, and it's definitely not limited to West Africa...Maggi cubes, for example, are quite popular in Latin American cooking too, where a host of other seasonings are surely being replaced. Thanks for reading, Stefanie!
∧ · ∨ · Reply · Share ›

 Alain Job → Laura@EYW · 6 months ago
People knew this long time ago, maybe convenience trends exported from the west added to lack of controls from governments are paving the way and perpetuating the journey of maggy now readily available on Tesco shelves as well . There is obviously an opportunity now for looking into a much healthier substitute but as it's always been poverty stricken countries that use it the most who can find value?
∧ · ∨ · Reply · Share ›

We live in a culture of response. New media technologies encourage rapid and widespread responses to the texts we encounter. Online newspapers and news sources provide opportunities for readers to respond to articles and editorials in comment sections. A comment feature accompanies YouTube videos, and YouTube supports posting video responses. Fan-made films, inspired by films, books, television shows, or other texts, are prolific on YouTube and other video sharing websites and are, in essence, fans' responses to texts. Through Facebook's comment feature, users can respond to status updates, links, videos, and photos. Even fan voting for reality television shows like *American Idol* and *Dancing with the Stars* reflects a kind of response.

In college, responding to texts is a central activity. Your academic work in college is based on the idea that your task is to respond to information that is delivered to you in a variety of formats: texts, discussions, lectures, and experiments, among others. That is, you are asked to think about, analyze, learn, and place yourself in relation to the information within a given context—the essential task of response.

11.1 Describe how and why you respond to texts in college

Writing to Respond

All writing is a response to a given rhetorical situation. Every situation provides the context for how you may respond. In one way or another, you respond to just about everything you read. You respond to an advertisement for a movie by deciding whether or not to watch the movie. When you read about or hear a new song, you respond by deciding whether or not to download it. When you read a chapter in a biology textbook, you respond by taking notes in case the material appears on a test.

In college, teachers commonly ask students to respond to various texts. English teachers often ask students to read a piece of literature and to respond to it in writing or in discussion. Law students may be asked to read a case and respond to it. The distinction between how we respond to a preview for a movie and to a short story our teacher has assigned lies in the form the response takes and the degree of critical work we devote to the response.

A response to a movie preview certainly relies on an unstated critical assessment of the preview. You watch the preview and analyze it to determine whether the movie appears to be potentially entertaining, yet you do not necessarily explain or articulate that analysis as you act on it. Academic response is more explicitly critical in that you must understand, analyze, evaluate, and situate the text that you have read. When teachers assign readings, they generally expect that you will form some kind of response to the reading: asking questions about it in class, participating in class discussion, referring to it in discussions or writing, or even recounting the information from it on an exam. Ultimately, responding to texts in college is directly linked to writing as a method of learning and is more likely to take the form of a written response. This chapter focuses on the written, critical response, but learning to write critical responses also influences how you respond to texts generally, no matter the situation.

David Leavitt has been called "one of the brightest stars of the gay literary world today." While he was enrolled as an undergraduate at Yale, *The New Yorker* published his short story "Territory" and soon after published his short story "Out Here." He has since published a number of short story collections and novels, including *The Lost Language of Cranes* on which the BBC based a film by the same title. Leavitt's writing is not limited to fiction, however, and he regularly responds to other writers' works, films, and political situations.

In the essay that follows, Leavitt responds to Ang Lee's 2005 film *Brokeback Mountain*. The film, which won numerous awards and Academy Award nominations, is based on Pulitzer Prize–winning author E. Annie Proulx's short story "Brokeback Mountain" and depicts the complex relationship between two men. Set in the American West, the film portrays the romantic and sexual relationship between Ennis del Mar (Heath Ledger) and Jack Twist (Jake Gyllenhaal). As you read Leavitt's response to the film, pay particular attention to what he summarizes about the film and how he organizes his response within the summary.

Men in Love: Is *Brokeback Mountain* a Gay Film?

David Leavitt

Big love, in stories about men, tends to be a cheat, a lost cause, or a chimera. In *Brokeback Mountain*—Ang Lee's moving, operatic film adaptation of Annie Proulx's story—it's exactly what the tag line for the film says: a force of nature. Herding sheep just above the tree line on a Wyoming mountain, two dirt-poor cowboys find themselves suddenly caught up in a passion for each other that they have no idea how to name, much less cope with. Neither thinks of himself as "queer." On the contrary, the mountain itself gets both the credit and the blame for the affair that over the next 20 years will endow their lives with an intermittent grandeur, even as in other ways it drags them to the ground.

Is *Brokeback Mountain*, as it's been touted, Hollywood's first gay love story? The answer—in a very positive sense, I think—is yes to the love story, no to the gay. Make no mistake: The film is as frank in its portrayal of sex between men as in its use of old-fashioned romance movie conventions. Its stars are unabashedly glamorous. The big-eyed Jake Gyllenhaal is a far cry from Proulx's small, bucktoothed

> Notice how Leavitt begins to provide a summary of the film without falling into a formulaic pattern of "this is what the movie is about." He provides the audience with some key information about the film: who directed it, what story it is based on, and a glimpse of the plot.

annotated example

Jack Twist, just as the blond, square-jawed Heath Ledger is nothing like her Ennis Del Mar, "scruffy and a little cave-chested." Yet, even if, in their tailored jeans and ironed plaid shirts, Gyllenhaal and Ledger sometimes look more like Wrangler models than teenagers too poor to buy a new pair of boots, the film neither feels synthetic (in the manner of the abysmal *Making Love*) nor silly (in the manner of gay porn). On the contrary, his stars' outsize screen presence provides Lee with a means of bringing to vivid cinematic life what is in essence a paean to masculinity.

> Notice the strength of the first sentence as Leavitt's way of stating his primary point about the film. Consider why Leavitt distinguishes the film's portrayal of the characters versus Proulx's short story version of the characters. Leavitt is clear that it is the film he responds to, not the story, and then provides details of the film that display his own critical reading.

And masculine the film is. Ledger's astonishing performance reveals an unsuspected vein of tenderness in a character more likely to express emotion through violence than words. His Ennis Del Mar is as monolithic as the mountainscape in which—with the same swiftness, brutality, and precision that he exhibits in shooting an elk—he has sex with Jack Twist for the first time. ("Gun's goin' *off*," Jack grunts in response—in the story, not the movie.) Ennis' surprise at the affair—at its inconvenience as much as at its intensity—reflects a fundamental humbleness that keeps butting up against Jack's willingness to take risks. It's Jack who proposes, over and over, that they start up a ranch together, a plan Ennis counters with pragmatism (not to mention fear), even after his wife, Alma, divorces him. Instead Ennis limits the relationship to fishing and hunting trips two or three times a year. It's as if he believes they don't deserve better.

> Again, Leavitt provides details of the film, summarizing key points of detail and plot without relying on a chronological organizational strategy, matching his summary to the needs of his response. In this paragraph, Leavitt begins to direct his focus on the characters in the film, here attentive to Ennis Del Mar.

As for Jack, the same cockiness that makes him dream of a "sweet life" with Ennis also leads him to pursue sex with other men, despite his own marriage—something Ennis never contemplates. In a key scene, Jack, disappointed at learning that, even after his divorce, Ennis has no intention of making a life with him, drives to a *louche* simulacrum of Juarez, where he picks up a hustler and disappears with him into the literal darkness of a back alley. The scene is unsettling because it presents such a stark contrast to Jack and Ennis' heady, exalted mountaintop lovemaking. For just a few seconds, we get a glimpse of the urban nightscape that was the locus of the very gay movies that might have been playing, in big cities, at the moment when the scene takes place—movies like *Nighthawks* and *Taxi zum Klo*, in which sexual profligacy is at once celebrated as a form of liberation and mourned as a pallid substitute for meaningful connection.

> Leavitt directs his attention to the other main character, Jack Twist, but in doing so uses the opportunity to place the film in context with other gay movies. Think about what this move does, not just in terms of Leavitt's ethos in this response, but in giving us a better view of *Brokeback Mountain* within a particular genre.

It goes without saying that *Brokeback Mountain* is an entirely different kind of film. Perhaps it takes a woman to create a tale in which two men experience sex and love as a single thunderbolt, welding them together for life; certainly Proulx's story is a far cry from such canonical gay novels as Edmund White's *The Farewell Symphony* or Allan Hollinghurst's *The Swimming Pool Library*, which poeticize urban promiscuity and sexual adventuring. Proulx, by contrast, exalts coupledom by linking it to nature. Her narration, with its echoes of Western genre fiction, is knobby and elliptical, driven by an engine as unpredictable as the one that runs Jack Twist's troublesome truck, with the result that it often backs into scenes that a more conventional writer would place front and center.

Though *Brokeback Mountain* may have the sheen of a Hollywood romance, it is anything but conventional. True, screenwriters Larry McMurtry and Diana Ossana have ironed out Proulx's kinks, but they haven't eliminated her eccentricities; instead, they've found a cinematic parallel in their appropriation of Hollywood conventions of masculinity. This is particularly the case in the last half of the film, which alternates scenes of quotidian domestic grief (and the rare emotional triumph) with the trips that Jack and Ennis make together into the mountains—trips during which, as they age, sex takes a back seat to bickering and what might best be described as a kind of conjugal ease. What both men want, it becomes clear, is what Ennis is afraid to let them have: the steadiness of each other's companionship. By the end, Ledger's Ennis has crow's feet, while Gyllenhaal's Jack has sprouted a prosthetic paunch and a heavy mustache. The result is a defense of gay marriage made all the more eloquent by its evasion of the banalities implied in the word "gay."

Indeed, with the one exception of the scene in Juarez, nothing in *Brokeback Mountain* cries "gay." Neither of the heroes eschews sex with women; instead, they simply assert that they prefer sex with each other. At one point in the story, Ennis asks Jack, "This happen a other people?" and Jack answers, "It don't happen in Wyomin and if it does I don't know what they do, maybe go to Denver." Interestingly, McMurtry and Ossana leave this lone mention of possible urban refuge out of the movie, the point of which seems to be less to subvert the conventions of male bonding than to extend them. "Lover" isn't a word Ennis and Jack ever utter. Instead they call each other "friend." When they kiss, their teeth hit. Respect for some burdensome ideal

> This is a great paragraph. Notice that Leavitt's discussion winds together three approaches in his response: situating the film in the context of gay narrative, synthesizing Proulx's story into the genre of gay stories, and then pulling the discussion into the context of Western genre fiction.

> Leavitt's response firms up its position that this is a response to the film, not the short story. Identifying how the screenwriters were able to adapt the short story to screen without losing its nuances, Leavitt is essentially telling readers that Proulx's story is noteworthy, but this response is about the film and what that film means to viewers. This film, he shows us, has political overtones.

annotated example

of masculine struggle underlies and at the same time undercuts their ability to love each other: an idea that Ledger in particular brings home by investing his performance with the deadpan, reticent tenderness of Hollywood Western stars from the 1950s. His stoicism drives the movie, and nowhere more movingly than when he utters its signature line: "If you can't fix it you've got to stand it."

Does the fact that none of the principals involved in *Brokeback Mountain* is openly gay have anything to do with the film's happy resistance to the stale clichés of gay cinema? Perhaps. In any case, McMurtry, Ossana, and Lee deserve as much credit for their tenacity (it took them seven years to get the movie made) as for the skill with which they've translated Proulx's spare, bleak story into a film with an epic sweep that nonetheless manages to be affectingly idiosyncratic in its portrayal of two men in love. In the end, *Brokeback Mountain* is less the story of a love that dares not speak its name than of one that doesn't know how to speak its name, and is somehow more eloquent for its lack of vocabulary. Ascending from plains where they lead lives of drudgery and routine humiliation, Ennis and Jack become the unwitting heroes of a story they haven't a clue how to tell. The world breaks their backs, but in this brave film, they're as iconic as the mountain.

Leavitt begins to directly answer the question posed in his title. Part of his purpose here seems to be to distinguish what "gay" might actually mean and that that meaning might be more complex than sex between two people of the same gender. Again, notice the detail of summary that Leavitt provides and how those details serve his purpose.

Think about how Leavitt concludes this response. Certainly, it offers praise to the filmmakers and the film itself. But how does it leave you as a reader with a final moment of response from the writer? That is, consider what Leavitt says in this conclusion.

student example

Alexandra Bargoot majors in English, minors in classics and dance, and plans to pursue a law degree. She serves as president of the student organization Volunteers for International Student Affairs. Given her active participation on her campus, Alexandra is particularly alert to conversations occurring around her. When a columnist for her school's newspaper wrote about the need for school funding to drastically reform in response to student opinion, Alexandra felt obligated to respond to the column to point out some of its inaccuracies. Using solid research, Alexandra refutes the columnist's claims methodically and through documented evidence. This essay is formatted and documented using the conventions of APA style.

Argument in Response to

"Importance of Education Lost in the Mix"

Alexandra Bargoot

On Thursday, September 15, 2011, columnist Akansha Mishra published

"Importance of Education Lost in the Mix" in which she attempts to assert the

idea that the funding mechanism of education needs "dramatic reform" because

students' "desire to obtain a valuable educational experience" is overpowered by

the fear that the profession a degree leads to won't provide the income to pay the

debt incurred in its acquisition. She argues that students are consequently angry

at the university and that a shift in attitudes toward education has occurred in

our generation. However, her evidence to support her argument is in some cases

factually inaccurate and in others logically spurious.

Mishra writes that the funding of our educational system needs reform

but that financing education is a secondary concern to policymakers in today's

economic climate. She claims such reforms "can help many of our troubles." This

assertion overlooks the fact that education is a long term investment for current

students to help create a promise of a better future on both personal and societal

levels. The return is not immediate. Funding education will not "alleviate" the

crises of foreclosure and job loss that so many Americans face today as Mishra argues. It would foster future economic growth through innovation and also raise the intellectual level of the country, but it would not immediately create employment opportunities and overall stability.

I agree with Mishra that students do worry about tuition costs, but the "relentless anger" and "hopelessness" that she claims students harbor towards the university because of these costs are observably not the posture of the entire student body. Last week, for example, I saw a student protesting against recent tuition increases. One student to whom the protestor handed a flyer made a point of telling the protestor that he was not at all upset by the new costs. Seeing one person on either side of the argument, and myself being neutral, all in one place at the same random moment is evidence that the opinions of the student body are much more varied than Mishra describes.

It is not accurate for Mishra to say that there is a change in the student population's sentiments, that "we have become" more preoccupied with saving money. Tuition has always been a large expenditure. Consequently most college students have always been concerned with saving money. This is not a new phenomenon due to any current tuition increase. Upper classmen are experiencing an increase in their tuition costs. That does not mean students were not money conscious before. The tuition Mishra writes about is still substantially less than the national average. According to the College Board (2012), the average cost per year at a public college for tuition and fees is $7,605. The cost at UF, after the increase, is still only $5,700 (University of Florida Student Financial Affairs, 2012).

Passion to acquire a professional degree is not replaced by fear of the financial burden as Mishra argues. The two exist simultaneously. The job market is more competitive with more students attending graduate schools, though the demand for professionals remains the same. Society can only support a certain percentage of lawyers even if the percentage of graduates increases. For example, according to *U.S. News and World Report* (2012), only 60.2% of the University of Florida Levin College of Law graduates were employed at the time of graduation and only 56.1% of the Law School at University of Miami were employed at the time of graduation. Both percentages are down from previous years. This trend is reflected at other schools as well. Thus a fear of being unable to repay loans is warranted.

However, there has been no drop in the number of students applying to schools, so Mishra's argument that the passion of students is dying is unfounded. According to Ruiz (2010), both the percentage of students taking the LSAT and

RESPONSE TO "EDUCATION LOST IN THE MIX"   4

the GRE have actually risen in the last few years, as well as the number of

law school applicants. Cornell University's Law School has had its applicant

pool increase by 44% in the last year (Ruiz, 2010). Changes could be made to

fund education more effectively, but for Mishra to say that we have become

students who are more preoccupied with the cost of our education rather than

the experiences it brings, and that the financial burden has taken away our

passion to become doctors and lawyers, is spurious. Mishra's further comment

that a recent shift in values of the current generation in the U.S., relative to the

preceding one, regarding education is partially to blame for "the failure of our

education system" is also false. It is true that college age students are now old

enough to elect officials, but most politicians are of our parents' generation.

The second half of the statement is easily proven factually inaccurate. Her

perception that our generation values education less due to this increase in

expenses inflicted upon us does not stand against reports by the College Board

Advocacy and Policy Center (Lee & Rawls, 2010). In the age bracket 25–64,

40.3% of the American population has at least an associate's degree (p. 7). We

are ranked sixth after Russia, Canada, Israel, Japan, and New Zealand. Of

people 25–34, 40.4% have at least their associate's degree (p. 8). Between the ages of 55–64, 38.5% of people in the U.S. have their associates degree or higher

(p. 8). The perception of education in the United States has not changed negatively

over the course of these generations.

In this second category, the 25–34 age bracket, the United States is

ranked in twelfth place compared to other countries. Note that in sixth place is

Ireland with 43.9% of people in those years having an education of an associate's

degree or higher, which is only 3.5% higher than the U.S. (Lee & Rawls, 2010, p.

8). She is wrong in saying that in the U.S. we do not value education as much as we

formerly did. The statistics indicate that we do not value education today as much

as some other countries, but this is due to a change on their part in policy and

cultural attitudes, not ours.

These statistics indicate that students are being given the opportunity to

excel refuting Mishra's concluding comment, "Let us not strip students of their

right to excel and provide for their country." Furthermore, being part of such an

institution is not a right but an opportunity earned. You make a decision to be

there and take on the financial responsibilities of the endeavor. An education is

a way to make a better life for oneself in the future. Mishra's assertion that the

government should provide money for our education because we will then provide for our country is a false appeal to patriotism. The primary result of education

is the improvement in the quality of life of the educated individual, which is

undeniably the core motivator to aspiring to earn a degree.

Mishra uses broad unsupported statements to construct her largely

emotive argument which does not stand to scrutiny. She erroneously connects the

funding of education, which would enhance the country's stability in the long-run,

to obviating immediate financial and employment crises. Today, even with the risk

of high financial obligation, students are still enrolling in programs demonstrating

a continuing passion for learning in our generation. The final punch of an

emotionally infused conclusion, connecting the advancement of the interests

of students to supporting the country, borders on propaganda and provides no

evidence for her arguments.

References

College Board. (2012). *Quick guide: College costs*. Retrieved from https://bigfuture
.collegeboard.org

Lee, J. M., & Rawls, A. (2010). *The college completion agenda 2010 progress
report*. Retrieved from the College Board website: http://completionagenda
.collegeboard.org

Mishra, A. (2011, September 15). Importance of education lost in the mix. *The
Independent Florida Alligator*. Retrieved from http://www.alligator.org

Ruiz, R. R. (2010, January 9). Recession spurs interest in graduate, law schools.
The New York Times. Retrieved from http://www.nytimes.com

University of Florida Student Financial Affairs. (2012). Basics: Cost of
attendance. Retrieved from http://www.sfa.ufl.edu/basics/cost-of-attendance

U.S. News and World Report. (2012). *U.S. News college compass best colleges*.
Retrieved from http://www.usnews.com

student example

Thinking about Alexandra's Essay

1. What is Alexandra's purpose in responding to Akansha Mishra's newspaper column? Does she achieve this purpose effectively? Why or why not?

2. What role does research play in Alexandra's response? Would her response be as effective without the inclusion of her research? Why or why not?

3. What does Alexandra's response provide the situation in which it participates? Do you see this as a valuable contribution to the situation? Why or why not?

student example

THE ROAD TO A
STRONG THESIS

SECOND THOUGHTS:
"It's not accurate and not what many of my friends think about college funding."

SECOND THOUGHTS:
"But how do I show that Mishra's underlying assumptions are wrong and don't give her claim any support?"

SECOND THOUGHTS:
"The research pretty clearly shows that Mishra's evidence in support of her claim is not accurate."

PURPOSE:
To respond to Akansha Mishra's claims in her newspaper column that there needs to be a "dramatic reform" to educational funding mechanisms because students' "desire to obtain a valuable educational experience" is overpowered by fear of post-graduation debt.

EXIGENCY:
"I need to respond to Mishra to show that her characterization of student fear is misrepresented and inaccurate."

RESPONSE:
"I wonder how much research Mishra conducted to see how her claims might be supported. I should probably conduct my own research to figure out not just how students feel about these issues, but what the professionals say about college funding and accrued debt when students go to professional schools."

ASSIGNMENT
To write a response to a reading

THESIS:
"The evidence Mishra uses to support her argument is in some cases factually inaccurate and in others logically spurious."

It is likely that Alexandra Bargoot had more than one reaction to Akansha Mishra's newspaper column, but to effectively respond, she needed to identify a specific claim she wanted to make in response to Mishra. Alexandra needed to develop a strong thesis for her response.

FINAL THOUGHTS:
"I have to concretely show these inaccuracies and explain the logical fallacies."

professional example

Ta-Nehisi Coates is senior editor for *The Atlantic*; his writing has appeared in *The Village Voice*, *Time*, *The New York Times*, and *The Atlantic*. He regularly writes about culture, politics, race, Black history, pop culture, and social issues. His acclaimed book *The Beautiful Struggle* is a memoir of his childhood in Baltimore and is a tribute to his father, a veteran of the Vietnam War and a Black Panther who started his own underground press. In "Nothing Is So Necessary for a Young Man …," Coates responds to Leo Tolstoy's classic novel *War and Peace*. Notice how Coates grounds his response in his experiences but also situates the response in a larger context.

Nothing Is So Necessary for a Young Man …

Ta-Nehisi Coates

Citizen E has been on me to read *War and Peace* for over a year now. He echoes my father, who has been on me to read *War and Peace* for the better part of twenty years. I'm having a hard time with it, and evidently, I am in good company. Henry James called it a "large loose baggy monster." I have found it much the same—emphasis on monster. It's tough to get a foothold on any one character, or any one set of events—there are many formal soirées where it feels like nothing, save gossiping over Napoleon's latest machinations, seems to happen.

And yet I am attracted to Tolstoy's seeming disrespect for plot and form even as I am not sure what, precisely, I'm reading. But more than that I'm attracted by my own limits, to the rather strict nature of my native aesthetic. Pops traces my days as a writer back to toddler-dom. He says when I was just two I would sit by the speaker and demand that he play the Last Poets' *Delights of the Garden* over and over again. I don't much remember what's on that record, but I have vague memories of being transfixed by the Last Poets.

I think it's about some deep sense that a sentence is really an instrument of percussion, that I hear all my favorite writers the way other people hear Max Roach. I finished *Rebecca* a few weeks back and as much I loved how, for most of the book, Du Maurier manages the suspense, how she turns your own fearful curiosity against you, what I really love is the rhythm of something like this:

> I wonder what she is doing now. She and Favell. I think it was the expression on her
> face that gave me my first feeling of unrest. Instinctively, I thought, "She is comparing
> me to Rebecca."; and sharp as a sword, the shadow came between us.

I read that, and, rightly or wrongly, I heard African drumming. Same for Doctorow. Same for Fitzgerald (especially in his Jazz Age essays.) Same for Komunyakaa. Same for Diaz. I see literature through an odd Afrocentric lens. What I love about the Western canon, I love because it takes me back to what I thought was beautiful all those days ago when I would troop to school thinking over and over,

> It's only one capable, breaks the unbreakable,
> Melodies unmakable, patterns unescapable.
> A haunt if you want the style I possess,
> I bless the Child, the Earth, the Gods and bomb the rest.

I read Tolstoy and don't hear drumming—or rather not the drumming that I am as yet qualified to recognize. And I think that's the point. I don't hope to love this book—if I do, that's great. But more so, I hope to understand why so many other people love this book, to appreciate their appreciation, if not to share it. I have said this before, but I would hate to grow old and become a prisoner to my own aesthetics. I do not despise those who inveigh against hip-hop and X-Boxes—but I fear, most powerfully, becoming them.

My Dad read *War and Peace* before he went off to Vietnam. He must have been about 16, a poor black kid trying to find his way out of Philadelphia. By the time he came to Tolstoy, he'd seen his father alive for the last time. He'd come home, as a six-year-old, and seen all of his home set out in the street. He'd lived in a truck for a week, and he'd come to believe that if he stayed in Philly, he would be killed. Still awaiting him was the murder of two of his older brothers, the service, the Panthers, and a tribe of children.

What moves someone like that to Tolstoy? What allows you to cross that long, dreamy bridge from the ghettos of America to the parlors of old Russia?

There is something out there. I'm going to find it.

Analyzing the Situation

1. Who do you suppose Coates imagines as his audience? In what ways does he address this audience?

2. How does Coates's early reference to Henry James help him situate his response?

3. In what ways might the fact that Coates published this response in *The Atlantic* constrain what he can and can't say in his response?

Analyzing the Rhetoric

1. How do you respond to Coates's tone in this essay? That is, does the way this piece "sounds" affect how you respond to it? In what ways?

2. "Nothing Is So Necessary for a Young Man ..." does not include much summary of *War and Peace*. Do you suppose that Coates's awareness of his audience allows him to assume that the majority of his readers will have read the novel or will know what it's about

professional example

so he doesn't need to provide much summary? Do readers—including you—need to know what *War and Peace* is about to connect with Coates's response?

3. Is this response really about *War and Peace*, or is it about a different issue? That is, does Coates really respond to *War and Peace* or his he just using the book as a vehicle to enter a different situation? Explain.

Discussing

1. How do you respond to Coates's response? As a class, discuss your individual responses to this essay, both to its content and to its effectiveness as a written response.

Writing

1. Coates's response exhibits some of the techniques of response identified in this chapter, but it also takes other approaches. Write a response to Coates that focuses on how he has written his response and on the effectiveness of his response.

2. Part of Coates's response is driven by the encouragement (maybe pressure) his father put on him to read *War and Peace*. Have you ever felt "encouraged" to read a particular book? Write a response to Coates that addresses your experience with such encouragement and the effect it had on your reading. Remember: you should write a response, not necessarily a personal narrative.

SIDE ᴮʸ SIDE

Each of the three previous examples responds to a specific text: the film *Brokeback Mountain*, a newspaper column, and *War and Peace*. But each of these responses is also about the situation in which the responded-to texts participate: the portrayal of sex between men, the costs of education, and the ways in which we read literature. Consider how each writer uses the opportunity of response to tie specific texts to "bigger" issues.

	annotated example David Leavitt, "Men in Love: Is *Brokeback Mountain* a Gay Film?"	**student example** Alexandra Bargoot, "In Response to 'Importance of Education Lost in the Mix'"	**professional example** Ta-Nehisi Coates, "Nothing Is So Necessary for a Young Man ..."
PURPOSE	To address how Hollywood films represent sex between men	To respond to a newspaper column about educational funding	To understand why his father and Citizen E find *War and Peace* important
AUDIENCE	Readers of *Slate*, a daily web magazine; those interested in Hollywood films; and those interested in discussions of homosexuality	Readers of the newspaper in which the column to which she responds originally appeared	Readers of *The Atlantic*
CONTENT	Leavitt examines both the film *Brokeback Mountain* and E. Annie Proulx's short story on which the film is based. He considers these texts in relation to gay films and expectations of gay films.	Alexandra identifies the original column writer's claims and then analyzes and refutes what the author claims. To do so, she provides and cites relevant information.	Coates describes how he came to be reading Tolstoy's *War and Peace* and his response to the book. He explains his own relationship with reading and writing, particularly, that he reads with a Afrocentric lens.
LANGUAGE	Leavitt's language is elegant, carrying the beauty of the film and Proulx's short story in his own writing. The tenor of his language carries his claims, not aggressively, but confidently.	Alexandra's language is conversational, yet confident. Her tone questions Mishra's logic but is not condescending. Part of her conviction—and the strength of her ethos—grows from her confidence in her research.	Coates's language is deeply personal. It carries a sense of wonder and exploration.
DISTRIBUTION	Circulated by *Slate,* an online daily magazine	Shared with her peers and submitted to the newspaper in which the original column appeared	Circulated by *The Atlantic* magazine
ORGANIZATION	Leavitt begins by posing a question. He then provides a summary of the film and parts of the short story on which the film is based, pointing out specific scenes that clarify the film's story. He also provides background information about the writing and making of the film. Only at the end of the essay does he respond to the initial question.	Alexandra begins by summarizing Mishra's claims in the original newspaper column. She then states her claims refuting Mishra's position and provides statistics and other information from reliable sources.	Coates begins by explaining how he came to be reading Tolstoy's *War and Peace*; he then offers anecdotes about his relationship to reading and writing. He frames his response to *War and Peace* and the impetus of so many people to read it in terms of what it means to read such a book through an Afrocentric mind-set.

11.2 Identify the characteristics of response

Characteristic	Preparing Your Response
Reading	Reading texts for response requires more than a cursory reading. A first reading may provide the opportunity for you to form initial responses, but more critical readings allow you to develop the more critical responses that are expected in college. Multiple readings break down into two kinds of reading: *surface reading* and *critical reading*. Surface readings provide a general understanding of the obvious facets of the text, but critical readings enable you to see the details of the text and the situation in which the text is presented.
Analysis	Analysis allows you to better understand what you have read. Through analysis, you can focus on the various parts of the text to understand the relations between those parts. Analysis can be thought of as breaking a whole into its parts to better understand how the whole works. The critical questions you ask about a text drive how you conduct a textual analysis.
Summary	The purpose of a summary is to provide a condensed, but accurate, version of an original text, which provides context for an audience who may not have read or viewed the text to which you are responding. In academic responses, summaries also provide an opportunity to show your audience that you understand the text in a particular way. In responses, summaries are generally presented two ways: either as a synopsis or as paraphrased text. Synopses are brief overviews of a text, conveying all of its primary points but not the details. In paraphrasing, you explain the text you are responding to in your own words.
Evaluation	Evaluation is an assessment of the worth or significance of the text that you have read, analyzed, and summarized. There's no single correct way to evaluate a text. The situation will dictate the procedure you use to evaluate. Your evaluation will draw on your own experiences, how you relate the text to other texts, and the value you identify in the text in a given situation.
Connection and Synthesis	Part of the objective of critical analysis of a text is to connect the text and your evaluation to other texts and other conversations, to suggest how that text is part of a situation, connected with other texts and ideas. Doing so requires that you learn to synthesize texts and situations, to bring them together in conversation.

11.3 Develop strategies for writing responses

Strategy	Developing Your Analysis
Read and reread	Consider developing a list of specific questions to ask about the reading (see "Questions for Reading Texts Critically"). Be sure to write your answers so you can refer to them when writing your response. Also consider using a critical reading worksheet to guide you through your reading (see "Critical Reading Worksheet for Responding to a Text").
Take notes	• *Annotating*—Record critical or explanatory comments in your notes or directly on the text you are reading. • *Highlighting*—Mark directly on a text (by highlighting or underlining) to identify key points or direct quotes you may want to return to. • *Making marginal notations*—Note ideas in the margins of the text to help you recall what you thought or what you wanted to explore further. • *Writing summary sentences*—Jot down concise sentences to summarize text as you read it. • *Journaling*—Try the dual-column journal approach for keeping notes: fold the page of the journal in half and use one side of the folded page to jot down information or quotes directly from the text you are reading; then use the other side of the folded page to write your thoughts about or responses to that information.
React	Take a few minutes after you first read a text to write down your initial reactions, what stood out for you, and what questions you have. Your initial reactions to a text may be your most insightful and may likely drive how you formulate your critical approach to the text.
Analyze	Use these questions to examine of the text. • *Subject*—What is the text about? • *Audience*—To whom is this text directed? • *Situation*—Where does the text fit in a rhetorical situation? • *Purpose*—What appears to be the writer's purpose? • *Genre*—What form does the text take and what expectations do you have from that form? • *Delivery*—How is the text circulated? What is its medium? • *Method*—How does the writer convey information? • *Style*—How does the writer approach the text stylistically? • *Effectiveness*—What works? What did the writer do in the text that makes it effective?
Focus	From among the many things you would like to respond to, select one or two related responses and focus on those ideas, maintaining a central theme. Guide your audience by providing a direct claim about the text you are responding to early in your response. Think of it as your thesis statement, explaining exactly what your response is about.
Summarize	When writing a summary, convey the text's purpose, main points, and details that are relevant to the purpose of your response. Look specifically for • Sentences in the text that identify main ideas • An introduction and conclusion • Visual guides and organizational tools that denote key points of information, for example, titles, headings, and graphics
Connect and synthesize	Connect the original text to your own experiences, to other texts related to the situation, to other texts that inform how you read the original text and vice versa, or to larger conversations about the content—all of which require you to think beyond the superficial, obvious points of the text and formulate complex, original ideas. Synthesize by combining information from various locations, identifying similarities and variations to form new explanations, ideas, and thoughts.
Organize	Refer to "Two Common Organizational Strategies for Writing Responses."

Two Common Organizational Strategies for Writing Responses

Organize your response so your audience can easily understand your position. Two common strategies are illustrated here. Both strategies begin with an introduction that identifies the text you are responding to and offers a preview of the claim you are making in your response. The key difference in the two strategies is that the first summarizes the entire text before offering a response, where the second works part by part or topic by topic through the text, offering a response at each step.

Modifying these organizational strategies can lead to even more dynamic and interesting responses, so consider diverging from these templates to come up with more interesting ways to respond. For instance, the second of these strategies implies a chronological movement through the text, providing a summary of one part with response, a summary of the next part with response, and so on. Consider modifying this pattern to provide a summary relating to one of your objectives, with response, then another summary related to an objective, with response, and so on.

Full Summary/Full Response

The writer provides a summary of the full original text followed by a response. This organization can be effective because it provides cohesion to the summary and allows the audience to grasp the original text as a whole. However, this approach may also cause difficulty for the reader, particularly with a complex summary, because the reader will need to recall summary details during the response segments of the document.

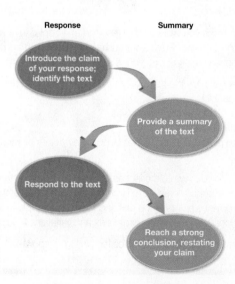

Alternating Summary and Response

The writer provides one part of the summary followed immediately by the response and then another part of the summary and another response. Writers using this pattern can move sequentially through the text from beginning to end, summarizing and responding to each part in order. This pattern can also be used to focus on particular themes or topics in the text, isolating key issues and responding to them one at a time.

This strategy can be effective because it links moments of summary with moments of response. It may fall short, however, if the writer does not provide connection between points of summary to help the reader gain a fuller sense of the total summary.

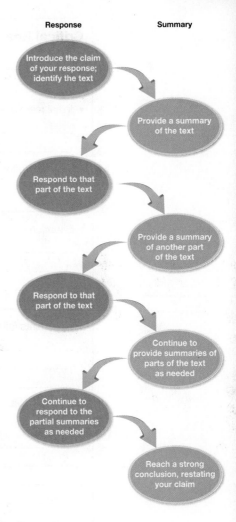

Response   Summary

Introduce the claim of your response; identify the text

Provide a summary of the text

Respond to that part of the text

Provide a summary of another part of the text

Respond to that part of the text

Continue to provide summaries of parts of the text as needed

Continue to respond to the partial summaries as needed

Reach a strong conclusion, restating your claim

Questions for Reading Texts Critically

- What is the title of the text?
- Who is the author of the text?
- How is the text circulated and distributed?
- What genre is the text? (Once you have established the genre of the text, develop questions about how the text fits or doesn't fit within the genre.)
- What role does the genre play in how you read and understand the text?
- Who is the text's audience and how did you come to this conclusion?
- What is your initial reaction to the text?
- From what point of view is the text presented?
- Is location important in the text?
- What are the main ideas of the text?
- How would you describe the style of the text?
- Does the text use visuals in a particular way?
- Are there parts of the text that are unclear or difficult to understand?
- How is the text organized?
- How does the organization affect how the text conveys information?
- Is there anything striking about the text?
- How does the text relate to other texts with which I'm familiar or to my own life?
- How does the text fit with other texts associated with this situation?

Critical Reading Worksheet for Responding to a Text

- Title _____

- Author _____

- Initial reactions (after first reading) _____
  _____
  _____

- Purpose (after subsequent critical readings) _____
  _____
  _____

- Situation (What do you learn about the situation from the text?) _____
  _____
  _____
  _____
  _____

- Key points (after subsequent critical readings) _____
  _____
  _____
  _____
  _____

- Summary (in your own words) _____
  _____
  _____
  _____
  _____
  _____

- Your critical insight (What do you notice?) _____
  _____
  _____
  _____
  _____
  _____

- Synthesis/Connection (How does the text tie to other texts/situations?) _____
  _____
  _____
  _____
  _____
  _____

MAPPING
YOUR SITUATION

NETWORKS
- In what networks will my response circulate?
- How is my response linked to other responses in the situation?
- How does my response change this situation?

WRITERS AND SPEAKERS
- Who are the other writers and speakers in this situation?
- How do the other writers respond?

RELATIONS
- What is my relation to the situation?
- What are the relationships between writers/speakers, audience, and players?
- What are the relationships to external forces, like culture, religion, or politics?
- What are the power relations?

AUDIENCE
- Who will read/see my response?
- What do I know about my intended audience?
- Who will the response affect directly and indirectly?

MEDIUM AND METHOD
- In what genre will I respond?
- What background information do my readers need?
- What method will I use to convey my response?
- How will I distribute my response?

CONTEXT
- From where does my response come?
- Where will the response appear?
- What limits how I can respond?
- Who knows about this situation and who needs to hear my response?

PURPOSE
- Why am I responding to this situation?
- What does my response need to convey?
- Does my response serve a specific purpose?

Mapping your situation will help you generate ideas you can use to compose. Start by answering these questions about each part of the situation. Begin with your purpose and work outward to relations and networks.

Writing Projects

Essay

Locate a copy of today's local newspaper, and find the editorial page. Read the first full editorial (not a letter to the editor) published in the newspaper and write a response to that editorial.

Responding to Visuals

In October 2010, *Elle* magazine featured actress Gabby Sidibe, who was nominated for an Academy Award for Best Performance by an Actress in a Leading Role for her performance in *Precious*. The magazine was accused of lightening the appearance of Sidibe's skin to appeal to a wider readership. At the time, *Elle* editor in chief Robbie Meyers explained, "At a photo shoot, in a studio, that is a fashion shoot, that's glamorous, the lighting is different. The photography is different than a red carpet shot from a paparazzi." She emphasized, "We absolutely did not lighten her skin. Retouching is when we take a piece of hair and move it out of her eye, so you can't compare a picture on a press line from what you do in a studio, where your job is to make them look beautiful."

Gabby Sidibe and Aishwarya Rai photographed at fashion events.

Three months later, in January 2011, *Elle* was again criticized for lightening the appearance of a cover model's skin tone on *Elle India*'s cover, this time, Miss World and Bollywood actress Aishwarya Rai, who was outraged over the cover photo and threatened lawsuits.

Do an online search to locate the *Elle* magazine covers, compare them to these two photos, and consider the situation. Then write a response to the situation.

Digital

YouTube makes it easy to respond to posted videos through either written comments or video responses. Typically, users create video responses to reply to videos already posted on the site. These responses most frequently take the form of an individual talking to a camera and don't usually include any kind of editing or effects. Although they are popular, video responses on YouTube are generally understood to be fairly useless and mostly pointless. In other words, YouTube viewers have embraced the video response but, for the most part, not as a mechanism for substantial response.

View an assortment of YouTube response videos; then write a document suggesting an approach to making response videos that might make them more meaningful in the video-sharing exchange. Comment on the potential for substantive responses in this medium.

Research

Chapter 27 includes readings about what it might mean to be a member of the millennial generation, members of which have a "mind-set that embraces instability, that tolerates—and even enjoys—recalibrating careers, business models and assumptions." Select and respond to one of the readings in that chapter.

Radical Revision

On January 3, 2013, The U.S. Joint Chiefs of Staff overturned a 1994 rule that banned women from being assigned to small ground combat units. Defense Secretary Leon Panetta identified that women are an "integral part" of the military and increasingly find themselves in the "reality of combat." The new ruling could open more than 230,000 jobs to women, mainly in Marine and Army infantry units. In response to the announcement, cartoonist Adam Zygus published the cartoon on the following page, "We Can Do It!" The cartoon relies on the U.S. cultural icon of Rosie the Riveter and the 1943 J. Howard Miller propaganda poster produced for Westinghouse Electric known as "We Can Do It!" to convey its response.

Zygus's cartoon is an image/text, combining the written and the visual. It would not function clearly without both the written text and the drawn images. But even so, the cartoon does not reach one particular audience: people who are visually impaired. Revise Zygus's cartoon to convey the response to a visually impaired audience. Do not describe the cartoon; instead, convey the information in the cartoon without relying on visual language. Use any media form you find effective, and be as detailed as possible in crafting your response.

Seeking Feedback

Peers, target audiences, and editors can offer valuable observations that will strengthen your writing. You will encourage more constructive feedback from these readers if you structure your questions for them carefully. Consider asking these kinds of questions to get feedback:

Writing Process
GUIDELINES

Use the guidelines in this chart to plan, review, and evaluate your process for writing. Each step in the process should support the overall purpose of your project.

SITUATE
- Understand your reasons for responding to the text or the situation (exigencies).
- Understand how relations might affect your response.
- Identify how your response is limited by constraints.
- Recognize the speakers or writers to whom you are responding.
- Identify and analyze the audiences involved in the situation.
- Consider what genres, media, and methods are used in the situation and which might be of use to you in your response.

PLAN
- Confirm your reason for responding in this situation (exigency).
- Clarify your purpose in responding.
- Consider your form of response to the situation.
- Consider what might be the best genre, media, and method for your response.
- Analyze what you know about the text and what you need to discover before responding.
- Begin to take notes.

RESEARCH
- Determine what kind of information you will need and the best ways to locate that information.
- Conduct research to gather the information you need.
- Confirm that your research will be valid within your response.
- Identify any visuals you may either need to provide or need to respond to.
- Organize your response.
- Evaluate your information in light of your response to determine whether you need to conduct further research.

DRAFT
- Confirm your purpose.
- Draft the summary of the text you plan to respond to.
- Draft and organize the content of your document.
- Use the visual process to develop any visuals you will need.
- Design your document.

REVIEW AND REVISE
- Review your response for clarity and concision.
- Review your response for accuracy.
- Review your response for degree of detail appropriate to the situation and purpose
- Review your response for extraneous information.
- Review your response for organizational approach.
- Review your response for explanations of key terms necessary within the situation.
- Review your response for style appropriate to the situation.
- Confirm your research and citations.
- Review your response for visual effectiveness and readability.
- Consider revising the title to most accurately reflect your response's purpose.

EDIT
- Proofread carefully.
- Correct all mechanical and grammatical errors.

EVALUATE
- Seek feedback from peers (take advantage of peer editing opportunities).
- Ask for feedback from a representative member of the target audience.
- Ask for feedback from an editor in whom you are confident.
- Evaluate the usefulness of any feedback you receive and revise accordingly.

DISTRIBUTE/CIRCULATE
- Consider technologies of circulation.
- Publish in a form that will be visible within the situation.
- Identify methods for increasing circulation (like search engine optimization) within and beyond the specific situation.
- Consider audience access.
- Identify possible sources of audience response.

Summary

All writing is a kind of response. Reading critically is probably the most important part of writing to respond because it allows you to better understand what you have read and, thus, prepares you to respond. The summary—a condensed, but accurate, version of an original text that is relevant to your purpose—is also vital because it helps your audience understand what you are responding to. Through evaluation and critical analysis of a text, your response should systematically

EVALUATION Guidelines

INITIAL REACTION

- What are your initial reactions to the response?
- What do you see as the purpose of the response?
- What are the strengths of the response?
- What are the weaknesses of the response?
- Does the response hold your interest?
- Generally speaking, what is the primary thing the writer must do to improve this document?

SITUATION

- Who do you understand this response to be written for, and what leads you to that conclusion?
- Does the response fulfill its purpose effectively?
- Has the writer accounted for the audience by explaining all that needs to be explained?

READABILITY

- Does the title provide an accurate, clear representation of the document?
- Did you understand the response?
- Which parts, if any, are difficult to follow or understand?
- What organizational strategy does the writer use to respond?
- Are you able to follow the organization of the response?

CONTENT

- Does the response make sense?
- Does the writer provide a concrete summary of the text or situation that is being responded to?
- Does the writer provide the necessary information to support the response?
- What, if anything, is particularly interesting in the response?
- What unnecessary or extraneous information, if any, is in the response?
- What details stand out for you?
- What details are extraneous or unnecessary?

VISUALS

- Does the writer use visuals to clarify or explain written information?
- If so, are the visuals appropriate to the purpose?
- Do the visuals work in conjunction with the writing or independently?
- Are the visuals clear and easy to read?
- Does the document design distract from or support the response's purpose and/or readability?
- What recommendations regarding visuals do you have for the writer?

MECHANICS

- Are there evident mechanical distractions in the response?
- Which sentences, if any, are unclear?
- Which sentences or paragraphs are particularly well written?
- Are all references cited appropriately?

connect the text's details and your evaluation to other texts and other conversations and suggest how that text is part of a situation. For that process, it is crucial to develop strong critical reading approaches and to cultivate sound note-taking skills, which can help you remember your ideas, distinguish points of interest in the text you want to address, identify points you should address in your summaries, and retain key information. By synthesizing and connecting texts to other experiences and texts, you demonstrate that you can think beyond the superficial, obvious points of the text and formulate more complex ideas. Finally, how you organize your response can affect how your audience understands your position and can affect the readability of your writing.

Chapter Review

1. Why do you respond to texts in college?

2. Why is reading considered an element of writing to respond?

3. What role does analysis play in writing to respond?

4. Why are summaries important when writing to respond?

5. What is the purpose of evaluation?

6. What is the purpose of connection/synthesis in writing to respond?

7. What are some strategies for rereading a text?

8. Identify three useful ways to take notes.

9. What is significant about how you react to a text when responding to that text?

10. How should you summarize a text you are responding to?

11. What are some methods for analyzing a text?

12. What are some strategies for synthesizing when responding to a text?

13. Identify the two primary forms of organizational strategies when writing to respond.

Thinking and Writing about the Chapter

Reflection

At the beginning of this chapter, you were asked to write in your journal or blog about what it means to respond to what others have written and why you might feel obligated to respond in particular situations and not in others. Now that you have read this chapter, return to your journal or blog and write a response to your original entry about response.

Discussion Threads

1. In what ways do you already write responses in college? As a class, discuss how response is already an active part of your engagement with texts in college.

2. This chapter addresses the importance of summary within responses, but summaries can also be important parts of other objectives of writing. Discuss how and when you might use summary in forms of writing other than response.

Collaboration

Working in pairs or groups of three, select a short literary text to discuss. Together, look for two or three points of agreement in how you respond to the text. Then, focusing on those responses, collaborate to write a single response to the text.

Writing

1. Argentinean writer Jorge Luis Borges wrote a remarkable piece of short fiction titled "The Library of Babel," a translation of which can be found online. Read Borges's story and then respond to it.

2. Chances are there is a situation on your campus that you want to respond to. Take this opportunity to respond, not to a text, but to that situation that you believe requires response.

Local Situation

Every semester, the administration at your college or university publishes texts that affect the lives of students on your campus. Some of these texts may explain new policies, some may describe opportunities on campus, and some may simply highlight or promote programs occurring on campus. Select a text that is part of your campus culture. Then, after reading and analyzing it, write a response to the text, assuming that your audience has not yet read the document. Be alert to how and why you summarize the document and how you organize the response.

Writing to Analyze

CHAPTER

12

Learning Objectives

12.1 Explain why analysis is important to your work in college

12.2 Differentiate between content analysis and rhetorical analysis

12.3 Use effective strategies to conduct textual and process analyses

12.4 Use effective strategies to analyze visuals

Before you read this chapter

What does it mean to analyze something? What kinds of things do you analyze in your personal life and your academic life? What role does analysis play in how you learn? In your blog or your journal, answer these questions and write about the kinds of analysis you perform regularly.

In 2007, a year before President Barack Obama was elected, it had become evident that the Internet would significantly influence the outcome of the election in ways that it couldn't possibly have in previous elections. In particular, YouTube's *Face the Candidates* page provided the sixteen presidential candidates the opportunity to maintain official campaign pages. Viewers could watch everything from debates to campaign stops to casual conversations, and they could do so just about anywhere using mobile technologies like mobile phones and other wireless network devices.

In December 2007, writer Mark Raby, writing for the online news source *TG Daily*, analyzed the "YouTube effect" and how it was, in fact, affecting the election. Raby's analysis revealed some intriguing information about the correlation between the numbers of views a candidate was amassing on his or her YouTube pages and the state of the candidate's popularity. Raby's article showed, among other interesting data, that according to the analysis of all six candidates' YouTube channels, "John Edwards, Barack Obama, and Hillary Clinton have all pulled out of the pack. Clinton is way out in front with more than 2.6 million views, followed by Obama and Edwards, right in line with where they fall on the primary poll." However, Obama had the greatest lead over all candidates with regard to the numbers of YouTube users actually subscribed to his pages. Obama had more than 13,000 subscribers, more than twice that of his closest competitor, Hillary Clinton.

Raby's analysis, published almost a year before the election, proved to be one of the most prophetic of the election. What is remarkable about Raby's analysis isn't just the data he gathered, but the scrutiny with which he analyzed the data and the clarity with which he presents his findings. Interestingly, Raby ends his analysis by concluding that the primary thing learned from the analysis wasn't a conclusive correlation between YouTube or Internet usage and the ability to win elections but that the impact of Internet resources like YouTube on elections remains uncertain. Where Raby succeeds in his scrutiny is providing us with a significant new understanding of digital media in our presidential election process.

12.1 Explain why analysis is important to your work in college

Analysis

To analyze is to examine something carefully to determine how all of its parts work together as a whole. Analysis also suggests a degree of critical reflection or a sense of evaluation and judgment. Some might understand "being critical" as a tendency to point out flaws; however, being critical more accurately means careful evaluation or scrutiny. Critical analysis is a process of scrutinizing something to become aware of details and how they relate to one another. Analysis is a central part of critical thinking and problem solving.

In college, you will be asked to analyze many kinds of things in a variety of disciplinary situations such as the following:

- Engineering—Analyze a systems development process
- Psychology—Analyze a cognitive process
- History—Analyze the causes of a historical event
- Drama—Analyze the plot structure of a play

Analysis is a central facet of college education because it requires that you scrutinize for the purpose of deeply understanding the object of your analysis.

Critical analysis is by no means a strictly academic activity; in fact, adept critical analysis will serve you most in your personal, professional, and civic lives outside of college. Most of the choices you will face—especially the really difficult choices—will require that you carefully analyze in order to solve problems and make decisions. For instance, in a professional setting you may need to analyze sales information before determining whether or not to support your company's push to expand to a global market. In your personal life, you may need to analyze treatment options for a medical situation, or you may need to analyze insurance policy options or mortgage options. In your civic life, you may need to analyze political candidates' platforms or local referendums. Ultimately, the approaches you learn for critical analysis in college will inform the strategies you use for analysis in the rest of your life.

Although critical analysis can be applied to just about any aspect of your life and to just about any object in any discipline, this chapter focuses on analyzing texts, written and visual. Certainly, many analytical strategies can be applied to other kinds of settings and objects, but this chapter focuses on how we analyze and write about things that are written (including visuals). Textual analysis is not an account of how you feel about a text; it is not about whether or not you agree with the text. Textual analysis examines the text and how the text works. College writers are asked to analyze texts for three specific reasons:

- *To participate.* Writers analyze texts to figure out where they want to fit and to derive meaning.
- *To practice.* Texts can be taken apart over and over again in a variety of ways to practice and develop analytical approaches.
- *To model.* Writers can learn more about their own choices by analyzing and mimicking choices others have made in their writing.

In the United States, we regularly tout the claim that everyone is entitled to his or her own opinion. There are two things we should acknowledge about this maxim: first, while we believe in the value of this claim, we must not forget that the right to having an opinion does not mean that one automatically has the right to voice that opinion in any situation or that others must also value that opinion. Second, critical analysis, the kind addressed in this chapter, is the process by which one develops informed opinions. Critical analysis, both rhetorical and situational, refines the value of an opinion in a given situation, making it valuable.

annotated example

Colonel Tim Collins delivered a speech in 2003 that has become known as one of the most powerful speeches of the Iraqi war. In 2005, Colonel Collins listened to Marie Fatayi-Williams deliver a speech which he regarded as genuinely emotional and unforgettable. *The Guardian*, a British daily newspaper, published the following commentary by Collins in which he analyzes her speech. Fatayi-Williams gave her speech in London, near the site where four days earlier a young terrorist had detonated a suicide bomb on a double-decker bus, killing himself and 13 others. Marie Fatayi-Williams's 26-year-old son Anthony was one of the 13 killed.

Straight from the Heart

Tim Collins

Caught in the spotlight of history, set on the stage of a very public event, Marie Fatayi-Williams, the mother of Anthony Fatayi-Williams, 26 and missing since Thursday, appeals for news of her son. Her words are a mixture of stirring rhetoric, heartfelt appeal and a stateswoman-like vision, and so speak on many levels to the nation and the world. Her appeal is a simple one—where is my son? If he has been killed, then why? Who has gained?

> Consider how much context the first sentence alone delivers. This paragraph introduces the frame of Collins's analysis, summarizes the text to be analyzed, and alerts us to Fatayi-Williams's use of pathos. Collins prepares his audience well for the coming analysis.

Marie has found herself, as I did on the eve of the invasion of Iraq, an unwitting voice, speaking amid momentous events. Her appeal, delivered on Monday not far from Tavistock Square, where she fears her son died in the bomb attack on the number 30 bus, gives a verbal form to the whirlpool of emotions that have engulfed society as the result of last week's bombings. I suspect Marie, like myself, had no idea that her words would find such wide recognition, have fed such an acute hunger for explanation, have slaked such a thirst for expression of the sheer horror of Thursday's events.

> Collins links Fatayi-Williams's situation to his own; this maneuver allows Collins to declare his position in this situation, personalizing his analysis by emphasizing his own emotional appeal and that of Fatayi-Williams.

This kind of speech is normally the preserve of the great orators, statesmen and playwrights, of Shakespeare, Churchill or Lincoln. It is often a single speech, a soliloquy or address from the steps of the gallows, that explains, inspires, exhorts and challenges. But always such addresses are crafted for effect and consciously intended to sway and influence, and often, as in the case of Shakespeare's *Henry V*, they are set in the mouth of a long dead hero or delivered by wordsmiths who are masters of their craft. It is rare in history that such oratory is

> Through comparison, Collins identifies and classifies the kind of speech Fatayi-Williams delivers. He describes her speech as unique within his classification. Again, he identifies the power of Fatayi-Williams's use of pathos.

the genuine article, springing from the heart and bursting forth to an unwitting audience. In Marie's case, her speech gains its power as a vehicle of grief and loss, and of the angst of a mother who yearns for her beloved son. In my case it was the opposite emotion from which I drew inspiration—an appeal to understand, to empathise, to give courage and purpose. I was motivated by a need to warn and teach as well as to encourage. Marie's motivation is a reflection on loss and that most powerful of all emotions, a mother's love.

The form the address takes is as poignant as the language used. There is an initial explanation of the extraordinary circumstances of the loss, a *cri de coeur* for the innocent blood lost, a rejection of the act by its comparison to the great liberators, and the assertion that her loss is all our loss in the family of humanity. It ends with her personal grief for her flesh and blood, her hopes and pride. The language echoes verses of the Bible as well as from the Koran. It has raw passion as well as heart-rending pathos.

> This paragraph addresses Fatayi-Williams's use of language, organizational strategies, summary, allusion, and argumentation. This analysis helps Collins situate the speech historically, making a connection to the preceding paragraph and adding to good paragraph cohesion.

With only a photograph of her son and a sheet of paper as a prompt, Marie's words burst out with as much emotion as anger. Her speech stands in stark contrast to the pronouncements of politicians, prepared by aides and delivered from copious notes. It is indeed the raw originality and authentic angst that give the delivery such impact, the plea such effect. No knighted veteran of the Royal Shakespeare Company could deliver such an address without hours or even days of rehearsal. I know from my own experience that only momentous events can provoke such a moment, only raw emotion can inspire such a spontaneous plea. I am often asked how long it took me to write my speech, delivered to my regiment, the Royal Irish, on the eve of the invasion of Iraq on March 19, 2003, at Fort Blair Mayne camp in the Kuwaiti desert. My answer is simple—not one moment. There was no plan; I spoke without notes. For me there was only the looming spectre of actual warfare and the certainty of loss and killing, and I was speaking to myself as well as to my men. I suspect for Marie there was only the yawning black void of loss, the cavern left behind in her life caused by the loss of a son who can never be replaced.

> Collins establishes Fatayi-Williams's speech as historically unique and identifies the authenticity of her pathos. Collins uses this paragraph to relate the situation of Fatayi-Williams's speech to his own experiences, contributing to his own ethos by confirming his qualifications to conduct and report the analysis.

What, then, can we take from this? Marie's appeal is important as it is momentous. Her words are as free from hatred as they are free from self-interest; it is clear that no man can give her her heart's desire—her son. I was also struck by the quiet dignity of her words, the clarity of her view and the weight of her convictions. She does not

> In the preceding paragraph, Collins shows how the use of pathos contributes to Fatayi-Williams's ethos. This paragraph takes up Fatayi-Williams's ethos. Collins identifies her sincerity, her lack of malice, and her lack of self-interest in achieving her purpose as a speaker–writer.

condemn, she appeals; her words act as an indictment of all war and violence, not just acts of terror but also the unnecessary aggression of nation states. Her message is simple: here is a human who only wanted to give, to succeed and to make his mother proud. Where is the victory in his death? Where is the progress in his destruction? In her own words: "What inspiration can senseless slaughter provide?"

I am certain that Marie's appeal will go down as one of the great speeches of our new century. It will give comfort to the families and friends of the dead and injured, both of this act and no doubt, regrettably, of events still to come. It should act as a caution to statesmen and leaders, a focus for public grief and, ultimately, as a challenge to, as well as a condemnation of, the perpetrators.

> Collins's analysis leads to a prediction, tied to the longevity of the situation; he clearly states what it is about the speech that leads to his prediction. Collins uses his analytical reading of Fatayi-Williams's speech as evidence for his position in the situation.

Marie is already an icon of the loss of Thursday July 7. Having travelled from Africa to find a better life, Anthony Fatayi-Williams carried the hopes and pride of his family. Now, as his mother has travelled to London, arguably one of the most cosmopolitan and integrated cities in the world, and standing nearby a wrecked icon of that city, a red double-decker bus, she has made an appeal which is as haunting as it is relevant, as poignant as it is appealing. It is a fact that such oratory as both Marie and I produced is born of momentous events, and inspired by hope and fears in equal measure.

> Collins establishes that Fatayi-Williams's speech has already solidified a position in a historical context. Think about the role that institutions (like textbooks) play in the situation and how they connect with Collins's analysis. Notice how Collins's analysis is served by his alignment of Fatayi-Williams's speech with his own.

But Marie's appeal is also important on another level. I have long urged soldiers in conflict zones to keep communicating with the population in order to be seen as people—it is easier to kill uniforms than it is to kill people. On July 7 the suicide bombers attacked icons of a society that they hated more than they loved life, the red London bus and the tube. Marie's speech has stressed the real victims' identities. They are all of us.

> Collins shifts to show how Fatayi-Williams's speech is also a moment of connection. The final sentence reminds us that icons are symbols that generically stand for the group of things they represent. This concluding sentence is Collins's ultimate analytical point: Marie Fatayi-Williams is talking about more than herself and her son.

Fatayi-Williams's Speech

Marie Fatayi-Williams's speech is presented here to provide you with more context for Collins's analysis. It appeared in *The Guardian* immediately following Tim Collins's analytical essay. Note that the speech is not analytical per se; it is a lament.

"This is Anthony, Anthony Fatayi-Williams, 26 years old, he's missing and we fear that he was in the bus explosion . . . on Thursday. We don't know. We do know from the witnesses that he left the Northern line in Euston. We know he made a call to his office at Amec at 9:41 from

Marie Fatayi-Williams speaks July 11, 2005, at Tavistock Square, London.

the NW1 area to say he could not make [it] by the tube but he would find alternative means to work.

Since then he has not made any contact with any single person. Now New York, now Madrid, now London. There has been widespread slaughter of innocent people. There have been streams of tears, innocent tears. There have been rivers of blood, innocent blood. Death in the morning, people going to find their livelihood, death in the noontime on the highways and streets.

They are not warriors. Which cause has been served? Certainly not the cause of God, not the cause of Allah because God Almighty only gives life and is full of mercy. Anyone who has been misled, or is being misled to believe that by killing innocent people he or she is serving God should think again because it's not true. Terrorism is not the way, terrorism is not the way. It doesn't beget peace. We can't deliver peace by terrorism, never can we deliver peace by killing people. Throughout history, those people who have changed the world have done so without violence, they have [won] people to their cause through peaceful protest. Nelson

Mandela, Martin Luther King, Mahatma Gandhi, their discipline, their self-sacrifice, their conviction made people turn towards them, to follow them. What inspiration can senseless slaughter provide? Death and destruction of young people in their prime as well as old and helpless can never be the foundations for building society.

My son Anthony is my first son, my only son, the head of my family. In African society, we hold on to sons. He has dreams and hopes and I, his mother, must fight to protect them. This is now the fifth day, five days on, and we are waiting to know what happened to him and I, his mother, I need to know what happened to Anthony. His young sisters need to know what happened, his uncles and aunties need to know what happened to Anthony, his father needs to know what happened to Anthony. Millions of my friends back home in Nigeria need to know what happened to Anthony. His friends surrounding me here, who have put this together, need to know what has happened to Anthony. I need to know, I want to protect him. I'm his mother, I will fight till I die to protect him. To protect his values and to protect his memory.

Innocent blood will always cry to God Almighty for reparation. How much blood must be spilled? How many tears shall we cry? How many mothers' hearts must be maimed? My heart is maimed. I pray I will see my son, Anthony. Why? I need to know, Anthony needs to know, Anthony needs to know, so do many others unaccounted for innocent victims, they need to know.

It's time to stop and think. We cannot live in fear because we are surrounded by hatred. Look around us today. Anthony is a Nigerian, born in London, worked in London, he is a world citizen. Here today we have Christians, Muslims, Jews, Sikhs, Hindus, all of us united in love for Anthony. Hatred begets only hatred. It is time to stop this vicious cycle of killing. We must all stand together, for our common humanity. I need to know what happened to my Anthony. He's the love of my life. My first son, my first son, 26. He tells me one day, "Mummy, I don't want to die, I don't want to die. I want to live, I want to take care of you, I will do great things for you, I will look after you, you will see what I will achieve for you. I will make you happy." And he was making me happy. I am proud of him, I am still very proud of him but I need to know where he is, I need to know what happened to him. I grieve, I am sad, I am distraught, I am destroyed.

He didn't do anything to anybody, he loved everybody so much. If what I hear is true, even when he came out of the underground he was directing people to take buses, to be sure that they were OK. Then he called his office at the same time to tell them he was running late. He was a multi-purpose person, trying to save people, trying to call his office, trying to meet his appointments. What did he then do to deserve this. Where is he, someone tell me, where is he?"

Emilia Maria "Nicky" Cadiz majors in both microbiology and cell science and East Asian languages and literatures as well as minors in business administration. Nicky's fascination with East Asian culture and languages stems from living in five countries during her childhood. After graduation she hopes to attend medical school and eventually incorporate into her medical practice holistic methods of healthcare learned through science and East Asian culture.

Nicky's essay analyzes a photograph featured on the cover of *Harper's Bazaar* fashion magazine. Nicky uses her analysis to support an argument about how visuals might be misused or misunderstood given the importance of visuals in contemporary culture. As you read Nicky's essay, think about how she conducts her analysis and how she also analyzes the situation of the photograph.

The Jersey Shore and *Harper's Bazaar*

Emilia Maria "Nicky" Cadiz

Visuals inhabit and enrich our daily lives. We encounter visual rhetoric in all forms of media through photographs, charts, and symbols, and society expects us to understand and inherently know what these visuals mean. In a world teeming with imagery, photographers, and graphic designers, their respective audiences must have some sort of visual literacy; they must know how to produce and interpret images. The pervasiveness of visuals has created the current "visual culture." Photojournalists and reporters use images to capture moments in time and to prove to their audience that events actually happened. Graphic designers construct computer generated visuals and mix them with photographs to make compelling arguments. They use photographs to support their arguments or even to help make their claims. Those who include visuals in their work expect their audiences to accept the image without question, and more often than not, audiences do. This phenomenon stems from our belief that "seeing is believing." No one questions the image. But is the image the truth? Sometimes we fail to realize that photographers and graphic designers, through their work, are themselves rhetoricians. The visuals they employ can persuade; they can evoke emotion. Tables, charts, and graphs adorn newspapers and science journals and serve to accentuate information from surveys or data from research. Images make statements. Tailoring an image—using different Photoshop features, angles, and lens focus points—mirrors how an experienced writer would cut, paste, and structure an argument. Therefore, all visuals are arguments whether or not they are effective and/or ethical. This tailoring alters the way an image is perceived and received by the masses. How the audience interprets a visual depends on the visual literacy of both the viewer and the image creator. Our culture is so overly saturated with visuals that we have become accustomed to blindly believing them. Photographers and designers take advantage of our naiveté and modify their visuals to cater to the three rhetorical appeals—ethos, pathos and logos—in order for us to believe them. For example, let us consider the April 2010 *Harper's Bazaar* cover image that featured the girls from *Jersey Shore.* How credible is it that both *Harper's Bazaar* and *Jersey Shore* were used in the same sentence?

For an audience to believe the *Harper's Bazaar* visual, the photographer must relate the image to the subject at hand. If the visual does not support the subject matter then there is no argument. *Harper's Bazaar* is one of the nation's high-class fashion magazines that targets upper class women who live in the city. In April 2010, *Harper's Bazaar* attempted to capitalize on *Jersey Shore*'s popularity by featuring the *Jersey Shore* girls—Jenni "JWoww" Farley, Nicole "Snooki" Polizzi, and Samantha "Sammi" Giancola—in their magazine. On the cover, JWoww, Snooki, and Sammi wore $6820, $7500, and $2850 designer evening gowns, respectively. If *Harper's Bazaar* associates itself with glitzy socialites, expensive designer clothing, and high fashion designers, then why are the "classy" *Jersey Shore* girls on the cover? Society knows these three girls as scantily-clad, potty-mouthed

Snooki, Sammi, and JWoww from *Jersey Shore*, before their *Harper's Bazaar* "extreme makeover."

"guidette" party animals with high-poofed hair, fresh extensions, and well-kept tans. How have these two opposites evidently joined forces? Many fashion gurus had this same logic and questioned the reason behind *Harper's Bazaar*'s decision to include the *Jersey Shore* girls.

Consequently, no fashion critic took this April 2010 edition seriously, and *Women's Wear Daily,* the "bible" of the fashion world, simply stated that the *Jersey Shore* cast was "Basking in, and hyperactively milking, their 15 minutes [of fame]" (5). It was extremely out of character for both *Harper's Bazaar* and the *Jersey Shore* girls. According to JWoww's tweet on the day of the shoot, she "never purchased one mag/and now [she's] in a lot of em!" Clearly she had never read the magazine, since she spelled Bazaar "Bizaar." How surprising. The entertainment world was buzzing in disbelief. Almost every tabloid and entertainment blog jokingly wrote something about JWoww, Snooki, and Sammi's appearance in the magazine.

What were the *Harper's Bazaar* editors thinking? They featured world-renown, trashy girls in their high class magazine. The *Jersey Shore* girls' feature article and pictures showed JWoww, Snooki, and Sammi attending charm and etiquette school with Lizzie Post, great-great-granddaughter of Etiquette School legend Emily Post. According to Emily Post's Etiquette Daily *Harper's Bazaar* asked The Emily Post Institute, an institute promoting etiquette in America since 1946, to participate in "an etiquette lesson photo shoot with the girls of *The Jersey Shore*" and to "teach the girls a little bit of etiquette and refinement." In the *Harper's Bazaar* video, Snooki states that she's "been to etiquette school" and that she "knows a couple things already, but [she] hasn't been using them." JWoww says that she "does know the lessons they're teaching very well," and similarly Sammi "feels like she already knows how to be a lady." Apparently all three girls have yet to watch a *Jersey Shore* episode. Spoiler Alert: There has not been a *Jersey Shore* episode to date that can validate any of those three statements.

Visuals create their own arguments. The audience sees the image from the perspective the photographer chooses. Altering images changes the way an image is viewed. A photographer constructs the image just as a writer would construct his or her argument. The image caters to its audience's liking. Images are structured to appeal to the audience's ethos, pathos, and logos. In visual arguments, photographers and graphic design artists edit the image to leave only what is important, only what is needed. They can crop out whatever is unnecessary and Photoshop the image to suit and support the argument. Visuals are everywhere—on billboards, posters, newspapers, advertisements—and well executed ones can stand alone as effective arguments. But do not in the least bit forget that every visual has a purpose and an angle from its creator. *Harper's Bazaar*'s attempt to make the girls from *Jersey Shore* classy did not resonate well with their upper-class, high-fashion audience. The *Jersey Shore* girls were just out of their element. JWoww said that on the show "they're being themselves." Clearly that is not seen in this refined photo shoot. After the shoot, the girls reverted back to their *Jersey Shore*-selves to record the second season of *The Jersey Shore* in South Beach, Miami. In the end, *Harper's Bazaar* failed to appeal to their posh, socialite audience, and thus, they failed to persuade their readers and make them believe.

student example

Works Cited

Britney, Free. "*Jersey Shore* Featured in . . . *Harper's Bazaar?*" *Hollywood Gossip.* SheKnows Entertainment, 4 Mar. 2010. Web. 7 May 2012.

Gorgan, Elena. "*Jersey Shore* Cast Looking Mighty Classy for *Harper's Bazaar.*" *Softpedia.* Softnews, 15 Apr. 2010. Web. 7 May 2012.

"*Jersey Shore* Makeover: Charm School." *Harper's Bazaar.com.* Hearst Communications, May 2011. Web. 7 May 2012.

"Memo Pad: Glamming the 'Jersey Shore'" *Women's Wear Daily.* 3 March 2010. Web. 7 May 2012.

Odell, Amy. "*Harper's Bazaar* Shot the *Jersey Shore* Girls." *New York Magazine.* New York Media, 3 Mar. 2010. Web. 7 May 2012.

Senning, Daniel Post. "Lizzie Post Visits the Jersey Shore: No, Really!" *Emily Post's Etiquette Daily.* Emily Post Institute, 16 Apr. 2010. Web. 7 May 2012.

Thinking about Nicky's Essay

1. Nicky Cadiz's analysis in this essay takes on a dual purpose: to scrutinize *Harper's Bazaar*'s decision to use a photograph of the *Jersey Shore* girls on its cover and to examine how, why, and whether readers accept photographs as inherently true. In essence, then, Nicky's analysis serves a more encompassing argumentative purpose. What are her analytical claims, and how do they support her argumentative claims? That is, in what ways does Nicky "use" analysis in this essay?

2. On what does Nicky base her analysis?

3. In many ways, Nicky Cadiz's analysis is not an analysis of the technical aspects of or content of the *Harper's Bazaar* cover photograph, but is an analysis of a situation in which the photograph participates. What does her analysis reveal, though, about the photograph that we might not gather from just the photograph?

student example

THE ROAD TO A
STRONG THESIS

SECOND THOUGHTS:
"I noticed that the recent cover of *Harper's Bazaar* features a photo of the *Jersey Shore* girls. That seems a bit unusual. Maybe I could analyze what *Harper's Bazaar* might be suggesting with that photo."

SECOND THOUGHTS:
"But asking that kind of question also suggests that I want to know why we find photographs interesting, or more to the point, why do we accept photographs as depicting something 'real'?"

SECOND THOUGHTS:
"Analyzing what we 'understand' seems a bit vague. Maybe I need to analyze what the photo means or what it suggests about the magazine."

RESPONSE:
"I need to understand the point of that cover photo and what it might suggest about how we understand photographs."

RESPONSE:
"Doing this would allow me to make an argument about how we interpret photographs. This way my analysis of the *Jersey Shore* girls cover could be an example of how readers tend to accept photographs representing reality."

RESPONSE
"This makes sense. Now my analysis has a point other than practicing analysis. Now that analysis can support my argument."

QUESTION
"What can I analyze? And why would I analyze something?"

ASSIGNMENT
"To write an analytical essay."

THESIS:
"Our culture is so saturated with visuals that we have become accustomed to blindly believing them."

Nicky Cadiz was assigned the task of writing an analytical essay. By looking at the cultural context in which the *Jersey Shore* girls' photograph circulated, Nicky was able to develop a thesis that she found to be more relevant and useful than just performing the analysis for the sake of analysis.

FINAL THOUGHTS:
"Now I have a position I can support using my analysis. This gives me a reason to conduct the analysis and a context in which to discuss it."

professional example

James Cameron's movie *Avatar* was the highest grossing film of all time. Self-described "biethnic" writer Annalee Newitz published a critical analysis of *Avatar* in *io9,* a popular futurism, science, and technology blog. Newitz, a former policy analyst for the Electronic Frontier Foundation, has contributed to *Wired*, *Popular Science*, *The Washington Post*, *New York Magazine*, and *New Scientist*, to name but a few. She has also published three books: *She's Such a Geek: Women Write about Science, Technology, and Other Nerdy Stuff*; *Pretend We're Dead: Capitalist Monsters in American Pop Culture*; and *White Trash: Race and Class in America*.

In "When Will White People Stop Making Movies Like *Avatar*?" Newitz analyzes *Avatar* as a familiar white narrative about colonization. As you read her essay, consider how Newitz synthesizes her analysis of *Avatar* with her analysis of other films and cultural characteristics. In what ways does this synthesis serve the analysis, and in what ways does the analysis serve the synthesis?

When Will White People Stop Making Movies Like *Avatar*?

Annalee Newitz

Critics have called alien epic *Avatar* a version of *Dances with Wolves* because it's about a white guy going native and becoming a great leader. But *Avatar* is just the latest scifi rehash of an old white guilt fantasy.

Spoilers . . .

Whether *Avatar* is racist is a matter for debate. Regardless of where you come down on that question, it's undeniable that the film—like alien apartheid flick *District 9*, released earlier this year—is emphatically a fantasy about race. Specifically, it's a fantasy about race told from the point of view of white people. *Avatar* and scifi films like it give us the opportunity to answer the question: What do white people fantasize about when they fantasize about racial identity?

Avatar imaginatively revisits the crime scene of white America's foundational act of genocide, in which entire native tribes and civilizations were wiped out by European immigrants to the American continent. In the film, a group of soldiers and scientists have set up shop on the verdant moon Pandora, whose landscapes look like a cross between Northern California's redwood cathedrals and Brazil's tropical rainforest. The moon's inhabitants, the Na'vi, are blue, catlike versions of native people: They wear feathers in their hair, worship nature gods, paint their faces for war, use bows and arrows, and live in tribes. Watching the movie, there is really no mistake that these are alien versions of stereotypical native peoples that we've seen in Hollywood movies for decades.

And Pandora is clearly supposed to be the rich, beautiful land America could still be if white people hadn't paved it over with concrete and strip malls. In *Avatar*, our white hero Jake Sully (sully—get it?) explains that Earth is basically a war-torn wasteland with no greenery or natural resources left. The humans started to colonize Pandora in order to mine a mineral called unobtainium that can serve as a mega-energy source. But a few of these humans don't want to crush the natives with tanks and bombs, so they wire their brains into the bodies of Na'vi avatars and try to win the natives' trust. Jake is one of the team of avatar pilots, and he discovers to his surprise that he loves his life as a Na'vi warrior far more than he ever did his life as a human marine.

Jake is so enchanted that he gives up on carrying out his mission, which is to persuade the Na'vi to relocate from their "home tree," where the humans want to mine the unobtanium. Instead, he focuses on becoming a great warrior who rides giant birds and falls in love with the chief's daughter. When the inevitable happens and the marines arrive to burn down the Na'vi's home tree, Jake switches sides. With the help of a few human renegades, he maintains a link with his avatar body in order to lead the Na'vi against the human invaders. Not only has he been assimilated into the native people's culture, but he has become their leader.

This is a classic scenario you've seen in non-scifi epics from *Dances With Wolves* to *The Last Samurai*, where a white guy manages to get himself accepted into a closed society of people of color and eventually becomes its most awesome member. But it's also, as I indicated earlier, very similar in some ways to *District 9*. In that film, our (anti)hero Wikus is trying to relocate a shantytown of aliens to a region far outside Johannesburg. When he's accidentally squirted with fluid from an alien technology, he begins turning into one of the aliens against his will. Deformed and cast out of human society, Wikus reluctantly helps one of the aliens to launch their stalled ship and seek help from their home planet.

If we think of *Avatar* and its ilk as white fantasies about race, what kinds of patterns do we see emerging in these fantasies?

In both *Avatar* and *District 9*, humans are the cause of alien oppression and distress. Then, a white man who was one of the oppressors switches sides at the last minute, assimilating into the alien culture and becoming its savior. This is also the basic story of *Dune*, where a member of the white royalty flees his posh palace on the planet Dune to become leader of the worm-riding native Fremen (the worm-riding rite of passage has an analog in *Avatar*, where Jake proves his manhood by riding a giant bird). An interesting tweak on this story can be seen in 1980s flick *Enemy Mine*, where a white man (Dennis Quaid) and the alien he's been battling (Louis Gossett Jr.) are stranded on a hostile planet together for years. Eventually they become best friends, and when the alien dies, the human raises the alien's child as his own. When humans arrive on the planet and try to enslave the alien child, he lays down his life to rescue it. His loyalties to an alien have become stronger than to his own species.

These are movies about white guilt. Our main white characters realize that they are complicit in a system which is destroying aliens, AKA people of color—their cultures, their habitats, and their populations. The whites realize this when they begin to assimilate into the "alien" cultures and see things from a new perspective. To purge their overwhelming sense of guilt, they switch sides, become "race traitors," and fight against their old comrades. But then they go beyond assimilation and become leaders of the people they once oppressed. This is the essence of the white guilt fantasy, laid bare. It's not just a wish to be absolved of the crimes whites have committed against people of color; it's not just a wish to join the side of moral justice in battle. It's a wish to lead people of color from the inside rather than from the (oppressive, white) outside.

Think of it this way. *Avatar* is a fantasy about ceasing to be white, giving up the old human meatsack to join the blue people, but never losing white privilege. Jake never really knows what it's like to be a Na'vi because he always has the option to switch back into human mode. Interestingly, Wikus in *District 9* learns a very different lesson. He's becoming alien and he can't go back. He has no other choice but to live in the slums and eat catfood. And guess what? He really hates it. He helps his alien buddy to escape Earth solely because he's hoping the guy will come back in a few years with a "cure" for his alienness. When whites fantasize about becoming other races, it's only fun if they can blithely ignore the fundamental experience of being an oppressed racial group. Which is that you are oppressed, and nobody will let you be a leader of anything.

This is not a message anybody wants to hear, least of all the white people who are creating and consuming these fantasies. Afro-Canadian scifi writer Nalo Hopkinson recently told the *Boston Globe:*

In the US, to talk about race is to be seen as racist. You become the problem because you bring up the problem. So you find people who are hesitant to talk about it.

She adds that the main mythic story you find in science fiction, generally written by whites, "is going to a foreign culture and colonizing it."

Sure, *Avatar* goes a little bit beyond the basic colonizing story. We are told in no uncertain terms that it's wrong to colonize the lands of native people. Our hero chooses to join the Na'vi rather than abide the racist culture of his own people. But it is nevertheless a story that revisits the same old tropes of colonization. Whites still get to be leaders of the natives—just in a kinder, gentler way than they would have in an old Flash Gordon flick or in Edgar Rice Burroughs' Mars novels.

When will whites stop making these movies and start thinking about race in a new way?

First, we'll need to stop thinking that white people are the most "relatable" characters in stories. As one blogger put it:

By the end of the film you're left wondering why the film needed the Jake Sully character at all. The film could have done just as well by focusing on an actual Na'vi native who comes into contact with crazy humans who have no respect for the environment. I can just see the explanation: "Well, we need someone (an avatar) for the audience to connect with. A normal guy will work better than these tall blue people." However, this is the type of thinking that molds all leads as white male characters (blank slates for the audience to project themselves on) unless your name is Will Smith.

But more than that, whites need to rethink their fantasies about race.

Whites need to stop remaking the white guilt story, which is a sneaky way of turning every story about people of color into a story about being white. Speaking as a white person, I don't need to hear more about my own racial experience. I'd like to watch some movies about people of color (ahem, aliens), from the perspective of that group, without injecting a random white (erm, human) character to explain everything to me. Science fiction is exciting because it promises to show the world and the universe from perspectives radically unlike what we've seen before. But until white people stop making movies like *Avatar*, I fear that I'm doomed to see the same old story again and again.

Analyzing the Situation

1. Who is Annalee Newitz's audience for this analytical reading of *Avatar*? What is it about the text itself that leads you to this conclusion?

2. In her synthesis, Newitz references movies that are contemporaries of *Avatar*, but she also references older films. What does she gain in referring to movies that are 20 and 25 years older than *Avatar*?

3. Newitz's essay participates in a situation in which there are a tremendous number of players. How would you identify and describe the players in this situation?

Analyzing the Rhetoric

1. What is Newitz's purpose in citing Nalo Hopkinson and the one unnamed blog?

2. In what ways does Newitz use synopsis and summary?

3. How does Newitz use the first person to establish her position in this essay?

Discussing

1. This chapter later suggests that when analyzing a text (or anything, for that matter) it helps to state your first reactions as questions, not statements, so you can avoid making judgments. As a class, state your first reactions to Newitz's essay about *Avatar* as questions and discuss.

2. Does Newitz convince you? Do you agree with her analysis? Take some time to discuss how you respond to Newitz's analysis and the ways in which her analysis does or does not support her contention.

3. In what ways does the success of *Avatar* provide Newitz an opportunity to respond to the film from the perspective she does? Discuss why Newitz might have chosen *Avatar* as the impetus for writing about films, in general, as she does.

Writing

1. Analyze the argument that Newitz makes and the evidence she uses to support it. That is, conduct a detailed content analysis of the essay. Then write an analytical essay of your own that scrutinizes how Newitz makes her argument. You may also want to conduct some rhetorical analysis.

2. Given the context that Newitz has provided—racial approaches to action films—consider another adventure movie that Newitz does not address. Then write your own analysis of the film you choose, addressing how that film may or may not depict the "fantasy" Newitz describes.

SIDE BY SIDE

Each of the three writing examples analyzes a particular kind of text: a speech, a photograph, and a movie. Each uses its analysis to explain a more complex context: terrorism and loss, visual culture, and representations of race. Consider how each writer conveys the analysis and how each uses the analysis toward an overall purpose.

	annotated example TIM COLLINS, "Straight from the Heart"	**student example** NICKY CADIZ, *"The Jersey Shore* and *Harper's Bazaar"*	**professional example** ANNALEE NEWITZ, "When Will White People Stop Making Movies Like *Avatar*?"
PURPOSE	To analyze Marie Fatayi-Williams's speech, its historical value, and its contribution to how we talk about terrorism and violence.	To argue that our culture is so saturated with visuals that we have become accustomed to blindly believing them.	To analyze the film *Avatar* to answer the question "What do white people fantasize about when they fantasize about racial identity?"
AUDIENCE	Readers of the UK's *The Guardian* newspaper.	Nicky's writing teacher and peers interested in visual culture.	Science fiction film fans.
CONTENT ANALYSIS	Collins identifies what is significant in Marie Fatayi-Williams's speech. He specifically explains the substantive information she conveys within the historical context of the speech.	Nicky questions the appearance of the *Jersey Shore* girls in the cover photo. Her analysis examines what might be suggested to readers by including the girls, dressed in expensive clothing, in the photo.	Annalee Newitz's analysis examines the content of *Avatar*, but does so as a means to a more encompassing analysis of science fiction films as reflecting larger, cultural characteristics like racism.
RHETORICAL ANALYSIS	Collins is deliberate in his examination of Fatayi-Williams's language and delivery. He notes, for example, that Fatayi-Williams's language echoes verses of the Bible and of the Koran.	Nicky's analysis considers the visual rhetoric of the photograph and the rhetoric the *Jersey Shore* girls and the *Harper's Bazaar* editors use to discuss the cover photo.	Newitz provides some visual rhetorical analysis, but her more significant rhetorical analysis focuses on the role of power and institution in this rhetorical situation.
DISTRIBUTION	Circulated through a widely read newspaper.	Shared with her classmates and teacher.	Posted on a popular technology blog.
ORGANIZATION	Collins uses his own experiences in giving emotionally charged speeches in trying times. He moves back and forth between discussing Fatayi-Williams's speech and clarifying his analysis by offering comparisons with his own experiences.	Nicky frames her analysis with introductory and concluding discussions about the role of visuals in contemporary culture.	Newitz provides an analytic overview of *Avatar*. She then compares particular aspects of her analysis and of *Avatar* with other films of the same genre.
LANGUAGE	Collins's language is confident and authoritative. He is not only a colonel but also an expert on language and speech delivery.	Nicky's language identifies specific details about the *Jersey Shore* girls' photo. She also carefully chooses her language to create a tone of playful critique.	Although Newitz's blog post presents an analysis that requires careful thought, her tone is conversational.

12.2 Differentiate between content analysis and rhetorical analysis

Type of Analysis	Prparing Your Analysis
CONTENT ANALYSIS	Content analysis is the examination of what a text is about. Content analysis takes into account information accuracy, meaning, substance, relevance, interpretation, and other such characteristics.
Questions for Content Analysis	Ask: What is the main idea of the text? What are the secondary ideas of the text? What interests me about the text? Who and what are the main characters of the text? How are those characters described? What information is conveyed by the text? How is the text similar to or different from other texts of the same theme or genre? Is the text logical?
RHETORICAL ANALYSIS	Rhetorical analysis is an examination of why the writer made particular rhetorical choices in composing a text and whether those choices were effective. This type of analysis examines rhetorical devices, linguistic or visual, to understand what effect they may have on the content and how the text works.
Questions about Purpose	What appears to be the purpose of the text? Is this purpose explicitly identified within the text or implied?
Questions about Situation	In what situation did this text arise? Who is the writer/speaker? What position does the writer have in the situation?
Questions about the Writer/Speaker	How does the writer/speaker establish ethos? Is the writer's voice evident in the document?
Questions about Audience	Who is the audience? What characteristics of the text lead you to this conclusion?
Questions about Organization	How is the text organized or arranged? Does the writer transition smoothly between different ideas?
Questions about Language	How do you describe the language the writer uses? Does the writer use jargon, formal language, technical language, slang, or idioms? Does the writer use words you are not familiar with? Are they defined? What kinds of style and tone does the text use? Are those choices effective for this document?
Questions about Medium and Method	What method does the text primarily exhibit; that is, is the text argumentative, persuasive, antagonistic, explanatory, descriptive, informative, emotional, and so forth? In what medium is the text presented? Does that medium affect how you read the text?
Questions about Genre	Can the text be categorized as a familiar genre? How does the genre work in conjunction with the content of the text?

12.3 Use effective strategies to conduct textual and process analyses

Strategy	Developing Your Analysis
Situate	Identify your purpose for analyzing the text and your purpose in writing that analysis so you can better devise how you will conduct your analysis.
Make a claim	By establishing a claim, you can focus your written analysis on a particular approach and guide your audience through that analysis.
Identify the expected	Identify what parts you would expect to find in the type of thing you are analyzing. For example, we would expect a novel to have plot, characters, and setting. When analyzing an image, we expect that image to have an optical center.
React carefully	Try framing your reactions not as statements but as questions. After reading an essay, rather than "That essay really interested me; it was insightful," ask "What was it about that essay specifically that interested me? What did I find insightful?"
Look for details	Clarify for yourself the details you identify so you can better clarify them for your audience. Identify what remains unclear, even after your attempts to clarify, and record that information in your notes. Details of a text may be unclear intentionally or problematically, which you may need to address.
Narrow your focus	When analyzing a text, tightly focus your approach on only those issues that are relevant to your purpose.
Identify the parts	Classify the parts you identify to figure out how they work together to form the whole. You may want to create a labeling system for yourself to identify the parts, how they work, and where they fit.
Examine the words	In addition to clarifying for yourself terms that are jargon, idioms, slang, and so on, make certain that you understand the nuances of words' meanings that can subtly alter the message.
Use concrete language	Concrete language (words that are either tangible or perceptible through the senses such as visual, audio, or tactile attributes) allows you to be clear about what your analyses reveal.
Summarize	Consider providing a complete summary before presenting the details of your analysis.
Synthesize	Synthesis involves analyzing a whole and its parts to determine how the whole or parts might contribute to developing a new idea. Considering your analysis in relation to other information and other texts also can strengthen how you synthesize.
Organize	• *Organize by importance.* Present the most relevant information first. • *Organize by criteria.* Organize your findings according to which criteria are most important. • *Organize by scope.* Organize your information beginning with broader conceptual information and tapering to more specific details. • *Organize by chronology.* Begin with what you noticed first and move through your analytical process as it unfolded.

MAPPING
YOUR SITUATION

NETWORKS
- In what networks will my analysis circulate?
- How is my analysis related to others' analyses?
- How might my analysis affect the situation?

WRITERS AND SPEAKERS
- Who are the other writers and speakers in this situation?
- What have they said about this situation?
- What other analyses are presented?

RELATIONS
- What is my relation to the situation?
- What are the relationships between writers/speakers, audience, and players?
- What are the relationships to external forces, like culture, religion, or politics?
- What are the power relations?

AUDIENCE
- Who will read/see my analysis?
- What do I know about my intended audience?
- Who will the analysis affect directly and indirectly?

MEDIUM AND METHOD
- In what genre will I deliver my analysis?
- What method will I use to convey my analysis?
- How will I distribute my analysis?

CONTEXT
- Where will my analysis take place?
- Where will my analysis appear?
- What limits are imposed on my analysis?

PURPOSE
- What am I analyzing?
- Why am I analyzing?
- What does my analysis need to convey?
- Does my analysis serve a larger purpose?

Mapping your situation will generate ideas you can use to compose your analysis. Start by answering these questions about each part of the situation. Begin with your purpose and work outward to relations and networks.

Writing Projects

Essay

Select a text—a film, a book, an essay, a blog page, and so on—and read it carefully. Then conduct a thorough content and rhetorical analysis of the text. Once you feel comfortable with your analysis and your understanding of the text, write an analytical essay that describes and explains the text you selected.

Visual Analysis

Using any one of the techniques discussed in this chapter, write an analysis of this image.

Digital

Google Analytics is a service provided by Google that analyzes how a website is visited and used. The service is designed to help businesses and organizations learn more about how clients use their websites. Take some time to learn more about Google Analytics, both what it does and how different organizations use it. Then identify three organizations that make their Google Analytic data public. Analyze the data each provides. Design a web page that uses your analysis to depict how Google Analytics may or may not improve a website's function.

Research

As digital technologies saturate academic disciplines, humanities scholars have begun to explore the possibilities of using computer technologies in humanities research and teaching. The "digital humanities" have emerged as a central area of studies within the humanities. However, there is little agreement as to what "digital humanities" might include. Conduct some research about the digital humanities, learning how various writers and institutions define "digital humanities." Analyze several of the definitions that you locate. What are the commonalities and differences among the definitions? Using your research, write a document that analyzes the various definitions and then synthesizes the parts of the definitions that you identify as most useful, elaborating what you see as a cohesive definition of the term.

Radical Revision

Act 2, Scene 2 from William Shakespeare's *Romeo and Juliet* is a rather famous scene; it is the well-known and often-performed balcony scene. Locate a copy of the written scene. Read the scene and then analyze it, taking into account both content analysis and rhetorical analysis. Write an analysis of the scene. Once you have written your analysis, consider how you might recreate the balcony scene in a contemporary setting using contemporary media. Using any animation storytelling application you find online (like Animoto, Muvizu, or GoAnimate), write and design an animated version of the scene that situates the conversation in a context familiar to you and your peers. Use your analysis to ensure that you retain key elements of the scene within your revised approach.

12.4 Use effective strategies to analyze visuals

Analyzing Visuals

Many of the analytical methods and strategies discussed earlier in this chapter about written texts can be applied to analyzing visuals; however, you should also develop analytical approaches that are unique to reading visuals. In this section, you can examine ways of thinking about visuals and develop strategies for analyzing visuals, particularly three key concepts: visual rhetoric, visual literacy, and visual analysis.

Visual rhetoric is the study of how visuals make and convey meaning. Visual rhetorical analysis often analyzes the relationship between writing and visuals as a way of better understanding how visuals communicate. Visual rhetorical analysis is different from design analysis in that it focuses on communication and meaning, whereas design tends to focus on the aesthetic.

Visual literacy refers to one's familiarity and ability to interpret meaning from visual texts. Like other forms of literacy, visual literacy is both learned and culturally influenced. Being adept at reading visuals within a cultural situation is visual literacy.

Visual analysis comprises many well-developed methods and processes, summarized in the following charts.

General Concepts about Visual Analysis	
Direct analysis	Looks at what is contained in a visual's content. Direct analysis may include identifying various subjects within the image, perspectives (like camera angles), patterns, and so on. Direct analysis questions should evolve from what you see in the visual.
Indirect analysis	Examines what is outside of the visual that helps audiences determine a visual's meaning. For example, if you have been asked to analyze an aerial photograph of the 2010 BP Deepwater Gulf of Mexico oil spill, an indirect analysis would likely reveal information about environmental disaster, ocean currents, oil drilling, and other similar subjects as influencing what an audience takes from the photograph but which are not directly depicted in the image itself.
Visual rhetorical analysis	Examines visual rhetorical tools at play in a visual, just as a writer does in a piece of writing. Visual rhetorical analysis makes conscious choices about how a visual will be designed, produced, and situated, breaking a visual into its parts. Visual rhetorical analysis applies written textual analysis, asking about purpose, audience, ethos, and so on, but it extends its analysis to visually specific rhetorics: use of color, use of space, flow, balance, repetition, and so on.

Within these three types of analysis, direct, indirect, and visual rhetorical, you can also approach your analysis using the strategies described in the following chart.

Strategies for Approaching Visual Analysis	
Technical analysis	Examines the techniques the writer/producer used to make the visual. Techniques for a photograph might include camera angle, hue and saturation, balance, center of interest, viewpoint, lighting, texture, tone, contrast, framing, and perspective. Techniques for a painting might include materials, brush use, color, shape, movement, perspective, tone, and contrast.
Social/situational analysis	Examines what a visual might mean in a given context. Social analysis, for example, might consider what meaning an audience interprets from a photograph of, say, the Changing of the Guard ritual at Buckingham Palace and what social/cultural understanding of that ritual the audience would have to have to interpret that visual. Situational analysis asks specifically how a given context imposes or changes the meaning of a visual.
Content analysis	Examines, through either direct or indirect analysis, what you see or don't see in a visual. Content analysis can scrutinize things like setting, composition, and characters.
Analysis of medium and method	Scrutinizes how a visual conveys meaning specifically because of how it was composed and the medium in which it is presented.
Semiotic analysis	Examines how the signs and symbols of a visual convey meaning.

Writing Process
GUIDELINES

Use the guidelines in this chart to plan, review, and evaluate your process for writing an analysis. Each step in the process should support the overall purpose of your analysis.

SITUATE
- Understand your reasons for conducting the analysis.
- Understand how relations affect your analysis.
- Identify how the constraints affect your analysis.
- Distinguish the role of location in your analysis.
- Recognize the speakers or writers in the situation and how they affect your analysis.
- Identify and analyze the audiences involved in the situation.
- Consider what genres, media, and methods are used in the situation.
- Acknowledge how various institutions and power affect the situation.
- Consider the ecological relationships.

PLAN
- Confirm your reason for conducting this analysis.
- Clarify your purpose in analyzing.
- Consider your form for delivering your analysis.
- Understand the purpose of the document in which your analysis will appear.
- Consider what might be the best genre, media, and method to deliver your analysis.
- Begin to take notes.

RESEARCH
- Determine what kind of information you will need to support your analysis.
- Conduct research to gather the information you need.
- Confirm that your research will be valid within the context of the analysis.
- Identify any visuals you may need to analyze or to depict your analysis.
- Organize your information.

DRAFT
- Confirm your purpose.
- Confirm that your choices in genre, media, and method will be effective within the situation.
- Draft and organize the content of your analysis.
- Use visual processes to develop any visuals you will need.
- Design your document.

REVIEW AND REVISE
- Review your document for clarity and concision.
- Review your document for accuracy.
- Review your document for degree of detail appropriate to the situation and purpose.
- Review your document for extraneous information.
- Review your document for organizational approach.
- Review your document for explanations of key terms necessary within the situation.
- Review your document for style appropriate to the situation.
- Confirm your research and citations.
- Review your document for visual effectiveness and readability.
- Consider revising the title to most accurately reflect the document's purpose.

EDIT
- Proofread carefully.
- Correct all mechanical and grammatical errors.

EVALUATE
- Seek feedback from peers (take advantage of peer-editing opportunities).
- Ask for feedback from a representative member of the target audience.
- Ask for feedback from an editor in whom you are confident.
- Evaluate the usefulness of any feedback you receive and revise accordingly.

DISTRIBUTE/CIRCULATE
- Consider technologies of circulation.
- Publish in a form that will be visible within the situation.
- Identify methods for increasing circulation (like search engine optimization) within and beyond the specific situation.
- Consider audience access.
- Identify possible sources of audience response.

Seeking Feedback

Peers, target audiences, and editors can offer valuable observations that will strengthen your writing. You will encourage more constructive feedback from these readers if you structure your questions for them carefully. Consider asking these kinds of questions to get feedback:

EVALUATION Guidelines

INITIAL REACTION

- What are your initial reactions to the analysis?
- What do you see as the purpose of the analysis?
- What are the strengths of the analysis?
- What are the weaknesses of the analysis?
- Does the analysis hold your interest?
- Generally speaking, what is the primary thing the writer must do to improve this document? Are there details the analysis does not present that you thought should be present? Is the analysis focused?

SITUATION

- Who do you understand this analysis to be written for, and what leads you to that conclusion?
- Does the analysis fulfill its purpose effectively?
- Has the writer accounted for the audience by explaining all that needs to be explained?

READABILITY

- Does the title provide an accurate, clear representation of the document?
- Did you understand the analysis?
- Are there parts that are difficult to follow or understand?
- What organizational strategy does the writer use to present the analysis?
- Are you able to follow the organization of the analysis?
- Is the degree of detail suitable for this analysis?

CONTENT

- Does the analysis make sense?
- Does the writer provide a concrete summary or description of the thing that is being analyzed?
- Does the writer provide the necessary information to support the analysis?
- Is there anything particularly interesting that the writer presents?
- Is there unnecessary or extraneous information in the analysis?
- What details stand out for you?
- Does the writer provide extraneous or unnecessary details?

VISUALS

- Does the writer use visuals to clarify or explain the analysis?
- If so, are the visuals appropriate to the purpose?
- Do the visuals work in conjunction with the writing or independently?
- Are the visuals clear and easy to read?
- Does the document design distract from or support the purpose and/or readability of the analysis?
- What recommendations regarding visuals do you have for the writer?

MECHANICS

- Are there evident mechanical distractions in the analysis?
- Are there sentences that are unclear?
- Are there sentences or paragraphs that are particularly well written?
- Are all references cited appropriately?

Summary

To analyze is to examine something carefully. College students analyze texts for three reasons: to participate, to practice, and to model. Analyzing texts involves conducting two kinds of analysis: content analysis and rhetorical analysis. Writing to analyze requires that you combine two important and detailed activities: writing and analyzing. Visuals, like any text, can be analyzed. Analyzing visuals involves the key concepts of visual rhetoric, visual literacy, and visual analysis.

Chapter Review

1. Why is **analysis** important to your work in college?

2. What is the distinction between **content analysis** and **rhetorical analysis?**

3. What are some strategies for conducting **textual and process analysis?**

4. What are some strategies for **analyzing visuals?**

5. How can you use **visuals** to support your analytical writing?

6. How might you adapt your **writing process** to address analytical writing specifically?

Thinking and Writing about the Chapter

Reflection

The prompt at the beginning of this chapter asked you to think and write about the role of analysis in how you learn. Now that you have read this chapter about writing to analyze, go back to the journal entry or blog post that you wrote in response to the Initial Thoughts prompt and analyze what you write. First, analyze the content of what you wrote in light of what this chapter discusses and then analyze the rhetoric of your writing. What does your analysis reveal about your initial thoughts about analysis?

Discussion Threads

1. *Situations of Writing* claims that we write in college for three primary reasons: to learn, to participate, and to express. Discuss the ways in which analysis and analytical writing contribute to each of those three reasons for writing.

2. Much of this chapter addresses methods and approaches for analyzing texts. In what ways might you be able to apply those methods and approaches to analyzing your own texts, your own writing? Discuss how you might become a better analytical reader of your own writing as a way of becoming a better analytical writer.

Collaboration

1. Because analytical essays—particularly essays that analyze literary works—are such a familiar college writing assignment, many online clearing houses advertise the sale of analytical term papers, essays, research papers, book reports, and exam responses. In small groups, take some time to search for sites that sell college-level analytical documents. You can easily find these sites by searching for terms like "analytical essay" or "critical literary analysis." Once you have found a few such sites, analyze what the sites offer users. Consider how they rhetorically represent their services, how they list the kinds of documents they make available, and how they assess the value of their documents. Identify what they mean by "analytical" in terms of the kinds of papers they have available. You may also want to scrutinize how they obtain the documents they are selling. With these questions in mind as a starting point, begin to develop more specific analytical questions, searching for details about how these companies market and distribute academic analytical documents. Then collaboratively write an essay that presents the analytical information you have gathered.

2. To the right you will find a graphic called "Anatomical man kicking a soccer ball." Working independently, analyze the graphic and develop a series of questions for analysis. Write a short analysis of the picture. Then, in small groups, compare your analysis with the analyses of others in your group. Collaboratively, examine elements common to each of your analyses and elements unique to each analysis. Then combine the elements of each analysis to write a single, collaborative (and more detailed) analysis of the picture.

Writing

1. The Declaration of Independence is one of the most significant documents in U.S. history. Schoolchildren in the United States are taught about the Declaration; some are asked to memorize parts of it. Yet, however familiar or unfamiliar the Declaration may be to you or others, the document itself warrants close textual analysis.

   You can find a transcript of the Declaration of Independence in the National Archive web pages. Using the analytical tools and approaches discussed in this chapter, write an analysis of the Declaration of Independence. You may want to conduct content analysis and rhetorical analysis, as well as situational analysis of the document. Keep in mind that the Declaration of Independence is complex in its content and form; be sure your analysis is focused.

2. Below you will find a photograph taken of a German film crew documenting the daily life of the Maasai people in Narok, Kenya. Using any of the methods or approaches discussed in this chapter, write an analysis of this photograph.

3. On June 27, 1969, New York City Police raided The Stonewall Inn, a noted gay bar in Greenwich Village. At the time, such raids were almost commonplace. However, during this particular raid, patrons of The Stonewall decided to fight back. A riot outside the Stonewall ensued, with thousands fighting the police force amid cries of "Gay Pride!" As the first time in American history that the homosexual community fought back, the incident is considered to be the catalyst moment that initiated the gay rights movement in the United States and worldwide.

Conduct some research to learn more about the Stonewall riot, the situation that led to the riot, the cultural atmosphere in the United States that contributed to the riot, and the effect of the riot. Then write a situational analysis of the riot itself, of the outcome of the riot, or the situation that led to the riot.

Local Situation

Most colleges and universities use their web pages to promote the mission of the school. College and university web pages also provide current students with information about degree requirements, course requirements, and curricular details. Analyze your school's mission statements and how they are expressed via the Web. Then examine how the web pages represent the curriculum for your major (or a major you might be interested in pursuing). Write an essay that analyzes the ways in which the major you select is represented and how it is ecologically connected with how the mission for the college or university is expressed through the Web.

Writing to Evaluate

13

Learning Objectives

13.1 Distinguish critical evaluation from everyday evaluation

13.2 Develop and apply critical, evaluative criteria

13.3 Write critical evaluations using effective strategies

13.4 Analyze visuals using effective criteria

13.5 Use visuals strategically in your evaluative writing

Before you read this chapter

Consider what it means to evaluate something. How do you evaluate? What does evaluation suggest? What is the difference between evaluation and analysis? In your journal or blog, write about your understandings of what evaluation entails.

Member since: Dec-30-97 in United States

Detail

Criter

Recent Feedback Ratings (last 12 months)

	1 month	6 months	12 months
Positive	715	3317	5220
Neutral	4	15	20
Negative	3	27	30

Item
Co
S
S

k as a buyer   All Fe

In 1999, software engineer John Swapceinski launched the web page *Teacher Ratings*, a site designed to let university students rate their professors. The site, which became *Rate My Professors*, included more than ten million ratings for close to one million professors, and students now use it not only to rate their professors but also to help them make decisions about what courses to register for in the future.

One of its developers explains the purpose of the site: "All we're doing is taking chatter that may be in the lunchroom or the dorm room and organizing it so it can be used by students." Ultimately, what the developers of *Rate My Professors* provide is information based on a series of criteria through which students evaluate professors.

As the site admits, there's really nothing statistically reliable about the ratings, nor do the ratings actually provide an accurate reflection of the quality of a professor's teaching. Nevertheless, the site remains popular and unquestionably contributes to many students' evaluative processes in selecting classes. *Rate My Professors* uses subjective criteria in its ratings, but in the context, that subjectivity is as valuable as any other kind of data. The rhetorical situation in which *Rate My Professors* participates requires these kinds of opinions as part of the evaluative process.

Evaluation

To evaluate is to judge, to assess a value by determining the worth, merit, and significance of something. Like analysis, evaluation depends on careful scrutiny and examination, and it contributes to problem solving and decision making. In fact, you make informal appraisals every day to help you make decisions: which clothes to wear, music to listen to, classes to register for, movies to see, company to keep, food to eat, and so on. You make most of your evaluative decisions without thinking about your criteria because you have internalized them throughout your life and have a tacit understanding of them.

In contrast, when conducting a formal evaluation, you will need to develop explicit criteria and explain how they guide your evaluation beyond what you do and don't like. Assertions, claims, and opinions are not evaluations—until you provide criteria for and evidence supporting your assertions. Formal evaluation depends on detailed analysis, specific criteria for how to conduct that analysis, and clearly articulated reasons for why and how you made the analysis.

Evaluative criteria are basically the standards we set to judge something. A chemistry teacher's evaluation of your lab work might be based on predetermined standards established by the chemistry department. NBA scouts evaluate a basketball player's value for their teams based on criteria established by the coaches and players. Identifying and articulating the criteria by which you evaluate something focuses your evaluation on what information you need to make an informed decision. In fact, it is the most important part of your evaluation.

Evaluation is an act of responsible participation because in doing it, you gather information, ask questions, and make relevant judgments that can affect others. When you write an evaluation and distribute it, you participate in a conversation that can influence how others make judgments.

Outside of college, written evaluations are likely to be an important part of your life. At work, you may have to learn how to respond to performance reviews, and you will likely have to write evaluations of others. In your community life, you may read and write evaluations about local interests like school board proposals, city planning proposals, or a homeowners' association's plans. In your personal life, you evaluate things such as brands of food products, real estate options, automotive performance, and cell phone carriers, all of which affect your decisions. In addition, you rely on reviews of books, movies, music, software, games, and products, all of which are forms of evaluation. Many online shopping sites such as Amazon or Best Buy include reviews of the products they sell. These reviews, written (we assume) by actual product users, judge and evaluate a product so others can make better-informed decisions—a purpose that ultimately applies to all forms of evaluation.

annotated example

Edward C. Baig writes the Personal Technology column in *USA Today* and cohosts *USA Today*'s weekly "Talking Tech" podcast. Baig has written for *Business Week*, *U.S. News & World Report*, and *Fortune Magazine*. He is also the coauthor of *iPhone for Dummies* and *iPad for Dummies*. Baig often writes to evaluate new computer products; his reviews inform and influence readers regarding the computer products they purchase and use. In the review reprinted here, Baig evaluates the Sony Tablet P, a two-screened tablet released by Sony in 2012. As you read the review, consider how and why Baig establishes the criteria he uses in his evaluation.

Review: Sony Tablet P Shows 2 Screens Aren't Better Than 1

Edward C. Baig

One constant of almost every tablet computer introduced since the original iPad is a slate-style design. That is why the dual-screen Sony Tablet P represents such a departure.

> Baig's opening paragraph sets the context for the review: what is being evaluated, what makes the tablet different from others, and why the review is timely.

The two 5.5-inch touchscreen displays on this Android tablet are hidden when you fold the entire thing into a clamshell that can fit an inside blazer pocket. It's Sony's second unique tablet design of late. The first was the Sony Tablet S that came out last year, which is meant to evoke a folded-back magazine.

Folded in your pocket, the Tablet P, which went on sale this week and is available through AT&T Wireless, is something altogether different. It's just over an inch thick, which makes it feel rather chunky. You also feel every bit of its 0.8 pounds too. Of course, you can't slip an iPad into a pocket, including the latest model that Apple unveiled Wednesday in San Francisco.

> Continuing to provide context, Baig begins to offer details about the tablet, conveying information about size and weight, as well as comparative information.

As for the clamshell, you don't immediately know what to make of the gray contraption with the black hinge on the bottom. It reminds you of a hard case for eyeglasses or for a fancy ballpoint pen. The presence of Sony and AT&T logos and a camera peephole (for one of the two mediocre cameras on board) provides the biggest hint that this is an electronic gadget of some sort. But you're still not sure of its purpose even if you look closely at its oval-shaped bottom and see the power button, AC-power port, volume buttons and micro USB connector.

> Baig's language is beginning to reveal his judgment about the tablet. He continues to provide details about the tablet, but in doing so begins to develop a tone of disapproval in his writing.

It becomes clearer when you unfold the device and see the two handsome screens, each with 1024×480 resolution. The design is vaguely similar to the Nintendo 3DS portable handheld. But the reason for two screens still isn't obvious.

You can lay the entire tablet flat or angle up just the panel with the upper screen, which lets you prop the tablet up on a desk or night table. Unfolded, the device is rectangular and just over 6×7 inches.

Under many scenarios, such as when you're browsing the Web, the two displays are effectively combined to form one larger viewing area. But the pivoting bezel, smack dab in the middle, obstructs your view and mars the experience.

In some instances, the displays can be used to show independent but related content, such as a virtual keyboard on the bottom screen you use to enter a Web address on the top screen. Too bad that keyboard lacks a dedicated ".com" key, a nicety found on numerous other tablets. Another unfortunate drawback: You cannot display separate apps on the two screens. That's in stark contrast to another dual-screen device I've reviewed, the Kyocera Echo smartphone.

Sony says 40 dual-screen optimized apps were available at launch. One two-screen app that works well is UStream. You can watch say the *PBS NewsHour* stream on the upper display while checking out viewer comments on the bottom.

I tried the *Virtual Table Tennis* app game in which you control your paddle on the bottom while watching the ping-pong action on the top.

If you're viewing a movie in the top screen, the play controls appear on the bottom. Similarly, while you can read the contents of a specific e-mail in that upper screen, the bottom screen might display your inbox or the keyboard you can use to compose a new message.

Tablet P is tied to Sony's own digital entertainment experiences, including the Music Unlimited subscription service and Video Unlimited, for movies and TV shows sales and rentals. You can use it as an e-reader. The device is also "PlayStation certified," so you could have a go, as I did, at *Crash Bandicoot* or other PlayStation games, with the controls familiar to gamers appearing on both screens.

But Tablet P is at its most frustrating when the two screens are meant to work as one. On some apps you have the option to view content that spans both screens or just employ a single screen (a waste, it seems, since the other screen is not used at all).

Again, Baig uses comparisons to situate his claims, and he makes clear evaluative statements explaining his perception of the tablet.

Baig uses description as a method for establishing what part of the tablet he is evaluating. Notice how the evaluative claims depend on this description of how the two screens work together.

Now Baig offers an evaluative statement about the two screens, a statement that may not have been clear without the previous paragraph establishing and explaining how the two screens work together.

Baig maintains his evaluative approach, identifying more negative characteristics of the tablet. This evaluation does not waiver; it is decided in its position.

The positive aspects of the tablet are really a few of the applications available for it. However, in addressing those applications, Baig still maintains a critical stance, identifying the difficulties with the device itself.

These two paragraphs work well in, first, identifying some of the characteristics of the tablet, and, then, identifying a primary negative aspect of the product.

annotated example

Worth noting:

- *Audio.* The lone external speaker is all-too-soft, evident when I listened to music without headphones inside Pandora.
- *Reception.* I had trouble holding onto a Wi-Fi signal in my house, though none of my other computers or tablets had difficulty on the same networks.
- *Memory.* Sony could be more generous. Before boarding a plane, I tried downloading a movie I had rented moments before from the Video Unlimited Store only to be told that I didn't have enough room on the device. A 2GB SD memory that can be expanded to 32GB is supplied.
- *Pricing.* The tablet costs $399.99 with a two-year AT&T data agreement; $549.99 without. AT&T's 3GB monthly data plan costs $35 and its 5GB plan $50. Though billed as a 4G device, Tablet P runs off AT&T's HSPA+ network, not its fastest LTE network.
- *Battery life.* I didn't conduct a formal test, but Sony claims about seven hours of general use. I got through a full day of mixed use without a problem. The battery is removable.
- *Software.* Though it currently runs the older Honeycomb version of Android, AT&T says Tablet P is upgradeable to Android 4.0 Ice Cream Sandwich. No timetable was given.

> Baig provides feedback about six important criteria. In this section, Baig categorizes specifically the features that he sees as "worth noting." This organizational structure can help guide readers through the specifics of his negative response to the product.

I give Sony brownie points for trying something new but am unconvinced that in most instances two screens are better than one.

The bottom line:

Store: sony.com/tablet

Price: $399.99 with two-year AT&T contract or $549.99 without.

Pro: Two very nice screens. Dual-screen optimized apps work well. Fits in pocket. Tied into Sony entertainment experiences with movies, music, books, and PlayStation games.

Con: Browsing and other apps marred by obstructed view. Spotty Wi-Fi. Older version of Android for now. No ".com" key on virtual keyboard. Design won't appeal to everybody.

> Baig clearly summarizes his evaluation, noting what is positive and what is negative, but in doing so confirms his overall negative judgment.

student example

Quang Ly is majoring in English and pursuing minors in business administration and entrepreneurship. When he graduates, he hopes to attend law school and study intellectual property rights. During his spare time Quang likes to blog about his personal life, writing about things like interpersonal relationships and the complications of love.

Quang is also a *Twilight* fan. After writing a manual for his English teacher about how to survive a vampire invasion, Quang was encouraged to write an evaluation to explain why the *Twilight* series has become so popular. His evaluation uses headings to identify specific areas of evaluation, and he uses a good deal of secondary information to support his evaluation. In fact, Quang's thorough use of research and analysis contribute much of the strength and effectiveness of the evaluation. Notice how Quang uses his research to support the evaluation, and notice, too, how he explains his choice of criteria.

Have You Been Bitten? Evaluating the Success of the *Twilight* Craze

Quang Ly

Craze is an understatement, and the word alone cannot begin to describe the enormous fan base the *Twilight* series has managed to gather since becoming a global hit. The *Twilight* book series has garnered much attention since its first novel appeared in 2005. Stephanie Meyer, the author behind the best-selling vampire-romance novels, is often compared to the widely acclaimed J. K. Rowling, author of the popular *Harry Potter* series. Meyer's *Twilight* books have accomplished popularity and commercial success, impacting not only American culture but also creating a worldwide phenomenon. While compelling, the claim about *Twilight*'s massive success is broad and sweeping. How can we, as critics ourselves, prove and validate this claim and perhaps other similar claims?

First, we must acknowledge that measuring "success" is difficult, particularly when dealing with a work of literature or art. Critics of the *Twilight* series have weighed in on both sides of the argument, some claiming the book a literary success, others criticizing it as shallow and unformed. When *Twilight*, the first book in the series, was published in 2005, reviews in *Publisher's Weekly*, *The Times*, *The Daily Telegraph*, and on Amazon.com, among many others, praised Meyers and the book. *Publisher's Weekly* identified Meyer's as one of the most "promising authors of 2005." However, other reviews, such as those published in the *Kirkus Review*, *The New York Times*, and *The Washington Post* found little to praise about the book. Writing in *The New York Times*, Elizabeth Spires criticized the novel, saying "The premise of *Twilight* is attractive and compelling—who hasn't fantasized about unearthly love with a beautiful stranger?—but the book suffers at times from overearnest, amateurish writing. A little more 'showing' and a lot less 'telling' might have been a good thing, especially some pruning to eliminate the constant references to Edward's shattering beauty and Bella's undying love." Similarly, writing for *The Washington Post*, Elizabeth Hand writes that "Meyer's prose seldom rises above the serviceable, and the plotting is leaden." Perhaps most telling, horror author Stephen King, in an interview published in *USA Weekend*, was asked to compare Meyer with Rowling; he responds: "Both Rowling and Meyer, they're speaking directly to young people. ... The real difference is that Jo Rowling is a terrific writer and Stephanie Meyer can't write worth a darn. She's not very good."

As the series progressed, criticism for the books and films continued, as did fan appreciation. Thus, evaluating the success of the *Twilight* series must be considered in terms of critics versus fans. By strictly literary criteria, the series may not be a successful piece of literature; however, from the fans' perspective, the series is hailed as excellent. Thus, evaluating the success of the series should be addressed from the fans' perspective simply because literary criteria and aesthetic evaluation are never cut and dry. However, fan-based success can be identified, quantified, and evaluated through four critically important criteria: copies sold, recognition/awards received, commercial success, and public's reception. These criteria provide a framework we can use to evaluate the success of a work or text from a fan perspective. These criteria can be used to evaluate the success of *Twilight* and provide the data needed to support the claim that the *Twilight* series is one of the most successful and influential young adult series in contemporary literature.

According to *Publishers Weekly*, the *Twilight* series has sold over 116 million copies worldwide, with translation into at least 37 different languages (Turan). Though these numbers do not compare to the *Harry Potter* series (having sold 450 million copies and translated into 67 languages ("Rowling")), Meyer's book sales have set their own records, making Meyer an instant best-selling author and *Twilight* an immediate hit with fans. When the first book of the series, *Twilight*, reached bookstores, it became the most popular reading fad of the time and sent waves of positive word-of-mouth promotion of the book all over the world. Young adults (the primary readers of *Twilight*) flocked to bookstores to try to get their hands on the "hot, new" book.

We can look at the sales of the entire book series to get a better idea of how the first sensational book led to the record-breaking sales of the other books: *Twilight* (17 million), *New Moon* (5.3 million), *Eclipse* (4.5 million), *Breaking Dawn* (6 million). These staggering numbers indicate the impact Stephanie Meyer's book has had on the world with her vampire-fantasy books. These sales figures also show how the books have influenced, and even inspired, people not only to read her books but also to encourage their friends to give Meyer's books a chance.

The *Twilight* books have consecutively set sales records in the publishing industry; likewise, they have achieved substantial recognition and awards. The first novel *Twilight*, for example, debuted at No. 5 on the *New York Times* Best Seller list within a month of its release in 2005 and later peaked at No. 1 ("Children's," 2007). That same year, *Twilight* was named one of *Publishers Weekly's* Best Children's Books of 2005. In addition, the novel was also the biggest selling book of 2008 (Cadden).

Meyer's sequels have also gained notable recognition. The second book, *New Moon*, debuted at #5 on the *New York Times* Best Seller List for Children's Chapter Books, and in its second week rose to the #1 position, where it remained for the next eleven weeks ("Children's," 2006). *New Moon* was also #1 on *USA Today's* Top 150 Bestsellers. The book also remained on the *USA Today* Best Seller list for over 150 weeks after entering the list two weeks after its release, later peaking at #1 (Rev. of *New Moon*). Moreover, *New Moon* was the best-selling book of 2009. The second novel followed in the footsteps of the first novel and finished the year strong with its loyal *Twilight* fans.

Eclipse was the fourth bestselling book of 2008, following only *Twilight*, *New Moon*, and *Breaking Dawn*. It, too, was ranked #1 on *Publishers Weekly's* list of "Bestselling Hardcover Backlist Children's Books" in 2008 (Cadden). *Eclipse* peaked at #1 on *USA Today's* top 150 best sellers list and went on to spend over 100 weeks on the list ("Eclipse"). The book replaced J. K. Rowling's *Harry Potter and the Deathly Hallows* on the top of bestseller lists around the globe, including *The New York Times* Best Seller list. For another book to replace one of Rowling's books as one of the bestselling books around the globe is more than significant. This particular accomplishment speaks to how well Meyer's story connects with its audience and is a great way to really pinpoint the massive impact of the *Twilight* series.

Finally, *Breaking Dawn* was the third best-selling novel of 2008 behind *Twilight* and *New Moon*. The novel was awarded the British Book Award for "Children's Book of the Year" and debuted at #1 on *USA Today's* top 150 best sellers list, spending over 58 weeks on the list ("Watch"). The 2009 "Children's Choice Book Awards" selected the novel as "Teen Choice Book of the Year" and at the same time, the *Twilight* series won the 2009 Kids' Choice Award for Favorite Book, where it competed against the *Harry Potter* series ("Breaking Dawn"). Whereas *Harry Potter* was once the favorite among teens, *Twilight* dethroned that series.

Given the number of *Twilight* books sold, in addition to the numerous awards the series received, it comes as no surprise that the series spawned a tremendously successful movie franchise. Adoption into film can be a good indicator that a book has been well-received by the public. There is a long-standing Hollywood practice of turning popular fiction with a large fan base into feature films. Such bestsellers-turned-movies include *Harry Potter*, *The Chronicles of Narnia*, and *Lord of the Rings*. Meyer's *Twilight* series entered the Hollywood radar, and her renowned vampire romance fantasy novels were adapted into movies that raked in millions of viewers and millions of dollars, rendering even further the immense impact the series has on the world.

student example

The first film, *Twilight* (2008), grossed $35.7 million on its opening day and has grossed $392 million worldwide. The film is fifth overall on online ticket service Fandango's list of top advance ticket sales (McClintock, "'Twilight'"). In addition, DVD sales grossed another $181 million, ranking it as the most purchased DVD of the year in 2008 ("Twilight"). The first movie became an instant success and paved the way for its sequels to achieve similar degrees of success.

The second film, *The Twilight Saga: New Moon* (2009) trumped *Twilight's* box office success, setting new records for advance ticket sales. The film is currently the biggest advance ticket seller on Fandango (Davis). The opening weekend of *The Twilight Saga: New Moon* is the fourth highest opening weekend in domestic history with $142 million ("Opening").

The third film of the series, *Twilight Saga: Eclipse* (2010), surpassed *The Twilight Saga: New Moon* in a variety of categories. The film is the first of the *Twilight Saga* films to be released in IMAX. In addition, the film also has the widest independent release. The film ended its box-office run in the U.S.A. and Canada having grossed $300 million to become the highest-grossing film of the franchise and the highest-grossing romantic fantasy, werewolf, and vampire movie of all time at the American and Canadian box office ("The Twilight Saga: Eclipse").

The next to last film, *Breaking Dawn–Part 1* (2011) earned a franchise-best $291 million on its worldwide opening weekend, marking it the 10th largest worldwide opening of all time (Subers). It reached $500 million worldwide in 12 days, record time for the franchise. It ranks as the 4th highest-grossing film of 2011 worldwide and the 2nd highest grossing film of the franchise (McClintock, "Box Office").

The *Twilight Saga* films have definitely raised the bar for other franchises to aim for. Their gross figures are beyond extraordinary. The *Twilight* films have accomplished rare feats, such as most purchased DVD in a year and widest independent releases. The incredible sales figures of these films confirms that *Twilight* has captured the hearts of millions of people, and it does not look like the *Twilight* craze is going to slow down anytime soon. Once a person is bitten by *Twilight,* there does not seem to be a cure for it, or at least not a desire to be cured from it.

Like any popular fiction book, *Twilight* has met with both support and opposition from the public. But Meyer's book has been praised more for its plot, which combines the right amount of romance and horror into one perfectly good story, than for its controversial relationship the books display between the characters. *Twilight* fans all over the world have fallen in love with Meyer's books and many claimed her books are the successor to *Harry Potter.*

In addition, because of Meyer's choice of setting in the books, the town of Forks, Washington, has been improving economically thanks to *Twilight*-related tourism (remember: you can't really get to Hogwarts). Die-hard fans want to immerse themselves in the same environment in which their favorite characters appear. Even the high school depicted in the *Twilight* movies is being renovated by way of public donations.

There have been other not-so-noticeable effects from *Twilight*. For example, there are multiple survival guides for how to survive a vampire attack. There are also different variations of shirts that say "Team Edward" and "Team Jacob"; the fast food chain Burger King recently used these shirts in a commercial campaign. Likewise, though there have been college courses about vampires and literary works like *Dracula* for a while now, the *Twilight* series has "revamped" the definition of vampires and has reintroduced the idea of vampires to a whole new generation, and now more colleges are offering more classes specifically about vampires.

Interest in vampires is sweeping the nation in a large part because of how popular *Twilight* has become over the years, and the entertainment industry is taking advantage of this fad by introducing vampire related television shows such as the *Vampire Dairies* and *My Babysitter's a Vampire* (though Joss Whedon's *Buffy the Vampire Slayer* (1996) predates *Twilight* by nearly a decade and was a very popular television show; likewise, Anne Rice's multi-book series *The Vampire Chronicles* had developed a large fan base beginning in 1976, and that Meyer has noted as influential in her writing). We may all have once considered vampires to be horrible creatures, but now we view them as something interesting and extraordinary in part due to *Twilight*.

Fan-based appreciation, made evident by the franchise's international popularity, serves as viable criteria for evaluating *Twilight*'s success. The series is, unquestionably, regarded as one of the most successful young adult series in recent times. To reiterate, using the four criteria copies sold, recognition/awards received, commercial success, and public's perception, and acknowledging the distinction between these fan-based criteria and aesthetic literary criteria, we can clearly see that the *Twilight* series is not only a successful series, it is one of the most successful series in popular literary history.

Works Cited

Amazon.com. "*Twilight*. (The *Twilight* Saga, Book 1): Editorial Review." Web. 18 Apr. 2012.

"Breaking Dawn." *eNotes.com*. eNotes.com, Inc., 2012. Web. 18 Apr. 2012.

Cadden, Mary, et al. "Best-Selling Books: The annual top 100 (2008)." *USA Today*. Gannett, 21 June 2011. Web. 18 Apr. 2012.

"Children's Books. (2006)" *New York Times*. New York Times, 22 Oct. 2006. Web. 18 Apr. 2012.

"Children's Books. (2007)" *New York Times*. New York Times, 17 Jun. 2007. Web. 18 Apr. 2012.

Craig, Amanda. (2006). "New-Age Vampires Stake Their Claim." *Times* [London]. Times Newspapers, Ltd., 14 Jan. 2006. Web. 19 Apr. 2012.

Davis, Erik. "'New Moon' Now Fandango's Biggest Advance Ticket Seller Ever!" *Freshly Popped: The Movie Blog*. Fandango, 16 Nov. 2009. Web. 18 Apr. 2012.

"Eclipse." *eNotes.com*. eNotes.com, Inc., 2012. Web. 18 Apr. 2012.

student example

"Exclusive: Stephen King on J. K. Rowling, Stephenie Meyer." *USA Weekend*. Gannett, 2 Feb. 2009.
    Web. 19 Apr. 2012.

Hand, Elizabeth. "Love Bites." *Washington Post*. Washington Post, 10 Aug. 2008. Web. 19 Apr. 2012.

"Harry Potter vs. Twilight." *Bookstove*. Bookstove.com, 8 Nov. 2009. Web. 18 Apr. 2012.

McClintock, Pamela. "'Twilight' shining bright at box office." *Variety*. Variety Media, 21 Nov. 2008.
    Web. 18 Apr. 2012.

---. "Box Office Report: 'Twilight: Breaking Dawn' Hits $500 Mil Worldwide in 12 Days." *Hollywood
    Reporter*. Hollywood Reporter, 29 Nov. 2011. Web. 18 Apr. 2012.

"Opening Weekends." *Box Office Mojo*. IMDB, n.d. Web. 18 Apr. 2012.

Rev. of New Moon. *Cakitches.com*. 2011. Web. 18 Apr. 2012.

"Rowling 'makes £5 every second.'" *BBCNews.com*. BBC, 3 Oct. 2008. Web. 18 Apr. 2012.

Subers, Ray. "Around-the-World Roundup: 'Breaking Dawn' Lights Up Overseas." *Box Office Mojo*.
    IMDB, 22 Nov. 2011. Web. 18 Apr. 2012.

Spires, Elizabeth. "'Enthusiasm,' by Polly Shulman and 'Twilight,' by Stephenie Meyer." *New York
    Times*. New York Times, 12 Feb. 2006. Web. 19 Apr. 2012.

Turan, Kenneth. "You wanna neck?" *Los Angeles Times*. Tribune Newspapers, 21 Nov. 2008. Web. 18
    Apr. 2012.

"Twilight." *Answers.com*. Answers Corporation, 2012. Web. 18 Apr. 2012.

"Twilight Review." *Publisher's Weekly*. PWxyz, 18 Jul. 2005. Web. 19 Apr. 2012.

"The Twilight Saga: Eclipse." *Box Office Mojo*. IMDB, n.d. Web. 18 Apr. 2012.

"Watch Breaking Dawn Online." *Watch Breaking Dawn Online*. Weebly, n.d. Web. 18 Apr. 2012.

Thinking about Quang's Essay

1. Quang Ly's analytical approach is not to evaluate the artistic quality of the *Twilight* series but, instead, to evaluate the series' popularity and influence. He accounts for this distinction at the beginning of his essay. In what ways do the criteria he establishes affect how you respond to his evaluation? How does his side-stepping of literary aesthetic criteria affect his evaluation? Why might he want to avoid an aesthetic evaluation?

2. Quang uses a good deal of research to provide quantitative information in support of his evaluation. How does Quang's use of research differ from the experiential, or hands-on, research that Baig uses in the previous example about the Sony two-screen tablet? Which approach do you find more reliable? Given that Baig is a professional technology commentator and that Quang is a student, how does each writer's ethos interact with the kind of research each uses?

3. Does the judgment that Quang levels in this evaluation convince you that his position is accurate? Reliable? Valuable? Why or why not?

student example

THE ROAD TO A
STRONG THESIS

SECOND THOUGHTS:
"As books and films, the series could be evaluated as literary works using aesthetic literary criteria to determine whether the books are successful or not."

SECOND THOUGHTS:
"A lot of literary reviews didn't like the writing in the books, but the fans liked the narratives."

SECOND THOUGHTS:
"If I do that, I'll need to be distinct in what criteria I am using to guide the evidence I gather."

RESPONSE:
"I could probably find reliable evidence to show how many copies of the book have sold, how many and what kinds of recognition and awards the books and films have received, what kind of commercial success the movies have had, and the public's response to the books and films."

RESPONSE:
"But literary criticism will probably rely on aesthetic literary criteria, and I'd have to have some concrete way of talking about the series as literature or as pop culture and figuring out whether the series is art or entertainment. I don't feel prepared to write about those kinds of big issues. Literary aesthetic seems to be a pretty uncertain way to indicate success."

RESPONSE:
"That means that any criteria I develop will have to distinguish between fans and critics. But once I make that distinction, I can show evidence of how fans respond to the series."

Question:
"What can be evaluated about *Twilight*?"

ASSIGNMENT:
"My teacher asked me to evaluate *Twilight*."

THESIS:
"Based on fan response, sales of books and films, and awards received, the *Twilight* series has been an exceptional success and has become one of the most influential franchises in recent young adult literature."

When Quang Ly's teacher asked him to evaluate the *Twilight* series, he was given an idea, or more specifically a subject, to write about. He was not given a thesis. Quang had to develop that thesis on his own.

FINAL THOUGHTS:
"I will really need to emphasize why I am not using more traditional literary criteria and why my focus on fan-based criteria is a legitimate indicator of the series' success."

professional example

Sean McCoy is a freelance photographer and writer based in Denver, Colorado. He is currently a Contributing Editor at Monopoint Media, home of GearJunkie.com. Before joining GearJunkie.com, McCoy was the chief photographer for *The Virgin Islands Daily News*. He was also owner of Three Amigos Tropical Adventures, a day cruise and overnight adventure service he ran aboard his 45-foot sailing trimaran. Along with two rock climbers from Minneapolis, Minnesota, he was also the cofounder of the rock and ice climbing magazine *Vertical Jones Magazine*. McCoy's evaluation "Square Water Bottle Raises $126K on Kickstarter. We Test It Out" was published on October 22, 2012, in the online magazine GearJunkie.com, an online publication that focuses on news, product reviews, and adventure stories from the outdoor world. Published in the category "Food/Hydration Reviews," "Square Water Bottle Raises $126K on Kickstarter. We Test It Out" evaluates a new kind of water bottle for outdoor enthusiasts. As you read this gear review, notice how McCoy synthesizes his descriptions of the bottle with his evaluative statements and criteria to maintain a conversational tone more than a technical tone.

Square Water Bottle Raises $126K on Kickstarter. We Test It Out

Sean McCoy

A novel idea can raise six-figure investment via crowd-source funding sites like Kickstarter. Clean Bottle recently proposed turning its popular hydration vessel square, and people responded in droves.

We got a first look at the stainless steel bottle last week. Beyond its stand-out shape, the Clean Bottle Square opens on both ends for easy washing, is dishwasher-safe, and it fits in average car cup holders for universal use.

While it may seem a little superfluous, the top-and-bottom openings are pretty darn convenient. They allow the bottle to be fully cleaned from either end, no reaching in to scrub.

The top and bottom caps fit snuggly on, and they close with a reassuring click in just a quarter turn. The caps are made of non-BPA plastic. Rubber gaskets seal them shut.

While the Square looks like a Thermos-type bottle, it is not. Don't make this mistake like we did—it is a single-walled bottle. Metal conducts heat, and I found out first-hand that hot liquids in this thing can burn fingers if you're not careful!

Style-wise, the bottle matches the look and feel of a metal Macbook Pro, which should bode

Exploded view of Clean Bottle Square

McCoy / Square Water Bottle Raises $126K on Kickstarter. We Test It Out

275

well for the coffee-shop set. As noted, it fits in a car cup holder, letting you take it easily along on trips or errands. It is very tall, though, so watch out because it can tip over easily.

A potential downfall, the bottle holds only 20 liquid ounces. To me that amount is the absolute minimum size a water bottle can be and still be worth carrying around.

As noted, the bottle is tall at 11 inches and it weighs about 10 ounces when empty. This is not a bottle meant for backpacking or serious outdoor pursuits.

Advantages to the square design? If dropped, the bottle cannot easily roll away. This is not a problem that I've faced a lot in my life, but maybe for kids it could be an advantage.

My take? Outside of the notable exception of use on sailboats, trains or other moving vehicles, I really don't see the big advantage to the square shape. On sailboats or other places with shifting angles and unstable surfaces the bottle might really shine.

At $40, the bottle is pricey. But with an eye-catching design and quality build it could fit nicely in a lot of Christmas stockings when it is released in December.

Analyzing the Situation

1. Why might a writer who writes for a gear review resource evaluate a water bottle?

2. Who is McCoy's audience here? How do you know?

3. Does McCoy's medium tell you anything about how conversations in this situation circulate? What might the medium reveal, too, about the audience?

Analyzing the Rhetoric

1. What does the title tell you about the evaluation, and how does the title prepare you for how the evaluation will be presented?

2. What role do the visuals play in how McCoy evaluates the bottle?

3. What language does McCoy use to clarify his evaluative position?

professional example

Discussing

1. McCoy's evaluation is not very long. Given that the evaluation is a product review for a water bottle—a product that is not really complicated—does McCoy provide enough information, definition, and evaluation to suit your needs as a reader? Discuss whether or not you want more information from McCoy in this review.

2. How do evaluations like McCoy's serve audiences? That is, McCoy evaluates a water bottle, a fairly mundane object. With things like water bottles, many people simply evaluate whether or not they like drinking from them; so, why does McCoy write this evaluation, and how does it serve its audience?

Writing

1. Using only the criteria McCoy uses in his evaluation, evaluate a different brand of water bottle. Then, using McCoy's evaluation, compare the Square with the water bottle you have evaluated.

2. Locate three other published reviews of water bottles online—even another review of the Square. By what criteria are those bottles evaluated? How do those reviews compare with McCoy's in terms of detail, criteria, medium, audience, purpose, and approach? Write a document that evaluates how water bottles are evaluated and how each review you use compares with McCoy's.

three examples

SIDE BY SIDE
Compare the way the three evaluations in this chapter make use of the elements of the rhetorical situation.

	annotated example Edward C. Baig, "Review: Sony Tablet P Shows 2 Screens Aren't Better Than 1"	**student example** Quang Ly, "Have You Been Bitten? Evaluating the Success of the *Twilight* Craze"	**professional example** Sean McCoy, "Square Water Bottle Raises $126K on Kickstarter. We Test It Out"
PURPOSE	To provide evaluative information about a new product	To evaluate why a book series might be considered successful	To evaluate a new version of a familiar product
AUDIENCE	Readers deciding whether or not to purchase a tablet with one or two screens	Readers who are interested in the success of the *Twilight* series	Readers who are outdoor enthusiasts
CRITERIA	Design, size, weight, usability, efficiency, reception, memory, pricing, battery life, software	Copies sold, recognition, commercial success, and public reception	Design, size, clean-ability, temperature retention, and cost
EVIDENCE	Based on observation, personal experience, and product testing	Based on research; uses and cites numerous Web resources	Based on observation, description, and personal experience with the product
METHODS	Reports outcomes of product testing; compares with other similar products	Uses research-based evidence to provide quantitative information	Describes features and characteristics and evaluates their effectiveness
OUTCOME	Judges the product to be inferior	Judges the book series to be successful	Judges the bottle to be attractive but limited in its usefulness
DISTRIBUTION	Circulated by way of mass media	Circulated by way of academic essay	Circulated by way of online review page
ORGANIZATION	Uses single and multiple paragraph schemes to address individual product characteristics. Uses listing to emphasize key points at the end	Uses fan-based criteria and organizes by each criteria: copies sold, recognition/awards received, commercial success, and public's reception	Uses short paragraphs to address each characteristic evaluated
LANGUAGE	Uses a critical tone to emphasize the negative evaluation. Words like *chunky, mediocre, obstructs, mars, too bad, unfortunately, frustrating, waste,* and *worth nothing* all maintain a negative tone	Uses formal, academic language	Uses first-person, conversational tone to connect with the audience

277

13.2 Develop and apply critical, evaluative criteria

Characteristic	Preparing Your Evaluation
Evaluation is not always safe	The judgments you may reach may not sit well with others. Sometimes evaluations reveal things you may not wish to have learned. A performance evaluation, for example, may expose weaknesses in your job performance, potentially affecting your path to a promotion or your sense of competence.
Evaluation must be transparent to be ethical	Evaluations done ethically do not pursue hidden agendas. The audience should understand why you are evaluating and how you arrived at your results.
Evaluation must have a purpose	Defining your purpose helps set the context for the evaluation, and it contributes to the transparency of your evaluation.
Evaluative writing should make a claim that leads to an outcome	Effective evaluations state a claim much like a thesis statement. They clearly explain the judgments based on the research and analysis. Outcomes may lead to a final decision or to further evaluative work.
Evaluation should be written for a specific audience	Knowing your audience in advance can affect how you conduct your analysis because you will understand what information the audience needs.
Evaluative writing should explain what is at stake	Evaluations have not only a purpose, a reason for evaluating, but also ramifications. Your audience should be able to discern what the implications of your evaluation are.
Evaluation must be conducted according to criteria	Criteria should be determined beforehand by the situation, that is, by the purpose of the evaluation and the audience. These criteria and why they are pertinent need to be clear.
Evaluations may require research	An academic evaluation may require that you conduct research to complete the evaluation. For example, a literature teacher may ask you to evaluate a selection of poetry, but to do so, you may have to conduct research about the poem or the poet to better understand the context or meaning of the poem.
Evaluations require evidence	Evaluations that don't provide evidence come across as assertions or opinions: "*Avatar* is the best movie of the decade." That evaluation provides a judgment that may or may not be accurate. Your audience will need supporting evidence such as "*Avatar* is the best movie of the decade because it grossed more money than any other movie, received consistently higher rankings, and received more Academy Award nominations than any other movie in this time period."
Evaluations should describe techniques and methods you used	In addition to details about the criteria you use, your evaluation should include an explanation of the techniques you use to gather the information and evidence.
Evaluations are based on analysis that is clearly explained	The analysis should logically connect the information, the criteria, the method, and the outcome.
Evaluations must be distributed	An evaluation must reach its audience to serve its purpose. For instance, posting a review of a product on a sales web page helps ensure that your evaluation will reach an interested audience.

Respond

Strategy	Developing Your Evaluation
Identify the thing to be evaluated	Be sure to describe and define for your audience what you are evaluating. Describe the parts and relations of the thing and any terms needed to understand it. These details also can become part of the evidence supporting your claim.
Ask questions	Ask critical research questions to lead you to a better understanding of the details of the thing being evaluated.
Consider the situation	How you evaluate and how you report the results of your evaluation depend on the situation of the evaluation. Your audience will affect the criteria for your evaluation, your method, and how you convey the results, including the medium you use. Also consider the constraints that limit your evaluation and the players who might be affected by your evaluation.
Define the criteria	Define the criteria and standards you choose to guide your evaluation, keeping in mind what your audience needs to know. Never change criteria in the midst of an evaluation or, if comparing like items, never measure one item by one set of criteria and the other item by another set. Criteria may be weighted; that is, some criteria may be more important than others.
Confirm needed resources beforehand	Ahead of time, make sure you have access to any equipment, tools, materials, or measuring rubrics that you might need to conduct the evaluation.
Provide evidence	Search out evidence such as statistical data, description, testimony, forensic data, and usability testing to support your evaluation.
Include visuals	Whenever possible, be sure to include visuals that help your audience comprehend the purpose, criteria, method, and/or result of your evaluation.
Be ethical	Remember: evaluations inform decisions that can affect people's lives. Be sure your results are not skewed. Adhere to the criteria you have established.
Organize	Organize your evaluative writing using one of the approaches described in this chapter.
Don't ignore your feelings	Stating how you feel about something is a valid form of evaluation. Explaining *why* you feel a certain way, however, will be most effective.
Reach a conclusion	Explicitly state an outcome, even if that outcome is a need for further evaluation. If your criteria and analysis don't lead to a definitive result, you may need to rethink the criteria and evaluation process you used and reevaluate.

Developing Criteria for an Evaluation

Each kind of subject that you might evaluate requires a different set of evaluative criteria. For instance, you would evaluate a software application differently than you would sushi restaurants. Thus, the criteria you select should reflect your evaluative purpose and relate to what you are evaluating. Answer the following questions and analyze your responses to identify relevant elements or characteristics that could become criteria.

Criteria	Questions
Initial Reactions	Questions regarding initial reactions: • What about this thing do I like or not like (support, agree with)? Why? • What did I notice first? • How do I feel about this thing?
Physical Attributes	Questions regarding physical attributes: • What can be said about size, color, taste, weight, sound, and smell? • What can be said about design and functionality?
Validity	Questions regarding validity: • If evaluating a text, who is the author? Is the author an expert? What is the author's reputation? • If evaluating a web page, who sponsors the page? Is there a conflict of interest? Is the sponsor reputable? Is the sponsor easily identifiable? • If there is research involved, is the research accurate? • Is the evidence presented in a nonbiased way, or does it seem weighted toward a particular conclusion? • Does the evidence appear to be encompassing, or is something missing? • Are there evident errors?
Cost and Value	Questions regarding cost and value: • How does the product cost compare with other similar products? • What is the monetary, personal, and cultural worth of what you are evaluating? • What are the immediate value and long-term value? The immediate cost and long-term cost?
Comparatives	Questions regarding comparatives: • Which is better? How do you define *better*? • Which is safer? • Which lasts longer? • Which is clearer, makes more sense?

Organizing an Evaluation

Evaluative writing needs to convey the following information:

- What is being evaluated, defined and described clearly
- What your judgment is, stated directly and based on the evaluation
- What criteria you used, defined and explained

- Why and how you reached your judgment
- What opposing evaluations might say (and what evidence refutes them)
- A concluding statement that emphasizes your judgment

You can organize your evaluation by following the preceding bulleted list, even using headings to distinguish these parts of an evaluative document.

Alternatively, depending on the situation, you may want to try either of the following two common approaches.

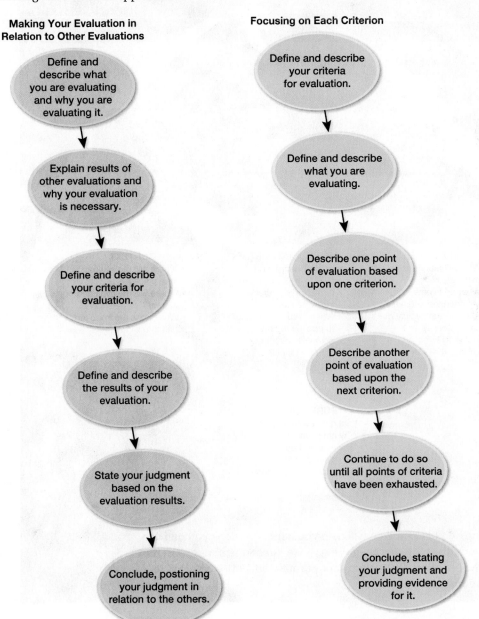

Making Your Evaluation in Relation to Other Evaluations

Define and describe what you are evaluating and why you are evaluating it.

↓

Explain results of other evaluations and why your evaluation is necessary.

↓

Define and describe your criteria for evaluation.

↓

Define and describe the results of your evaluation.

↓

State your judgment based on the evaluation results.

↓

Conclude, positioning your judgment in relation to the others.

Focusing on Each Criterion

Define and describe your criteria for evaluation.

↓

Define and describe what you are evaluating.

↓

Describe one point of evaluation based upon one criterion.

↓

Describe another point of evaluation based upon the next criterion.

↓

Continue to do so until all points of criteria have been exhausted.

↓

Conclude, stating your judgment and providing evidence for it.

MAPPING
YOUR SITUATION

NETWORKS
- In what networks will my evaluation circulate?
- How is my evaluation related to other evaluations?
- How might my evaluation affect future evaluations in this situation?

WRITERS AND SPEAKERS
- Who are the other writers and speakers in this situation?
- What have they said about the situation?
- Why are they in the position to speak in this situation?

RELATIONS
- What is my relation to the situation?
- What are the relationships between writers/speakers, audience, and players?
- What are the relationships to external forces, like culture, religion, or politics?
- What are the power relations?

AUDIENCE
- Who will read/see my evaluation?
- What do I know about my intended audience?
- Who will the evaluation affect directly and indirectly?

MEDIUM AND METHOD
- In what genre will I deliver my evaluation?
- What are my criteria for evaluation?
- What method will I use to convey my evaluation?
- How will I distribute my evaluation?

CONTEXT
- Where will my evaluation take place?
- Where will my evaluation appear?
- What limits are imposed on my evaluation?

PURPOSE
- What am I evaluating?
- Why am I evaluating?
- How should I approach my evaluation to accomplish my purpose?

Mapping your situation will help you generate ideas you can use to compose. Start by answering these questions about each part of the situation. Begin with your purpose and work outward to relations and networks.

Writing Projects

Essay

Any of the subjects in the following list might be evaluated from various perspectives. Select one of them and develop a detailed set of criteria by which to conduct an evaluation. After establishing your criteria, conduct the evaluation, and use one of the organizational strategies discussed in this chapter to write an evaluation of the subject you picked.

General:

- Your dietary/nutritional habits
- A movie currently showing
- Effectiveness of public transportation in your area
- Land use in your community
- Radio stations in your community
- Sustainability efforts in your community

On your campus:

- The school newspaper
- The availability of technology
- Library accessibility
- Dining choices
- Energy consumption
- Recycling efforts

Visual Evaluation

13.4 Analyze visuals using effective criteria

Edward C. Baig's review of the Sony tablet (see page 264) uses the Android operating system, which was developed by a consortium of companies to compete with Apple's iPads. Using online resources, identify four features that both Android tablets and iPads have. Then conduct some research to compare these features between the two types of tablet platforms. Next, design a graphic (chart or graph) that conveys the information in an evaluative fashion (see "Visuals and Evaluation" in this chapter).

Digital

An increasingly popular feature of online commerce enables customers and users to provide feedback about companies, products, and services. Develop a set of criteria and evaluate a product you have recently purchased or a service you have recently used. Post your evaluation either to a site such as Yelp, Angie's List, or Epinions, or directly into the customer comments portion of the website through which you made the purchase.

Research

Locate three web pages that provide information about pollution in your state. Evaluate those three sites for their accuracy, effectiveness in presenting information, clarity, reliability, and accessibility. You may use your library's suggestions for evaluating Web resources in addition to the suggestions provided in this chapter and in the chapter on evaluating sources.

Radical Revision

Look back to the other prompts for writing projects provided here. Select one of these prompts for which you have already written a response and radically revise the document to be published as a YouTube video. Be alert to (a) how you will need to revise your evaluation to address a public audience instead of an academic audience and (b) how the difference in media will affect how you present your evaluation. Also keep ethics in mind.

13.5 Use visuals strategically in your evaluative writing

Visuals and Evaluation

Visuals can be evaluated much like text. In addition, visuals can be used as tools to help you figure out, organize, and convey your evaluations.

Evaluating Visuals

Visuals, like any text, can be evaluated. In fact, on a daily basis, you already evaluate countless visuals that compete for your attention, including advertisements, web pages, instructions, directions, films, television broadcasts, icons, logos, photographs, graffiti, videos, and sign lettering. Evaluating a visual can consider straightforward criteria such as readability, effectiveness, genre, and so on, but certain visuals such as works of art may also be evaluated from an aesthetic perspective. Because aesthetic criteria are difficult to identify and confirm, aesthetic evaluation often uses less specific criteria.

Visuals that Evaluate

In addition to evaluating visuals, we can use visuals as tools for helping the audience to comprehend information. Visuals can reinforce the information in your evaluation or can function independent of written text. In general, graphics and images can be effective for evaluative purposes. As the following chart shows, graphics, including graphs and charts, depict information symbolically, and images, including photographs, depict information in more realistic ways than text alone can.

Type of Visual | Use for Conveying Evaluative Information

Graphics

Graphs

A graph is a diagram that represents the relationship between two or more kinds of quantifiable information, often in relation to time. Thus, graphs might assist in showing how two or more items compare in an evaluation. Bar graphs such as the one shown here are common forms.

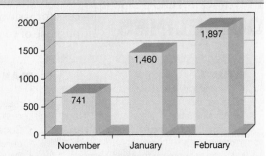

Charts

Charts, closely related to graphs, represent information visually, but not usually in relation to time. Pie charts (shown here) and flowcharts are common forms. Some flowcharts show a process linearly in time, but they do not specifically quantify time.

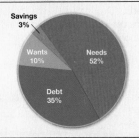

Tables

Tables simply list data in a system of rows and columns, providing easy access to specific information that might be difficult to find in a graphic relationship. The table shown here provides data that shows the population growth of South Bend, Indiana, as it relates to the surrounding county.

Year	South Bend	Percent of County	St. Joseph County
2005	107,889	40.5	266,371
2010	108,368	40.1	270,266
2015	109,158	39.5	276,679
2020	110,045	38.8	283,885
2025	110,914	38.1	290,946

Source: IBRC

Images

Photographs

Because of their realistic representational qualities, photographs can accurately depict evidence and examples to assist an evaluation. For example, before and after photographs can show convincing effects of a process. The photographs found here show the effect of trawling on the seabed.

Photo manipulation applications, like Adobe's Photoshop, allow users to customize and alter photographs through cropping; adjusting colors; adding callouts or captions; and highlighting, adding, or deleting particular parts of a photograph. Close attention to ethical considerations is critical when using these applications.

Writing Process
GUIDELINES

Use the guidelines in this chart to plan, review, and evaluate your process for writing. Each step in the process should support the overall purpose of your project.

SITUATE
- Understand your reasons for evaluating.
- Understand how constraints might limit your evaluation.
- Distinguish the role of location in your analysis.
- Match your criteria to your audience's needs.
- Consider what genres, media, and methods might assist you.

PLAN
- Confirm and clarify your reason/purpose for evaluating.
- Consider your form for delivering your analysis.
- Develop your criteria.
- Begin to take notes.

RESEARCH
- Determine what kind of information you will need to evaluate.
- Conduct research to gather the information you need.
- Confirm that your research will be valid and useful.
- Identify any visuals you may need to evaluate or depict your evaluation.
- Organize your evaluation.

DRAFT
- Confirm your purpose.
- Define and explain your criteria.
- Define and explain the reason for the evaluation.
- Define and explain the subject being evaluated.
- Draft and organize the content of your document.
- Use the visual process to develop any visuals you will need.
- Design your document.

REVIEW AND REVISE
Review your evaluation for
- clarity and concision.
- accuracy.
- degree of detail appropriate to the situation and purpose.
- extraneous information.
- organizational approach.
- style appropriate to the situation.
- visual effectiveness and readability.
- Confirm your research and citations.
- Consider revising the title to most accurately reflect the document's purpose.

EDIT
- Proofread carefully.
- Correct all mechanical and grammatical errors.

EVALUATE
- Seek feedback from peers (take advantage of peer editing opportunities).
- Self-evaluate.
- Ask for feedback from a representative member of the target audience.
- Ask for feedback from an editor in whom you are confident.
- Evaluate the usefulness of any feedback you receive and revise accordingly.

DISTRIBUTE/CIRCULATE
- Consider technologies of circulation.
- Publish in a form that will be visible within the situation.
- Identify methods for increasing circulation (like search engine optimization) within and beyond the specific situation.
- Consider audience access.
- Identify possible sources of audience response.

Seeking Feedback

Peers, target audiences, and editors can offer valuable observations that will strengthen your writing. You will encourage more constructive feedback from these readers if you structure your questions for them carefully. Consider asking these kinds of questions to get feedback.

EVALUATION Guidelines

INITIAL REACTION

- Do you agree with the evaluation? Why or why not?
- Did the evaluation provide all you needed to get a clear picture of the item evaluated?
- Does the author provide enough details? What details stand out for you?
- How clearly are the criteria and method of evaluation explained?
- What is the purpose of the evaluation?
- What are the strengths of the evaluation?
- What are the weaknesses of the evaluation?
- Generally speaking, what is the primary thing the writer must do to improve this document?
- What details, if any, does the evaluation not include that you thought should be present?

SITUATION

- Who do you understand this evaluation to be written for, and what leads you to that conclusion?
- Does the evaluation fulfill its purpose effectively?

READABILITY

- Did you understand the evaluation?
- Were the judgments clearly explained?
- What parts, if any, are difficult to follow or understand?
- What organizational strategy does the writer use to present the evaluation?
- Are you able to follow the organization of the evaluation?

CONTENT

- Does the evaluation reach a judgment based on the criteria?
- Does the writer describe and define the criteria?
- Does the writer describe and define the item being evaluated?
- What particularly interesting information, if any, does the writer present?
- What unnecessary or extraneous information, if any, appears in the evaluation?
- What details stand out for you?

VISUALS

- Does the writer use visuals to clarify or explain the evaluation?
- If so, are the visuals appropriate to the purpose?
- Do the visuals work in conjunction with the writing or independently?
- Are the visuals clear and easy to read?
- Does the document design distract from or support the purpose and/or readability of the evaluation?
- What recommendations regarding visuals do you have for the writer?

MECHANICS

- What evident mechanical distractions, if any, are in the document?
- Which sentences are unclear, if any?
- Which sentences or paragraphs are particularly well written, if any?
- Are all references cited appropriately?

Summary

To evaluate is to assess something to determine its worth, merit, and significance and to articulate that assessment in a clear claim. Evaluation is an act of responsible participation because the evaluator gathers information, asks questions, and makes relevant judgments that can affect others. As a result, evaluation is not always safe, but to be ethical and valid, it must be transparent. Evaluation should be intended for a specific audience and should explain to that audience what is at stake. It must be conducted using relevant criteria and may require resources, research, and evidence, which should be described and explained. All evaluations are based on analysis that leads to an outcome. Visuals can also be evaluated; in addition, visuals themselves can be used as tools for conveying evaluative information.

Chapter Review

1. What are the primary differences between critical evaluations and everyday evaluations?

2. What are the evaluative characteristics of explicit, rigorous evaluation?

3. Identify and explain eight strategies for writing critical evaluations.

4. What are some methods for developing critical, evaluative criteria?

5. What kinds of visuals evaluate?

Thinking and Writing about the Chapter

Reflection

Now that you have learned more about writing to evaluate, look back to the blog post or journal entry you wrote in response to the prompt at the beginning of this chapter. How has your understanding of evaluation changed? Write a follow-up post or entry to explain your new understanding of evaluation.

Discussion Threads

1. What do you informally evaluate in your college life? How do you conduct those evaluations? What criteria do you use, and how did you select them? Do you evaluate the same way each time?

2. Review what this chapter says about the ethics of evaluation. Then discuss the role of ethics in evaluating in a college setting. What are the ethical ramifications of your evaluations of classes, teachers, majors, events, activities, residential and dining facilities, and resources?

3. This chapter asserts that evaluation is an act of responsible participation because evaluation gathers information, asks questions, and makes relevant judgments that can affect others. Discuss how writing to evaluate and responsible participation converge in your life and your classmates' lives.

Collaboration

1. It is likely that the teacher in the class for which you are using *Situations of Writing* will ask you to evaluate your own and your classmates' writing. Working in small groups, develop a set of criteria that might be useful for your class to use as guidelines when conducting such evaluations. Once each group has completed the task, collaborate as a class to synthesize these sets into a single set of evaluation criteria.

2. The shopping.com network includes a well-used evaluation site called Epinions. Working in groups, explore the Epinions pages and analyze the evaluative mechanisms there. What kinds of things are evaluated on Epinions? How does Epinions help establish evaluative criteria for its users? How does it allow users to develop their own evaluative criteria?

Writing

1. Many websites and organizations offer "Top 100" lists, which are forms of evaluation. Yet, often, the reports of the lists do not include any explanation of criteria or method for the evaluation. Explore one of the following web pages and then write an evaluation of the top 100 list, addressing the criteria for the list's evaluation when you can locate it or speculating on the criteria when you can't.

   - Top 100 Speeches
   - Top 100 Films
   - Top 100 Songs
   - Top 100 Music Videos
   - Top 100 Blogs
   - Top 100 Websites
   - Top 100 Universities

2. What was the last movie you saw? The last book you read? The last music you purchased? The last app you added to your phone? Using the guidelines provided in this chapter, write a critical evaluation of any one of these choices.

3. From a student's perspective, write an evaluation of each of the chapters in this part of *Writing Situations*. Establish evaluative criteria that allow you to compare each chapter's examples, exercises, and readability. Consider how interesting (or boring) each chapter is. Address consistencies and inconsistencies. Identify which chapters you found to be most useful or informative and why. Then, based on your evaluation, make a list that ranks the chapters according to your evaluation.

Local Situation

Chances are your college or university has developed and published policies regarding Internet use. These policies likely include protocols concerning privacy, accessibility, e-mail use, security, identity, passwords, harassment, and intellectual property. Locate your school's Internet policies. Write an evaluation either of these policies in general or of one specific policy, particularly in relation to students.

14 | Writing to Argue

Learning Objectives

14.1 Explain the difference between formal and informal arguments

14.2 Identify elements of argumentative writing

14.3 Organize your arguments in effective ways

14.4 Explain the three types of rhetorical appeals: ethos, pathos, and logos

14.5 Name and apply a range of strategies for writing to argue

14.6 Use visuals persuasively, as evidence, and as methods of persuasion

Before you read this chapter

Do you like to argue? What makes a good argument? Who do you argue with? Take some time to think about the kinds of arguments you have. In your journal or blog, write about what it means to you to argue and when and why you argue.

In 2006, the Canadian band Nickelback released the single "If Everyone Cared"; the band also released a music video to accompany the song. The video, which intercuts shots of the band performing and images of four influential human rights activists, makes a poignant argument about activism and the need for individuals to let their voices be heard when injustice arises. The video integrates written text, still images, filmic images, music, and lyrics to articulate its position. What makes the video's argument so poignant is not the use of these various textual forms or the power of the lyrics or music, but the directness and brevity of the argument.

The video itself is constructed much like an argumentative essay, providing a statement of position, reasons for the claim, and evidence of the claim. It addresses social justice, specifically, peaceful solutions to conflicts like human rights violations, arguing for solving arguments differently.

Argument

14.1 Explain the difference between formal and informal arguments

To argue is to take a position and justify it. Aristotle defined rhetoric as the art of persuasion, as the skill in moving an audience to action. In this way, argumentation and rhetoric are inseparable, and this chapter addresses argumentative writing from a rhetorical perspective. You are probably already familiar with most facets of arguments simply because we are surrounded by arguments in our daily lives: arguments about what to purchase, what to wear, political events, what television shows to watch, and so on.

We could make a case that aspects of argument are built into much of what conveys information: an advertisement argues for you to purchase a sports drink; the label on the sports drink argues for its use, its effectiveness, and the quality of its ingredients; even the design of the bottle can be read as a particular kind of argument within a specific context. Art, music, and literature can be argumentative: think about the Nickelback song and the novels of George Orwell or Alice Walker and the arguments each makes about social conditions. Within specific contexts, even the design of a chair might be read as a particular kind of argument. Analyzing these arguments is an important part of how we understand our world. But understanding our world is only part of the objective; participating is the other. Learning how to make responsible, strong arguments is a critical part of learning how to participate in college and beyond.

In college writing, an argument is generally considered the statement of a main idea or a claim—sometimes called a "thesis statement"—followed by reasons and evidence in support of that claim. Good academic writing is most often a fluid presentation of an idea, the reasons for the idea, and evidence in support of that idea. Successful academic writing shows that you have an investment in the material and can take a position in the disciplinary conversation. Not all assignments will directly ask you to "argue," but most implicitly require that you take a position and provide evidence in support of that position.

14.2 Identify elements of argumentative writing

Formal Argumentation

Academic writing generally requires formal argumentation that relies on evidence, proof, and logic. Formal arguments begin by making a specific claim. They then provide a thorough sequence of evidence that logically and clearly leads to a conclusion.

Formal arguments are persuasive when the writer/speaker is able to clearly show the audience how the evidence reasonably leads to the conclusion.

Academic arguments are one kind of formal argument; academic arguments commonly include these characteristics:

An arguable claim. In order for an argument to unfold, there has to be a point of disagreement. If everyone in the audience is in agreement with the speaker/ writer, then no argument can unfold.

A rational argument. Formal arguments are based on the analysis and evaluation of evidence and data. Academic arguments are not centered on emotional responses.

A cohesive logic. Formal arguments must direct the audience from claim through evidence to conclusion. The logic of an argument is made evident through the transitions a writer uses to guide readers from one piece of evidence to the next.

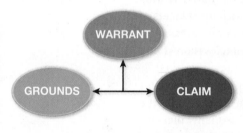

Keep in mind, too, that academic audiences anticipate and expect writers to provide citations for the evidence they use when writing.

British philosopher Stephen Toulmin influenced how we think about the formal argumentative structure, clarifying the claim→evidence→conclusion model. Toulmin wanted a more practical way to exhibit practical reasoning in argumentation. Toulmin's basic model looks like this:

The **claim** is the position that the writer argues for; this is the conclusion the writer strives to reach. The claim answers the question, "what's your point?" The **grounds** (also called reasons or evidence) are the reasons or supporting evidence used to support the claim. The **warrant** is the sequence of reasoning that connects the grounds to the claim. Warrants can be thought of as connections, the things that tie the grounds and the claims together logically.

As an example, Toulmin provides this argument:

CLAIM: Harry is a British subject.

GROUNDS: Harry was born in Bermuda.

WARRANT: A man born in Bermuda will be a British subject.

What Toulmin's model provides us is a dynamic method for analyzing arguments and for thinking about how we structure our own formal arguments. However, Toulmin's model should not be used as a formula for devising arguments. Every argument—formal and informal—must be constructed for the situation in which it participates in order for it to be effective.

annotated example

Slate magazine is a daily online magazine covering politics, news, business, technology, and culture. *Slate*'s popular "Dialogue" segment engages two experts to debate a newsworthy topic by way of an e-mail exchange. *Slate* publishes each e-mail as an independent entry in the order of the exchange. In this way, each e-mail can be read either independently as an argument or in conjunction with the rest of the debate. The e-mail reprinted here is the opening text of an exchange on animal rights between Peter Singer, a Princeton University bioethics professor, and Richard A. Posner, judge of the U.S. Court of Appeals for the Circuit and senior lecturer at the University of Chicago Law School. This entry is written by Singer. As you read this initiation of the exchange, pay particular attention to how Singer clarifies his claim to establish the specific position he wishes to argue.

Animal Rights

Peter Singer

Dear Judge Posner,

I'm not a lawyer, let alone a judge, but I've noticed increasing interest in legal circles in the topic of the legal status of animals. This seems to have been triggered in part by the efforts of the Great Ape Project, by the publication of Steven Wise's *Rattling the Cage*, and by the fact several law schools, including Harvard, are now teaching courses on law and animals. You reviewed *Rattling the Cage* in the *Yale Law Journal*, and while you were critical of Wise's argument that the law should recognize chimpanzees and other great apes as legal persons, your tone was respectful, and you took his argument seriously. That has encouraged me to attempt to persuade you that—for I am an ethicist, not a lawyer—there is a sound *ethical* case for changing the status of animals.

> Singer's strategy for establishing credibility is to acknowledge that he is not an expert in legal matters, but an expert in issues of ethics. Note that Singer is direct in making his claim, using a thesis-statement approach.

Before the rise of the modern animal movement there were societies for the prevention of cruelty to animals, but these organizations largely accepted that the welfare of nonhuman animals deserves protection only when human interests are not at stake. Human beings were seen as quite distinct from, and infinitely superior to, all forms of animal life. If our interests conflict with theirs, it is always their interests which have to give way. In contrast with this approach, the view that I want to defend puts human and nonhuman animals, *as such*, on the same moral footing. That is the sense in which I argued, in *Animal Liberation*, that "all animals are equal." But to avoid common misunderstandings, I need to be careful to

annotated example

spell out exactly what I mean by this. Obviously nonhuman animals cannot have equal rights to vote and nor should they be held criminally responsible for what they do. That is not the kind of equality I want to extend to nonhuman animals. The fundamental form of equality is *equal consideration of interests*, and it is this that we should extend beyond the boundaries of our own species. Essentially this means that if an animal feels pain, the pain matters as much as it does when a human feels pain—if the pains hurt just as much. How bad pain and suffering are does not depend on the species of being that experiences it.

> Singer explains his first reason for making the claim that he does, answering "why" he takes the position he does. Singer uses this opportunity to carefully define and explain a key term of his argument: *equal*.

People often say, without much thought, that *all* human beings are infinitely more valuable than any animals of any other species. This view owes more to our own selfish interests and to ancient religious teachings that reflect these interests than to reason or impartial moral reflection. What ethically significant feature can there be that *all* human beings but *no* nonhuman animals possess? We like to distinguish ourselves from animals by saying that only humans are rational, can use language, are self-aware, or are autonomous. But these abilities, significant as they are, do not enable us to draw the requisite line between *all* humans and nonhuman animals. For there are many humans who are not rational, self-aware, or autonomous, and who have no language—all humans under 3 months of age, for a start. And even if they are excluded, on the grounds that they have the potential to develop these capacities, there are other human beings who do not have this potential. Sadly, some humans are born with brain damage so severe that they will never be able to reason, see themselves as an independent being, existing over time, make their own decisions, or learn any form of language.

> Singer specifically invokes a sense of reason and logic. Think about how this strategy is an appeal to logos. Singer is using his evidence to tease out a nuanced definition of "all humans."

If it would be absurd to give animals the right to vote, it would be no less absurd to give that right to infants or to severely retarded human beings. Yet we still give equal consideration to their interests. We don't raise them for food in overcrowded sheds or test household cleaners on them. Nor should we. But we do these things to nonhuman animals who show greater abilities in reasoning than these humans. This is because we have a prejudice in favor of the view that all humans are somehow infinitely more valuable than any animal. Sadly, such prejudices are not unusual. Like racists and sexists, speciesists say that the boundary of their own group is also a boundary that marks off the most valuable beings from all the rest. Never mind what you are like, if you are a member of my group, you are superior to all those who are not members of my group. The speciesist favors a larger group than the racist and so has a large circle of concern; but all these prejudices use an arbitrary and morally irrelevant fact—membership of a race, sex, or species—as if it were morally crucial. The only acceptable limit to our moral concern is the point at which there is no awareness of pain or pleasure, and no preferences of any kind. That is why pigs count, but lettuces don't. Pigs can feel pain and pleasure. Lettuces can't.

One closing caution: I have been arguing against the widely accepted idea that we are justified in discounting the interests of an animal merely because it is not a member of the species *Homo sapiens*. I have not argued against the more limited claim that there is something special about beings with the mental abilities that normal humans possess, once they are past infancy, and that when it is a question of life or death, we are justified in giving greater weight to saving their lives. Of course, some humans do not possess these mental abilities, and arguably some nonhuman animals do—here we return to the chimpanzees and other great apes with which I began. But whatever we decide about the value of a life, this is a separate issue from our decisions about practices that inflict suffering. Unfortunately a great deal of what Americans do to animals, especially in raising them for food in modern industrialized farms, does inflict prolonged suffering on literally billions of animals each year. Since we can live very good lives without doing this, it is wrong for us to inflict this suffering, irrespective of the question of the wrongness of taking the lives of these animals.

Singer stays focused on a particular aspect of animal rights, focusing his reasons and evidence on the distinction between all people and animals, working to convince Posner (and the *Slate* audience) that sweeping claims and definitions don't accurately depict what is a much more complex issue.

In concluding, Singer clarifies his argument, making sure his audience stays focused on his position. Singer identifies what he is not claiming and why, which helps him direct his audience's potential responses.

student example

Brooke Horn is an active writer who spends a good deal of time thinking about her writing and the role of writing in people's lives. Brooke majors in English and minors in classical studies. In the essay that follows, Brooke asks the important question as to whether or not first-year college students should be required to take an entry-level writing class. Her answer is definitive: the first-year writing class should be required for all first-year college students. However, part of her argument is that if such a class were to be universally required, the course itself would require some conceptual rethinking. As you read Brooke's essay, think about how she constructs her argument, and think about how the tone of her essay works with that argumentative structure.

The First-Year Dilemma: To Write or Not to Write?

Lauren Brooke Horn

Teachers, scholars, and administrators alike have been pondering over a question that has been vexing the education system for quite some time: should all first-year college students be required to take an entry-level writing course? And if so, what exactly should be covered in the curriculum? The following essay provides support for the argument favoring the mandatory inclusion of composition in the first-year-level college curriculum and includes ways in which this essential course can be altered to increase its educational value. Unsurprisingly, the answer to the critical question proposed above is yes; all first-year college students should be required to take an entry-level writing course. However, to determine what improvements need to be made to the curriculum, the current needs of first-year college students should be assessed. This involves understanding: (a) what information is already ingrained in incoming students' mental databases of knowledge, (b) how they currently use that knowledge, and (c) what refinements to that knowledge base are necessary to prepare for the future.

When considering first-year writing, current methods of communication among students and, more importantly, *future* methods of communication must be examined. Today, people use e-mails, phone calls, text-messages, status updates, Tweets, and a multitude of other methods to communicate. These transmissions often occur in a condensed textual form and are accompanied by visualizations (examples include emoticons, memes, Instagram and Pinterest). More and more frequently, young generations are relying more heavily on these visuals than written and spoken language to communicate. Informal language has devolved into abbreviated, minimally punctuated

student example

short-form to keep pace with the speed in which information circulates. This evolution has watered down language and contributed to the breakdown of written skills.

While most high school students spend an adequate amount of scholastic discourse learning how to construct a proper essay, they arrive in college unprepared for the higher expectations to which college professors and professionals will hold them. Most high school seniors begin their college experience without the faintest idea of what standards to meet concerning written assignments. The truth is, despite their previous education, many incoming college students have not mastered the set of skills necessary to write at the college level. This lack of skill extends to such rudimentary skills as proper citations, correct grammar, and use of tone—all of which can be efficiently addressed in a beginning writing course. A broad, entry-level writing course alleviates much of the stress (and answers many of the questions) created by the transition to college expectations while simultaneously allowing students to shape their skills, goals, and ideals through both oral and written exercises.

There is much debate in academia about whether or not first-year composition is a necessary component in the college curriculum. Those who teach the curriculum in question (as well as curriculums more advanced than first-year composition) are divided over the issue and have been for quite some time. D. G. Kehl, a professor of first-year composition at Arizona State University, is one of those that support first-year composition. In his article "An Argument against Abolishing Freshman Composition," Kehl states that he is "in defense of a course which deals with 'composition' only peripherally, a course which sets its goals beyond the mere instruction of written expression and seeks necessarily to provide sociological, psychological, political, cultural, historical, and literary approaches to communication" (60). Kehl is not only arguing for the continued inclusion of first-year composition, he is arguing that the curriculum of such a course needs to address more than technical skill.

One of the arguments against the continued inclusion of a beginning writing course is the strain it puts on the budget and educators. The first-year composition curriculum is usually taught by those teachers who are unqualified to teach higher level English courses. Those same teachers are also often grossly underpaid. According to Salary.com, the median income for assistant English professors is between $42,308 and $71,092 ("Job Details for Asst. Professor—English")—compared to what the site reports as the median income of assistant law professors, which is between $67,106 and $117,513 ("Job Details for Asst. Professor—Law"). In most schools, however, the burden of teaching first-year composition has been delegated to graduate assistants, adjuncts, and part time educators—all of whom make considerably less than quoted above for teaching the same classes. Due to the high volume of students, the sheer number of educators required to instruct them requires a significant portion of the budget. This combination, along with the high cost of educating that many students and employing that many teachers, has caused first-year composition to top the list of ways to save money and streamline during budget cuts.

A compromise between the two opposing views—(a) keeping first-year composition a mandatory part of every first-year curriculum and (b) abolishing it completely—is to keep the course, but to drop the mandate to those select majors that are writing intensive. This allows students who are not pursuing writing-intensive majors/careers to focus on those courses that will better prepare them for their chosen paths. Because not as many students will be required to take the course, fewer educators would be required and salaries could be increased. This solution would permit those students who feel that their writing skills are insufficient (but are not in writing intensive disciplines) to take the course for personal improvement at their discretion. This solution is a good compromise to both sides of the argument, but it ultimately undermines the purpose of the course: to prepare all incoming college students for communication in both their academic and professional pursuits. Composition not only teaches students how to write an essay with intelligence and style, it teaches them how to communicate with the world.

However, if first-year composition is to be kept as a required course for all first-year students, considerable changes and revisions are necessary. There needs to be more of an emphasis on arguing a point using logos (logic) instead of arguing based upon pathos (emotions and opinions). The backbone of college writing is based upon research, and it is absolutely critical that students become accustomed to conducting research and writing clear, concise arguments early on—even if they conflict with the student's personal views. In addition, there needs to be a far greater emphasis on peer-to-peer communication skills that will be immediately applicable, so that, should the student choose to not pursue any further instruction in writing, the student is more than competent in several venues of writing—whether it be e-mails at work, a report about research, a statement regarding company policy, and so forth. There is certain etiquette when it comes to written communication, and that etiquette is dying in the hands of our generation. It is the responsibility of the education system to prepare students for the workplace and for the rest of their careers in academia, and there is no place more appropriate to do so than in first-year composition.

First-year composition is a fundamental tool in the education system's toolbox that cannot be replaced. However, this "tool" has, over time, become a bit rusty and outdated. Consequently, this imperative "tool" needs to be polished and certain parts need to be replaced. Such replacements are necessary because as our culture and the ways that we communicate evolve, so should the ways in which communication is taught to the college generation. If first-year writing courses were removed from the curriculum entirely, or even made optional, many new students would lose the opportunity to learn valuable skills necessary for success in casual, academic, and professional settings. With some minor cuts and the implementation of new ideas, first-year composition has the potential to be one of the most useful and the most influential courses a college student can take. First-year composition is not simply a basic writing course; it is a building block, and one which provides students the opportunity to "compose" their writing style. First-year students are quite literally, for perhaps the first time, writing their own tale, and what kind of instruction they receive early on determines just how well written that story of self-discovery will be.

Works Cited

Kehl, D. G. "An Argument against Abolishing Freshman Composition." *College English* 32.1 (1970): 60–65. Print.

"Job Details for Asst. Professor—English." *Salary.com*. Kenexa, n.d. Web. 8 Oct. 2012.

"Job Details for Asst. Professor—Law." *Salary.com*. Kenexa, n.d. Web. 8 Oct. 2012.

Thinking about Brooke's Essay

1. Brooke argues that all first-year students should be required to take a first-year writing course. Given her argument and your own experiences, do you agree with her? Explain your response. Keep in mind that Brooke does not address whether the course itself should be abolished, but whether the course should be required of all students.

2. Brooke's argument is fundamentally a statement of her opinion on the question of whether first-year students should or should not be required to take a first-year composition course. But, through uses of evidence and examples, Brooke constructs an argument that moves well beyond a simple statement of opinion to a crafted, developed argument. What strategies does she use to support her claim and make it part of an argument rather than a statement of opinion or assertion?

student example

THE ROAD TO A
STRONG THESIS

SECOND THOUGHTS:
"This is something that has been addressed pretty widely among professionals, which is good because I can situate my argument in a larger debate. I agree with those people who have said that all college students should take an entry-level writing class."

SECOND THOUGHTS:
"Those things seem pretty obviously connected. Why am I interested in them? What is it about them that I think needs to be addressed more?"

SECOND THOUGHTS:
"But is that something that just happens here, or is it more wide-ranging?"

EXIGENCY:
"At my school, not everyone has to take a first-year writing class, and from what some of my friends and classmates say, they really aren't ready for the writing assignments they get in other classes, which seems pretty important to me."

PURPOSE:
"I need to write about the relationship between writing and education."

RESPONSE:
"Maybe the professionals who teach college writing have already addressed this. I suppose I could do some research."

ASSIGNMENT
To write an argumentative essay

THESIS:
"All first-year college students should be required to take a compulsory composition class."

As a writer and student, Brooke certainly had a topic about which she wanted to write: learning to write. But a topic is not the same as a claim. Through careful consideration, Brooke was able to develop a claim through an internal conversation that may have unfolded along a path like this.

FINAL THOUGHTS:
"Now I just have to defend my position by explaining why."

professional example

Between 1997 and 1999, seventeen Latino and African-American high school students filed lawsuits against the University of Michigan for discriminatory admissions practices, bringing to light a controversial affirmative action plan used by the University of Michigan that would cause debate for several years. On January 15, 2003, President George W. Bush intervened in the situation, proclaiming his opposition to the University of Michigan's affirmative action policy on admissions, calling the policy a "quota system" that rejects or accepts students "based solely on race" and a method that is fundamentally flawed. The president and his administration then filed a friend-of-the-court brief that outlined their opposition to the UM program.

Three days after President Bush filed his brief, writer and activist Tim Wise published the following argumentative essay, "Whites Swim in Racial Preference" in *Z Magazine*, an online, independent magazine dedicated to "resisting injustice, defending against repression, and creating liberty." Wise's activism, speaking, and writing have drawn much attention from both conservative and liberal camps. Wise's essay addresses the University of Michigan situation and the president's response, but in doing so, it makes an argument about the larger situation of racial discrimination. As you read this argumentative essay, pay particular attention to how Wise meticulously makes connections in his argument.

Whites Swim in Racial Preference

Tim Wise

Ask a fish what water is and you'll get no answer. Even if fish were capable of speech, they would likely have no explanation for the element they swim in every minute of every day of their lives. Water simply is.

Fish take it for granted.

So too with this thing we hear so much about, "racial preference."

While many whites seem to think the notion originated with affirmative action programs, intended to expand opportunities for historically marginalized people of color, racial preference has actually had a long and very white history.

Affirmative action for whites was embodied in the abolition of European indentured servitude, which left black (and occasionally indigenous) slaves as the only unfree labor in the colonies that would become the U.S.

Affirmative action for whites was the essence of the 1790 Naturalization Act, which allowed virtually any European immigrant to become a full citizen, even while blacks, Asians and American Indians could not.

Affirmative action for whites was the guiding principle of segregation, Asian exclusion laws, and the theft of half of Mexico for the fulfillment of Manifest Destiny.

In recent history, affirmative action for whites motivated racially restrictive housing policies that helped 15 million white families procure homes with FHA loans from the 1930s to the '60s, while people of color were mostly excluded from the same programs.

In other words, it is hardly an exaggeration to say that white America is the biggest collective recipient of racial preference in the history of the cosmos. It has skewed our laws, shaped our public policy, and helped create the glaring inequalities with which we still live.

White families, on average, have a net worth that is 11 times the net worth of black families, according to a recent study; and this gap remains substantial even when only comparing families of like size, composition, education, and income status.

A full-time black male worker in 2003 makes less in real dollar terms than similar white men were earning in 1967. Such realities are not merely indicative of the disadvantages faced by blacks, but indeed are evidence of the preferences afforded whites—a demarcation of privilege that is the necessary flipside of discrimination.

Indeed, the value of preferences to whites over the years is so enormous that the current baby-boomer generation of whites is currently in the process of inheriting between $7 and $10 trillion in assets from their parents and grandparents—property handed down by those who were able to accumulate assets at a time when people of color by and large could not.

To place this in the proper perspective, we should note that this amount of money is more than all the outstanding mortgage debt, all the credit card debt, all the savings account assets, all the money in IRAs and 401k retirement plans, all the annual profits for U.S. manufacturers, and our entire merchandise trade deficit combined.

Yet few whites have ever thought of our position as resulting from racial preferences. Indeed, we pride ourselves on our hard work and ambition, as if somehow we invented the concepts.

As if we have worked harder than the folks who were forced to pick cotton and build levies for free; harder than the Latino immigrants who spend 10 hours a day in fields picking strawberries or tomatoes; harder than the (mostly) women of color who clean hotel rooms or change bedpans in hospitals, or the (mostly) men of color who collect our garbage.

We strike the pose of self-sufficiency while ignoring the advantages we have been afforded in every realm of activity: housing, education, employment, criminal justice, politics, banking, and business. We ignore the fact that at almost every turn, our hard work has been met with access to an opportunity structure denied to millions of others. Privilege, to us, is like water to the fish: invisible precisely because we cannot imagine life without it.

It is that context that best explains the duplicity of the President's recent criticisms of affirmative action at the University of Michigan.

President Bush, himself a lifelong recipient of affirmative action—the kind set aside for the mediocre rich—recently proclaimed that the school's policies were examples of unfair racial preference. Yet in doing so he not only showed a profound ignorance of the Michigan policy, but made clear the inability of yet another white person to grasp the magnitude of white privilege still in operation.

The President attacked Michigan's policy of awarding 20 points (on a 150-point evaluation scale) to undergraduate applicants who are members of underrepresented minorities (which at U of M means blacks, Latinos, and American Indians). To many whites such a "preference" is blatantly discriminatory.

Bush failed to mention that greater numbers of points are awarded for other things that amount to preferences for whites to the exclusion of people of color.

For example, Michigan awards 20 points to any student from a low-income background, regardless of race. Since these points cannot be combined with those for minority status (in other words poor blacks don't get 40 points), in effect this is a preference for poor whites.

Then Michigan awards 16 points to students who hail from the Upper Peninsula of the state: a rural, largely isolated, and almost completely white area.

Of course both preferences are fair, based as they are on the recognition that economic status and even geography (as with race) can have a profound effect on the quality of K–12 schooling that one receives, and that no one should be punished for things that are beyond their control. But note that such preferences—though disproportionately awarded to whites— remain uncriticized, while preferences for people of color become the target for reactionary anger. Once again, white preference remains hidden because it is more subtle, more ingrained, and isn't called white preference, even if that's the effect.

But that's not all. Ten points are awarded to students who attended top-notch high schools, and another eight points are given to students who took an especially demanding AP and honors curriculum.

As with points for those from the Upper Peninsula, these preferences may be race-neutral in theory, but in practice they are anything but. Because of intense racial isolation (and Michigan's schools are the most segregated in America for blacks, according to research by the Harvard Civil Rights Project), students of color will rarely attend the "best" schools, and on average, schools serving mostly black and Latino students offer only a third as many AP and honors courses as schools serving mostly whites.

So even truly talented students of color will be unable to access those extra points simply because of where they live, their economic status, and ultimately their race, which is intertwined with both.

Four more points are awarded to students who have a parent who attended the U of M: a kind of affirmative action with which the President is intimately familiar, and which almost exclusively goes to whites.

Ironically, while alumni preference could work toward the interest of diversity if combined with aggressive race-based affirmative action (by creating a larger number of black and brown alums), the rollback of the latter, combined with the almost guaranteed retention of the former, will only further perpetuate white preference.

So the U of M offers 20 "extra" points to the typical black, Latino, or indigenous applicant, while offering various combinations worth up to 58 extra points for students who will almost all be white. But while the first of these are seen as examples of racial preferences, the second are not, hidden as they are behind the structure of social inequities that limit where people live, where they go to school, and the kinds of opportunities they have been afforded. White preferences, the result of the normal workings of a racist society, can remain out of sight and out of mind, while the power of the state is turned against the paltry preferences meant to offset them.

Very telling is the oft-heard comment by whites, "If I had only been black I would have gotten into my first-choice college."

Such a statement not only ignores the fact that whites are more likely than members of any other group—even with affirmative action in place—to get into their first-choice school, but it also presumes, as anti-racist activist Paul Marcus explains, "that if these whites were black, everything else about their life would have remained the same."

In other words, that it would have made no negative difference as to where they went to school, what their family income was, or anything else.

The ability to believe that being black would have made no difference (other than a beneficial one when it came time for college), and that being white has made no positive difference, is rooted in privilege itself: the privilege that allows one to not have to think about race on a daily basis; to not have one's intelligence questioned by best-selling books; to not have to worry about being viewed as "out of place" when driving, shopping, buying a home, or for that matter, attending the University of Michigan.

So long as those privileges remain firmly in place and the preferential treatment that flows from those privileges continues to work to the benefit of whites, all talk of ending affirmative action is not only premature but a slap in the face to those who have fought, and died, for equal opportunity.

Analyzing the Situation

1. We might say that Tim Wise wrote this essay in 2003 in response to President Bush's intervention in the University of Michigan situation, but he really uses that situation as an opportunity to address an even larger situation. How do you respond to his argumentative tactic in this essay to use one event to make a claim about the larger issue at hand?

2. Given the prominence of President Bush's intervention into this situation, why do you suppose that Tim Wise opted to publish his response in *Z Magazine*? Do you think that was a good choice of media? Why or why not?

Analyzing the Rhetoric

1. What contributes to Tim Wise's ethos in this argument? What evidence in the essay can you point to as exemplifying how he establishes his ethos? How does Wise's role as director of AWARE and as a well-known activist and writer affect his ethos in this essay specifically?

2. Of the three types of persuasive appeals—ethos, pathos, logos—which do Wise employ in this essay, and how does he do so?

Discussing

1. Of course, racial discrimination is a deeply contested issue, and it might be difficult to discuss all of the intricacies of that topic in a college classroom. Yet Wise uses the situation of his essay to address many facets of racial discrimination, ranging from the historical to the economic to the educational. Rather than debate your positions in response to Wise's claims and evidence, take some time to discuss his method in making his argument. Is his essay persuasive? Is his evidence informative and reliable? Is his logic sound?

2. It's one thing to discuss Wise's rhetorical approach to making his argument—something that is necessary in this chapter—but it's an entirely different thing to discuss his claim, his reasons, and his evidence. In fact, it's something we should not avoid; this is, after all, an incredibly important subject, no matter where you stand on such issues. So, have at it. Discuss Wise's claim. But remember, argue responsibly and respectfully.

Writing

1. Write an argumentative essay that responds to Wise's claim in "Whites Swim in Racial Preference." Be sure to focus on ensuring that the evidence you use in support of your claim is comparable in rigor and use to Wise's to ensure that your response works in conversation—whether in agreement, disagreement, or otherwise—with Wise's essay.

2. Take some time to read your school's policies about admissions. Then write an argumentative essay that makes a claim about their effectiveness and their fairness. Do not feel obligated to look for or write about your school's admission policies from the same perspective as Wise did, though you are welcome to. Look for other points that you recognize as debatable issues. Develop a focused claim, provide good, logical reasons for your claim, and support them with substantial, reliable evidence.

three examples

SIDE BY SIDE

Each of the three examples on the previous pages provides distinct, explicit arguments. Each essay relies on careful organization of support for its claims, yet each author approaches making his or her argument differently than do the others. This comparison of the three essays provides an overview of the authors' varying approaches.

	annotated example Peter Singer, "Animal Rights"	**student example** Lauren Brooke Horn, "The First-Year Dilemma: To Write or Not to Write?"	**professional example** Tim Wise, "Whites Swim in Racial Preference"
PURPOSE	To address an argument to Judge Richard A. Posner of the U.S. Court of Appeals for the Circuit as part of *Slate* magazine's "Dialogue" segment	To address the need for writing instruction in the first-year college curriculum	To address racial preference in the United States
AUDIENCE	Readers of *Slate* magazine	Peers and classmates	Readers interested in issues of race in the United States
CLAIM	There is a sound *ethical* case for changing the legal status of animals.	All first-year college students should be required to take a first-year composition course.	White America is the biggest collective recipient of racial preference in history.
EVIDENCE	Grounded in the author's work and reputation as an ethicist and author	Both professional research and personal observation to support the author's claim	Provides historical information to situate his position and then supports his claim with information from recent legal news
DISTRIBUTION	Worldwide via *Slate*'s online site	Limited to classmates and others she chose to share the essay with	Accessible worldwide through Znet, a regularly updated website that generally focuses on politics from a left-wing perspective
ORGANIZATION	Uses a point-by-point explanation of the reasons for the claim	Provides some background information and then makes the claim. Brooke then situates her claim in the professional discussions and next offers explanations and examples to support her claim.	Begins by providing historical background and then uses current data to support his position
LANGUAGE	Singer's language seems friendly and explanatory rather than aggressive and argumentative.	Brooke's language is definitive and strong. She takes an authoritative or confident tone in defense of her position.	Uses a direct, evidence-based tone to convey information matter-of-factly

MAPPING
YOUR SITUATION

NETWORKS
- In what networks will my argument circulate?
- How is my argument related to others' positions?
- How does my argument change this situation?

WRITERS AND SPEAKERS
- Who are the other writers and speakers in this situation?
- What have others argued in this situation?
- Why do they get to make these arguments?

RELATIONS
- What is my relation to the situation?
- What are the relationships between writers/speakers, audience, and players?
- What are the relationships to external forces, like culture, religion, or politics?
- What are the power relations?

AUDIENCE
- Who will read/see my argument?
- What do I know about the audience that I want to read my argument?
- Who might my argument affect directly and indirectly?

MEDIUM AND METHOD
- In what genre will I deliver my argument?
- What method will I use to convey my argument?
- How will I distribute and circulate my argument?

CONTEXT
- Where will my argument unfold?
- Where will my argument appear?
- What limits are imposed on my argument?

PURPOSE
- Why do I want to make an argument?
- What am I going to argue?
- How can my argument accomplish my purpose?

Mapping your situation will help you generate ideas you can use to compose. Start by answering these questions about each part of the situation. Begin with your purpose and work outward to relations and networks.

Prepare

Characteristic	Preparing Your Argument
A clearly defined position	All arguments include a claim. Defining your position and making the claim establish exactly what you are arguing about. You may refine that claim more specifically as you research, analyze, and write.
An arguable position	A claim has value only if its scope is adequate to allow argument. If it is too broad, you will have no feasible way to address the subject with any real rigor. Adequate scope also includes definable, defendable terms. Focus your claim on specifics, not large topics.
Relevant background information	Your audience will need a context—relevant background information—through which they can understand your position. Determining what background information to provide depends on what you know about your audience.
A reason	An argument requires reasons to support the claim or position.
Evidence	Reasons for a position also need to be supported. Evidence of the reasons can include identifiable facts, statistical data, description, testimony (including anecdotes and personal narrative, often acquired through interviews and surveys), forensic data, case studies, textual evidence and citation, and visual evidence.
An appeal	Writers create an appeal through the language they use, the evidence they provide, and the approach they take in making an argument. • *Ethos*—The appeal to character and credibility, established through the tone of the language, accuracy of information, the speaker/writer's reputation and trustworthiness, and the presentation and medium of the argument. • *Pathos*—The appeal to emotion to motivate action, most often established through language and tone, but also enacted through visuals and even the organizational structure of an argument. • *Logos*—The appeal to reason, grounded in explaining connections between points.
Acknowledgment and consideration of other positions and counterpositions	A strong argument anticipates counterarguments and other positions and addresses their claims. If one's claim cannot stand up against other arguments, it will have no power to persuade.

Strategy	Developing Your Argument
Develop a central and identifiable position	Take a stand on a *specific* argument. Ambiguous claims don't persuade an audience.
Present background information	Background information might include definitions of key terms, explanations of issues, or summaries of events or texts.
Define key terms	Some arguments are built around definitions, for example, what constitutes *murder* or what is economic *improvement*.
Define the situation	Explain the situation in which you propose your claim. Validity of claims can change depending on the situation.
Appeal to the audience	Be alert to how you use appeals of ethos, pathos, and logos to persuade your audience. Remember that these appeals work differently depending on the situation and often work best when used in conjunction with one another.
Consider the unstated	Do not assume your audience understands key parts of your claim. For example, in the claim "We should eat only organic foods because organic foods do not contain pesticides," the unstated part of the premise is that pesticides are bad for you.
Argue responsibly	• Provide reliable information and evidence. • Do not silence or attack counterpositions; engage them. • Do not skew information or distort evidence. • Recognize other positions. • Be respectful.
Make sure your claim is arguable	Make sure your claim is driven by reasons that are stronger than opinions or assertions. Show *why* you have taken your position on the subject.
Focus	Focus your claim on one specific facet of your position. For example, the argument "*Star Wars* is the most influential science fiction movie of all time" would likely be unwieldy and too subjective. To focus, ask questions about that position like, What makes it influential?
Be invested	Identify what specifically interests you and why.
Consider what you already know	Outline or list what you already know and assume about the topic and your position. Use these notes as a working framework to begin writing to identify gaps you need to fill and to identify your potential claims.
Provide reasons	As you develop your claim, ask yourself *why* for every aspect of your claim. Identify which reasons are relevant and interesting, which are irrelevant, or which do not support your claim.
Provide evidence	Support your reasons with evidence to show that they are correct, accurate, and valuable. Evidence can be in the form of well-researched and documented identifiable facts, statistical data, description, testimony, forensic data, case studies, textual evidence, and visual evidence.
Conduct research	Search for additional information, no matter what you already know about a position or a situation. Carefully record your notes as well as information about citations and attributions of materials.
Establish authority	Consider how your tone and language affect your ethos.
Address other claims and counterarguments	Add credibility to your argument by addressing legitimate questions or positions and briefly accounting for illegitimate or weak counterarguments.

14.3 Organize
your arguments in
effective ways

Organizational Approaches to Argument

There are three basic strategies to consider when writing to argue. All strategies, of course, can be modified to fit your needs, but the key to presenting any argumentative writing is making certain your audience sees the connection between your claim, your reasons, and your evidence.

The basic organizational approach for an argument moves efficiently from introducing an issue, through reasons and evidence, to a strong conclusion.

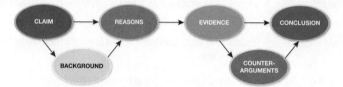

A variation of the basic approach organizes provides evidence for each claim in succession. This approach is often used in scholarly and scientific arguments that favor careful, logical development of a claim.

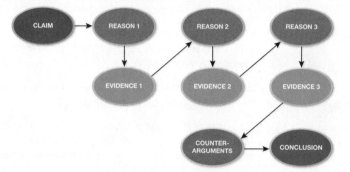

A third organizational strategy pays more attention to counterpositions, questions, and criticisms. This strategy is often used in arguments that are highly charged or emotional, because this strategy responds to possible objections at each step in the argument.

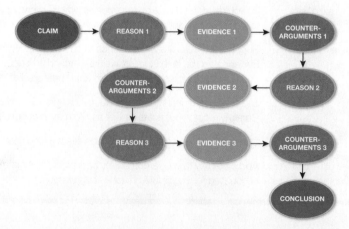

Writing Projects

Essay

Using the information provided in this chapter, select one of the topic questions listed below, make a focused claim in response to that question, and write an argumentative essay about that topic. Be sure to establish a strong, specific claim within the topic, conduct research to learn more about the topic beyond what you may already know, provide substantial reasons for your claim, and supply reliable evidence in support of that claim.

- Should sustainability be an integral part of all college curricula?
- How important are visuals in contemporary culture?
- How important is or isn't the consumption of meat to good nutrition?
- How has information technology "improved" your life?
- Is it acceptable to use animals in scientific research?
- Is a college degree really valuable in the current economic climate?
- Should colleges begin using electronic textbooks rather than print textbooks?
- Should college students be required to demonstrate proficiency in a second language?
- Should animals be kept in zoos?

Visual Argumentation

Each of the flags shown here makes an argument. Select one, make a claim about what argument it presents, and support that claim with good reasons and evidence.

Digital

The flags in the preceding assignment are fairly well known and used widely; thus, their argument is likely to be familiar or more easily understood. But flags are often used to make less-familiar arguments or to argue against the argument of another flag.

For this assignment, design a flag that conveys an argument—political, academic, cultural, civic, campus-based, or whatever. Using image software available to you on your campus or on your own computer, create a new flag. As a class, display your flags, either on screen or in print, and discuss the arguments made in each before each creator explains his or her intended arguments.

Research

Lauren Brooke Horn's "The First-Year Dilemma: To Write or Not to Write?" makes a specific argument about whether first-year students should be required to take a first-year composition course. Her argument, of course, is only one position among many within this topic. In fact, the question of whether first-year composition should be a universal requirement for college students has been and continues to be debated extensively. Conduct some research to learn more about these conversations, then position yourself in the larger conversation. Write a research-based essay in which you answer the question, Should first-year college students be required to take a first-year writing course?

Radical Revision

As this chapter explains, we encounter arguments in many forms throughout the day. One of the most prevalent forms of argument in American culture is the argument of advertising. For this assignment, select a television commercial that argues that viewers should purchase a particular product. Watch the commercial and analyze its argumentative components. What is its claim? How does it support its claim? Once you are comfortable with your analysis, revise the commercial as a traditional academic essay that conveys the same argument.

14.6 Use visuals persuasively, as evidence, and as methods of persuasion

Visuals and Argumentation

The effects of visuals in argument can be powerful both for audiences and speakers/writers. In daily life, you and others are inundated with images that make arguments. To understand and respond to those arguments, you must be able to read them critically. Visuals are remarkable tools for making arguments; appealing to emotion, logic, and a sense of credibility; and providing evidence, so you need to know how to make,

take, and change visuals for those purposes.

On February 11, 1968, 1,300 Black sanitation workers went on strike in Memphis, Tennessee. Citing discrimination and dangerous working conditions, the protesters sought to join a union. The men participating in the protest carried signs that simply read "I Am a Man." These signs made a powerful argument, but readers of the signs had to first understand the unstated premise, one grounded in the opening line of the Declaration of Independence: "all men are created equal."

The following chart shows the many purposes visuals can serve in your argumentative writing.

Purpose of Visual	Comments
Provide evidence	Visuals such as photographs, video, courtroom sketches, radar or satellite imagery, or sonography (like a mammogram or ultrasound) can provide visual evidence of a claim. For example, during the British Petroleum Deepwater Horizon oil spill disaster in the Gulf of Mexico, photography and video provided evidence of the environmental destruction the spill caused. 
Appeal to emotion	Visuals can make powerful appeals to emotion. Through visuals, in order to persuade us, advertisements appeal to our humor, anger, frustration, and desire; political organizations appeal to our sense of patriotism; environmental groups appeal to our empathy and disgust; and social justice organizations often appeal to our sense of grief and horror. 
Appeal to logic	Visuals can contribute to a sense of logic, too. Forensic evidence is often identified visually in photographs and diagrams. Graphics like tables and charts can help an audience see connections between points of evidence. 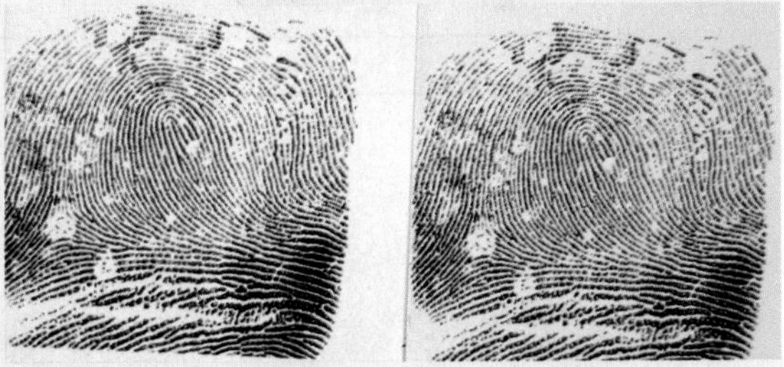
Appeal to ethos	Often, including visuals such as charts, tables, and diagrams can contribute to a sense of authority. The newspaper *USA Today* regularly uses charts and diagrams on its front page to help persuade its readers through a sense of information authority.

Student Visual Example

A Day in the Life of Your Child on Adderall
Ian Rowe

Ian Rowe has been fascinated by comics since he was in elementary school. He was particularly interested in the ways that comics like Bill Watterson's *Calvin and Hobbes* could use the medium to provide arguments about societal norms. Ian majors in English and hopes to earn his Teaching English as a Second Language certificate so he can teach overseas. In the example here, Ian uses his skills as a cartoonist to create an argument that relies primarily on visual expression.

Student Visual Example

The Multiple Sources of Self-Esteem
Hyesu Grace Kim

Hyesu Grace Kim majors in both health science and English. She aspires to go to law school when she graduates. Grace is a dedicated writer who blogs regularly. Grace became interested in the ways in which subtle statements contribute to sustainable arguments. In the example that follows, Grace provides an argument that combines both visuals and text to show how statements that were not necessarily uttered as arguments form ecologies to create an argument. Her argument is interesting in that none of the implied speakers appears to have intended a particular argument, but when their words are taken in conjunction with each other's words, their audience interprets a direct argument.

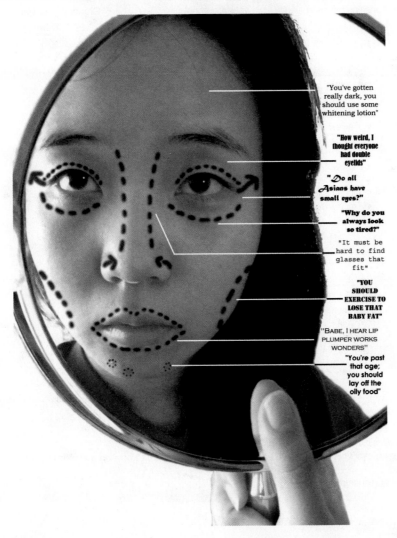

Writing Process
GUIDELINES

Use the guidelines in this chart to plan, review, and evaluate your process for writing. Each step in the process should support the overall purpose of your project.

SITUATE

- Understand your reasons for taking a position in the situation (exigencies).
- Consider who your argument will affect (players).
- Understand how relations affect your claim.
- Indentify how your claim is limited by constraints.
- Recognize the speakers or writers of counterarguments.
- Identify and analyze the audiences involved in the situation.
- Consider what genres, media, and methods have been used to make claims in this situation.
- Acknowledge how various institutions and power affect the argument.
- Consider the ecological relationships between your position and others.

PLAN

- Confirm your reason for taking a position (exigency).
- Clarify your purpose in writing or speaking the claim.
- Consider what might be the best genre, media, and method for you to make your argument.
- Analyze what you know and what you need to discover before voicing your argument.
- Begin to take notes.

RESEARCH

- Determine what kind of evidence you will need and the best ways to locate it.
- Conduct research to gather the evidence you need.
- Identify how your evidence supports your reasons and claim.
- Confirm that your evidence will be valid within the situation.
- Identify any visuals you may need.
- Organize your evidence.

DRAFT

- Confirm your purpose.
- Confirm that your choices in genre, media, and method will be effective within the situation.
- Draft and organize the content of your argument.
- Employ the visual process to develop any visuals you will need.
- Design your document.

REVIEW AND REVISE

- Review your argument for clarity and concision.
- Review your argument for accuracy.
- Review your argument for extraneous or irrelevant information.
- Review your argument for organizational approach.
- Review your argument for explanations of necessary key terms.
- Review your argument to confirm you have not used fallacy.
- Review your argument for style appropriate to the situation.
- Confirm your research and citations.
- Review your argument for visual effectiveness and readability.

EDIT

- Proofread carefully.
- Correct all mechanical and grammatical errors.

EVALUATE

- Seek feedback from peers (take advantage of peer editing opportunities).
- Ask for feedback from a representative member of the target audience.
- Ask for feedback from an editor in whom you are confident.
- Evaluate the usefulness of any feedback you receive and revise accordingly.

DISTRIBUTE/CIRCULATE

- Consider technologies of circulation.
- Publish in a form that will be visible within the situation.
- Identify methods for increasing circulation (like search engine optimization) within and beyond the specific situation.
- Consider audience access.
- Identify possible sources of audience response.

Seeking Feedback

Peers, target audiences, and editors can offer valuable observations that will strengthen your writing. You will encourage more constructive feedback from these readers if you structure your questions for them carefully. Consider asking these kinds of questions to get feedback:

EVALUATION Guidelines

INITIAL REACTION

- Is the argument persuasive?
- What is the writer's claim?
- What are the writer's reasons for making that claim?
- What are the strengths of the argument?
- What are the weaknesses of the argument?
- Does the argument hold your interest?
- Generally speaking, what is the primary thing the writer must do to improve this document?
- Is the argument focused?

SITUATION

- Who do you understand this argument to be written for, and what leads you to that conclusion?
- What is the role of the argument in its situation?
- Has the writer accounted for the audience by explaining all that needs to be explained?

READABILITY

- Does the title provide an accurate, clear representation of the document?
- Did you understand the argument?
- Are there parts that are difficult to follow or understand?
- What organizational strategy does the writer use to present the argument?

CONTENT

- Does the argument make sense?
- Does the writer provide necessary background information?
- Does the writer provide sufficient evidence?
- Is it clear how the evidence supports the claim?
- Does the arguement make logical sense?
- Do you recognize any fallacies in the argument?
- What appeals does the writer use?
- Are the appeals used effectively?

VISUALS

- Does the writer use visuals as evidence for the claim?
- If so, are the visuals appropriate to the purpose?
- Do the visuals work in conjunction with the writing or independently?
- Are the visuals clear and easy to read?
- Does the document design distract from or support the purpose and/or readability of the argument?
- What recommendations regarding visuals do you have for the writer?

MECHANICS

- Are there evident mechanical distractions in the document?
- Are there sentences that are unclear?
- Are there sentences or paragraphs that are particularly well written?
- Are all references cited appropriately?

Summary

To argue is to take a position that is supported with evidence. You will need to analyze and make arguments in your personal, professional, college, and civic lives. All arguments begin with a claim, a statement about where you stand on an issue, and include clearly explained reasons to support the claim or position. Those reasons need to be supported with evidence, which determines the value of your claim. Sound argumentation relies on appeals to ethos, pathos, and logic. Misusing these appeals can seriously weaken the effectiveness of an argument. In addition, a strong argument also anticipates counterarguments and other positions and respectfully considers them. No matter what you already know about a position or a situation, you should learn more to be as informed as possible as you articulate your argument. Daily life is inundated with images that make arguments in remarkable ways because they appeal to emotion, logic, and a sense of credibility, and they can provide convincing evidence.

Chapter Review

1. Define the differences between formal and informal arguments.

2. How will you likely encounter argumentation in your college, personal, professional, and civic lives?

3. Identify five elements of argumentative writing.

4. What is the relationship between claims, reasons, and evidence?

5. Explain the three types of rhetorical appeals:
   - Appeals based on credibility
   - Appeals to emotion
   - Appeals to logic

6. List and explain six logical fallacies.

7. How does good argumentation account for counterarguments, criticisms, and questions?

8. What are five strategies for writing to argue?

9. What is a common way to organize an argument?

10. How are visuals used to persuade?

Thinking and Writing about the Chapter

Reflection

Now that you have read about argumentation, how are you going to change the ways in which you argue? Look back at the journal entry or blog post you wrote in response to the prompt at the beginning of this chapter. How will the argumentative strategies found in this chapter affect the ways you think about arguing?

Discussion Threads

1. Where do arguments unfold in your daily life? Discuss the kinds of arguments you most frequently encounter. Remember, think beyond personal disagreements, and think about where you witness attempts at persuasion.

2. Of the three appeals—logos, pathos, ethos—which do you most often find to be most effective? In what contexts do they work best? Discuss how the three appeals work and which you find to be effective and why.

3. In what kinds of texts do you most often recognize fallacies? Discuss what fallacies are used most often and in which kinds of texts you find them.

4. When King Abdulla of Saudi Arabia was a royal guest in the United Kingdom, the Welsh Guard was faced with a dilemma. The Welsh Guard has the duty of playing music to honor the arrival of guests at Buckingham Palace; however, members of the band were opposed to many of the social and political positions of the Saudi king, whose country has a terrible record for treatment of women. The band decided to play the Imperial March theme from *Star Wars* (also known as "Darth Vader's Theme"), fulfilling their duty while making an underhanded argument about the Saudi King. The Guard Band provided no thesis, no claim, no evidence within their argument, merely an audible rhetoric portraying the King as dictatorial and oppressive. As a class, discuss the effectiveness of such kinds of "guerilla argument."

Collaboration

1. Individually, locate two essays: one that you find to be persuasive and one that you don't. Make a few copies of each essay, or locate them online and keep the URLs accessible. Then write a short assessment describing why you characterize one essay as persuasive and the other as not persuasive. Working in small groups, share copies of the essays and your assessments of them. Read each person's selected original essays and his or her response, and discuss what similar and different characteristics emerge in each of your analyses.

2. Arguing responsibly and respectfully requires careful awareness of how you make an argument. Working in small groups, develop a list of things you consider necessary in respectful and responsible argumentation. Then, as a class, develop a more comprehensive list, and consider how you, as a class, might use that list to help establish parameters for how you and your classmates should argue in the context of the class.

Writing

1. MTV's first season of *Jersey Shore*, a reality-based television series, became a breakout hit, garnering much publicity, both positive and negative. When MTV renewed the *Jersey Shore* contract, the cast decided to argue for raises together, as a collective. This strategy proved effective, and the *Jersey Shore* cast successfully persuaded MTV executives to substantially increase their compensation.

Other groups, including political organizations, clubs, businesses, and communities, also find strength in collective argument. For this assignment, consider circumstances in which people support one another's positions and argue together. Then identify one situation in which collective argument was used—either successfully or unsuccessfully—and make a case for whether it was or was not an effective strategy in that situation.

2. Joan Lowy is a reporter who has worked for both Scripps Howard News Service and the Associated Press. In April 2004, she published the article "America's 18,000 Golf Courses are Devastating the Environment: Thirsty Golf Courses Drive Environmental Protests." Find the article online. Given the claim made in the title of the article, is the article an argument? Does it support the title in reason and evidence? Write an analysis of Lowy's article as a piece of argumentative writing.

3. The online journal *Adbusters* publishes a segment of spoofs of popular advertisements. The parodies are themselves arguments that play on the familiarity of highly visible ads. Take some time to go to the *Adbusters* Spoof Ads pages and study the spoof ads. Then locate a well-known advertisement and create your own parody ad. Once you have completed your ad, write an explanation of the argument you forward in it.

Local Situation

Responsible, respectful arguments are an important part of a community's decision-making process. At any given time, it is likely that your campus community or the local surrounding community is engaged in an argument or debate over some issue, often revolving around a proposed change or improvement. Identify an argument that is taking place in your campus community in which at least two parties have different claims about the situation. Learn as much as you can about the argument, and then write an argumentative essay in which you make a claim in the situation.

Writing to Propose

CHAPTER 15

Learning Objectives

15.1 Explain and use the elements of writing to propose

15.2 Apply multiple strategies for writing to propose

15.3 Write college research and topic proposals

15.4 Write grant proposals

15.5 Discuss the role of requests for proposals (RFPs)

15.6 Synthesize visuals into proposals

Before you read this chapter

What does it mean to propose something? When are proposals made to us and when do we propose things to others? In your journal or blog, consider what is involved in proposing and what strategies might lead to successful proposals.

In July 2009, Thomas Z. Freedman, a representative of the Democratic Leadership Council, published a controversial proposal titled "A Kindle in Every Backpack: A Proposal for eTextbooks in American Schools." In it, he proposes giving every student in America an e-book reader so they will have better access to current, interactive learning materials and up-to-date technologies.

To make this proposal, Freedman first establishes that amid the important debates about education reform, the United States is missing an opportunity to improve education. He then addresses three aspects of the situation. First, he describes various benefits to students, such as access to rapidly updated materials; more exciting, interactive textbooks; health benefits (reduced backpack loads); and environmental benefits. Second, Freedman addresses the economics of such a plan, acknowledging that he has only sketchy estimates available. Third, he shows how the plan could be implemented and supported. Freedman's proposal identifies several facets of a problem and proposes a solution.

The ten-page proposal provides data to support the proposed concept, and its formality and professional delivery lend to its credibility. However, the proposal was seen as controversial and received considerable criticism for several reasons. First, given the political affiliation of the writer and sponsoring organization, the proposal was seen as partisan. Second, because the proposal referred to the generic technology of e-readers by a single brand name (the Amazon Kindle), critics noted favoritism within a competitive market. And, third, its incomplete solution for addressing costs created doubt about its feasibility.

Despite the well-founded criticism, the "Kindle in Every Backpack" proposal serves as an important example. It identifies and defines a problem that many may not have recognized as a problem, and its proposed solution is founded on valid information. Although it may not have persuaded relevant players to immediately adopt the proposal, it has, through debate and criticism, accomplished the other task of writing to propose: to define and explain a problem and to call an audience to action in response to that problem.

15.1 Explain and use the elements of writing to propose

Proposals

To propose is to present an idea for consideration, expecting that it will be scrutinized, analyzed, and evaluated. Proposals offer solutions and a plan, so they are important in decision making and problem solving. Writing to propose is closely related to argumentative, analytical, and evaluative writing.

- *Argumentative*—For any proposal to succeed, it must persuade an audience that its solutions are feasible, effective, and accurate.
- *Analytical*—Proposals dissect problems to determine solutions.
- *Evaluative*—Writers and audiences judge the value of a proposed solution.

The overarching purpose of any proposal is to bring an audience to action by providing its members with the information needed to adopt or reject a proposed solution.

Proposals may be formal, like the "A Kindle in Every Backpack" proposal, or informal, like your classmate's proposal that a group meet for coffee after class to discuss an assignment. Whether formal or informal, all proposals must give the audience adequate information so they may act. The Kindle proposal, for instance, had to provide details about anticipated results of the program, budget requirements, and long-term effects. Your classmate needs to identify where and when you would meet for coffee.

Proposals must be focused. Big problems—like the destruction of rain forests, global warming, overfishing, or poverty—aren't going to be solved with single proposals; those kinds of problems are too complex, requiring sophisticated solutions and rigorous debates about how to define those situations. Thus, effective proposals focus on realistically solvable problems. They define what they do and what they don't do—their scope—and they focus on providing solutions only for specified problems. However, proposals must also be dynamic. You don't necessarily craft a good proposal by proposing the obvious or the easy; instead, you must think through problems and often formulate new, creative ways to solve those problems. In fact, the "problem" your proposal addresses shouldn't be thought of as a problem in the negative sense, but as an opportunity or possibility. Most audiences would much rather hear that an opportunity presents itself than face a problem.

Proposals are common to college, workplace, and civic writing. They come in many forms: grant proposals, contract proposals, sales proposals, marketing proposals, research proposals, budget proposals, funding proposals, architectural or construction proposals, and so on. In your career, you will likely have to write many formal and technical proposals, especially within industries and fields that rely on systems of proposals and bidding for contracts. In college writing, you will likely be asked to write proposals, too. Your civil engineering professor may ask you to propose a solution to a construction problem; your political science professor, to propose a solution to a local electoral problem; your English professor, to propose a topic to write about in a research paper. And in your civic, community life, you may read and even write proposals for local issues such as building new schools or changing a local sales tax structure.

annotated example

Joan Didion is a noted American essayist and novelist. Didion graduated from the University of California, Berkeley. During her senior year, she entered and won an essay contest sponsored by *Vogue* magazine; the prize for the competition was a job at the magazine's New York office, where she remained on staff for two years. While at *Vogue*, Didion wrote her first novel *Run, River* (1963). In 1968, she published her first collection of essays, *Slouching Toward Bethlehem*, that describes her experiences in California during the 1960s. Her second collection of essays, *The White Album*, provides a personal look at life. Many of Didion's essays, including "In Bed," reprinted here from *The White Album*, address her own psychological and physical battles.

"In Bed" is an essay; it is not a proposal in the formal sense. Yet, it clearly defines a problem and proposes a solution. As you read "In Bed" and the commentary provided, think about how Didion's essay functions as a proposal and about how a proposal, particularly an informal proposal, can function in essay form rather than structured proposal form.

In Bed

Joan Didion

Three, four, sometimes five times a month, I spend the day in bed with a migraine headache, insensible to the world around me. Almost every day of every month, between these attacks, I feel the sudden irrational irritation and the flush of blood into the cerebral arteries which tell me that migraine is on its way, and I take certain drugs to avert its arrival. If I did not take the drugs, I would be able to function perhaps one day in four. The physiological error called migraine is, in brief, central to the given of my life. When I was 15, 16, even 25, I used to think that I could rid myself of this error by simply denying it, character over chemistry. "Do you have headaches sometimes? frequently? never?" the application forms would demand. "Check one." Wary of the trap, wanting whatever it was that the successful circumnavigation of that particular form could bring (a job, a scholarship, the respect of mankind and the grace of God), I would check one. "Sometimes," I would lie. That in fact I spent one or two days a week almost unconscious with pain seemed a shameful secret, evidence not merely of some chemical inferiority but of all my bad attitudes, unpleasant tempers, wrong-think.

For I had no brain tumor, no eyestrain, no high blood pressure, nothing wrong with me at all: I simply had migraine headaches, and migraine headaches were, as everyone who did not have them knew, imaginary. I fought migraine then, ignored the warnings it sent,

> In this paragraph, Didion opens by defining the problem, explaining its history and situation. She explains how often the problem arises and the results of the problem: her confinement to bed.

> In this paragraph, Didion reviews the history of previously applied solutions. Notice that her language does not necessarily take on the role of a technical proposal. Rather, her language is narrative in structure, setting context by providing a history of the previously defined problem.

went to school and later to work in spite of it, sat through lectures in Middle English and presentations to advertisers with involuntary tears running down the right side of my face, threw up in washrooms, stumbled home by instinct, emptied ice trays onto my bed and tried to freeze the pain in my right temple, wished only for a neurosurgeon who would do a lobotomy on house call, and cursed my imagination.

It was a long time before I began thinking mechanistically enough to accept migraine for what it was: something with which I would be living, the way some people live with diabetes. Migraine is something more than the fancy of a neurotic imagination. It is an essentially hereditary complex of symptoms, the most frequently noted but by no means the most unpleasant of which is a vascular headache of blinding severity, suffered by a surprising number of women, a fair number of men (Thomas Jefferson had migraine, and so did Ulysses S. Grant, the day he accepted Lee's surrender), and by some unfortunate children as young as two years old. (I had my first when I was eight. It came on during a fire drill at the Columbia School in Colorado Springs, Colorado. I was taken first home and then to the infirmary at Peterson Field, where my father was stationed. The Air Corps doctor prescribed an enema.) Almost anything can trigger a specific attack of migraine: stress, allergy, fatigue, an abrupt change in barometric pressure, a contretemps over a parking ticket. A flashing light. A fire drill. One inherits, of course, only the predisposition. In other words I spent yesterday in bed with a headache not merely because of my bad attitudes, unpleasant tempers and wrong-think, but because both my grandmothers had migraine, my father has migraine and my mother has migraine.

> In this paragraph, we see Didion further defining the problem, showing historical context, previously attempted solutions, and description of whom the problem affects.

No one knows precisely what it is that is inherited. The chemistry of migraine, however, seems to have some connection with the nerve hormone named serotonin, which is naturally present in the brain. The amount of serotonin in the blood falls sharply at the onset of migraine, and one migraine drug, methysergide, or Sansert, seems to have some effect on serotonin. Methysergide is a derivative of lysergic acid (in fact Sandoz Pharmaceuticals first synthesized LSD-25 while looking for a migraine cure), and its use is hemmed about with so many contraindications and side effects that most doctors prescribe it only in the most incapacitating cases. Methysergide, when it is prescribed, is taken daily, as a preventive; another preventive

> Didion continues to outline the problem, providing details as evidence.

which works for some people is old-fashioned ergotamine tartrate, which helps to constrict the swelling blood vessels during the "aura," the period which in most cases precedes the actual headache.

Once an attack is under way, however, no drug touches it. Migraine gives some people mild hallucinations, temporarily blinds others, shows up not only as a headache but as a gastrointestinal disturbance, a painful sensitivity to all sensory stimuli, an abrupt overpowering fatigue, a stroke like aphasia, and a crippling inability to make even the most routine connections. When I am in a migraine aura (for some people the aura lasts fifteen minutes, for others several hours), I will drive through red lights, lose the house keys, spill whatever I am holding, lose the ability to focus my eyes or frame coherent sentences, and generally give the appearance of being on drugs, or drunk. The actual headache, when it comes, brings with it chills, sweating, nausea, a debility that seems to stretch the very limits of endurance. That no one dies of migraine seems, to someone deep into an attack, an ambiguous blessing.

> In this paragraph, Didion details the effects of the problem. Notice that she provides a discussion of general effects on many sufferers and then provides her own situation and effects as a personal detail.

My husband also has migraine, which is unfortunate for him but fortunate for me: perhaps nothing so tends to prolong an attack as the accusing eye of someone who has never had a headache. "Why not take a couple of aspirin," the unafflicted will say from the doorway, or "I'd have a headache, too, spending a beautiful day like this inside with all the shades drawn." All of us who have migraine suffer not only from the attacks themselves but from this common conviction that we are perversely refusing to cure ourselves by taking a couple of aspirin, that we are making ourselves sick, that we "bring it on ourselves." And in the most immediate sense, the sense of why we have a headache this Tuesday and not last Thursday, of course we often do. There certainly is what doctors call a "migraine personality," and that personality tends to be ambitious, inward, intolerant of error, rather rigidly organized, perfectionist. "You don't look like a migraine personality," a doctor once said to me. "Your hair's messy. But I suppose you're a compulsive housekeeper." Actually my house is kept even more negligently than my hair, but the doctor was right nonetheless: perfectionism can also take the form of spending most of a week writing and rewriting and not writing a single paragraph.

> Didion aligns herself with the problem, showing that, although she does not fit the standard definition of a migraine sufferer, her alignment with the problem comes in similar, yet distinct forms. Until this point in the essay, Didion's overarching goal has been to establish the reality of the problem, convincing the audience that this problem is real, that she suffers from it, as do others. It is difficult to refute her claim of problem given the thoroughness and the various ways in which she provides evidence of it.

But not all perfectionists have migraine, and not all migrainous people have migraine personalities. We do not escape heredity.

I have tried most of the available ways to escape my own migrainous heredity (at one point I learned to give myself two daily injections of histamine with a hypodermic needle, even though the needle so frightened me that I had to close my eyes when I did it), but I still have migraine. And I have learned now to live with it, learned when to expect it, how to outwit it, even how to regard it, when it does come, as more friend than lodger. We have reached a certain understanding, my migraine and I. It never comes when I am in real trouble. Tell me that my house is burned down, my husband has left me, that there is gunfighting in the streets and panic in the banks, and I will not respond by getting a headache. It comes instead when I am fighting not an open but a guerrilla war with my own life, during weeks of small household confusions, lost laundry, unhappy help, canceled appointments, on days when the telephone rings too much and I get no work done and the wind is coming up. On days like that my friend comes uninvited.

> Didion reaches her proposal in this paragraph. Her solution may not seem to solve the problem in the sense that we might expect. We probably expect Didion to propose: here is how I avoid migraines, or here is how I get rid of migraines. Instead, her proposal is more feasible: here is how I have learned to cope with the problem.

And once it comes, now that I am wise in its ways, I no longer fight it. I lie down and let it happen. At first every small apprehension is magnified, every anxiety a pounding terror. Then the pain comes, and I concentrate only on that. Right there is the usefulness of migraine, there in that imposed yoga, the concentration on the pain. For when the pain recedes, ten or twelve hours later, everything goes with it, all the hidden resentments, all the vain anxieties. The migraine has acted as a circuit breaker, and the fuses have emerged intact. There is a pleasant convalescent euphoria. I open the windows and feel the air, eat gratefully, sleep well. I notice the particular nature of a flower in a glass on the stair landing. I count my blessings.

> In this final moment, Didion shows us the benefit of her proposal. Notice, too, that Didion is not flagrant in her proposal. She does not tell others directly how to deal with their migraines; rather she shows the success of how she has learned to cope with her own. Though a subtle strategy, Didion convincingly suggests a solution of migraine management.

student example

Eric Trotta is an English major who plans to attend law school after graduation. Eric reads many kinds of literature and is particularly fond of Ernest Hemingway. Eric's connection to Hemingway seems evident because, like Hemingway, Eric has a passion for wildlife, in particular for fish. Eric hopes to combine his love of fish and fishing with his law school pursuits and become an environmental lawyer to work specifically with fisheries management policy. In his essay "Handling the Snakehead Invasion," Eric proposes that more research be conducted about the invasive species of northern snakehead fish that have taken up residence in the Potomac River. As you read Eric's essay, notice how he presents the details of his research in support of his proposal.

Handling the Snakehead Invasion

Eric Trotta

In the past decade, sensationalized reports of "Frankenfish" have surfaced across the eastern seaboard of the United States. The monstrous fish these reports discuss are actually a species of fish from Southeast Asia called the Northern Snakehead, *Channa argus*. The media has portrayed the snakehead as a destructive, hell-bent fish with a bottomless appetite for anything that fits in its mouth and the ability to crawl on land to search for new bodies of water to terrorize. It should come as no surprise that the popular response to finding snakeheads is to kill them on sight and eradicate them from any location they are found. This solution works when the snakeheads are found in small ponds and lakes because those are isolated populations that can be dealt with easily. However, from 2003–2006, there was a large increase in reported snakehead sightings throughout the states of Virginia, Maryland, and Delaware and many of those reports came from the Potomac River, an economically important watershed in the Washington, D.C. area. The large recreational and commercial fishing industries which rely on the Potomac River felt threatened by the impending invasion of snakeheads which they feared would collapse the river's ecosystem.

The biggest problem facing the fisheries management officers of the Potomac River is the lack of information regarding the impact of snakeheads. While there is a wealth of information on the northern snakehead's biology and ecological role, all of that research has been conducted in the species' native ecosystem. Very little is known about the snakehead's impact on native fish populations in the Potomac River. What is known is that the northern snakehead has already begun breeding throughout the river and the population is nearly established, if it has not become established already. Once a species has become established in a location, it is infinitely more difficult to eradicate because of successful breeding and widespread distribution. Wildlife management authorities, such as the Maryland Department of Natural Resources and the Virginia Department of Game and Inland Fisheries, lack enough knowledge about the northern snakehead's interaction with the native ecosystem to make informed decisions regarding what to do about their presence.

I suggest that the wildlife management departments that oversee the Potomac River conduct thorough research about the impact that snakeheads have on the river. The first step to adequately control the introduction of a new species into an ecosystem is to fully understand the way in which the new species interacts with the native species. An appropriate response to the snakehead problem can only be made by gathering a wealth of knowledge about the lifestyle of the northern snakehead population in the Potomac River. This solution lays the groundwork for methods of controlling the snakehead population. Knee-jerk responses to the snakehead threat may seem appropriate, but the scale of the snakehead incursion needs to be recognized first and foremost. I propose that wildlife management officials increase efforts to research snakehead ecology because there is a clear lack of knowledge surrounding the species' impact in the Potomac River. While the proposed solution does not directly affect the current population of snakeheads in the river, it will bolster future efforts to manage the species due to the valuable information gathered from the research.

The time to do this research is now, before the population grows too large to control. The consequences of failing to act early can be seen in the Midwest where Asian carp, *Hypophthalmichthys molitrix,* have completely taken over many tributaries of the Illinois River. The carp have outcompeted native species for food and space and as a result, vast stretches of the Illinois are almost devoid of fish other than the carp. This has resulted in the collapse of many fishing industries which rely on the native species to survive. Research about the snakehead population should be conducted in order to avoid the destruction that currently faces the Illinois River. If northern snakeheads prove to have strong negative impacts on the Potomac River ecosystem, efforts to control the population need to be made before it grows too large to handle.

Once more information about the ecological impacts of northern snakeheads on the Potomac River is identified, the appropriate response can be determined. If the impact of the northern snakehead is not as damaging as the media speculated, expensive eradication measures could be avoided. Further research into the role of the snakehead in the ecosystem could reveal that the species is economically beneficial. An example of a non-native fish becoming economically valuable in the United States is the introduction of Peacock bass, *Cichla ocellaris,* into the waters of South Florida. Originally introduced to control other species of invasive fish, the peacock bass has become an important economic resource for Florida, generating over 5 million dollars a year for Broward and Miami-Dade counties through the recreational fishing industry. With snakeheads already possessing the status of a highly valued game fish in their native range, and well-established recreational and commercial fisheries capitalizing on them, it is possible that they could reach that status in the Potomac River. However, until researchers fully understand the impact that northern snakeheads have on native fish populations, the economic impacts cannot be determined.

There are a few steps that must be taken to enact my proposed solution to the snakehead problem. First, government funding for snakehead research must be increased. There is simply not enough awareness or concern for the consequences of northern snakeheads taking over the Potomac River. While funding for wildlife management is already low, research about the snakehead population will not be expensive. The research methods which I suggest be used are low cost but effective. In order to better understand the impact that northern snakeheads have on the Potomac River, fisheries biologists should use population sampling to determine the role that snakeheads have in the ecosystem. One of the easiest ways to do this is through the examination of stomach contents. Dissecting snakeheads caught in the Potomac River will reveal what they feed on and in what quantity. Researchers should also examine the stomach contents of other predatory fish as well to determine if they feed on juvenile snakeheads and if their diet overlaps with that of the adult snakeheads. Information like this is incredibly valuable to assessing the snakehead's impact on native species because one of the biggest concerns regarding snakeheads is the lack of natural predators to keep the population in check. Researchers should also conduct studies about the spawning behavior of the northern snakeheads in the Potomac River to reveal which habitats and water qualities they prefer for breeding. The combined results of researching the feeding and breeding habits of the northern snakehead, as well as determining if they have any natural predators, will allow better decisions to be made to control the population in the Potomac River.

Opponents of my proposal may claim that researching the ecological impacts of the northern snakeheads is a waste of time. Many people believe that snakeheads are destructive and have negative impacts on the native fish populations in the Potomac River, and because of this they should be removed. Rushing to make a decision about how to control the snakehead population could cause more harm than good. Many eradication methods, such as poison and electroshocking, while effective, cause collateral damage to the ecosystem they were intended to save. Before deciding to kill the snakeheads off, the value of the native fish that will also be killed during the eradication must be considered. On the other hand, failure to take any action could be equally destructive. As the example of the Asian carp in the Illinois River shows, waiting too long to make a decision about what to do with an invasive species could allow the population to grow too large to effectively handle and result in the collapse of the entire ecosystem.

While there has been much concern regarding the impacts that northern snakeheads will have on the Potomac River, very little is understood about their role in the river's ecosystem. Before decisions about methods of controlling the population can be made, adequate research must be conducted. I have proposed that the wildlife management authorities which oversee the Potomac River increase the research that they are conducting about the snakehead population in order to fully understand their role in the ecosystem and so an informed decision about what to do might be rendered. By researching the feeding and breeding habits of the northern snakeheads in the Potomac River wildlife biologists will be able to adequately determine the impact that they have on the ecosystem, and reckless removal efforts can be substituted with informed decisions.

Thinking about Eric's Essay

1. Why do you suppose Eric makes this proposal? What might his exigency be?

2. Eric is straightforward in his proposal, identifying clearly that he proposes a particular plan of action. In what way does this directness affect how you read his proposal? Does his directness contribute to your sense of whether to accept his proposal or reject his proposal?

3. What role does background information play in Eric's proposal? Could he make the same proposal without providing the context in which he makes the proposal?

THE ROAD TO A
STRONG THESIS

SECOND THOUGHTS:
"There are lots of problems that require solutions within conversations about fisheries. Which problems interest me the most?"

SECOND THOUGHTS:
"But even that is an expansive question, and no single solution I propose will be feasible to solve the snakehead problem."

SECOND THOUGHTS:
"Maybe that is the problem: that we don't know enough about the problem to propose effective or feasible solutions."

RESPONSE:
"Is there really a snakehead 'problem'? There's not much research out there that shows that snakeheads are necessarily a problem, only that they are an invasive species. So how do I propose to solve the problem if it isn't clearly defined?"

RESPONSE:
"I'm interested in how we think about invasive species, but that's too broad of a subject to propose a solution for. Which invasive species scenario is most pressing?"

EXIGENCY:
"I need to write about the snakehead population in the Potomac River because the situation has been getting attention recently in the national press."

Purpose:
"To propose a solution to a fisheries problem."

ASSIGNMENT:
To write a proposal

THESIS:
"I propose that there needs to be more research conducted about the effects of the introduction of the northern snakehead into the Potomac River ecosystem."

Eric Trotta had a good idea about the subject he wanted to address and what he wanted to propose, but having an idea is not the same as having a thesis. To successfully make his proposal and fulfill his purpose, Eric had to develop a strong thesis. He probably followed a path much like this one to develop that thesis.

FINAL THOUGHTS:
"Now I can examine why there needs to be more research before other solutions are proposed."

Compulsory education is a form of education that students are required to participate in. In the United States, compulsory education is generally determined by age. Elementary school children are required to go to school, but some high school students can drop out and are not required to continue schooling. Although compulsory education has had many supporters, it has also had a number of critics. Paul Goodman was one of the most outspoken critics of compulsory education, and education policy in general. He was vocal in establishing what was known as the "deschooling movement."

The well-known essay "A Proposal to Abolish Grading" proposes that grading at the college level serves little purpose other than ranking students for the benefit of graduate and professionals schools and potential employers. As you read "A Proposal to Abolish Grading," pay particular attention to how Goodman defines the problem and proposes a solution.

A Proposal to Abolish Grading

Paul Goodman

Let half a dozen of the prestigious universities—Chicago, Stanford, the Ivy League—abolish grading, and use testing only and entirely for pedagogic purposes as teachers see fit.

Anyone who knows the frantic temper of the present schools will understand the trans-valuation of values that would be affected by this modest innovation. For most of the students, the competitive grade has come to be the essence. The naïve teacher points to the beauty of the subject and the ingenuity of the research; the shrewd student asks if he is responsible for that on the final exam.

Let me at once dispose of an objection whose unanimity is quite fascinating. I think that the great majority of professors agree that grading hinders teaching and creates bad spirit, going as far as cheating and plagiarizing. I have before me the collection of essays, *Examining in Harvard College*, and this is the consensus. It is uniformly asserted, however, that the grading is inevitable; for how else will the graduate schools, the foundations, the corporations know whom to accept, reward, hire? How will the talent scouts know whom to tap?

By testing the applicants, of course, according to the specific task-requirements of the inducting institution, just as applicants for the Civil Service or for licenses in medicine, law and architecture are tested. Why should Harvard professors do the testing for corporations and graduate schools?

The objection is ludicrous. Dean Whitla, of the Harvard Office of Tests, points out that the scholastic-aptitude and achievement tests used for admission to Harvard are a superexcellent index for all-around Harvard performance, better than high-school grades or particular Harvard course-grades. Presumably, these college-entrance tests are tailored for what Harvard and similar institutions want. By the same logic, would not an employer do far better to apply his own job aptitude test rather than to rely on the vagaries of Harvard section-men? Indeed, I doubt that many employers bother to look at such grades; they are more likely to be interested merely in the fact of a Harvard diploma, whatever that connotes to them. The grades have most of their weight with the graduate schools—here, as elsewhere; the system runs mainly for its own sake.

It is really necessary to remind our academics of the ancient history of Examination. In the medieval university, the whole point of the grueling trial of the candidate was whether or not to accept him as a peer. His disputation and lecture for the Master's was just that, a masterpiece to enter the guild. It was not to make comparative evaluations. It was not to weed out and select for an extra-mural licensor or employer. It was certainly not to pit one young fellow against another in an ugly competition. My philosophic impression is that the medieval thought they knew what a good job of work was and that we are competitive because we do not know. But the more status is achieved by largely irrelevant competitive evaluation, the less will we ever know.

(Of course, our American examinations never did have this purely guild orientation, just as our faculties have rarely had absolute autonomy; the examining was to satisfy Overseers, Elders, distant Regents—and they as paternal superiors have always doted on giving grades rather than accepting peers. But I submit that this set-up itself makes it impossible for the student to become a master, to have grown up, and to commence on his own. He will always be making A or B for some overseer. And in the present atmosphere, he will always be climbing on his friend's neck.)

Perhaps the chief objectors to abolishing grading would be the students and their parents. The parents should be simply disregarded; their anxiety has done enough damage already. For the students, it seems to me that a primary duty of the university is to deprive them of their props, their dependence on extrinsic valuation and motivation, and to force them to confront the difficult enterprise itself and finally lose themselves in it.

A miserable effect of grading is to nullify the various uses of testing. Testing, for both student and teacher, is a means of structuring, and also of finding out what is blank or wrong and what has been assimilated and can be taken for granted. Review—including high-pressure review—is a means of bringing together the fragments, so that there are Rashes of synoptic insight.

There are several good reasons for testing, and kinds of test. But if the aim is to discover weakness, what is the point of downgrading and punishing it, and thereby inviting the student to conceal his weakness, by faking and bulling, if not cheating! The natural conclusion of synthesis is the insight itself, not a grade for having had it. For the important purpose of placement, if one can establish in the student the belief that one is testing not to grade and make invidious comparisons but for his own advantage, the student should normally seek his own level, where he is challenged and yet capable, rather than trying to get by. If the student dares to accept himself as he is, a teacher's grade is a crude instrument compared with a student's self-awareness. But it is rare in our universities that students are encouraged to notice objectively their vast confusion. Unlike Socrates, our teachers rely on power-drives rather than shame and ingenuous idealism.

Many students are lazy, so teachers try to goad or threaten them by grading. In the long run this must do more harm than good. Laziness is a character-defense. It may be a way of avoiding learning; in order to protect the conceit that one is already perfect (deeper, the despair that one never can). It may be a way of avoiding just the risk of failing and being downgraded. Sometimes it is a way of politely saying, 'I won't.'

But since it is the authoritarian grown-up demands that have created such attitudes in the first place, why repeat the trauma? There comes a time when we must treat people as adults, laziness and all. It is one thing courageously to fire a donothing out of your class; it is quite another thing to evaluate him with a lordly F.

Most important of all, it is often obvious that balking in doing the work, especially among bright young people who get to great universities, means exactly what it says. The work does not suit me, not this subject, or not at this time, or not in this school, or not in school altogether. The student might not be bookish; he might be school-tired; perhaps his development ought now to take another direction. Yet unfortunately, if such a student is intelligent and is not sure of himself, he can be bullied into passing, and this obscures everything. My hunch is that I am describing a common situation. What a grim waste of young life and teacherly effort! Such a student will retain nothing of what he has 'passed' in. Sometimes he must get mononucleosis to tell his story and be believed.

And ironically, the converse is also probably commonly true. A student flunks and is mechanically weeded out, who is really ready and eager to learn in a scholastic setting, but he has not quite caught on. A good teacher can recognize the situation, but the computer wreaks its will.

Analyzing the Situation

1. We can assume that Paul Goodman did not envision you as his audience when writing "A Proposal to Abolish Grading." Yet you are now his audience. Recalling that we cannot always anticipate who all of our audiences will be, how do you respond as an unintended audience to Goodman's proposal? Are there any specific points in the proposal that indicate that Goodman did not anticipate you or your classmates being his audience?

2. Power, institution, and constraint all appear as important parts of Goodman's proposal. In what ways does he account or not account for each in his proposal?

3. "A Proposal to Abolish Grading" was originally published in Goodman's book *Compulsory Miseducation* in 1962. That book is now out of print and difficult to find in hard copy. Yet the book is now available as a PDF on a number of different web pages. In what ways does the media form and circulation of the essay change how we come to know the essay and how have the media and circulation changed the essay's audience?

professional example

Analyzing the Rhetoric

1. How would you describe Goodman's tone in this essay? How does his tone contribute to his ethos, and, in turn, to the degree you find his proposal convincing?

2. How does Goodman use evidence in "A Proposal to Abolish Grading" to support his proposal? What kinds of evidence does he use?

3. How does Goodman incorporate the parts of a proposal discussed in this chapter into "A Proposal to Abolish Grading"?

Discussing

1. Students are commonly asked to read Goodman's essay "A Proposal to Abolish Grading" and then write an analysis of the essay. In fact, these assignments are so common a simple Web search reveals sites that sell prewritten analytical essays about "A Proposal to Abolish Grading." Discuss why "A Proposal to Abolish Grading" might be so commonly assigned, and then discuss how you think Goodman might respond to the fact that clearinghouses are selling prewritten analytical essays about his essay and that students—we can assume—purchase and submit these prewritten essays as responses to class assignments for which they are evaluated.

2. How do you respond to Goodman's proposal? Discuss the effectiveness of his proposal as a proposal, addressing in particular whether you are convinced by his proposal in your own college situation.

3. Noting that "A Proposal to Abolish Grading" was first published in 1962, is its proposal still relevant? Discuss whether or not Goodman's claims in his proposal are still valid points of concern.

Writing

1. Consider the college situation in which you now participate: the role of grades on your campus, the role of grades and ranking in our culture, the role of ranking in a career field you might be interested in, the kinds of grades you earn, your family's understanding of the worth of grades, and so on. Then write your own proposal recommending that grades be either abolished or maintained in American colleges.

2. What factors besides grading play a role in how students are evaluated and ranked between college and their post-college lives? Write a proposal that suggests using other forms of assessment.

3. Write a proposal to your college administration recommending that they consider Goodman's essay in thinking about how grades function on your campus.

SIDE BY SIDE

Each of these three essays provides a different kind of proposal, and two of them do not necessarily propose solutions to problems. Didion indirectly proposes a method of convalescence for migraine sufferers, but her proposal is neither definitive nor comprehensive. Trotta proposes a need for further research about the invasive species snakehead before enacting any definitive response to their presence in rivers. His proposal asks for more information before a solution can be proposed. Goodman proposes the abolishment of grading systems in education, explaining the negative effects of grading. Despite their differences in approach, each proposes realistic possibilities in response to the identified problem. The following table helps identify how each writer approaches different aspects of his or her proposal.

	annotated example Joan Didion, "In Bed"	**student example** Eric Trotta, "Handling the Snakehead Invasion"	**professional example** Paul Goodman, "A Proposal to Abolish Grades"
PURPOSE	To describe living with migraines and propose a realistic solution for dealing with them	To propose action in regard to the presence of the northern snakehead in the Potomac River	To propose that traditional forms of grading in American universities be abolished
AUDIENCE	Readers who read magazines like *Life*, *The Saturday Evening Post*, *The New York Times*, and *Esquire*	Individuals interested in marine biology, marine ecology, invasive species, fisheries, and similar subjects	College administrators and teachers, and, perhaps, college students
PROPOSAL	To find a way to live with migraine headaches rather than futilely trying to avoid or conquer them	To conduct much more research regarding the effect of the northern snakehead's presence in the Potomac River	To abolish grading in American colleges and universities
ORGANIZATION	Didion provides substantial context about the problem, defining what migraines are and her experiences with them. Only then does she offer her proposal.	Eric provides background information about the problem to create context for his proposal. After making his proposal, he then shows why and how it is necessary within the context.	Goodman begins by making his proposal. He then provides information as to why he makes his proposal, and next anticipates criticisms, which he refutes.
LANGUAGE	Didion's language ranges from personal to authoritative as she alternates between clinical details about migraines and expressions of personal experiences.	Eric's language is professional, not pleading, confusing, or aggressive. Eric provides concrete, professional information and makes a direct, unambiguous proposal.	Goodman's language is authoritative and critical. At points, his language seems to convey a sense of superiority; it can, also, be dismissive at times. Yet Goodman makes clear why he makes such a proposal.
DISTRIBUTION	Circulated in her book *The White Album*	Shared with peers and teachers	Circulated in his book *Compulsory Miseducation*

Prepare

Characteristic	Preparing Your Proposal
The problem	Before you can propose a solution, you have to identify and understand the problem. Clearly understanding the problem will help you convince your audience of that problem and how it might be solved. An audience that recognizes a problem but has no investment in it is less likely to act on your proposal.
The scope	Some problems, such as global warming or poverty, are too big or complex to be addressed in a single proposal. Showing an audience what a proposal offers and what it doesn't helps define the limits, or scope, of the proposal. How you define the scope—whether in a sentence or in a long, detailed passage—depends on the purpose of the proposal.
The solutions	Ultimately, a proposal offers solutions. Problems often can be solved in various ways, so a proposal needs to specifically define the solution it offers. Solutions should be realistic and feasible.
The methods	Many audiences want to know not just the solution you offer but by what method that solution can be achieved. Defining the methods can mean explaining how a solution could be implemented. Defining your methods in some proposal situations may be one of the most significant parts of your overall proposal.
The plan of action	Detailing your plan of action shows your audience that you understand the specific demands of what you are proposing. A well-designed plan works in conjunction with a well-designed method and serves to help validate that method. Visuals such as flowcharts, schedules, calendars, or organizational charts can walk your audience through the plan and help them visualize it. Plans are best delivered chronologically in a step-by-step fashion.
The conclusion (or recommendation)	Proposals should reach a conclusion regarding a problem and its solution, then call an audience to action. Be explicit in showing what your proposal calls for. In some situations—like corporate/business situations—audiences do not have time to read all of the details of a proposal and, so, may read only the conclusion. Thus, the conclusion has to be specific in its recommendation, leaving no question about what is being proposed.

15.2 Apply multiple strategies for writing to propose

Strategy	Developing Your Proposal
Identify the problem	Where is the problem? How did it come to be? What is its history? Its context? Its value? Who does it affect? How has it been addressed in the past?
Define the problem	Convince your audience that the problem is real and important. If your audience does not believe there is a problem, they will have no need for your solution.
Define the scope	Show your audience what your proposal covers and what it does not.
Identify solutions	Before you can convince your audience to adopt a particular solution, you have to understand what the possible solutions are or can be. What causes the problem? What happens if it's solved? What happens if it's not solved? Are there similar problems that have already been solved that you can study for possible solutions?
Consider multiple solutions	Some proposals may offer a few solutions for the reader to choose from. Some may offer multiple solutions as a strategy for emphasizing a particular solution. When writing a proposal that offers a single approach, you should explore multiple solutions to determine which one really is the best for the situation.
Believe in the solution	As you develop your solution, be confident in it. It will be difficult to convince your audience that it is the right solution if you don't believe that it is.
Identify the method and plan	Be sure to explain what steps are necessary to complete a solution. Show what should be done as well as when, where, and how it should be done.
Explain feasibility	Convince your audience that the solution is, in fact, feasible—that it is doable within the circumstances. In many government, business, or grant proposals, an explanation of feasibility may include statements of budget or cost effectiveness.
Recommend a solution	Statements like "I recommend" or "you should" help guide an audience to a clear understanding of what the solution is. Good proposals lead to action because they are deliberate in recommending a solution.
Convince the audience that the solution is valid	Convince your audience that the proposed solution is the right one, which will lead to action.
Provide evidence	Like any good argumentative, analytical, or evaluative writing, proposals need to show an audience that there is evidence supporting the recommendation.
Anticipate questions and criticisms	Identify the potential criticisms and adjust the proposal to account for them. Acknowledge and refute the criticism, showing how your proposal is superior to the criticism and why the criticisms do not influence your solutions.
Address alternative solutions	One of the most convincing strategies you can use is showing how your proposed solution is superior to alternative solutions. Compare and contrast your solution either with other proposed solutions or with solutions that have been used historically with the problem or similar problems.
Propose ethically	Don't exaggerate claims of what your solution will provide. Don't promise to solve problems you can't solve.
Organize	There are two basic organizational strategies for presenting a proposal. Some proposals such as business or grant proposals follow a predefined template. Informal proposals are less regimented in their proposing and may take on an essayistic or narrative approach.

Organizational Approaches to Writing to Propose

The order in which you present your proposal can affect how your audience evaluates the proposal. Keep in mind that some proposals, like business or grant proposals, often follow defined or template organization strategies for ease of access and situational or contextual conventions. Informal proposals are less regimented in their structures and may take on an essayistic or narrative approach. Some proposals are guided in their organization by what the person or organization who has requested the proposal identifies as necessary to the proposal, as is the case in Requests for Proposals (RFPs).

No matter how you organize your proposal, you should begin by identifying and defining the details of the problem the proposal addresses. Without the context of the problem, the audience will not be able to situate the solution.

When proposing multiple solutions for an audience to evaluate, you may want to adopt this organizational approach. Begin by identifying the problem, then describe a range of possible solutions. From among those solutions, recommend one course of action and address possible concerns before concluding with a call to action.

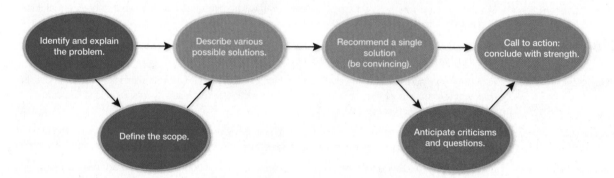

When recommending a single solution, consider organizing your proposal to establish your proposed solution first; then provide evidence, address possible questions or objections, and then conclude with a call to action.

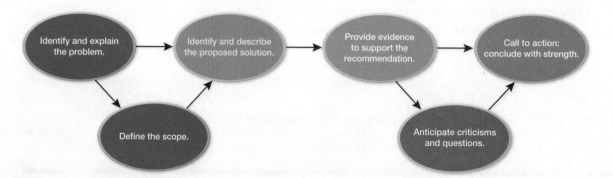

MAPPING
YOUR SITUATION

NETWORKS
- In what networks will my proposal circulate?
- How is my proposal related to other proposals?
- How might my proposal change the situation?

WRITERS AND SPEAKERS
- Who are the other writers and speakers in this situation?
- What other proposed solutions have they presented?
- Why have they been able to propose these solutions?

RELATIONS
- What is my relation to the situation?
- What are the relationships between writers/speakers, audience, and players?
- What are the relationships to external forces, like culture, religion, or politics?
- What are the power relations?

AUDIENCE
- Who will read my proposal?
- What do I know about my intended audience?
- Who will the proposal affect directly and indirectly?

MEDIUM AND METHOD
- What background information do my readers need to understand my proposal?
- In what genre will I propose a solution?
- What method will I use to convey my proposal?
- How will I distribute and circulate my proposal?

CONTEXT
- From where will my proposal emanate?
- Where will the proposal appear?
- What limits what I can propose?

PURPOSE
- Why am I making this proposal?
- What does my proposal need to accomplish?
- Does my proposal serve a specific purpose?

Mapping your situation will help you generate ideas you can use to compose. Start by answering these questions about each part of the situation. Begin with your purpose and work outward to relations and networks.

College Research and Topic Proposals

In many college courses, your teachers will ask you to write proposals identifying what you want to write about and how you plan to conduct your research. These research proposals can help you focus and can give you and your teacher the opportunity to discuss your ideas and plans before you write your papers. Good feedback on a research proposal can help you to situate your writing for the class and a specific assignment.

When writing a research proposal, first be sure to understand the situation: what does the assignment require? What do you think the instructor wants you to get out of the assignment? Second, understand the assignment as a situational problem that must be solved: what am I going to write about? Then be sure to include the following information:

Elements of a Research Proposal

Element	What to Include
Statement of the subject	Begin with a concise overview of the subject, identifying the area within which you propose to write. Identify key questions, debates, or controversies within the subject that you plan to address in your project.
Statement of scope	Like the statement of the subject, state the scope concisely, defining explicitly what you plan to focus on in your proposed project. Clearly explain what you plan to do. Consider this section in terms of a simple statement: "In the proposed project, I plan to _____."
Statement of rationale	Simply put, explain why you plan to do what you propose to do. You should explain what interests you about the topic, why you think it is important within the subject and situation, and why you see the topic as valid.
Statement of method	Explain how you plan to complete the assignment—what kinds of research you will conduct, what resources you will use, and how you will approach the writing and organization of the final paper. The statement of method helps teachers show you where and how to locate and evaluate suitable resources.
Annotated bibliography	Demonstrate your understanding of the situation by including an annotated bibliography of the resources you have already identified as useful and informative so your instructor will see that you have already begun to consider a topic or research approach in a formal way before proposing to write about that subject. An annotated bibliography—a summary or annotation of each work identified in a bibliographic list of sources—displays that you know how to locate and evaluate resources, that they are available, that they are appropriate to the situation, that you understand them, and that you have begun to consider how you will use them to further your research.

Grant Proposals

In college, you may write proposals to seek funding for a student organization to which you belong, and you may write or collaborate in writing grant proposals to gain funding for research projects. Grants are usually provided by government organizations, foundations, and corporations to support academic research. Grant proposals generally contain six parts:

Elements of a Grant Proposal

15.5 Discuss the role of requests for proposals (RFPs)

Element	What to Include
The statement of need or opportunity	Explains the context of the proposed research. It defines the problem within the situation. Grant proposals are usually written to audiences unfamiliar with the situation, so you need to explain the details of the situation and the problem in ways that someone unfamiliar with the situation will understand. Good grant proposals explain problems as opportunities, focusing on the positive rather than the negative.
The statement of goals and objectives	Outlines what you plan to accomplish in the proposed research. The goals of a project are the more general things you hope to achieve through the project; the objectives are the specific, measurable, accountable outcomes. Because many funding organizations provide support so they can benefit from your outcomes, this section is crucial because it explains what you hope to achieve. Be as detailed as possible.
The statement of activities	Details how you plan to accomplish your goals and objectives. This section provides the specifics of how you plan to complete the research, including your methods, resources, and activities. This section often includes a time line showing what you plan to do and when.
The statement of evaluation	Describes how you plan to evaluate your research to show that you met the proposed goals and objectives. In short, the statement of evaluation shows that you understand how to report your results and the success or failures of the project should you be granted funding and that you have a plan to provide that information.
The statement of organization	Explains who you or the group writing the proposal are. Grants are often awarded based on previous research success, so the statement of organization is, in essence, a résumé statement, explaining why you or the organization is qualified to conduct the proposed research.
Attachments	Are also included in many grant proposals to provide information like proposed budgets, tax information, or anything else relevant, but not critically important, to the grant.

Writing Projects

Essay

At some point this semester, your teacher will likely assign a research-based writing assignment for this class. In anticipation of that assignment and using the information provided in this chapter, write a topic/research proposal explaining what you would like to write about. Consult your course syllabus and your teacher for the assignment details so the proposal fits the assignment.

Visual Proposal

On page 345, read about how visuals can be used to support a written proposal and how visuals themselves can make proposals. Then complete this assignment. Consider the classroom in which you are using this book. From your perspective as a student, how might the room be better designed? Create a visual that proposes a new classroom designed specifically for the class that you are taking.

Digital

This chapter begins with a summary of Thomas Z. Freedman's proposal "A Kindle in Every Backpack: A Proposal for eTextbooks in American Schools," which proposes placing e-readers in elementary schools and high schools. The issue of e-textbooks is, of course, of equal importance for college students. In fact, you may be reading this text as an e-book. Investigate how digital textbooks are thought of and addressed on your campus, and consider how you think digital textbooks ought to be available to students. Write to your school administrators to propose an e-textbook program that you think might be more efficient and beneficial to students and faculty.

Research

Colleges or departments often conduct exit interviews with graduating seniors to gather feedback about their experiences in the college or department. These students often express a desire for greater connections between classroom/curricular experiences and the realities of job market needs. Identify one or two majors that you have considered or might consider for study. Look closely at the requirements for that major and what courses are required and recommended for it. Research what kinds of jobs in that field are really available and what those jobs generally expect in a new employee. Compare those needs with what the major offers, looking for inconsistencies or problems between the major and the jobs (keep in mind that not all majors are career driven). Then write a proposal that recommends one or more solutions for how the college or department could address the inconsistency. Consider how you define the problem as either a problem or an opportunity.

Radical Revision

In 1729, Jonathan Swift anonymously published one of the most famous proposals of all times: "A Modest Proposal for Preventing The Children of Poor People in Ireland From Being A burden to Their Parents or Country, and For Making Them Beneficial to The Public." The essay, of course, is satirical. If you are not familiar with the essay, which is commonly known simply as "A Modest Proposal," you can read it online. After reading the essay, create a visual media production—any medium you choose— that conveys Swift's proposal.

Visuals and Proposals

Visuals can be used many ways when writing to propose. In proposals that include spatial information—such as a proposal to construct an addition to a building or to alter school or voting districts—visuals can be used to show how that new space might look. Figure 15.1, for instance, identifies proposed elementary and middle school attendance areas for the Baltimore school district for the 2010–2011 school year.

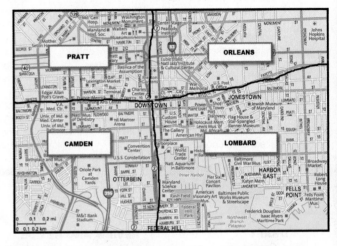

FIGURE 15.1 Proposed elementary and middle school attendance areas for the Baltimore school district.

Likewise, some proposals—such as architectural design proposals—may rely predominantly or solely on renderings, models, drawings, or other visuals to propose how something—for example, a new building or memorial—might look if built. In this way, some visuals are themselves propositions of what something might look like. Digital rendering technologies have enhanced the possibility of visually proposing. Look, for example, at Figure 15.2, which shows a digital rendering of a proposed construction at Eagles Watch Resort in Hampstead, North Carolina.

FIGURE 15.2 A digital rendering proposing a construction at Eagles Watch Resort in Hampstead, North Carolina.

Writing Process
GUIDELINES

Use the guidelines in this chart to plan, review, and evaluate your process for writing. Each step in the process should support the overall purpose of your project.

SITUATE

- Understand your reasons for proposing a solution in the situation (exigencies).
- Consider who your proposal will affect (players).
- Understand how relations affect your proposal.
- Indentify how your proposal is limited by constraints.
- Recognize the speakers or writers of counter-proposals.
- Identify and analyze the audiences involved in the situation.
- Consider what genres, media, and methods have been used to make claims in this situation.
- Acknowledge how various institutions and power affect the proposal.
- Consider the ecological relationships between your solution and others.

PLAN

- Confirm your reason for proposing a solution (exigency).
- Clarify your purpose in writing or speaking the proposal.
- Consider what might be the best genre, media, and method for you to make your proposal.
- Analyze what you know and what you need to discover before voicing your proposal.
- Begin to take notes.

RESEARCH

- Determine what kind of evidence you will need and the best ways to locate it.
- Conduct research to gather the evidence you need.
- Identify how your evidence supports your proposal.
- Confirm that your evidence will be valid within the situation.
- Identify any visuals you may need.
- Organize your evidence.

DRAFT

- Confirm your purpose.
- Confirm that your choices in genre, media, and method will be effective within the situation.
- Draft and organize the content of your proposal.
- Employ the visual process to develop any visuals you will need.
- Design your document.

REVIEW AND REVISE

- Review your proposal for clarity and concision.
- Review your proposal for accuracy.
- Review your proposal for extraneous or irrelevant information.
- Review your proposal for organizational approach.
- Review your proposal for explanations of necessary key terms.
- Review your proposal for style appropriate to the situation.
- Confirm your research and citations.
- Review your proposal for visual effectiveness and readability.

EDIT

- Proofread carefully.
- Correct all mechanical and grammatical errors.

EVALUATE

- Seek feedback from peers (take advantage of peer editing opportunities).
- Ask for feedback from a representative member of the target audience.
- Ask for feedback from an editor in whom you are confident.
- Evaluate the usefulness of any feedback you receive and revise accordingly.

DISTRIBUTE/CIRCULATE

- Consider technologies of circulation.
- Publish in a form that will be visible within the situation.
- Identify methods for increasing circulation (like search engine optimization) within and beyond the specific situation.
- Consider audience access.
- Identify possible sources of audience response.

Seeking Feedback

Peers, target audiences, and editors can offer valuable observations that will strengthen your writing. You will encourage more constructive feedback from these readers if you structure your questions for them carefully. Consider asking these kinds of questions to get feedback:

EVALUATION Guidelines

INITIAL REACTION
- What are your initial reactions to the proposal?
- Are you convinced that the problem defined in the proposal is really a problem?
- Is the proposal convincing?
- Does the proposal seem feasible?
- What are the strengths and weaknesses of the proposal?
- Generally speaking, what is the primary thing the writer must do to improve the proposal?

SITUATION
- Who do you understand the proposal to be written for?
- Does the proposal seem appropriately detailed for the situation?

READABILITY
- Do you understand the proposal, particularly how the solution fits the problem?
- Does the proposal flow from description of the problem to description of the solution?
- Does the proposal's conclusion make a strong argument?

CONTENT
- Has the writer clearly defined the problem?
- Has the writer clearly identified whom the problem affects or the situation of the problem?
- Has the writer clearly explained the proposed solution?
- Is it clear what the proposal recommends?
- Does the proposal provide adequate evidence in support of the usefulness of the solution?
- Does the proposal leave the audience in a position to act?
- Has the writer provided a clear scope in the proposal?

VISUALS
- Does the writer use visuals to propose?
- If so, are the visuals appropriate to the purpose?
- Do the visuals work in conjunction with the writing or independently?
- Are the visuals clear and easy to read?
- Does the document design distract from or support the proposal's purpose and/or readability?
- What recommendations regarding visuals do you have for the writer?

MECHANICS
- What, if any, evident mechanical distractions are in the proposal?
- Which sentences, if any, are unclear?
- Which sentences or paragraphs are particularly well written?
- Are all references cited appropriately?

Summary

To propose is to present for consideration. The overarching purpose of any proposal is to bring an audience to action by providing the information needed to adopt (or reject) the proposed solution. In this way, proposals are closely related to argumentative writing, analytical writing, and evaluative writing. Before you can propose a realistic and feasible solution, however, you have to identify and understand the problem. In addition, you must clarify the scope of the proposal, your methods, and your plan of action as well as provide evidence supporting the recommendation. Finally, a strong proposal anticipates and addresses a reader's questions or criticism.

In your college courses, you may write proposals identifying what you want to write about and how you plan to conduct your research. In other college activities, you may write proposals to seek funding for a student organization, and you may write, or collaborate in writing, grant proposals to gain funding for research projects. Visuals can be used when writing to propose, for example, to show how a proposed physical change might look. In addition, graphics such as charts and graphs can be used to estimate projected numerical information. Some proposals—such as architectural design proposals—may rely predominantly on visuals to propose a new area or structure.

Chapter Review

1. What is the function of a proposal?

2. What three rhetorical approaches are generally synthesized in a proposal?

3. Identify and explain three characteristics of proposal writing.

4. Identify and explain eight strategies for writing to propose.

5. What are two reasons your teacher might ask you to write a research or topic proposal to propose what you might write about in a significant writing assignment?

6. What are the six primary parts of a grant proposal?

7. How might you use visuals in a proposal?

Thinking and Writing about the Chapter

Reflection

Now that you have read about writing to propose, look back at the journal entry or blog post you wrote in response to the prompt at the beginning of the chapter. Now how would you explain strategies for proposing? Would they be the same explanations as before?

Discussion Threads

1. What kinds of proposals—either formal or informal—do you encounter? Where do you encounter them? Discuss the role of proposals in your personal life, your civic life, and your college life.

2. What role do proposals play in your college life? Do you and your teachers negotiate assignment requirements and due dates based on proposals students make in class? Do you propose topics to write about or readings for class assignments? Discuss how proposals might provide opportunities for discussion and collaboration between students and teachers and why, perhaps, teachers might accept or deny students' proposals in such matters.

3. The beginning of this chapter introduces Thomas Z. Freedman's proposal "A Kindle in Every Backpack: A Proposal for eTexbooks in American Schools." You can download the proposal from the Democratic Leadership Council website. Once you have read the proposal, consider what your initial reactions are to the idea proposed in "A Kindle in Every Backpack." Discuss with your classmates how you respond to the proposal and why you reach those conclusions.

Collaboration

1. On April 20, 2010, the British Petroleum (BP) offshore drilling rig Deepwater Horizon exploded in the Gulf of Mexico, creating one of the largest oil spills in U.S. history. BP attempted several times to stop the oil flow, but the extreme depth of the well hampered its efforts. Many people and organizations began to propose solutions for capping the well, cleaning up the leaked oil, and preventing future spills. Working in groups, locate three to five proposals dealing with a single aspect of the Deepwater Horizon oil spill. These proposals can be ones made by professionals or amateurs, can be formal or informal, and may be written or presented in other media. Analyze the ways in which the proposals define the problem and try to convince an audience that their solution is feasible. Write an assessment of what you find in your analysis.

2. In the aftermath of the September 11, 2001, attacks on the World Trade Center in New York, the Lower Manhattan Development Corporation (LMDC) was established to oversee the rebuilding of Ground Zero locations. In January 2002, the LMDC solicited proposals from 50 artists and architects to propose designs for an on-site memorial. Those proposals relied on visuals to depict what the proposed constructions would look like. The 50 proposals were then displayed at a gallery in New York. Twice the LMDC attempted to identify finalists from the proposals, and twice the public rejected the proposed finalists. Consequently, the LMDC had to reissue its call for design proposals.

In small groups, take some time to learn about the proposals that were submitted and the process through which the LMDC finally found its final design. Then write a short analysis of how the original proposals were presented and evaluated.

Writing

1. Has your campus adopted a sustainability program, a green program, or a similar program to encourage sustainability on your campus? If so, investigate how your campus promotes that program. Consider the differences between what the program proposes to do and what really happens on campus. Then write a proposal suggesting how those gaps might be closed. If you understand the program as working, then write a proposal about extending or expanding the program. If your campus does not have such a program, write a proposal to initiate one.

2. On February 27, 2007, author Richard Louv provided testimony before the U.S. House of Representatives Interior and Environmental Subcommittee about the way children understand and interact with the environment. His testimony, titled "Leave No Child Inside," was based on an article by the same title published in the March/April 2007 edition of *Orion* magazine. In both documents, Louv proposes methods for increasing children's interaction with, education about, and respect for natural environments. You can find Louv's testimony on the Interior Department and *Orion* magazine websites. Read these two pieces and analyze them as proposals. Then write an assessment of how each functions as a proposal.

3. What is the biggest problem you face on a regular basis? Why does it continue to be a problem? Who does the problem affect besides you? Analyze the problem and formulate a list of possible solutions. Then write a proposal that offers the most feasible solution for solving the problem. Consider problems you encounter in your personal life, your college life, your work life, or your community life.

Local Situation

As a student, you have a different perspective of your campus than do the school's teachers, administrators, and staff members, yet most of the problems that arise on campus are likely addressed by those other populations. In fact, campus employees and administrators are often not aware of particular problems until students inform them. In many instances, simply reporting a problem is appropriate. For example, a student may report a plumbing problem in a dorm restroom without having to propose solutions for solving that problem. However, in some situations, you should want to have a voice in how campus problems get solved. In those situations, proposing solutions can be an important part of your participation in the campus community.

For this assignment, identify a problem affecting students on your campus that goes unnoticed by campus employees and administrators. Then write a formal proposal that offers a solution. Remember to focus the proposal on a single, realistically solvable problem. Direct the proposal to the audience on your campus that has the authority to address and solve the problem. Part of your task will be convincing the audience that the problem is real and worth addressing. Once you and your teacher have agreed that the assignment is complete, consider presenting it to that audience.

Writing Visuals

16 | Finding, Adapting, and Making Visuals

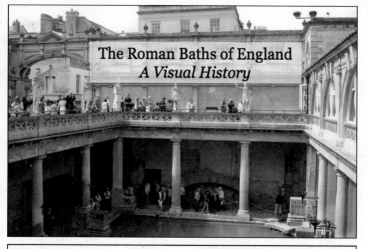

The Roman Baths of England
A Visual History

The Roman Empire
27 B.C.–410 A.D.

After the assassination of military leader Julius Caesar in 44 B.C., Augustus seizes power and officially forms the Roman Empire in 27 B.C. For the next 200 years Rome will flourish, experiencing relative stability and prosperity. But around 300 A.D., the empire begins to weaken due to economic difficulties, persistent invasions, and ineffective leaders. In 410 A.D., the steadily declining Roman Empire shows its inability to protect itself when the Visigoths, a Germanic tribe, sack Rome.

Julius Caesar leads first Roman invasion of Britain

Caesar is assassinated

The reign of Augustus

The height of the Roman Empire

Political and economic instability

The end of the Roman Empire

| 54 B.C. | 44 B.C. | 29 B.C.–14 A.D. | 100–250 A.D. | 4th Century A.D. | 410 A.D. |

Learning Objectives

16.1 Use databases, web searches, and other resources to locate and obtain visuals from other sources

16.2 Change, revise, or modify visuals as needed to meet the needs of your rhetorical situation

16.3 Use visuals ethically by applying principles of accuracy, clarity, and responsibility to specific situations

16.4 Create visuals to meet your own needs and situation by understanding and applying a multistep composing process

Before you read this chapter

Think about the role visuals play in the writing you do. Do you put visuals in your academic writing? If so, where do you find those visuals? How do you decide which visuals to put in a document? If you don't use visuals in your documents, why don't you? What are the constraints you face that contribute to your decision not include visuals? In your blog or journal, write about how you use or don't use visuals when you write in response to academic assignments.

Processes for finding, adapting, making, and using visuals, like writing processes, require analytic thought, situational understanding, and recursive steps. Because writers find and repurpose visuals from other sources (like an image search on the Web), alter preexisting visuals, or make new visuals, and because visuals can encompass a wide range of elements and forms—drawings, photographs, videos, animations, and infographics—we need to understand the act of making and using visuals as similar to the way we understand the act of writing. We can understand processes of finding or making visuals as much like writing processes: they begin with planning and designing (like planning and drafting), then undergo a phase of testing and evaluation, then require careful analyses of the visual and the results of the evaluation, and finish with redesigning or revising the visual.

We can think of the way that most writers approach visuals in three ways:

- *Finding* refers to locating a visual that someone else has made for a similar or other purpose and using it to meet your needs. Finding may also refer to identifying design ideas and using them to influence your designs.
- *Adapting* is related to finding in that you locate a visual or design to use for your own purposes, but you alter it in ways to make it more applicable to your needs.
- *Making* refers to creating an original visual, to starting with a blank screen or page and designing a visual to fit your needs specifically.

This chapter provides details about each of these approaches, including guidelines for finding, adapting, and making visuals. Throughout the chapter, you will see a number of examples by student author Mariah O'Toole, who composed an image essay, "The Roman Baths of England: A Visual History," which appears at the end of the chapter.

Finding and Adapting

Writing in college often requires that you address some visual element of your document, whether the design of a printed document or the inclusion of visuals to accompany a written report. Because writing classes don't often teach students how to make visuals but may ask students to include visuals—like infographics or diagrams or charts—students frequently locate and include visuals that others have made. Finding a visual entails locating a visual, like an image, that someone else has made and published, taking that visual from its original context, and using it for a purpose or in a context other than for what it was originally intended. A visual can also be located and used simply as an example, not altering its purpose but identifying it as an example of that purpose. For example, in order to create the image in Figure 16.1 for her image essay about the Roman baths, Mariah O'Toole located six visuals in an online image database and adapted them to suit her needs in the image essay.

Often writers who take visuals and repurpose them for their own uses also adapt the visuals to more appropriately suit their purposes. Adapting a visual can include

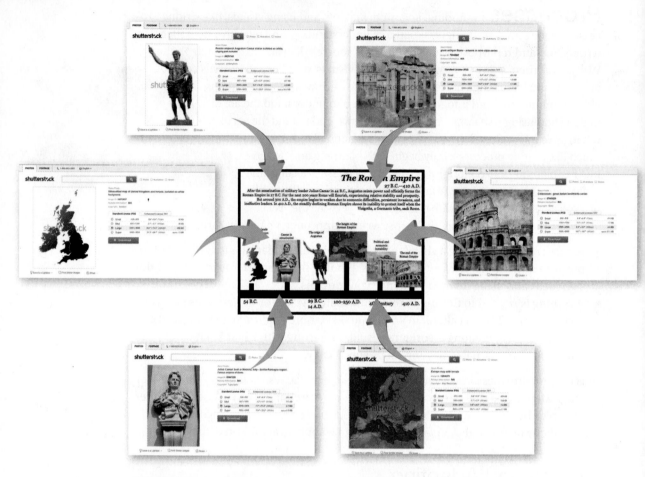

FIGURE 16.1 Mariah O'Toole adapted images she found online to fit her needs.

cropping, resizing, altering colors, using only details, reframing, distorting, or anything you do to alter the original image for your needs. In fact, simply by taking a visual from one context and placing it in another, you have changed that visual because it will be seen differently. Finding and adapting visuals requires that you engage in processes for locating, altering, and using visuals.

1. Understand the situation; be certain you understand your purpose and audience.
2. Conduct research in order to best understand how visuals have been used already in the situation.
3. Take notes regarding the kind of visual you need to include.
4. Locate multiple visuals that might serve your needs.

5. Create drafts of your text using the visuals.

6. Seek feedback about the visuals; ask specifically about whether they convey the information or serve the purpose as you intend them.

7. Revise based on the feedback by either changing the visuals further or replacing them with others you have located.

8. Solicit more feedback.

9. Revise and render final copies.

Finding Visuals

There are a many accessible and useful resources for finding visuals. Keep in mind that finding visuals requires careful analyses in order to locate the most appropriate visuals. Likewise, most search mechanisms used in locating visuals require that you enter search terms to describe what you are looking for. Search terms are a form of descriptive writing, and learning how to describe the visuals you want can affect your ability to locate those visuals. You can generally locate the visuals you may need from four basic kinds of sources:

16.1 Use databases, web searches, and other resources to locate and obtain visuals from other sources

- *Internet and web searches*—Keep in mind that many of the visuals you find online are copyright protected; if you use a visual you take from the Web or Internet, it is your responsibility to seek permission to use that visual and to acknowledge its source. Common sources include Google Image Search, Yahoo! Image Search, Ask Images, Picsearch, and Pixsy. Symbols.com is useful for locating symbols; Animation Factory is a good resource for animation, PowerPoint backgrounds, and video backgrounds. Most web searches will also identify visuals found in databases and hosting sites.

- *Databases*—Databases provide numerous kinds of visuals ranging from art reproductions to stock photography to drawings to photojournalism images to videos and animations. Databases provide such a vast range of visual possibilities that advertising agencies, web designers, publishers, and just about anyone who uses visuals professionally will use database visuals for their work when they can. Look back, for instance, at Mariah O'Toole's visual in Figure 16.1, which she created by combining multiple images from a single database.

- *Hosting sites*—Visual hosting sites, like Flickr, are used to house and share various kinds of visuals, like photos and videos. Hosting sites are also often used by bloggers and other web writers to house the visuals they embed in their work rather than storing them on their own hardware. Many hosting sites are searchable, and you can find useful visuals to use on many hosting sites.

- *Clip art*—Clip art refers to pictures that you clip or copy from previously printed material. The term refers to physically cutting a picture from a paper document to use in another context, but in the digital age it also refers to precrafted graphics that are made available for public use. Nearly every word processing and publishing application contains libraries of clip art, and many businesses and industries maintain context-specific clip art libraries. Even though a number of commercial galleries do sell their clip art, electronic clip art was developed to provide nonartists with simple graphics that are not bound by copyright and licensing restrictions. Most clip art is considered to be in the public domain, but you should confirm that any clip art you use does not require permission. Although electronic clip art is readily available and easy to locate, it usually conveys an amateur look.

16.2 Change, revise, or modify visuals as needed to meet the needs of your rhetorical situation

Adapting Visuals

Often just taking a visual from one situation and reconstituting it in another may not fully satisfy your needs. You may need to adapt visuals to more fully serve the purpose of your document (see Figure 16.2). Editing software, like Photoshop, GIMP, or iPhoto, offers tools to change visuals. When adapting visuals, you will still need to identify the original source of the visual, but you can alter the visual to better suit your

FIGURE 16.2 Original image (outlined in red) changed multiple ways for various uses.

needs. Locating and adapting visuals inherently imposes some constraints and limits in what you can convey visually. Sometimes taking and changing visuals is a lot like using the wrong tool to get a job done: sometimes it might work; sometimes it won't.

Some common changes include:

- Resizing
- Changing colors
- Altering perspective
- Cropping
- Distorting
- Removing details
- Applying filters

Using Visuals Ethically

As you locate and adapt visuals, you will want to be alert to several ethical considerations:

16.3 Use visuals ethically by applying principles of accuracy, clarity, and responsibility to specific situations

- *Manipulation*—Digital manipulation offers you the opportunity to change visuals in such a way that they become more applicable to your purpose. However, manipulated images can also present false or inaccurate representations of information. Image manipulation can be used to misinform, alter opinions, and convey inaccurate or incorrect information. In academic work, some forms of manipulation might be construed as plagiarism or other violations of academic honesty. Manipulating a visual is different from adapting a visual in that manipulation implies a devious alteration that is intended to influence an audience for your advantage.
- *Permission*—Copyright holders have the right to place restrictions on how their visuals can be used in order to ensure that they are not misused and do not discredit the owner or maker. In many contexts, using a visual without permission is not only unethical but may also result in legal action.

    For most college class assignments, you may use copyrighted material without seeking permission. Keep in mind, though, that just because something is legal does not mean that it is also ethical. You should consider the ethical implications of fair use and permissions, not just the legality. Keep in mind, too, that in most academic settings, taking and changing visuals is considered the equivalent of taking or changing someone's written work: be sure to cite any visual you take or change.
- *Citation*—If you capture an image from a web page or database and use it in a class assignment, you should identify the source with a citation, even if you have changed the image to apply to your situation. Often academic writing assignments require that you use visuals that others have produced—like a government chart or a scientific diagram—in order to show accurate and meaningful information.

In such instances, it is always best to cite the source of those visuals. Failure to cite the source of a visual you have taken or changed is a form of plagiarism.

- *Accuracy*—The visuals you present should accurately represent the information you wish to convey. Be sure to carefully evaluate your visuals to ensure that they accurately represent information. One common way in which writers unintentionally present inaccurate information is by not confirming relationships between captions and visuals; be sure your captions and visuals correlate.

- *Representation*—Consider how the visuals you use represent you as a writer or the organization from which you have taken a visual. Visuals contribute to ethos and to representation of others in the situation. For example, imagine that you have been asked to design a document for a digital imaging supply company. How differently would an audience perceive the quality of the product you were representing if you used the visual in Figure 16.3(a) versus Figure 16.3(b)? Consider how the aesthetic and quality of the visual represents the product, the company, and the writer.

- *Obfuscation*—Visuals are used to clarify information; however, they can also be used to obfuscate information. For example, in March 2005, one of the top news stories in the United States was a court decision to remove the feeding tube from Terri Schiavo following a seven-year legal battle between her parents and her husband about whether or not to continue life support. Schiavo had been diagnosed as being in a fixed vegetative state and unlikely to recover. When covering the story, a major news site published a chart depicting the results of a poll that asked "Based on what you have heard or read about the case, do you agree with the court's decision to have the feeding tube removed?" The poll showed that 62 percent of Democrats polled agreed, 54 percent of Republicans polled agreed, and 54 percent of Independents polled agreed. Consider the way the bar graph in Figure 16.4 reports the information from the poll. Following complaints about the visual representation of the poll, the site replaced the original graph with one similar to Figure 16.5. This example shows how easily visual representation can lead readers to see information in ways that might obfuscate.

(a)   (b)

FIGURE 16.3 Varying quality of representation linked to choice of visuals.

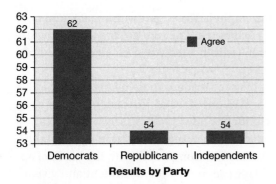

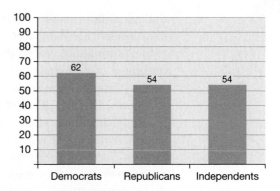

FIGURE 16.4 Graph depicting information from a March 2005 poll. Notice the scale on the left, which begins at 53 percent.

FIGURE 16.5 Revised bar graph, with the vertical scale on the left adjusted to begin at zero. Revised, this graph tells a different visual story than the original.

- *Concealment*—Visuals can also conceal information. One obvious method of concealing is through cropping. Sometimes cropping can remove key information and thereby conceal the context or details of the visual information. Consider Figure 16.6(a), for example, which was reported to depict a polar bear resting near Arctic Village, Alaska. The original picture in Figure 16.6(b), however, clearly indicates that the picture was taken in a zoo. In this case, the image cropping and the caption used conceal contextual information in order to influence how readers perceive the visual.
- *Clarity*—Three primary factors affect visual clarity: size, readability, and resolution. Intentionally including visuals that are too small to be read can be an unethical way of hiding information from readers. Presenting visuals that are either

(a) Photograph claiming to show polar bear resting near Arctic Village, Alaska.

(b) Original, uncropped picture revealing more contextual information

FIGURE 16.6 Cropped visual used to conceal information and original photograph.

difficult or impossible to read because of their placement within a document or because they are too cluttered may prevent readers from getting a clear picture of the information. Visuals that are not easily located when noted in the text of a document may confuse readers.

- *Access*—In order for your visuals to be of use to readers, those readers must be able to access the visuals. Be alert to the formats and sizes of the visuals you use. Keep in mind that some servers may have difficulty downloading large visual files and some software applications may have trouble reading less-used image or graphic formats. Make sure your visual file formats are compatible with the kinds of applications your audience will most likely use to read the document and visuals. Presenting oversized or unusually formatted visuals might be interpreted as an attempt to keep information from readers.

16.4 Create visuals to meet your own needs and situation by understanding and applying a multistep composing process

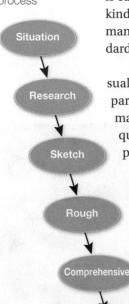

Situation

Research

Sketch

Rough

Comprehensive

Revise

Render

Making Visuals

The best way to obtain visuals that specifically fit your needs may be to make your own. Taking digital photographs is fairly simple, and the hardware—digital cameras—is easily available and simple to use. In addition, most computers now contain some kind of basic paint and draw programs that allow users to make simple graphics, and many word processors and publishing applications contain basic draw tools as standard features.

No matter what tools you use to make your visuals, we can think of making visuals as being a seven-part process, but like the phases of any writing process, the parts of processes used to make visuals never occur as linearly as they appear. You may find yourself combining phases or engaging several at once or in different sequences. We can think of the process of making visuals as generally following this pattern:

Understand the Situation

You can use many of the same approaches you would use to analyze and understand a rhetorical situation in order to produce visuals for that situation. Visual design and production are about solving problems. Like writing, making visuals requires that you be attentive to the functional problems you face—how the visual will solve or contribute to solving the problem at hand—and the rhetorical problems you face—what choices you make in creating your visual. You might include visual elements in order to increase comprehension, clarify, illustrate, organize, emphasize, highlight, establish authority, reach a broader audience, gain attention, or add aesthetic or stylistic sophistication to your work. No matter the reason for using visuals, you need to be confident that the visuals will serve your overall purpose and reach your audience.

Conduct Research

In order for you to solve the visual rhetorical problems to ensure that your visual will solve functional problems, you must first know all you can about the situation. One of the most important parts of conducting research prior to making a visual is to determine the range of possibilities of what is appropriate or useful to the situation. The resources available to you and the situation itself can constrain what visuals will and won't be effective in a given situation.

You probably already have strategies for locating information and keeping track of notes you take when you write; you may want to develop similar strategies for keeping up with visuals. Professional artists and designers often use "morgue files" for this kind of visual research. The idea of morgue files originated with police investigators and news reporters. For police investigators, morgue files were the boxes of evidence and files kept about unsolved murder cases, in case they might be needed later—hence, the name "morgue files." Thus, we can think of morgue files as kinds of archives or databases. Of course, now, this kind of filing, archiving, and researching occurs digitally rather than with clippings and boxes. Artists and designers adopted the idea of morgue files as a way of gathering ideas and examples to help them create their own works. Visual morgue files can include photos, magazine clippings, drawings, videos, infographics, web designs, product labels, products, sculptures, or anything that might inform or inspire your own visual work.

Tech Tip

You may want to consider using a web-based file hosting service or other cloud computing service to store your morgue file. Using such a service can help alleviate storage pressure on your computer memory; likewise, most file hosting services maintain backup copies of your files, making it nearly impossible to lose your files. Most file hosting services are capable of storing any kind of file: text-based, image, video, and audio. And you can access your files from anywhere with an Internet connection. File hosting services like Dropbox and Evernote offer free file hosting with limited memory space, though you can purchase additional space as needed.

Make Drafts

Just like writing, making visuals requires that you draft your ideas before creating a final product. These are some strategies for drafting visuals:

- *Write*—Before you begin making your visuals, it is a good idea to begin by writing about the visuals you need to make. Writing can help you flesh out your ideas, identify details, and discover possible approaches. Lists are often a good way to think through what needs to be included in your visual. For example, if you are working with the design of a specific document, you might want to list the details and ideas you want to work with: typography, layout, page size, margins, and so on.

- *Use sketches, thumbnails, and wireframes* —Although visuals are most likely to be rendered digitally, many graphic artists and designers agree that it's always best to begin creating visuals by sketching or thumbnailing your ideas. Thumbnailing should be thought of as a method for exploring ideas. Thumbnails are rough sketches of your ideas. Sketches are also preliminary drawings, but you can think of the thumbnails as different from sketches in that thumbnails attempt to show complete designs, whereas sketches may depict details or parts. Wireframes are similar to thumbnails and sketches in that they are rough drawings for layout and designs. Sketching, thumbnailing, and wireframing are so similar that it's often difficult to distinguish between the activities.

You can think about sketching, thumbnailing, and wireframing as being similar to note taking or writing early drafts of a document; the idea isn't to make the final copy in the first attempt, but to get ideas and concepts down to work with. Sketching doesn't require that you know how to draw with great artistic flair, only that you be able to convey to yourself visually the ideas you have. Mariah O'Toole, whose image essay appears in this chapter, used both wireframes and sketches to plan and produce her image essay (see Figure 16.7).

Sketching, thumbnailing, and wireframing can help you:[1]

- *Quickly explore ideas*—Sketching is much quicker than designing on a computer, so within limited amounts of time, you can explore multiple ideas through rough sketches, saving you time.
- *Explore layout and composition possibilities*—Sketching can assist you in developing layout ideas quickly and can help you recall ideas and plans. Like all sketching, your preliminary ideas don't have to look exactly like your final product. Mariah O'Toole's wireframe in Figure 16.7, for example, helped her determine the organization and layout of her image essay.
- *Explore variations*—Sketching allows you to make multiple versions of an idea so you can compare them in order to decide which might work best. By sketching, you can consider multiple solutions to visual rhetorical and functional problems. The more variations you develop, the more solutions you have to work with toward a final, dynamic visual.
- *Seek feedback*—Using your sketches—particularly when you sketch multiple approaches to a visual—can serve as a method for gathering initial feedback before you invest the time in producing the final visual. Seeking feedback early in your process for making visuals can save lots of time throughout the process and can help you ensure that your visuals successfully reach your audience. Show your sketches to friends, classmates, colleagues, coworkers, and representative audience members and ask for their input. The best visuals grow

---

[1] Many of the concepts regarding sketching found here are adapted from Sean Hodge's tutorial "The Role of Sketching in the Design Process" on the Tuts + video tutorial Photoshop channel.

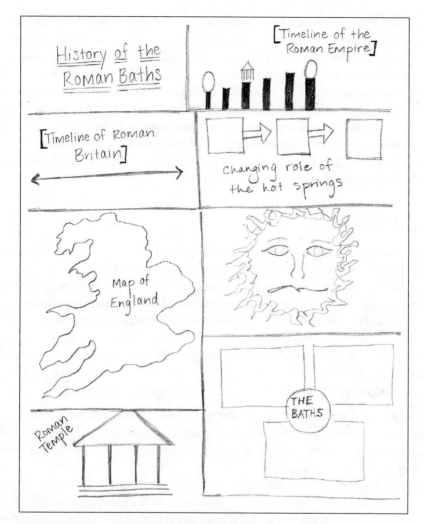

FIGURE 16.7 Mariah O'Toole's wireframe used to design her image essay "The Roman Baths of England: A Visual History."

from an interactive process involving writer–designers and their audiences. Mariah O'Toole, for example, explains about her image essay that "My original version suffered from a lack of clarity and coherence. My peer reviewers also mentioned that I needed to communicate to my audience the significance of Roman occupation at Aquae Sulis in relation to British history. I realized that they were completely right—I needed to add more text to my image essay to better communicate the importance of my visuals in regard to their connection with the Roman Empire and British history."

- *Refine*—Because sketches are created with minimal commitment to their success and with very few materials, it is easier to refine your visual designs early in the process than once you have begun rendering final visual products. You can use your sketches to adjust elements, add new parts, or delete parts fairly effortlessly. Many designers, writers, and graphic artists sketch and resketch until they flesh out the ideas they really want to convey.

- *Experiment*—You should use early stages of making visuals as opportunities to test solutions, to try new ideas, and to experiment with your visuals. Of course, your visuals should work toward their purpose, but creative, dynamic visuals often evolve from experimentation with form, style, design, and all of the other possibilities in the realm of visual composition. In these early phases, don't be afraid to take chances.

Make Roughs

Roughs can be thought of as rough drafts. They are a transitional phase of the process, moving your work from sketches to comprehensive designs. Roughs are more refined than sketches, thumbnails, and wireframes, but they are not yet complete, final versions. In roughs, you should bring your various sketches together to develop layout and design of the entire visual. You can make roughs by hand or digitally. Roughs can be useful for seeing the whole project instead of just fragments. Roughs also allow you to get feedback on the whole visual, not just concepts and details. As with thumbnails, it's a good idea to make multiple versions of your roughs to experiment with various approaches. Consider these guidelines when making roughs:

- *Use your thumbnails as guides*—Just as you would use your notes when writing, use your sketches and thumbnails to guide your roughs. Your sketches likely include important information or details you might forget or overlook if you don't refer to them.
- *Work toward final size*—Because roughs influence your final visual, it is a good idea to make your roughs as close as possible to the size you anticipate the final being (of course, if you're making a large visual like a billboard or oversized poster, you may only be able to work in more manageable sizes). Making a rough the same size as the final form of the visual will let you get a better sense of space, contrast, readability, relationships, and clarity. When working digitally with actual-size visuals, keep in mind that variations in resolution will affect the visibility and clarity of a visual as it is made larger.
- *Make multiple versions*—As you did with your sketches, consider making multiple versions of your roughs as well. Multiple versions are useful for teasing out ideas, soliciting feedback, and trying different approaches.
- *Add text*—Note in your roughs where any text should appear. Roughs are a good place to test various typographic approaches.
- *Get feedback*—Use your roughs to gather feedback from friends, classmates, colleagues, and potential audience members. Audience understanding and satisfaction are central to designing effective visuals.

Make Comprehensives

Comprehensives are refined, full-size versions of your visuals. Comprehensives provide the opportunity to refine and adjust your visuals from your roughs. Comprehensives also offer you the opportunity to get feedback on more fully developed versions of your visuals. Writers often develop several comprehensives that they and others analyze before determining the final design. Consider the following when creating comprehensive layouts:

- *Work in your final medium*—Comprehensives can be thought of as the transition from ideas and concepts to final product. Therefore, you should work in your final medium in order to best see how the visual will end up. Working in your final medium will also reveal limits and possibilities you have not yet anticipated but that are made evident by the medium.
- *Follow your process*—When making comprehensives, be sure to go back to your early sketches and roughs to consider the transitions you have made. There may be ideas in the original sketches that you overlooked, or you may recognize details that you want to include in your comprehensives and finals.
- *Get feedback*—Just as you have in previous parts of your process, be sure to solicit feedback on your comprehensives. They will provide potential audience members with as close to accurate a version of the final project as possible.

Revise

Just like in writing, revision really occurs throughout any process of making visuals. You revise sketches, roughs, and comprehensives. Yet, like writing, revising visuals is so important to making successful visuals that revision should be addressed as a deliberate, critical part of the process. Like revising your writing, revising your visuals is one of the most important aspects of making visuals. Unlike writing, though, writers not familiar with making visuals often rely on their first version of a visual approach without considering that the visual approach might benefit from revision. Remember, processes for making visuals should emphasize testing, analyzing, and redesigning visuals in order to improve their ability to convey information clearly and accurately. Consider these guidelines when revising your visuals:

- *Reconfirm your purpose*—Check your visual to be sure it fulfills the purpose you set out to fulfill. Sometimes as you design and revise your visuals, your visual may drift from its original purpose as you add and revise features and details.
- *Analyze your visual*—Once you have made your comprehensives, take some time to carefully analyze your visual. Analysis can be thought of as a kind of dissection during which you look carefully at the parts to see how they comprise a whole.

When analyzing your visuals toward the end of revising them, be alert to the following:

- Purpose—Does the visual fulfill its purpose, as far as you can tell?
- Satisfaction—Are you satisfied with the image?
- Aesthetics—Do you like how the visual looks?
- Content and inventory—What is in the visual?
- Composition—How is the visual put together? What elements are used? How do the parts work together to form the whole?
- Rhetoric—How does the visual convey information or meaning?
- Literacy—What does the audience need to know in order to understand the visual?
- Visual cues—How do elements like color, form, lines, light, and so on contribute to the visual's purpose?
- Technical—How do technical aspects of the visual—like, materials, point of view, lighting, texture, perspective, tone, and contrast—function to make the visual "work"?
- Social and situational—Can the visual be interpreted differently in different contexts? How have you ensured that it will be understood as you intend it in the situation in which it will appear?
- Cognitive elements—How do cognitive elements like memory, selectivity, and habituation effect how the visual conveys meaning?

- *Seek feedback*—Sometimes a writer-designer's understanding of what a visual conveys may not coincide with how an audience actually reads the visual. Gathering reader input can serve as a way of testing and analyzing your visual before redesigning or finalizing it. Just as you would ask peer reviewers specific questions to guide the direction of their comments on your writing, it is also a good idea to provide reviewers a series of questions about your visual in order to gather information that can contribute to your revision plans. Although you may want to ask questions specific to your visual, consider asking your reviewers to respond to these kinds of questions when providing feedback about your visuals:

- Do you find the visual appealing, attention getting, or provocative?
- Does the visual clearly convey information?
- Does the visual match the information in the written document?
- Does the visual fit the space where it is located?
- Does the format of the visual seem appropriate to the situation?
- Would the information be better communicated through another format?
- Does the style of the visual seem appropriate to the situation?
- What does the visual represent?
- Are the visual metaphors clearly understood?
- Are the details of the visual evident?
- Is the visual well designed?
- Are there design elements that might be approached differently or more effectively?

- Are there technical aspects of the visual that might be revised?
- Are there typographic aspects of the visual that might be revised?
- Are the colors used in the visual effective?

Render

Once you have revised your comprehensives and you know what you want the final version to accomplish, make the final version. To render a visual is to give it its final form. When rendering your final visual, consider these guidelines:

- *Carefully execute the final design*—Be meticulous in transferring all design ideas from your comprehensives to the final version. Be sure to create all components you intended to include.
- *Pay attention to the details*—Sometimes it is easy to overlook the details you intended to include in your final version because you have made so many early versions of the visual. Be alert to the smallest detail.
- *Consult thumbnails, roughs, and comprehensives*—Use your notes and early designs to guide your final visual.
- *Adjust to fit*—Make sure that your final version fits spatially within the delivery or presentation medium. Be alert to issues like whether the color should be rendered as cmyk or rgb colors based on the final media (cmyk refers to the color scheme used in print documents; c = cyan, m = magenta, y = yellow, k = key [black]. rgb refers to the color scheme used in digital documents; r = red, g = green, b = blue). Check file sizes and projection sizes. Confirm that visuals embedded in other texts fit and relate visually to the final context.

student example

Mariah O'Toole is a student at a mid-sized public university where she majors in English and minors in business administration. She plans to work in educational publishing when she graduates but also has long-term aspirations to become a master calligrapher and organic farmer. Mariah is a student athlete who plays field hockey for her school. Mariah writes a lot in school but also enjoys writing poetry and blogging. In the image essay that follows, Mariah responds to a writing assignment in her British history class that asked students to explore the impact of the Roman Empire on British history. Using a range of visuals and captions, Mariah's essay explores the historical uses of the Roman baths in England.

The Roman Baths of England: A Visual History

Mariah O'Toole

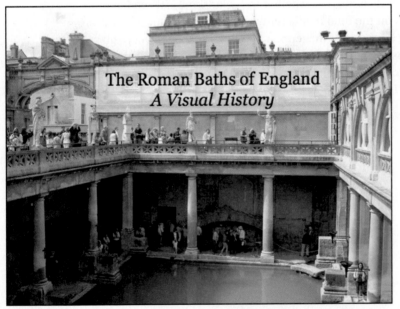

Title Screen
Notice how Mariah provides a clear title and uses a dynamic lead visual both to draw the reader's attention and to provide visual context for the essay.

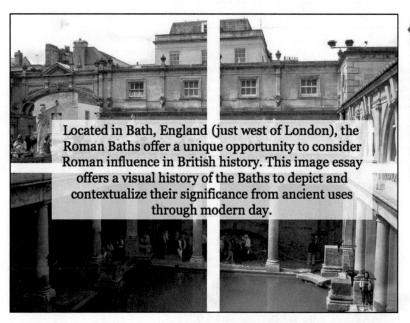

Located in Bath, England (just west of London), the Roman Baths offer a unique opportunity to consider Roman influence in British history. This image essay offers a visual history of the Baths to depict and contextualize their significance from ancient uses through modern day.

Repetition
Notice how Mariah uses the same image from the Title Screen to create continuity and flow.

Image/Text
Notice how Mariah blends the use of written text and photographic image to introduce her readers to the context of her image essay.

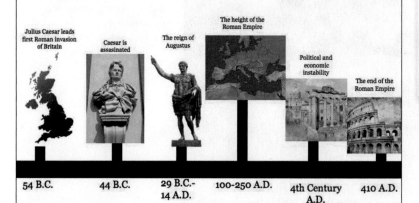

The Roman Empire
27 B.C.—410 A.D.

After the assasination of military leader Julius Caesar in 44 B.C., Augustus seizes power and officially forms the Roman Empire in 27 B.C. For the next 200 years Rome will flourish, experiencing relative stability and prosperity. But around 300 A.D., the empire begins to weaken due to economic difficulties, persistent invasions, and ineffective leaders. In 410 A.D., the steadily declining Roman Empire shows its inability to protect itself when the Visigoths, a Germanic tribe, sack Rome.

Julius Caesar leads first Roman invasion of Britain

Caesar is assasinated

The reign of Augustus

The height of the Roman Empire

Political and economic instability

The end of the Roman Empire

54 B.C.   44 B.C.   29 B.C.-   100-250 A.D.   4th Century   410 A.D.
                                   14 A.D.   A.D.

Explanatory Text
Notice how Mariah uses text and captions to bring together the information her visuals and writing convey.

Images and Graphics
Notice that Mariah blends her use of image and graphics and written text to create this time line to guide her readers through the history of the Roman Empire.

Roman Britain
54 B.C.—410 A.D.

Led by Julius Caesar, the first Roman conquest of Britain occured in 54 B.C. The construction of Hadrian's Wall in 122 A.D. secured Britain's northern border and cemented Britain's place as part of the Roman Empire. Roman occupation led to the development of a vibrant Romano-British culture which fostered the construction of Roman baths, amphitheaters, and temples. The once vibrant Roman Britain would officially end in 410 A.D., as Emperor Constantine III pulled the last remaining Roman troops out of Britain.

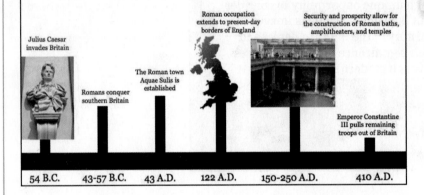

Julius Caesar invades Britain

Romans conquer southern Britain

The Roman town Aquae Sulis is established

Roman occupation extends to present-day borders of England

Security and prosperity allow for the construction of Roman baths, amphitheaters, and temples

Emperor Constantine III pulls remaining troops out of Britain

| 54 B.C. | 43-57 B.C. | 43 A.D. | 122 A.D. | 150-250 A.D. | 410 A.D. |

> **Continuity**
> Notice that Mariah uses the same time line approach and blended image and graphic style for conveying information about the history of Roman Britain as she did for the Roman Empire.

Aquae Sulis
43 A.D.—410 A.D.

The Romans established Aquae Sulis on the site of natural hot springs in 43 A.D. Prior to Roman occupation, the hot springs were used by the Britons as a shrine to the goddess Sulis. The Romans identified Sulis with their goddess, Minerva, and encouraged her worship. The similarities between Sulis and Minerva are said to have helped the Britons adapt to Roman culture.

> **Captions**
> Notice that Mariah uses captions to explain her visuals, create continuity between the visuals, and create flow between images.

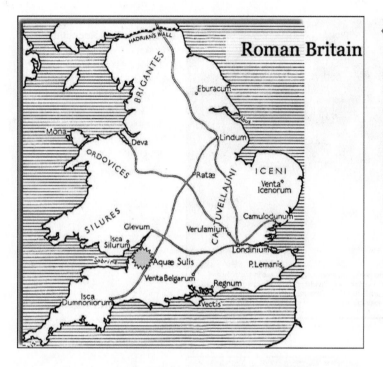

Graphics

Although most of Mariah's image essay relies on photographs, Mariah also uses graphics like this map to create visual distinction among the kinds of information she conveys.

Color

Notice how Mariah uses the blue-colored symbol within this black and white map to highlight the location of Bath, UK.

The Roman Temple

Late 1st Century A.D.

The Roman Temple at Aquae Sulis was built in the late 1st century A.D. to honor the goddess Sulis Minerva who was revered for her healing powers. This goddess combined the British goddess Sulis with the Roman goddess Minerva and reflected the establishment of a Romano-British culture. Coins were thrown into the hot springs, located next to the temple, as offerings to the goddess.

Graphics

Notice in this part of the image essay that Mariah has hand drawn the two graphics she needs in order to be able provide exactly the information she needs readers to have. Often, it is much better and much more efficient to make the visuals you need than to try to find them already made.

The Roman Baths
2nd Century A.D.

The Roman bathing complex, consisting of three lead-lined pools, was constructed sometime in the early 2nd century A.D. The baths were constructed around the sacred spring—the site where offerings were made to the goddess Sulis Minerva. This spring pumped an astonishing quarter of a million gallons of water per day, at a temperature of 120 F. The baths acted as the center of Roman life, a place not only to bathe, but also to socialize and worship.

Variation and Repetition

Notice in these three parts of the image essay how Mariah uses typography to maintain consistency through repetition but also how she varies the designs of each image in order to maintain a dynamic visual appeal and flow.

Bathe

The Baths

Socialize

Worship

Balance

Notice how Mariah uses the three photographs, the written text and the shapes in this visual to create a sense of visual balance rather than haphazardly placing each element in the visual.

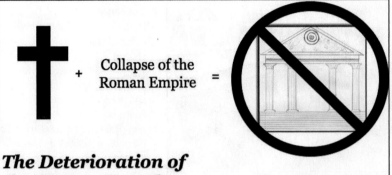

+ Collapse of the Roman Empire =

The Deterioration of the Roman Temple

Late 4th Century A.D.

As the Roman Empire weakened and Christianity gathered strength, traditional pagan religions were marginalized. In 391 A.D., the Christian emperor, Theodosius, ordered that pagan temples be abandoned throughout the Roman Empire. The Roman Temple at Aquae Sulis subsequently fell into a state of disrepair, leading to its eventually collapse.

Visual Echo
Notice that Mariah repeats the same original drawing that she used earlier but in a different size. This graphic echoes the larger one she used earlier, helping to create a connection for readers between this information and earlier information.

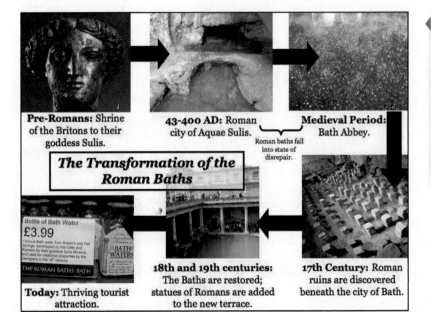

Pre-Romans: Shrine of the Britons to their goddess Sulis.

43-400 AD: Roman city of Aquae Sulis.

Roman baths fall into state of disrepair.

Medieval Period: Bath Abbey.

The Transformation of the Roman Baths

Bottle of Bath Water
£3.99
Famous Bath water from Britain's only Hot Springs, worshipped by the Celts and Romans for their goddess Sulis Minerva and used for medicinal properties by the Georgians in the 18th century
BATH WATERS
THE ROMAN BATHS·BATH

Today: Thriving tourist attraction.

18th and 19th centuries: The Baths are restored; statues of Romans are added to the new terrace.

17th Century: Roman ruins are discovered beneath the city of Bath.

Color
Notice that Mariah consistently uses the color black to add information to the visuals. For instance, in the previous image she uses the circle/slash NO symbol, which we are used to seeing as red, in black as well as the directional arrows that guide the audience's reading path and all of the written text.

student example

Today: The Roman Baths of Bath, England, are a popular tourist attraction.

Conclusion
Notice that Mariah's final image echoes the lead visual and the second visual. Though this final visual is not the exact same picture, it is visually familiar and helps create a sense of conclusion to the essay by providing what amounts to visual bookends within which the essay is contained.

Summary

- We can understand processes of making visuals as much like writing processes.
- We can think of the way that most writers approach visuals in three ways: locating, adapting, and making.
- There are many accessible and useful resources for locating visuals.
- Often just taking a visual from one situation and reconstituting it in another may not fully satisfy your needs. You may need to change visuals to more fully serve the purpose of your document.
- The best way to obtain visuals that specifically fill your needs may be to make your own.
- Processes for making visuals generally follow the pattern of understanding the situation, conducting research, making drafts, making roughs, making comprehensives, revising, and rendering.
- As you locate, adapt, and make visuals, you should be alert to ethical considerations.

Chapter Review

1. In what ways are processes for making visuals similar to writing processes?

2. What three approaches do writers most often take in order to include visuals in their work?

3. What is the best way to obtain a visual you need for your work?

4. Identify the seven parts of the process described for making visuals.

5. Why do writers commonly take visuals that have already been made?

6. Identify four primary sources for locating and using visuals.

7. Identify five ethical issues you should consider when using visuals.

Thinking and Writing about the Chapter

Discussion Threads

1. Whether you include images or graphics in the writing you submit for assignments in college, you always make choices about visual elements of your writing: typographical, layout, and medium, for example. As a class, talk about how you usually make these choices. Are they constrained by the situation? (For example, do your instructors require that you use particular fonts or media?) Do you make visual changes when you draft, after you draft, or not at all? Do you rely on the technologies you use—like your word processor and printers—to guide your visual choices? In short, talk about your experiences and approaches to making, taking, and changing visuals.

2. This chapter considers the processes through which writers make, take, and change visuals, processes we often engage in, but that we don't often think about as formal processes, as we might our writing processes. Discuss what it might mean to you as a writer to think about the visual aspects of your writing as a series of processes and how those processes might integrate with your regular writing processes.

3. Designer Chris Spooner was asked to design a new logo for Vivid Ways, a unique company that helps people lead more exciting, colorful lives. On completion of the Vivid Ways logo, Spooner detailed his design process for making the logo on his blog spoongraphics. Take some time to read Spooner's case study of his process for making the logo, and then discuss his process in conjunction with the suggestions made in this chapter.

Collaboration

Often, writers may write down ideas for visuals they wish to create or include in their writing. In collaborative writing, for instance, one collaborator may describe a visual to the other collaborators so they might help craft it. In many business situations, too, writers are often given descriptions of visuals someone else wants to include in a document or other project. For this assignment, write a description of a visual; this might be a graphic or an image. Then make the visual that you have described. Without showing your visuals to each other, exchange descriptions with a collaborator. Next, use the other person's description to guide you in making his visual. Then compare visuals with the descriptions and discuss the approaches each of you took to make the visuals.

Writing

1. Identify an audience that has many different characteristics from you. Look for a group that is of a different age, educational background, economic standing, and so forth. Then write a set of parameters that might guide you in designing a visual for that audience. What things must you account for in the visual, regardless of its objective or medium?

2. Select a product package—a candy bar wrapper, a wireless phone package, a toothbrush package, or anything else—and analyze the visual elements of the packaging. Consider the material choices in the packaging, the typography used on the package, the visual organization, images and graphics used, and so on. Write an analysis of the original package, explaining how you read the package. Then create a series of ten thumbnails showing ten other approaches you might create for that packaging. Focus on the product logo and the material delivery of the package.

3. In August 1990, comic book scholar Scott McCloud challenged himself to write and draw a 24-page comic in 24 hours. He then challenged comic book artist Steve Bissette to do the same thing. Both artists successfully fulfilled the challenge. The 24-hour comic then became a popular challenge among professional and amateur comic book artists. Variations of the challenge have since evolved, including the one-hour comic. Some comic book artists, in fact, have used the one-hour comic as a personal challenge to rapidly increase their portfolio by, say, writing 70 one-hour comics over the course of a month. Others use the exercise to help develop their invention and revision strategies. Using the techniques described in this chapter, write and draw a one-hour comic. The subject can be anything; the goal is to move through the process of making a visual as rapidly as possible. Think of this as a training exercise.

Designing Documents

CHAPTER 17

Learning Objectives

17.1 Design your documents in more dynamic ways

17.2 Address the reader experience through design thinking and information architecture

17.3 Make design part of your overall writing processes

Before you read this chapter

When you read a document, whether digital or print, how does the design of the document contribute to how you read the document? How does the design of the document contribute to what you expect from the document? In your journal or blog, write about how the design of a document contributes to how one reads the document and how designing a document might contribute to how you think about writing documents.

Design, simply put, is planning and making something. In our contemporary world, nearly everything we encounter has been designed (some things better than others). The keys on the keyboards on our computers were designed, as were the tiles in our bathrooms. Every doorknob or faucet we ever touch was designed. The floor plan of every building on your campus was designed, as was every window, every door, and every light and light switch; the configuration of streets and traffic flow in your community were designed. We live in a design era, a time when—literally—nearly everything we encounter has been designed—even much of the food we eat and the filtered air we breathe in indoor environments. To design is to plan, organize, and make. Design, like writing, is at all times situational. We can think of design as how writers guide readers' experiences with texts.

Document design (also known as layout), though, is not just about adjusting fonts and headings after the document has been written; it is a much more dynamic way of organizing and presenting content to respond to a reader's needs in a particular situation. Good document design is always aware of reader experience. Exceptional and effective document design draws on *design thinking* and *information architecture*. Design thinking is a form of analytical problem solving through which writers analyze situations in order to develop creative and efficient design solutions. Closely related to design thinking, information architecture is a way of thinking about how writers categorize, organize, and structure information to deliver to readers. Together, design thinking and information architecture guide readers' experiences as they navigate a document.

Document design is a dynamic part of the rhetorical choices you make in conveying information. Visual design, whether the design of a document or of a specific graphic or image, is a primary factor in how your audience sees and reads your document. Visual design can be a complex part of your visual processes and your writing processes, but simplicity should trump complexity in design. Repetition and familiarity are memorable and comforting.

In the pages that follow, you will find two versions of the first ten pages of a report published by the United Nations Human Settlements Program called "Guide to Monitoring Target 11: Improving the Lives of 100 Million Slum Dwellers." The first fabricated version of the report is designed as a standard college writing assignment might be designed. The second version appears as an "Extreme Design Makeover," revealing a new, dynamic version of the report. The second version was designed and laid out by Michael Jones Software, an advertising and marketing firm in Kenya. It was originally published both in print and as a PDF. Both versions presented here contain the same written text, the same information, and both are well designed for specific situations. However, the academic version reveals missed opportunities to convey the information in clearer, more memorable ways for the reader. The Extreme Design Makeover version creates a different experience for the reader.

Before: Traditional Report Format

Guide to Monitoring Target 11:
Improving the lives of
100 million slum dwellers
Progress towards the Millennium Development Goals, Nairobi,
May 2003

Presented by:
United Nations Human Settlements Programme
UN-Habitat
Global Urban Observatory

Genre Recognition

The formatting of this cover sheet indicates that this is a particular kind of document. Everything from the paper it is printed on to the typeface and the layout of the title page screams "boring academic paper!" These design choices probably don't draw many readers in, other than perhaps a few specialists intereted in the subject.

Optical Center

In many visuals, particularly documents, key information is placed at the optical center of the visual. The optical center of a visual, through, is not the physical center. Optical center is approximately one third of the distance from the top of the document. Readers' eyes are drawn to the optical center of a visual.

Contents

The designations employed and the presentation of material in this publication do not imply the expression of any opinion whatsoever on the part of the Secretariat of the United Nations concerning the legal status of any country, territory, city or area or of its authorities, or concerning the delimitation of its frontiers or boundaries or regarding its economic system or degree of development. The analysis, conclusions and recommendations of the report do not necessarily reflect the views of the United Nations Human Settlements Programme (UN-HABITAT), the Governing Council of UN-HABITAT or its Member States.

Excerpts from this publication may be reproduced without authorization, on condition that the source is indicated.

© United Nations Human Settlements Programme (UN-HABITAT), 2003

ISBN: 92-1-131682-0
HS/690/03E

United Nations Human Settlements Programme publications can be obtained from UN-HABITAT Regional and Information Offices or directly from:

P.O. Box 30030
Nairobi, Kenya
Fax: +(254-20) 624060
E-mail: unhabitat@unhabitat.org
Website: http://www.unhabitat.org

Typography

Variation in typeface can help readers identify various levels of information. In this document, the writers have used boldfaced type to indicate heading levels. The writers use boldface to indicate a section heading.

Margins/Alignment

Margins can contribute to a sense of visual clarity and organization. Although word processors are great for working with writing and revision, they aren't always the best tools for document design.
Notice how the right side margin with the page numbers is not consistently straight.

White Space/Negative Space

White space is also known as negative space. It is the space within a document or visual that is not occupied. You can think of it as the blank space. White space can be used to group items together, isolate items, create visual clarity, attract a reader's attention, or create a general aesthetic quality. White space can be created through margins, line spacing, indentation, paragraph length, and headings.

Foreword

3

This guide represents a milestone in the efforts of the United Nations to monitor the Millennium Development Goals adopted by the UN member states in the year 2000. These goals address essential dimensions of poverty and their effects on people's lives. They constitute, in themselves, a commitment by the world's leaders to the world's poor, addressing the most pressing issues related to poverty such as health, gender equality, education and environmental sustainability.

UN-HABITAT has been assigned the responsibility to assist United Nations Members States in monitoring and eventually attaining the global "Cities without Slums" target of improving the lives of at least 100 million slum dwellers by the year 2020. To proceed with this task, UN-HABITAT has consulted a number of experts to develop generic and operational definitions of terms and concepts related to urban poverty and slums for use by National Governments, policy makers and their advisors, planners, local authorities, statisticians, survey specialists and the academics. This guide offers not only the definitions but also a hierarchy of indicators at the operational level and specific ways to measure them.

Each country should use this guide to understand the issues and to set its own goals and targets in relation to recognized slum conditions, trends and needs. The "Cities without Slums" targets established by countries should then be carried forward through coordinated policies and actions related to slum-upgrading, environmental management, infrastructure development, service delivery and poverty-reduction at large.

This practical guide, published in conjunction with the first meeting of the Governing Council of the United Nations Human Settlements Programme (UN-HABITAT), promises to contribute to our collective effort to monitor the Millennium Development Goals and to enable the world's cities to improve the lives of slum dwellers. It merits special attention by all partners of the Habitat Agenda at a time when slums are being clearly identified as a crucial development issue around the world.

Mrs. Anna Kajumulo Tibaijuka

Executive Director
United Nations Human Settlements Programme (UN-HABITAT)

The Millennium Development Goals

4

Setting goals for the Millennium

The Millennium Development Goals adopted by the UN member states in the year 2000 are broad goals for the entire world. They address essential dimensions of poverty and their effects on people's lives attacking pressing issues related to poverty reduction, health, gender equality, education and environmental sustainability. By accepting these goals, the international community has made a commitment to the world's poor, the most vulnerable, in precise terms, established in quantitative targets.

In order to assist Member States realize the eight goals of the Millennium Declaration, the United Nations System has set numerical targets for each goal. Further, it has selected appropriate indicators to monitor progress on the goals and attain corresponding targets. A list of 18 targets and more than 40 indicators corresponding to these goals ensure a common assessment and appreciation of the status of MDGs at global, national and local levels.

The United Nations System assigned UN-HABITAT the responsibility to assist Members States monitor and gradually attain the "Cities without Slums" Target, also known as "Target 11". One of the three targets of Goal 7 "Ensure Environmental Sustainability," Target 11 is: "By 2020, to have achieved a significant improvement in the lives of at least 100 million slum dwellers".

Goal 7 Target 11 comes in response to one of the most pressing challenges of the Millennium. By dealing with the people living in the most depressed physical conditions in the world's cities, Target 11 is a direct recognition that slums are a development issue which needs to be faced. Slums cannot simply be considered as an unfortunate consequence of urban poverty but need to be treated as a major issue.

In an effort to advance the monitoring of this target, UN-HABITAT has undertaken the task of defining and articulating relevant indicators, in consultation with activists, practitioners and policy makers with demonstrated experience in reducing urban poverty. The Agency is also keen to collect data globally in order to generate statistically-valid figures and estimates that quantify the magnitude and characteristics of slums as a necessary first step for formulating policy recommendations and actions at the global level. Future steps are envisioned to assist Members States with advocacy instruments, such as the Global Campaigns

Consistency through Repetition

The writers use consistent typeface choices for section headings, margins, white space. The clean, clinical feel of this consistency emphasizes content over form rather than letting the two work together to convey information.

Alignment

Design expert Robin Williams identifies that amateur designers frequently place things on the page wherever there happens to be space; instead, she says, "nothing should be placed arbitrarily." Alignment contributes to visual cohesiveness.

There are three basic forms of alignment: flush left, flush right, and centered. Center alignment is most commonly used and is generally safe, but it offers very little beyond the ordinary. Consider the different appearances of these three allignments:

Centered

TERESA COX

OFFWRLD GAME DESIGN

WWW.OFFWRLD.NET

Flush Left

TERESA COX

OFFWRLD GAME DESIGN

WWW.OFFWRLD.NET

Flush Right

TERESA COX

OFFWRLD GAME DESIGN

WWW.OFFWRLD.NET

for Secure Tenure and on Urban Governance, and with technical co-operation on slum upgrading and urban management.

Goals are not imposed, they are an international call for action
Each country need to set its own goals and targets in relation to recognized conditions, trends and needs. Targets should be considered as commitments made by countries with the support of the international community. Target 11 calls for coordinated policies and actions related to slum-upgrading, environmental management, infrastructure development, service delivery and poverty-reduction at large.

What are the obstacles?
Poor policies. The failure to plan the city to cater for urban demographic trends. The failure to address people's needs, inequities in access to services, insecurity of tenure, and inequalities between men and women. But there are also other broader issues to consider: the burden of debt, the decline in development aid and, sometimes, inconsistencies in donor policies which hinders faster progress.

What will it take to overcome these obstacles?
Dialogue to understand the poor's needs and include them in planning the city. Understanding the slum phenomena in its own context, the conditions in which men and women live in slums, through collecting and analyzing adequate information, is part of the response to the problem. City managers and stakeholders should be able to plan slum interventions with a reliable information that should be understood and acknowledged by all.

If some countries have made great progress in improving the lives of slum dwellers, other can as well.
Target 11 on slums can be met. But it will take hard work. Success will require stronger voices for the poor that lead to improving their security of tenure, adequate planning and economic stability that favour the development of basic services. It will also take political will to make it a high priority for the Millennium.

The present guidelines provide advice to UN-HABITAT's partners, which include National Governments, the policy makers and their advisors, planners, at the city level, statisticians or survey specialists at the National Statistical Offices, or the academic milieu, in providing the agreed generic and the operational definitions of the concepts of secure tenure and slums. To this aim, the guidelines offer not only the definitions, but also a hierarchy of indicators at the operational level, and the specific ways to measure them.

Target 11 in the Overall Development Framework

Target 11 is only a piece of the larger development framework
Within the context of several development goals competing with each other for the attention of policy makers and the world's limited financial resources for international development, it is important to note the selection of goals and targets adopted by the international development community.

Improving the lives of slum dwellers will be achieved by considering the overall picture
Target 11 deals more specifically with the issue of slums and the improvement of the lives of slum dwellers. However, in order to face the challenge of slum dwellers, one needs to consider the other facets of the problem through the other goals and targets. The conditions of slum dwellers will not improve worldwide if no action is taken in order to eradicate poverty and hunger (goal 1), to reduce child mortality (goal 4), combat HIV-AIDS (goal 6) and develop a global partnership for development (goal 8).

Each country and city should look at the overall development framework proposed in the MDGs and decide which of the goals and targets should be considered in order to improve the lives of slum dwellers. One practical way to go about it is to select key related goals and targets and to measure progress made in achieving each goal in the slum areas. Additional targets and indicators can be selected by countries in order to complete the diagnostic of slum conditions.

Example: Target 3. Ensure that all boys and girls complete a full course of primary schooling. Is this achieved in slums as compared to other areas of the city? If not, what should be the next target for years x and y?

Scope of Millennium Development Goals and Targets

Goal 1. Eradicate extreme poverty and hunger
    Target 1. Reduce by half the proportion of people living on less than a dollar a day
    Target 2. Reduce by half the proportion of people who suffer from hunger

Goal 2. Achieve universal primary education
    Target 3. Ensure that all boys and girls complete a full course of primary schooling

---

Typography
The writers introduce a new level of information, which they indicate with italicized type. Though it is not visually dynamic, writers need to use heading level indicators consistently so as not to confuse readers. When used consistently, such visual markers help readers navigate verious levels of information within the document.

Consistency through Repetition
Notice that the writers do not vary their design choices in any way. They provide absolutely nothing unexpected or different on any page.

Lists
Lists can be effective in conveying information in a way that suggests a relationship between the different parts of the information. Likewise, lists suggest a type of organization within the information.

7

Goal 3. Promote gender equality and empower women
    Target 4. Eliminate gender disparity in primary and secondary education preferably by 2005, and at all levels by 2015

Goal 4. Reduce child mortality
    Target 5. Reduce by two thirds the mortality rate among children under five

Goal 5. Improve maternal health
    Target 6. Reduce by three quarters the maternal mortality ratio

Goal 6. Combat HIV/AIDS, malaria and other diseases
    Target 7. Halt and begin to reverse the spread of HIV/AIDS
    Target 8. Halt and begin to reverse the incidence of malaria and other major diseases

Goal 7. Ensure environmental sustainability
    Target 9. Integrate the principles of sustainable development into country policies and programmes; reverse loss of environmental resources
    Target 10. Reduce by half the proportion of people without sustainable access to safe drinking water
    Target 11. Achieve significant improvement in lives of at least 100 million slum dwellers, by 2020

Goal 8. Develop a global partnership for development
    Target 12. Develop further an open trading and financial system that is rule-based, predictable and non-discriminatory. Includes a commitment to good governance, development and poverty reduction - nationally and internationally
    Target 13. Address the least developed countries' special needs. This includes tariff- and quota-free access for their exports; enhanced debt relief for heavily indebted poor countries; cancellation of official bilateral debt; and more generous official development assistance for countries committed to poverty reduction
    Target 14. Address the special needs of landlocked and small island developing States
    Target 15. Deal comprehensively with developing countries' debt problems through national and international measures to make debt sustainable in the long term
    Target 16. In cooperation with the developing countries, develop decent and productive work for youth

---

Tabs/Indentation

Like other uses of negative space, writers can use indentation and tabs to indicate varying levels of information.

8

    Target 17. In cooperation with pharmaceutical companies, provide access to affordable essential drugs in developing countries
    Target 18. In cooperation with the private sector, make available the benefits of new technologies - especially information and communications technologies

Global Trends on Slums

Almost two billion people currently live in urban regions of the developing world. This figure is projected to double over the next 30 years, at which time urban dwellers will account for nearly half the global population1. Moreover, most of these new urban dwellers are likely to be poor – resulting in a phenomenon termed as the 'urbanization of poverty'. Slums are a physical and spatial manifestation of increasing urban poverty and intra-city inequality. However, slums do not accommodate all of the urban poor, nor are all slum dwellers always poor.

It is estimated that up to one-third of the World's urban population lives in slums. The comparatively more rapid growth in the urban areas of developing countries suggests that the problems associated with slum dwelling will worsen in those areas that are already most vulnerable. More than 70% of the least developed countries' (LDCs) and of Sub-Saharan Africa's urban population lived in slums in 2001 and this is set to increase unless there is substantial intervention. Regardless of the characterization of slums, slum dwellers face higher developmental challenges such as higher morbidity and infant mortality rates than either non-slum dwellers or the rural population.

Although the term 'slum' is considered an easily understandable catchall, it disguises the fact that within this and other terms lie a multitude of different settlements and communities. However, slums can be said to divide into two broad classes:
• Slums of hope: 'progressing' settlements, which are characterized by new, normally self-built structures, usually illegal (e.g. squatters) that are in, or have recently been through, a process of development, consolidation and improvement; and
• Slums of despair: 'declining' neighborhoods, in which environmental conditions and domestic services are undergoing a process of degeneration.
Slums are now viewed more positively by public decision-makers than in the past. They are increasingly seen as places of opportunity, as 'slums of hope' rather than 'slums of despair'. National approaches to slums have generally shifted from negative policies such as forced eviction, benign neglect and involuntary resettlement, to more positive policies such as self-help and in situ upgrading, enabling and rights-based policies.

Tables

Tables provide readers with an easy way to access information that might otherwise be difficult to locate and see relationally. However, writers should pay particular attention the design of their tables to ensure that readers can easily navigate the tables.

9

Population living in slums (UN-HABITAT, 2001 estimates)

Major area	Total population (millions)		Total Urban population (millions)		Urban population as % of total population		% Urban Slum	Urban slum Population (millions)
	1990	2001	1990	2001	1990	2001	2001	2001
WORLD	5,255	6,134	2,286	2,923	43.5	47.7	31.6	924
Developed regions	1,148	1,194	846	902	73.7	75.5	6.0	54
Developing regions	4,106	4,940	1,439	2,022	35.0	40.9	43.0	870
Least Developed Countries (LDCs)	515	685	107	179	20.8	26.2	78.2	140

Sources:
1/ Total and urban population: UN Population Division, World Urbanization Prospects: The 2001 Revision, Table A.1;
2/ Slum percentages: DHS (1987–2001); MICS (1995–2000); WHO/UNICEF JMP (1998–1999)

People Living in Slums

UN-HABITATS estimates, 2001

Developed regions	54 million
Transition countries	25 million
Latin American & Caribbean	128 million
Asia Pacific	570 million
Africa	188 million
World	924 million

1. United Nations (2002), "World Urbanization Prospects: The 2001 Revision, Data Tables and Highlights", Population Division, Department of Economic and Social Affairs, United Nations Secretariat, 20 March 2002, ESA/P/WP.173, page 1.

10

Population living in slums (UN-HABITAT, 2001 estimates)

	Total Urban population (millions)	Urban population as % of total population	Urban slum Population (millions)	Slum population as % of total Urban population
WORLD	2,923	47.7	924	31.6
Developed regions	902	75.5	54	6.0
Europe	534	73.6	33	6.2
Other	367	78.6	21	5.7
Developing regions	2,022	40.9	870	43.0
Northern Africa	76	52.0	21	28.2
Sub-Saharan Africa	231	34.6	166	71.9
Latin America and the Caribbean	399	75.8	128	31.9
Eastern Asia	533	39.1	194	36.4
Eastern Asia excluding China	61	77.1	16	25.4
South-central Asia	452	30.0	262	58.0
South-eastern Asia	203	38.3	57	28.0
Western Asia	125	64.9	41	33.1
Oceania	2	26.7	0	24.1
Transition countries	259	62.9	25	9.6
Commonwealth of Independent States	181	64.1	19	10.3
Other Europe	77	60.3	6	7.9
Least Developed Countries (LDCs)	179	26.2	140	78.2

Sources:
UN-HABITAT, Global Urban Observatory, 2003. Estimations based on:
1/ Total and urban population: UN Population Division, World Urbanization Prospects: The 2001 Revision, Table A.1;
2/ Slum percentages: DHS (1987–2001); MICS (1995–2000).

After: Report Design Makeover

17.2 Address the reader experience through design thinking and information architecture

Guide to Monitoring Target 11:

Improving the lives of 100 million slum dwellers

Progress towards the Millennium Development Goals, Nairobi, May 2003

UN-HABITAT

GL★BAL
URBAN
OBSERVATORY

Visuals

Visuals can be eye catching, like this cover. They can help set context and help readers situate the document. Why do you suppose these writers chose a photograph instead of a line drawing, cartoon, or graphic?

Pathos

Visuals can convey powerful appeals to emotion, as this image of two children playing in a polluted river does.

Repetition/Visual Echo

Notice that the writers chose to repeat the orange color from the top of the photo in their title design. Repetition, like this, creates a sense of visual cohesion and helps create a sense of visual flow from the top of the page to the lower part of the page.

Depth

Depth refers to distance. In most visuals, depth is not literal but perceived. Because most print and digital visuals are actually two dimensional, depth can be created through visual distinctions. In this image, for example, we interpret the size of the boys in the foreground and the people in the background to suggest proximity and distance to create a sense of depth.

Contrast, Variation, and Emphasis

Notice how the writers' choice of contrasting-color text in the title emphasizes the title, drawing readers' eyes to it. Consider, also, how the title text differs from the other text on the page.

Ethos

Notice how the inclusion of the icons of the two organizations that support the publication of this document add to the document's credibility.

Contents

ISBN: 92-1-131682-0
HS/690/03E

United Nations Human Settlements Programme publications can be obtained from UN-HABITAT Regional and Information Offices or directly from:
P.O. Box 30030
Nairobi, Kenya
Fax: +(254-20) 624060
E-mail: unhabitat@unhabitat.org
Website: http://www.unhabitat.org

Report designed and laid out by Michael Jones Software - mjs@ftltd.co.ke
Cover photo by Thierry Geenen for the Nairobi River Basin Project, UNEP

Repetition/ Consitency

Notice the use of the same color and font as the title from the front page. This kind of repetition helps create a sense of cohesion and consistency between pages.

White Space

Notice how the table of contents page uses white space to create clarity and separation between the contents and disclaimer and copyright information.

Foreword

This guide represents a milestone in the efforts of the United Nations to monitor the Millennium Development Goals adopted by the UN member states in the year 2000. These goals address essential dimensions of poverty and their effects on people's lives. They constitute, in themselves, a commitment by the world's leaders to the world's poor, addressing the most pressing issues related to poverty such as health, gender equality, education and environmental sustainability.

UN-HABITAT has been assigned the responsibility to assist United Nations Members States in monitoring and eventually attaining the global "Cities without Slums" target of improving the lives of at least 100 million slum dwellers by the year 2020. To proceed with this task, UN-HABITAT has consulted a number of experts to develop generic and operational definitions of terms and concepts related to urban poverty and slums for use by National Governments, policy makers and their advisors, planners, local authorities, statisticians, survey specialists and the academics. This guide offers not only the definitions but also a hierarchy of indicators at the operational level and specific ways to measure them.

Each country should use this guide to understand the issues and to set its own goals and targets in relation to recognized slum conditions, trends and needs. The "Cities without Slums" targets established by countries should then be carried forward through coordinated policies and actions related to slum-upgrading, environmental management, infrastructure development, service delivery and poverty-reduction at large.

This practical guide, published in conjunction with the first meeting of the Governing Council of the United Nations Human Settlements Programme (UN-HABITAT), promises to contribute to our collective effort to monitor the Millennium Development Goals and to enable the world's cities to improve the lives of slum dwellers. It merits special attention by all partners of the Habitat Agenda at a time when slums are being clearly identified as a crucial development issue around the world.

Mrs. Anna Kajumulo Tibaijuka
Executive Director
United Nations Human Settlements Programme (UN-HABITAT)

| 1

Visual
Notice how the inclusion of the visual helps readers connect with the page and how the visual draws readers into the writing. The size of the visual is important here, too, as it does not dominate the page. Notice, as well, the effect the visual has in creating a variation in margins within the page's more dominant margins.

Optical Center
Notice effective use of the optical center.

Margins
Margins contribute to the use of negative space and visually frame the document. Margins that are too small overcrowd a page with text; margins too large create a sense of emptiness. In most academic or professional documents, writers use margins of one to one and a half inches.

Narrow Margins   Medium Margins   Wide Margins

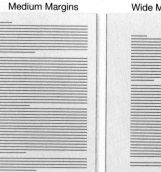

The Millennium Development Goals

Setting goals for the Millennium

The Millennium Development Goals adopted by the UN member states in the year 2000 are broad goals for the entire world. They address essential dimensions of poverty and their effects on people's lives attacking pressing issues related to poverty reduction, health, gender equality, education and environmental sustainability. By accepting these goals, the international community has made a commitment to the world's poor, the most vulnerable, in precise terms, established in quantitative targets.

In order to assist Member States realize the eight goals of the Millennium Declaration, the United Nations System has set numerical targets for each goal. Further, it has selected appropriate indicators to monitor progress on the goals and attain corresponding targets. A list of 18 targets and more than 40 indicators corresponding to these goals ensure a common assessment and appreciation of the status of MDGs at global, national and local levels.

The United Nations System assigned UN-HABITAT the responsibility to assist Members States monitor and gradually attain the "Cities without Slums" Target, also known as "Target 11". One of the three targets of Goal 7 "Ensure Environmental Sustainability," Target 11 is: "By 2020, to have achieved a significant improvement in the lives of at least 100 million slum dwellers".

Goal 7 Target 11 comes in response to one of the most pressing challenges of the Millennium. By dealing with the people living in the most depressed physical conditions in the world's cities, Target 11 is a direct recognition that slums are a development issue which needs to be faced. Slums cannot simply be considered as an unfortunate consequence of urban poverty but need to be treated as a major issue.

In an effort to advance the monitoring of this target, UN-HABITAT has undertaken the task of defining and articulating relevant indicators, in consultation with activists, practitioners and policy makers with demonstrated experience in reducing urban poverty. The Agency is also keen to collect data globally in order to generate statistically-valid figures and estimates that quantify the magnitude and characteristics of slums as a necessary first step for formulating policy recommendations and actions at the global level. Future steps are envisioned to assist Members States with advocacy instruments, such as the Global Campaigns for Secure Tenure and on Urban Governance, and with technical co-operation on slum upgrading and urban management.

Goals are not imposed, they are an international call for action

Each country need to set its own goals and targets in relation to recognized conditions, trends and needs. Targets should be considered as commitments made by countries with the support of the international community. Target 11 calls for coordinated policies and actions related to slum-upgrading, environmental management, infrastructure development, service delivery and poverty-reduction at large.

| 2

"By 2020, to have achieved a significant improvement in the lives of at least 100 million slum dwellers".

What are the obstacles?

Poor policies. The failure to plan the city to cater for urban demographic trends. The failure to address people's needs, inequities in access to services, insecurity of tenure, and inequalities between men and women. But there are also other broader issues to consider: the burden of debt, the decline in development aid and, sometimes, inconsistencies in donor policies which hinders faster progress.

What will it take to overcome these obstacles?

Dialogue to understand the poor's needs and include them in planning the city. Understanding the slum phenomena in its own context, the conditions in which men and women live in slums, through collecting and analyzing adequate information, is part of the response to the problem. City managers and stakeholders should be able to plan slum interventions with a reliable information that should be understood and acknowledged by all.

If some countries have made great progress in improving the lives of slum dwellers, other can as well.

Target 11 on slums can be met. But it will take hard work. Success will require stronger voices for the poor that lead to improving their security of tenure, adequate planning and economic stability that favour the development of basic services. It will also take political will to make it a high priority for the Millennium.

The present guidelines provide advice to UN-HABITAT's partners, which include National Governments, the policy makers and their advisors, planners, at the city level, statisticians or survey specialists at the National Statistical Offices, or the academic milieu, in providing the agreed generic and the operational definitions of the concepts of secure tenure and slums. To this aim, the guidelines offer not only the definitions, but also a hierarchy of indicators at the operational level, and the specific ways to measure them.

Line Breaks

Line breaks use white space to help create an uncluttered design. Notice how this page uses line breaks between paragraphs to visually distinguish between chunks of information and contribute to readability.

Emphasis

Sometimes you may need to place special emphasis on particular words, phrases, or even sentences. Using boldface, italicized, colored, or CAPITALIZED text can signal emphasis.

Organization

Headings can be useful for identifying organizational patterns. Various heading levels might be identified through textual variations, like the changes in text color the writers use on this page.

Balance

Balance is the way in which elements within a visual or document are arranged and aligned to create a unified whole. Readers tend to find satisfaction when there is a sense of equilibrium among visual elements. Balance is the way in which visual elements are distributed on the page and the "weight" each carries. Notice on this page how the columns and the two colored boxes contribute to a sense of balance.

Headers

Headers, or running heads, appear at the top of pages to indicate document titles, sections, authors, or other organizational information about the document.

Sample Document

GL🌐BAL
OBSERVATORY

Target 11 in the overall development framework

Target 11 is only a piece of the larger development framework

Within the context of several development goals competing with each other for the attention of policy makers and the world's limited financial resources for international development, it is important to note the selection of goals and targets adopted by the international development community.

Improving the lives of slum dwellers will be achieved by considering the overall picture

Target 11 deals more specifically with the issue of slums and the improvement of the lives of slum dwellers. However, in order to face the challenge of slum dwellers, one needs to consider the other facets of the problem through the other goals and targets. The conditions of slum dwellers will not improve worldwide if no action is taken in order to eradicate poverty and hunger (goal 1), to reduce child mortality (goal 6), combat HIV-AIDS (goal 6) and develop a global partnership for development (goal 8).

Each country and city should look at the overall development framework proposed in the MDGs and decide which of the goals and targets should be considered in order to improve the lives of slum dwellers. One practical way to go about it is to select key related goals and targets and **to measure progress made in achieving each goal in the slum areas**. Additional targets and indicators can be selected by countries in order to complete the diagnostic of slum conditions. *Example: Target 3. Ensure that all boys and girls complete a full course of primary schooling. Is this achieved in slums as compared to other areas of the city? If not, what should be the next target for years x and y?*

...select key related goals and targets and to measure progress made in achieving each goal in the slum areas.

Scope of Millennium Development Goals and Targets

Goal 1. Eradicate extreme poverty and hunger
Target 1. Reduce by half the proportion of people living on less than a dollar a day
Target 2. Reduce by half the proportion of people who suffer from hunger

Goal 2. Achieve universal primary education
Target 3. Ensure that all boys and girls complete a full course of primary schooling

Goal 3. Promote gender equality and empower women
Target 4. Eliminate gender disparity in primary and secondary education preferably by 2005, and at all levels by 2015

Goal 4. Reduce child mortality
Target 5. Reduce by two thirds the mortality rate among children under five

Goal 5. Improve maternal health
Target 6. Reduce by three quarters the maternal mortality ratio

Goal 6. Combat HIV/AIDS, malaria and other diseases
Target 7. Halt and begin to reverse the spread of HIV/AIDS
Target 8. Halt and begin to reverse the incidence of malaria and other major diseases

Goal 7. Ensure environmental sustainability
Target 9. Integrate the principles of sustainable development into country policies and programmes; reverse loss of environmental resources
Target 10. Reduce by half the proportion of people without sustainable access to safe drinking water
Target 11. Achieve significant improvement in lives of at least 100 million slum dwellers, by 2020

Goal 8. Develop a global partnership for development
Target 12. Develop further an open trading and financial system that is rule-based, predictable and non-discriminatory. Includes a commitment to good governance, development and poverty reduction - nationally and internationally
Target 13. Address the least developed countries' special needs. This includes tariff- and quota-free access for their exports; enhanced debt relief for heavily indebted poor countries; cancellation of official bilateral debt; and more generous official development assistance for countries committed to poverty reduction
Target 14. Address the special needs of landlocked and small island developing States
Target 15. Deal comprehensively with developing countries' debt problems through national and international measures to make debt sustainable in the long term
Target 16. In cooperation with the developing countries, develop decent and productive work for youth
Target 17. In cooperation with pharmaceutical companies, provide access to affordable essential drugs in developing countries
Target 18. In cooperation with the private sector, make available the benefits of new technologies - especially information and communications technologies

3 l

Annotations

Consistency
Notice that this banner maintains the same color as the two boxes from the preceding page. Using color consistently builds cohesion within a document.

Emphasis
Visually distinct type draws a reader's eyes to the text and signals that emphasized information is important.

Pull Quotes
Writers may emphasize key information by pulling an important quote from the body of the text and highlighting it in the page design.

Balance
Notice the inclusion of this visual in relation to the visual on the preceding page. Note, in particular, the relative position on the pages, the sizes of the images, and the visual tone of each.

Page Numbers
Page numbers help readers locate information within a document and track their own location within a document. You should place page numbers consistently in either the header or footer so as not to interfere with the body text of the document.

Lists
Lists may be useful for organizing and visually discerning categories of information.

Global trends on slums

Almost two billion people currently live in urban regions of the developing world. This figure is projected to double over the next 30 years, at which time urban dwellers will account for nearly half the global population[1]. Moreover, most of these new urban dwellers are likely to be poor – resulting in a phenomenon termed as the 'urbanization of poverty'. Slums are a physical and spatial manifestation of increasing urban poverty and intra-city inequality. However, slums do not accommodate all of the urban poor, nor are all slum dwellers always poor.

It is estimated that up to one-third of the World's urban population lives in slums. The comparatively more rapid growth in the urban areas of developing countries suggests that the problems associated with slum dwelling will worsen in those areas that are already most vulnerable. **More than 70%** of the least developed countries' (LDCs) and of Sub-Saharan Africa's urban population lived in slums in 2001 and this is set to increase unless there is substantial intervention. Regardless of the characterization of slums, slum dwellers face higher developmental challenges such as higher morbidity and infant mortality rates than either non-slum dwellers or the rural population.

Although the term 'slum' is considered an easily understandable catchall, it disguises the fact that within this and other terms lie a multitude of different settlements and communities. However, slums can be said to divide into two broad classes:

- **Slums of hope:** 'progressing' settlements, which are characterized by new, normally self-built structures, usually illegal (e.g. squatters) that are in, or have recently been through, a process of development, consolidation and improvement; and

- **Slums of despair:** 'declining' neighborhoods, in which environmental conditions and domestic services are undergoing a process of degeneration.

Slums are now viewed more positively by public decision-makers than in the past. They are increasingly seen as places of opportunity, as 'slums of hope' rather than 'slums of despair'. National approaches to slums have generally shifted from negative policies such as forced eviction, benign neglect and involuntary resettlement, to more positive policies such as self-help and in situ upgrading, enabling and rights-based policies.

Population living in slums (UN-HABITAT, 2001 estimates)

Major area	Total population (millions)		Total Urban population (millions)		Urban population as % of total population		% urban slum	Urban slum population (millions)
	1991	2001	1990	2001	1990	2001	2001	2001
WORLD	5,255	6,134	2,286	2,923	43.5	47.7	31.6	924
Developed regions	1,148	1,194	846	902	73.7	75.5	6.0	54
Developing regions	4,106	4,940	1,439	2,022	35.0	40.9	43.0	870
Least Developed Countries (LDCs)	515	685	107	179	20.8	26.2	78.2	140

Sources:
1/ Total and urban population: UN Population Division World Urbanization Prospects: The 2001 Revision, Table A.1;
2/ Slum percentages: DHS (1987-2001), MICS (1995-2000), WHO/UNICEF JMP (1998-1999)

1. United Nations (2002), "World Urbanization Prospects: The 2001 Revision, Data Tables and Highlights", Population Division, Department of Economic and Social Affairs, United Nations Secretariat, 20 March 2002, ESA/P/WP.173, page 1.

4

Bullets
Using bulleted lists can help readers visually distinguish between chunks of information.

Consistency
Notice that the use of similarly sized visuals remains consistent from page to page.

Tables
Tables provide readers with an easy way to access information that might otherwise be difficult to locate and see relationally.

Footnotes
Footnotes provide further information, like citation information or clarifications. They provide quick access to information, so the reader does not have to navigate to other locations within the document, such as a bibliography. Footnotes can also contribute to the ethos of the document by readily providing acknowledgment of valid, reliable sources.

Color Variation and Connection
By varying the color, the writers have distinguished the function of this box from the box used in the header. However, by including the single stripe of the same color as the header box, the writers create a sense of connection to the overall page. Likewise, the repeated color stripe also delineates a specific kind of information in the table. And, of course, the deep red color is eye catching, pulling readers to the information in the table.

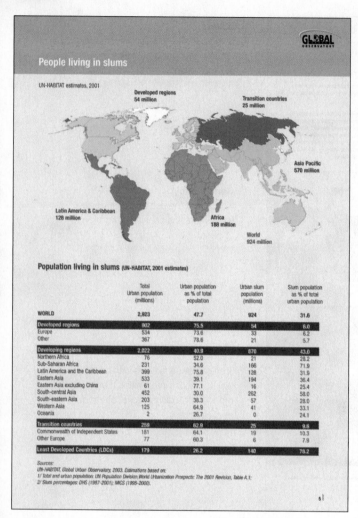

People living in slums

GL⊕BAL OBSERVATORY

UN-HABITAT estimates, 2001

Developed regions 54 million
Transition countries 25 million
Asia Pacific 570 million
Latin America & Caribbean 128 million
Africa 188 million
World 924 million

Population living in slums (UN-HABITAT, 2001 estimates)

	Total Urban population (millions)	Urban population as % of total population	Urban slum population (millions)	Slum population as % of total urban population
WORLD	2,923	47.7	924	31.6
Developed regions	902	75.5	54	6.0
Europe	534	73.6	33	6.2
Other	367	78.6	21	5.7
Developing regions	2,022	40.9	870	43.0
Northern Africa	76	52.0	21	28.2
Sub-Saharan Africa	231	34.6	166	71.9
Latin America and the Caribbean	399	75.8	128	31.9
Eastern Asia	533	39.1	194	36.4
Eastern Asia excluding China	61	77.1	16	25.4
South-central Asia	452	30.0	262	58.0
South-eastern Asia	203	38.3	57	28.0
Western Asia	125	64.9	41	33.1
Oceania	2	26.7	0	24.1
Transition countries	259	62.9	25	9.6
Commonwealth of Independent States	181	64.1	19	10.3
Other Europe	77	60.3	6	7.9
Least Developed Countries (LDCs)	179	26.2	140	78.2

Sources:
UN-HABITAT, Global Urban Observatory, 2003. Estimations based on:
1/ Total and urban population. UN Population Division, World Urbanization Prospects: The 2001 Revision, Table A.1;
2/ Slum percentages: DHS (1987-2001); MICS (1995-2000).

s|

Maps

Maps can be useful for conveying geographical or spatial information. Maps depict vast areas, like universes, or small spaces, like a room or park. Maps can be integrated with other visuals like charts or line drawings to more clearly convey information. Maps can be presented as simple line drawings or as detailed photographs.

Color Palette

When writers and designers choose a color palette or color scheme for their document, they choose colors that coordinate to create complements or contrasts. Palettes should be kept simple; you don't want to overwhelm your readers by using too many colors in a single design. If, for example, you use different colors to indicate different heading levels, using more than three colors can make it difficult for readers to recall what each color indicates. Many kinds of software include palette generators to help users select colors that work well together.

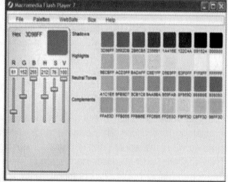

Tables

Notice the difference between the design of this table and the one on the preceding page.

Balance

Though different in approach, the two graphics on this page work together to convey detailed informtion. Despite their visual differences, their spacing and placement create a balanced page.

Highlight

Notice how the only use of the color red on the page highlights the total population information on the map.

Photo Citation

Notice how the writers have chosen to include the photo citation within the photo, rotating the text, rather than as a standard caption.

Typographical Alterations

Notice how the writers shift typographical choices throughout this page, using a standard body text, a red text to highlight, a white text to indicate meta information, bold bulleted lists to highlight in a different way, a larger font to separate, and italicized text to indicate the availability of further information. Note, too, the writers' use of the shaded text box to further distinguish separation.

Bold Typeface:
emphasized text

Larger Font Size:
separates text

Text Box:
separates text

White Typeface:
meta information

Black Typeface:
body text

Red Typeface:
emphasized text

Italicized Typeface:
emphasized text

Monitoring Target 11

At its January 2002 meeting in New York, the UN-Inter-Agency Development Group (UNDG) on MDGs expressed concerns that tenure and sanitation did not adequately constitute a complete response to the target of 'improving the lives of 100 million slum dwellers'. UN-HABITAT therefore also proposed to develop a definition and an operational measurement of slum improvement in order to respond more directly to Target 11.

An Expert Group Meeting was held in Nairobi in November 2002 on 'Defining Slums and Secure Tenure'. Experts agreed on the following generic definition of slums:

A slum is a contiguous settlement where the inhabitants are characterized as having inadequate housing and basic services. A slum is often not recognised and addressed by the public authorities as an integral or equal part of the city.

The Expert Group Meeting recommended that the adequate monitoring of Target 11 be undertaken through five components, reflecting conditions that characterize slums:

- **Insecure residential status;**
- **Inadequate access to safe water;**
- **Inadequate access to sanitation and other infrastructure;**
- **Poor structural quality of housing;**
- **Overcrowding.**

It was also recommended that a slum index be developed on the basis of the above components through networks of activists, policy makers, scholars and practitioners.

The Expert Group Meeting also agreed on the following definition of secure tenure:

Secure Tenure is the right of all individuals and groups to effective protection by the State against unlawful evictions.

Operational definitions and questionnaires are developed further below.

The United Nations system initially assigned two indicators for Target 11:

- **Indicator 31: Proportion of people with secure tenure;**
- **Indicator 32: Proportion of people with access to improved sanitation.**

However, up to recently, there was no internationally recognized operational definition of slums. Other notions were used instead to document the existence of slums: percentage of population living in informal settlements, the durability, quality and size of housing units, the level of basic services, etc. The same applies for security of tenure, indicator 31.

What is a slum household?

A slum household is a group of individuals living under the same roof that lack **one or more** of the conditions listed on the opposite page. According to the situation in the city this can be locally adapted. For example, in cities like Rio de Janeiro where living area is insufficient for both the middle classes and the slum population alike, it could be formulated as two or more of the conditions.

6

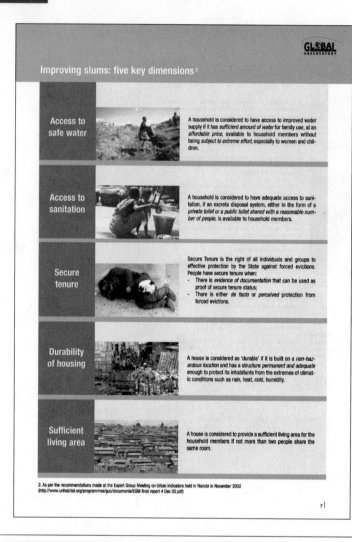

Improving slums: five key dimensions[2]

Access to safe water	A household is considered to have access to improved water supply if it has *sufficient amount of water* for family use, at an *affordable price*, available to household members without being *subject to extreme effort*, especially to women and children.
Access to sanitation	A household is considered to have adequate access to sanitation, if an excreta disposal system, either in the form of a *private toilet* or *public toilet shared with a reasonable number of people*, is available to household members.
Secure tenure	Secure Tenure is the right of all individuals and groups to effective protection by the State against forced evictions. People have secure tenure when: - There is *evidence of documentation* that can be used as proof of secure tenure status; - There is either *de facto* or *perceived* protection from forced evictions.
Durability of housing	A house is considered as 'durable' if it is built on a *non-hazardous location* and has a structure *permanent and adequate* enough to protect its inhabitants from the extremes of climatic conditions such as rain, heat, cold, humidity.
Sufficient living area	A house is considered to provide a sufficient living area for the household members if not more than two people share the same room.

2. As per the recommendations made at the Expert Group Meeting on Urban Indicators held in Nairobi in November 2002 (http://www.unhabitat.org/programmes/guo/documents/EGM final report 4 Dec 02.pdf)

7 |

Repetition/Visual Echo
The same visual elements are repeated to depict relationships between various parts of the visual. Visual repetition can create a sense of harmony within a visual. On this page, the writers depict a relationship between the five key dimensions by repeating the color scheme of the boxes; the size and placement of the photgraphs; and the placement, style, and typography of the written text.

Variation
Variation works in opposition to repetition. That is, variation allows writers to show distinctions between visual elements by emphasizing their differences. Variation can be used to draw a reader's attention, create a hierarchy among parts of a document, or indicate a change or break in a document.

Typographic Variation
Typographic variation changes the size, weight, or color of a font (or alters the position of text, as the writers have done here) to distinguish between levels of information: subtitle and content.

Grouping
Grouping visual elements together can convey a sense of relationship between elements. Readers can make connections between visual elements not just because of their similarities, but specifically because of their arrangement in evident groups. Grouping is achieved through proximity. Items grouped close together appear to be part of the same group, whereas items separated by larger spaces appear to be not grouped together. Grouping can be particularly useful when writing because by dividing and grouping pieces of text on the page or screen, writers visually cue readers that some information is grouped together for a reason.

The spacing of these dots conveys a sense of two groups.

Understanding Design Processes

17.3 Make design part of your overall writing processes

Document design can be thought of as integral to writing processes and central to reader experience. The design process always begins and ends with clear communication.

Unfortunately, there are rarely set rules about design beyond the parameters established by a rhetorical situation. Generally speaking, design thinking encourages creativity and originality but does so within the constraints of the situation. For example, most college writing situations constrain your design and layout possibilities through situational expectations like turning in documents on 8½ × 11 paper with black printer ink (like the first version of the UN report) or through particular electronic course management applications. Just as with writing, in every situation there is effective design and there is ineffective design. Like writing processes and processes for finding, adapting, and making visuals, design processes can be described as a series of steps, and like writing processes and processes for making visuals, these steps should always be thought of as open, nonlinear methods. In short, design processes change depending on the designer and on the situation. Good designers develop good design habits and then learn to adjust them in each situation:

- *Understanding the situation*—Writers and designers need to understand everything about the situation in which their documents, designs, and visuals will participate. This includes identifying and confirming the purpose of the document and the constraints the situation imposes. This part of the process requires asking critical questions and taking lots of notes. What is the purpose of my design and the visuals I am making? What kinds of designs and visuals will the situation allow and not allow?
- *Research and analysis*—Consider what approaches have been used before in this and similar situations. What works and what doesn't work?
- *Design specifications*—Identify all of the details you must include. It is often a good idea to write out design specifications as a list or outline to refer to.
- *Conceptualization*—Begin to draft ideas, to develop concepts and plans. Think of this part of the process as brainstorming, as using the information you have gathered to spark ideas.
- *Development*—Begin drafting and revising your design. Try various approaches. Test ideas on colleagues, peers, and representative audiences. Test the design; test the visual. Seek feedback. Remember, how you design a document helps influence readers' experiences, so it is a good idea to solicit feedback from readers about design effectiveness.
- *Implementation*—Bring your design into the environment where it will function. If, for example, your design is for a research project in a biology class, combine your content and design to begin to see how they work together. Remember, don't add design to your content, create both together, constructing each to serve the other.

- *Evaluation*—Carefully consider what works and what doesn't work with your design. Seek feedback—as much as possible. Your designs and visuals must reach their audiences and serve their purposes. The only true way to test this is to involve readers and ask for their input.
- *Redesign*—At all stages of your design processes, you should be ready to redesign, to adjust, and to revise. Like in all aspects of writing, revision is probably the most important activity you can engage in.

Notice

As you think about and use color in your writing, keep in mind that about 8 percent of all men and 0.5 percent of all women are color blind. Color blindness is a mild disability that prevents people from distinguishing between some colors. It is more prevalent among men because it is associated with the Y chromosome. Although you may not have to account for colorblindness in all of your writing, you should be aware that color blindness does limit how some readers will encounter your writing.

Summary

- Designing is planning and making something.
- Design and layout can be thought of as processes.
- The choices you make in how you put various parts of a visual together affect how your audience reads your documents.
- White space is the space within a document or visual that is not occupied.
- Balance is the way in which elements within a visual or document are arranged and aligned to create a unified whole.
- Grouping visual elements of a document or other visual together can convey a sense of relationship between elements.
- Repetition means using the same visual elements repeated in various parts of a visual to depict relationships between various parts of the visual.
- Variation allows you to show distinctions between visual elements by emphasizing their differences.
- Flow is the ways in which a designer places various visual elements together in order to guide a reader's eyes through the document or visual.

Chapter Review

1. Why is design important?

2. What is the relationship between design and document design?

3. How can we think of design as process?

4. Why is it important to understand how color functions?

5. Identify three forms we respond to visually.

6. If visuals generally occur in two-dimensional presentations, how do they convey depth?

7. How do still visuals convey movement?

8. Identify five design features that are useful in document design.

9. What are some guidelines concerning the size of visuals in document design?

10. What are four identifiable relationships between visuals and written text?

11. What typographical features can be used to create emphasis in your writing?

12. In what ways are templates both useful and possibly detrimental in document design?

Thinking and Writing about the Chapter

Reflection

Now that you have read a bit about document design, look back to the journal entry or blog post you wrote in response to the prompt at the beginning of the chapter. Write a follow-up entry to your orginal response that describes what you now see as the key aspects of document design and the importance of those elements for writers and readers.

Discussion Threads

1. The beginning of this chapter introduces the idea that nearly everything we come in contact with on a daily basis has been designed. Take some time to think about the things with which you interact regularly, particularly those things that include some component of writing, and what kinds of design elements make them effective or ineffective, useful or not. Think, for instance, about the interaction between written text and objects in the bus you ride, the car you drive, the train you take, or any other form of transportation you use regularly. Think about the differences between how the design uses writing and icons. Then, as a class, discuss how you think about the designs of things. Talk about how often you don't consider the design of some things that you use and why it does or doesn't matter if you recognize or acknowledge that some things are designed.

2. On January 10, 2011, the Bowl Championship Series (BCS) National Championship football game pitted the Auburn University Tigers against the University of Oregon Ducks. Auburn won the game 22 to 19. The day after the game, Todd Van Horn, one of Nike's top football uniform designers, described the role of visual design in making the University of Oregon's uniforms. A blog entry posted on the *Fast Company* design blog, titled "How Nike's Visual Tricks Made the Oregon Ducks Look Fast (Despite Defeat)," offered an analysis and commentary on the design of the Oregon uniforms.

As a class, discuss this blog post, considering the power of design in the situation described and how that discussion might inform how you think about design elements in your writing. Is it fair for a team to use their uniforms to distract their opponents, as the Oregon helmet was designed to do, or intimidate them, or confuse them? Do such uniforms give teams an advantage? Consider the differences—if there are any—between the Oregon uniforms and the decision of FINA, the international governing body of competitive swimming, to ban the LZR high-technology swimwear fabric design because it provided swimmers with an unfair advantage.

FIGURE 17.1 An excerpt from a wordless graphic novel.

3. In 1999, French comic book publisher L'Association published an international collection of wordless comics called *Comix 2000*. The book is written and designed to reach across transnational audiences, so none of the comics in it include any words. It is designed to have exactly 2,000 pages, and it contains the work of 324 writers from 29 different countries. The book also includes an introduction that is presented in ten different languages. The book contains no color comics, only black and white. As a class, discuss what challenges writers and designers face in creating wordless visuals, like comics, for a distinctly transnational audience.

4. As a class, discuss some of the design considerations you would need to account for when designing print and electronic documents for these audiences: elderly readers, readers with little time, young readers, and readers with minimal computer experience.

Collaboration

1. Form groups of three or four students; base your divisions on common majors or similar professional interests. As a group, then, identify four primary textual forms used to exchange information within the major or profession your group chooses. You may want to look at trade publications like magazines, newsletters, or web pages. You may want to look at documentation of professional organizations like a governing agency or licensing association. Consider examining professional journals, databases, and archives. You may also want to look to less formal publications like in-field blogs, wikis, and Facebook pages. Once you have located four different forms, use the design features addressed in this chapter to analyze each for design elements. Are there commonalities that seem pertinent to the field? Do the various forms vary in design? Are the designs more indicative of the form or the field? Do the designs seem effective in how they communicate information for the field? Once you have completed your analysis, write a document that reports what you have found in your analysis. When writing the document, pay particular attention to how you design your document to reflect what you have found and how you report the information. Consider how you might use examples from your analysis in the design of your document. Think, too, about how your design will interact with your audience.

2. You probably haven't given it much thought, but a lot of effort was dedicated to creating the design for the chapters of *Writing Situations*. Every design element of the book is the result of collaboration between the writer, editors, and design team. This group created many designs of the book and revised the design often before agreeing on the version you now see. The book is designed to be visually appealing and easily accessible. Its features are demarcated visually. Chapter openers and end-of-chapter materials look different from the rest of the chapters, but look like other chapter openers and end-of-chapter materials. It uses a consistent color palette to denote different heading levels and features in conjunction with typographical variation. Yet, with as much thought as was given to designing the book, the design is also constrained by the physical size of each page and the overall number of pages. Part of this constraint is exacerbated by cost: bigger pages and more pages cost more money to produce. Likewise, visuals taken from elsewhere could only be included if copyright permission could be obtained, or the visuals had to be made specifically for the book. That is to say, the book was designed for a particular situation and the designers carefully considered all of the facets of that situation.

   Despite all of the effort dedicated to the design, other writers, editors, and designers probably would have designed the book differently. In fact, you probably have your own ideas about what would make the design of *Writing Situations* more effective, more aesthetically pleasing, and even more accessible or useful. In small collaborative teams, evaluate the design of the first six pages of this chapter. Using the information found in this chapter, revise the design of the first six pages of the chapter, imagining that your design will then be applied to the rest of the book. Once you have finalized and rendered your design, write an explanation of the choices you made in your redesign. Be sure to upload images of your design and your written explanations to the *Writing Situations* Pavilion to share with other students using *Writing Situations*. The writer, editors, and designers would love to see your design concepts here, too!

3. *Writing Situations* uses numerous headings and other design elements to help its visual organization. Examine any two pages in the book. Notice the number of different design elements used on these pages. To better understand how document design functions, undesign the two pages of the book you have examined. To undesign the pages, take all of the content of the two pages and retype the information in a simple, standard font. Do not divide any of the sections; do not include headings, titles, or other design elements that distinguish between parts of the content. Once you have an undesigned version, exchange your undesigned version with a partner (hint: it's probably easiest to exchange electronic files to work with). Don't tell your partner which two pages you've un-designed (though you should be able to easily tell which pages you've been given based on content). Then, using the content of the undesigned pages you've been given, design the two pages as you would just based on the content you've been given and the design strategies addressed in this chapter. Once you and your partner complete your designs, share them with each other and compare them with the original pages. Discuss your responses to each other's designs and to the process of undesigning.

4. In April 2011, visual designers Geoff Sawers and Bridget Hannigan published a hand-drawn map called "US Literary Map" that uses typography to locate different American authors within their geographical locations. This was Sawers and Hannigan's second literary map;

FIGURE 17.2 Geoff Sawers works on "UK Literary Map."

their first was of British literary figures. The photograph above (Figure 17.2) shows Sawers working on the UK Literary Map. When the U.S. version (see Figure 17.3) was released, Sawers addressed the choices he and Hannigan made in making the maps:

> Now that our US literary map is out, I thought I'd say a word or two about how I did it. The first one (the UK map) was quite eclectic in its selection of authors; it was just my personal favourites, although it covered most of the big names. If anyone were to ask 'Where is so-and-so?' I could just say, 'I'm sorry, I've never read them.'
>
> This time, however, on the USA map, although we have not attempted to be definitive—I think that's impossible—we have tried to be a little more representative. We worked with our old friend Bridget Hannigan, who produced long lists of possible names, partly from her own knowledge (she is an American herself) and partly by going through lists of Pulitzer Prize winners and so on. I added mine, and Matthew in the office supplied several more. There are still one or two high-profile omissions; Ayn Rand and Norman Mailer for instance are both writers who have sold hugely and been widely influential, but at the end of the day you cannot please everybody and to include them would have meant leaving out someone else about whom we felt more strongly.
>
> Once I had chosen an orthographic projection of the contiguous states that cinched in the north a little so that it would all fit on the paper, we divided up the names we had, state by state. They all have some kind of connection to where they are placed; it might be where they were born, lived and died, but in other cases it is just from a single book or poem. Very few people could only be placed in one

FIGURE 17.3 "US Literary Map," Geoff Sawers and Bridget Hannigan.

location. The state boundaries are still visible in some places, although California has spilled over into Nevada, for instance, and New England is so crowded that the names for Maryland, Virginia, and a couple of other states have been displaced to the West and South. Hawaii and Alaska would not fit graphically, so I chose to just draw them at the extreme North- and South-West. Finally, on the East, I included a spray of names coming out from New York who are largely Americans who have made their name in Europe (James Baldwin, Gertrude Stein) or immigrants.

I love the way the relative density of the coasts and interior tells its own story about America; the Native American names that crop up in the mid-West, the Hispanic names further south. And then I settled down to ink it all in; a process that took some weeks. I amazed myself by doing it all without a single correction; on the UK map I mis-spelt the very first word.

The literary maps are interesting projects both in terms of what they convey and in how they are designed. The choice, for instance, to use textual representations of each author instead of, say, portraits, for example, changes drastically how we read the map. In fact, because Sawers chose to use written text, we literally read this map, not just look at it.

Working in small groups, design and produce a similar kind of text-based map, but not one of literary figures. Instead choose another framing concept. Consider, for instance, using sports teams, agricultural production, recreational activities, wildlife inhabitants, musicians, artists, athletes, local television affiliates, and so on. Once you design and produce your map, explain, in a brief essay, why you made all of the visual rhetorical choices you made in designing your map as you did.

Writing

1. Using your word processor, examine the list of fonts available to you. Select one that appeals to you visually. Take some time to learn about the history of that font through web-based research. Then identify five examples of where that font is used and acquire a visual of the font used in those locations. Write a history of the font, showing the locations of its use that you have identified and any other visual you feel might help clarify your historical record of the font.

2. Books that are reprinted in newer editions over time are often redesigned with each new edition. Likewise, different publishers may publish their own versions of classic books, creating designs unique to their editions. Select one of the books listed at the end of this assignment. Locate at least four different editions of the same book. Vary the editions you select based on a range of years and, if possible, various publishers. Analyze the differences in design in each version, paying particular attention to typographic choices. Consider, too, the material differences of each edition, like the size of the pages and the quality of the paper. Once you have examined the four versions, write a comparison of the design of the four versions. Be sure to address how the various design approaches affect how you respond to the book and how you read it.

Books:

The Aeneid
David Copperfield
Being and Time
The Compleat Angler
Lectures on Rhetoric and Belles Lettres
The Plays of William Shakespeare
Tom Sawyer
The Prince
The Great Gatsby
Slaughterhouse-Five
1984
The Republic
Brothers Karamazov
The Catcher in the Rye
The Wealth of Nations
For Whom the Bell Tolls
The Picture of Dorian Gray

The Grapes of Wrath
Brave New World
How to Win Friends and Influence People
The Call of the Wild
Swiss Family Robinson
Dharma Bums
The Iliad and the Odyssey
Catch-22
Walden
Lord of the Flies
The Master and Margarita
Atlas Shrugged
The Metamorphosis
Ulysses
The Young Man's Guide
Seek: Reports from the Edges of America & Beyond

Crime and Punishment

The Art of Warfare

Don Quixote

The Hobbit

The Rough Riders

East of Eden

Leviathan

Adventures of Huckleberry Finn

The Politics

The Boy Scout Handbook

Cyrano de Bergerac

The Crisis

Invisible Man

The Divine Comedy

3. Often, writers and document designers need to use the same content in multiple media forms. Design requirements for print documents, web pages, blogs, and promotional materials like pamphlets are likely to vary. Select a document you have recently written for an academic assignment. Create three versions of the document using the design approaches addressed in this chapter: a print document, a web-based document, and a blog entry.

4. We have all encountered documents that have been overdesigned: documents that use too many colors, too many different fonts, too many variations. We read documents that overuse emphasis elements like boldface, italics, capitalization, underscore, and colored lettering. Locate an example of an overdesigned document. Analyze the document for the information it works to convey and for the flaws you see in its design approach. Then redesign the text to make it more efficient.

5. As you have seen in this chapter, document design is constrained by the material elements of the situation. For instance, when writing a traditional research paper for one of your classes, the standard 8½ × 11-inch paper constrains what you can and cannot do with your design on that page. For this assignment, design the "document" that appears on the six sides of a milk or juice carton, like the one pictured here. Have fun creating your product, but keep in mind what kinds of information should be included in the rhetorical situation of a milk or juice carton. Be sure to include what needs to be there while also including what you think makes the document aesthetically pleasing and functional. Pay attention to color choice, readability, legibility, and content delivery.

6. Designer Shepard Fairey started as a street artist known for his street art campaign: "André the Giant Has a Posse," which featured a stencil of the face of World Wrestling Federation super star André the Giant and the word "obey." For the 2008 United States Presidential campaign, Fairey used a similar design to create the now famous Hope poster of Barack Obama. As Fairey's poster earned fame as the icon for Obama's campaign, many parodies and remixes of the poster also emerged, helping the poster become more iconic. In the designs of the André the Giant poster and the Obama poster, Fairey uses a combination of text and graphic, creating an interesting balance both visually and in terms of information between the word and the graphic.

For this assignment, design a full-color poster that combines a picture of something widely recognizable—like a famous person, place, event, or object—and a single word that establishes a meaningful relationship between word and picture. When you design your poster, consider the ways you might change the picture you use to create a specific feel to your poster. Consider altering tint, saturation, and tone, but be sure your changes don't eliminate the ability to recognize the person, place, event, or thing. Pay close attention to the colors you use, the typographical choices you make, the balance and symmetry of the design, and the meaning you convey. Your poster may be ironic, humorous, argumentative, informative, inspirational, motivational, demotivational, or any other purpose you wish to assign it.

7. For this assignment, begin by identifying the ten most populated cities in the United States. Then locate the local government web pages for each of the ten cities and, if your hometown is not one of the ten cities, your own local government's web pages. Analyze the web pages for design approaches, noting design strategies and evaluating design effectiveness. How does your city's web page compare to the most populated cities' web pages? Next, examine the web pages for the major newspapers in each of the most populated cities and your own hometown. Once you have conducted your analysis and evaluation, write an assessment of how your city is represented through the design of both the local government web pages and the local newspaper web pages.

Local Situation

College campuses around the country produce large numbers of documents for a wide range of audiences and situations. Materials for recruiting students, attracting donors, publicizing events, acknowledging achievements, and reporting policies are written, designed, and updated regularly by writers from a range of locations on every campus. In order to help retain consistency among the range of documents circulated, many colleges develop templates and even policies about what and how information is to be disseminated.

Think about how information is conveyed to new students on your campus. Develop a template for a document to be used to inform first-year students on your campus of news, policy changes, deadlines, and other important information. Think not only about how such documents work to convey information for pragmatic reasons but also how those documents might be used to help build a sense of community on campus for new students. Consider what elements of your template must appear on all documents, what design structures should be adhered to, and what elements allow writers to make adjustments.

Writing Research

18 | Planning and Conducting Research

Learning Objectives

18.1 Describe academic research as a nonlinear process of critical scholarly investigation

18.2 Conduct research using an analytical and evaluative approach

18.3 Develop criteria for evaluating research resources

18.4 Use library resources such as catalogs and databases effectively

18.5 Use online resources such as search engines efficiently and effectively

18.6 Conduct primary research and field research

Before you read this chapter

What is "research"? When and how do you conduct research? Is research something you only do or use in academic settings? In your journal or blog, compose an entry about what research means to you.

Research is the careful and systematic search for information and evidence in the pursuit of learning. Research requires asking questions through a process that is central to learning about rhetorical situations. Each stage of research locates information that not only helps answer relevant questions but also leads to new questions. Research is always a critical process, one that requires you to analyze and evaluate information to determine its value and reliability. The research process also reveals how others contribute to a situation as well as what is accepted and not accepted as legitimate information in a situation.

Primary research is the collection of original information through methods such as experiments, interviews, field research, surveys, and questionnaires. Primary research might also include examining original documents, like historical records, literary works, or images. Secondary research involves examining what others have already contributed to someone's primary research. Secondary research materials include books that convey information about a subject, scholarly journal articles, textbooks, biographies, and documentaries. If you were writing an essay and used a quotation from Nathaniel Hawthorne's essay "Chiefly about War Matters," you would be using a primary source. If you referred to James Bense's book *Nathaniel Hawthorne's Intention in "Chiefly About War Matters,"* you would be referring to a secondary source.

Some research takes place in libraries, including special parts of a library like an archive or a special collection. Much research now takes place online. Some research requires firsthand learning in laboratories or in the field. Different disciplines approach research differently, and in each area of study you pursue, you will need to learn what research approaches are accepted and expected. Scientific research, for example, relies on approaches that are different from research in the humanities. Searching for the information we need can be daunting simply because there is so much of it. Various active reading strategies can help you navigate the mass of information available.

Traditionally, academic research was defined as a six-step process:

1. Identify the question you need to answer or the problem you need to solve.
2. Locate all of the literature (relevant information) already written about the subject, a process called a "literature review."
3. Identify the purpose of your own research.
4. Gather information relevant to your research purpose.
5. Analyze or interpret the data you gathered.
6. Evaluate the information and report your findings.

Although this process served its purposes for a long time in the age of print, contemporary methods modify this process to adapt to the age of digital information and ever-expanding knowledge.

It would likely be impossible to locate and review all of the literature pertinent to a given research endeavor, particularly when responding to a college writing assignment in a limited amount of time. Likewise, first gathering vast amounts of research and then evaluating it is rather inefficient. Instead, analysis and evaluation should permeate research processes so you can refine your searching smoothly and efficiently in an ongoing process.

18.1 Describe academic research as a nonlinear process of critical scholarly investigation

Critical Scholarly Investigation

Research in college can be thought of as critical scholarly investigation. Each of these terms—*critical, scholarly, investigation*—evokes a particular aspect of how academic research is conducted:

Critical—Academic research should involve a process of critique that includes questioning and judging. It should always be critical, analytical, and evaluative. Academic research requires skeptical reading.

Scholarly—Academic research is grounded in scholarly methodologies and uses sound resources. It respects scholarly and intellectual values and builds ethically on the work of others.

Investigation—Academic research requires close study and observation. It is systematic and methodic in its inquiry. Academic research asks more than the surface-level questions. It delves into details to reveal new information.

Evaluation and analysis should always be central to research. Evaluation is not the final stage of a research process but the atmosphere in which research unfolds.

Like writing processes, research processes are not linear (see Figure 18.1). What research reveals alters thinking, planning, and the next questions that need to be

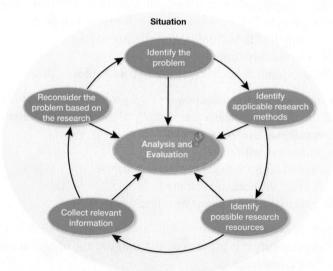

FIGURE 18.1 A visual model of research as a nonlinear process.

asked. Ideally, research never ends, but realistically, research stops when you have discovered enough useful and reliable information to fulfill the needs of the situation in which you participate. You can approach research as an ongoing process.

Analyzing and Evaluating Sources

18.2 Conduct research using an analytical and evaluative approach

Analysis is careful examination, a process of breaking something down to observe how all of its parts work together as a whole. Analysis requires critical reflection as well as evaluation and judgment. Analyzing research materials involves carefully examining each resource and asking many questions about it, including the following:

Question	Comments
Who wrote it?	Knowing the credentials and authority of an author can help you quickly assess the value and reliability of a work. Look specifically for bylines and author affiliations.
What else has the writer written?	Is this person an expert? Experts write about subjects more than once and may be more reliable writers than others who have written only a single piece about a subject.
Where was it published?	Identifying the publisher of a text can indicate whether the publication was vetted by professionals and whether the publication has a bias toward a particular political position.
Where was it published?	The relevance of some information may be time sensitive, and some research may have been updated or refuted since publication. Always consider the most recent and relevant information, but also consider the field-defining, canonical works that are still relevant.
What does the content convey?	After reading the text, explain to yourself what the content says and take notes about how you draw that conclusion from the writing.
What argument does the writer make?	What stance does the writer take on the issue? Is it sound and logical? Does the writer provide ample evidence to support the argument? Do the sources of evidence suggest reliability?
Who is the intended audience?	The reliability of a piece may be affected by who the intended audience is.
What have others said about it?	Research is only as valid as the situation allows it to be. Research that is often cited may be of greater relevance than research that isn't. Likewise, consider how others related to the situation respond to the research: do they embrace it, reject it, or criticize it?

Analytical questions don't always lead to immediate answers. Instead, analytical questions often lead to more questions, and good analysis and research follow the leads those questions reveal. Evaluating a resource involves asking and answering analytical questions. To evaluate is to judge by determining something's worth, merit, and significance. Like analysis, evaluation depends on careful scrutiny and examination. Detailed analysis works best when you establish specific criteria to investigate. Criteria are the standards used to judge something.

18.3 Develop criteria for evaluating research resources

The criteria you use to analyze and evaluate research materials will always be influenced by the situation. College writing situations, for example, require that research materials be judged based on scholarly criteria. Although they change with methods and with time, scholarly criteria are established by the academic situation. Thus, when you conduct research in college, you do not have to create criteria; instead, you learn and adhere to criteria appropriate to the situation.

Every academic discipline has its own kinds of research criteria. The criteria for research in biology, for example, vary from criteria in English, history, physics, mathematics, and every other discipline. It is the researcher's responsibility to understand those criteria and apply them when conducting research. Part of this task is simplified by the fact that reliable, validated information circulates through specific kinds of publications. Focusing your research efforts on these kinds of resources can help simply because they have usually been evaluated by scholarly criteria and are understood as reliable. Many kinds of documents fall into this category:

- Scholarly books
- Biographies
- Scholarly articles
- Sponsored web pages
- Interviews
- Tests, observations, experiments

Other kinds of documents may also be reliable but may require a greater degree of scrutiny:

- Trade books (for general readers)
- Newspapers and online news sources
- E-mails
- Individual websites
- Internet chat forums
- Blogs
- Wikis

Some kinds of documents may not be accepted as valid college-level research and should be avoided simply because they do not meet scholarly criteria:

- Encyclopedias
- Clearinghouses for term papers and essays

Even though you may have confidence in specific types of sources, always evaluate the particular resource and its content to ensure that it meets scholarly criteria. Analyzing and evaluating involves not only validating the reliability of the source but also evaluating the information, the research itself. Consider, for example, the researcher who locates an interesting and important article in a reputable scholarly journal, written by a reputable expert in the field. The researcher then cites the article in her own research only to later discover that the cited article had been disputed and proven invalid in other research. In this situation, the researcher failed to carefully evaluate the information, relying simply on the fact that it appeared in a reputable resource.

Because college-level research and writing are inseparable and because they are understood to meet scholarly criteria, students should expect to meet the same kinds of criteria. These criteria should be used to analyze and evaluate the materials you use in your research, and they should be applied to your own writing. You can think of the following criteria as "scholarly":

Criterion	Comments
Substantive	Research materials must carry weight and should include substantial information.
Relevant	Research materials should clearly relate to your research objectives; your research objectives should clearly relate to the task you have been assigned.
Authoritative	Research materials should be published and circulated through mechanisms that have histories and reputations as authorities within the subject area. Likewise, the authors should either have an established record as an authority or establish themselves as authoritative through the resource.
Accurate	Research materials should convey their correctness through professional validation like peer-review processes, as most scholarly journals and scholarly books do, or they should prove their validity within the content.
Timely	Research materials should be current in their information. Even historical documents or documents about historical information should be accurate in their timeliness.

Using these criteria as guidelines and developing critical analytical and evaluative questions to investigate those criteria throughout your research process will lead to more effective, reliable, and relevant research. Conduct your research—no matter what kind or for what purpose—in an atmosphere of analysis and evaluation.

Conducting Research

Academic research is far more than a quick Google search. There are many ways to conduct research and many methodologies and resources to use. Moreover, in each subject you study, you will need to adjust your research approaches to adhere to the criteria of that discipline—and the criteria your teachers establish. Meeting those criteria requires that you be rigorous in your research approaches.

18.4 Use library resources such as catalogs and databases effectively

Using Library Resources

When it comes to academic research, there really is no better resource than your school's library (see Figure 18.2). Evaluating research materials in a college library can be much easier simply because most of the materials housed in academic libraries are assumed to be already evaluated, reliable, and in accordance with many scholarly criteria. Successful college writers and researchers develop good working relationships with their libraries. Start by taking a tour of your library, wandering around, and learning what resources are available. Above all, get to know the librarians—the most important assets libraries have.

Many resources allow you to ask librarians questions about your research online. For example, the online Ask a Librarian resource at the Library of Congress allows users to submit questions or conduct virtual chats with librarians to solve research problems. Many state library systems maintain similar online tools for researching materials available in that state, and most college library web pages allow you to send queries to librarians.

In the past, learning your library required going to the physical library spaces on your campus—which is still an important thing to do. Today, you can wander around your library from your computer, tablet, or smartphone no matter where you are (see Figure 18.3). Through your library's web pages you can easily contact a librarian or check the availability of books, journal articles, reference materials, and other information the library maintains. In many instances, you can even download or check out electronic copies of the documents you need.

Tech Tip

Many resources allow you to ask librarians questions about your research online. For example, the online Ask a Librarian resource at the Library of Congress allows users to submit questions or conduct virtual chats with librarians to solve research problems. Many state library systems maintain similar online tools for researching materials available in that state, and most college library web pages allow you to send queries to librarians.

FIGURE 18.2 Rule one of library research should always be "ask a librarian."

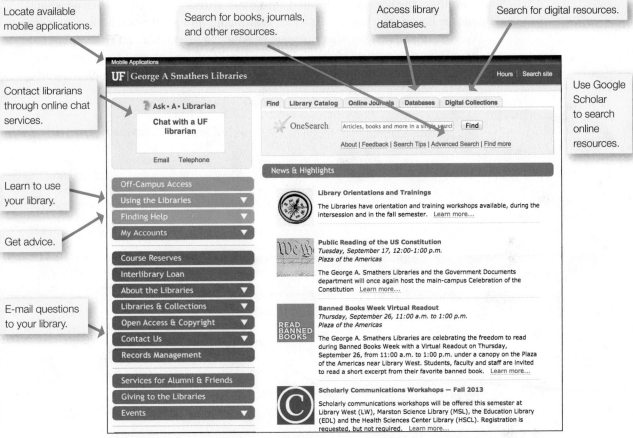

Locate available mobile applications.

Search for books, journals, and other resources.

Access library databases.

Search for digital resources.

Contact librarians through online chat services.

Use Google Scholar to search online resources.

Learn to use your library.

Get advice.

E-mail questions to your library.

FIGURE 18.3 You can use many of your library's resources just by learning what the library has available online.

Using the Library's Catalogs

Most library catalogs can now be found online, so you can browse these resources from just about anywhere. Digital catalogs can make finding resources convenient, but as a researcher, you will need to learn how to best use the digital catalogs available to you.

Locating books.   Book catalogs identify all of the books a library has available. Online catalogs allow users to search for books by title, author, subject, series, International Standard Book Number (ISBN), International Standard Serial Number (ISSN), Online Computer Library Center Numbers (OCLC), and even the book's library call numbers (see page 412). Catalogs show users whether a library houses a specific book, where in the library it is located, and other critical information such as what editions the library has, whether the book is available, and publication information.

As an example, imagine that you were conducting research about visual images. You heard about Ron Burnett's book *How Images Think* and wanted to examine the book yourself. Figures 18.4 and 18.5 show what information you could gather about the book by using the library's online catalog.

Use the catalog search engine to conduct a title search for the book.

You can save these catalog listings in a folder in case you want to look for other resources and return to these later.

You can add each catalog listing to a folder, print the listing, e-mail the listing to yourself or someone else, text message the listing to yourself or someone else, get a citation for the listing, or export the listing into other citation genertors.

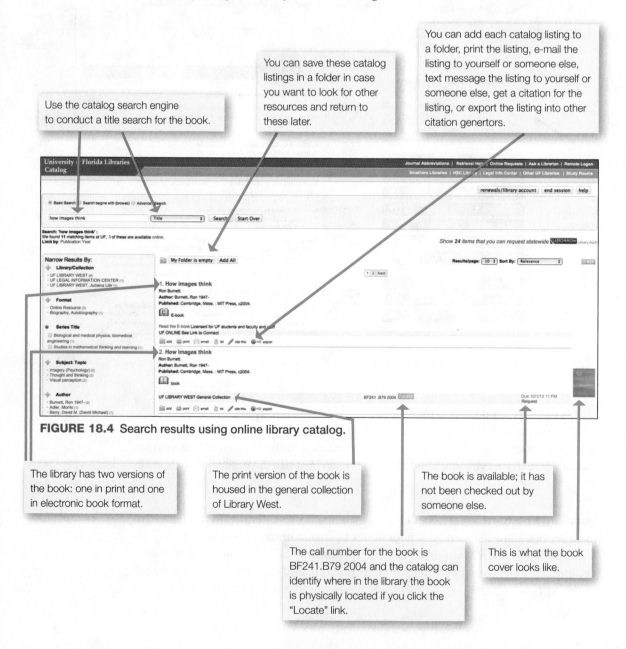

FIGURE 18.4 Search results using online library catalog.

The library has two versions of the book: one in print and one in electronic book format.

The print version of the book is housed in the general collection of Library West.

The book is available; it has not been checked out by someone else.

The call number for the book is BF241.B79 2004 and the catalog can identify where in the library the book is physically located if you click the "Locate" link.

This is what the book cover looks like.

Export this catalog information to a citation generator

Text this catalog listing to yourself or someone else

Print this catalog listing

Add the catalog listing to your research folder

View all catalog listings in your research folder

E-mail this catalog listing to yourself or someone else

Get a citation for this book

Author's name and birthdate link to all works by the author housed in the library

Publication information

ISBN

Subjects under which the book is cataloged

Media format (book)

Book's table of contents

Location of the book: library in which it is located, the call number for locating the book, and a link to show the physical location of the book within the library

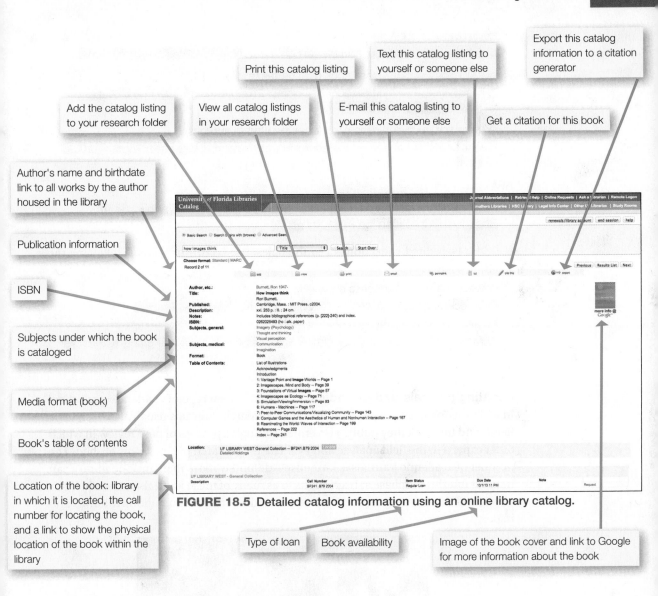

FIGURE 18.5 Detailed catalog information using an online library catalog.

Type of loan

Book availability

Image of the book cover and link to Google for more information about the book

How to Cite Books

MLA

Author or Editor's Last Name, First Name, Middle Initial. *Book Title.* Place of Publication: Publisher, Year of Publication. Medium.

Note: If the book is an edited collection or anthology, use "ed." or "eds." after the editor's name(s).

Note: For books with more than three authors or editors, use "et al."—the abbreviation for the Latin "et alii" (and others).

EXAMPLE FOR SINGLE-AUTHORED BOOK

Steinbeck, John. *The Log from the Sea of Cortez.* New York: Penguin, 1995. Print.

EXAMPLE FOR MULTI-AUTHORED BOOK (TWO OR THREE AUTHORS)

Williams, Joseph M., and Gregory G. Colomb. *Style: Lessons in Clarity and Grace.* New York: Longman, 2010. Print.

EXAMPLE FOR MULTI-AUTHORED BOOK (MORE THAN THREE AUTHORS)

Bloom, Lynn Z., et al. *The New Assertive Woman.* Gretna, LA: Selfhelp Success, 2009. Print.

APA

Author or Editor's last name, First initial, Middle initial. (Date of publication). *Book title.* Publication location: Publisher.

Note: For edited collections or anthologies, use "(Ed.)" or "(Eds.)" following the editor's name(s).

EXAMPLE FOR SINGLE-AUTHORED BOOK

Steinbeck, J. (1995). *The log from the Sea of Cortez.* New York: Penguin.

EXAMPLE FOR MULTI-AUTHORED BOOK

Williams, J. M., & Colomb, C. G. (2010). *Style: Lessons in clarity and grace.* New York: Longman.

Locating journals and periodicals. Journals are a type of academic periodical in which scholars and experts publish their research. Journals usually serve specific fields, and the work they publish is verified through a process of peer review in which other experts in the field analyze and evaluate the research before it is published. The number of academic journals is immense—definitely more than any one library can house. Libraries purchase subscriptions to as many of these journals as their budgets allow, and they catalog these resources, including information about volumes and issues.

In addition to academic journals, many libraries also maintain large collections of periodicals such as newspapers and magazines. Some magazines, like *Nature* or *Science*, have the reputation of publishing important, validated research. Some kinds of periodicals report on news and other events.

Many library catalogs now provide direct links to digital versions of specific articles and provide searches for journal titles and article titles (see the section about databases below). Advanced search mechanisms may also allow you to search within selected parameters such as specific publication dates.

As an example, consider that in your research you wanted to locate information found in the journal *Journal of Thought*. The library catalog can provide detailed information about how to find the journal in the library and online (see Figure 18.6).

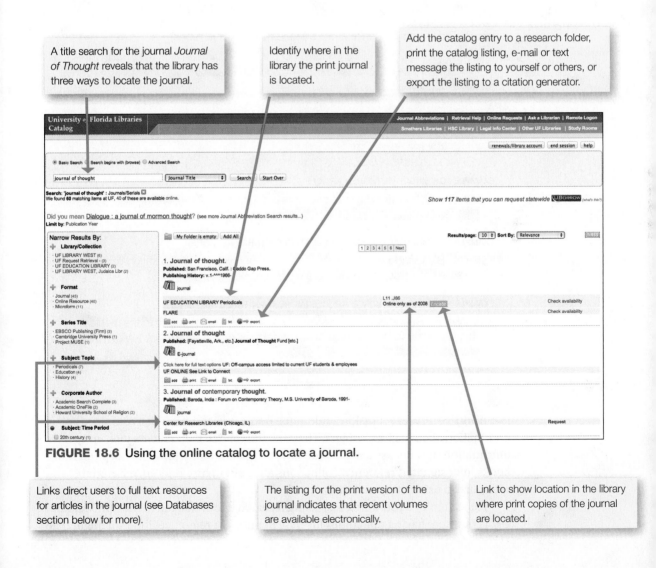

A title search for the journal *Journal of Thought* reveals that the library has three ways to locate the journal.

Identify where in the library the print journal is located.

Add the catalog entry to a research folder, print the catalog listing, e-mail or text message the listing to yourself or others, or export the listing to a citation generator.

FIGURE 18.6 Using the online catalog to locate a journal.

Links direct users to full text resources for articles in the journal (see Databases section below for more).

The listing for the print version of the journal indicates that recent volumes are available electronically.

Link to show location in the library where print copies of the journal are located.

How to Cite Journal Articles

MLA

Author's Last Name, First Name, Middle Initial. "Article Title." *Journal Title* Volume. Issue Number (Year of Publication): Page Range. Medium.

EXAMPLE FOR SINGLE-AUTHORED ARTICLE

Dobrin, Sidney I. "Ecology and Concepts of Technology." *Journal of the Council of Writing Program Administrators.* 35.1 (2011): 175–98. Print.

EXAMPLE FOR MULTI-AUTHORED ARTICLE (TWO OR THREE AUTHORS)

Halbritter, Bump, and Julie Lindquist. "Time, Lives, and Videotape: Operationalizing Discovery in Senses of Literacy Sponsorship." *College English* 75.2 (2012): 171–98. Print.

EXAMPLE FOR MULTI-AUTHORED ARTICLE (MORE THAN THREE AUTHORS)

Jaeschke, Roman, et al. "Users' Guides to the Medical Literature: How to Use an Article About a Diagnostic Test." *Journal of the American Medical Association* 271.9 (1994): 703–07. Print.

APA

Author's last name, First initial, Middle initial. (Date of publication). Title of article. *Title of Journal, Volume*(issue), page numbers.

EXAMPLE FOR SINGLE-AUTHORED ARTICLE

Dobrin, S. I. (2011). Ecology and concepts of technology. *Journal of the Council of Writing Program Administrators, 35*(1), 175–198.

EXAMPLE FOR MULTI-AUTHORED ARTICLE (TWO OR THREE AUTHORS)

Halbritter, B., & Lindquist, J. (2012). Time, lives, and videotape: Operationalizing discovery in senses of literacy sponsorship. *College English, 75*(2), 171–198.

EXAMPLE FOR MULTI-AUTHORED ARTICLE (MORE THAN THREE AUTHORS)

Jaeschke, R., Guyyatt, G. H., & Sackett, D. L. (1994). Users' guides to the medical literature: How to use an article about a diagnostic test. *Journal of the American Medical Association, 271*(9), 703–707.

Locating reference books. Reference books are comprehensive collections of information about a given subject. They are designed to help readers look up specific information, not necessarily be read cover to cover. Many libraries keep reference books in designated reference collections and, often, hire reference librarians who specialize in using these materials.

For example, if you were conducting research about Kenyan author Dr. Margaret Ogola but were having difficulties locating her book, a reference librarian might help you use the library's catalog to locate the reference work *Kenya Books in Print* to look up information about Ogola's book (see Figure 18.7).

FIGURE 18.7 Using the online catalog to locate reference materials.

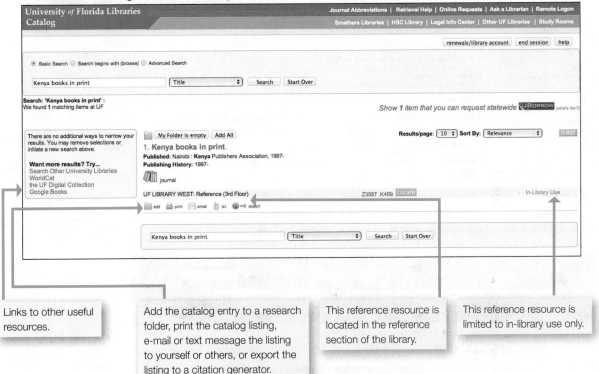

Links to other useful resources.

Add the catalog entry to a research folder, print the catalog listing, e-mail or text message the listing to yourself or others, or export the listing to a citation generator.

This reference resource is located in the reference section of the library.

This reference resource is limited to in-library use only.

Searching archives. Archives are collections of historical records such as documents that are of particular value or that are rare. Many libraries maintain archives of their college or university documents, preserving the history of the institution; some also maintain archives or special collections of distinct materials. Archives and special collections are often kept separate from a library's general collection and are likely to be restricted from general circulation and use because of their value or age. However, many libraries have begun digitizing their archives and special collections to make them more accessible, and you can search them through catalogs.

Searching bibliographies. Bibliographies are lists of books, articles, and other documents that are compiled to show works related to a given subject or by a specific author. Bibliographies can be of great use in conducting research because they make it easier for researchers to identify possible resources. Although libraries usually house a variety of bibliographies (see Figure 18.8), many of which are updated regularly, online bibliographies are able to provide more up-to-date bibliographic information (see Figure 18.9).

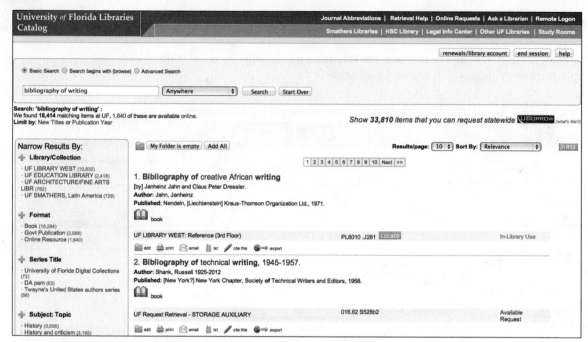

FIGURE 18.8 Using the online catalog to locate bibliographies.

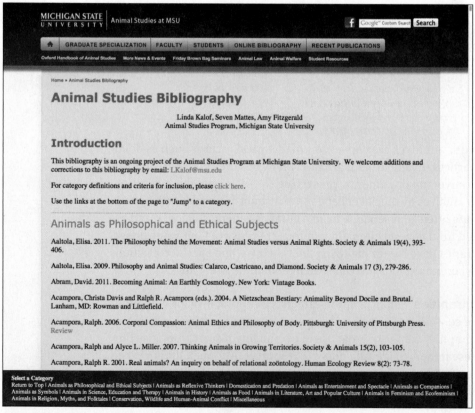

FIGURE 18.9 An online bibliography.

Using catalog links, interlibrary loan, and library networks. Because space and economics limit the overall number of resources a single library can house, many library catalogs include links to other reliable sources through which you might find useful information. Similarly, many libraries belong to library networks that allow patrons at one library to search other libraries in the network for resources and, in most cases, allow patrons to borrow those resources through interlibrary loans (see Figure 18.10).

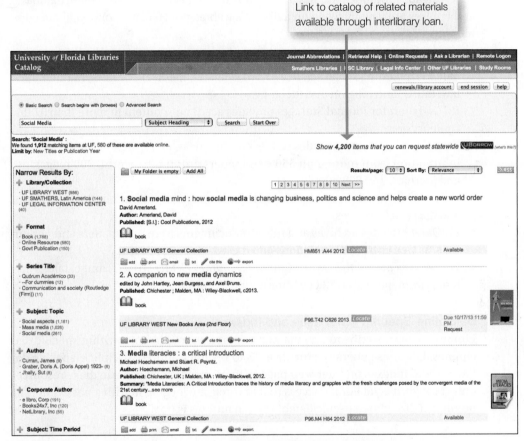

FIGURE 18.10 Link to materials available through interlibrary loan.

Using Databases and Indexes

Databases and indexes are comprehensive collections of information, some that are general purpose and some that are discipline specific. Indexes provide specific citations for where to locate articles in periodicals and other publications. Some indexes include abstracts or summaries of the publications to help you determine whether the publication serves your needs. These databases and indexes help libraries save space by providing patrons with direct links to texts they need without having to physically store the texts in the library. For researchers, databases and indexes are convenient because they provide information about and quick access to journals, articles, and other documents.

General Purpose-Databases and Indexes

General-purpose databases and indexes provide information across disciplines. They are useful for initiating a research project because they can provide an overview of the kinds of resources that are available. Reference librarians can help you determine which database or index will best suit your research needs. Links to general databases and indexes are usually listed on a library's web pages. Here are some that are commonly used:

- *Academic Search Complete* provides direct links to full-text journals in a wide range of fields including social sciences, hard sciences, medical sciences, mathematics, law, music, and religion and theology.
- *JSTOR* (short for Journal Storage) provides academic content in more than 57 disciplinary areas.
- *LexisNexis Academic* provides full text for business, legal, medical, and reference information from more than 350 newspapers around the world, 300 magazines and journals, and 600 newsletters.
- *Project Muse* provides online access to peer-reviewed journals in the humanities and the social sciences.
- *ProQuest* provides archives and full-text documents from newspapers and periodicals, as well as from dissertations and theses.
- *WorldCat* is part of the *Online Computer Library Center* (OCLC) and catalogs materials from more than 72,000 libraries in 170 countries.

Discipline-Specific Databases and Indexes

Libraries also subscribe to and maintain databases and indexes within specific disciplines. Libraries generally provide links to several hundred discipline-specific databases and indexes on their web pages. Often, researchers can use these resources only through special library access that may require logging in with a password. The number of discipline-specific databases and indexes is huge.

Accessing Government Publications

Indexes and databases can also be useful for locating government documents. Local, state, and federal government agencies all publish a variety of documents, including reports, factsheets, and surveys. The Federal Depository Library Program (FDLP) distributes federal government publications to libraries through the U.S. Government Printing Office (GPO), which publishes documents produced by and for the federal government. Among its resources, the GPO publishes the *Federal Register*, a daily-updated publication of rules and policies for federal agencies and organizations; the *Congressional Record*, the official record of U.S. Congressional proceedings; and the

Code Laws of the United States of America, which compiles all U.S. federal laws. You can link to FDLP resources through most library web pages or access the online Catalog of U.S. Government Publications (see Figure 18.11).

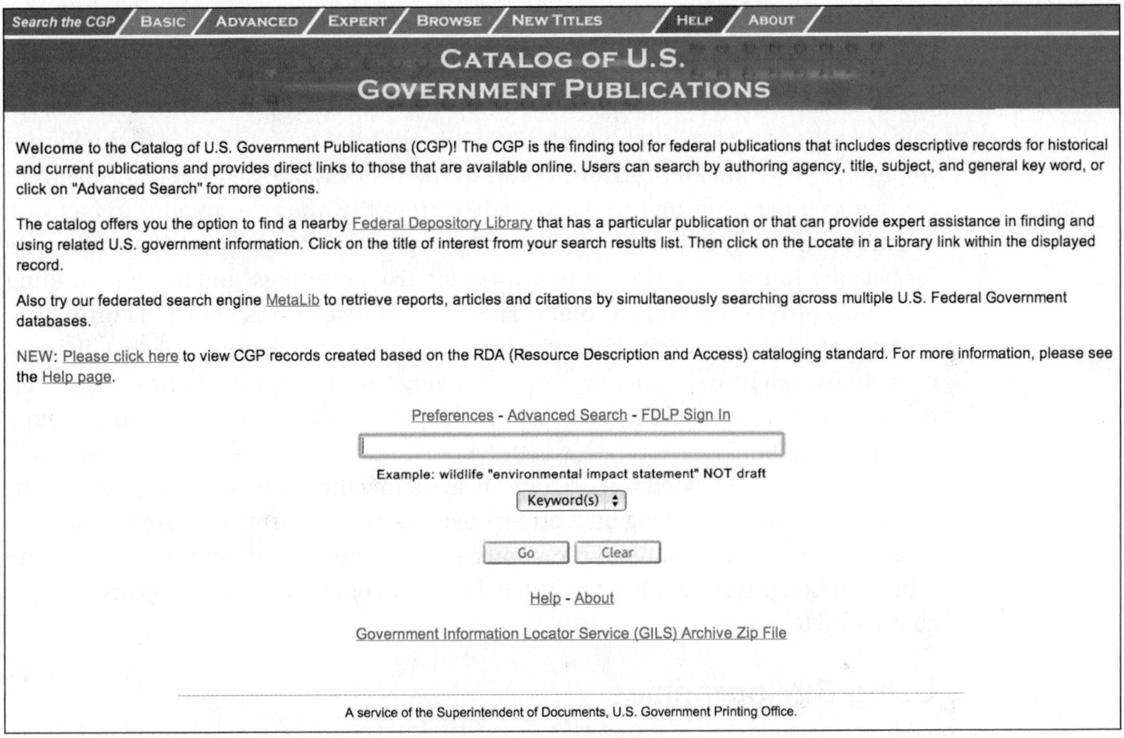

FIGURE 18.11 The Catalog of U.S. Government Publications; www.gpo.gov.

Using Biographies

Some research requires that you learn about and account for biographical information. In addition to general catalog searches, you can use a number of other research tools to locate specific biographical resources. Some of these tools may provide short biographies, and some provide citations for where to locate biographies. Because biographies are published in many forms—books, articles, interviews—using these print and electronic tools to locate biographies can make your research more efficient. Commonly used biography resources are listed here:

- *Biography Index* provides index listings for biographies that have been published in books and magazines.
- *Biographical Dictionaries* provide alphabetic listings of biographies and short biographical statements for each listing.
- *Biography Reference Bank* provides biographical information for more than 660,700 individuals and links to more than 380,000 related, full-text articles.

- *Current Biography* is a monthly magazine that publishes biographical profiles of newsworthy individuals.
- *Contemporary Authors* part of the Gale Network, provides biographical information about more than 120,000 modern writers.

Browsing

Before libraries began cataloging their holdings in digitally accessible formats, researchers had to locate documents in the library's holdings by going to the library to physically locate and retrieve them. In the process, a researcher's eyes might wander to other titles on the shelves adjacent to the ones she sought. In fact, she might intentionally look at the books and journals surrounding the ones she came for because library materials are organized in like groupings, and the surrounding titles may also be of interest to her. This form of research is known as browsing. Browsing the library, casually looking at or reading through the items in a library's collections, can be a productive—and satisfying—form of research. Browsing often turns up useful materials and can spark thoughts and ideas for how to approach a research project.

Patient and dedicated researchers always allow themselves time to browse a library's stacks when working on a project because that unstructured approach lets a researcher roam in unplanned directions. Because most academic libraries use the Library of Congress Classification System (see box), books of similar subjects are typically found together.

Using Bibliographies

Chances are that many of the resources you locate in your research will include bibliographies of the resources the writer cites. Thorough researchers always examine bibliographies to locate other sources. Bibliographies can also reveal information about the reliability of the work in which the bibliography appears. In fact, many researchers examine a work's bibliography first, before reading any of the work, to gather information about the work and its reliability and relevance. Bibliographies that identify other reliable sources are likely to indicate that the work itself is reliable. Likewise, if particular works appear in several bibliographies across your research, you might infer that the cited work is important and relevant. The dates of works listed in a bibliography can suggest whether the work is addressing recent information or whether it is outdated.

18.5 Use online resources such as search engines efficiently and effectively

Using Online Resources

In addition to the many resources available through libraries, researchers now use the World Wide Web and other Internet resources to conduct research. Online research of the Internet's remarkable amount of information can be productive, but beware: a lot of the information is not useful, and a good deal of it is not reliable. The first rule of online research is to confirm reliability. You can best ensure reliability if you use the resources to which the library provides links, but libraries don't have all of the resources that you might find online, so you may need to search for other online resources. However, never rely strictly on online research. Always use library resources in conjunction with online resources—the second rule of online research. The following sections provide suggestions and guidelines for conducting research online.

Two Rules of Online Research

1. Confirm reliability of the source.
2. Always use library resources in conjunction with online resources.

Using Search Engines and Web Directories

Search engines locate information housed on the Web. Search engines can return results for web pages, images, document files, and other file types. Search engines use highly sophisticated algorithms and automated web crawlers to locate and index information related to the keywords or search terms a user provides. Some of the most commonly used search engines include Google, Yahoo!, Bing, AltaVista, Lycos, and Ask. Search engines can be useful, but they can also be chaotic and unreliable. Because each search engine uses its own algorithms and web crawling approaches, each can return different results for the same searches. For example, consider the different search returns for information about Caribbean writer Jamaica Kincaid delivered by Google and Bing in Figure 18.12. Likewise, a search engine may not search all of the content in a web page or may not search all web pages, potentially overlooking information that may be of use. Some search engines such as Google and Yahoo! also give priority to sponsored links. Consequently, some returns appear just because their owners have paid for them to appear in the results, which alters what results you receive.

Because general search engines can be unpredictable and return such an array of often unreliable or irrelevant results, it is better to use either search engines designed for academic research or discipline-specific search engines. For example, instead of using Google to conduct academic research, try using Google Scholar, which searches within scholarly publications. Compare the search results from Google Scholar in Figure 18.13 and those in the Google and Bing general search returns in Figure 18.12.

Search engines work by locating information according to the search terms you enter. Entering a general search term such as "sustainability" or "writing" can return millions, even billions, of results, far too many for efficient research. By narrowing your terms to more specific descriptions, search engines will return fewer and more relevant results. For example, the search term "sustainability at the University of

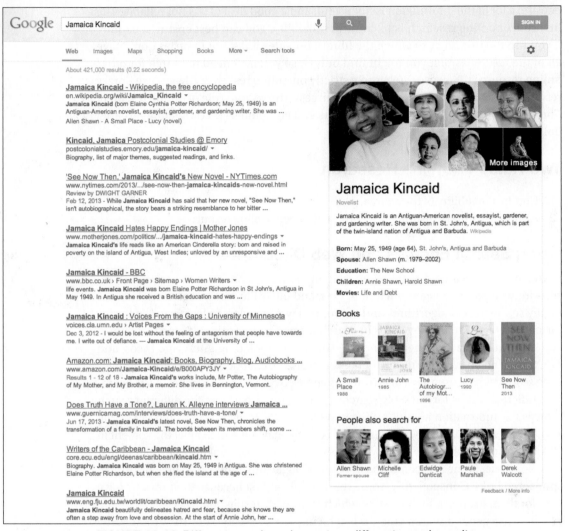

FIGURE 18.12 Different search engines return different search results.

Maryland" still returns more than 29,000 results, but the first returns are specifically useful to that search.

Use quotation marks for specific word orders. Search engines will search for multiple-word key terms in no particular order unless you place them in quotation marks, in which case the engine will look for those words in that order. For example, a search for digital photography handbook will return different results than will "digital photography handbook."

Use Boolean search tools. Boolean searches use the connectors and, or, and not to make sets. The connector and requires that both search terms be located in

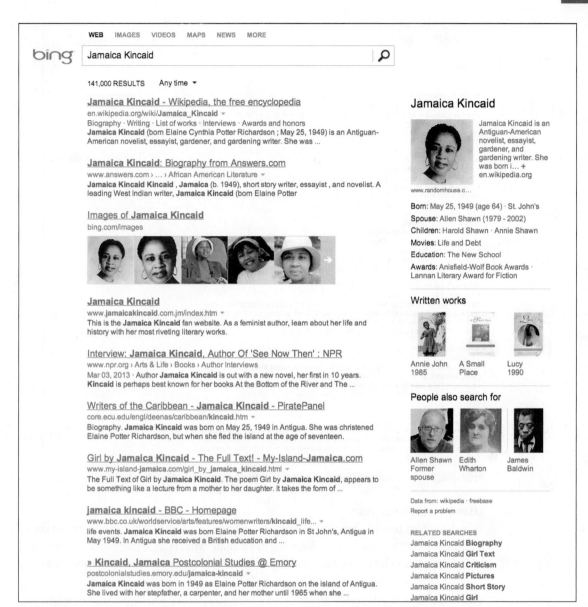

FIGURE 18.12 Compare these search results from Bing with the Google results on the facing page.

the search result, which can narrow search results (Example: marketing and branding). The connector or can expand a search by having the search engine look for one search term or another (Example: marketing or branding). The connector not can narrow a search by asking the search engine to return results for the first word of a search, but only when the second word is not included in the record (Example: marketing *not* branding).

FIGURE 18.13 Google Scholar provides more academically relevant links.

Using Web Resources

Search engines provide access to many types of resources, and as noted earlier, the key to making use of Web resources is learning to evaluate what is legitimate and valuable and what is not. Consider using the following nine kinds of Web sources in your research.

Web Pages

Web pages provide some of the most divergent content on the Web and are generally considered full and independent texts. Anyone can write and post web pages, so confirming reliability is always a priority. Recognized reliable web pages include those maintained by government agencies, official organizations, legitimate businesses, and educational institutions. Many individuals also maintain web pages, and their reliability is often judged based on ethos and reputation. Keep in mind, too, that unlike books and periodicals, web page, content can be updated frequently, so content may change between when you first access a web page and when you next access it. Thus, when citing web pages, you must include an access date.

MLA citation no longer requires the use of URLs in web citation. MLA explains that website addresses are not static and because web documents often appear in multiple locations, readers should be able to locate web sources using search engines by way of title or author.

How to Cite a Web Page

MLA

Author. *Title of Page.* Sponsoring Organization or Publisher, Date of Publication or Last Update. Medium of Publication. Access Date.

EXAMPLE

United States. Environmental Protection Agency. *Science and Technology: Land, Waste and Cleanup Science.* United States Environmental Protection Agency, 26 July 2013. Web. 18 Feb. 2014.

APA

Author. (Date published). *Title of website.* Retrieved from URL.

Note: If publication date is not available, use n.d.

EXAMPLE

U.S. Environmental Protection Agency. (2013). *Science and technology: Land, waste and cleanup science.* Retrieved from http://www2.epa.gov/science-and-technology /land-waste-and-cleanup-science

Journal Articles

Journal articles are often housed on the Web, and locating them can be an efficient research approach. Many academic journals now maintain archives and current issues online. Many provide online content in addition to their print content, whereas some journals may be found strictly online.

How to Cite Journal Articles Located on the Web

MLA

Author. "Article Title." *Journal Title,* Volume. Number (Date): Page Numbers. Medium. Date of Access.

Note: If page numbers are not available, use "n. pag."

EXAMPLE

Malhi, Yadvinder. "The Productivity, Metabolism, and Carbon Cycle of Tropical Forest Vegetation." *Journal of Ecology,* 100.1 (2012): 65–75. Web. 10 Feb. 2014.

APA now includes a digital object identifier (DOI) as a standard part of citation when it is available.

APA

Author's name(s). (Year). Title of article. *Title of periodical, volume,* Page numbers. doi: (if available)

Note: If there is no author listed or the author is unknown, begin the entry with the work's title.

Note: If there are more than six authors, list the first six and "et al." to indicate there are additional authors.

EXAMPLE (WITH DOI)

Malhi, Y. (2012). The productivity, metabolism and carbon cycle of tropical forest vegetation. *Journal of Ecology, 100*(1), 65–75. doi: 10.1111/j.1365-2745.2011.01916.x

EXAMPLE (WITHOUT DOI)

Malhi, Y. (2012). The productivity, metabolism and carbon cycle of tropical forest vegetation. *Journal of Ecology, 100*(1), 65–75. Retrieved from http://web.ebscohost.

Periodicals and News Outlets

Periodicals and other news sources provide information online in many forms and of varying degrees of reliability. Information may be posted in legitimate online publications like some Web magazines, or zines, and reliable, well-known news sites. Some print periodicals may also maintain online versions of their publications that include content found only online.

How to Cite Online Magazines and News Sources

MLA

Author. "Article Title." *Publication Title.* Publisher, Date of Publication. Medium of Publication. Access Date.

Note: If the site's publisher is not listed, use "N.p."

EXAMPLE

Jarvis, Jeff. "Bring Back the Busy Signal." *Huffington Post.* 12 Jan. 2012. Web. 10 Feb. 2014.

APA

Author's name(s). Date (Year, Month Date). Title of article. *Title of Publication.* doi or Retrieved from URL

EXAMPLE

Jarvis, J. (2012, January 12). Bring back the busy signal. *Huffington Post.* Retrieved from http://www.huffingtonpost.com/jeff-jarvis/email-communication_b_1200838.html

Digital Books

Digital books are now available from a number of resources. Your library may provide access to many e-books, which require special reading devices, but you can also find books and substantial parts of books online. One of the best resources for books online is Google Books. Likewise, book sales sites like Amazon.com often provide tools for looking at select parts of a book such as the table of contents and the index. These tools can let you identify citations, look for information, and help you decide whether a book offers the resources you need.

How to Cite an Online Book or E-book

MLA

Author. *Title.* Publication Information (if available). Title of the Website Where Book Was Found. Medium of Publication. Access Date.

EXAMPLE

Fouts, Janet. *Social Media Success!: Practical Advice and Real-World Examples for Social Media Engagement.* Books24x7. Web. 21 Mar 2012.

APA

Author's name(s). (Year of publication). *Title.* Retrieved from URL

Note: When the URL leads to information on how to obtain the book rather than to the book itself, use "Available from" instead of "Retrieved from."

EXAMPLE

Fouts, J. (2012) *Social media success!: Practical advice and real-world examples for social media engagement.* Retrieved from http://library.books24x7.com/toc.aspx?bookid=38021

Blogs and Posted Comments

Blogs, Web logs created by individuals and containing personal reflections, observations, and opinions, have become an important part of how information circulates. Many news outlets, in fact, use blogs as primary sources for the information they report. Blogs can be useful sources, but you need to carefully analyze and evaluate each blog you use, including the blogger's credentials and reputation, because blogs—and the comments others post in response to a blogger's postings—are not validated through any formal process.

How to Cite a Blog or Posted Comment

MLA

Last Name, First Name, "Title of Individual Blog Entry." *Title of Weblog.* Sponsoring/Publishing Organization (if available), Date Posted. Medium of Publication. Date accessed.

Note: If the sponsor/publisher of the site is unavailable, use "N.p."

EXAMPLE

Kibby, Brian. "Leaders and Confidence: A Habit Worth Forming." *If Not Now … When?* 9 Jan. 2012. Web. 16 Jan. 2012.

APA

Author. Date (Year, Month Date). Re: Title [Web log post]. Retrieved from URL

Note: When there is no author listed or the author is unknown, begin the entry with the work's title.

Note: Use [web log post] for messages posted to the blog and [web log comment] when citing a comment to a blog.

EXAMPLE

Kibby, B. (2012, January 9). Re: "Leaders and confidence: A habit worth forming." [Web log post]. Retrieved from http://www.briankibbyblog.com/2012/01/09/leaders-and-confidence-ahabit-worth-forming/

Wikis

A wiki is a website that allows its users to add, modify, or delete its content. Wikis pose some of the biggest difficulties for researchers. Because wikis are communally written, it can be difficult to identify who contributed to the entry. Likewise, many wikis rely on the community that writes the wiki post to confirm accuracy and validation. Thus, false or inaccurate information can find its way into a wiki entry. Wikipedia is a commonly used example of the problems with wikis as research resources (see p. 000 for more about Wikipedia). Although some wikis do generate important information, wikis are not generally considered legitimate college-level research sources. However, many wikis provide links and bibliographic citations that might direct you to more reliable resources.

In addition, note that the wiki format can be particularly useful as a tool for collaborative writing because it permits multiple users to edit a single document. Wiki generators allow you to create your own wikis for research purposes.

How to Cite a Wiki

MLA

"Title of Work." *Wiki Title.* Name of Sponsoring Organization, Day, Month, Year of Publication. Medium. Date of Access.

Note: If the author name is not provided, begin the citation with the title of the web page, article, or document.

Note: If the sponsoring institution or publisher is not available, use N.p.

Note: If the date of publication is not available, use n.d.

EXAMPLE

"Writing." *Wikipedia*. Wikimedia, 6 Jan. 2012. Web. 12 Jan 2012.

APA

Article Title. (Date). Retrieved from (wiki title): URL

Note: For material that may change over time, APA requires the inclusion of a retrieval date.

EXAMPLE

Writing. (2012, January 6). Retrieved January 12, 2012, from Wikipedia:
   http://en.wikipedia.org/wiki/Writing

Online Images

As visuals overtake writing as the primary method of conveying information in many public arenas, academic situations are also seeing an increase in the value and use of visuals in college writing. Thus, being able to find, adapt, and make visuals may be important within your research; in fact, visuals may often be required. However, like any other form of information found on the Web, you will need to analyze and evaluate the validity of each visual that you use. Be certain to use visuals from reliable sources, always cite the locations from which you take images, and when possible, credit the visual's creator. Digital manipulation of images is easy and simple, so confirm that the images you use are official versions that have not been altered or manipulated.

How to Cite an Online Image

MLA

Artist's Last Name, First Name. "Description or Title of Image." Date. Online image. *Title of larger site*. Date of download. <URL>.

EXAMPLE

Erdmann, Anita. "Photograph from Yellowstone National Park." N.d. Online image. No Caption needed. 13 Jan, 2012. <http://www.nocaptionneeded.com/wp-content/uploads/2011/12/Lone-tree-Yellowstone.jpg>

APA

Primary Contributor(s') name(s) (Indicate Type of contribution). (Date). *Image Title* [Photograph or Image]. Retrieved from URL

Note: When no date is available, use n.d.

Note: List the primary contributors in the author position and use parentheses to identify their contribution (Director, Producer, etc.).

Note: Begin with the image title when no primary contributor is listed.

EXAMPLE

Erdmann, Anita. (Photographer). (n.d.). *Photograph from Yellowstone National Park* [photograph]. Retrieved from http://www.nocaptionneeded.com/wp-content/uploads /2011/12/Lone-tree-Yellowstone.jpg

Online Film or Video

Your library may have a collection of downloadable videos and films, and numerous hosting sites provide access to all kinds of videos and films online, many of which can contribute to research. For example, websites like *Top Documentary Films* and *Free Documentaries* provide access to informative documentaries. Subscription services such as Netflix also house films and videos that might be of use in your research. Likewise, many websites embed informative videos. News outlets, educational sites, research-driven sites, and video sharing sites such as Vimeo and YouTube provide videos that may aid your research.

How to Cite an Online Film or Video

MLA

Title of Film. Director. Distributor, Year of Publication. Web. Access Date. <URL>.

Note: Indicate the roles of contributors with these abbreviations:
Director = Dir., Performers = Perf., Producers = Prod., Writer = Screenplay by.

EXAMPLE

Alamar. Screenplay by Pedro González-Rubio, Dir. Mantarraya Productions, 2009. Web. 28 July 2011. <http://www.hulu.com/watch/264550/alamar>

APA

Director or Writer (indicate type of contribution [see note below]). (Date). *Title* [Format]. Available from URL

Note: Along with the writer's name, identify the primary contributors in the author position and indicate their contribution in parentheses (Director, Producer, etc.).

EXAMPLE

González-Rubio, P. (Writer and Director). (2009). *Alamar.* [Film]. Available from http://www .imdb.com/title/tt1502396/

Podcasts

Podcasts are digital audio or video files, usually part of a themed series, that can be downloaded from a website. They can be quick to create, upload, and circulate on the Internet, so many people use them to convey information to large and/or specific audiences. Although you must scrutinize them carefully, there are lots of informative and reliable podcasts available about many subjects that can be useful resources for conducting research.

How to Cite a Podcast

MLA

Author's Name, Host, or Producer. "Title of Podcast." *Title of Program*. Release Date. Name of Database. Web. Date of access.

EXAMPLE

Foster, John. "This Week in Media 85: Later Clarke." *This Week in Media*. 20 Mar. 2008. Podcast.com. Web. 11 Aug. 2011.

APA

Primary Contributor(s') name(s) (Indicate type of contribution [see note below]). Date (Year, Month Date). *Podcast title* [Audio podcast]. Retrieved from URL

Note: Use n.d. when the date is not available.

EXAMPLE

Foster, J. (Moderator). 2008, March 20. *This week in media 85: Later Clarke* [Audio Podcast]. Retrieved from http://www.podcast.com/Technology/I-475570.htm

Note: Identify primary contributors in the author position and use parentheses to identify their contribution (Director, Producer, etc.).

Cautions and Possibilities in Using *Wikipedia*

Generally speaking, it is probably a good idea to limit using *Wikipedia* in your college research and writing, not because there is something inherently wrong with *Wikipedia*, but because it does not adhere to the evaluative criteria of the scholarly writing situation. Some teachers, departments, and even entire colleges ban students from using *Wikipedia* because it may contain inaccurate and incomplete information. Moreover, *Wikipedia* is a type of general encyclopedia, and college-level research demands more substantive, critical information than encyclopedias provide.

Despite its limitations, *Wikipedia* can be a very useful resource—if you use it the right way. *Wikipedia* can offer a fast, general overview of a subject for readers who are unfamiliar with

the subject. At the bottom of each *Wikipedia* entry, readers can find a list of bibliographic citations and links to sources from which the *Wikipedia* entry was developed. Researchers can use *Wikipedia*'s bibliographies as starting points to initiate research searches. In most cases, these sources contain reliable, authoritative versions of the information from which *Wikipedia* draws. Most students who use *Wikipedia* use it in conjunction with other research.

18.6 Conduct primary research and field research

Conducting Field Research

Field research is one important way to conduct primary research. The value of primary research is that it produces original information that may change what we know about a subject and may lead to secondary materials that will be written about it. Primary research is also valuable in that the researcher discovers firsthand knowledge.

Field research originated as a scientific research approach in which researchers would literally "go into the field" to make observations and collect data. Now, field research refers to many kinds of data gathering that take place away from traditional research locations such as libraries and laboratories. Field research produces "raw data," or information that has yet to be interpreted in terms of a particular question. Most disciplines use some form of field research to generate original information. For example, marketing researchers conduct lots of field research to study how marketing information is conveyed and received. Anthropologists study culture by observing particular cultural settings. Archaeologists dig for artifacts at various locations worldwide. Although every discipline has its own field research protocols, tools, and methods, the three approaches of observing, issuing surveys and questionnaires, and conducting interviews are commonly used by many.

Observing

All field research requires some degree of observation, of paying attention. The objective of observation is to identify factual information and to keep that information independent of your reaction to or analysis of that information. For example, imagine that for your anthropology course you have been assigned to observe the dress styles of students attending a campus job placement event. You may observe that most of the students in attendance dress in familiar business attire, except for a few who wear jeans and running shoes. Noting the specifics of the attire, like jeans and running shoes, is factual observation; commenting that these students dressed inappropriately for the event is not observation but is interpretation.

Conducting valuable observation includes planning your observation approaches. Expert observers do not enter an observation situation thinking "I'm just going to watch and see what happens." Instead, they plan what they will look for. Planning an approach can help focus an observation, allowing the researcher to pay closer attention to details that most affect the research rather than look at a wider panorama. Likewise, observers acknowledge their position in the situation as an observer; where they position themselves—as an outsider or insider, for example— affects how they will observe and how they will report their observations. Thus, planning an observation approach for each situation is always necessary.

Element	Questions
Participation	Am I watching as an outsider or as an insider? Should I participate or just observe? How will my degree of participation affect what I observe?
Purpose:	What am I looking for? What do I want to find? What do I expect to find? How might those expectations affect what I find and how might those findings affect my purpose?
Method	How will I observe? How will I record my observations? What will I do with my observations when I have completed them?
Detail	How do I remain focused on the details I need to observe? Can visuals—like photographs or sketches—help record details? Can audio recordings help me recall details?
Participants:	Who or what am I observing? How do I describe them and explain their roles?

Ultimately, the most important part of observing is recording your observations. When taking notes during an observation, you may want to consider using a dual-column approach. In one column, write only objective observations; in the other column, note your immediate interpretations. This approach can help you distinguish between observation and interpretation, and each part might contribute to how you use the information in your writing.

Issuing Surveys and Questionnaires

Surveying is a way of collecting focused information from general audiences, usually through a formal mechanism designed to target specific details. Questionnaires are designed to identify specific information within a designated population. Both surveys and questionnaires can be useful tools for soliciting information, but to retrieve reliable and useful information, they must be designed and written to elicit relevant responses from the research population.

Keep in mind that surveys/questionnaires can be disseminated and received in print, digitally, and over the phone, and the media you use may affect the answers you receive. For example, responders to a printed questionnaire may not write as much as you would like in response to questions, particularly if the questionnaire is lengthy. Digital survey tools like Survey Monkey can make circulating surveys and questionnaires easy, but they also limit the ways in which you can circulate them. For example, if you are conducting research about the customer service at a community clinic, asking clinic patients to log on to the online survey page when they get home will likely yield fewer responses compared with handing them the survey in the clinic lobby and asking them to respond at that time.

Guideline	What You Can Do
Keep surveys and questionnaires short.	Identify the primary information you want to target. Focus your questions to that purpose. Limit questions by considering what you need to know, would like to know, and don't need to know.
Use simple, direct language.	Given that surveys are usually intended to solicit information from large groups, you need to ensure that the survey is clear and simple so a diverse audience can understand it.
Use common explanations.	Because surveys reach large audiences, don't assume that all readers will understand concepts, abbreviations, or jargon you use. Make sure to explain all concepts, abbreviations, and technical or professional terms.
Organize questions to maintain flow.	Group questions within a subject and/or organize them to move readers from one idea to the next. If you have several categories of questions, consider using section headings to clarify what the groups of questions are about.
Don't lead your audience.	Ethically, to encourage valid answers, you should avoid asking leading questions, ones that influence responders to respond in a particular way. Otherwise, you may skew the results.
Balance rating scales.	If your questions ask responders to rate something, create a rating scale that provides as many positive as negative response choices. For example a scale of 1 = negative experience, 2 = neutral experience, 3 = positive experience, 4 = exceptional experience is not balanced because it provides only one way to express a negative experience and two ways to express positive experiences.
Offer limited but clear choices.	If you provide responders with choices such as in multiple-choice questions, limit the number of possible responses and clearly differentiate them. Too many choices or choices that seem overly similar may confuse readers.
Avoid long-term recall questions.	People have a more difficult time remembering things from long ago than they do from recent events, so focus on more recent events. For example, instead of asking "How many books have you read on an e-reader in the last two years?" ask "How many books have you read on an e-reader in the last four weeks?"
Write closed-ended questions.	Open-ended questions are ones to which people can respond with anything. Open-ended responses decrease your chances that the response will address what you are examining in the research. Instead, write closed-ended questions that direct responders to think about the objective of the survey (for example, "You have indicated that you oppose the recently proposed health care measures. Are your oppositions based on cost, access, or availability?").
Test and revise your survey before full release.	Ask readers who represent the population you are researching to read and evaluate the document, then use their evaluations to make revisions. You may also want to ask a target group to answer the draft survey/questionnaire; then review their answers to determine whether some of the questions caused confusion or unusable answers, revising as necessary.
Title the survey.	A title on a survey/questionnaire helps your audience identify what it is they will be asked about.
Include an introduction.	Surveys/questionnaires should include a brief introduction that explains the purpose of the document, which helps the audience understand why they are responding. Often, these introductions also motivate the audience to participate in the survey/questionnaire.

Conducting Interviews

Interviews, a kind of firsthand information gathering, involve direct contact with a person who can provide information that is either not available in published form or that provides a unique insight into a situation. Some interviews may be conducted just to learn more about the person being interviewed. Interviews must be conducted in a professional, critical manner to be a useful form of research. Simply chatting with

Stage	What You Can Do
1. Prepare	Understand the purpose for the interview.
	Identify who might best provide you the information you need.
	Request an interview with the person, let him or her know your objectives and intent as well as how long it will be, and arrange a time and place to meet.
	Learn as much as you can about the person and the situation so you can interview the person from an informed position, able to bypass the obvious questions and focus on the details.
	Plan what questions you want to ask and the order in which you should ask them so you can obtain worthwhile information.
	Base your questions on what you have learned about the situation, and keep them short and clear.
	Remember: the person you are interviewing will likely respond to you more favorably if you present yourself as having some background knowledge about the subject.
2. Conduct	Take notes. Throughout the interview, be sure to record as much information as you can, but don't let your note taking distract from the interview's flow. If possible, use a recording device to record the entire conversation.
	Organize your questions to flow from one subject to the next. Don't ask questions randomly, but in a sequence that makes sense and logically moves from one idea to the next.
	Add impromptu questions if the person being interviewed says something that you think leads to another question. (Strong preparation will help you to follow up in this way.)
	Adjust the order of your questions if the person being interviewed moves between subjects in ways other than what you planned.
	Ask for clarification if you have questions or need clarification about something the interviewee has said.
	Stick to the time limit you agreed to.
3. Conclude	Thank the person you interviewed immediately and with a follow-up e-mail or note.
	Review your plan for the interview with the person.
	Consider arranging for the interviewee to see/hear/read the interview in advance if you are going to make the interview accessible in its entirety.
	Analyze the content of the interview to evaluate how it fits your purpose and what parts of the interview you want to use in your writing.

a person may solicit some information, but the best interviews are carefully planned to target the information you need, then recorded and analyzed. Interviews can be conducted in writing, by phone, by Internet, or face to face. You might publish an interview in its entirety, or you might use key information from it, either quoted or paraphrased, within the context of your own writing.

Summary

Research is the careful and systematic search for information and evidence in the pursuit of learning. In college, research is integral to writing. Academic research can be thought of as critical scholarly investigation that can be either (a) primary research that collects or examines original information or (b) secondary research that examines what others have contributed to particular primary research. Analyzing research materials involves carefully examining each resource and asking many questions about it. Detailed analysis works best when you establish specific criteria to investigate.

Your school's library is the best resource for academic research. Online and print catalogs in academic libraries provide information about books, journals, reference materials, archives, and bibliographies. Databases and indexes are comprehensive collections of information that gather general or discipline-specific information; they can be particularly useful for locating government documents and biographical information. Simply browsing the library can also be a productive—and satisfying—form of research. Researchers now use the World Wide Web and other Internet resources to conduct research, but it is a good idea to strictly limit using *Wikipedia* in your college research and writing because the information is not always verified. Conducting your own primary research can involve field research, which includes observing, issuing surveys and questionnaires, and conducting interviews.

Chapter Review

1. What is the difference between primary research and secondary research?

2. In what ways is academic research a nonlinear process?

3. Describe why college-level research should be thought of as critical scholarly investigation instead of "looking up stuff."

4. Within what kind of atmosphere should all scholarly research be situated?

5. Why is it important to adhere to criteria for evaluating research resources?

6. What is the first rule of using library resources to conduct research?

7. What are three resources available to you through your campus library's web pages?

8. In what efficient and effective ways should you use online resources such as search engines in your research?

9. Identify three ways to conduct primary research.

Thinking and Writing about the Chapter

Reflection

Now that you have had some time to consider the function of research, revisit the journal entry or blog post you wrote in response to the prompt at the beginning of this chapter. Now how would you describe of the role of research in academic writing? What are some key approaches to conducting research to which you should now be alert?

Local Situation

Learn your library. Complete the following table to learn how to better use your campus library.

Task	Result
Where on your campus is the library located?	
How can you get in touch with the reference librarians at your campus's library?	
What is the URL for your library web page and online catalog?	
Using the library's catalog, locate and check the availability of William Gibson's book *Neuromancer*.	
Using the library's catalog, locate and check the availability of the journal *College English*. What volumes are available in print? Can you access full articles through the library's digital resources?	
Using your library's resources, locate the *Oxford English Dictionary* and provide definitions for these words: *physics*, *commercial*, and *rhetoric*.	
Does your library maintain any archives or special collections? If so, where are they kept? How do you access them? And what subject areas do they cover?	
Locate *The Bedford Bibliography for Teachers of Writing*.	
To which of these databases does your library provide access: Academic Search Complete, JSTOR, LexisNexis Academic, Project Muse, ProQuest, WorldCat?	

(Continued)

Task	Result
To what databases in these disciplines does your library provide access: art, business, computers and technology, education, medicine and nutrition, history? What are the requirements for accessing these databases?	
Does your library provide access to videos and podcasts?	
Where might you locate a biographical dictionary or a longer biography?	
What is the call number for the book *Junkware* by Thierry Bardini? If you browse the stacks surrounding Bardini's work, what else do you find of interest?	

Evaluating and Synthesizing Information

Learning Objectives

19.1 Select research that supports your own ideas

19.2 Synthesize your research and your ideas to produce new and meaningful work that reads smoothly

19.3 Avoid plagiarism in your writing when synthesizing research that supports your ideas

Before you read this chapter

What does it mean to synthesize? In what contexts do you synthesize? What strategies do you use to synthesize in those contexts? In your journal or blog, write about the kinds of synthesis you already engage in and your strategies for effectively synthesizing.

To synthesize is to form a new whole from carefully evaluated, selected, and relevant parts.

Unlike analysis, in which you dissect a whole into parts to better sense how the parts work together, the process of synthesis brings together various parts to make a fluid, new whole. Effective research writing brings research together in smooth, polished ways to support a writer's purposes. Less-effective research writing patches sources together in a quilt-like fashion without fully integrating all the pieces as a whole.

The process of synthesis parallels cooking: blending together various ingredients to make a new, independent dish. Each ingredient on its own may produce a distinct taste, but when carefully combined with other ingredients, will produce a new, more complex dish.

Gloria Bley Miller, author the most comprehensive and widely read Chinese cookbook for Western readers, explains that Chinese cooking always starts with ingredients that are combined and rarely cooked alone. Only in being brought together through particular methods can these ingredients bring out the best in one another.[1]

In writing, synthesizing research works much the same way. Rather than simply throwing together pieces of information, research writers carefully select the pieces of research that best contribute to their purpose and plan. They then blend the research into their own writing. Synthesizing research within your writing can produce more readable writing, provide readers with a clear understanding as to why you have used the research, and ultimately create a more pleasurable reading experience.

Not everything blends together well, however. As in cooking, including something that is incompatible might undermine, even ruin, the entire creation. Likewise, using too much or too little of something can either overpower a composition or leave it lacking. Effective synthesis involves deciding not only what to leave out but also what to include. Individual audience needs and expectations as well as the situational constraints also affect how writers synthesize.

Although the primary purpose of synthesis is to integrate research into your writing, synthesis also serves a more encompassing agenda to build relationships between your writing and other texts. Cut-and-paste approaches to integrating research into writing—methods that present the different parts as parts rather than unifying them—are often used by beginning writers and are usually less effective. Synthesis invites a conversation between your research and your ideas; cut-and-paste composition promotes fragmentation and confusion.

---

[1] Miller, Gloria Bley. *The Thousand Recipe Chinese Cookbook*. New York: Fireside Books, 1966. Print. p. 12.

Looking Beyond: Mashups

Mashups can be viewed as a kind of synthesis. In music, mashups create new songs by blending parts of other songs. Video mashups edit together video clips from multiple sources to create the appearance of a single video. Media mashups blend sound, video, graphics, writing, and animation in various proportions, often modifying the original sources to render unique, independent products. In essence, mashups combine parts to make a new whole. How a writer combines the parts in a mashup contributes to whether readers or viewers accept the mashup as an innovative new text or as a patchwork of sources. A great example of a mashup of the Beatles with Fatboy Slim, along with many others, can be found on YouTube.

Supporting Your Own Ideas

19.1 Select research that supports your own ideas

Many kinds of college-level research writing require that writers report information gathered through research. This kind of reporting can be valuable in many kinds of academic and public situations, but it doesn't always provide smooth, flowing writing that provides new perspectives. Patchwork reporting of information emphasizes the various parts of research over the writer's own work and thought. Writing that effectively synthesizes research supports the writer's purpose, ideas, and approaches. The most difficult part of synthesizing research is to make sure you support your voice and position with research rather than simply agree or disagree with the research or report the research.

As you conduct your research, think about why particular information stands out to you. How does that information connect to your thinking about the situation and subject? How does it support or conflict with your ideas? Does it offer a different perspective from yours? Of course, as you read and learn more about the subject and situation, you may alter your ideas, but your ideas should drive not only your purpose for writing but also how you use the research to support your position.

Because writing is always an act of taking a position within a situation, you can think of your writing as entering into a conversation within the situation. Your research helps you locate and stake your position in the larger conversation of the situation. Thorough research provides a glimpse of the larger conversation; your ideas express your place in that conversation. Bringing your position together with your research establishes your place in the conversation. Consider the distinction between the following original and revised paragraphs. The first version uses a patchwork research approach that obscures the writer's voice; the revised version presents a more effective synthesis and emphasizes the writer's ideas and position.

ORIGINAL VERSION: According to Gunther Kress, a British education expert, literacy needs to be thought of in terms of "the broad move from the now centuries-long dominance of writing to the new dominance of the image and, on the other hand, the move from the dominance of the medium of the book to the dominance of the medium of the screen" (1). In their book *The World of the Image*, Trudy Smoke and Alan Robbins say that "Everywhere you look in the modern world, images are becoming more common, more present, and more pervasive. We are immersed in a world of images" (ix). Bruce E. Gronbeck explains that "Because of the explosion of mediated spectacle and the public's seemingly insatiable hunger for it, the 19th and 20th centuries have been called *ocularcentric*, or eye centered" (xxi). Therefore, images are important in understanding how we learn about the world.

REVISED FOR SYNTHESIS: Ours is a world of images. Everywhere we look, we see images. Images that convey information, like traffic signs; images that make arguments, like advertisements; images that portray identity, like clothes or tattoos; images that attract attention, like art or posters; and images that inform, like news photographs. How we see our world has a lot to do with the images we see every day. Image experts Trudy Smoke and Alan Robbins say it plainly in their book *The World of the Image*: "Everywhere you look in the modern world, images are becoming more common, more present, and more pervasive. We are immersed in a world of images" (ix). Because we are immersed in a world of images, it is important to be careful and critical in how we understand images because images are central to how we now learn. Education experts like Gunther Kress identify just how important images are in learning, showing how literacy now needs to be thought of in terms of "the broad move from the now centuries-long dominance of writing to the new dominance of the image and, on the other hand, the move from the dominance of the medium of the book to the dominance of the medium of the screen" (1).

The revised paragraph focuses on the writer's ideas; the research is secondary and serves as support for the writer's ideas. The writer's voice guides the paragraph and connects the two cited sources. Notice, that the writer has opted not to include the Gronbeck citation; often, a writer's point can be clarified with less research.

When synthesizing research into your work, always begin by writing your ideas, claims, and thoughts. Once you express your ideas and objectives, then add your relevant research to support your position. But don't add too much. You don't need to include every relevant quote or resource; provide enough research to confirm and support your position. Maintain your voice as the guiding force in the writing. Although the research a writer conducts beforehand informs how she will approach writing her ideas, the writer's ideas should remain paramount. Thus, writers who synthesize research into their writing often draft their documents first with no research included, which allows them to flesh out their ideas and objectives first. Once they are satisfied with their position, then they incorporate relevant research.

19.2 Synthesize your research and your ideas to produce new and meaningful work that reads smoothly

Synthesizing Research

Learning how to bring your research into relationship with your writing is crucial if you want to make the best use of your research. The following guidelines about taking notes; responding to research; connecting, quoting, paraphrasing, and summarizing research; and avoiding common synthesizing mistakes can help you develop practices for smoothly integrating your research and your writing.

Taking Notes

Thorough note taking is the starting point for strong synthesis. Notes can help you recall why you found a piece of research interesting, valuable, or in need of critique. Writing down not just the information and citations you find in your research but also your thoughts about the research can help you connect the research to your own thinking. A common research dilemma among college writers is to return to a piece of noted research and not be able to recall why the research was relevant in the first place because their notes were not clear or specific.

Responding to Research

When including research information in your writing, be sure to respond to that information, showing readers how it is relevant—an important part of synthesis. Good notes can remind you of your early response to the research and make responding easier to do. Novice writers will often include research in their writing, but without explanation, so readers are left to develop their own connections and responses to it. This "writing in faith" approach is risky because the audience may not interpret the research the same way you do. Consider the effect of the following two examples, the original version with no response to the included research and the revision with the author's response.

ORIGINAL VERSION: College-level research in America requires copious attention to appropriate citation forms more so than to the ethics of citation and authorship. Rebecca Moore Howard, in her article "Plagiarism, Authorship, and the Academic Death Penalty," explains that "American academic culture demands that writers who use the exact words of a source supply quotation marks at the beginning and end of the quotation, so that the reader can know where the voice of the source begins and ends" (799).[1] Over attention to citation forms in college classrooms can lead to college-level writers understanding little more than how to cite information, rather than why citation is important.

REVISED VERSION: College-level research in America requires copious attention to appropriate citation forms more so than to the ethics of citation and authorship. Rebecca Moore Howard, in her article "Plagiarism, Authorship, and the Academic Death Penalty," explains that "American academic culture demands that writers who use the exact words of a source supply quotation marks at the beginning and end of the quotation, so that the reader can know where the voice of the source begins and ends" (799).[2] What Howard identifies in the

> The direct quote from Howard seems to interrupt the writer's two sentences about citation. If we removed Howard's quote from the paragraph, the two sentences flow more fluidly. However, Howard's position brings something valuable to the discussion.

---

[1] The full citation that would appear in the Works Cited list would look like this:

Howard, Rebecca M. "Plagiarism, Authorship, and the Academic Death Penalty." *College English.* 57.7 (1995): 788–806. Web. 14 Feb. 2014.

In the revised version, the writer responds to Howard's claim, guiding readers to see a nuanced interpretation of Howard's claim that strengthens the writer's position. The writer's response, steers the audience smoothly toward the synthesis of the research information within the writer's overall agenda.

example of quotation marks is an institutional coding system that emphasizes the importance of students complying with cultural standards for the sake of compliance rather than understanding why such standards are in place. Howard's subtle recognition of this distinction reveals much about how college students understand citation.

Connecting Research

Responding to research is one way to connect the research to writing. Strong synthesis works to integrate research and writing smoothly, connecting both in more than superficial ways. This integration includes connection not only between your writing and your research but also between different parts of your research. Simply stringing together different bits of information, whether from the same or different sources, does not usually result in smooth synthesis. Any research you use in your writing must connect with your writing and with any other research. A writer's responsibility is to interconnect research and writing in logical and beneficial ecosystems. Fundamentally, you can connect research in six ways. Each of these ways may be approached differently—stylistically and methodologically—and each may be used in conjunction with the others.

1. Use individual pieces of research to support your position.

2. Use multiple pieces of research to support your position.

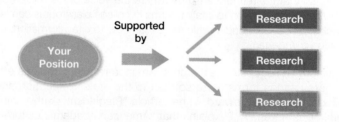

---

[2]The full citation that would appear in the Works Cited list would look like this:
Howard, Rebecca M. "Plagiarism, Authorship, and the Academic Death Penalty." *College English.* 57.7 (1995). 788–806. Web. 14 Feb. 2014.

3. Use research to confirm the specific research that supports your position.

4. Use multiple pieces of research to form a synthetic support for your position.

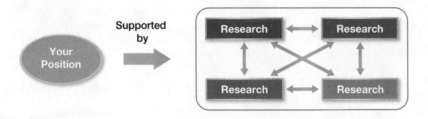

5. Use your position to refute research.

6. Use your position and supporting research to refute other research.

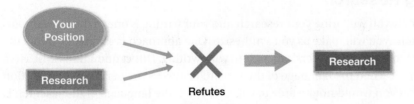

Using Effective Connection Words

When making connections in their writing, college writers often repeat the same connection words too frequently, which makes for tedious reading and indefinite or vague connections. Most commonly, writers default to the verb *says* to connect research within their writing: "the author says," "Smith says," "the article says," and so on. One way to create more sophisticated connections in your writing, and more dynamic writing overall, is to use a variety of attribution verbs—verbs that attribute information to a source. Each of the attribution verbs listed here has a distinct meaning, and one cannot simply be substituted for another. You should learn what each verb means, and then use a good variety of them to make connections in your writing.

accepts	claims	endorses	proposes
accounts for	comments	explains	questions
acknowledges	compares	expresses	realizes
addresses	complains	finds	reasons
adds	concedes	grants	refutes
admits	concludes	hypothesizes	rejects
advises	concurs	illustrates	remarks
affirms	confesses	implies	replies
agrees	confirms	indicates	reports
alleges	considers	insinuates	responds
allows	contends	insists	reveals
analyzes	criticizes	interprets	sees
answers	deals with	introduces	shows
argues	decides	lists	speculates
asks	declares	maintains	states
asserts	defines	mentions	suggests
assumes	denies	notes	supports
believes	describes	objects	supposes
categorizes	disagrees	observes	thinks
challenges	discusses	offers	uses
charges	disputes	opposes	verifies
cites	emphasizes	points out	writes

Quoting Research

Deciding how you will bring your research into your writing is one of the most important decisions you will make as you synthesize. One approach is to directly quote the research. Quoting brings others' voices into your writing. Direct quotations best serve your synthesis when the language of the research conveys the pertinent information in a way that you would not be able to capture, when the language of the research is itself part of what makes the information relevant, or when you need the audience to be aware of the research language or the source of particular language.

Working Quotes into Writing

Quoting research requires that you carefully represent the research through its exact wording. Fitting quoted material smoothly into your writing is difficult to do. The attribution verbs listed above can be helpful, but sometimes you may have to adjust the quote so it flows within your writing. These adjustments include removing language and adding or clarifying information. The following chart shows three strategies for seamlessly including quotes.

Strategy for Incorporating a Quote	Example
To remove language from a quote, use ellipses to indicate that something has been removed.	**Original Quote:** "One of the most important innovations in contemporary American education as distinguished from European and Asian education practices since the late 1800s as reported in various journals and indexes has been the democratization of information distribution." **Revised Quote:** "One of the most important innovations in contemporary American education … has been the democratization of information distribution. Note that removing some of the words does not alter the core meaning of the sentence but, instead, emphasizes what is relevant to the situation. It is imperative when removing information from a direct quote that you not alter the original meaning. Doing so would misrepresent the source of your research.
Use brackets to add or clarify information within a direct quote.	**Original Quote:** "If the administrator had been present as required, the engineers would have been alerted to the change of plans." **Revised Quote:** "If the administrator [Mrs. Lisa Louw] had been present as required, the engineers would have been alerted to the change of plans."
Also use brackets to indicate an alteration in verb tense.	**Original Quote:** According to Muswell, "Michael Graves, Philip Johnson, Robert Venturi, and Charles Moore have been regularly identified as the leading figures in postmodern architecture" (138). **Revised Quote:** According to Muswell, "Michael Graves, Philip Johnson, Robert Venturi, and Charles Moore [are] regularly identified as the leading figures in postmodern architecture" (138).

In some situations, you may want to include longer direct quotations than in other situations. Short and long quotes are indicated differently in academic writing, and how each is identified depends on which formal writing style you use.

In MLA style, if the quoted material is fewer than four complete, typed lines, the material should be indicated by using quotation marks at the beginning and end of the quoted material, which should be incorporated directly into the body of your writing. If the quoted material is longer than four complete, typed lines, the material should be offset from the body of the text by indenting the quoted material by one inch from the left margin, or two standard tab indents of one-half inch each. Do not use quotation marks for longer, indented quotes.

Short and Long Quotations in MLA Format

SHORT QUOTATION

Otaku culture refers to people, generally in younger populations, who participate in a Japanese subculture that is characterized by its attachment to video games, anime, science fiction, computers, special-effects movies, anime figurines, and other similar cultural artifacts. As Hiroki Azuma defines it in *Otaku: Japan's Database Animals*, "Otaku culture, as exemplified through comics and anime, still often maintains an image of youth culture" (3). But Otaku culture is also populated by a large number of men in Japan over the age of 40.

THE SOURCE FOR THIS QUOTE IS CITED IN MLA THIS WAY

Azuma, Hiroki. *Otaku: Japan's Database Animals*. Minneapolis: U of Minnesota P, 2009. Print.

LONG QUOTATION

Because different people have different concepts of what might and might not be considered obscene, obscenity standards fluctuate depending on historical moments and varying contexts. For example, at various times, books like D. H. Lawrence's *Lady Chatterley's Lover*, J. D. Salinger's *Catcher in the Rye*, and Walt Whitman's *Leaves of Grass* each have been considered obscene and, at other times, have been considered great works of literature. Because perceptions of obscenity can be so problematic from a legal perspective, in 1957, the United States Supreme Court issued clarifications regarding freedoms of expression:

> Sex and obscenity are not synonymous. Obscene material is material which deals with sex in a manner appealing to prurient interest. The portrayal of sex in art, literature and scientific works, is not itself sufficient reason to deny material the constitutional protection of freedom of speech and press. Sex, a great and mysterious motive force in human life, has indisputably been a subject of absorbing interest to mankind through the ages; it is one of the vital problems of human interest and public concern. (476)

The court was also adamant that in order to determine whether a piece of media was to be understood as obscene, the entire media had to be considered, not just part of it.

THE SOURCE FOR THIS QUOTE IS CITED IN MLA THIS WAY

Roth v. United States. 354 U.S. 476. Justia US Supreme Court Center. *US Law, Case Law, Codes, Statutes and Regulations: Justia US Supreme Court Center.* Web. 29 Jan. 2012.

Short and Long Quotations in APA Format

SHORT QUOTATION

The Italian cheese Pecorino is identified by a two-letter abbreviation of the town in which it is made. For example, Pecorino GR is made only in Grosetto, and Pecorino PE is from Pesaro. Unfortunately, most of the Pecorinos are not available in the United States. As cheese expert and author Steven Jenkins puts it, "These name-controlled Pecorino Toscanos are sold in a number of variations—all grand. Currently only Pecorino Toscano is sold in the U.S., while Pecorino dell'Umbria and Pecorina Marchigiano are rarely found outside of central Italy" (243). Controlling the naming of cheese may contribute to maintaining regional specialties, but it also limits ranges of distribution.

THE SOURCE FOR THIS QUOTE IS CITED IN APA THIS WAY

Jenkins, S. (1996). *Cheese primer*. New York: Workman Publishing.

LONG QUOTATION (40 OR MORE WORDS)

Research on web design needs to take into account how and when users are engaging with a particular site. Hall (2013), for example, describes a type of causal research:

> Once you have implemented the solutions you proposed, and have a website or application up and running out in the world, you might start noticing that people are using it in a certain way, possibly a way that isn't exactly what you'd hoped. Or perhaps, something really terrific is happening and you want to replicate the success in other parts of your operation. For example, you've noticed that ever since the Fantastic Science Center redesign launched, tickets for the Friday evening science-loving singles event are selling better, but ticket sales have completely dropped off for the Sunday afternoon film program. You need to do some causal research. (p. 15).

THE SOURCE FOR THIS QUOTE IS CITED IN APA THIS WAY:

Hall, E. (2013). *Just enough research.* New York: A Book Apart.

If you are using APA style, then short quotes of no more than forty words are included directly in the body of the writing and are indicated using quotation marks at the beginning and end of the quoted material. Longer quotes of more than forty words should be indented one-half inch from the left margin. Do not use quotation marks for longer, indented quotes.

Punctuating Quotes

When using quotations in your writing, follow these four basic rules:

1. In short quotes, periods and commas always go inside quotation marks unless you use parenthetical citation, in which case the period or comma follows the closing parenthesis.

   "If we want to know where good ideas come from**,**" Steven Johnson writes, "we have to put them in context" (17).

2. Because indented long quotes do not use any quotation marks, the parenthetical citation follows the final period, as is shown in the examples for long quotations.

3. Question marks and exclamation points go inside quotation marks when they are part of the quoted material; they are placed outside of the quotation marks if they are not part of the quoted material. If the question mark or exclamation point is part of the quoted material (and thus appears inside the quotation mark), then the parenthetical citation is placed outside of the quotation mark, followed by a period. If the question mark or exclamation point is not part of the quoted material, then it is placed after the citation.

   There are many urban myths about unusual questions asked at job interviews. One of the most interesting is ascribed to be a common question IBM asks its job applicants: "How do you weigh an elephant without using a weight scale**?"**

   Who first said "We have nothing to fear but fear itself"**?**

   The inquiry, then, must ask questions like "What effect do these things and artifacts have on us**?"** (Verbeek 1).

   Why, then, does Gershenfeld claim that "there's a very real sense in which the things around us are infringing on a new kind of right that has not needed protection until now" (102)**?**

4. Colons and semicolons should always be placed outside of quotation marks.

   Peggy Teeter, who began her career writing about her experiences in World War II and the Korean War, used to say that "the only way to learn to write is to write"**;** this kind of pragmatic advice can be useful for a number of reasons.

Paraphrasing Research

Paraphrasing involves explaining all or part of the research information in your own words rather than quoting it. Paraphrasing can contribute to the synthesis of your research because it presents the information in your language, blending it with the rest of your writing. Paraphrasing can help you avoid relying too heavily on direct quotes, which can distract the audience from your voice. However, just because paraphrased information is stated in your language does not mean that the ideas you convey have become yours. Paraphrased information must be attributed to the sources from which it is derived. Paraphrased text is generally shorter than the original material because you have condensed the ideas, but in doing so, you should neither alter nor misrepresent the original information.

Follow these rules when paraphrasing:

- Make certain you understand the work you are paraphrasing. You can't clearly convey information you don't understand.
- Avoid looking at the original text as you write the paraphrase so you are not tempted to rely on the original language.
- Indicate with quotation marks any words or unique language you borrow from the original.
- Provide citations for any research you paraphrase.

Consider this example of original text that is then paraphrased.

ORIGINAL TEXT

High-speed rail has hit another milestone, this time in China, with the opening of the world's longest bullet train line.

The 1,425-mile high-speed rail system runs from Beijing to Guangzhou, reducing the time travelers would spend commuting between the capital and the manufacturing city from 22 hours to a scant 8 hours.

Traveling at an average speed of 186 mph, the line stops in Shijiazhuang, Zhengzhou, Wuhan and Changsha before arriving at its final destination in Guangzhou.

The opening of this newest high-speed rail line is just the latest in a string of bullet trains that have begun to infiltrate the country after the network began operation in 2007. There are currently 5,779 miles of high-speed track in the country, and the state-run China Daily newspaper says that's set to expand to over 31,000 miles of track by 2020.

But this latest milestone hasn't come without its problems. According to the AFP, safety concerns have been a regular issue since 2008, with one high-speed rail collision occurring in 2011 that claimed the lives of 40 people.

"We can't make sure it's error-proof in the future, and we have been subject to a lot of pressure from the public," Zhao Chunlei, deputy chief of the ministry's transportation department, told the Global Times newspaper.

The timing of the high-speed rail line correlates with China's Lunar New Year holiday celebration, which takes place this February, and will see hundreds of millions of people traveling across the country to visit their ancestral homes in what's described by the *AFP* as "the world's largest annual migration."

PARAPHRASE

The world's longest bullet train line opened in China, running 1,425 miles from Beijing to Guangzhou at an average speed of 186 mph, reducing travel time for the trip from 22 hours to 8 hours. China currently has 5,779 miles of high-speed train track and hopes to expand to over 31,000 miles of track by 2020. There have been some safety concerns with the new trains since 2008, including concerns involving a 2011 high-speed rail collision that killed 40 people. The opening of the new train line coincides with China's lunar New Year holiday celebration, during which hundreds of millions of people travel across the country to visit their ancestral homes.

THE SOURCE ARTICLE IS CITED IN MLA THIS WAY:

Lavrinc, Damon. "World's Longest Bullet Train Line Opens in China." *Wired.com*. Web. 26 Dec. 2012.

THE SOURCE ARTICLE IS CITED IN APA THIS WAY:

Lavrinc, D. (2012). World's longest bullet train line opens in China. *Wired.com*. Retrieved from http://www.wired.com/autopia/2012/12/worlds-longest-bullet-train/.

Summarizing Research

When the research is long and the overall concepts are more relevant to your writing than are the details, you will want to summarize the information. Summaries simply report or describe information, but they do not convey the degree of details that paraphrasing might. Think of summarizing as distilling information to a minimal explanation of the main ideas. The following chart presents effective strategies for summarizing.

Summarizing Strategy	Comments
Identify what you are summarizing and include an in-text citation.	Even though you write summaries in your own words, they still convey others' ideas. So you need to acknowledge that the summary includes someone else's work and provide attribution to the source.
Make sure you understand what it is you are summarizing.	It is difficult to reduce a text that you don't understand, and doing so may produce an inaccurate summary. Before writing your summary, be sure you understand each part of the text, the relationships between each part, and the organization of the text.
Provide the main ideas.	Summaries do not include details. Focus on the big, overarching ideas.
Use your words and writing styles.	Of course, you will need to use some of the key phrases of the research, but your own language should dominate the summary.
Quote and attribute any exact phrases you use from the original.	If you do use exact wording from the source, be sure to cite it properly.
Write your summary without looking at the source text.	Base your summary on what you recall from the text, but afterward, go back to the source text and make sure that you have represented it accurately.

Consider the following examples of summaries:

SAMPLE SUMMARY OF "WORLD'S LONGEST BULLET TRAIN LINE OPENS IN CHINA":

Although there are some safety concerns, China opened the world's longest bullet train line as part of a plan to continue extending their bullet train system before 2020.

SAMPLE SUMMARY OF HERMAN MELVILLE'S MOBY DICK:

Herman Melville's novel *Moby Dick*, told from the perspective of Ishmael, a whaler who joins Captain Ahab's crew aboard the *Pequod*, focuses on Ahab's obsession with a white whale known as Moby Dick and the captain's willingness to sacrifice everything, including his ship and crew, to destroy the whale.

MOBY DICK IS CITED IN MLA THIS WAY:

Melville, Herman, Hershel Parker, and Harrison Hayford. *Moby-Dick*. New York: Norton, 2002. Print.

MOBY DICK IS CITED IN **APA** THIS WAY:

Melville, H. (2002). *Moby-Dick* (H. Parker & H. Hayford, Eds.). New York: Norton.

Avoiding Common Mistakes in Synthesizing Research

One way to improve synthesis is to understand what contributes to poor synthesis and avoid it. Student writers often commit these common synthesis mistakes[3] throughout their research and writing.

Synthesis Mistake	Consequence
Mistakes while choosing research resources	
1. Not including key research such as information from the leading expert on a subject	Might ignore important, expected information
2. Simply including the first research you find or a random choice of research without checking whether it is the most relevant or related information	Can make it difficult to bring research together smoothly
Mistakes while analyzing and evaluating research	
3. Carelessly or not rigorously evaluating research sources	Can result in using irrelevant or contested research
4. Carelessly or not rigorously evaluating research details	Can lead to misrepresenting whole research sources and/or specific research details
5. Using only one source (instead of multiple sources) to confirm a position	Creates a logical fallacy akin to begging the question
6. Forcing research to fit your needs when it does not	Is unethical and will seem forced and difficult to follow
7. Being unaware of or overlooking critiques of the research you use	Can reflect weak research evaluation and can leave audiences questioning the validity of the connections you make
Mistakes while bringing research together in writing	
8. Intentionally not addressing conflicting research to more easily fit particular research into your synthesis	Is unethical in academic writing
9. Failing to provide enough research or evidence to support your ideas in a situation	Pressures the audience to accept your position without receiving substantial links to the situation
10. Plagiarizing information	Misrepresents others' ideas and primary research as your own
11. Making any of the above common mistakes	Inevitably leads to other mistakes writers make in their own positions, their own claims, their own arguments and information

---

[3] These errors are adapted from Durkin, Michael J. "Types of Errors in Synthesizing Research in Education." *Review of Educational Research* Vol. 66 No. 2 (1996): 87–97.

19.3 Avoid plagiarism in your writing when synthesizing research that supports your ideas

Avoiding Plagiarism

One of the most important parts of synthesizing research in your writing is ensuring that your writing is *your writing* and that any research you use is clearly identified as someone else's. Certainly, all of your research will influence what you write, the positions that you take, and the ideas you convey; however, direct repetition of someone else's ideas, words, or methods is plagiarism. In college, plagiarism is considered a violation of academic standards; college-level research respects scholarly values and builds ethically on the work of others. Part of this ethic requires that writers and researchers always acknowledge when they rely on others' ideas, approaches, words, and methods.

Definition of Plagiarism

Plagiarism varies from situation to situation. College students are expected to adhere to institutional and disciplinary definitions of plagiarism. Many colleges and universities have strict definitions and penalties for plagiarism; others may have limited or more liberal policies and definitions. Some universities have different policies for different colleges and disciplines within the institution. Often academic situations define *plagiarism* in relation to whether writers "intentionally" represent someone else's work or ideas as their own. Other definitions make a distinction between using "common knowledge" and someone else's intellectual property. But these kinds of definitions are ambiguous, and it really isn't always clear what constitutes "common knowledge" or whether a writer "intentionally" uses someone else's work. These kinds of ambiguities can leave writers unsure as to whether or not they have plagiarized and can lead to worry and anxiety—particularly in college settings where penalties for plagiarizing can be hefty.

It may be best to think of plagiarism as a set of standards specific to each situation in which you write. For college writers, those procedures contribute to academic integrity and academic standards.

Basically, plagiarism is representing someone else's words and/or ideas as your own. This definition is simple; the act and consequences, however, are not. In college writing situations, the following six practices are more often than not identified as plagiarism:

1. Buying a piece of writing and presenting it as your own paper.
2. Copying and pasting exact language from a source without citing the source.
3. Changing words in another person's sentence or phrase but retaining the same idea/structure without citing the source.
4. Collaborating with another student or other students to produce a text that was supposed to be produced individually.
5. Seeking assistance from an expert or authority that would change the fundamental ideas or language of your paper, for example, having a paid tutor contribute to your essay.
6. Failing to use the proper documentation required by disciplinary standards.

It is wise to find out what your institution's definitions of plagiarism are as well as what policies and consequences it has established.

Determining Usability and Plagiarism

Plagiarism is a matter of ethics. Ethics are the rules of conduct we choose to adhere to in any given situation. Plagiarism, then, is a matter of violating an academic rule of conduct. Attribution, documentation, and citation are all tied to professional standards and professional codes of ethics. Academics have numerous documentation styles and standards, each affiliated with particular disciplines (for example, in English, MLA style is preferred; in engineering, IEEE style is preferred). Outside of the academic world, many professional disciplines have their own ethical guidelines regarding plagiarism and their own style guides. Journalists, for example, might use the *Associated Press Stylebook and Briefing on Media Law,* which addresses not only plagiarism but also copyright infringement and other legal and ethical issues for journalists. Business professionals might use the *FranklinCovey Style Guide* or the *IBM Styleguide,* both of which address ethical concerns for business writers.

In many situations, including academic writing, plagiarism can have an effect on viability of publication and possibly on profitability. More important, however, is that plagiarism affects the usability of the writing product. Failure to accurately and completely document source material jeopardizes the usability and the integrity of the product. If professional academics cannot assure that a writer's research comes from acceptable places, then they cannot support or endorse the arguments or findings in the writing.

Usability, then, is simply a matter of confirming that your writing is usable within a given situation. In academic writing situations, your research must comply with the ethical codes and professional standards your college or university maintains. It is, then, every college writer's responsibility to locate, read, and abide by his or her college's policies about plagiarism and academic integrity.

Plagiarism, Remix, and Mashup

In November 2012, Turnitin.com, one of the most widely used Internet-based services for plagiarism prevention in colleges, released a report and an infographic called "The Plagiarism Spectrum: Tagging 10 Types of Unoriginal Work." This report, based on an international survey of nearly 900 instructors in secondary and higher education, identifies ten forms of plagiarism that result from the prevalent role of digital media in student writing. Among these ten, the report identifies mashup as the fourth most frequent and problematic form of plagiarism and remix as the seventh most frequent.

Although mashup and remix are considered plagiarism in specific situations such as academic writing, they are seen as innovative, creative methods of expression in other situations. They are also popular methods of production. Even so, in many nonacademic situations, remix and mashups risk being identified as copyright violations or misappropriation of intellectual property. The key is to be alert to when and where remix and mashup are accepted forms and in what situations they are deemed plagiarism. As a basic rule, assume that remix and mashup qualify as plagiarism according to most academic honesty standards. Submit remix or mashup projects in your college work only after consulting with your instructor, and always be alert to the academic standards of your institution.

Accepting Responsibility

By entering into an academic community, every student has, in essence, signed an agreement with the institution to submit to its terms of conduct. Part of that agreement relates to complying with academic writing standards, including understanding and avoiding plagiarism.

Unfortunately, some institutional policies tell students to avoid plagiarism but do little to show them how to avoid it. It is, then, your responsibility to develop strategies to ensure you do not plagiarize and that you understand exactly what constitutes plagiarism in your institution's writing situations. As you write and think about your writing, ask yourself these kinds of questions:

- Am I required to use source materials in this class?
- If so, do they include only sources we've read in class or outside sources, too?
- Should I use citations on the in-class sources?
- What documentation style am I required to use? Am I to observe conventions only for citing sources in the text and works cited at the end of the paper or, in addition, style conventions such as formatting, footnoting, etc.?
- Where can I find a brief overview of the important in-text and bibliographic conventions I should use?
- Are there any restrictions on getting assistance with editing and revising?
- Are there any restrictions on collaboration?
- Should I be aware of or incorporate any other discipline-specific citation procedures that have not been covered by the university's plagiarism policy?

Summary

To synthesize is to form a new whole from carefully evaluated, selected, and relevant parts. Synthesis builds ecological relationships among your writing, the situation, and other texts. The most difficult part of synthesizing research is writing about the research in ways that support your voice and position. When synthesizing research into your work, always begin by writing your ideas, claims, and thoughts. Thorough note taking enables strong synthesis, helping you to respond to the research, show readers how the research is relevant, and connect research information and your ideas in logical and beneficial ecosystems. Direct quotations best serve your synthesis when you want your readers to encounter the exact language of the research. Paraphrased information is best when research content is important, but the language of the research is not as relevant. Summarizing research is appropriate when the research is long and the overall concepts are more relevant to your writing than are the details. One way to improve synthesis is to avoid making the 11 key mistakes that undermine it. Although the mistake of plagiarism is defined differently in various situations, it basically involves representing someone else's words and/or ideas as your own. In college, plagiarism is considered a violation of academic standards. You must accept the responsibility to avoid plagiarism by asking careful questions about source materials and documentation formats.

Chapter Review

1. Where should you begin when synthesizing your research and your writing?

2. Identify five ways you can bring your research and your writing together.

3. Why should you avoid plagiarizing?

4. How can you avoid plagiarizing?

Thinking and Writing about the Chapter

Local Situation

How does your university or college define plagiarism? Where does the definition appear? Do different departments or programs have their own definitions of plagiarism? Are there any parts of the definition that are ambiguous or unclear? What are the penalties for plagiarism? First, write a summary of your institution's plagiarism policies. Next, write a paraphrase of your institution's plagiarism policies.

20 | Presenting and Documenting Research

Before you read this chapter

When you conduct research, how do you integrate what you discover into your writing? How do you make your research and your writing work together? How do you determine what to include and what not to include? In your journal or blog, explain what you do to make research you conduct useful to your readers.

Learning Objectives

20.1 Prepare a research plan

20.2 Locate and evaluate resources

20.3 Integrate sources smoothly into a formal research paper

20.4 Avoid plagiarism and document sources

While you are in college, you will most likely have to write some

form of research paper. Writing research papers requires not only good research skills, including scholarly critical investigation, but also careful attention to using that research to support your position, whether your rhetorical purpose is informative, evaluative, argumentative, or analytical.

This chapter begins with a careful examination of one student's research paper. The analysis of this paper will show you how the student conscientiously uses substantial information to support her position. She integrates research into her writing without allowing it to take over the essay or become a patchwork of research that shows little or no clear relationship with her purpose.

The remainder of the chapter provides guidelines for developing a research plan, locating and evaluating resources, and synthesizing research into your writing. These guidelines are designed to be revised and adjusted each time you enter into a rhetorical situation that requires you to conduct research and integrate that research into your writing. Finally, the chapter presents guidelines for attributing your research to its sources in MLA and APA styles.

student example

Summer Woods is majoring in English and history on a pre-law track and plays on her school's Division I soccer team. When she graduates, she plans to tour the world, taking photographs and writing about the different kinds of people and places she encounters. After traveling, she hopes to attend law school and become an international human rights lawyer, working with organizations like the United Nations to ensure all people are given the basic freedoms they deserve. Summer loves reading anything from novels to newspapers. Her favorite author is Kurt Vonnegut, and her favorite book is *To Kill a Mockingbird*. She also writes short fiction stories and poetry. You can read one of Summer's narratives in Chapter 8. Summer is also a longboarder and a wakeboarder, and she loves classic rock greats such as Bob Dylan, the Beatles, Tom Petty, and the Rolling Stones. Summer wrote the research paper reprinted here for her Post–1945 European History class. In it she compares the 1968 student protests in France with the more violent 1968 Red Faction Army protests in Germany, showing how the nonviolent French protests and the violent German protests both failed in some aspects. As you read Summer's paper, be alert to how Summer uses research to support her position throughout the essay and how her paper both informs and argues. Note, too, the various ways in which she synthesizes her research into her essay to create a smoothly flowing paper.

Summer Woods

Professor Marlin

History 212

14 February 2014

From Protest to Resistance: Evaluating the Evolution and Ultimate Success of the Non-Violent 1968 May Protests and the Violent Red Army Faction

Summer uses this opening paragraph to establish context and to situate her claim within that context. Notice how this paragraph exemplifies the move from topic to thesis.

Summer directly states her thesis in the final sentence of this first paragraph.

1968 saw the unprecedented rise of revolution from Third World nations to the industrialized world of Europe. In France, student protests threatened to undermine the Fifth Republic while the German government struggled to subdue the terrorist actions of the Red Army Faction (RAF). While most demonstrations started peacefully, none of the movements could have continued without starting to resemble the violent state they claimed to be against. In the long run the RAF failed as a revolution because it succumbed to such pressures, while peaceful demonstrations ended sooner but still effectively changed culture by encouraging society to question the state around them. The moderation of the May 1968 Protests allowed them to be a successful revolution as they facilitated gradual overall change of French society, while the terrorism of the RAF that evolved from the German Student Movement had positive initial goals but became too radical to instill any lasting change.

While neither of the movements started out with a strategy of violent

aggression, the May 1968 Protests in France never evolved past reciprocal actions

against the police, yet almost caused the collapse of President Charles de Gaulle's

government. The protests began at the University of Nanterre in France, a suburban

outpost of the Sorbonne that was built to hold post-war rising student enrollment.

It was a reflection of bourgeois family life, "full of young people whose future

was staked in the success of capitalism, arch-consumers of a consumer culture"

(Feenberg 3). However, it was also located on the outskirts of Paris and therefore

fostered an environment in which students were frustrated by their sense of isolation.

Conflict began when a student, Daniel Cohn-Bendit, attempted to instigate reforms

by verbally criticizing the university system. This May 22nd movement was different

from the RAF and other Left-wing organizations that relied on centralization and

personality cults as it was initially leaderless. Cohn-Bendit believed the presence

of an organization was detrimental to a successful revolt as a universal movement

that allowed any kind of protest was the key to a true revolution. After the police

crushed a brief student occupation, Nanterre was shut down, and the dissent spread

to Paris at the Sorbonne. The students were joined by the workers movement and

newspaper and television reporters who were protesting the lack of democratic

> Summer uses a direct quotation and the MLA internal citation approach of listing author name and page number.

> Summer uses comparison and contrast to help synthesize the two parts of her thesis into a single approach.

> Notice how Summer uses summary to condense complex information for the purpose of her claim.

channels allowed by the state. While the demonstrations eventually turned violent as police were sent in to oppress the students with tear gas, Cohn-Bendit claimed, "No one can point to any person or leader as responsible.... It is the system that is violent. Of course we have resisted government power; after all it is this power which has sent its police against us" (Feenberg 13). Police actions trapped students in the Latin Quarter and the violence the protestors reacted with was driven by the necessity over the movement and the impossibility of retreat, not by an ideology that promoted forcefulness as means to an end. The demonstrators had much less access to guns and other weapons than did the police and were forced to resort to handmade, defensive options (Seidman 43-44). Their lack of prepared resources indicates that they did not initiate their demonstration with the intent of it escalating, but were forced to adapt to the violence of the state that would not even allow peaceful protests as a form of expression. However, even with provocation, the movement disbanded before student groups reached a state of violence and the divisions died out without any reaching the radical level of the RAF.

The May 1968 protests were unique compared with any other demonstrations of the time as they fought "not only against the regime, but

---

Summer uses a direct quotation and the MLA internal citation approach of listing author name and page number.

This detailed paragraph begins with a qualifying phrase that Summer uses to establish contrast between the two events she addresses. Pay particular attention to how she integrates the research into her writing to support her claims without losing her voice in the writing or disrupting her flow.

against revolution.… It was the libertarian value of the movement, refusing no

one the floor, denying nothing but constraint" (Feenberg 38). The movement,

without a focused leadership, didn't seek to liberate any specific political or social

group, but sought the total liberation of the human being. The ambiguity of the

protests allowed it to reach a large range of groups, such as industrial workers

and newspaper reporters, as it did not link the demonstrators by social-economic

standards but instead by a feeling of being repressed by "the man." The protests

reached such a height that the government feared civil war or revolution and De

Gaulle even fled the country. Yet, the violence evaporated as quickly as it arose,

and by 1969 the Gaullist party emerged stronger than before. The ambiguity that

gave Cohn-Bendit's movement mass appeal was also its downfall, as it could only

continue to instill supporters for so long without a single rallying and organizing

cause behind it.

  While the May 1968 Movement sought a new form of revolution entirely,

student unrest in West Germany was modeled after political theorists such

as Herbert Marcuse, who predicted violence was a necessary evil to achieve

revolutionary ends. His essay, *Repressive Tolerance,* argues that the contemporary

governments had failed to be democratic as they practiced violence as a state

This paragraph continues to provide an overview of the 1968 protests, but Summer is careful to show the relevance of her overview to her own claim, specifically, through the final two sentences. Note, too, Summer's synthesis of research at the beginning of the paragraph to support the focus of the paragraph.

response to dissent and used suppression to prevent any ideas that went against the goals of the state (Marcuse 95-96). Those who held power therefore determined what constituted violence, and tolerance of democratic expression was nothing more than "a means for perpetuating the struggle for existence and suppression the alternatives" (98). In a true democratic society, by definition, there would be ways for a subversive minority to develop; however, if these means are blocked by organized repression and indoctrination of the supposed democratic state itself, groups may have to resort to violent and undemocratic means to reopen them. A failure to do so is what Marcuse refers to as "the danger of destructive tolerance and benevolent neutrality"; that is, passive non-action is more harmful than active violence. Non-violence is "not only preached to, but exacted from the weak—it is a necessity rather than a virtue, and normally it does not seriously harm the case of the strong" (105). These ideas, along with the inspiration of revolutionary leaders like Che Guevara, inspired the student movements of the 1960s who hoped to reveal the violence inherent in the state by eliciting brutal police response to the demonstrations.

The German Student Movement was the best realization of Marcuse's ideals put into practice but failed due to factional divisions following the death of the student movement's leader, Rudi Dutschke. In West Germany, the protest movement was not only a reaction against the perceived authoritarianism and hypocrisy of the government, but also a response to the failure of the early generation to deal with their Nazi past. These feelings culminated in a demonstration organized by the SDS in 1967 against a visit by the Shah of Iran to Berlin. Many students saw it as an explicit example of the German government supporting a dictatorship that brutally oppressed its own people (Kurlansky 28). The death of one of the protestors, Benno Ohnesorg, increased the spread of demonstrations in response to police brutality. Dutschke and his supporters were fascinated by the idea of subjectivity and the ability of individual actions to change the course of history ("Socialist Worker"). While he didn't advocate proactive violence, he believed that police brutality would reveal the true nature of the state and raise public support for their cause as, "Revolutionaries must not just wait for the objective conditions for a revolution. By creating a popular 'armed focus' they can create the objective conditions for a revolution by subjective initiative" ("Socialist Worker"). His ideas culminated in the 1968 International Vietnam Congress in which participants expressed their sense of the strength of anti-imperialist movements worldwide and the urgent need for military protest. At

Summer uses a paraphrase and the MLA internal citation approach of listing the name of the source when no author name or page number is available.

the congress Dutschke gave an urgent speech, imploring, "Comrades we don't have much time.... How this period of history ends depends primarily on our will" (Varon 67). He did not, however, promote violence beyond that instigated by the police and instead advocated a "long march through the institutions of power to create radical change from within" (34). He explains:

> Only since we have begun, however cautiously, to speak the language of the
> system we have made ourselves understandable to works and a danger to
> Springer. That language is violence. The system speaks it, because the system
> is constituted by violence ... the attack on Rudi Dutschke was the spark.
> Dutschke is distinguished among us for maintaining from the outset that it
> is not a purely moral–intellectual choice that compels us to fight our system;
> rather our physical and spiritual existence is threatened by this system, which
> we cannot reform but must destroy. (Dutschke, "Gewalt" 25-26)

Soon after, Dutschke barely survived an assassination attempt, which radical students blamed on an anti-student campaign in the "pogrom" papers of the Springer publishing company. More Leftist groups attempted to blockade the distribution of the newspapers all over Germany, which led to major street violence with the police. As the press continued to feed a climate of anti-student hysteria,

---

Summer uses a long, direct quotation and the MLA internal citation approach of listing author name and page number. She insets the long quotation, as per MLA style guidelines, to identify the material as a direct quotation.

the reaction of the media to the new Left itself became a major object of protest (Varon 39). Dutschke had rejected such radicalized student protests, as he feared it would cause the dissolution of the student movement. His fears were realized as the SDS split in 1969 and many New Leftists became dispirited and unable to identify with each other. The divide over the strategy for broadening power of the movement gave rise to small Marxist-Leninist parties and the armed Red Army Faction.

The Red Army Faction also rose out of a faction of the SDS following the Dutschke shooting but quickly evolved from mere demonstrations to terrorist acts that continued through the 1980s. Ulrike Meinhof, one of the founding members of the RAF, believed that the only distinction between the violent "so-called radicals" and the peaceful "well-meaning groups," like the French May 1968 protests, was that the former was not willing to stop until their desired reforms were achieved ("Everybody Talks" 186). She differentiated between the two: "Protest is when I say I don't like this. Resistance is when I put an end to what I don't like" ("From Protest to Resistance" 1). She cited the protests against the Easter attack on Rudi Dutschke as the first time people massively crossed the line between verbal protest and physical resistance, but advocated that further action had to be taken. For Meinhof, those who promoted nonviolence as means

Summer begins this substantial paragraph by reminding readers which of the two protests she is discussing. This clarification helps readers keep track of the essay's flow.

Notice that Summer relies heavily on her research in this paragraph—necessary because she is conveying information that is not common knowledge. Yet, even though most of the paragraph conveys research information, Summer's synthesis—through direct quotations, paraphrasing, short quotations, and long quotations—does not distract from her position or voice because it meshes seamlessly into the essay without becoming too repetitive.

to oppose the state were hypocritical as they actually represented a system that had produced hypocrisies such as the Springer papers and the Vietnam War. Instead, she praised people who are "reading and able to engage in resistance—so that others finally understand that things cannot go on this way" (241). She, along with Andreas Baader, Gundrun Ensslin, Horst Mahler, began to shift the German movement towards accomplishing these more radical concepts of revolutionary change through guerrilla warfare.

The Red Army Faction began to wage guerrilla campaigns in 1969 in order to create a catalyst for larger revolts but could never attract a following, as their violence became a tactical failure itself. Even other Leftists denounced them as "everything from self-indulgent fools living out Bonnie-and-Clyde fantasies to left-wing adventurists hopelessly cut off from the masses" (Varon 3). The RAF sought to punish Germany for the sins of its Nazi past and used armed rebellion to compensate for the virtual absence of violent resistance against the Third Reich. The group quickly escalated their violence by engaging in terrorist acts such as bombing and arson. Their efforts increased in intensity through the 1970s as they committed brutal acts of violence to free jailed members, but their ideology was rarely articulated (Kurlansky 54).

They were able to gain some public sympathy for their treatment by the state while imprisoned, but it decreased as members escalated guerrilla terrorism. Baader's writings during the time were fragmentary, sloganistic and often contradictory, and amounted to little more than "ex post facto justifications for actions not guided by a properly political agenda" (Varon 65). He, along with Meinhof and other leaders, were soon killed while in prison but the RAF remained active in some form until the 1980s, although support rapidly disintegrated throughout the previous decade. Their revolution was unsuccessful as it attempted to change a society without extreme problems by using extreme measures and, by resorting to the extreme of dissent, became equivalent to the extreme fascism of the past generation they were rejecting (Nepstad 57). Ultimately, the RAF was doomed from the beginning, as its attempt to convert the tantalizing sense of possibility of revolution into reality was undermined by its denigration of critical thinking and glorification of violence.

While the German Student Movement and the RAF eventually failed because of its turn to radicalism, the May Events were successful as a revolution despite many historical arguments that they failed because they didn't instill direct political change. For example, Seidman argues that the events were an "imaginary revolution" and simply represented a continuity of social and political trends that have occurred

Like the previous paragraph, Summer begins this paragraph announcing specifically what the paragraph addresses, which helps to guide readers. Summer continues to balance her discussion with enough research so she supports her position without allowing the research to dominate the tone or flow of the essay.

throughout history. Contrary to revolution, these events actually demonstrated the power of the centralized state and the attracters of a consumer society that have effectively smothered revolution (265). While the success of the movement is judged by its juxtaposition with groups like the RAF, whose radicalism alienated it from mass society; its true accomplishment can be seen if it's removed from these counterparts. The defining characteristic of a revolution is not that it is stronger than the state, but that it is able to call existing society into question and press it into action. The May Events accomplished this and united different social groups such as workers and students into one common goal. Their only mistake was giving up on their revolution too soon, as many became passive as the violence of the government increased and public support decreased (Kurlansky 87). They failed to see in the long run the nature of their success as one former protestor reflected, "Why couldn't we see our victory? Because our victory had been brought by a rising tide of radicalism, we expected it to look like a rising tide. But having power is not the same thing as having all the power" (Cluster 146). While peaceful revolutions could not accomplish radical goals as they did not resort to radical means, they still subtly shifted the relationship of power towards a fully realized democratic state.

Summer continues to use her research in this paragraph to inform readers and to lead them to her point. The final sentence of this paragraph summarizes the paragraph while also confirming her overall claim. Although Summer relies on her research in this paragraph, notice that she concludes the paragraph with a strong statement made in her own voice.

The May 1968 Protests and the RAF diverged into extremely different paths but both demonstrations evolved from similar conditions from the New Left. They originally held a similar goal of rejecting the imperialism of the West and challenging the inherent suppression of democracy and were led by students inspired by revolutionary movements in the Third World. The revolutions of 1968 represented a turning point in history as people weren't revolting against their governments because they had no other choice due to external conditions of poverty or totalitarian dictatorships, but because they were unhappy with democratic limitations on expression or the conditions of citizens in Third World countries. The students at the Sorbonne all came from affluent families of privilege, yet they still were willing to throw it all away for an abstract future, "We refuse a world where the assurance of not dying from hunger is exchanged for the risk of dying from boredom" (Freenberg 38).

As the protestors were fighting for a change of mind, not change of government, it is impossible to quantitatively measure how successful they were. But, in a sense of cultural change, they were successful in instilling a new sense of consciousness that not only desired democratic expressions of freedom, but had begun to demand it.

Summer begins this paragraph with a strong transition from the previous paragraph. Her research does not overwhelm the paragraph, but supports the points she wishes to make.

Summer concludes her research paper with a definitive return to her claim. She summarizes her position, reminding readers about the comparative work she has done to show the relationships between the two events and how that comparison lends to her claim.

Works Cited

Cluster, Dick. "It Did Make a Difference: The Anti-War Movement." *They Should*
    Have Served That Cup of Coffee. Boston: South End, 1979. 131-47. Print.

Feenberg, Andrew, and Jim Freedman. *When Poetry Ruled the Streets: The French*
    May Events of 1968. Albany: State University of New York, 2001. Print.

Kurlansky, Mark. *1968: The Year That Rocked the World.* New York:
    Ballantine, 2004. Print.

Marcuse, Herbert. "Repressive Tolerance." *A Critique of Pure Tolerance.*
    Boston: Beacon, 1965. 95-137. Print.

Meinhof, Ulrike. "From Protest to Resistance." 1968. *Everybody Talks About*
    the Weather ... We Don't: The Writings of Ulrike Meinhof. Ed. Karin
    Bauer. New York: Seven Stories, 2008. 239-43. Print.

---. "Everybody Talks About the Weather." 1969. *Everybody Talks About the*
    Weather ... We Don't: The Writings of Ulrike Meinhof. Ed. Karin Bauer.
    New York: Seven Stories, 2008. 184-89. Print.

Nepstad, Sharon Erickson. *Nonviolent Revolutions: Civil Resistance in the Late*
    20th Century. Oxford: Oxford UP. 2011. Print.

"Rudi Dutschke and the German Student Movement in 1968." *Socialist Worker*
    [London] 03 May 2008, 2099th ed.: *Worker Online.* Web. 2 Nov. 2012.

Seidman, Michael. *The Imaginary Revolution: Parisian Students and Workers in*
    1968. New York: Berghahn, 2004. Print.

Varon, Jeremy. *Bringing the War Home: The Weather Underground, the Red*
    Army Faction, and Revolutionary Violence in the Sixties and Seventies.
    Berkeley: University of California, 2004. Print.

Summer includes a complete list of works cited in her research paper. This works cited list is presented in MLA style to remain consistent with her in-text citation.

student example

THE ROAD TO A STRONG THESIS

QUESTION
"There are many issues surrounding the 1968 protests that could be addressed, but what distinguishes the different protests from each other?"

RESPONSE
"There was a distinction between protests that turned violent and those that did not, but in either case, the protests never achieved their overall objectives. This is important: does violence aid or deter a protest?"

RESPONSE
"That might be the direction of the paper: show how two different protests unfolded, one non-violent and one violent, to inform my readers about the historical events and to compare the outcomes. Did violence or non-violence achieve more as a protest strategy?"

PURPOSE
"To convey information beyond classroom discussions about the 1968 protests in Europe."

SECOND THOUGHTS
"Did specific protests accomplish what they intended? Did it matter whether the protests turned violent or not? That seems worth discussing."

SECOND THOUGHTS
"I'll need to show how a non-violent protest unfolded and how a violent protest unfolded. If I show an example of a violent and a non-violent protest, can I use that approach to inform my audience about the conditions under which the protests emerged?"

ASSIGNMENT
To write a research essay.

THESIS
"The moderation of the May 1968 Protests allowed them to be a successful revolution as they facilitated gradual overall change of French society, whereas the terrorism of the RAF that evolved from the German Student Movement had positive initial goals but became too radical to instill any lasting change."

Summer Woods was assigned the task of writing a research paper for her history class. By synthesizing her sources, considering her purpose, and reflecting on her audience, she was able to develop a strong thesis for her paper.

FINAL THOUGHTS
"Now I can create my comparison of the events to show this outcome."

20.1 Prepare
a research plan

Developing a Research Plan

Research requires that you plan not only what you will research but also why, how, and when you will conduct it. Not all research is conducted in the same way, nor does it require the same amount of time or the same use of time. Instead, it is always constrained and directed by the situation in which you conduct it. Various elements of the rhetorical situation such as your intended audience and your purpose have direct effect on your research. Likewise, you should account for the timing (kairos) of your research in terms of what research is chronologically important within the situation and when in the situation you voice your research. Commonly, student researchers begin their research by just "looking up stuff," but research involves much more careful planning within the context of the situation. The following guidelines will show you how to develop a research plan. Think of these guidelines as a template that can, and should, be adjusted and revised to suit the needs of the various writing/research situations in which you participate.

Guidelines for Developing a Research Plan

Step	Comments
Make a schedule	Develop a detailed research schedule that allots time for all steps in the research task. Be sure to build in some extra time in case you run into any glitches along the way.
Identify a topic	Select topics that are of interest to you and that are pertinent to your writing situation. Consider how the assignment or purpose itself helps guide your topic choice. A broad topic such as organic foods will have to be narrowed and focused throughout your research and writing process, but remember that a topic, even a narrowed one, is not a thesis or claim.
Generate ideas	Once you have a topic, begin to generate ideas about the topic so you can better understand your research needs as well as revise and tighten the focus of your topic toward a claim. Consider using these strategies to generate ideas: • *Reading*—to discover new information and connections • *Thinking*—particularly to compare and contrast or recall what you already know about a subject • *Questioning*—to push the boundaries of what you know • *Writing*—to clarify, organize, and flesh out thoughts • *Remembering*—to connect your own experiences to the topic • *Wandering*—to prompt connections by going someplace real, exploring online, or just browsing through the library • *Discussing* ideas with others—to explore the topic • *Viewing and listening*—including viewing art, photography, movies or listening to music, podcasts, or spoken audio, to prompt connections

Step	Comments
Conduct preliminary research	Preliminary research can help you generate ideas, narrow your focus, and develop a claim. Begin with resources such as reference books that contain general information about your topic. Remember that although print and online encyclopedias are unacceptable sources for college-level research, you can use them in preliminary research to get a basic understanding of a subject and find bibliographies that point to other sources. You can also use web pages and introductory texts as starting points. During your preliminary research, start to identify key terms and concepts, as well as predominant authors and texts tied to your research subject, all of which can be used as search terms in catalogs, databases, and online.
Develop a working research question	Once you have begun to understand and narrow your topic, identify particular areas of interest. Develop your research question within these areas, and use it to frame your investigation. A good research question will guide what kind of research you do and what your objectives will be as well as lead to a focused claim. For example, you may discover in your preliminary research for the topic of organically grown foods that the USDA's National Organic Program oversees legal definitions of *organic* in the United States and certifies growers. You might develop a research question such as "By what criteria does the National Organic Program certify growers?"
Establish a provisional thesis	Use your research question to develop an initial claim. For example, if your research question is "By what criteria does the National Organic Program certify growers?" your provisional thesis might become "The criteria used by the National Organic Program to certify organic growers are too lenient and need to be redrafted to meet more stringent standards." You will likely refine your thesis as you conduct more detailed research and revise your research question, so don't assume you have to stick with either.
Develop a working bibliography	As you begin your research, keep track of all of the sources you examine. You may not use all of the sources you look at, but maintain a record of them in case you need to go back to them or you decide to include them in your writing. It doesn't matter where you keep your working bibliography—in a notebook or in an electronic medium—but keep it all in one place and in the citation format you intend to use in your document.
Draft an outline	Once you have your research question and a provisional thesis, develop a tentative outline, which can help you think through your overall approach, organize your ideas, and track your progress. Your outline does not need to be formal or terribly detailed. You may begin with just a list of topics to address within the framework of the provisional thesis.

MAPPING
YOUR SITUATION

NETWORKS
- In what networks will my research circulate?
- How is my research related to others' research?
- How might my research affect the situation?

WRITERS AND SPEAKERS
- Who are the other writers and speakers in this situation?
- What have they said about this situation?
- What other analyses are presented?

RELATIONS
- What is my relation to the situation?
- What are the relationships between writers/speakers, audience, and players?
- What are the relationships to external forces, like culture, religion, or politics?
- What are the power relations?

AUDIENCE
- Who will read my research?
- Who do I want to hear/read my research?
- What do I know about the audience that I want to read my research?
- Who might my research affect directly and indirectly?

MEDIUM AND METHOD
- How will I present my research?
- In what genre will I deliver my research?
- What tone will my research take?
- How will I distribute and circulate my research?

CONTEXT
- Where will my research unfold?
- Where will my research appear?
- What limits are imposed on my research?

PURPOSE
- Why do I want to or need to conduct research?
- What am I going to conduct research about and why?
- What does my research need to accomplish?
- How will I convey my research?

Mapping your situation will help you generate ideas you can use to compose. Start by answering these questions about each part of the situation. Begin with your purpose and work outward to relations and networks.

Locating and Evaluating Resources

Once you have a working research plan—a schedule, a topic, a working research question, a provisional thesis, and a tentative outline—you should begin conducting your detailed research. The following guidelines, along with the information found elsewhere in this book, will help you develop an approach to conducting research and should be a central part of your overall research plan. You should think of these guidelines as a template that can, and should, be adjusted and revised to suit the needs of the various writing/research situations in which you participate.

20.2 Locate and evaluate resources

20.3 Integrate sources smoothly into a formal research paper

Guidelines for Conducting Research

Strategy	Comments
Analyze and evaluate	Your work to analyze and evaluate sources should begin even before you start to locate resources. First, determine the criteria you will use to analyze and evaluate any sources you find. Academic criteria, for example, require that you use particular kinds of sources, which will temper how you locate resources and what kinds of resources you engage. Then, as you conduct your research, continue to analyze and evaluate resources as you encounter them.
Initiate searches	Relying on your criteria for evaluating sources, begin to locate resources that will be of use to you, adding to the information you encountered during your preliminary research. For academic research, there is no better resource than your school's library. Most—not all—of the materials housed in academic libraries are reliable and meet many scholarly criteria. To obtain sources not available through your library, consider using library networks and inter-library loan to secure them. In addition, search online databases and indexes, government publications, and biographies.
Browse	Just browsing can lead to important research discoveries. As you search for a specific book on the shelves, look at the other books that surround it—a strategy called "browsing the stacks." Similarly, when using your library's online catalog, follow the catalog links to other similar publications.
Use bibliographies	Thorough researchers always examine bibliographies to locate other sources. In addition, a bibliography that identifies reliable sources likely indicates that the work itself is reliable. Likewise, if a particular work appears in several bibliographies across your research, you might infer that the cited work is relevant. The dates of works listed in a bibliography can suggest whether the work is addressing recent information or is outdated.
Search online	First, follow two important rules of online research: (a) confirm reliability and (b) use online resources only in conjunction with library resources. Use general search engines such as Google with caution, and instead, try using academic search engines, like Google Scholar.
Conduct primary research	Primary research produces original information. In some research situations, you may need to generate information that cannot be located in library or online resources or that simply hasn't yet been scrutinized and published. Primary research can include field research, observation, surveys, questionnaires, and interviews.
Take notes	Thorough notes can help you recall why you found a piece of research interesting, valuable, or in need of critique.

Attributing and Documenting Sources

Within college writing situations and many other writing situations, professional standards require that you fully acknowledge any resource you use in your own work. *Attribution* literally means the act of assigning; in the case of research, you will assign credit to the source from which you adapt or quote information. Attributing source credit is a crucial part of ethically conducting and using research.

Avoiding Plagiarism

One of the most important parts of conducting and referring to research is ensuring that you clearly identify others' work as theirs and not as yours. Ideas and words are thought of as a writer's intellectual property, and in academic writing, using some-one else's intellectual property without attribution can be considered akin to theft. Carefully attributing research to its source can help you avoid plagiarism, the act of appropriating others' ideas or work as your own, whether intentionally or uninten-tionally. In college, plagiarism is considered a violation of academic standards and is not tolerated. Remember, college-level research respects scholarly values and builds ethically on the work of others, so acknowledgment of others' work is a critical part of integrating research into your writing.

Plagiarism can take many forms, and you should always understand how your college or university defines it. In most academic settings, the following forms are generally understood as plagiarism, so you should not use them as strategies in your writing:

- *Cut and paste*—Copying large segments of a text written by someone other than you and pasting it into your own writing without attributing the pasted text to its real author
- *Wholesale copying*—Copying an entire document (or most of a document) from another author, including copying from published texts, digital texts, unpublished texts, even texts your friend or roommate wrote
- *Failure to cite*—Not acknowledging the source of an idea or piece of text you use in writing your document
- *Patchwriting*—Explained by plagiarism expert Rebecca Moore Howard as not copying a text exactly, but paraphrasing it too closely, which can be considered plagiarism, even if you provide a source citation
- *Paper mill plagiarism*—Purchasing a paper from a paper mill—an online source that databases and sells academic papers of all kinds—and submitting it as your own work; can also be considered academic cheating
- *Collusion*—Claiming a work as your own even though someone else substantially helped you complete it; also considered to be academic dishonesty (usually does not include help from a writing center or school-approved tutoring center)

Documenting Sources

In academic research, you must attribute credit to every research source you use, whether you directly quote it, paraphrase it, summarize it, or rely on it in any way. Fortunately, contemporary digital technologies make source citation simple through a variety of easily accessible tools. Many college and university library web pages now include citation generators and citation management tools that will automatically build and store a properly formatted bibliography of your sources. Likewise, various web pages and mobile applications will generate citations from information you enter into a form. Certainly use these tools when you can; however, make sure you understand the documentation process completely so you do not misuse them. Also be aware that some citation generator applications may not be 100 percent accurate in their citation construction.

All citation forms are designed to provide readers with particular information that will assist them in locating the cited sources:

- Name of the author
- Title of the work
- Page numbers
- Date of publication
- Place of publication
- Publisher
- Location of published work
- Type of work (genre)

Various style guides establish different organizational formats for presenting these pieces of information.

Formatting Documentation

There are two parts of source attribution: an in-text citation that is abbreviated and a detailed source citation for each source you refer to, usually placed at the end of the document. The following chart provides an overview of in-text citation styles for the Modern Language Association (MLA) and the American Psychological Association (APA) citation styles, two of the most widely used citation forms in academic writing.

The following table provides an overview of proper full source citation formats for MLA and APA citation styles. Works Cited lists and Reference lists should be formatted as hanging indents in which all lines except the first are indented 0.5 inches. In Microsoft Word, you can easily format hanging indents by simply highlighting or clicking on the citation entry and pressing CTRL+T in Windows. In Macintosh, click the dropdown line spacing button in the menu area at the top of the document and select Line Spacing Options from the drop down menu. Select "Hanging" under the heading "Special" and "Double under "Line Spacing." All entries within the Works Cited or Reference lists should be organized alphabetically, except in those instances noted in the chart below.

In-text Citations in MLA Style

The MLA citation style uses a parenthetical, in-text citation system to direct readers to the Works Cited bibliography at the end of the document, which provides full citation information. These in-text citations provide only necessary information, often limited to only an author's last name and a page number. Parenthetical citations should be placed in the text as close to the cited material as possible and should appear at punctuated breaks in the sentence such as at the point just before a comma or terminal punctuation mark. Parenthetical citations should not repeat information already provided in the text; if in the text you have named the author, for example, then you do not need to include the author's name in the parenthetical citation. Page numbers should be represented by inclusive numbering, which does not repeat key numbers (107-10, not 107-110), and a hyphen should separate page ranges.

AUTHOR IDENTIFIED IN TEXT: W.J.T. Mitchell provides a more nuanced definition (98-112).

AUTHOR IDENTIFIED IN CITATION: One image theorist provides an even more nuanced definition (Mitchell 98-112).

MULTIPLE AUTHORS: This is made evident in the idea of becoming animal (Deleuze and Guattari 213-15).

TWO LOCATIONS IN A SINGLE CITED TEXT: Smith elaborates this point later in the work (118-23, 132).

TWO WORKS CITED: Theoretically speaking, the approach seems well-received (Sanchez 68; Hardin 108).

PAGES IN MULTIVOLUME WORK: The Network, then, supersedes the influence of society (Castells 2:37-39).

ENTIRE MULTIVOLUME WORK: This lends to a rigorous consideration of the Network (Castells vol. 2).

ORGANIZATIONAL AUTHORS: Providing easily accessible family planning in developing nations could reduce the costs of newborn and maternal healthcare (United Nations, *State of World Population 2012* 45-46).

NO AUTHOR: As the joint commission reported (*Report* 19-23).

In-Text References in APA Style

The APA citation style is similar to MLA style but varies in the way it formats citation information in text and at the end of the document. In-text citations are parenthetical, like MLA, but the full citations at the end of the documents are called References. The content of in-text citations and how they are inserted in the text is also similar to MLA style; however, a key difference is that when multiple sources are listed within an in-text citation, they should be presented in alphabetical order. Page ranges are represented using full numbering (112–114, not 112–14), and an en dash is used to separate page ranges.

SINGLE AUTHOR IDENTIFIED IN TEXT: Pritchard (1969) first suggested the possibility.

SINGLE AUTHOR IDENTIFIED IN CITATION: When the possibility was first suggested, few researchers took the proposition seriously (Pritchard, 1969).

TWO AUTHORS IDENTIFIED IN CITATION: The approach to job search strategies was promising (Keller & Weisser, 2011).

Note: In the citation, use an ampersand (&) to join names.

TWO AUTHORS IDENTIFIED IN TEXT: Keller and Weisser (2011) proposed a promising approach to job search strategies.

Note: In the text, use *and* to join the names.

THREE OR MORE AUTHORS IDENTIFIED IN TEXT: Bawarshi, DeSantis, Carpenter, and Bossing (2013) first reported the case.

Note: Cite all authors when the reference first appears; in subsequent in-text references use the first last name and et al.:

Bawarshi et al. (2013) first reported the case.

ORGANIZATIONAL AUTHORS: Providing easily accessible family planning in developing nations could reduce the costs of newborn and maternal healthcare (United Nations [UN], 2012).

Subsequent citations: (UN, 2012)

Note: Organizational names (corporations, government, or other agencies) that are used as author names are usually spelled out when they appear in an in-text citation. Some organizational names, however, may be spelled out the first time they appear in a citation and abbreviated in following instances. When deciding whether an organizational name can be abbreviated, keep in mind that both the shortened or abbreviated form of the name must provide enough information in the citation for the reader to locate the entry in the reference list. Organizational names that are already short or that would produce an unfamiliar abbreviation if shortened should be written out each time.

UNKNOWN AUTHOR: Using a direct quotation: The article "Transnational Communication" (2013) calls to question the "idea that the web is English dominated" (p. 3).

USING PARAPHRASED INFORMATION: More Asian-language web pages appear every day, calling to question the idea that the Web is English dominated ("Transnational Communication," 2013).

Works Cited Entries in MLA Style

Book

SINGLE-AUTHORED BOOK:

Steinbeck, John. *The Log from the Sea of Cortez.* New York: Penguin 1995. Print.

MULTI-AUTHORED BOOK (TWO OR THREE AUTHORS):

Williams, Joseph M. and Gregory G. Colomb. *Style: Lessons in Clarity and Grace.* New York: Longman, 2010. Print.

MULTI-AUTHORED BOOK (MORE THAN THREE AUTHORS):

Bloom, Lynn Z., et al. *The New Assertive Woman.* Gretna, LA: Selfhelp Success 2009. Print.

Journal article

SINGLE-AUTHORED ARTICLE:

Dobrin, Sidney I. "Ecology and Concepts of Technology." *Journal of the Council of Writing Program Administrators* 35.1 (2011): 175-98. Print.

MULTI-AUTHORED ARTICLE (TWO OR THREE AUTHORS):

Halbritter, Bump, and Julie Lindquist. "Time, Lives, and Videotape: Operationalizing Discovery in Senses of Literacy Sponsorship." *College English* 75.2 (2012): 171-98. Print.

MULTI-AUTHORED ARTICLE (MORE THAN THREE AUTHORS):

Jaeschke, Roman, et al. "Users' Guides to the Medical Literature: III. How to Use an Article About a Diagnostic Test: B. What Are the Results and Will They Help Me in Caring for My Patients?" *Journal of the American Medical Association* 271.9 (1994): 703-707. Print.

Multiple works by the same author

Houston, Pam. *A Little More about Me.* New York: Norton, 1999. Print

---. "Contents May Have Shifted #49-#60." *Iowa Review* 41.1 (2011), 48-62. Print.

---. *Cowboys Are My Weakness.* New York: Norton, 1992. Print.

---. "Our Own Bloomsbury." *O, The Oprah Magazine* 8.1 (2007). 143. Print

Note: List works by the same author alphabetically by title. Spell the author's full name in the first entry, but use three hyphens in subsequent entries to indicate works by the same author.

Article in a periodical

Weakley, Jeff. "The Tipping Point." *Florida Sportsman* Dec. 2012:43-45.

Web page

United States. Environmental Protection Agency. *Science and Technology: Land, Waste and Cleanup Science.* United States Environmental Protection Agency, 26 July 2013. Web. 18 Feb. 2014.

Online journal article

Malhi, Yadvinder. "The Productivity, Metabolism and Carbon Cycle of Tropical Forest Vegetation." *Journal of Ecology,* 100.1 (2012): 65–75. Web. 10 Feb. 2014.

Periodical or news outlet

Jarvis, Jeff. "Bring Back the Busy Signal." *Huffington Post.* 12 Jan. 2012. Web. 10 Feb. 2014.

Digital book

Fouts, Janet. *Social Media Success!: Practical Advice and Real-World Examples for Social Media Engagement.* Books24x7. Web. 21 Mar. 2012.

Blogs and comments

Kibby, Brian. "Leaders and Confidence: A Habit Worth Forming." *If Not Now ... When?* 9 Jan. 2012. Web. 16 Jan. 2012.

Wikis

"Writing." *Wikipedia.* Wikimedia Foundation, 6 Jan. 2012. Web. 12 Jan. 2012.

Online images

Erdmann, Anita. "Photograph from Yellowstone National Park." N.d. Online image. No Caption Needed. 13 Jan. 2012. <http://www.nocaptionneeded.com/wp-content/uploads/2011/12/Lone-tree-Yellowstone.jpg>

Online video

Alamar. Screenplay by Pedro González-Rubio, Dir. Mantarraya Productions, 2009. Web. 28 July 2011. <http://www.hulu.com/watch/264550/alamar>

Podcast

Foster, John. "This Week in Media 85: Later Clarke." *This Week in Media.* 20 Mar. 2008. Podcast.com. Web. 11 Aug. 2011.

References in APA Style

Book

SINGLE-AUTHORED BOOK:

Steinbeck, J. (1995). *The log from the Sea of Cortez.* New York: Penguin.

MULTI-AUTHORED BOOK:

Williams, J. M., & Colomb, C. G. (2010). *Style: Lessons in clarity and grace.* New York: Longman.

Journal article

SINGLE-AUTHORED ARTICLE:

Dobrin, S. I. (2011). Ecology and concepts of technology. *Journal of the Council of Writing Program Administrators, 35*(1), 175–198.

Note: Include the journal issue number (in parentheses) if the pagination begins again with each issue.

MULTI-AUTHORED ARTICLE (TWO OR THREE AUTHORS):

Halbritter, B., & Lindquist, J. (2012). Time, lives, and videotape: Operationalizing discovery in senses of literacy sponsorship. *College English, 75*(2), 171–198.

MULTI-AUTHORED ARTICLE (MORE THAN THREE AUTHORS):

Roman, J., Guyatt, G. H., & Sackett, D. L. (1994). Users' guides to the medical literature: III. How to use an article about a diagnostic test: B. What are the results and will they help me in caring for my patients? *The Journal of the American Medical Association, 271*(9), 703–707.

Multiple works by the same author

Houston, P. (1992). *Cowboys are my weakness.* New York: W.W. Norton.

Houston, P. (1999). *A little more about me.* New York: W. W. Norton.

Houston, P. (2007, January). Our own Bloomsbury. *O, The Oprah Magazine, 8*(1), 143.

Houston, P. (2011). Contents may have shifted #49–#60. *Iowa Review, 41*(1), 48–62.

Note: If the works are published in different years, list them chronologically with the earliest first. If they are from the same year, list them alphabetically by title and insert "a" "b" and so on after the dates to indicate the order:

(2014a)

(2014b)

Entries for the author and a coauthor (e.g., Houston & Jones) would come after the entries for that author alone and would be ordered alphabetically by the coauthor's last name.

Article in a periodical

Weakley, J. (2012). The tipping point. *Florida Sportsman, 44*(12), 43–45.

Web page

U.S. Environmental Protection Agency. (2013). *Science and technology: Land, waste and cleanup science.* Retrieved from http://www2.epa.gov/science-and-technology/land-waste-and-cleanup-science

Online journal article

WITH DOI:

Malhi, Y. (2012). The productivity, metabolism and carbon cycle of tropical forest vegetation. *Journal of Ecology, 100*(1), 65–75. doi: 10.1111/j.1365-2745.2011.01916.x

WITHOUT DOI:

Malhi, Y. (2012). The productivity, metabolism and carbon cycle of tropical forest vegetation. *Journal of Ecology, 100*(1), 65–75. Retrieved from http://web.ebscohost.com

Periodical or news outlet

Jarvis, J. (2012, January 12). Bring back the busy signal. *Huffington Post.* Retrieved from http://www.huffingtonpost.com/jeff-jarvis/email-communication_b_1200838.html

Digital book

Fouts, J. (2012). *Social media success!: Practical advice and real-world examples for social media engagement.* Retrieved from http://library.books24x7.com/toc.aspx?bookid=38021

Blogs and comments

BLOG ENTRIES:

Kibby, B. (2012, January 9). Leaders and confidence: A habit worth forming [Web log post]. Retrieved from http://www.briankibbyblog.com/2012/01/09/leaders-and-confidence-a-habit-worth-forming/

BLOG COMMENTS:

Norman Mailer. (2012, March 19). Re: "Leaders and confidence: A habit worth forming." [Web log post]. Retrieved from http://www.briankibbyblog.com/2012/01/09 /leaders-and-confidence-a-habit-worth-forming/

Wikis

Writing. (2012, January 6). Retrieved January 12, 2012, from Wikipedia: http://en.wikipedia .org/wiki/Writing

Online images

Erdmann, Anita. (Photographer). (n.d.). *Photograph from Yellowstone National Park*. [photograph]. Retrieved from http://www.nocaptionneeded.com/wp-content /uploads/2011/12/Lone-tree-Yellowstone.jpg

Online video

González-Rubio, P. (Writer and Director). (2009). *Alamar*. [Film]. Available from http://www .imdb.com/title/tt1502396/

Podcast

Foster, J. (Moderator). 2008, March 20. *This week in media 85: Later Clarke* [Audio Podcast]. Retrieved from http://www.podcast.com/Technology/I-475570.htm

Summary

While you are in college, you will probably have to write some form of research paper. In research-based writing, your research should always support the claim you make in the document. Research requires that you plan not only what you will research but also why, how, and when you will conduct that research. Once you have a working research plan, you should begin conducting your detailed research through careful, systematic investigation. After you have collected research materials, you can begin to synthesize the research and your writing by bringing ideas, concepts, language, and work of others into your own work to support your claims. Be careful to acknowledge the sources you use in your own writing, through in-text citations and complete bibliographic information at the end of the document, so you do not plagiarize someone else's work. This information must be presented in the appropriate format of whatever writing style you are using, for instance, MLA or APA.

Chapter Review

1. Why is it important to develop a strong research plan?

2. What are some strategies for generating ideas?

3. If research isn't just "looking up stuff," then what is research?

4. What does it mean to synthesize your research?

5. Why is it important to attribute your sources?

Thinking and Writing about the Chapter

Reflection

Now that you have read this chapter, how might you revise what you said you would do to make your research more useful to your readers? Respond in your journal or blog.

Essay Exams

Learning Objectives

21.1 Prepare for college-level essay exams

21.2 Develop strategies for successfully taking essay exams

Before you read this chapter

How many of your classes this semester will require that you write essays in class in response to exam questions? How many exam essays did you have to write to apply for college? How do you prepare for and write essays in response to exam questions? In your journal or blog, write about your experience thus far with writing essays in response to exam questions and what you see as their purpose in college-level education.

Timed compositions and on-demand writing have become a regular part of educational assessment. For example, many colleges and universities require the writing portion of standardized tests like the SAT, ACT, or GRE for admission. Timed writing assessments like these usually truncate your writing processes, allowing virtually no time for invention or revision, focusing instead on rapid, single-draft writing. In these kinds of test situations, writers spend less time inventing since the exams usually provide a topic and they often have no time for revision.

More frequently than not, college-level essay exams require more dynamic approaches than do standardized writing tests. Essay exams share some characteristics with timed writing tests—like the constraint of time—but they differ in that they don't often ask you to write about impromptu subjects and they are likely to anticipate more substantive answers. Essay exams in college, that is, are not off-the-cuff responses. They require preparation and planning and ask students to display breadth of knowledge. They ask the writer to recall course information and research beyond the course materials. They require students to establish a position within a conversation and to carefully synthesize what they know with what they claim. The college-level essay exam is not simply a regurgitation of information but an opportunity to display rigorous engagement with ideas, texts, and situations.

Preparing for Essay Exams

21.1 Prepare for college-level essay exams

One of the primary distinctions between timed writing assessments and college-level essay exams is that you can prepare more directly for essay exams. Most of the time, students don't know what they will write about in a timed writing assessment until they are handed the writing prompt. For essay exams in college, however, students have a good idea as to what will be on the exam. This means that you can develop specific strategies for preparing for essay exams.

Confirm the Exam's Form and the Coverage

Teachers want you to do your best on exams and will usually provide ample information about the exam, including the form it will take and the content it will cover. If your instructor doesn't supply this information, ask. Ask how many questions will be on the exam. Ask how long responses are anticipated to be. Ask what material will be covered. Ask about what criteria the teacher will use to evaluate the written responses. Once you have a clear idea as to what you might be asked and what is to be expected of you in your responses, then you can prepare more efficiently. Knowing what is expected gives you a target to aim for in your preparation.

Review Material

Once you know what material the exam will cover, you should begin to review the material. Read your notes, the text, and any other materials that you have used in class. As you review the relevant material, consider organizing the material into manageable parts, organized by similarity. For example, if you are preparing for an exam in an American literature course, you might want to organize the information by author or by date or by region. Organizing your materials in this way not only makes the material manageable, but it also helps you anticipate the kinds of questions you might be asked on the exam. For example, if your American literature instructor has emphasized characteristics of various authors' writing, then you should organize your materials by author. You can also anticipate questions about specific authors' writing or questions that ask you to compare and contrast the characteristics of different writers.

Summarize Material

Once you gather, organize, and review the material you anticipate the exam to cover, write summaries of the different portions you have created. Writing summaries will help you recall overall concepts and general overviews of your various units of information. Summaries convey generalities; they do not convey details. Think of summarizing as distilling information to a minimal explanation of the main ideas. Write summaries from memory of the material, and then compare your summary with your notes. What aspects should you add to your summary? What details would you want to add to the summary to make it more relevant to an essay? Use the generalities of the summary to help you recall the details of the material.

Collaborate and Ask Questions

One of the best ways to remember information is to talk with others about that material. Collaborating for exam preparation can be beneficial in a number of ways:

- You and your classmates may share notes that you or they missed.
- You and your classmates might share creative ways for remembering specific information.
- How someone talks about specific information may trigger your memory during the exam.
- Conversation about the material can help build your confidence in recalling and talking about the material.
- Together, you and your classmates can anticipate what kinds of questions might appear on the exam.
- You and your classmates can identify what might be primary, imperative information to know and what might be secondary.

Practice Writing

Nothing can help you prepare more for an essay exam than practicing writing essay exam responses. Of course, you can't recreate the exam situation exactly, but you can practice in ways that will help better prepare you for that situation. To practice writing essay exams:

- Select a topic that you anticipate will be on the exam.
- Don't avoid the topics you have the most difficulty with. In fact, you should focus on writing about the topics you are less comfortable with.
- Write without looking back at your notes; use what you have memorized to write.
- Set a time limit on your writing and stick to it.
- Write in whatever format you will use for the exam: with pen on paper, in a blue book, on-screen, etc.
- Write continuously until your time limit is complete.
- Write practice essays about several of the topics that might appear on the exam; do not return to your notes between prompts.
- When you finish writing, compare the details of your responses with your notes and course materials. What did you do well? What did you forget or leave out?
- Consider practicing writing in collaborative groups, assigning each other prompts and responding to each other's answers.

Taking Essay Exams

21.2 Develop strategies for successfully taking essay exams

The key to taking an essay exam is being prepared for the exam. Know the material you are to be examined on, and know how to take an essay exam. If you have prepared sufficiently, then the essays on the exam should provide an opportunity for you to display your knowledge and ability. Knowing how to take an essay exam can help you be more efficient and focused in your writing. This section provides a number of guidelines for taking essay exams.

Relax

It is normal to feel anxious before—and during—an exam. Being confident that you are prepared for the exam can help reduce anxiety. If you are nervous before an essay exam, remind yourself that you are prepared. Take several deep breaths. Relax. Remind yourself that you know and understand the material that will be on the exam and that you know how to take an essay exam. Don't let stress or anxiety determine the atmosphere in which you take the exam. Keep in mind that lack of sleep can both contribute to test anxiety and reduce your ability to focus on the exam tasks. Be sure to be well rested for your exams. As they say, "you got this."

Read the Entire Exam

By reading the exam completely, you will better be able to anticipate what you have to do next. If you begin a response to the first question without reading the rest of the exam, you might find yourself rushed to finish questions at the end of the exam. Reading the whole exam can help you get into the right frame of mind, as well. In the few minutes it takes you to read the exam, you will begin to analyze the questions and to think about possible approaches and answers.

Analyze the Situation

Just like every rhetorical situation into which you enter, each essay exam you take is its own unique rhetorical situation. Thus, like any writing scenario, you need to take into account as much as you can about the situation.

- What, in addition to successfully completing the exam, is my exigency for responding as I do to the situation?
- Who is my audience? Does the exam designate writing to a particular audience, or is a general audience or an audience of the instructor assumed?
- What constraints—like time, space, and media—limit what I can and cannot do in my response?
- What relations do I need to account for in my response?
- How do the genre and medium of the essay exam affect the methods I should use?

Analyze the Question

By carefully analyzing the question, you can determine what kind of response is expected for the prompt. Read the exam questions carefully; read them at least twice, making sure you understand the question. Identify key terms in the prompt to determine what must be addressed and what kind of response is anticipated. Essay exams most frequently ask for these kinds of responses:

Response	Example
Analysis Essay exams often ask that you analyze something, identifying its parts and explaining both how those parts work together and how the whole relates to a larger situation. Analysis is a careful examination. Analysis is a kind of dissection, a process of disassembling something to determine how all of its parts work together as a whole. Analysis also suggests a degree of critical reflection or a sense of evaluation and judgment. Essay exams might ask you to analyze an idea, a theory, a text, or an event.	Europe witnessed a number of failed revolutions in 1848. Most commonly known as the "Spring of Nations," the "Springtime of the Peoples," and the "Year of Revolution," these revolutions failed for a number of reasons. Analyze the events of the Revolutions of 1848 that ultimately led to their failures.

Response	Example
Application Essay exams may ask you to apply a theory, concept, or process to a specific situation or context. The goal of application exam prompts is to get you to show not only that you understand the process, concept, or theory but also that you can apply it or use it. Application essay prompts require that you explain the process, concept, or theory in detail; explain the context for the application; and apply the process, theory, or concept to the situation.	There are a number of water treatment filtration processes that are used independently or in conjunction with one another in the treatment of municipal drinking water worldwide. Identify one such process and apply it to uses in filtration for waterborne disease in developing nations.
Argument Essay exams may ask you to defend, justify, support, or prove a position. Prompts that ask you to make an argument are designed to assess two things: your ability to make a cogent claim and your ability to support that claim with evidence. Essay exams that ask you to make arguments anticipate that you will be able to use information you have gathered prior to the exam as evidence in support of your position. Keep in mind that many types of academic writing require some degree of argumentation, so an argument-based essay exam question may not include the word "argument."	Traditional educational certification has recently been challenged by education reformers who propose a new system of certification known as "Badges." In the context of our discussions about educational reform, are Badges a viable alternative to traditional education?
Classification Essay exams may ask you to show how a group of things are related by classifying them. Classification strategies group items, ideas, phenomena, or events together according to their similarities. These strategies often use carefully defined categories to classify various items. Scientific taxonomy—like the system used to classify organisms into kingdom, phylum, class, order, family, genus, and species—is a familiar classifications strategy.	The terms *media*, *new media*, *digital media*, *old media*, and even *new new media* are umbrella terms used to describe a range of kinds of media. Using these terms, classify the various media we have examined thus far in the semester.
Comparison/Contrast Essay exams may ask you to compare or contrast two ideas, events, texts, or theories to show that you understand the details of each and how each relates to the other. Comparison/contrast exam prompts are designed so you can identify similarities and/or differences between things.	Within a geographic framework and using M. King Hubbert's peak theory, compare and contrast peak oil production and peak copper production.
Critique Essay exams may ask you to critique a text, an idea, or a theory. Critique requires critical thought, and instructors who assign critique in an essay exam will be looking for more than superficial, obvious responses. Criticism, though often understood as pointing out negative aspects, is really an act of identifying, analyzing, and evaluating details. Critique can show the positive as well as the negative. The key to writing responses to essay exam questions that ask for critique is to provide details that display more than surface-level observations.	In 1986, Deirdre McCloskey published *The Rhetoric of Economics* in which she argues that "The Mathematization of Economics" was a good thing, but that economic modernism went too far in using equilibrium model building and econometrics. McCloskey's critique targets three Nobel Prize–winning economists: Paul Samuelson, Lawrence Klien, and Jan Tinbergen. McCloskey provides a number of interesting criticisms, many of which have been questioned. Offer a critique of McCloskey's argument, providing specific examples from the text and from other sources to support your claim.

(continued)

Response	Example
Definition Essay exams may ask you to define terms and concepts that are of particular import to a discipline. Although definitions may range from short dictionary-like definitions to more detailed explanatory definitions often found in professional or disciplinary dictionaries, essay exam definition questions ask that you display a detailed understanding of the thing being defined. Definition essays, then, need to provide a clear definition and relevant supporting examples. Essay exam definitions prompts encourage extended definitions.	*Ethics* can be a problematic concept, particularly when used in popular media and conversation. However, within philosophy, there are a number of specific definitions that establish ethics as "moral philosophy" and guide specific intellectual inquiries. Within the framework of philosophy, define *ethics*.
Description Essay exams may ask you to describe a process, an event, a phenomenon, or an idea. To describe is to depict, to portray details. The purpose of describing is to encourage an audience to "see" the thing described, so we might think of description as providing a visual account. No matter what an exam asks you to describe, whether it is mundane or unusual, the objective is to show that thing to your audience in interesting, vivid ways. Providing details is an essential part of writing descriptions.	Describe the offshore construction process for the Barrow Offshore Wind Farm.
Evaluation Essay exams may ask you to evaluate a text, an idea, a theory, an event, or a phenomenon. Evaluation is a kind of judgment. Evaluation assesses value and determines the worth, merit, and significance of something. Like analysis, evaluation is dependent on careful scrutiny and examination. Evaluation depends on detailed analysis, establishing specific criteria for how to conduct that analysis, and the ability to articulate why and how you made the analysis. Remember, when writing an evaluation in response to an essay exam, to identify and explain the criteria you used to conduct your evaluation.	Companies often redesign their web pages for a number of reasons: branding initiatives, identity makeovers, changes in services, or interface upgrades. Companies assume that their redesigns will improve their sites, but sometimes redesigns fail. Identify a recognizable company that has redesigned its web page and evaluate the redesign in light of the design standards addressed thus far.
Explanation Essay exams that ask you to explain something may not explicitly ask you to explain. Instead, look for terms like "why" or "how" as indicating a need for explanation. Explanatory writing is similar to informative writing. Explanatory essay exam prompts ask you to demonstrate your knowledge about a subject. These kinds of exam prompts are designed to get you to provide details, to show that you have a sophisticated understanding of the subject. Explanatory writing should provide examples, clarifications, and reasons.	Explain how Jean-Bertrand Aristide rose to power in Haiti and was elected to his first term as Haiti's president.
Response some prompts provide a quote, statement, or summary and ask you to respond. These are particularly common with placement exams and other forms of assessment exams.	Mahatma Gandhi once said that "poverty is the worst form of violence." Given what we have discussed regarding poverty and economic policies, how do you respond to Gandhi's words?
Summary Essay exams may ask you to summarize a text, a process, an idea, or an event. Summary prompts ask you to provide a general overview of the main ideas of the thing to be summarized. Summary prompts are designed to let you show that you understand the overall concept or text but do not require that you address the more nuanced details.	Summarize the conditions of the 1783 Treaty of Paris.

Plan Your Response

Rarely do students have the opportunity to write multiple drafts in response to an essay exam prompt. It is more likely that your first draft will also be your final draft. For this reason, planning your response becomes a crucial part of writing your response. Writers who just start writing without a plan often find themselves either running out of time or writing an essay that wanders with little sense of purpose. SCUBA divers often use the motto "plan your dive; dive your plan," to describe the importance of knowing what it is they will do when underwater. Divers who diverge from the plan risk a number of possible dangers

like getting lost or separated from the dive group, missing the objective of the dive, or even running out of air. Of course, divers may need to adjust their plan once in the water if the conditions aren't exactly what they anticipated, but sticking to the plan is always the best bet. The same holds true for responding to essay exams. Formulate a plan for responding to the writing prompt and stick to it. If you start to wander away from the plan, you might lose your train of thought, fail to fulfill the purpose of the response, or even run out of time and not complete your answer.

Planning a response requires that you account for what you want to say in your essay and how you will budget your time to answer the question. Budget your time in light of how much time is allotted and how many tasks the exam asks you to complete. Be sure to include time for evaluating and possibly making minimal changes to it before you turn it in. Most important, though, plan what you want to be sure to include in your response. Once you have read and analyzed the question, make a list of the things you know you should include. Note key concepts, events, texts, and other relevant information you want to be certain to include. Then identify the order in which you want to present the information. Don't just write about things as they come to mind; create an outline and be alert to organizational strategies.

Identify Your Claim

Once you have read the exam, analyzed the situation and the question, and planned your response, you should formulate a claim to make in your answer. Think of the claim as the thesis statement of your answer. Your answer should support this claim. One strategy for developing a claim in response to an essay exam prompt is to restructure the question as a statement. Doing so ensures that your answer targets the question directly and that you provide an explicit claim in relation to the prompt.

> **EXAMPLE PROMPT:** The terms *speed* and *velocity* are often used interchangeably; however, there are some distinct differences between the two. In what ways are *speed* and *velocity* different?

> **EXAMPLE CLAIM:** Speed and velocity differ from one another in that speed is a scalar quantity and velocity is a vector quantity.

Begin Writing

The purpose of an essay exam is to provide you with an opportunity to display your knowledge and understanding. Essay exams generally have a specific audience: your instructor. Therefore, responses to prompts don't require that you draw an audience into the essay as you might in other forms of writing. Instead, you should write your claim statement as the first sentence of the essay and begin to support it with your position and evidence. Use the plan you crafted to do so. Keep in mind, though, that the essay exam still requires adherence to standards of academic essay writing and should, therefore, be written in an organized manner. One way to accomplish this is to begin with your claim statement and then complete the opening paragraph by using the plan you developed to show your reader what you plan to cover. In this way your claim statement and your plan serve as the introduction to your response.

Claim + Plan = Introduction

Develop the Essay

Once you have developed the introduction based on the claim statement and plan, develop the essay just as the introduction identifies it will unfold. Provide evidence for each of the points of the plan. Stick to the plan, adjusting only when absolutely necessary. Make sure your response provides answers to all parts of the prompt; be thorough. Don't pad the essay with extraneous or irrelevant information. Use language and terms relevant to the discipline. Avoid repetition, particularly in word choice.

Synthesize

Even though you are likely to craft your plan as a list of things to cover, and you should work your way through that plan, don't simply patch your support together one piece at a time. Synthesize your evidence into the writing so support for your claim is the predominant part of the essay. Show your familiarity with the materials, but also show how those materials support your answer to the prompt by synthesizing them into your writing.

Evaluate the Essay

If you've planned well and have some remaining time once you've finished writing your response, you should read and evaluate your essay before submitting it. As you read over it:

- Revise, proofread, and edit the essay. Correct any mistakes you notice.
- Ask: Did I answer the whole question? Did I stay focused?
- Ask: Are my ideas clearly conveyed?
- Ask: Have I used valid examples and references?
- Ask: Have I provided a sufficient number of examples or evidence?
- Ask: Have I met the criteria the instructor explained and that I'll be evaluated on?

Be sure to correct any errors or oversights you might encounter.

Summary

- Essay exams in college are not off-the-cuff responses; they require preparation and planning.
- Essay exams are generally given for a confined amount of information or content coverage.
- You can develop specific strategies for preparing for essay exams.
- Once you have a clear idea about the exam's form and coverage, you can prepare more efficiently.
- Once you know what material the exam will cover, you should begin to review the material.
- Writing summaries will help you recall overall concepts and general overviews of information.
- One of the best ways to remember information is to talk with others about the material.
- Nothing can help you prepare more for an essay exam than practicing writing essay exam responses.
- The key to taking an essay exam is being prepared for the exam.
- Being confident that you are prepared for the exam can help reduce anxiety.
- Make sure you know exactly what you have to do to complete the entire exam.
- Each essay exam you take is its own unique rhetorical situation.
- There is only a limited number of things an essay exam prompt can ask you to do in the amount of time allotted.
- Formulate a plan for responding to the writing prompt, and stick to it.
- Formulate a claim to make in your answer.
- Your claim statement and your plan serve as the introduction to your response.
- Provide evidence for each of the points of the plan.
- Synthesize your evidence into the writing so support for your claim is the predominant part of the essay.
- Read and evaluate your essay before submitting it.

Chapter Review

1. Identify five things you can do to prepare for an essay exam.

2. Identify six things you should do when taking an essay exam.

Reflection

Look back at the journal entry or blog post you wrote in response to the prompt at the beginning of this chapter. Now look back at the journal entry or blog post you wrote in response to the prompt at the beginning of this chapter. Write a new entry in which you discuss what you see as the purpose of writing essays in response to college-level exams and strategies for doing so effectively.

Readings

22 | Technology

Before you read this chapter

What is technology? What are some different ways you might define technology? How do you view technology's effects in your life? In culture and society? Do you regard technology as generally beneficial or generally detrimental? In your journal or blog, write about what you think technology is and how it affects your life.

WIKILEAKS CABLES - DAY 1

More than 250,000 documents, given to media groups by WikiLeaks, provide candid and at times critical views of foreign leaders as well as sensitive information on terrorism and nuclear proliferation filed by U.S. diplomats

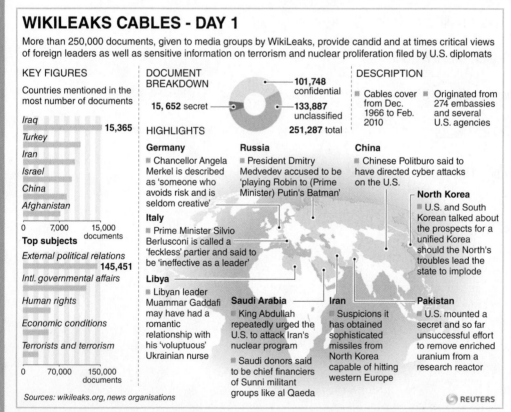

KEY FIGURES

Countries mentioned in the most number of documents

Iraq — 15,365
Turkey
Iran
Israel
China
Afghanistan

0   7,000   15,000 documents

Top subjects

External political relations — 145,451
Intl. governmental affairs
Human rights
Economic conditions
Terrorists and terrorism

0   70,000   150,000 documents

Sources: wikileaks.org, news organisations

DOCUMENT BREAKDOWN

15, 652 secret
101,748 confidential
133,887 unclassified
251,287 total

HIGHLIGHTS

Germany
■ Chancellor Angela Merkel is described as 'someone who avoids risk and is seldom creative'

Italy
■ Prime Minister Silvio Berlusconi is called a 'feckless' partier and said to be 'ineffective as a leader'

Libya
■ Libyan leader Muammar Gaddafi may have had a romantic relationship with his 'voluptuous' Ukrainian nurse

Russia
■ President Dmitry Medvedev accused to be 'playing Robin to (Prime Minister) Putin's Batman'

Saudi Arabia
■ King Abdullah repeatedly urged the U.S. to attack Iran's nuclear program
■ Saudi donors said to be chief financiers of Sunni militant groups like al Qaeda

Iran
■ Suspicions it has obtained sophisticated missiles from North Korea capable of hitting western Europe

DESCRIPTION

■ Cables cover from Dec. 1966 to Feb. 2010

■ Originated from 274 embassies and several U.S. agencies

China
■ Chinese Politburo said to have directed cyber attacks on the U.S.

North Korea
■ U.S. and South Korean talked about the prospects for a unified Korea should the North's troubles lead the state to implode

Pakistan
■ U.S. mounted a secret and so far unsuccessful effort to remove enriched uranium from a research reactor

REUTERS

Technology can be a tricky concept, but we usually accept its meaning without much thought. Technology can be a general, encompassing concept, or it can be specific as in computer technology, medical technology, or information technology. We tend to think of technology as progressive, as advancing how we think about and do things. We tend to want the latest technologies over older technologies. Technology, in this way, might suggest a sense of improvement: as the technologies become more complex and sophisticated, the tasks we accomplish through those technologies become easier to achieve or we're able to accomplish more complex tasks.

Technology evolves. We even categorize technology as either high-tech or low-tech. High-tech represents progress, and low-tech is the obsolete, or at least that which is destined to be obsolete. Clinging to the low-tech is often thought of as being nostalgic, quaint, old school, or even oblivious. Even technologies that were at one time marvels of advancement are now obsolete. Consider NASA's space shuttles, once described as the most technologically complex and advanced piece of equipment humans ever developed. Yet, In February 2011, NASA launched the final space shuttle mission, retiring the remaining five shuttles after the last mission to develop new, more effective space vehicles.[1] Our culture values high-tech and devalues low-tech. And we are complicit in our technological consumerism and cravings for newer, faster, sleeker, more advanced technologies. What we want from technology today will be obsolete soon as we demand even newer, faster, sleeker, more advanced technologies tomorrow.

The word *technology* is derived from the Greek word *techné*, which is usually understood as craftsmanship, art, or craft. Techné is understood to be very different from yet tied to *episteme*, which means "to know." That is, techné suggests how things are done and episteme suggests how things are known. In this way, then, technology is understood as getting stuff done. But the word *technology* has meant different things at different times in history. For the Greeks, techné was an art, but in the United States in the late nineteenth and early twentieth centuries, *technology* was understood to refer to the industrial arts, how we make things from wood or metal using power or machine tools. Now we tend to use the general term *technology* to mean primarily computer or digital technologies. A tech geek, for instance, is someone who has great skills and knowledge about all things digital and computer based.

Our definitions of *technologies* and those technologies themselves affect how we interact with the world. Technologies are responsible for advances, and they are responsible for setbacks. Technologies have contributed to industrial growth, to class development and distinction, to economic failure and success, to medical advancement and health risks, and to environmental protection and destruction. Communication technologies like the printing press, the telephone, and the Internet have been praised by many as aiding open, more democratic communications the world over.

---

[1]NASA constructed seven space shuttles; two were lost in accidents: *Challenger* (1/28/86) and *Columbia* (2/1/03).

Some people even identify writing as a specific kind of technology that changed the world. Technologies have been used for peaceful ends and technologies have fueled combative, destructive ends as well. Some technologies have even served both.

The readings in this chapter are not technological. That is, they are not technical or about technical subjects. Rather they are about how we interact with various technologies. They are about the idea of technology and its interaction with culture, society, and daily life. They are gathered here not to teach you about specific technologies, but to help you think about how you interact with all kinds of technologies. The readings are about concepts of technologies. Some of the readings in this chapter are about old technologies and some are about new technologies. Some are about change and some are about resistance to change. Some cheer on technological developments and some question them. But all of them ask you to consider the role of technology in your life.

The Telephone

Anwar F. Accawi

Anwar F. Accawi was born in Magdaluna, near Sidon, a coastal city in southern Lebanon. As a high-school student, Accawi attended an American missionary school in Sidon and won a scholarship to attend Warren Wilson College in Asheville, North Carolina. After college, he returned to Lebanon, where he taught English as a second language at the American University in Beirut. While teaching there, he married a woman from Tennessee. In 1975, when civil war broke out in Lebanon, he and his wife and two children fled to her hometown of LaFollette, Tennessee, and Accawi became a full-time instructor in the English Language Institute at The University of Tennessee at Knoxville.

In writing and talking about growing up in Lebanon, Accawi has explained that his village was a "pre-industrial self-sufficient village with about a hundred people. There were none of the modern amenities that we take for granted today. In fact, there wasn't even a road in or out of the village. We walked everywhere we had to go or we rode our little donkeys and mules." During World War II, his village was introduced to the radio, the telephone, and the car, and his village was thrust into the twentieth century, changing forever the order of what village life had been for hundreds of years prior. The essay found here, "The Telephone," recounts Accawi's memory of what happened to his village when the first telephone was installed. As you read the essay, think specifically about how the technology of the telephone affected the culture of the village. Think, too, about how you think about a telephone and how telephone technologies have changed since Accawi's village got its telephone. How do you respond to the situation of Accawi's telephone and the contemporary situation in which telephones are ubiquitous? How does technology in this essay participate in the situation of Accawi's writing?

When I was growing up in Magdaluna, a small Lebanese village in the terraced, rocky mountains east of Sidon, time didn't mean much to anybody, except maybe to those who were dying, or those waiting to appear in court because they had tampered with the boundary markers on their land. In those days, there was no real need for a calendar or a watch to keep track of the hours, days, months, and years. We knew what to do and when to do it, just as the Iraqi geese knew when to fly north, driven by the hot wind that blew in from the desert, and the ewes knew when to give birth to wet lambs that stood on long, shaky legs in the chilly

March wind and baaed hesitantly, because they were small and cold and did not know where they were or what to do now that they were here. The only timepiece we had need of then was the sun. It rose and set, and the seasons rolled by, and we sowed seed and harvested and ate and played and married our cousins and had babies who got whooping cough and chickenpox—and those children who survived grew up and married *their* cousins and had babies who got whooping cough and chickenpox. We lived and loved and toiled and died without ever needing to know what year it was, or even the time of day.

It wasn't that we had no system for keeping track of time and of the important events in our lives. But ours was a natural—or, rather, a divine—calendar, because it was framed by acts of God. Allah himself set down the milestones with earthquakes and droughts and floods and locusts and pestilences. Simple as our calendar was, it worked just fine for us.

Take, for example, the birth date of Teta Im Khalil, the oldest woman in Magdaluna and all the surrounding villages. When I first met her, we had just returned home from Syria at the end of the Big War and were living with Grandma Mariam. Im Khalil came by to welcome my father home and to take a long, myopic look at his foreign-born wife, my mother, Im Khalil was so old that the skin of her cheeks looked like my father's grimy tobacco pouch, and when I kissed her (because Grandma insisted that I show her old friend affection), it was like kissing a soft suede glove that had been soaked with sweat and then left in a dark closet for a season. Im Khalil's face got me to wondering how old one had to be to look and taste the way she did. So, as soon as she had hobbled off on her cane, I asked Grandma, "How old is Teta Im Khalil?"

Grandma had to think for a moment; then she said, "I've been told that Teta was born shortly after the big snow that caused the roof on the mayor's house to cave in."

"And when was that?" I asked.

"Oh, about the time we had the big earthquake that cracked the wall in the east room."

Well, that was enough for me. You couldn't be more accurate than that, now, could you? Satisfied with her answer, I went back to playing with a ball made from an old sock stuffed with other, much older socks.

And that's the way it was in our little village for as far back as anybody could remember: people were born so many years before or after an earthquake or a flood; they got married or died so many years before or after a long drought or a big snow or some other disaster. One of the most unusual of these dates was when Antoinette the seamstress and Saeed the barber (and tooth puller) got married. That was the year of the whirlwind during which fish and oranges fell from the sky. Incredible as it may sound, the story of the fish and oranges was true, because men—respectable men, like Abu George the blacksmith and Abu Asaad the mule skinner, men who would not lie even to save their own souls—told and retold that story until it was incorporated into Magdaluna's calendar, just like the year of the black moon and the year of the locusts before it. My father, too, confirmed the story for me. He told me that he had been a small boy himself when it had rained fish and oranges from heaven. He'd gotten up one morning after a stormy night and walked out into the yard to find fish as long as his forearm still flopping here and there among the wet navel oranges.

The year of the fish-bearing twister, however, was not the last remarkable year. Many others followed in which strange and wonderful things happened: milestones added by the hand of Allah to Magdaluna's calendar. There was, for instance, the year of the drought, when the heavens were shut for months and the spring from which the entire village got its drinking water slowed to a trickle. The spring was about a mile from the village, in a ravine that opened at one end into a small, flat clearing covered with fine gray dust and hard, marble-sized goat droppings, because every afternoon the goatherds brought their flocks there to water them. In the year of the drought, that little clearing was always packed full of noisy kids with big brown eyes and sticky hands, and their mothers—sinewy, overworked young women with protruding collarbones and cracked, callused brown heels. The children ran around playing tag or hide-and-seek while the women talked, shooed flies, and awaited their turns to fill up their jars with drinking water to bring home to their napping men and wet babies. There were days when we had to wait from sunup until late afternoon just to fill a small clay jar with precious, cool water.

Sometimes, amid the long wait and the heat and the flies and the smell of goat dung, tempers flared, and the younger women, anxious about their babies, argued over whose turn it was to fill up her jar. And sometimes the arguments escalated into full-blown, knockdown-dragout fights; the women would grab each other by the hair and curse and scream and spit and call each other names that made my ears tingle. We little brown boys who went with our mothers to fetch water loved these fights, because we got to see the women's legs and their colored panties as they grappled and rolled around in the dust. Once in a while, we got lucky and saw much more, because some of the women wore nothing at all under their long dresses. God, how I used to look forward to those fights. I remember the rush, the excitement, the sun dancing on the dust clouds as a dress ripped and a young white breast was revealed, then quickly hidden. In my calendar, that year of drought will always be one of the best years of my childhood, because it was then, in a dusty clearing by a trickling mountain spring, I got my first glimpses of the wonders, the mysteries, and the promises hidden beneath the folds of a woman's dress. Fish and oranges from heaven . . . you can get over that.

But, in another way, the year of the drought was also one of the worst of my life, because that was the year that Abu Raja, the retired cook who used to entertain us kids by cracking walnuts on his forehead, decided it was time Magdaluna got its own telephone. Every civilized village needed a telephone, he said, and Magdaluna was not going to get anywhere until it had one. A telephone would link us with the outside world. At the time, I was too young to understand the debate, but a few men—like Shukri, the retired Turkish-army drill sergeant, and Abu Hanna the vineyard keeper—did all they could to talk Abu Raja out of having a telephone brought to the village. But they were outshouted and ignored and finally shunned by the other villagers for resisting progress and trying to keep a good thing from coming to Magdaluna.

One warm day in early fall, many of the villagers were out in their fields repairing walls or gathering wood for the winter when the shout went out that the telephone-company truck had arrived at Abu Raja's *dikkan*, or country store. There were no roads in those days, only footpaths and dry streambeds, so it took the telephone-company truck almost a day to work its way up the rocky terrain from Sidon—about the same time it took to walk. When the truck came into view, Abu George, who had a huge voice and, before the telephone, was Magdaluna's only long-distance communication system, bellowed the news from his front porch. Everybody dropped what they were doing and ran to Abu Raja's house to see what was happening. Some of the more dignified villagers, however, like Abu Habeeb and Abu Nazim, who had been to big cities like Beirut and Damascus and had seen things like telephones and telegraphs, did not run the way the rest did; they walked with their canes hanging from the crooks of their arms, as if on a Sunday afternoon stroll.

It did not take long for the whole village to assemble at Abu Raja's *dikkan*. Some of the rich villagers, like the widow Farha and the gendarme Abu Nadeem, walked right into the store and stood at the elbows of the two important-looking men from the telephone company, who proceeded with utmost gravity, like priests at Communion, to wire up the telephone. The poorer villagers stood outside and listened carefully to the details relayed to them by the not-so-poor people who stood in the doorway and could see inside.

"The bald man is cutting the blue wire," someone said.

"He is sticking the wire into the hole in the bottom of the black box," someone else added.

"The telephone man with the mustache is connecting two pieces of wire. Now he is twisting the ends together," a third voice chimed in.

Because I was small and unaware that I should have stood outside with the other poor folk to give the rich people inside more room (they seemed to need more of it than poor people did), I wriggled my way through the dense forest of legs to get a firsthand look at the action. I felt like the barefoot Moses, sandals in hand, staring at the burning bush on Mount Sinai. Breathless, I watched as the men in blue, their shirt pockets adorned with fancy lettering in a foreign language, put together a black machine that supposedly would make it possible to talk with uncles, aunts, and cousins who lived more than two days' ride away.

It was shortly after sunset when the man with the mustache announced that the telephone was ready to use. He explained that all Abu Raja had to do was lift the receiver, turn the crank on the black box a few times, and wait for an operator to take his call. Abu Raja, who had once lived and worked in Sidon, was impatient with the telephone man for assuming that he was ignorant. He grabbed the receiver and turned the crank forcefully, as if trying to start a Model T Ford. Everybody was impressed that he knew what to do. He even called the operator by her first name: "Centralist." Within moments, Abu Raja was talking with his brother, a concierge in Beirut. He didn't even have to raise his voice or shout to be heard.

If I hadn't seen it with my own two eyes and heard it with my own two ears, I would not have believed it—and my friend Kameel didn't. He was away that day watching his father's goats, and when he came back to the village that evening, his cousin Habeeb and I told him about the telephone and how Abu Raja had used it to speak with his brother in Beirut. After he heard our report, Kameel made the sign of the cross, kissed his thumbnail, and warned us that lying was a bad sin and would surely land us in purgatory. Kameel believed in Jesus and Mary, and wanted to be a priest when he grew up. He always crossed himself when Habeeb, who was irreverent, and I, who was Presbyterian, were around, even when we were not bearing bad news.

And the telephone, as it turned out, was bad news. With its coming, the face of the village began to change. One of the first effects was the shifting of the village's center. Before the telephone's arrival, the men of the village used to gather regularly at the house of Im Kaleem, a short, middle-aged widow with jet-black hair and a raspy voice that could be heard all over the village, even when she was only whispering. She was a devout Catholic and also the village *shlikki*—whore. The men met at her house to argue about politics and drink coffee and play cards or backgammon. Im Kaleem was not a true prostitute, however, because she did not charge for her services—not even for the coffee and tea (and, occasionally, the strong liquor called arrack) that she served the men. She did not need the money; her son, who was overseas in Africa, sent her money regularly. (I knew this because my father used to read her son's letters to her and take down her replies, as Im Kaleem could not read and write.) Im Kaleem was no slut either—unlike some women in the village—because she loved all the men she entertained, and they loved her, every one of them. In a way, she was married to all the men in the village. Everybody knew it—the wives knew it; the itinerant Catholic priest knew it; the Presbyterian minister knew it—but nobody objected. Actually, I suspect the women (my mother included) did not mind their husbands' visits to Im Kaleem. Oh, they wrung their hands and complained to one another about their men's unfaithfulness, but secretly they were relieved, because Im Kaleem took some of the pressure off them and kept the men out of their hair while they attended to their endless chores. Im Kaleem was also a kind of confessor and troubleshooter, talking sense to those men who were having family problems, especially the younger ones.

Before the telephone came to Magdaluna, Im Kaleem's house was bustling at just about any time of day, especially at night, when its windows were brightly lit with three large oil lamps, and the loud voices of the men talking, laughing, and arguing could be heard in the street below—a reassuring, homey sound. Her house was an island of comfort, an oasis for the weary village men, exhausted from having so little to do.

But it wasn't long before many of those men—the younger ones especially—started spending more of their days and evenings at Abu Raja's *dikkan*. There, they would eat and drink and talk and play checkers and backgammon, and then lean their chairs back against the wall—the signal that they were ready to toss back and forth, like a ball, the latest rumors going around the village. And they were always looking up from their games and drinks and talk to glance at the phone in the corner, as if expecting it to ring any minute and bring news that would change their lives and deliver them from their aimless existence. In the meantime, they smoked cheap, hand-rolled cigarettes, dug dirt out from under their fingernails with big pocketknives, and drank lukewarm sodas that they called Kacula, Seffen-Ub, and Bebsi. Sometimes, especially when it was hot, the days dragged on so slowly that the men turned on Abu Saeed, a confirmed bachelor who practically lived in Abu Raja's *dikkan*, and teased him for going around barefoot and unshaven since the Virgin had appeared to him behind the olive press.

The telephone was also bad news for me personally. It took away my lucrative business—a source of much-needed income. Before the telephone came to Magdaluna, I used to hang around Im Kaleem's courtyard and play marbles with the other kids, waiting for some man to call down from a window and ask me to run to the store for cigarettes or arrack, or to deliver a message to his wife, such as what he wanted for supper. There was always something in it for me: a ten- or even a twenty-five-piaster piece. On a good day, I ran nine or ten of those errands, which assured a steady supply of marbles that I usually lost to Sami or his cousin Hani, the basket weaver's boy. But as the days went by, fewer and fewer men came to Im Kaleem's, and more and more congregated at Abu Raja's to wait by the telephone. In the evenings, no light fell from her window onto the street below, and the laughter and noise of the men trailed off and finally stopped. Only Shukri, the retired Turkish-army drill sergeant, remained faithful to Im Kaleem after all the other men had deserted her; he was still seen going into or leaving her house from time to time. Early that winter, Im Kaleem's hair suddenly turned gray, and she got sick and old. Her legs started giving her trouble, making it hard for her to walk. By spring she hardly left her house anymore.

At Abu Raja's *dikkan*, the calls did eventually come, as expected, and men and women started leaving the village the way a hailstorm begins: first one, then two, then bunches. The army took them. Jobs in the cities lured them. And ships and airplanes carried them to such faraway places as Australia and Brazil and New Zealand. My friend Kameel, his cousin Habeeb, and their cousins and my cousins all went away to become ditch diggers and mechanics and butcher-shop boys and deli owners who wore dirty aprons sixteen hours a day, all looking for a better life than the one they had left behind. Within a year, only the sick, the old, and the maimed were left in the village. Magdaluna became a skeleton of its former self, desolate and forsaken, like the tombs, a place to get away from.

Finally, the telephone took my family away, too. My father got a call from an old army buddy who told him that an oil company in southern Lebanon was hiring interpreters and instructors. My father applied for a job and got it, and we moved to Sidon, where I went to a Presbyterian missionary school and graduated in 1962. Three years later, having won a scholarship, I left Lebanon for the United States. Like the others who left Magdaluna before me, I am still looking for that better life.

Analyzing the Situation

1. One of the connections Accawi makes in "The Telephone" is a sense of the relationship between "civilization" and technology. First, what does it mean for a place—like Magdaluna—to be "civilized"? Second, how does understanding what "civilized" means and the role technology plays in civilization affect how you understand the situation in which Accawi writes and the situation about which he writes?

2. Are there players in the situation in which Accawi writes? Can you identify them? Do those players suggest, too, an ecological relationship between Magdaluna's situation with the telephone and other similar, small communities worldwide? How might acknowledging such an ecology affect how we read and understand "The Telephone"?

3. What role do institution and power play in "The Telephone"? Think beyond Accawi's mention of schools and religion, and consider how institution and power are manifest in the very idea of technology, ranging from the "official" telephone installers to the distant institutions that influence Magdaluna's community once the telephone is installed. Is technology itself, both the idea of technology and the technological gadgets—in this essay in the form of the telephone—a form of institution and power?

Analyzing the Rhetoric

1. Could "The Telephone" have been written in the third person instead of the first person, as it is? What does Accawi gain rhetorically in writing the essay in the first person?

2. What role does description play in "The Telephone"? What role does argumentation play? What is the relationship between description and argumentation in "The Telephone"?

3. What role do names play in this essay? That is, what does Accawi gain by providing us with as many names as he does?

4. What is the effect of the final sentence of "The Telephone"? What does this sentence contribute to the essay's overall address of technology?

Discussing

1. Why do you suppose that Anwar Accawi begins this essay by addressing time? How does time connect to his discussion of the telephone and technology? What is the distinction Accawi makes between "natural time" and technological time? What role does time play at the end of the essay? Discuss the relationship between time, technology, and culture as Accawi describes it.

2. When Accawi describes the process of installing the telephone in Abu Raja's house, he points out that the wealthier villagers could watch the installation from inside the home and the remaining observers lined up by a decreasing degree of wealth. How does this description contribute to a sense of the relationship between wealth and technological access? Discuss the implications of what Accawi seems to suggest when writing about the scene of installation.

3. What is the message Anwar Accawi conveys in "The Telephone" about technology? Discuss what the author tells us about the telephone itself and what we might understand the telephone to represent.

Writing

1. Accawi writes, "And the telephone, as it turned out, was bad news." How is technology bad news, not in Accawi's situation per se, but generally? That is, is Accawi's situation unique, or are there more general "bad news" scenarios related to technology? Write an essay that addresses situations in which technological advancements might contribute to cultural bad news.

2. Has your life been changed by technology? Have you observed how your community has been changed by a specific kind of technology? Write a personal account of how you or you and your community have been affected by the introduction of a specific kind of technology or a specific technological device.

3. Conduct some research using online resources to learn more about the history of the telephone as a technology. Then, after you have learned about the telephone generally, focus your research to learn about how and when telephone service first came to your community. Dig a bit deeper and trace the history of how telephone technologies and use evolved since telephones were introduced in your community. Consider examining coverage areas, access, and cultural uses of the telephone. Then, dig even deeper, and extend your research to examine what else was happening in your community at various stages of the telephone history you have discovered. Are there correlations between the arrival of and development of telephone service in your community? Are they evident, or do you have to extrapolate the connection between the two histories? Write an informative essay that describes the history of telephones in your community relative to both the general history of telephones and the history of your community.

4. As a class, develop a wiki that provides information about the development of telephone technology, its spread worldwide, and its effect on various cultures, regions, and nations.

Is Google Making Us Stupid? What the Internet Is Doing to Our Brains

Nicholas Carr

Nicholas Carr writes about technology and its effects on society, economics, and business. He is the author of *Does IT Matter?* and *The Big Switch: Rewiring the World from Edison to Google*, which made the 2008 *Wall Street Journal* bestseller list. The *Christian Science Monitor* explains that *The Big Switch* is "widely considered to be the most influential book so far on the cloud computing movement." His latest book, *The Shallows: What the Internet is Doing to Our Brains* extends the argument he makes in the essay reprinted here.

"Is Google Making Us Stupid?" was first published as the cover story for *Atlantic Monthly*'s Idea Issue in the summer of 2008. The essay attracted a good deal of attention, sparking many other writers to respond to Carr's claims. In "Is Google Making Us Stupid?" Carr contends that Internet technologies are changing not just the ways we read but the ways we think as well. He worries that human cognitive processes are being altered by the technologies we engage and suggests that such changes are negative. In order to make his claim, Carr weaves together research and personal narrative to form an intriguing argument. As you read "Is Google Making Us Stupid?" pay particular attention to how Carr merges the personal with research and how that combination works in support of his purpose. Consider, too, how Carr casts Internet technologies in relation to print technologies.

"Dave, stop. Stop, will you? Stop, Dave. Will you stop, Dave?" So the supercomputer HAL pleads with the implacable astronaut Dave Bowman in a famous and weirdly poignant scene toward the end of Stanley Kubrick's *2001: A Space Odyssey*. Bowman, having nearly been sent to a deep-space death by the malfunctioning machine, is calmly, coldly disconnecting the memory circuits that control its artificial "brain." "Dave, my mind is going," HAL says, forlornly. "I can feel it. I can feel it."

I can feel it, too. Over the past few years I've had an uncomfortable sense that someone, or something, has been tinkering with my brain, remapping the neural circuitry, reprogramming the memory. My mind isn't going—so far as I can tell—but it's changing. I'm not thinking the way I used to think. I can feel it most strongly when I'm reading. Immersing myself in a book or a lengthy article used to be easy. My mind would get caught up in the narrative or the turns of the argument, and I'd spend hours strolling through long stretches of prose. That's rarely the case anymore. Now my concentration often starts to drift after two or three pages. I get fidgety, lose the thread, begin looking for something else to do. I feel as if I'm always dragging my wayward brain back to the text. The deep reading that used to come naturally has become a struggle.

I think I know what's going on. For more than a decade now, I've been spending a lot of time online, searching and surfing and sometimes adding to the great databases of the Internet. The Web has been a godsend to me as a writer. Research that once required days in the stacks or periodical rooms of libraries can now be done in minutes. A few Google searches, some quick clicks on hyperlinks, and I've got the telltale fact or pithy quote I was after. Even when I'm not working, I'm as likely as not to be foraging in the Web's info-thickets, reading and writing e-mails, scanning headlines and blog posts, watching videos and listening to podcasts, or just tripping from link to link to link. (Unlike footnotes, to which they're sometimes likened, hyperlinks don't merely point to related works; they propel you toward them.)

For me, as for others, the Net is becoming a universal medium, the conduit for most of the information that flows through my eyes and ears and into my mind. The advantages of having immediate access to such an incredibly rich store of information are many, and they've been widely described and duly applauded. "The perfect recall of silicon memory," *Wired*'s Clive Thompson has written, "can be an enormous boon to thinking." But that boon comes at a price. As the media theorist Marshall McLuhan pointed out in the 1960s, media are not just passive channels of information. They supply the stuff of thought, but they also shape the process of thought. And what the Net seems to be doing is chipping away my capacity for concentration and contemplation. My mind now expects to take in information the way the Net distributes it: in a swiftly moving stream of particles. Once I was a scuba diver in the sea of words. Now I zip along the surface like a guy on a Jet Ski.

I'm not the only one. When I mention my troubles with reading to friends and acquaintances—literary types, most of them—many say they're having similar experiences. The more they use the Web, the more they have to fight to stay focused on long pieces of writing. Some of the bloggers I follow have also begun mentioning the phenomenon. Scott Karp, who writes a blog about online media, recently confessed that he has stopped reading books altogether. "I was a lit major in college, and used to be [a] voracious book reader," he wrote. "What happened?" He speculates on the answer: "What if I do all my reading on the web not so much because the way I read has changed, i.e. I'm just seeking convenience, but because the way I THINK has changed?"

Bruce Friedman, who blogs regularly about the use of computers in medicine, also has described how the Internet has altered his mental habits. "I now have almost totally lost the ability to read and absorb a longish article on the web or in print," he wrote earlier this year. A pathologist who has long been on the faculty of the University of Michigan Medical School, Friedman elaborated on his comment in a telephone conversation with me. His thinking, he said, has taken on a "staccato" quality, reflecting the way he quickly scans short passages of text from many sources online. "I can't read *War and Peace* anymore," he admitted. "I've lost the ability to do that. Even a blog post of more than three or four paragraphs is too much to absorb. I skim it."

Anecdotes alone don't prove much. And we still await the long-term neurological and psychological experiments that will provide a definitive picture of how Internet use affects cognition. But a recently published study of online research habits, conducted by scholars from University College London, suggests that we may well be in the midst of a sea change in the way we read and think. As part of the five-year research program, the scholars examined computer logs documenting the behavior of visitors to two popular research sites, one operated by the British Library and one by a U.K. educational consortium, that provide access to journal articles, e-books, and other sources of written information. They found that people using the sites exhibited "a form of skimming activity," hopping from one source to another and rarely returning to any source they'd already visited. They typically read no more than one or two pages of an article or book before they would "bounce" out to another site. Sometimes they'd save a long article, but there's no evidence that they ever went back and actually read it. The authors of the study report:

> It is clear that users are not reading online in the traditional sense; indeed there are signs that new forms of "reading" are emerging as users "power browse" horizontally through titles, contents pages and abstracts going for quick wins. It almost seems that they go online to avoid reading in the traditional sense.

Thanks to the ubiquity of text on the Internet, not to mention the popularity of text-messaging on cell phones, we may well be reading more today than we did in the 1970s or 1980s, when television was our medium of choice. But it's a different kind of reading, and behind it lies a different kind of thinking—perhaps even a new sense of the self. "We are not only *what* we read," says Maryanne Wolf, a developmental psychologist at Tufts University and the author of *Proust and the Squid: The Story and Science of the Reading Brain*. "We are *how* we read." Wolf worries that the style of reading promoted by the Net, a style that puts "efficiency" and "immediacy" above all else, may be weakening our capacity for the kind of deep reading that emerged when an earlier technology, the printing press, made long and complex works of prose commonplace. When we read online, she says, we tend to become "mere decoders of information." Our ability to interpret text, to make the rich mental connections that form when we read deeply and without distraction, remains largely disengaged.

Reading, explains Wolf, is not an instinctive skill for human beings. It's not etched into our genes the way speech is. We have to teach our minds how to translate the symbolic characters we see into the language we understand. And the media or other technologies we use in learning and practicing the craft of reading play an important part in shaping the neural circuits inside our brains. Experiments demonstrate that readers of ideograms, such as the Chinese, develop a mental circuitry for reading that is very different from the circuitry found in those of us whose written language employs an alphabet. The variations extend across many regions of the brain, including those that govern such essential cognitive functions as memory and the interpretation of visual and auditory stimuli. We can expect as well that the circuits woven by our use of the Net will be different from those woven by our reading of books and other printed works.

Sometime in 1882, Friedrich Nietzsche bought a typewriter—a Malling-Hansen Writing Ball, to be precise. His vision was failing, and keeping his eyes focused on a page had become exhausting and painful, often bringing on crushing headaches. He had been forced to curtail his writing, and he feared that he would soon have to give it up. The typewriter rescued him, at least for a time. Once he had mastered touch-typing, he was able to write with his eyes closed, using only the tips of his fingers. Words could once again flow from his mind to the page.

But the machine had a subtler effect on his work. One of Nietzsche's friends, a composer, noticed a change in the style of his writing. His already terse prose had become even tighter, more telegraphic. "Perhaps you will through this instrument even take to a new idiom," the friend wrote in a letter, noting that, in his own work, his "'thoughts' in music and language often depend on the quality of pen and paper."

"You are right," Nietzsche replied, "our writing equipment takes part in the forming of our thoughts." Under the sway of the machine, writes the German media scholar Friedrich A. Kittler, Nietzsche's prose "changed from arguments to aphorisms, from thoughts to puns, from rhetoric to telegram style."

The human brain is almost infinitely malleable. People used to think that our mental meshwork, the dense connections formed among the 100 billion or so neurons inside our skulls, was largely fixed by the time we reached adulthood. But brain researchers have discovered that that's not the case. James Olds, a professor of neuroscience who directs the Krasnow Institute for Advanced Study at George Mason University, says that even the adult mind "is very plastic." Nerve cells routinely break old connections and form new ones. "The brain," according to Olds, "has the ability to reprogram itself on the fly, altering the way it functions."

As we use what the sociologist Daniel Bell has called our "intellectual technologies"—the tools that extend our mental rather than our physical capacities— we inevitably begin to take on the qualities of those technologies. The mechanical clock, which came into common use in the 14th century, provides a compelling example. In *Technics and Civilization*, the historian and cultural critic Lewis Mumford described how the clock "disassociated time from human events and helped create the belief in an independent world of mathematically measurable sequences." The "abstract framework of divided time" became "the point of reference for both action and thought."

The clock's methodical ticking helped bring into being the scientific mind and the scientific man. But it also took something away. As the late MIT computer scientist Joseph Weizenbaum observed in his 1976 book, *Computer Power and Human Reason: From Judgment to Calculation*, the conception of the world that emerged from the widespread use of timekeeping instruments "remains an impoverished version of the older one, for it rests on a rejection of those direct experiences that formed the basis for, and indeed constituted, the old reality." In deciding when to eat, to work, to sleep, to rise, we stopped listening to our senses and started obeying the clock.

The process of adapting to new intellectual technologies is reflected in the changing metaphors we use to explain ourselves to ourselves. When the mechanical clock arrived, people began thinking of their brains as operating "like clockwork." Today, in the age of software, we have come to think of them as operating "like computers." But the changes, neuroscience tells us, go much deeper than metaphor. Thanks to our brain's plasticity, the adaptation occurs also at a biological level.

The Internet promises to have particularly far-reaching effects on cognition. In a paper published in 1936, the British mathematician Alan Turing proved that a digital computer, which at the time existed only as a theoretical machine, could be programmed to perform the function of any other information-processing device. And that's what we're seeing today. The Internet, an immeasurably powerful computing system, is subsuming most of our other intellectual technologies. It's becoming our map and our clock, our printing press and our typewriter, our calculator and our telephone, and our radio and TV.

When the Net absorbs a medium, that medium is re-created in the Net's image. It injects the medium's content with hyperlinks, blinking ads, and other digital gewgaws, and it surrounds the content with the content of all the other media it has absorbed. A new e-mail message, for instance, may announce its arrival as we're glancing over the latest headlines at a newspaper's site. The result is to scatter our attention and diffuse our concentration.

The Net's influence doesn't end at the edges of a computer screen, either. As people's minds become attuned to the crazy quilt of Internet media, traditional media have to adapt to the audience's new expectations. Television programs add text crawls and pop-up ads, and magazines and newspapers shorten their articles, introduce capsule summaries, and crowd their pages with easy-to-browse info-snippets. When, in March of this year, *The New York Times* decided to devote the second and third pages of every edition to article abstracts, its design director, Tom Bodkin, explained that the "shortcuts" would give harried readers a quick "taste" of the day's news, sparing them the "less efficient" method of actually turning the pages and reading the articles. Old media have little choice but to play by the new-media rules.

Never has a communications system played so many roles in our lives—or exerted such broad influence over our thoughts—as the Internet does today. Yet, for all that's been written about the Net, there's been little

consideration of how, exactly, it's reprogramming us. The Net's intellectual ethic remains obscure.

About the same time that Nietzsche started using his typewriter, an earnest young man named Frederick Winslow Taylor carried a stopwatch into the Midvale Steel plant in Philadelphia and began a historic series of experiments aimed at improving the efficiency of the plant's machinists. With the approval of Midvale's owners, he recruited a group of factory hands, set them to work on various metalworking machines, and recorded and timed their every movement as well as the operations of the machines. By breaking down every job into a sequence of small, discrete steps and then testing different ways of performing each one, Taylor created a set of precise instructions—an "algorithm," we might say today—for how each worker should work. Midvale's employees grumbled about the strict new regime, claiming that it turned them into little more than automatons, but the factory's productivity soared.

More than a hundred years after the invention of the steam engine, the Industrial Revolution had at last found its philosophy and its philosopher. Taylor's tight industrial choreography—his "system," as he liked to call it—was embraced by manufacturers throughout the country and, in time, around the world. Seeking maximum speed, maximum efficiency, and maximum output, factory owners used time-and-motion studies to organize their work and configure the jobs of their workers. The goal, as Taylor defined it in his celebrated 1911 treatise, *The Principles of Scientific Management*, was to identify and adopt, for every job, the "one best method" of work and thereby to effect "the gradual substitution of science for rule of thumb throughout the mechanic arts." Once his system was applied to all acts of manual labor, Taylor assured his followers, it would bring about a restructuring not only of industry but of society, creating a utopia of perfect efficiency. "In the past the man has been first," he declared; "in the future the system must be first."

Taylor's system is still very much with us; it remains the ethic of industrial manufacturing. And now, thanks to the growing power that computer engineers and software coders wield over our intellectual lives, Taylor's ethic is beginning to govern the realm of the mind as well. The Internet is a machine designed for the efficient and automated collection, transmission, and manipulation of information, and its legions of programmers are intent on finding the "one best method"—the perfect algorithm—to carry out every mental movement of what we've come to describe as "knowledge work."

Google's headquarters, in Mountain View, California—the Googleplex—is the Internet's high church, and the religion practiced inside its walls is Taylorism. Google, says its chief executive, Eric Schmidt is "a company that's founded around the science of measurement," and it is striving to "systematize everything" it does. Drawing on the terabytes of behavioral data it collects through its search engine and other sites, it carries out thousands of experiments a day, according to the *Harvard Business Review*, and it uses the results to refine the algorithms that increasingly control how people find information and extract meaning from it. What Taylor did for the work of the hand, Google is doing for the work of the mind.

The company has declared that its mission is "to organize the world's information and make it universally accessible and useful." It seeks to develop "the perfect search engine," which it defines as something that "understands exactly what you mean and gives you back exactly what you want." In Google's view, information is a kind of commodity, a utilitarian resource that can be mined and processed with industrial efficiency. The more pieces of information we can "access" and the faster we can extract their gist, the more productive we become as thinkers.

Where does it end? Sergey Brin and Larry Page, the gifted young men who founded Google while pursuing doctoral degrees in computer science at Stanford, speak frequently of their desire to turn their search engine into an artificial intelligence, a HAL-like machine that might be connected directly to our brains. "The ultimate search engine is something as smart as people—or smarter," Page said in a speech a few years back. "For us, working on search is a way to work on artificial intelligence." In a 2004 interview with *Newsweek*, Brin said, "Certainly if you had all the world's information directly attached to your brain, or an artificial brain that was

smarter than your brain, you'd be better off." Last year, Page told a convention of scientists that Google is "really trying to build artificial intelligence and to do it on a large scale."

Such an ambition is a natural one, even an admirable one, for a pair of math whizzes with vast quantities of cash at their disposal and a small army of computer scientists in their employ. A fundamentally scientific enterprise, Google is motivated by a desire to use technology, in Eric Schmidt's words, "to solve problems that have never been solved before," and artificial intelligence is the hardest problem out there. Why wouldn't Brin and Page want to be the ones to crack it?

Still, their easy assumption that we'd all "be better off" if our brains were supplemented, or even replaced, by an artificial intelligence is unsettling. It suggests a belief that intelligence is the output of a mechanical process, a series of discrete steps that can be isolated, measured, and optimized. In Google's world, the world we enter when we go online, there's little place for the fuzziness of contemplation. Ambiguity is not an opening for insight but a bug to be fixed. The human brain is just an outdated computer that needs a faster processor and a bigger hard drive.

The idea that our minds should operate as high-speed data-processing machines is not only built into the workings of the Internet, it is the network's reigning business model as well. The faster we surf across the Web—the more links we click and pages we view—the more opportunities Google and other companies gain to collect information about us and to feed us advertisements. Most of the proprietors of the commercial Internet have a financial stake in collecting the crumbs of data we leave behind as we flit from link to link—the more crumbs, the better. The last thing these companies want is to encourage leisurely reading or slow, concentrated thought. It's in their economic interest to drive us to distraction.

Maybe I'm just a worrywart. Just as there's a tendency to glorify technological progress, there's a countertendency to expect the worst of every new tool or machine. In Plato's *Phaedrus*, Socrates bemoaned the development of writing. He feared that, as people came to rely on the written word as a substitute for the knowledge they used to carry inside their heads, they would, in the words of one of the dialogue's characters, "cease to exercise their memory and become forgetful." And because they would be able to "receive a quantity of information without proper instruction," they would "be thought very knowledgeable when they are for the most part quite ignorant." They would be "filled with the conceit of wisdom instead of real wisdom." Socrates wasn't wrong—the new technology did often have the effects he feared—but he was shortsighted. He couldn't foresee the many ways that writing and reading would serve to spread information, spur fresh ideas, and expand human knowledge (if not wisdom).

The arrival of Gutenberg's printing press, in the 15th century, set off another round of teeth gnashing. The Italian humanist Hieronimo Squarciafico worried that the easy availability of books would lead to intellectual laziness, making men "less studious" and weakening their minds. Others argued that cheaply printed books and broadsheets would undermine religious authority, demean the work of scholars and scribes, and spread sedition and debauchery. As New York University professor Clay Shirky notes, "Most of the arguments made against the printing press were correct, even prescient." But, again, the doomsayers were unable to imagine the myriad blessings that the printed word would deliver.

So, yes, you should be skeptical of my skepticism. Perhaps those who dismiss critics of the Internet as Luddites or nostalgists will be proved correct, and from our hyperactive, data-stoked minds will spring a golden age of intellectual discovery and universal wisdom. Then again, the Net isn't the alphabet, and although it may replace the printing press, it produces something altogether different. The kind of deep reading that a sequence of printed pages promotes is valuable not just for the knowledge we acquire from the author's words but for the intellectual vibrations those words set off within our own minds. In the quiet spaces opened up by the sustained, undistracted reading of a book, or by any other act of contemplation, for that matter, we make our own associations, draw our own inferences and analogies, foster our own ideas. Deep reading, as Maryanne Wolf argues, is indistinguishable from deep thinking.

If we lose those quiet spaces, or fill them up with "content," we will sacrifice something important not only in our selves but in our culture. In a recent essay, the playwright Richard Foreman eloquently described what's at stake:

> I come from a tradition of Western culture, in which the ideal (my ideal) was the complex, dense and "cathedral-like" structure of the highly educated and articulate personality—a man or woman who carried inside themselves a personally constructed and unique version of the entire heritage of the West. [But now] I see within us all (myself included) the replacement of complex inner density with a new kind of self—evolving under the pressure of information overload and the technology of the "instantly available."

As we are drained of our "inner repertory of dense cultural inheritance," Foreman concluded, we risk turning into "'pancake people'—spread wide and thin as we connect with that vast network of information accessed by the mere touch of a button."

I'm haunted by that scene in *2001*. What makes it so poignant, and so weird, is the computer's emotional response to the disassembly of its mind: its despair as one circuit after another goes dark, its childlike pleading with the astronaut—"I can feel it. I can feel it. I'm afraid"—and its final reversion to what can only be called a state of innocence. HAL's outpouring of feeling contrasts with the emotionlessness that characterizes the human figures in the film, who go about their business with an almost robotic efficiency. Their thoughts and actions feel scripted, as if they're following the steps of an algorithm. In the world of *2001*, people have become so machinelike that the most human character turns out to be a machine. That's the essence of Kubrick's dark prophecy: as we come to rely on computers to mediate our understanding of the world, it is our own intelligence that flattens into artificial intelligence.

Analyzing the Situation

1. Carr writes that "the Net is becoming a universal medium." Given that Carr published "Is Google Making Us Stupid?" in the summer of 2008, has the situation of the Net's universal quality changed at all?

2. What do you suppose Carr's exigency was in writing this article? Does the fact that he published in *The Atlantic* online reveal anything about that exigency?

3. How is "Is Google Making Us Stupid?" ecologically connected to other texts? For instance, Carr cites many other documents, including Clay Shirky's "Does the Internet Make You Smarter?" How does Carr's essay connect to these other writings and how do they connectively contribute to the situation in which Carr writes?

Analyzing the Rhetoric

1. The word *stupid* is negative; it is not a word used to praise something. It can also be rather insulting. What does Carr accomplish by using the word *stupid* in the title of this essay about the Internet's effect on reading and thinking?

2. Why do you suppose Carr uses the reference to *2001: A Space Odyssey* to introduce and conclude his essay? Are you familiar with the film? Does the reference serve a particular purpose in terms of Carr's position?

3. Notice that Carr says that neurological and psychological experiments will "provide a definitive picture of how Internet use affects cognition." What does he gain in making his claim by asserting that these studies will provide "definitive" conclusions?

4. In what ways does Carr use research to support his claims? How does that research also contribute to his ethos in making those claims? In what ways does he use personal narrative to support his claims? How does his use of the personal contribute to his ethos? How does Carr negotiate between the personal writing and his research-based writing within a single essay?

5. Does "Is Google Making Us Stupid?" imply a judgment about which is better, screen or page? How does the essay express its judgment and how does that judgment affect the message conveyed in the essay?

Discussing

1. Carr seems to imply a difference in value between reading from the page and reading from the screen; that is, he seems to distinguish between print culture and screen culture. Discuss the differences you see between screen and print and what the differences in those technologies might suggest about reading.

2. Carr writes that reading by way of the Internet may not only alter how we read and think but may reveal "even a new sense of the self." Discuss the implications of what Carr means in suggesting this.

3. Citing sociologist Daniel Bell, Carr identifies a distinction between "intellectual technologies" and technologies that extend physical capabilities. In your own thinking what are the distinctions between these kinds of technologies? This is not a question of identification: do not focus on identifying what technologies might be labeled physical and which might be labeled intellectual. Instead, discuss the implications of identifying technologies by these categorizations and the values we assign to each concept.

4. What is this essay really about regarding technology? Do you agree with Carr's assessment? Discuss your response to Carr's claims.

Writing

1. Carr's essay "Is Google Making Us Stupid?" implies a transition from one kind of reading—the page—to another—the screen—as altering how he engages in reading and thinking. That is, part of Carr's position is based on the idea that some readers have had to change how they engage written media as the media around them have changed. Chances are that you have not had to make the same kinds of transitions Carr has had to simply because you

have grown up with print technologies and Internet technologies as part of how you have always read. With Carr's essay in mind, write an account of how you read, focusing on the roles print reading and Internet reading each play in how you engage information.

2. Is, as Carr reports Google's view, information a kind of commodity? Why or why not? Write an article about whether or not information is a commodity and how it is or is not commoditized.

3. Carr quotes Nietzsche as claiming that "our writing equipment takes part in the forming of our thoughts." Do you agree with this claim? Write an essay that considers the relationship between writing technologies—like typewriters, pens, smart

phones, word processors—and how people think when they write. Keep in mind, too, Carr's discussion of Plato's reaction against writing in *Phaedrus*.

4. As you might imagine, the debate regarding the value of Internet technologies and their effects on how we think, read, work, and live are far ranging. Using the social news website Digg, conduct some research to find out how the Internet's effects on cognition and similarly related processes—like reading—have been addressed in the media over the last year. Don't limit your search to just written text; consider how new media productions and Web 2.0 texts have also taken up this conversation. Write an assessment of what you find in your research.

Does the Internet Make You Smarter?

Clay Shirky

Clay Shirky has been a theater director, a professor, a consultant, and a designer. He teaches in the Interactive Telecommunications Program at New York University and was the first Professor of New Media Studies at Hunter College, where he created the college's first undergraduate and graduate programs in new media. As a consultant, he has worked with groups addressing network design, including Nokia, the BBC, Newscorp, Microsoft, BP, Global Business Network, the Library of Congress, the U.S. Navy, the Libyan government, and Lego. He is also a prolific writer whose articles, essays, books, and blogs consider the interaction between social networks and technological networks.

The essay reprinted here, "Does the Internet Make You Smarter?" was first published in *The Wall Street Journal* in the summer of 2010. The essay makes a claim for the

importance of the evolution of digital information technologies, but at the same time it acknowledges that like other technological advances, digital technologies will also provide an abundance of less-than-useful artifacts. As you read "Does the Internet Make You Smarter?" consider how Shirky represents the idea of technology in a situation that is often resistant to technological development.

Digital media have made creating and disseminating text, sound, and images cheap, easy and global. The bulk of publicly available media is now created by people who understand little of the professional standards and practices for media.

Instead, these amateurs produce endless streams of mediocrity, eroding cultural norms about quality and acceptability, and leading to increasingly alarmed predictions of incipient chaos and intellectual collapse.

But of course, that's what always happens. Every increase in freedom to create or consume media, from paperback books to YouTube, alarms people accustomed to the restrictions of the old system, convincing them that the new media will make young people stupid. This fear dates back to at least the invention of movable type.

As Gutenberg's press spread through Europe, the Bible was translated into local languages, enabling direct encounters with the text; this was accompanied by a flood of contemporary literature, most of it mediocre. Vulgar versions of the Bible and distracting secular writings fueled religious unrest and civic confusion, leading to claims that the printing press, if not controlled, would lead to chaos and the dismemberment of European intellectual life.

These claims were, of course, correct. Print fueled the Protestant Reformation, which did indeed destroy the Church's pan-European hold on intellectual life. What the 16th-century foes of print didn't imagine—couldn't imagine—was what followed: We built new norms around newly abundant and contemporary literature. Novels, newspapers, scientific journals, the separation of fiction and non-fiction, all of these innovations were created during the collapse of the scribal system, and all had the effect of increasing, rather than decreasing, the intellectual range and output of society.

To take a famous example, the essential insight of the scientific revolution was peer review, the idea that science was a collaborative effort that included the feedback and participation of others. Peer review was a cultural institution that took the printing press for granted as a means of distributing research quickly and widely, but added the kind of cultural constraints that made it valuable.

We are living through a similar explosion of publishing capability today, where digital media link over a billion people into the same network. This linking together in turn lets us tap our cognitive surplus, the trillion hours a year of free time the educated population of the planet has to spend doing things they care about. In the 20th century, the bulk of that time was spent watching television, but our cognitive surplus is so enormous that diverting even a tiny fraction of time from consumption to participation can create enormous positive effects.

Wikipedia took the idea of peer review and applied it to volunteers on a global scale, becoming the most important English reference work in less than 10 years. Yet the cumulative time devoted to creating Wikipedia, something like 100 million hours of human thought, is expended by Americans every weekend, just watching ads. It only takes a fractional shift in the direction of participation to create remarkable new educational resources.

Similarly, open source software, created without managerial control of the workers or ownership of the product, has been critical to the spread of the Web. Searches for everything from supernovae to prime numbers now happen as giant, distributed efforts. Ushahidi, the Kenyan crisis mapping tool invented in 2008, now aggregates citizen reports about crises the world over. PatientsLikeMe, a website designed to accelerate medical research by getting patients to publicly share their health information, has assembled a larger group of sufferers of Lou Gehrig's disease than any pharmaceutical agency in history, by appealing to the shared sense of seeking medical progress.

Of course, not everything people care about is a high-minded project. Whenever media become more abundant, average quality falls quickly, while new institutional models for quality arise slowly. Today we have *The World's Funniest Home Videos* running 24/7 on YouTube, while the potentially world-changing uses of cognitive surplus are still early and special cases.

That always happens too. In the history of print, we got erotic novels 100 years before we got scientific journals, and complaints about distraction have been rampant; no less a beneficiary of the printing press than Martin Luther complained, "The multitude of books is a great evil. There is no measure of limit to this fever for writing." Edgar Allan Poe, writing during another surge in publishing, concluded, "The enormous multiplication of books in every branch of knowledge is one of the greatest evils of this age; since it presents one of the most serious obstacles to the acquisition of correct information."

The response to distraction, then as now, was social structure. Reading is an unnatural act; we are no more evolved to read books than we are to use computers. Literate societies become literate by investing extraordinary resources, every year, training children to read. Now it's our turn to figure out what response we need to shape our use of digital tools.

The case for digitally-driven stupidity assumes we'll fail to integrate digital freedoms into society as well as we integrated literacy. This assumption in turn rests on three beliefs: that the recent past was a glorious and irreplaceable high-water mark of intellectual attainment; that the present is only characterized by the silly stuff and not by the noble experiments; and that this generation of young people will fail to invent cultural norms that do for the Internet's abundance what the intellectuals of the 17th century did for print culture. There are likewise three reasons to think that the Internet will fuel the intellectual achievements of 21st-century society.

First, the rosy past of the pessimists was not, on closer examination, so rosy. The decade the pessimists want to return us to is the 1980s, the last period before society had any significant digital freedoms. Despite frequent genuflection to European novels, we actually spent a lot more time watching "Diff'rent Strokes" than reading Proust, prior to the Internet's spread. The Net, in fact, restores reading and writing as central activities in our culture.

The present is, as noted, characterized by lots of throwaway cultural artifacts, but the nice thing about throwaway material is that it gets thrown away. This issue isn't whether there's lots of dumb stuff online—there is, just as there is lots of dumb stuff in bookstores. The issue is whether there are any ideas so good today that they will survive into the future. Several early uses of our cognitive surplus, like open source software, look like they will pass that test.

The past was not as golden, nor is the present as tawdry, as the pessimists suggest, but the only thing really worth arguing about is the future. It is our misfortune, as a historical generation, to live through the largest expansion in expressive capability in human history, a misfortune because abundance breaks more things than scarcity. We are now witnessing the rapid stress of older institutions accompanied by the slow and fitful development of cultural alternatives. Just as required education was a response to print, using the Internet well will require new cultural institutions as well, not just new technologies.

It is tempting to want PatientsLikeMe without the dumb videos, just as we might want scientific journals without the erotic novels, but that's not how media works. Increased freedom to create means increased freedom to create throwaway material, as well as freedom to indulge in the experimentation that eventually makes the good new stuff possible. There is no easy way to get through a media revolution of this magnitude; the task before us now is to experiment with new ways of using a medium that is social, ubiquitous and cheap, a medium that changes the landscape by distributing freedom of the press and freedom of assembly as widely as freedom of speech.

Analyzing the Situation

1. Part of Shirky's argument is a historical argument, one about how culture has responded to technological development in other situations. How does Shirky connect these varying situations in order to establish exactly what he sees as the situation of the development of digital technologies?

2. Does it matter that Shirky published "Does the Internet Make You Smarter?" in *The Wall Street Journal* and that it was circulated even further by *The Wall Street Journal* online? How does the location of its publication affect how we read Shirky's essay?

3. What does "Does the Internet Make You Smarter?" imply about the role of institution and power in media?

Analyzing the Rhetoric

1. Throughout "Does the Internet Make You Smarter?" Shirky uses the phrase "cognitive surplus." What does he mean by this term and how does he use it to support his position?

2. Shirky begins this essay by comparing the resistance to unmediated use of digital media with the development of the moveable-type printing press, a comparison he turns back to at several points in the essay. What does he gain in his own argument by making such a historical comparison? Is it a useful comparison?

3. Toward the end of his essay, Shirky provides three beliefs about why integrated literacy will fail in the age of the Internet. What is his purpose in articulating these three assumptions about the stance he argues against? Do they help guide his position and the remainder of his essay? In what ways?

Discussing

1. One of the points Shirky makes in "Does the Internet Make You Smarter?" is that the collaborative characteristics of Internet technologies improve how we make and circulate knowledge. He identifies a number of examples to support his claim. How do you respond to the claim that increased collaboration is a benefit? Discuss the role of collaboration and your assessment of the value of collaboration in terms of digital information technologies.

2. Shirky cites Martin Luther as decrying, "The multitude of books is a great evil. There is no measure of limit to this fever for writing." But Shirky does not provide the full quote from Luther: "The multitude of books is a great evil. There is no limit to this fever for writing; every one must be an author; some out of vanity, to acquire celebrity and raise up a name, others for the sake of mere gain." First, how do you respond to Martin Luther's quote—either Shirky's abbreviated version of it or the more complete version? Second, given the time period in which Luther made this claim and his own leadership role in the Protestant Reformation, how are his words applicable in the context in which Shirky invokes them?

3. One of the most provocative claims that Shirky makes is that "The Net, in fact, restores reading and writing as the central activities in our culture." Discuss the implications of such a claim.

Writing

1. Shirky provides a brief summary of how people responded to the development of the movable-type printing press, but his summaries are general. Conduct some research to learn more about the responses to the printing press and the effects it had historically. Write a research paper about the effect of the printing press on culture and the responses that were voiced about it.

2. Shirky makes a distinction between "throwaway materials" and materials of intellectual value. Yet distinguishing between those things can be a matter of situation and context. For example, for some, comics might be throwaway material, whereas for others they are a legitimate intellectual medium. With Shirky's argument in mind, write about how we might culturally distinguish between throwaway material and legitimate material.

3. How do you respond to Shirky's claim? Write a response essay that contributes to this situation.

A Death on Facebook: Intimacy and Loss in the Age of Social Media

Kate Bolick

Kate Bolick is a former new media editor at *The Atlantic Monthly* and senior editor at *Domino Magazine*. Her writing has appeared in the Ideas section of *The Boston Globe*, *The Atlantic Monthly*, *The New York Times*, and *Vogue*. She regularly writes about social media. Her essay reprinted here, "A Death on Facebook: Intimacy and Loss in the Age of Social Media," asks us to think about the role of friendship and intimacy as it is mediated by social networks like Facebook. The essay is less about technology and media per se than it is about the cultural and social effects of the mass use of such technologies. As you read this powerful piece, think about the kinds of relationships you have developed via social media that might not have evolved without the technological connection.

I met "S" several years ago, when she was hired by the magazine where I worked as an editor. She was an assistant in a different department, so we had very little day-to-day contact. I somehow learned that she went to nightclubs a lot, and I once overheard her tell a colleague that she wanted to be the editor in chief of a magazine someday. It was a snippet that stayed with me, as her partying lifestyle seemed contrary to such a career goal, and for a while whenever I passed her desk I would worry over the incongruity. Eventually I found resolution in the idea of Bonnie Fuller, doyenne of celebrity journalism. That's what S meant, I decided: she would be an editor like Fuller, rather than someone bookish, like the legendarily reticent *New Yorker* editor William Shawn. She even had a haircut like Fuller's.

Eventually S quit the magazine. There must have been a goodbye party, with the customary boutique cupcakes and plastic Champagne flutes. Months wore on, maybe even years. Much to our collective shock, one Wednesday morning our parent company announced it was shutting down the magazine, and by Friday we no longer had jobs. At first I was intoxicated by the novelty of solitude: it was late January, a nice time of year to spend the day reading on the sofa. But in the weeks to come, I started to miss popping into colleagues' offices to get their daily romantic updates, or just making absentminded loops through the corridors, halfheartedly hunting for chocolates.

So it came to pass that I started logging on to Facebook. And, like seemingly everyone else I'd ever met, eventually S "friended" me. My policy has been always to accept whoever asks, no question, and never to friend anyone myself. (In this way I maintain the fiction that I'm not an active user.) I glanced at S's picture—that pretty smile and Bonnie Fuller shag—clicked "confirm," and unconsciously relegated her to the vast, benign category of "friends" with whom I never interact, but who constitute a comforting background chorus.

S would accept no such fate. Straightaway, photos of her nightlife dominated my news feed. Her status updates were bubbly shrieks of uppercase letters and exclamation points. I considered "hiding" her—this is the function

that allows you to make a friend invisible without going so far as to "defriend" her—but that seemed excessive. S was, after all, my envoy to an alternate universe of abandon. Twenty-five years old and barelegged in winter was a variety of fun I'd never known before.

Then, in the spring, a man—G—entered the frame. At first he appeared with other men, the whole group at a table in a bar, offering pints of beer to the camera. But quickly everyone else fell away and he emerged in photographs with S alone, his arm thrown around her. At first the gesture was friendly and drunk, but over time I could track the way his arm both relaxed and tightened, his hand cupping her shoulder, and see him taking possession.

It turned out that G lived in London, and in the fall S posted images from a visit: the couple in a crowded pub, or on a bridge at sunset. By now I habitually clicked through S's photo albums, a diversion far better than popping into a colleague's office for a romantic update. Here, I had the satisfaction of a love plot unfolding right in my living room, complete with revolving backdrops and the suspense inherent in a long-distance relationship. When was her next trip? Oh look, G is coming to town! At this I felt relief: I took it as evidence that he was as committed to her as she was to him.

But that was nothing compared to my delight the December morning I logged on to Facebook and was greeted by a photo of S and G grinning madly on an enormous gray sofa, S presenting the back of her hand to the camera to show off the diamond on her finger. I have never known that kind of happiness with a man. Without thinking, I started to type a note of congratulations into the comment box, but midway through I erased it and logged off. I hardly knew this person. When had I become such a voyeur?

Still, I continued to devour her fairy tale. Here G was introducing her to his parents; here she was introducing him to hers. A year had passed since S had friended me. We never exchanged messages, or commented on one another's postings, or saw each other in person (save for one early, awkward encounter in a furniture store, during which it took me a moment to place who she was). Yet I thought about her often, even when I wasn't on Facebook, as I would any close friend in a similar joyful circumstance. More, in fact: her news thrummed inside my chest as if it were my own. I wondered where the wedding might take place, what she would wear. Being a voyeur isn't so bad, I decided, as long as you've been invited—and you don't tell anyone.

In late January, I traveled from my Brooklyn apartment to a remote Vermont farmhouse belonging to a friend of a friend. She was leaving the country for two weeks, and I'd agreed to take care of her animals. It was a brave little house with a big, tumbledown barn and fields that sloped into forests beyond. The days were bright with snow, the nights forbiddingly dark. I had to drive 20 miles to get Internet access. But one evening I made an exciting discovery: balanced just so on a windowsill, my iPhone had snatched a stray sliver of signal and garnered 50 e-mails. News from beyond! As the messages downloaded, excruciatingly slowly, I boiled water for tea, stoked the furnace, and settled into an armchair, pleased to see a message from a former colleague with S's name in the subject line: had I actually been invited to the wedding shower?

It was a mass e-mail. "It's my great displeasure to be the bearer of such horrible news, but S passed away on Sunday," it read. "It was very sudden and I believe it happened in her sleep. I don't have any other details; a friend of hers sent me a message via Facebook."

A loud sob broke out of me, like a bark. It was a frightening sound in that too-quiet house. I stood up, heart racing, and paced the rooms, switching on any lamp I could find. But the rooms weren't familiar to me, and their features—shelves sagging with books I'd never read; ropes of garlic garlanding a cupboard; decades of dirt caking the floor seams—only enlarged my sense of unreality. Even the smudged windows framed a night so black that I could see nothing there but my own pale face. How do you cry for someone you hardly know? And for what was I crying? S or her story?

Analyzing the Situation

1. What role does gender play in this essay (beyond the simple fact that we know the genders of the narrator and of "S")?

2. In what ways does the narrator's lack of familiarity with her physical surroundings when she learns of S's death affect the situation and her reaction?

3. Is the situation in which "A Death on Facebook: Intimacy and Loss in the Age of Social Media" participates an unusual situation or is it familiar and commonplace?

Analyzing the Rhetoric

1. Why do you suppose Kate Bolick opted to relate this story and pose her inquiry about intimacy by way of a personal narrative? Could she have engaged the same critical questions in other ways?

2. If questions usually leave a reader wanting answers, how do the final three questions of the essay function as a conclusion?

3. "A Death on Facebook: Intimacy and Loss in the Age of Social Media" is a relatively short essay, yet it takes on a rather complex and potentially big subject: intimacy and social media. How does the essay's brevity contribute to its success in engaging its subject?

Discussing

1. How do you respond to this essay? Focus your discussion on the ramifications of how social networking alters concepts of friendship and intimacy rather than on the events of the narrative.

2. Are Facebook friends and other social network contacts really friends? Discuss the varying degrees of how you think about your online relationships versus your face-to-face relationships.

3. What seems to be Kate Bolick's attitude toward Facebook and social media in general? That is, what does she seem to suggest the purpose of social networks is? Do you agree with her portrayal of them?

Writing

1. Although you may or may not have had a similar experience regarding the death of someone you knew via Facebook, MySpace, or another social network, you may have encountered other situations in which you reacted to an intimate detail or event posted to a social network by someone with whom you were not close. How did you respond to that situation? What was it about the situation that you reacted to? Write your own narrative about an experience you have had on a social network that left you wondering why you reacted as you did given the degree of intimacy you shared with that person.

2. Most social network users develop some form of personal philosophy about how they use such sites. Some, Like Kate Bolick, never friend anyone, some never post any personal information, others post only personal details. What's your social network philosophy? Write a description of how you use social networking, the philosophies you have developed for yourself, and your reasons for developing those philosophies.

Small Change: Why the Revolution Will Not Be Tweeted

Malcolm Gladwell

Malcolm Gladwell is one of the coolest writers writing today. He has been a staff writer with *The New Yorker* since 1996. Prior to that, he worked as a reporter for *The Washington Post*. In 1999 he won a National Magazine Award for his biographical profile of the inventor and marketing personality Ron Popeil, founder of Ronco. In 2005 *Time* magazine named Gladwell one of its 100 Most Influential People. Gladwell has published four books, including in 2009 *What the Dog Saw*, which is a compilation of his *New Yorker* articles and stories.

The essay "Small Change: Why the Revolution Will Not Be Tweeted," originally appeared in *The New Yorker* on October 4, 2010. It is a provocative piece about the differences between social activism in the 1960s and in the era of social networking. As you read this essay, consider how Gladwell's historical comparatives help support his claim.

At four-thirty in the afternoon on Monday, February 1, 1960, four college students sat down at the lunch counter at the Woolworth's in downtown Greensboro, North Carolina. They were freshmen at North Carolina A. & T., a black college a mile or so away.

"I'd like a cup of coffee, please," one of the four, Ezell Blair, said to the waitress.

"We don't serve Negroes here," she replied.

The Woolworth's lunch counter was a long L-shaped bar that could seat sixty-six people, with a standup snack bar at one end. The seats were for whites. The snack bar was for blacks. Another employee, a black woman who worked at the steam table, approached the students and tried to warn them away. "You're acting stupid, ignorant!" she said. They didn't move. Around five-thirty, the front doors to the store were locked. The four still didn't move. Finally, they left by a side door. Outside, a small crowd had gathered, including a photographer from the Greensboro *Record*. "I'll be back tomorrow with A. & T. College," one of the students said.

By next morning, the protest had grown to twenty-seven men and four women, most from the same dormitory as the original four. The men were dressed in suits and ties. The students had brought their schoolwork, and studied as they sat at the counter. On Wednesday, students from Greensboro's "Negro" secondary school, Dudley High, joined in, and the number of protesters swelled to eighty. By Thursday, the protesters numbered three hundred, including three white women, from the Greensboro campus of the University of North Carolina. By Saturday, the sit-in had reached six hundred. People spilled out onto the street. White teen-agers waved Confederate flags. Someone threw a firecracker. At noon, the A. & T. football team arrived. "Here comes the wrecking crew," one of the white students shouted.

By the following Monday, sit-ins had spread to Winston-Salem, twenty-five miles away, and Durham, fifty miles away. The day after that, students at Fayetteville State Teachers College and at Johnson C. Smith College, in Charlotte, joined in, followed on Wednesday by students at St. Augustine's College and Shaw University, in Raleigh. On Thursday and Friday, the protest crossed state lines, surfacing in Hampton and Portsmouth, Virginia, in Rock Hill, South Carolina, and in Chattanooga, Tennessee. By the end of the month, there were sit-ins throughout the South, as far west as Texas. "I asked every student I met what the first day of the sit-downs had been like on his campus," the political theorist Michael Walzer wrote in *Dissent*. "The answer was always the same: 'It was like a fever. Everyone wanted to go.'" Some seventy thousand students eventually took part. Thousands were arrested and untold thousands more radicalized. These events in the early sixties became a civil-rights war that engulfed the South for the rest of the decade—and it happened without e-mail, texting, Facebook, or Twitter.

The world, we are told, is in the midst of a revolution. The new tools of social media have reinvented social activism. With Facebook and Twitter and the like, the traditional relationship between political authority and popular will has been upended, making it easier for the powerless to collaborate, coordinate, and give voice to their concerns. When ten thousand protesters took to the streets in Moldova in the spring of 2009 to protest against their country's Communist government, the action was dubbed the Twitter Revolution, because of the means by which the demonstrators had been brought together. A few months after that, when student protests rocked Tehran, the State Department took the unusual step of asking Twitter to suspend scheduled maintenance of its Web site, because the Administration didn't want such a critical organizing tool out of service at the height of the demonstrations. "Without Twitter the people of Iran would not have felt empowered and confident to stand up for freedom and democracy," Mark Pfeifle, a former national-security adviser, later wrote, calling for Twitter to be nominated for the Nobel Peace Prize. Where activists were once defined by their causes, they are now defined by their tools. Facebook warriors go online to push for change. "You are the best hope for us all," James K. Glassman, a former senior State Department official, told a crowd of cyber activists at a recent conference sponsored by Facebook, A. T. & T., Howcast, MTV, and Google. Sites like Facebook, Glassman said, "give the U.S. a significant competitive advantage over terrorists. Some time ago, I said that Al Qaeda was 'eating our lunch on the Internet.' That is no longer the case. Al Qaeda is stuck in Web 1.0. The Internet is now about interactivity and conversation."

These are strong, and puzzling, claims. Why does it matter who is eating whose lunch on the Internet? Are people who log on to their Facebook page really the best hope for us all? As for Moldova's so-called Twitter Revolution, Evgeny Morozov, a scholar at Stanford who has been the most persistent of digital evangelism's critics, points out that Twitter had scant internal significance in Moldova, a country where very few Twitter accounts exist. Nor does it seem to have been a revolution, not least because the protests—as Anne Applebaum suggested in the *Washington Post*—may well have been a bit of stagecraft cooked up by the government. (In a country paranoid about Romanian revanchism, the protesters flew a Romanian flag over the Parliament building.) In the Iranian case, meanwhile, the people tweeting about the demonstrations were almost all in the West. "It is time to get Twitter's role in the events in Iran right," Golnaz Esfandiari wrote, this past summer, in *Foreign Policy*. "Simply put: There was no Twitter Revolution inside Iran." The cadre of prominent bloggers, like Andrew Sullivan, who championed the role of social media in Iran, Esfandiari continued, misunderstood the situation. "Western journalists who couldn't reach—or didn't bother reaching?—people on the ground in Iran simply scrolled through the English-language tweets post with tag #iranelection," she wrote. "Through it all, no one seemed to wonder why people trying to coordinate protests in Iran would be writing in any language other than Farsi."

Some of this grandiosity is to be expected. Innovators tend to be solipsists. They often want to cram every stray fact and experience into their new model. As the historian Robert Darnton has written, "The marvels of communication technology in the present have produced a false consciousness about the past—even a sense that communication has no history, or had nothing of importance to consider before the days of television and the Internet." But there is something else at work here, in the outsized enthusiasm for social media. Fifty years after one of the most extraordinary episodes of social upheaval in American history, we seem to have forgotten what activism is.

Greensboro in the early nineteen-sixties was the kind of place where racial insubordination was routinely met with violence. The four students who first sat down at the lunch counter were terrified. "I suppose if anyone had come up behind me and yelled 'Boo,' I think I would have fallen off my seat," one of them said later. On the first day, the store manager notified the police chief, who immediately sent two officers to the store. On the third day, a gang of white toughs showed up at the lunch counter and stood ostentatiously behind the protesters, ominously muttering epithets such as "burr-head nigger." A local Ku Klux Klan leader made an appearance. On Saturday, as tensions grew, someone called in a bomb threat, and the entire store had to be evacuated.

The dangers were even clearer in the Mississippi Freedom Summer Project of 1964, another of the sentinel campaigns of the civil-rights movement. The Student Nonviolent Coordinating Committee recruited hundreds of Northern, largely white unpaid volunteers to run Freedom Schools, register black voters, and raise civil-rights awareness in the Deep South. "No one should go

anywhere alone, but certainly not in an automobile and certainly not at night," they were instructed. Within days of arriving in Mississippi, three volunteers—Michael Schwerner, James Chaney, and Andrew Goodman—were kidnapped and killed, and, during the rest of the summer, thirty-seven black churches were set on fire and dozens of safe houses were bombed; volunteers were beaten, shot at, arrested, and trailed by pickup trucks full of armed men. A quarter of those in the program dropped out. Activism that challenges the status quo—that attacks deeply rooted problems—is not for the faint of heart.

What makes people capable of this kind of activism? The Stanford sociologist Doug McAdam compared the Freedom Summer dropouts with the participants who stayed, and discovered that the key difference wasn't, as might be expected, ideological fervor. "*All* of the applicants—participants and withdrawals alike—emerge as highly committed, articulate supporters of the goals and values of the summer program," he concluded. What mattered more was an applicant's degree of personal connection to the civil-rights movement. All the volunteers were required to provide a list of personal contacts—the people they wanted kept apprised of their activities—and participants were far more likely than dropouts to have close friends who were also going to Mississippi. High-risk activism, McAdam concluded, is a "strong-tie" phenomenon.

This pattern shows up again and again. One study of the Red Brigades, the Italian terrorist group of the nineteen-seventies, found that seventy per cent of recruits had at least one good friend already in the organization. The same is true of the men who joined the mujahideen in Afghanistan. Even revolutionary actions that look spontaneous, like the demonstrations in East Germany that led to the fall of the Berlin Wall, are, at core, strong-tie phenomena. The opposition movement in East Germany consisted of several hundred groups, each with roughly a dozen members. Each group was in limited contact with the others: at the time, only thirteen per cent of East Germans even had a phone. All they knew was that on Monday nights, outside St. Nicholas

Church in downtown Leipzig, people gathered to voice their anger at the state. And the primary determinant of who showed up was "critical friends"—the more friends you had who were critical of the regime the more likely you were to join the protest.

So one crucial fact about the four freshmen at the Greensboro lunch counter—David Richmond, Franklin McCain, Ezell Blair, and Joseph McNeil—was their relationship with one another. McNeil was a roommate of Blair's in A. & T.'s Scott Hall dormitory. Richmond roomed with McCain one floor up, and Blair, Richmond, and McCain had all gone to Dudley High School. The four would smuggle beer into the dorm and talk late into the night in Blair and McNeil's room. They would all have remembered the murder of Emmett Till in 1955, the Montgomery bus boycott that same year, and the showdown in Little Rock in 1957. It was McNeil who brought up the idea of a sit-in at Woolworth's. They'd discussed it for nearly a month. Then McNeil came into the dorm room and asked the others if they were ready. There was a pause, and McCain said, in a way that works only with people who talk late into the night with one another, "Are you guys chicken or not?" Ezell Blair worked up the courage the next day to ask for a cup of coffee because he was flanked by his roommate and two good friends from high school.

The kind of activism associated with social media isn't like this at all. The platforms of social media are built around weak ties. Twitter is a way of following (or being followed by) people you may never have met. Facebook is a tool for efficiently managing your acquaintances, for keeping up with the people you would not otherwise be able to stay in touch with. That's why you can have a thousand "friends" on Facebook, as you never could in real life.

This is in many ways a wonderful thing. There is strength in weak ties, as the sociologist Mark Granovetter has observed. Our acquaintances—not our friends—are our greatest source of new ideas and information. The Internet lets us exploit the power of these kinds of distant connections with marvelous efficiency. It's terrific at the diffusion of innovation, interdisciplinary collaboration, seamlessly matching up buyers and sellers, and the logistical functions of the dating world. But weak ties seldom lead to high-risk activism.

In a new book called "The Dragonfly Effect: Quick, Effective, and Powerful Ways to Use Social Media to Drive Social Change," the business consultant Andy Smith and the Stanford Business School professor Jennifer Aaker tell the story of Sameer Bhatia, a young Silicon Valley entrepreneur who came down with acute myelogenous leukemia. It's a perfect illustration of social media's strengths. Bhatia needed a bone-marrow transplant, but he could not find a match among his relatives and friends. The odds were best with a donor of his ethnicity, and there were few South Asians in the national bone-marrow database. So Bhatia's business partner sent out an e-mail explaining Bhatia's plight to more than four hundred of their acquaintances, who forwarded the e-mail to their personal contacts; Facebook pages and YouTube videos were devoted to the Help Sameer campaign. Eventually, nearly twenty-five thousand new people were registered in the bone-marrow database, and Bhatia found a match.

But how did the campaign get so many people to sign up? By not asking too much of them. That's the only way you can get someone you don't really know to do something on your behalf. You can get thousands of people to sign up for a donor registry, because doing so is pretty easy. You have to send in a cheek swab and—in the highly unlikely event that your bone marrow is a good match for someone in need—spend a few hours at the hospital. Donating bone marrow isn't a trivial matter. But it doesn't involve financial or personal risk; it doesn't mean spending a summer being chased by armed men in pickup trucks. It doesn't require that you confront socially entrenched norms and practices. In fact, it's the kind of commitment that will bring only social acknowledgment and praise.

The evangelists of social media don't understand this distinction; they seem to believe that a Facebook friend is the same as a real friend and that signing up for a donor registry in Silicon Valley today is activism in the same sense as sitting at a segregated lunch counter in Greensboro in 1960. "Social networks are particularly effective at increasing motivation," Aaker and Smith write. But that's not true. Social networks are effective at increasing *participation*—by lessening the level of motivation that participation requires. The Facebook page of the Save Darfur Coalition has 1,282,339 members, who have donated an average of nine cents apiece. The next biggest Darfur charity on Facebook has 22,073 members, who have donated an average of thirty-five cents. Help Save Darfur has 2,797 members, who have given, on average, fifteen cents. A spokesperson for the Save Darfur Coalition told *Newsweek*, "We wouldn't necessarily gauge someone's value to the advocacy movement based on what they've given. This is a powerful mechanism to engage this critical population. They inform their community, attend events, volunteer. It's not something you can measure by looking at a ledger." In other words, Facebook activism succeeds not by motivating people to make a real sacrifice but by motivating them to do the things that people do when they are not motivated enough to make a real sacrifice. We are a long way from the lunch counters of Greensboro.

The students who joined the sit-ins across the South during the winter of 1960 described the movement as a "fever." But the civil-rights movement was more like a military campaign than like a contagion. In the late nineteen-fifties, there had been sixteen sit-ins in various cities throughout the South, fifteen of which were formally organized by civil-rights organizations like the N.A.A.C.P. and CORE. Possible locations for activism were scouted. Plans were drawn up. Movement activists held training sessions and retreats for would-be protesters. The Greensboro Four were a product of this groundwork: all were members of the N.A.A.C.P. Youth Council. They had close ties with the head of the local N.A.A.C.P. chapter. They had been briefed on the earlier wave of sit-ins in Durham, and had been part of a series of movement meetings in activist churches. When the sit-in movement spread from Greensboro throughout the South, it did not spread indiscriminately. It spread to those cities which had preexisting "movement centers"—a core of dedicated and trained activists ready to turn the "fever" into action.

The civil-rights movement was high-risk activism. It was also, crucially, strategic activism: a challenge to the establishment mounted with precision and discipline. The N.A.A.C.P. was a centralized organization, run from New York according to highly formalized operating procedures. At the Southern Christian Leadership Conference, Martin Luther King, Jr., was the unquestioned authority. At the center of the movement was the black church, which had, as Aldon D. Morris points out in his superb 1984 study, "The Origins of the Civil Rights Movement," a carefully demarcated division of labor, with various standing committees and disciplined groups. "Each group was task-oriented and coordinated its activities through authority structures," Morris writes. "Individuals were held accountable for their assigned duties, and important conflicts were resolved by the minister, who usually exercised ultimate authority over the congregation."

This is the second crucial distinction between traditional activism and its online variant: social media are not about this kind of hierarchical organization. Facebook and the like are tools for building *networks*, which are the opposite, in structure and character, of hierarchies. Unlike hierarchies, with their rules and procedures, networks aren't controlled by a single central authority. Decisions are made through consensus, and the ties that bind people to the group are loose.

This structure makes networks enormously resilient and adaptable in low-risk situations. Wikipedia is a perfect example. It doesn't have an editor, sitting in New York, who directs and corrects each entry. The effort of putting together each entry is self-organized. If every entry in Wikipedia were to be erased tomorrow, the content would swiftly be restored, because that's what happens when a network of thousands spontaneously devote their time to a task.

There are many things, though, that networks don't do well. Car companies sensibly use a network to organize their hundreds of suppliers, but not to design their cars. No one believes that the articulation of a coherent design philosophy is best handled by a sprawling, leaderless organizational system. Because networks don't have a centralized leadership structure and clear lines of authority, they have real difficulty reaching consensus and setting goals. They can't think strategically; they are chronically prone to conflict and error. How do you make difficult choices about tactics or strategy or philosophical direction when everyone has an equal say?

The Palestine Liberation Organization originated as a network, and the international-relations scholars Mette Eilstrup-Sangiovanni and Calvert Jones argue in a recent essay in *International Security* that this is why it ran into such trouble as it grew: "Structural features typical of networks—the absence of central authority, the unchecked autonomy of rival groups, and the inability to arbitrate quarrels through formal mechanisms—made the P.L.O. excessively vulnerable to outside manipulation and internal strife."

In Germany in the nineteen-seventies, they go on, "the far more unified and successful left-wing terrorists tended to organize hierarchically, with professional management and clear divisions of labor. They were concentrated geographically in universities, where they could establish central leadership, trust, and camaraderie through regular, face-to-face meetings." They seldom betrayed their comrades in arms during police interrogations. Their counterparts on the right were organized as decentralized networks, and had no such discipline. These groups were regularly infiltrated, and members, once arrested, easily gave up their comrades. Similarly, Al Qaeda was most dangerous when it was a unified hierarchy. Now that it has dissipated into a network, it has proved far less effective.

The drawbacks of networks scarcely matter if the network isn't interested in systemic change—if it just wants to frighten or humiliate or make a splash—or if it doesn't need to think strategically. But if you're taking on a powerful and organized establishment you have to be a hierarchy. The Montgomery bus boycott required the participation of tens of thousands of people who depended on public transit to get to and from work each day. It lasted a *year*. In order to persuade those people to stay true to the cause, the boycott's organizers tasked each local black church with maintaining morale, and put together a free alternative private carpool service, with forty-eight dispatchers and forty-two pickup stations. Even the White Citizens Council, King later said, conceded that the carpool system moved with "military precision." By the time King came to Birmingham, for the climactic showdown with Police Commissioner Eugene (Bull) Connor, he had a budget of a million dollars, and a hundred full-time staff members on the ground, divided into operational units. The operation itself was divided into steadily escalating phases, mapped out in advance. Support was maintained through consecutive mass meetings rotating from church to church around the city.

Boycotts and sit-ins and nonviolent confrontations—which were the weapons of choice for the civil-rights movement—are high-risk strategies. They leave little room for conflict and error. The moment even one protester deviates from the script and responds to provocation, the moral legitimacy of the entire protest is compromised. Enthusiasts for social media would no doubt have us believe that King's task in Birmingham would have been made infinitely easier had he been able to communicate with his followers through Facebook, and contented himself with tweets from a Birmingham jail. But networks are messy: think of the ceaseless pattern of correction and revision, amendment and debate, that characterizes Wikipedia. If Martin Luther King, Jr., had tried to do a wiki-boycott in Montgomery, he would have been steamrollered by the white power structure. And of what use would a digital communication tool be in a town where ninety-eight per cent of the black community could be reached every Sunday morning at church? The things that King needed in Birmingham—discipline and strategy—were things that online social media cannot provide.

The bible of the social-media movement is Clay Shirky's "Here Comes Everybody." Shirky, who teaches at New York University, sets out to demonstrate the organizing power of the Internet, and he begins with the story of Evan, who worked on Wall Street, and his friend Ivanna, after she left her smart phone, an expensive Sidekick, on the back seat of a New York City taxicab. The telephone company transferred the data on Ivanna's lost phone to a new phone, whereupon she and Evan discovered that the Sidekick was now in the hands of a teen-ager from Queens, who was using it to take photographs of herself and her friends.

When Evan e-mailed the teen-ager, Sasha, asking for the phone back, she replied that his "white ass" didn't deserve to have it back. Miffed, he set up a Web page with her picture and a description of what had happened. He forwarded the link to his friends, and they forwarded it to their friends. Someone found the MySpace page of Sasha's boyfriend, and a link to it found its way onto the site. Someone found her address online and took a video of her home while driving by; Evan posted the video on the site. The story was picked up by the news filter Digg. Evan was now up to ten e-mails a minute. He created a bulletin board for his readers to share their stories, but it crashed under the weight of responses. Evan and Ivanna went to the police, but the police filed the report under "lost," rather than "stolen," which essentially closed the case. "By this point millions of readers were watching," Shirky writes, "and dozens of mainstream news outlets had covered the story." Bowing to the pressure, the N.Y.P.D. reclassified the item as "stolen." Sasha was arrested, and Evan got his friend's Sidekick back.

Shirky's argument is that this is the kind of thing that could never have happened in the pre-Internet age—and he's right. Evan could never have tracked down Sasha. The story of the Sidekick would never have been publicized. An army of people could never have been assembled to wage this fight. The police wouldn't have bowed to the pressure of a lone person who had misplaced something as trivial as a cell phone. The story, to Shirky, illustrates "the ease and speed with which a group can be mobilized for the right kind of cause" in the Internet age.

Shirky considers this model of activism an upgrade. But it is simply a form of organizing which favors the weak-tie connections that give us access to information over the strong-tie connections that help us persevere in the face of danger. It shifts our energies from organizations that promote strategic and disciplined activity and toward those which promote resilience and adaptability. It makes it easier for activists to express themselves, and harder for that expression to have any impact. The instruments of social media are well suited to making the existing social order more efficient. They are not a natural enemy of the status quo. If you are of the opinion that all the world needs is a little buffing around the edges, this should not trouble you. But if you think that there are still lunch counters out there that need integrating it ought to give you pause.

Shirky ends the story of the lost Sidekick by asking, portentously, "What happens next?"—no doubt imagining future waves of digital protesters. But he has already answered the question. What happens next is more of the same. A networked, weak-tie world is good at things like helping Wall Streeters get phones back from teen-age girls. *Viva la revolución.*

Analyzing the Situation

1. Why does Malcolm Gladwell situate his critique of social networks within situations of social protest?

2. What do you see as Malcolm Gladwell's purpose in this essay? Does he succeed in fulfilling it?

3. What role does institution play in the situation in which Malcolm Gladwell writes?

Analyzing the Rhetoric

1. How would you characterize the tone of "Small Change: Why the Revolution Will Not Be Tweeted"?

2. What does the title of this essay refer to in saying "the revolution will not be tweeted"? In what way does that reference contribute to how we read the essay?

3. Why do you suppose Malcolm Gladwell included the last section about Clay Shirky's book? What does that final segment of Gladwell's essay accomplish in his overall agenda?

Discussing

1. How do you respond to Malcolm Gladwell's comparison of the 1960 Woolworth's sit-in to the activism broadcast via social networking? Discuss the comparison.

2. Do you participate in any kind of activism? Does your activism involve any social networking strategies? Discuss with others in your class your own experiences with activism and social networking.

3. On a local scale, do students on your campus use social networking to promote campus organization or activism? In what ways do or don't they?

Writing

1. After reading "Small Change: Why the Revolution Will Not Be Tweeted," how would you describe the relationship between activism—at any level and for any cause—and social networking?

2. Using your Twitter account or your Facebook account (or creating a new one), friend or follow a cause that interests you. This can be any cause from large-scale global political causes to local community causes or even personal causes. Spend a week monitoring the tweets, wall posts, and status updates that are posted for that cause. Then write an analysis of how you understand the social networking facet of that cause to function. Is it effective? Is it part of a larger effort beyond social networking? How many people follow that cause? What is the population like that follows or friends? Is there a noticeable demographic?

3. Given the genre in which Malcolm Gladwell writes "Small Change: Why the Revolution Will Not Be Tweeted" and given his purpose in writing the essay, his coverage of the 1960 sit-ins can only be cursory. Yet their role in U.S. history is very important. Conduct some research to learn more about the sit-in protests and write a research paper about that part of the civil rights movement.

Thinking and Writing about the Chapter

Discussion Threads

1. Is technology more abundant now than it was 100 years ago, or is it merely different? Discuss how U.S. culture tends to see technology and its role in contemporary culture as opposed to U.S. culture of 100 years ago. You may want to consider what the major technological advances of 100 years ago were and what technologies most people did or did not have access to.

2. Select any two or three of the readings found in this chapter and discuss the similarities and/or differences in how those readings describe or understand the idea of technology.

Collaboration

Defining *technology* can be problematic. The word has numerous historical definitions and different people understand the word to mean different things. As a class, establish a wiki dedicated to defining *technology*, or more precisely, establish a wiki dedicated to exploring the variety of ways that *technology* can be defined. Consider how you might want to organize the wiki and how you might want to use examples to support your various definitions.

Writing

1. On a daily basis, how do you interact with technology? Write a chronological narrative of your daily interaction with technology—in whatever way you chose to define that concept. Describe the technologies and how they affect your life.

2. There are many blogs that follow and share information about current trends in technology. Mashable, for example, is a well-circulated blog dedicated to providing information about the latest trends and news in social networking. Others include Slashdot, BoingBoing, Engadget, TechCrunch, How-To Geek, Crunch Gear, and Gizmodo. Likewise, online tech magazines like *Wired* and online news magazines like *The Huffington Post* house many blogs and articles about specific technology subjects. Locate and follow a technology blog; then write an assessment and critique of what that blog provides its readers.

Local Situation

Most college campuses now have specific divisions dedicated to maintaining various technologies on campus. For example, it is likely that your campus has an office of information technology (or some other similarly named division) that oversees how communications technologies are maintained on campus. Your college may also have groups that oversee classroom technologies or computer labs for student use. You probably also have many academic programs dedicated to various technologies. Take some time to locate one such entity on your campus and explore the ways in which that organization talks about technology in its publicity materials (like its web pages). Don't be as concerned with what the office provides as with the rhetorical choices it makes and the way that those choices convey a sense of what constitutes technology. Then write a document that analyzes the rhetoric of the entity in such a way so as to make a claim about how that group projects an understanding of what technology is.

23 | Image/Culture

What does it mean to say that we "live in a visual culture"? In what ways is our culture visual? In what ways is our culture more visual than other cultures? In what ways is our culture more visual now than in the past? In your blog or journal, write about what it means to identify something as a visual culture and what you understand that claim to mean.

We live in a culture of images, a visual culture, a screen

culture. Countless images vie for our attention every day. We learn to be visually literate. We learn to read, analyze, and make images in ways that are similar to but also different from how we read, analyze, and write written language (writing).

Images are likenesses; they are representations made visible. Images depict. A photograph of a narwhal is not a narwhal; a photograph of a narwhal is a depiction of a narwhal. An image lets us make an association between what is depicted and what we know of the thing itself. This is clearly seen in Belgian painter René Magritte's famous painting "The Treachery of Images," the text of which translates to "This is not a pipe."

Imagery is a mental image. Imagery is what we picture in our minds, what we "see" of an object when we don't actually see the object. For example, the words "a blue orange" might lead you to picture what a blue orange might look like. What you see, what you imagine, is imagery. Writers use imagery to help readers "see" what the writer describes or explains. Imagery is often a result of successful description and can be tied to different senses or perceptions:

- visual imagery—what something looks like
- auditory imagery—what something sounds like
- olfactory imagery—what something smells like
- gustatory imagery—what something tastes like
- tactile imagery—what something feels like to the touch
- kinesthetic imagery—what something moves like
- organic imagery—what something feels like to the body (like hunger)

Both writing and images can elicit imagery for a reader/viewer. Thus, it is important to recognize that when we read writing or view images, there is a difference between what we see in the writing or image and what we "see" in our minds. In a culture of images, then, it is important to note that our interpretations of images are at least twice removed from the thing itself, once in the image and once in the imagery. To understand images, you should be able to distinguish between images and imagery.

Images can be captured—like a photograph—or they can be rendered—like a drawing. Images can be static—like a painting—or they can be kinetic—like a video. Images may be two dimensional—like a photo—or they may be three dimensional—like a model. Some images are temporary—like the images on a television or a mobile phone screen. We call these *volatile images*. Some images have been made more permanent through the materiality of their transmittal and circulation—like a photograph or a drawing on paper. We call these *fixed images*. Both types of images convey meaning, or, perhaps more accurately, we assign meaning to images when we read them.

This chapter contains readings that ask us to think about how we draw meaning out of images and how that meaning contributes to how we see the world in which we live. To consider image/culture is no simple task. The role of images in contemporary culture has become so ubiquitous that scholars have claimed that images now compete with writing as the primary mode of public communication. Examining the relationship between images and culture requires some consideration of rhetoric, technology, literacy, psychology, history, education, and so on. The readings in this chapter are gathered to help you think about an array of issues that emerge in our image culture:

- What is the power of photography and photographers?
- What should and shouldn't be seen?
- What should and shouldn't be looked at?
- Who should determine what we see and don't see?
- Do images convey a reliable sense of reality?
- Why do we invest so much in images?
- What role do images play in cultural politics?
- Are images used as weapons?
- Should we trust the images we see as being accurate?
- What can be done legally when malicious images circulate?
- How are visually impaired people affected by living in an image culture?
- How can images bring a community together?

As you read the essays and images in this chapter, think about how each of these readings contributes to and questions what it means to live in an image culture. Think, too, about how each specific reading reveals questions that might be asked of other specific situations.

Graven Images

Saul Bellow

Saul Bellow was one of the most distinguished American authors of the twentieth century. He won the Nobel Prize for Literature in 1976, the Pulitzer Prize in 1975, and the National Medal of Arts in 1988. He is the only author to win the National Book Award for Fiction three times. Reprinted here is Bellow's 1997 essay "Graven Images," Bellow's commentary about the power of photography. Bellow wrote "Graven Images" when he was 82 years old and had been photographed countless times throughout his life. The essay speculates as to the ways in which photographs represent an individual and whether that representation projects a different view of a person than the person has of himself. As you read "Graven Images," consider why Bellow, a renowned literary figure, might have felt the need to write about the power of photography.

Harry S. Truman liked to say that as president of this country he was its most powerful citizen—but sometimes he added, smiling, the photographers were even more powerful. They could tell the commander in chief where to go, make him move his chair, cross his legs, hold up a letter, order him to smile or to look stern. He acknowledged their power and, as a political matter, deferred to their judgment. What the people thought of their chief executive would to some extent be decided by the photographers and the picture editors. Photographers may claim to be a priesthood interpreting the laws of light, and light is a universal mystery that the picture takers measure with their light meters. "In nature's book of infinite mystery, a little I can read," says the Egyptian soothsayer in *Antony and Cleopatra*. Pictures taken in the light must be developed in the shallow mystery of darkrooms. But photographers have nothing in common with soothsayers. Their interests, apart from the technical one, are social and political. To some extent, it is they who decide how you are to be publicly seen. Your "visual record" is in their hands.

Broadly speaking, your *amour propre* is the territory invaded by the picture takers. You may wish or not wish to be in public life. Some people have not the slightest desire to be in the papers or on TV. Others feel that papers and TV screens confer immortality. TV crews on a city street immediately attract big crowds. The arrival of television cameras offers people the opportunity each and every one of them has dreamt of—a shot at eternity. Not by deeds, not by prayers, but solely by their faces, grinning and mugging.

But this aspect of modern image-making or idolatry is not, for me, the most interesting one. What I discover when I search my soul is that I have formed a picture of myself as I wish to be seen, and that while photographers are setting up their lights and cameras I am summoning up and fortifying that picture. My intent is to triumph over the photographers' vision of me—their judgment as to what my place in photographic reality is to be. They have *technics*—Science—on their side. On my side there is vanity and deceit—there is, as I have already said, *amour propre*; there is, moreover, a nagging sense that my powers of candor are weakening

and sagging, and that my face betrays how heavily it is mortgaged to death. *Amour propre*, with all its hypocritical tricks, is the product of your bourgeois outlook. Your aim is to gain general acceptance for your false self, to make propaganda, concealing your real motives—motives of personal advantage. You persuade people to view you as you need to be viewed if you are to put it over on them. We all are, insofar as we live for our *amour propre*, loyal to nothing except our secret, crippled objectives—the objectives of every "civilized" man.

Et cetera.

Yes, we're all too familiar with *amour propre*, thanks to the great romantic writers of the nineteenth century. But give clever people something to understand and you can count on them to understand it. So in facing the photographers it's not the exposure of my *amour propre* that concerns me. What I feel in making innumerable last-minute ego arrangements is that the real me will decide to withhold itself. I know that the best picture instruments of Germany or "state-of-the-art" Japan are constructed for ends very different from mine. What need is there to bring these powerful lenses up to the very tip of my nose? They will meaninglessly enlarge the pores of my skin. You will supply them with shots that remind viewers of the leg of a mosquito photographed through a microscope. The truth about you is that you have lost more hair than you thought and that your scalp is shining through—the truth is that you have huge paisley-shaped bruises under your eyes and that your bridgework when you smile is far from "photogenic." You are not simply shown—you are exposed. This exposure cannot be prevented. One can only submit to the merciless cruelty of "pure objectivity," which is so hard on your illusions.

Then, too, from a contemporary point of view, the daily and weekly papers—to say nothing of television—do not feel that they are honoring the truth if they do not tear away the tatters of vanity that cover our imperfections. No one is safe from exposure except the owners, the main stockholders, and the leading advertisers of the great national papers. Things weren't always like this. The "gentlemen" described by Aristotle are immune to shame—they are made that way; nothing shameful can touch these aristocrats. But Adam and Eve, when they had eaten the apple of self-consciousness, sewed fig leaves together to cover their nakedness.

It is the (not always conscious) premise of the photographer that his is the art of penetrating your private defenses. We, his subjects, can learn not to care. But we are not by any means an Aristotelian class, trained in the virtues. We are democrats and lead our petty lives in the shadow of shame. And for this as for all our weaknesses and vices there arise, in all civilized countries, entire classes of people, categories of specialists who specialize in *discovery* and exposure.

Their slogan is: Let the Record Show. And what the record shows is, of course, change and decay, instability, weakness and infirmity, darkness as endless and winding as the Malabar Caves as E. M. Forster years ago described them in *A Passage to India*.

A photograph that made me look worse than the Ruins of Athens was published by *Time* together with a line from William Blake: "The lineaments of gratified desire." Nowhere in the novel *Time* was reviewing had I so much as hinted that my face, with its lineaments, was anything like the faces Blake had in mind (faces of prostitutes, as his text explicitly tells us). But there was my dreary, sullen, tired, and aging mug. I was brought low by Blake's blazing words. But it is the prerogative of the mass media to bring you down when they think that you have gotten ahead of yourself—when they suspect you of flying too high. It doesn't damage us to be exposed, to appear in distorted shapes on film or slick paper or newsprint. I often remember how at the age of ninety-nine Freud's grandmother complained that in the paper "they made me look a hundred years old."

But picture editors and journalists often seem to feel that they are the public representatives of truth, and even that they are conferring some sort of immortality on you by singling you out. But you had better be prepared for rough treatment. Often your "privacy" is to them a cover for the lies and manipulations of *amour propre*.

Who would have thought that minor vanities might lead to such vexations. Your secrets will die in the glare of publicity. When the police strip Dimitri Karamazov to

his foul underpants, he says to them, "Gentlemen, you have sullied my soul."

But the world has undergone a revolutionary transformation. Such simple, romantic standards of personal dignity and of the respect due to privacy are to be found today only in remote corners of backward countries. Maybe in the Pyrenees or in the forgotten backlands of Corsica—places where I shouldn't care to live. Everywhere else, the forces of insight are on the lookout. The function of their insights is to make your secrets public, for the public has a right to know, and it is the duty of journalists to deliver the secrets of people "in the news" to their readers. For every story has a story behind it—which is to say that your face, in its own way a story, the story that you present, has another, sometimes very different story underlying it, and it is through the skill of the photographer that these layers of story are revealed.

Painters and sculptors, whose publics are smaller, also approach our heads and faces with insight. They class themselves as artists and are more intellectually sophisticated—better educated than photographers. They have generally absorbed a certain amount of twentieth-century psychology, and their portraits may be filled or formed by their ideas and they may have a diagnostic intent. Do you want to know whether X, our subject, is a violent narcissist? Or whether his is a real, a human face, not a false ideological mask or disguise.

The photograph—to narrow it down—reduces us to two dimensions and it makes us small enough to be represented on a piece of paper or a frame of film. We have been trained by the camera to see the external world. We look *at* and not *into*, as one philosopher has put it. We do not allow ourselves to be *drawn* into what we see. We have been trained to go by the externals. The camera shows us only those, and it is we who do the rest. What we do this *with* is the imagination. What photographs have to show us is the external appearance of objects or beings in the real world, and this is only a portion of their reality. It is after all a convention.

I have known—and still know—many excellent photographers whose work I respect. There are demonic, sadistic camera technicians, too. All trades are like that. But neither the kindly nor the wicked ones can show us the realities we so hope—or long—to see.

Finally, there is the ancient Jewish rule forbidding graven images. My maternal grandfather refused to have his picture taken. But when he was dying my mother brought in a photographer and hid him behind the bushes.

This faded picture is one of my Old World legacies. I also inherited the brass family samovar and my mother's silver change purse. In this purse I now carry Betapace, Hytrin, and Coumadin tablets.

My grandfather's picture was taken in the late 1890s. He is sitting, dying in an apple orchard, his beard is spread over his upper body. His elbow rests on the top of his walking stick and his hand supports his head. His big eyes tell you that he is absorbed in *olam ha-bo*—the world to come, the next life. My mother used to say, "He would have been very angry with me. To make pictures was sinful [an *averah*], but I took the *averah* on myself."

When we were very young, my parents told us that until we came of age they would be responsible for our transgressions. But that is an altogether different matter. What I am saying here is that nowadays not even the nobs have their portraits painted, and the masses preserve the faces of ancestors in daguerreotypes and Kodaks. The critical mind sees an insignificant photographer hidden in the bushes, inserting a plate and pulling the cloth over his head. Perhaps the old man knew perfectly well that his picture was being taken. My mother was then old enough to bear the burden of this sin. She committed it because she loved him and was afraid of forgetting what he had looked like.

In any case, I have been not only photographed but cast in bronze and also painted. Since I am too impatient to sit still, painters and sculptors have worked from photographs. The Chicago Public Library exhibits the busts of bookish local boys. The artist who did my head was obliged to measure it while I was watching the Chicago Bulls on television. It was an important game and I didn't intend to miss it.

Considering the bronze head on display in the Harold Washington Library, I think that Pablo Picasso would have done it better. He might perhaps have given me a third eye and two noses. I'd have loved two noses.

But for a one-nose job, the bust in the Chicago library isn't at all bad.

Analyzing the Situation

1. Why do you suppose Saul Bellow, a famed writer, decided to write this short essay about photography? What is his position as speaker/writer in this situation?

2. Is the situation in which "Graven Images" participates still relevant? Why or why not?

3. Bellow begins "Graven Images" by addressing the power of the photographer. What role does power then play in the situation in which "Graven Images" participates?

Analyzing the Rhetoric

1. Several times in "Graven Images," Bellow refers to literary texts to explain and clarify what he means in his discussion of photographs. Why do you suppose Bellow relies on fictional texts to explain the points he makes?

2. What is *amour propre* and why does Bellow use this term to convey his point?

3. What role does the story about Bellow's grandparents play in Bellow's claim in "Graven Images"?

Discussing

1. Bellow's essay suggests that photographs represent "us," the figure in a photograph and that people who view photographs interpret the pictures to provide a kind of understanding about the person who appears in the picture. Do photographs provide information about a subject? Can people really know something about you by seeing your picture?

2. What does Bellow mean when he says that photographs reduce us to two dimensions?

3. How does Bellow feel about photographers?

Writing

1. Obviously, Saul Bellow wrote "Graven Images" before digital cameras, social media, and photo sharing applications like Flickr and Photobucket became ubiquitous parts of our daily lives. Given what Bellow says about photography in "Graven Images," how do you suppose Bellow might address the current role of digital photography in our lives? Write an essay that speculates as to how Saul Bellow might write "Graven Images" today.

2. One of Saul Bellow's provocative ideas in "Graven Images" is that photographs expose their subjects. We can certainly see this premise in contemporary culture's fascination with pictures that depict celebrities in less-than-ideal ways: without makeup, stumbling, intoxicated, fighting, disheveled, crying, angry, and so on. We tend, too, to circulate similar kinds of images of people who are not celebrities: our friends, strangers, and even family. Why might we be fascinated with pictures that expose? Taking into account Bellow's claims about photography and exposure, write an essay that addresses our cultural fascination with exposure.

3. Using Internet resources, locate between five and ten photographs of Saul Bellow. Given how he describes himself and photographs of himself in "Graven Images," describe what the images you located tell you about Bellow. That is, write a descriptive essay about Saul Bellow based on the pictures of him that you find online.

4. The title "Graven Images" refers to the Judeo-Christian tradition articulated in the Judeo-Christian Bible in the book *Exodus* in the delivery of the Ten Commandments: "Thou shalt not make unto thee any graven image, or any likeness of anything that is in heaven above, or that is in the earth beneath, or that is in the water under the earth. Thou shalt not bow down thyself to them, nor serve them: for I the Lord thy God am a jealous God, visiting the iniquity of the fathers upon the children unto the third and fourth generation of them that hate me" (20:4–6). The passage is understood to be a statement against idolatry, the worship of idols or images. Like the Judeo-Christian tradition, Islam also maintains strict doctrines against idolatry. In recent years, a number of volatile situations have emerged in which depictions of Allah have circulated in newspapers, at art exhibits, and on the Internet. Take some time to learn about why Islamic belief shuns the depiction of Allah. Write an essay that explains these beliefs and then considers how such beliefs conflict with concepts of freedom of expression and why such conflicts inevitably result in animosity.

Richard Drew, The Falling Man

Tom Junod

Tom Junod is an award-winning journalist and magazine writer who has twice won the American Society of Magazine Editors' National Magazine Award, the most prestigious award for magazine writers. Reprinted here is Junod's essay "Richard Drew, The Falling Man," which originally appeared in the September 8, 2009, edition of *Esquire*. The essay is about photographer Richard Drew's infamous photo "The Falling Man," taken during the September 11, 2001, attacks on the World Trade Center buildings in New York City. The 9/11 attacks are often referred to as the most photographed and videotaped event in history. As you read this essay, consider what Junod is saying not only about the "Falling Man" photo specifically, but also about the role of images in contemporary culture. Note his distinction between "iconic" photographs and other images, as well.

In many ways, "Richard Drew, The Falling Man" is about more than the 9/11 attacks, about more than Richard Drew and his photograph, and about more than the man in the picture. The essay is really about what culture says we should and shouldn't see, what we should and shouldn't have images of. As you read Tom Junod's essay, think about this aspect of his position and how he uses the situation of the Falling Man image to address this more-encompassing issue.

In the picture, he departs from this earth like an arrow. Although he has not chosen his fate, he appears to have, in his last instants of life, embraced it. If he were not falling, he might very well be flying. He appears relaxed, hurtling through the air. He appears comfortable in the grip of unimaginable motion. He does not appear intimidated by gravity's divine suction or by what awaits him. His arms are by his side, only slightly outriggered. His left leg is bent at the knee, almost casually. His white shirt, or jacket, or frock, is billowing free of his black pants. His black high-tops are still on his feet. In all the other pictures, the people who did what he did—who jumped—appear to be struggling against horrific discrepancies of scale. They are made puny by the backdrop of the towers, which loom like colossi, and then by the event itself. Some of them are shirtless; their shoes fly off as they flail and fall; they look confused, as though trying to swim down the side of a mountain. The man in the picture, by contrast, is perfectly vertical, and so is in accord with the lines of the buildings behind him. He

splits them, bisects them: Everything to the left of him in the picture is the North Tower; everything to the right, the South. Though oblivious to the geometric balance he has achieved, he is the essential element in the creation of a new flag, a banner composed entirely of steel bars shining in the sun. Some people who look at the picture see stoicism, willpower, a portrait of resignation; others see something else—something discordant and therefore terrible: freedom. There is something almost rebellious in the man's posture, as though once faced with the inevitability of death, he decided to get on with it; as though he were a missile, a spear, bent on attaining his own end. He is, fifteen seconds past 9:41 a.m. EST, the moment the picture is taken, in the clutches of pure physics, accelerating at a rate of thirty-two feet per second squared. He will soon be traveling at upwards of 150 miles per hour, and he is upside down. In the picture, he is frozen; in his life outside the frame, he drops and keeps dropping until he disappears.

*****

The photographer is no stranger to history; he knows it is something that happens later. In the actual moment history is made, it is usually made in terror and confusion, and so it is up to people like him—paid witnesses—to have the presence of mind to attend to its manufacture. The photographer has that presence of mind and has had it since he was a young man. When he was twenty-one years old, he was standing right behind Bobby Kennedy when Bobby Kennedy was shot in the head. His jacket was spattered with Kennedy's blood, but he jumped on a table and shot pictures of Kennedy's open and ebbing eyes, and then of Ethel Kennedy crouching over her husband and begging photographers—begging him—not to take pictures.

Richard Drew has never done that. Although he has preserved the jacket patterned with Kennedy's blood, he has never not taken a picture, never averted his eye. He works for the Associated Press. He is a journalist. It is not up to him to reject the images that fill his frame, because one never knows when history is made until one makes it. It is not even up to him to distinguish if a body is alive or dead, because the camera makes no such distinctions, and he is in the business of shooting bodies, as all photographers are, unless they are Ansel Adams. Indeed, he was shooting bodies on the morning of September 11, 2001. On assignment for the AP, he was shooting a maternity fashion show in Bryant Park, notable, he says, "because it featured actual pregnant models." He was fifty-four years old. He wore glasses. He was sparse in the scalp, gray in the beard, hard in the head. In a lifetime of taking pictures, he has found a way to be both mild-mannered and brusque, patient and very, very quick. He was doing what he always does at fashion shows—"staking out real estate"—when a CNN cameraman with an earpiece said that a plane had crashed into the North Tower, and Drew's editor rang his cell phone. He packed his equipment into a bag and gambled on taking the subway downtown. Although it was still running, he was the only one on it. He got out at the Chambers Street station and saw that both towers had been turned into smokestacks. Staking out his real estate, he walked west, to where ambulances were gathering, because rescue workers "usually won't throw you out." Then he heard people gasping. People on the ground were gasping because people in the building were jumping. He started shooting pictures through a 200mm lens. He was standing between a cop and an emergency technician, and each time one of them cried, "There goes another," his camera found a falling body and followed it down for a nine- or twelve-shot sequence. He shot ten or fifteen of them before he heard the rumbling of the South Tower and witnessed, through the winnowing exclusivity of his lens, its collapse. He was engulfed in a mobile ruin, but he grabbed a mask from an ambulance and photographed the top of the North Tower "exploding like a mushroom" and raining debris. He discovered that there is such a thing as being too close, and, deciding that he had fulfilled his professional obligations, Richard Drew joined the throng of ashen humanity heading north, walking until he reached his office at Rockefeller Center.

There was no terror or confusion at the Associated Press. There was, instead, that feeling of history being manufactured; although the office was as crowded as he'd ever seen it, there was, instead, "the wonderful calm that comes into play when people are really doing their jobs." So Drew did his: He inserted the disc from his digital camera into his laptop and recognized, instantly, what only his camera had seen—something iconic in the extended annihilation of a falling man. He didn't look at any of the other pictures in the sequence; he didn't have to. "You learn in photo editing to look for the frame," he says. "You have to recognize it. That picture just jumped off the screen because of its verticality and symmetry. It just had that look."

He sent the image to the AP's server. The next morning, it appeared on page seven of *The New York Times*. It appeared in hundreds of newspapers, all over the country, all over the world. The man inside the frame—the Falling Man—was not identified.

*****

They began jumping not long after the first plane hit the North Tower, not long after the fire started. They kept jumping until the tower fell. They jumped through windows already broken and then, later, through windows they broke themselves. They jumped to escape the smoke and the fire; they jumped when the ceilings fell and the floors collapsed; they jumped just to breathe once more before they died. They jumped continually, from all four sides of the building, and from all floors above and around the building's fatal wound. They jumped from the offices of Marsh & McLennan, the insurance company; from the offices of Cantor Fitzgerald, the bond-trading company; from Windows on the World, the restaurant on the 106th and 107th floors—the top. For more than an hour and a half, they streamed from the building, one after another, consecutively rather than en masse, as if each individual required the sight of another individual jumping before mustering the courage to jump himself or herself. One photograph, taken at a distance, shows people jumping in perfect sequence, like parachutists, forming an arc composed of three plummeting people, evenly spaced. Indeed, there were reports that some tried parachuting, before the force generated by their fall ripped the drapes, the tablecloths, the desperately gathered fabric, from their hands. They were all, obviously, very much alive on their way down, and their way down lasted an approximate count of ten seconds. They were all, obviously, not just killed when they landed but destroyed, in body though not, one prays, in soul. One hit a fireman on the ground and killed him; the fireman's body was anointed by Father Mychal Judge, whose own death, shortly thereafter, was embraced as an example of martyrdom after the photograph—the redemptive tableau—of firefighters carrying his body from the rubble made its way around the world.

From the beginning, the spectacle of doomed people jumping from the upper floors of the World Trade Center resisted redemption. They were called "jumpers" or "the jumpers," as though they represented a new lemming like class. The trial that hundreds endured in the building and then in the air became its own kind of trial for the thousands watching them from the ground. No one ever got used to it; no one who saw it wished to see it again, although, of course, many saw it again. Each jumper, no matter how many there were, brought fresh horror, elicited shock, tested the spirit, struck a lasting blow. Those tumbling through the air remained, by all accounts, eerily silent; those on the ground screamed. It was the sight of the jumpers that prompted Rudy Giuliani to say to his police commissioner, "We're in uncharted waters now." It was the sight of the jumpers that prompted a woman to wail, "God! Save their souls! They're jumping! Oh, please God! Save their souls!" And it was, at last, the sight of the jumpers that provided the corrective to those who insisted on saying that what they were witnessing was "like a movie," for this was an ending as unimaginable as it was unbearable: Americans responding to the worst terrorist attack in the history of the world with acts of heroism, with acts of sacrifice, with acts of generosity, with acts of martyrdom, and, by terrible necessity, with one prolonged act of—if these words can be applied to mass murder—mass suicide.

*****

In most American newspapers, the photograph that Richard Drew took of the Falling Man ran once and never again. Papers all over the country, from the *Fort Worth Star-Telegram* to the *Memphis Commercial Appeal* to *The Denver Post,* were forced to defend themselves against charges that they exploited a man's death, stripped him of his dignity, invaded his privacy, turned tragedy into leering pornography. Most letters of complaint stated the obvious: that someone seeing the picture had to know who it was. Still, even as Drew's photograph became at once iconic and impermissible, its subject remained unnamed. An editor at the *Toronto Globe and Mail* assigned a reporter named Peter Cheney to solve the mystery. Cheney at first despaired of his task; the entire city, after all, was wallpapered with Kinkoed flyers advertising the faces of the missing and the lost and the dead. Then he applied himself, sending the digital photograph to a shop that clarified and enhanced it. Now information emerged: It appeared to him that the man was most likely not black but dark-skinned, probably Latino. He wore a goatee. And the white shirt billowing from his black pants was not a shirt but rather appeared to be a tunic of some sort, the kind of jacket a restaurant worker wears. Windows on the World, the restaurant at the top of the North Tower, lost seventy-nine of its employees on September 11, as well as ninety-one of its patrons. It was likely that the Falling Man numbered among them. But which one was he? Over dinner, Cheney spent an evening discussing this question with friends, then said goodnight and walked through Times Square. It was after midnight, eight days after the attacks. The missing posters were still everywhere, but Cheney was able to focus on one that seemed to present itself to him—a poster portraying a man who worked at Windows as a pastry chef, who was dressed in a white tunic, who wore a goatee, who was Latino. His name was Norberto Hernandez. He lived in Queens. Cheney took the enhanced print of the Richard Drew photograph to the family, in particular to Norberto Hernandez's brother Tino and sister Milagros. They said yes, that was Norberto. Milagros had watched footage of the people jumping on that terrible morning, before the television stations stopped showing it. She had seen one of the jumpers distinguished by the grace of his fall—by his resemblance to an Olympic diver—and surmised that he had to be her brother. Now she saw, and she knew. All that remained was for Peter Cheney to confirm the identification with Norberto's wife and his three daughters. They did not want to talk to him, especially after Norberto's remains were found and identified by the stamp of his DNA—a torso, an arm. So he went to the funeral. He brought his print of Drew's photograph with him and showed it to Jacqueline Hernandez, the oldest of Norberto's three daughters. She looked briefly at the picture, then at Cheney, and ordered him to leave.

What Cheney remembers her saying, in her anger, in her offended grief: "That piece of shit is not my father."

*****

The resistance to the image—to the images—started early, started immediately, started on the ground. A mother whispering to her distraught child a consoling lie: "Maybe they're just birds, honey." Bill Feehan, second in command at the fire department, chasing a bystander who was panning the jumpers with his video camera, demanding that he turn it off, bellowing, "Don't you have any human decency?" before dying himself when the building came down. In the most photographed and videotaped day in the history of the world, the images of people jumping were the only images that became, by consensus, taboo—the only images from which Americans were proud to avert their eyes. All over the world, people saw the human stream debouch from the top of the North Tower, but here in the United States, we saw these images only until the networks decided not to allow such a harrowing view, out of respect for the families of those so publicly dying. At CNN, the footage was shown live, before people working in the newsroom knew what was happening; then, after what Walter Isaacson, who was then chairman of the network's news bureau, calls "agonized discussions" with the "standards guy," it was shown only if people in it were blurred and unidentifiable; then it was not shown at all.

And so it went. In *9/11*, the documentary extracted from videotape shot by French brothers Jules and Gedeon Naudet, the filmmakers included a sonic sampling of the booming, rattling explosions the jumpers made upon impact but edited out the most disturbing thing about the sounds: the sheer frequency with which they occurred. In *Rudy*, the docudrama starring James Woods in the role of Mayor Giuliani, archival footage of the jumpers was first included, then cut out. In *Here Is New York*, an extensive exhibition of 9/11 images culled from the work of photographers both amateur and professional, there was, in the section titled "Victims," but one picture of the jumpers, taken at a respectful distance; attached to it, on the *Here Is New York* Website, a visitor offers this commentary: "This image is what made me glad for censuring [*sic*] in the endless pursuant media coverage." More and more, the jumpers—and their images—were relegated to the Internet underbelly, where they became the provenance of the shock sites that also traffic in the autopsy photos of Nicole Brown Simpson and the videotape of Daniel Pearl's execution, and where it is impossible to look at them without attendant feelings of shame and guilt. In a nation of voyeurs, the desire to face the most disturbing aspects of our most disturbing day was somehow ascribed to voyeurism, as though the jumpers' experience, instead of being central to the horror, was tangential to it, a sideshow best forgotten.

It was no sideshow. The two most reputable estimates of the number of people who jumped to their deaths were prepared by *The New York Times* and *USA Today*. They differed dramatically. The *Times*, admittedly conservative, decided to count only what its reporters actually saw in the footage they collected, and it arrived at a figure of fifty. *USA Today*, whose editors used eyewitness accounts and forensic evidence in addition to what they found on video, came to the conclusion that at least two hundred people died by jumping—a count that the newspaper said authorities did not dispute. Both are intolerable estimates of human loss, but if the number provided by *USA Today* is accurate, then between 7 and 8 percent of those who died in New York City on September 11, 2001, died by jumping out of the buildings; it means that if we consider only the

North Tower, where the vast majority of jumpers came from, the ratio is more like one in six.

And yet if one calls the New York Medical Examiner's Office to learn its own estimate of how many people might have jumped, one does not get an answer but an admonition: "We don't like to say they jumped. They didn't jump. Nobody jumped. They were forced out, or blown out." And if one Googles the words "how many jumped on 9/11," one falls into some blogger's trap, slugged "Go Away, No Jumpers Here," where the bait is one's own need to know: "I've got at least three entries in my referrer logs that show someone is doing a search on Google for 'how many people jumped from WTC.' My September 11 post had made mention of that terrible occurance [sic], so now any pervert looking for that will get my site's URL. I'm disgusted. I tried, but cannot find any reason someone would want to know something like that.... Whatever. If that's why you're here—you're busted. Now go away."

*****

Eric Fischl did not go away. Neither did he turn away or avert his eyes. A year before September 11, he had taken photographs of a model tumbling around on the floor of a studio. He had thought of using the photographs as the basis of a sculpture. Now, though, he had lost a friend who had been trapped on the 106th floor of the North Tower. Now, as he worked on his sculpture, he sought to express the extremity of his feelings by making a monument to what he calls the "extremity of choice" faced by the people who jumped. He worked nine months on the larger-than-life bronze he called *Tumbling Woman,* and as he transformed a woman tumbling on the floor into a woman tumbling through eternity, he succeeded in transfiguring the very local horror of the jumpers into something universal—in redeeming an image many regarded as irredeemable. Indeed, *Tumbling Woman* was perhaps the redemptive image of 9/11— and yet it was not merely resisted; it was rejected. The day after *Tumbling Woman* was exhibited in New York's Rockefeller Center, Andrea Peyser of the *New York Post* denounced it in a column titled "Shameful Art Attack,"

in which she argued that Fischl had no right to ambush grieving New Yorkers with the very distillation of their own sadness ... in which she essentially argued the right to look away. Because it was based on a model rolling on the floor, the statue was treated as an evocation of impact—as a portrayal of literal, rather than figurative, violence.

"I was trying to say something about the way we all feel," Fischl says, "but people thought I was trying to say something about the way they feel—that I was trying to take away something only they possessed. They thought that I was trying to say something about the people they lost. 'That image is not my father. You don't even know my father. How dare you try telling me how I feel about my father?'" Fischl wound up apologizing—"I was ashamed to have added to anybody's pain"—but it didn't matter.

Jerry Speyer, a trustee of the Museum of Modern Art who runs Rockefeller Center, ended the exhibition of *Tumbling Woman* after a week. "I pleaded with him not to do it," Fischl says. "I thought that if we could wait it out, other voices would pipe up and carry the day. He said, 'You don't understand. I'm getting bomb threats.' I said, 'People who just lost loved ones to terrorism are not going to bomb somebody.' He said, 'I can't take that chance.'"

*****

Photographs lie. Even great photographs. Especially great photographs. The Falling Man in Richard Drew's picture fell in the manner suggested by the photograph for only a fraction of a second, and then kept falling. The photograph functioned as a study of doomed verticality, a fantasia of straight lines, with a human being slivered at the center, like a spike. In truth, however, the Falling Man fell with neither the precision of an arrow nor the grace of an Olympic diver. He fell like everyone else, like all the other jumpers—trying to hold on to the life he was leaving, which is to say that he fell desperately, inelegantly. In Drew's famous photograph, his humanity is in accord with the lines of the buildings. In the rest of the sequence—the eleven outtakes—his humanity stands apart. He is not augmented by aesthetics; he is merely human, and his humanity, startled and in some cases horizontal, obliterates everything else in the frame.

In the complete sequence of photographs, truth is subordinate to the facts that emerge slowly, pitilessly, frame by frame. In the sequence, the Falling Man shows his face to the camera in the two frames before the published one, and after that there is an unveiling, nearly an unpeeling, as the force generated by the fall rips the white jacket off his back. The facts that emerge from the entire sequence suggest that the Toronto reporter, Peter Cheney, got some things right in his effort to solve the mystery presented by Drew's published photo. The Falling Man has a dark cast to his skin and wears a goatee. He is probably a food-service worker. He seems lanky, with the length and narrowness of his face—like that of a medieval Christ—possibly accentuated by the push of the wind and the pull of gravity. But seventy-nine people died on the morning of September 11 after going to work at Windows on the World. Another twenty-one died while in the employ of Forte Food, a catering service that fed the traders at Cantor Fitzgerald. Many of the dead were Latino, or light-skinned black men, or Indian, or Arab. Many had dark hair cut short. Many had mustaches and goatees. Indeed, to anyone trying to figure out the identity of the Falling Man, the few salient characteristics that can be discerned in the original series of photographs raise as many possibilities as they exclude. There is, however, one fact that is decisive. Whoever the Falling Man may be, he was wearing a bright-orange shirt under his white top. It is the one inarguable fact that the brute force of the fall reveals. No one can know if the tunic or shirt, open at the back, is being pulled away from him, or if the fall is simply tearing the white fabric to pieces. But anyone can see he is wearing an orange shirt. If they saw these pictures, members of his family would be able to see that he is wearing an orange shirt. They might even be able to remember if he owned an orange shirt, if he was the kind of guy who would own an orange shirt, if he wore an orange shirt to work that morning. Surely they would; surely someone would

remember what he was wearing when he went to work on the last morning of his life....

But now the Falling Man is falling through more than the blank blue sky. He is falling through the vast spaces of memory and picking up speed.

*****

Neil Levin, executive director of the Port Authority of New York and New Jersey, had breakfast at Windows on the World, on the 106th floor of the World Trade Center's North Tower, on the morning of September 11. He never came home. His wife, Christy Ferer, won't talk about any of the particulars of his death. She works for New York mayor Mike Bloomberg as the liaison between the mayor's office and the 9/11 families and has poured the energy aroused by her grief into her work, which, before the first anniversary of the attack, called for her to visit television executives and ask them not to use the most disturbing footage—including the footage of the jumpers—in their memorial broadcasts. She is a close friend of Eric Fischl's, as was her husband, so when the artist asked, she agreed to take a look at *Tumbling Woman.* It, in her words, "hit me in the gut," but she felt that Fischl had the right to create and exhibit it. Now she's come to the conclusion that the controversy may have been largely a matter of timing. Maybe it was just too soon to show something like that. After all, not long before her husband died, she traveled with him to Auschwitz, where piles of confiscated eyeglasses and extracted tooth fillings are on exhibit. "They can show that now," she says. "But that was a long time ago. They couldn't show things like that then ...."

In fact, they did, at least in photographic form, and the pictures that came out of the death camps of Europe were treated as essential acts of witness, without particular regard to the sensitivities of those who appeared in them or the surviving families of the dead. They were shown, as Richard Drew's photographs of the freshly assassinated Robert Kennedy were shown. They were shown, as the photographs of Ethel Kennedy pleading with photographers not to take photographs were shown. They were shown as the photograph of the little

Vietnamese girl running naked after a napalm attack was shown. They were shown as the photograph of Father Mychal Judge, graphically and unmistakably dead, was shown, and accepted as a kind of testament. They were shown as everything is shown, for, like the lens of a camera, history is a force that does not discriminate. What distinguishes the pictures of the jumpers from the pictures that have come before is that we—we Americans—are being asked to discriminate on their behalf. What distinguishes them, historically, is that we, as patriotic Americans, have agreed not to look at them. Dozens, scores, maybe hundreds of people died by leaping from a burning building, and we have somehow taken it upon ourselves to deem their deaths unworthy of witness—because we have somehow deemed the act of witness, in this one regard, unworthy of us.

*****

Catherine Hernandez never saw the photo the reporter carried under his arm at her father's funeral. Neither did her mother, Eulogia. Her sister Jacqueline did, and her outrage assured that the reporter left—was forcibly evicted—before he did any more damage. But the picture has followed Catherine and Eulogia and the entire Hernandez family. There was nothing more important to Norberto Hernandez than family. His motto: "Together Forever." But the Hernandezes are not together anymore. The picture split them. Those who knew, right away, that the picture was not Norberto—his wife and his daughters—have become estranged from those who pondered the possibility that it was him for the benefit of a reporter's notepad. With Norberto alive, the extended family all lived in the same neighborhood in Queens. Now Eulogia and her daughters have moved to a house on Long Island because Tatiana—who is now sixteen and who bears a resemblance to Norberto Hernandez: the wide face, the dark brows, the thick dark lips, thinly smiling—kept seeing visions of her father in the house and kept hearing the whispered suggestions that he died by jumping out a window.

He could not have died by jumping out a window.

All over the world, people who read Peter Cheney's story believe that Norberto died by jumping out a window. People have written poems about Norberto jumping out a window. People have called the Hernandezes with offers of money—either charity or payment for interviews—because they read about Norberto jumping out a window. But he couldn't have jumped out a window, his family knows, because he wouldn't have jumped out a window: not Papi. "He was trying to come home," Catherine says one morning, in a living room primarily decorated with framed photographs of her father. "He was trying to come home to us, and he knew he wasn't going to make it by jumping out a window." She is a lovely, dark-skinned, brown-eyed girl, twenty-two years old, dressed in a T-shirt and sweats and sandals. She is sitting on a couch next to her mother, who is caramel-colored, with coppery hair tied close to her scalp, and who is wearing a cotton dress checked with the color of the sky. Eulogia speaks half the time in determined English, and then, when she gets frustrated with the rate of revelation, pours rapid-fire Spanish into the ear of her daughter, who translates. "My mother says she knows that when he died, he was thinking about us. She says that she could see him thinking about us. I know that sounds strange, but she knew him. They were together since they were fifteen." The Norberto Hernandez Eulogia knew would not have been deterred by smoke or by fire in his effort to come home to her. The Norberto Hernandez she knew would have endured any pain before he jumped out of a window. When the Norberto Hernandez she knew died, his eyes were fixed on what he saw in his heart—the faces of his wife and his daughters—and not on the terrible beauty of an empty sky.

How well did she know him? "I dressed him," Eulogia says in English, a smile appearing on her face at the same time as a shiny coat of tears. "Every morning. That morning, I remember. He wore Old Navy underwear. Green. He wore black socks. He wore blue pants: jeans. He wore a Casio watch. He wore an Old Navy shirt. Blue. With checks." What did he wear after she drove him, as she always did, to the subway station and watched him wave to her as he disappeared down the stairs? "He changed clothes at the restaurant," says Catherine, who worked with her father at Windows on the World. "He was a pastry chef, so he wore white pants, or chef's pants—you know, black-and-white check. He wore a white jacket. Under that, he had to wear a white T-shirt." What about an orange shirt? "No," Eulogia says. "My husband did not have an orange shirt."

There are pictures. There are pictures of the Falling Man as he fell. Do they want to see them? Catherine says no, on her mother's behalf—"My mother should not see"—but then, when she steps outside and sits down on the steps of the front porch, she says, "Please—show me. Hurry. Before my mother comes." When she sees the twelve-frame sequence, she lets out a gasping, muted call for her mother, but Eulogia is already over her shoulder, reaching for the pictures. She looks at them one after another, and then her face fixes itself into an expression of triumph and scorn. "That is not my husband," she says, handing the photographs back. "You see? Only I know Norberto." She reaches for the photographs again, and then, after studying them, shakes her head with a vehement finality. "The man in this picture is a black man." She asks for copies of the pictures so that she can show them to the people who believed that Norberto jumped out a window, while Catherine sits on the step with her palm spread over her heart. "They said my father was going to hell because he jumped," she says. "On the Internet. They said my father was taken to hell with the devil. I don't know what I would have done if it was him. I would have had a nervous breakdown, I guess. They would have found me in a mental ward somewhere ...."

Her mother is standing at the front door, about to go back inside her house. Her face has already lost its belligerent pride and has turned once again into a mask of composed, almost wistful sadness. "Please," she says as she closes the door in a stain of morning sunlight. "Please clear my husband's name."

*****

A phone rings in Connecticut. A woman answers. A man on the other end is looking to identify a photo that ran in *The New York Times* on September 12, 2001.

"Tell me what the photo looks like," she says. It's a famous picture, the man says—the famous picture of a man falling. "Is it the one called 'Swan Dive' on Rotten. com?" the woman asks. It may be, the man says. "Yes, that might have been my son," the woman says.

She lost both her sons on September 11. They worked together at Cantor Fitzgerald. They worked on the equities desk. They worked back-to-back. No, the man on the phone says, the man in the photograph is probably a food-service worker. He's wearing a white jacket. He's upside down. "Then that's not my son," she says. "My son was wearing a dark shirt and khaki pants."

She knows what he was wearing because of her determination to know what happened to her sons on that day—because of her determination to look and to see. She did not start with that determination. She stopped reading the newspaper after September 11, stopped watching TV. Then, on New Year's Eve, she picked up a copy of *The New York Times* and saw, in a year-end review, a picture of Cantor Fitzgerald employees crowding the edge of the cliff formed by a dying building. In the posture—the attitude—of one of them, she thought she recognized the habits of her son. So she called the photographer and asked him to enlarge and clarify the picture. Demanded that he do it. And then she knew, or knew as much as it was possible to know. Both of her sons were in the picture. One was standing in the window, almost brazenly. The other was sitting inside. She does not need to say what may have happened next.

"The thing I hold was that both of my sons were together," she says, her instantaneous tears lifting her voice an octave. "But I sometimes wonder how long they knew. They're puzzled, they're uncertain, they're scared—but when did they know? When did the moment come when they lost hope? Maybe it came so quick ...."

The man on the phone does not ask if she thinks her sons jumped. He does not have it in him, and anyway, she has given him an answer.

The Hernandezes looked at the decision to jump as a betrayal of love—as something Norberto was being accused of. The woman in Connecticut looks at the decision to jump as a loss of hope—as an absence that we, the living, now have to live with. She chooses to live with it by looking, by seeing, by trying to know—by making an act of private witness. She could have chosen to keep her eyes closed. And so now the man on the phone asks the question that he called to ask in the first place: Did she make the right choice?

"I made the only choice I could have made," the woman answers. "I could never have made the choice not to know."

Catherine Hernandez thought she knew who the Falling Man was as soon as she saw the series of pictures, but she wouldn't say his name. "He had a sister who was with him that morning," she said, "and he told his mother that he would take care of her. He would never have left her alone by jumping." She did say, however, that the man was Indian, so it was easy to figure out that his name was Sean Singh. But Sean was too small to be the Falling Man. He was clean-shaven. He worked at Windows on the World in the audiovisual department, so he probably would have been wearing a shirt and tie instead of a white chef's coat. None of the former Windows employees who were interviewed believe the Falling Man looks anything like Sean Singh.

Besides, he had a sister. He never would have left her alone.

A manager at Windows looked at the pictures once and said the Falling Man was Wilder Gomez. Then a few days later he studied them closely and changed his mind. Wrong hair. Wrong clothes. Wrong body type. It was the same with Charlie Mauro. It was the same with Junior Jimenez. Junior worked in the kitchen and would have been wearing checked pants. Charlie worked in purchasing and had no cause to wear a white jacket. Besides, Charlie was a very large man. The Falling Man appears fairly stout in Richard Drew's published photo but almost elongated in the rest of the sequence.

The rest of the kitchen workers were, like Norberto Hernandez, eliminated from consideration by their outfits. The banquet servers may have been wearing white and black, but no one remembered any banquet server who looked anything like the Falling Man.

Forte Food was the other food-service company that lost people on September 11, 2001. But all of its male employees worked in the kitchen, which means that they wore either checked or white pants. And nobody would have been allowed to wear an orange shirt under the white serving coat.

But someone who used to work for Forte remembers a guy who used to come around and get food for the Cantor executives. Black guy. Tall, with a mustache and a goatee. Wore a chef's coat, open, with a loud shirt underneath.

Nobody at Cantor remembers anyone like that.

Of course, the only way to find out the identity of the Falling Man is to call the families of anyone who might be the Falling Man and ask what they know about their son's or husband's or father's last day on earth. Ask if he went to work wearing an orange shirt.

But should those calls be made? Should those questions be asked? Would they only heap pain upon the already anguished? Would they be regarded as an insult to the memory of the dead, the way the Hernandez family regarded the imputation that Norberto Hernandez was the Falling Man? Or would they be regarded as steps to some act of redemptive witness?

Jonathan Briley worked at Windows on the World. Some of his coworkers, when they saw Richard Drew's photographs, thought he might be the Falling Man. He was a light-skinned black man. He was over six five. He was forty-three. He had a mustache and a goatee and close-cropped hair. He had a wife named Hillary.

Jonathan Briley's father is a preacher, a man who has devoted his whole life to serving the Lord. After September 11, he gathered his family together to ask God to tell him where his son was. No: He demanded it. He used these words: "Lord, I demand to know where my son is." For three hours straight, he prayed in his deep voice, until he spent the grace he had accumulated over a lifetime in the insistence of his appeal.

The next day, the FBI called. They'd found his son's body. It was, miraculously, intact.

The preacher's youngest son, Timothy, went to identify his brother. He recognized him by his shoes: He was wearing black high-tops. Timothy removed one of them and took it home and put it in his garage, as a kind of memorial.

Timothy knew all about the Falling Man. He is a cop in Mount Vernon, New York, and in the week after his brother died, someone had left a September 12 newspaper open in the locker room. He saw the photograph of the Falling Man and, in anger, he refused to look at it again. But he couldn't throw it away. Instead, he stuffed it in the bottom of his locker, where—like the black shoe in his garage—it became permanent.

Jonathan's sister Gwendolyn knew about the Falling Man, too. She saw the picture the day it was published. She knew that Jonathan had asthma, and in the smoke and the heat would have done anything just to breathe ....

The both of them, Timothy and Gwendolyn, knew what Jonathan wore to work on most days. He wore a white shirt and black pants, along with the high-top black shoes. Timothy also knew what Jonathan sometimes wore under his shirt: an orange T-shirt. Jonathan wore that orange T-shirt everywhere. He wore that shirt all the time. He wore it so often that Timothy used to make fun of him: When are you gonna get rid of that orange T-shirt, Slim?

But when Timothy identified his brother's body, none of his clothes were recognizable except the black shoes. And when Jonathan went to work on the morning of September 11, 2001, he'd left early and kissed his wife goodbye while she was still sleeping. She never saw the clothes he was wearing. After she learned that he was dead, she packed his clothes away and never inventoried what specific articles of clothing might be missing.

Is Jonathan Briley the Falling Man? He might be. But maybe he didn't jump from the window as a betrayal of love or because he lost hope. Maybe he jumped to fulfill the terms of a miracle. Maybe he jumped to come home to his family. Maybe he didn't jump at all, because no one can jump into the arms of God.

Oh, no. You have to fall.

Yes, Jonathan Briley might be the Falling Man. But the only certainty we have is the certainty we had at the start: At fifteen seconds after 9:41 a.m., on September 11, 2001, a photographer named Richard Drew took a picture of a man falling through the sky—falling through time as well as through space. The picture went all around the world, and then disappeared, as if we willed it away. One of the most famous photographs in human history became an unmarked grave, and the man buried inside its frame—the Falling Man—became the Unknown Soldier in a war whose end we have not yet seen. Richard Drew's photograph is all we know of him, and yet all we know of him becomes a measure of what we know of ourselves. The picture is his cenotaph, and like the monuments dedicated to the memory of unknown soldiers everywhere, it asks that we look at it, and make one simple acknowledgment.

That we have known who the Falling Man is all along.

Analyzing the Situation

1. What role does kairos—timing—play in the situation in which Tom Junod writes this essay? Think, for instance, about why Junod's essay did not appear until eight years after the Falling Man photograph was taken. Think, too, about the photograph's "timelessness" and the fleeting moment it preserves.

2. If we understand part of Tom Junod's essay to be about what should be seen and not seen, shown and not shown, can we also ask whether Junod should or shouldn't write about the image? What is the ecological relationship between the Falling Man photograph and Junod's essay and how we "read" each one?

3. On September 9, 2011, ten years after Richard Drew took the Falling Man photograph and two years after Tom Junod published "Richard Drew, Falling Man," Junod published a follow-up article in *Esquire* called "Surviving the Fall: Ten Years later, Putting the Falling Man to Rest," which can be found on the *Esquire* web pages. Take some time

to read this follow-up article and consider what the more recent piece contributes to the situation in which the first essay participated.

Analyzing the Rhetoric

1. What does Junod mean by the final sentence of the essay? Is this an effective way to end this essay? Why or why not?

2. When Tom Junod's essay first appeared in *Esquire* on September 8, 2009, Richard Drew's "The Falling Man" photograph appeared at the beginning of the essay just as it does here. What is the rhetorical effect of including the photo with the essay? What is the effect of placing the photo at the beginning of the essay rather than in the middle or at the end of the essay?

3. At several points in his essay, Junod provides visual rhetorical analysis of the Falling Man photograph. What is the rhetorical purpose of Junod's visual rhetorical analysis within his essay?

Discussing

1. We often compare events in our lives—particularly tragic, unbelievable events—as being "like a movie." The phrase suggests a degree of unreality, something beyond belief. In his essay, Junod writes: "And it was, at last, the sight of the jumpers that provided the corrective to those who insisted on saying that what they were witnessing was 'like a movie,' for this was an ending as unimaginable as it was unbearable." Why do you suppose we explain things as being like movies? Why does Junod say that the jumpers would not let us see the 9/11 events as being "like a movie"?

2. When discussing Norberto Hernandez's sister Milagros seeing the Falling Man photograph, Junod writes "Now she saw, and she knew." What is the relationship between seeing and knowing? Why do we understand seeing as leading to—or even equating—knowing?

3. Without pictures like the Falling Man, without countless pictures and videotapes of the 9/11 events, what becomes of those events?

Writing

1. Tom Junod concludes "Richard Drew, The Falling Man" by provocatively saying that we have always known who the falling man was. But does it matter who the falling man was? Why do we culturally have the need to name the falling man? Why do we want to give the falling man identity? Write an essay that considers why we need to know who the falling man in the picture is.

2. In "Richard Drew, The Falling Man," Tom Junod tells us about Eric Fischl's controversial sculpture *Tumbling Woman*, which drew significant criticism because it reminded viewers of those who died when falling from the World Trade Center buildings. Certainly, Fischl intended for his sculpture to be connected to those terrible events, but was public response to the sculpture warranted? Was the museum director's response to the criticism responsible? Consider the situation of Fischl's sculpted image and write a response to the situation. Should Fischl's sculpture be visible publically?

3. Richard Drew's "The Falling Man" is not the only photograph taken during the 9/11 attacks and aftermath that became iconic. Conduct some research and identify three other photographs that are iconic of the 9/11 events. Analyze each photograph, and write an informative essay that explains why each attained the recognition and status it did.

4. Junod writes: "In the most photographed and videotaped day in the history of the world, the images of people jumping were the only images that became, by consensus, taboo—the only images from which Americans were proud to avert their eyes. All over the world, people saw the human stream debouch from the top of the North Tower, but here in the United States, we saw these images only until the networks decided not to allow such a harrowing view, out of respect for the families of those so publicly dying." Consider this attitude toward the families of the dying. Then conduct some research and consider how images of the dying and dead were handled during Hurricane Katrina. Why might such respect not have been granted during that tragic event, as well?

Debate Grows over Use of Sexual Assault Photo

Michelle Goldberg

Michelle Goldberg is senior contributing writer for *The Daily Beat/Newsweek*. In 2007, her first book, *Kingdom Coming: The Rise of Christian Nationalism*, was a finalist for the 2007 New York Public Library Helen Bernstein Award for Excellence in Journalism. Goldberg spent two years traveling the world conducting research that would result in the publication of her second book, *The Means of Reproduction: Sex, Power, and the Future of the World*, which addresses international arguments over reproductive rights. In addition to her books, her writing has appeared in *Salon.com*, *Glamour*, *Rolling Stone*, *The Nation*, *New York Magazine*, and many newspapers.

In April 2002, Michelle Goldberg published the article reprinted here in *Women's eNews*, a nonprofit news service that covers "issues of particular concern to women and providing women's perspectives on public policy." The article, "Debate Grows over Use of Sexual Assault Photo," tells the story of a photograph taken of a sexual assault during Seattle's 2001 Mardi Gras celebration. The article asks as to the ethics of what kinds of photographs should and shouldn't be published and the ethics of media representation. As you read the article, be alert to the ways in which Goldberg transitions from the conversation of the Seattle Mardi Gras photograph in question to more encompassing discussions about media depictions of victims.

There was nothing photographer Mike Urban could do except snap.

A staff photographer for the *Seattle Post-Intelligencer*, Urban was in downtown Seattle's Pioneer Square covering the 2001 Mardi Gras celebration, which had erupted into rioting that would leave one man dead.

From his perch on a fire escape, he saw a group of young men start up the typical Mardi Gras chant demanding that a woman bare her breasts. She refused and they attacked. In an incident that, according to the newspaper, echoed several others that night, her clothes were ripped off and she was groped by dozens of hands before escaping. Urban caught it all on film.

Until recently, none of the pictures Urban took of the assault were ever published. Like most newspapers, the *Seattle Post-Intelligencer* has a policy against naming rape and sexual assault victims, and, as executive editor Ken Bunting said, "If the intent in not publishing the name of a rape victim is not to subject her to further trauma and humiliation, certainly publishing her likeness, her partially unclad body, is taking it several steps too far." Instead, the paper turned the photos over to the police and ran a front-page story that described the attacks without printing details that might identify the victims.

But last month, one of Urban's pictures won first place in the National Press Photographers Association Best of Photojournalism contest in the domestic newspaper category. The contest's winning photographs have been published on the association's Web site and will appear on CD-ROM and in a book. The picture of the assaulted woman, splayed out like a sacrifice, hands grabbing her breasts and genitals, is among them.

Though her face is digitally distorted so she can't be easily recognized, the photographers association's decision to release the picture has spurred controversy, pitting journalism's duty to disseminate the truth against the privacy rights of a violated woman.

The Poynter Institute, the Florida journalism school where the contest was judged, decided to leave the picture off its Web site, where all the other contest winners are displayed. Bunting said, "We are gratified that the Poynter Institute chose not to publish it. We thought it was inappropriate in March 2001 and I still think it's inappropriate for publication."

Aly Colon, a member of the Ethics Faculty at Poynter, opposed publishing the photo because of the "additional harm you may be causing this individual, seeing herself again in this experience, being forced to relive it." In Colon's view, the picture doesn't serve a compelling enough journalistic purpose to justify potentially hurting the woman in it. The newspaper's description of what happened to this young woman was fairly complete and graphic, he said, and therefore the community knew that this occurred. "If there had been no other description or if there had been a counter-argument that this didn't happen at all, that might offer an argument for publishing it because without it, people will not know the truth."

But the press photographer's group insists that the disturbing picture contributes to awareness of sexual violence, thus meriting their unusual decision to give a journalism award to an unpublished photo and to risk upsetting the woman in it, should she ever see it. After all, the brutal image does more than just capture an isolated event. In addition to the other Mardi Gras attacks, the rowdy, leering men pawing at a stripped woman recall similar assaults at Woodstock 1999 and at the 2000 Puerto Rican Day Parade in Manhattan.

The picture "symbolizes some very frightening trends in our society," said Cheryl Hatch, a Seattle Associated Press photographer who was one of the contest's judges.

Hatch has worked with sexual abuse victims, and at first she was against publishing the picture. "If I was going to err, I was going to err on the side of the woman," she said. "I didn't want to do anything that would subject this woman to more degradation, exploitation, traumatization."

Yet like the other judges, she finally decided that the picture captured something words couldn't. The sight of an ordinary, clean-cut crowd descending into viciousness speaks "about the level of violence in our society and how it's a very thin line between civility and brutality, between calm and riot," she said.

Besides, she added, people tend to dismiss charges of sexual abuse at events like Mardi Gras that are known for public lasciviousness. "People would say, 'Oh, Mardi Gras, people go there to lift up their tops.'" Urban's image, she felt, made the horror of what happened explicit. After discussing the issue with a relative who had been sexually assaulted, she decided that publishing the picture with the woman's face hidden was a fair compromise.

Hatch said the judges' unanimous decision to publish the picture with the woman's face digitally obscured came after days of intense debate. One thing they discussed was what they saw as news organizations' double standard for pictures of foreigners and of Americans. Nick Ut's photo of a naked girl fleeing napalm in Vietnam has been widely reproduced, as have countless shots of starving, half-clothed Africans. According to Hatch, contest judge Horacio Villalobos, director of photography at Diario Popular in Buenos Aires, pointed out that American papers "run pictures all the time of people from other countries suffering and being abused and exploited. We publish pictures from abroad showing people's faces without regard to the issues debated in that room."

Yet according to Bunting, "It's a bogus comparison. It strikes me as an academic discussion that has no validity in the real world. We consider the story a picture will tell and the impact it will have on our audience. You can't look at a picture from 25 years ago and compare it to something that happened a year ago in Seattle."

As for the impact the photograph will have on the woman in it, no one knows. She has not come forward or been identified, nor any of her attackers charged. She might not have any idea of the controversy brewing over her image.

Analyzing the Situation

1. Goldberg's writing participates in a difficult and complex situation. It involves the Mardi Gras event, the victim, the photographer, the photograph, the award, the press association, the editor, and so on. What would you describe as the central or most important event within this situation?

2. What role do power and institution play in this situation? What institutions are prevalent in this situation?

3. How is this situation important from an ecological standpoint? That is, how does it affect other situations?

Analyzing the Rhetoric

1. What is the relevance of Goldberg's final paragraph?

2. Obviously, Goldberg's essay does not include Mike Urban's photograph. What is the visual rhetorical objective in not including the image in the essay? How would the essay itself have been altered if the image had been included? Should Goldberg have included the image? Should the image appear here in *Writing Situations* even without Goldberg's consent? Why or why not?

3. What role does dialogue play in Goldberg's essay?

Discussing

1. Michelle Goldberg reports that Cheryl Hatch "finally decided that the picture captured something words couldn't." Consider this distinction between the ability of words and images to convey information. Can pictures capture and convey something that words can't? Can words capture and convey something that images can't? Discuss how we distinguish between and assign value to words and images.

2. Who do you agree with, the journalists and editors who argued against publishing the photograph or the press photographer's group that argued for and did publish the photo?

3. In 2002, when the National Press Photographer Association announced that Mike Urban's photo had been awarded first prize in its Best of Photojournalism contest, *The Seattle Times*, a competitor of *The Seattle Post-Intelligencer* where Urban worked, published an article entitled "Mardi Gras news photo that wasn't published wins prize" by Florangela Davila and Carol M. Ostrom, which you can find by searching for the title on *The Seattle Times* web pages. Take a few minutes to read the article, then, as a class, discuss *The Seattle Times*'s article in relation to Michelle Goldberg's.

Writing

1. The editor at the *Seattle Post-Intelligencer* decided that readers should not see Mike Urban's photograph; the Poynter Institute also opted not to post the image on their web pages. Cheryl Hatch, a Seattle Associated Press photographer, though, argued that it should be seen. Should editors and others have the power to determine what readers can and can't see? Is this kind of editorial control a good thing or a bad thing? Write an essay that addresses who should have the power to determine what the public has access to see. Should people depicted in photographs have any say in who sees and doesn't see the pictures?

2. How do you respond to Ken Bunting's argument as Goldberg depicts it throughout the essay? Write a response to Bunting and his position regarding the publication of Mike Urban's photograph specifically and such editorial positions generally.

Citizens Protesting Anti-Semitic Acts, Billings, Montana

Frederic Brenner

Frederic Brenner was born in Paris in 1959. For more than 25 years he has traveled the world photographing the Jewish diaspora. His exhibits have appeared in New York, Paris, and Rome. Brenner's photograph was originally published in the *Billings Gazette* in Billings, Montana, on December 11, 1993, and was accompanied by this text:

"On December 2, 1993, someone twisted by hate threw a brick through the window of the home of one of our neighbors: a Jewish family who chose to celebrate the holiday season by displaying a symbol of faith—a menorah—for all to see. Today, members of religious faiths throughout Billings are joining together to ask residents to display the menorah as a symbol of something else: our determination to live together in harmony, and our dedication to the principle of religious liberty embodied in the First Amendment to the Constitution of the United States of America. We urge all citizens to share in this message by displaying this menorah on a door or a window from now until Christmas. Let all the World know that the national hatred of a few cannot destroy what all of us in Billings, and in America, have worked together so long to build."

The photo depicts the broken window with local religious and civic leaders standing outside holding menorahs as symbols of their community's commitment to religious freedom. The *Billings Gazette* estimated that by the end of the week when the photo was published between six and ten thousand families decorated their homes with menorahs.

Analyzing the Situation

1. Can readers address the situation of this photograph without the caption with which it was originally published?

2. What roles do power, institution, and participation play in this situation?

3. What role does location play in this situation?

Analyzing the Rhetoric

1. Frederick Brenner's photograph was taken with the intent of making an argument. How does it make that argument?

2. How does the original caption included with Brenner's photograph in the *Billings Gazette* affect how we read this photograph? Can we read this photograph without the caption?

3. Does pathos play a role in this image? If it does, how is it used?

Discussing

1. Understanding this photograph may require its relationship with the caption with which it was originally published, but it also requires that the reader of this picture be familiar with other cultural visual references. What should a reader of this photograph know in order to understand the photo?

2. Why do you suppose Brenner took this photograph in black and white rather than in color? Discuss the ways in which the choice to use black and white affects how we read the image.

3. Brenner's photograph is a response to a particular situation that is connected to many other situations of hate and fear. How do you respond to Brenner's response to the situation? Is a photograph an appropriate response for a community like this?

Writing

1. Write a visual rhetorical analysis of Brenner's photograph.

2. Brenner's photograph, "Citizens Protesting Anti-Semitic Acts, Billings Montana," is not really a famous photograph. Yet, it conveys many of the same messages about community, about hate, and about tolerance that other famous photographs have conveyed. Locate a famous photograph that has been used as an argument against acts of hatred. Analyze the image you have selected and Brenner's image and write an evaluation of the two examining why the photo you selected is better known than Brenner's.

3. How would you describe the situation in which Brenner's photograph participates? Without using Brenner's photo or any other image, describe the situation and the photo and the ecology they form.

Thinking and Writing about the Chapter

Reflection

The prompt at the beginning of this chapter asked you to write about what you thought living in a "visual culture" might suggest. Now that you have read some of the readings gathered in this chapter, revisit your journal or blog and write another entry or post about what you now think living in a visual culture might entail.

Discussion Threads

1. Tom Junod's essay "Richard Drew, The Falling Man" and Michelle Goldberg's article "Debate Grows over Use of Sexual Assault Photo" both address how U.S. media will show

pictures of victims' bodies with little censorship if the bodies are not American bodies. Why is the mass media hesitant to show American bodies but not "foreign" bodies?

2. Are photography and writing similar? In what ways? Do photographers and writers have the same kinds of cultural influence? Discuss the similarities and differences between photography and writing.

3. Why are images so important in contemporary culture?

Collaboration

1. Working in small groups, select one of the following topics and locate as many images as possible that relate to that subject. Then, by way of the images you locate, consider how you might characterize the image/culture of that topic. Collaboratively, write a document that explains the image/culture of the topic you have selected. Keep in mind you are writing about images, not about the words we use to describe the images. Be sure to include examples to support your explanation.

cupcakes	science fiction
digital technology	simulation
Friday	sleep
gaming	the color white
language	things
light	time
motion	travel
music	wildlife
possibility	writing

2. In 1906, American banker J. P. Morgan paid photographer Edward S. Curtis $75,000 to produce a 20-volume collection of photographs of Native Americans. The project would include more than 1,500 photographs and would take Curtis more than 20 years to complete. Curtis ultimately took more than 40,000 photographs. Curtis hired a number of people to help him with the project, including Frederick Webb Hodge, a Smithsonian Institution anthropologist, to edit each of the volumes of photographs. Curtis's photographs (a few of which are reprinted here) not only provided the world with images of cultures they had never seen before, but also helped document ways of life that were rapidly disappearing. In many instances, Curtis's photographs are the only records we have of particular Native American groups.

Six Navajo on horseback, ca. 1904

Working in teams, conduct research to locate Curtis's photographs (a substantial number of them are available through the Library of Congress). Then create a "collection" of 100 of his images that represents the visual heritage Curtis left. Write an introduction to accompany your collection.

At left, Yellow Bull of the Nez Perce. At right, a Hopi Girl, ca. 1905.

At left, Zosh Clishn, Apache, ca. 1906. At right, Bear Bull, illustrating an ancient Blackfoot method of arranging the hair.

Writing

1. On May 2, 2011, militant Islamist Osama Bin Laden was killed by U.S. armed forces. Photographs of Bin Laden's body and burial were suppressed by the U.S. government, which had claimed that there are three sets of photographs of the body. Similar situations have arisen in relation to photographs of well-known criminals or terrorists. The ethical questions that such situations demand are difficult to address, but require our critical consideration. Given the importance of photographs in our culture, should certain photographs be censored and restricted from circulation? Write an essay responding to the question "Should the government be able to repress controversial images?"

2. What do you consider to be the ten most important photographs of our time? That is, what ten photographs do you think best represent contemporary culture? Locate the ten images you identify. Write an image essay that depicts the ten you have selected and provides enough written text to both contextualize your selection of the images and provide information about each.

3. In 2008, Gerd Schuster, Willie Smits, and Jay Ullal published the book *Thinkers of the Jungle: The Orangutan Report* which accounts for the daily lives of orangutans in Borneo and Sumatra. The book contains many remarkable photographs, like the one found here, to both help readers see what the authors describe and to help make the authors' emotional appeal more powerful. Take some time to consider the image, which is known as "Thinkers of the Jungle Spear." What do you learn from this visual? How might others interpret this visual? Write an essay describing what this visual conveys.

4. Amsterdam-based photographer Claire Felicie's photo series "Here are the Young Men" asks about whether our experiences, particularly our life-altering experiences, affect the way we look. Over the course of one year, Felicie photographed twenty Dutch Marines of the 13th infantry company of the Royal Netherlands Marine Corps before, during, and after their deployment to Uruzgan, Afghanistan. As Slate.com blogger Heather Murphy has pointed out, "From first to last photo, only 12 months passed, but a great deal happened in those young men's lives."[1] Reprinted here are two of the triptychs of Felicie's photos; you can see the full photo series by entering "Claire Felice Here are the young men" in your search engine and clicking the search result for "Claire Felice Photography." Take some time to consider what you view in these photos and how the context in which they have been framed here affects how you view these images. Write a short essay explaining how and why knowing what the subjects of these photos are affects how you view them.

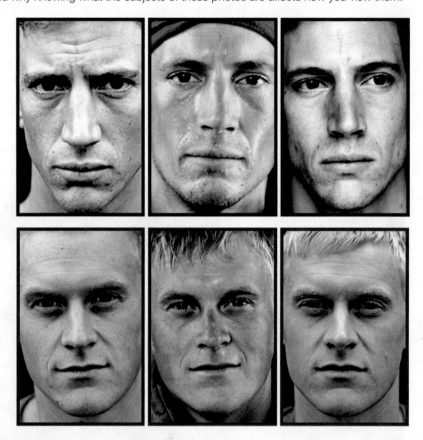

Local Situation

How is the culture of your campus conveyed visually? Analyze the image culture of your campus, and write an assessment/evaluation of what you discover.

---

[1] Murphy, Heather. "Marines' Faces Before, During, and After Serving in Afghanistan." *Slate*. The Slate Group, 17 Oct. 2012. Web. 14 Nov. 2013.

Sustainability

CHAPTER 24

Before you read this chapter

Ask yourself how you think about sustainability. What does the term mean to you? What is your attitude toward sustainability? Does your attitude influence your daily behavior, the way you live your life, the choices you make, your plans for the future, your career plans, or your interests? Do you have experience with learning about sustainability? With these questions in mind, write a personal narrative about your thoughts about and experiences with sustainability.

Sustainability refers to the ability to last, the ability to endure. The term has come to mean many things to different people, ranging from how to protect and sustain biological systems to how to maintain the availability of resources to how to ensure that a business, company, or organization endures through changing situations. Sustainability has become a popular way of talking about how to allow for development while protecting natural resources and ecosystems. Sustainability is generally understood as ideas and methods that work to reduce negative human impact on the world's ecosystems. From this perspective, then, sustainability can be seen as both an approach to environmental management—which is most often informed by the sciences—and consumption management—which is generally informed by economics. Recently, sustainability has been tied to "green" movements and the greening of many kinds of businesses, industries, and institutions.

Many definitions of sustainability identify the core idea that something must *sustain*. Problematically, *sustain* is defined by a series of concepts like *maintain*, *endure*, and *support*. In contemporary conversation, we tend to interpret these definitions as suggesting the maintenance, support, and endurance of human interests. Perhaps the most widely accepted definition of *sustainability* is the one that was forwarded in the 1987 United Nations World Commission on Environment and Development report *Our Common Future*, also known as the *Brundtland Report*. The *Brundtland Report* defines "sustainable development" as "development that meets the needs of the present without compromising the ability of future generations to meet their own needs." The definition has been criticized by some as focusing too much on economic development above other concerns. In September 2005, the United Nations held a world summit to continue work in creating development policies that had been initiated in the UN's 2000 Millennium Summit. Participants in the 2005 World Summit in New York City proposed that sustainability requires recognition of three ideas: economy, society, and environment, what have become known as the "three pillars of sustainability." The three pillars are often depicted visually to suggest the relationships between the three parts. The first representation nests economy within society and both economy and society within environment. The second suggests that sustainability occurs where the three parts converge; all three must be accounted for (see Figure 24.1).

Of course, neither the *Brundtland Report* definition nor the UN Summit Report definition is universally accepted as definitive. There are many groups and organizations that find fault with these definitions. Many environmentalists, for example, find the definitions to place environmental concerns in service of economic concerns. The Earth Charter Initiative, whose mission is "to promote the transition to sustainable ways of living and a global society founded on a shared ethical framework that includes respect and care for the community of life, ecological integrity, universal human rights, respect for diversity, economic justice, democracy, and a culture of peace," for example, proposes a model of sustainability "founded on respect for nature, universal human rights, economic justice, and a culture of peace."

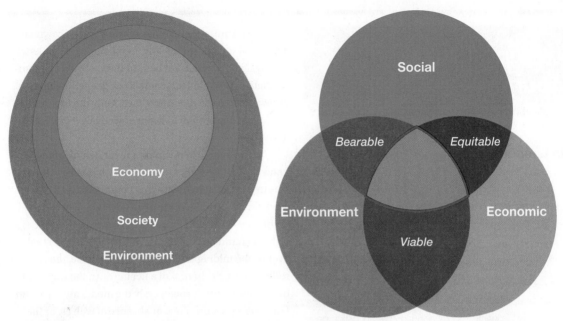

FIGURE 24.1 Visual representations of the three pillars of sustainability. The graphic on the left shows the nested version and the graphic on the right shows the confluent version.

Part of the difficulty in defining *sustainability* is that sustainability has to account for a tremendous number of complex parts. Just imagine trying to encapsulate everything you can think of relating to environment, economy, and society in a single definition. Likewise, because sustainability is always context specific, differences in location, belief, culture, government, resources, and need lead to various approaches to sustainability among different groups and populations worldwide. Thus, agreeing on a universally accepted definition is more than difficult.

Likewise, addressing sustainability in a single book—let alone a single book chapter like this one—is impossible; there are just too many contributing concepts that ought to be discussed. Thus, this chapter is not really about sustainability in any comprehensive way. Instead, this chapter offers a selection of readings that encourage you to think about specific concepts within the vast umbrella conversation of sustainability. Colleges and universities across the United States have begun to address sustainability as both curricular objectives (preparing students to live and work sustainably) and as a physical action on their campuses. This chapter contributes to that effort by asking you to think, talk, and write about subjects that relate to sustainability. Part of the agenda of this chapter, then, is to encourage you to think about sustainability as it relates to your own life.

Thinking Like a Mountain

Aldo Leopold

Aldo Leopold was a professor at the University of Wisconsin; he is also considered one of the most influential and important writers and thinkers in modern environmental ethics and wilderness conservation. Leopold was born in Burlington, Iowa, in 1887, and he died in 1947, a year before his award-winning book *A Sand County Almanac and Sketches Here and There* was published. *A Sand County Almanac* is considered to be one of the most influential books about nature and wilderness ever published, and in 1978, Leopold was posthumously awarded the John Burroughs Medal for the book. The book is often compared with the work of Henry David Thoreau. Leopold's work was some of the first to insist that all considerations of nature, wilderness, and environment never exclude a sense of ethics. To this end, the final section of *A Sand County Almanac*, "The Land Ethic," is considered landmark in establishing the idea of environmental ethics, as is the essay reprinted here, "Thinking Like a Mountain."

Originally published in 1949, a year after Leopold died, "Thinking Like a Mountain" was considered the most significant selection in *A Sand County Almanac*. As you read "Thinking Like a Mountain," consider the ways Leopold encourages readers to see land as a "community to which we belong."

A deep chesty bawl echoes from rimrock to rimrock, rolls down the mountain, and fades into the far blackness of the night. It is an outburst of wild defiant sorrow, and of contempt for all the adversities of the world. Every living thing (and perhaps many a dead one as well) pays heed to that call. To the deer it is a reminder of the way of all flesh, to the pine a forecast of midnight scuffles and of blood upon the snow, to the coyote a promise of gleanings to come, to the cowman a threat of red ink at the bank, to the hunter a challenge of fang against bullet. Yet behind these obvious and immediate hopes and fears there lies a deeper meaning, known only to the mountain itself. Only the mountain has lived long enough to listen objectively to the howl of a wolf.

Those unable to decipher the hidden meaning know nevertheless that it is there, for it is felt in all wolf country, and distinguishes that country from all other land. It tingles in the spine of all who hear wolves by night, or who scan their tracks by day. Even without sight or sound of wolf, it is implicit in a hundred small events: the midnight whinny of a pack horse, the rattle of rolling rocks, the bound of a fleeing deer, the way shadows lie under the spruces. Only the ineducable tyro can fail to sense the presence or absence of wolves, or the fact that mountains have a secret opinion about them.

My own conviction on this score dates from the day I saw a wolf die. We were eating lunch on a high rimrock, at the foot of which a turbulent river elbowed its way. We saw what we thought was a doe fording the torrent, her breast awash in white water. When she climbed the bank toward us and shook out her tail, we realized our error: it was a wolf. A half-dozen others, evidently grown pups, sprang from the willows and all joined in a welcoming melee of wagging tails and playful maulings. What was literally a pile of wolves writhed and tumbled in the center of an open flat at the foot of our rimrock.

In those days we had never heard of passing up a chance to kill a wolf. In a second we were pumping lead into the pack, but with more excitement than accuracy: how to aim a steep downhill shot is always confusing. When our rifles were empty, the old wolf was down, and a pup was dragging a leg into impassable slide-rocks.

We reached the old wolf in time to watch a fierce green fire dying in her eyes. I realized then, and have known ever since, that there was something new to me in those eyes—something known only to her and to the mountain. I was young then, and full of trigger-itch; I thought that because fewer wolves meant more deer, that no wolves would mean hunters' paradise. But after seeing the green fire die, I sensed that neither the wolf nor the mountain agreed with such a view.

•••

Since then I have lived to see state after state extirpate its wolves. I have watched the face of many a newly wolfless mountain, and seen the south-facing slopes wrinkle with a maze of new deer trails. I have seen every edible bush and seedling browsed, first to anaemic desuetude, and then to death. I have seen every edible tree defoliated to the height of a saddlehorn. Such a mountain looks as if someone had given God a new pruning shears, and forbidden Him all other exercise. In the end the starved bones of the hoped-for deer herd, dead of its own too-much, bleach with the bones of the dead sage, or molder under the high-lined junipers.

I now suspect that just as a deer herd lives in mortal fear of its wolves, so does a mountain live in mortal fear of its deer. And perhaps with better cause, for while a buck pulled down by wolves can be replaced in two or three years, a range pulled down by too many deer may fail of replacement in as many decades.

So also with cows. The cowman who cleans his range of wolves does not realize that he is taking over the wolf's job of trimming the herd to fit the range. He has not learned to think like a mountain. Hence we have dustbowls, and rivers washing the future into the sea.

•••

We all strive for safety, prosperity, comfort, long life, and dullness. The deer strives with his supple legs, the cowman with trap and poison, the statesman with pen, the most of us with machines, votes, and dollars, but it all comes to the same thing: peace in our time. A measure of success in this is all well enough, and perhaps is a requisite to objective thinking, but too much safety seems to yield only danger in the long run. Perhaps this is behind Thoreau's dictum: In wildness is the salvation of the world. Perhaps this is the hidden meaning in the howl of the wolf, long known among mountains, but seldom perceived among men.

Analyzing the Situation

1. At the end of "Thinking Like a Mountain," Aldo Leopold invokes the name of Thoreau. Seemingly, he does so not only to quote Thoreau's dictum but also to acknowledge the influence Thoreau had on his thinking about such matters. Because Leopold ends the essay with the reference to Thoreau, we can assume that Thoreau's influence is present throughout the essay. We also know that "Thinking Like a Mountain" has been incredibly influential in the development of thinking in contemporary environmental ethics and land ethics. In this way, then, how does "Thinking Like a Mountain" contribute to the ecology of the situation in which Leopold writes?

2. Aldo Leopold's "Thinking Like a Mountain" was published in 1949, more than sixty years ago. Has it exceeded its situation? Has its moment of kairos passed?

3. Is there a sense of institutional power in "Thinking Like a Mountain"? If so, what reveals that sense in the essay, and what would you identify as institutional power that influences the essay?

Analyzing the Rhetoric

1. In the second paragraph of "Thinking Like a Mountain," Aldo Leopold lists the ways both animals and humans respond to the echoing cry. What does Leopold accomplish rhetorically by placing both humans and animals in this list?

2. Twice in "Thinking Like a Mountain," Aldo Leopold suggests that the wolf's howl has "meaning." Can the wolf's howl have meaning the same way the statesmen's pen writes things with "meaning"? Does Leopold's language give meaning to the howl in any way?

3. Why do you suppose Leopold divided the essay into sections? Does the visual demarcation of the sections suggest anything to you as you read? Are there distinctions between the sections? If so, do they affect how you read and understand this piece?

Discussing

1. Early in "Thinking Like a Mountain," Aldo Leopold writes, "Only the mountain has lived long enough to listen objectively to the howl of a wolf." What do you suppose Leopold means by this? Discuss what this sentence might mean and what it contributes to an essay called "Thinking Like a Mountain."

2. Now that you have read "Thinking Like a Mountain," consider what Leopold suggests by way of his title. Discuss the ways we might think differently about the various roles of nature and our interactions with them.

Writing

1. In an essay modeling Aldo Leopold's strategies in "Thinking Like a Mountain," write about how we might think like another kind of formation that is familiar to you—other than a mountain. For instance, you may want to write an essay called "Thinking Like a Valley," "Thinking Like an Island," "Thinking Like an Isthmus," or "Thinking Like a Prairie." Use this as an opportunity not to mimic Leopold but to consider how you can think about your own local environments from a perspective and a strategy similar to Leopold's.

2. Aldo Leopold's "Thinking Like a Mountain" influenced many writers and thinkers and contributed to a larger understanding of conservation ethics and land ethics. Take some time to conduct some research to learn more about writers and thinkers who this essay influenced. Then write a research-based paper that explores some of the ecological connections "Thinking Like a Mountain" has stimulated. You may want to look for other writings that have appropriated Leopold's titles, or you may want to look for other writers who write about the kinds of things addressed in "Thinking Like a Mountain."

3. What does Leopold recount that he learned from shooting the wolf? Have you ever had an encounter with an animal that changed the ways in which you think about animals? Write a narrative that details such an experience and explains what you learned from that experience and why.

The Story of Stuff

Annie Leonard

A graduate of Barnard College, Annie Leonard is a vocal proponent of sustainability. Leonard has worked for Greenpeace International and for Essential Information, Ralph Nader's citizen action organization. Her animated documentary "The Story of Stuff" started as a lecture Leonard delivered about sustainability and the excesses of consumerism. Because of high demand for the lecture, working with a number of foundations, including Tides Foundation and Free Range Studios, Leonard released "The Story of Stuff" as a 20-minute animated feature in December of 2007. The documentary is available on The Story of Stuff Project web page and on You-Tube. The documentary has become very popular; the *Los Angeles Times* reported in July 2010 that the documentary has been viewed by more than 12 million people and has been translated into 15 languages.[1] "The Story of Stuff" is used in schools, as well as in corporate sustainability training programs and even places of worship.[2] But "The Story of Stuff" has also received a good deal of criticism; it has been labeled anti-consumer, anti-capitalist, and even anti-American in the way that it depicts the American consumer. Fox News and other groups have argued that the numbers used in the video are misleading.[3]

Because of the overwhelming attention that "The Story of Stuff" garnered, Annie Leonard and The Story of Stuff Project

---

[1] Roosevelt, Margot. "Teaching 'Stuff' about Ecology." *Los Angeles Times.* July 13, 2010.

[2] "Studying "Stuff" Examining "The Story of Stuff" with a Critical Eye." *The New York Times.* May 15, 2009.

[3] "Viral Video 'The Story of Stuff' Is Full of Misleading Numbers." *FoxNews.com.* Fox News Network, 14 May 2009. Web. 14 Nov. 2013.

have produced other similar videos, including "The Story of Cap and Trade," "The Story of Bottled Water," "The Story of Cosmetics," and "The Story of Electronics," all of which can be viewed on The Story of Stuff Project web page. As you watch "The Story of Stuff," pay particular attention to how Leonard uses visuals in conjunction with her narrative to clarify and explain. Think about how "The Story of Stuff" functions as an image essay.

Annie Leonard's documentary, "The Story of Stuff," focuses on sustainability and the excesses of consumerism.

Analyzing the Situation

1. Why do you suppose Annie Leonard chose to present "The Story of Stuff" as an animated video made available online? What does the medium provide her? Could she have delivered the same message in another form other than video with the same results? Likewise, why do you suppose she chose to animate the video rather than including other kinds of visuals? In what ways does the animation serve the video format and the online distribution?

2. "The Story of Stuff" presents a lot of numbers, statistics, and details. What does the delivery of this kind of information require of the situation, particularly of the audience?

3. What role do institution and power play in the situation in which "The Story of Stuff" participates? Which institutions and power structures are most evidently present in the situation?

Analyzing the Rhetoric

1. How would you describe Annie Leonard's delivery to her audience?

2. In what ways do Annie Leonard's former positions with Essential Information and Greenpeace affect her ethos in "The Story of Stuff"?

3. Early in "The Story of Stuff," Annie Leonard describes the "textbook" story of stuff as being only

part of the story and her ten years of world-traveling experience as providing her with the missing information (0:33–0:50). How does Leonard's critique of the "textbook" story, in conjunction with her own experience, help her establish authority to speak on the subject of production—particularly since she is not introduced in any formal way in the video?

4. How does Annie Leonard use the appeal of pathos in "The Story of Stuff"? Is it an effective appeal?

Discussing

1. How do you respond to "The Story of Stuff"? As a class, discuss your reactions to the image essay.

2. "The Story of Stuff" has received a good deal of criticism, including responses from Glenn Beck and from Fox News. Take some time as a class to consider these critiques of Annie Leonard and "The Story of Stuff" and discuss them in light of the documentary.

3. "The Story of Stuff" addresses the difference between *planned obsolescence* and *perceived obsolescence*. As a class, discuss these concepts as they are presented in the video. How do planned obsolescence and perceived obsolescence affect your life?

Writing

1. On May 10, 2009, *The New York Times* published a story on the front page of its Education section by Leslie Kaufman about "The Story of Stuff," titled "A Cautionary Video About America's 'Stuff'" in which Kaufman writes about how "The Story of Stuff" is used in classrooms across the country. In May 2009, *The New York Times* also published a short article called "Studying 'Stuff,'" which provides a curriculum for working with "The Story of Stuff."

Take some time to read these articles and write a response to them.

2. In "The Story of Stuff," Annie Leonard refers to economist and retail analyst Victor Lebow as saying, "Our enormously productive economy … demands that we make consumption our way of life, that we convert the buying and use of goods into rituals, that we seek our spiritual satisfaction, our ego satisfaction, in consumption … we need things consumed, burned up, replaced and discarded at an ever accelerating rate." Lebow's theory is only one of many economic theories of how the American economy might have rebuilt after World War II. Conduct some research into the economic strategies that were proposed in the United States after World War II and consider why Leonard chose Lebow's to cite. What other approaches might Leonard have reported about? Using your research, write a research-based essay about other theories contemporary to Lebow's and how they might have served or hurt Leonard's argument.

3. Select a single item from your stuff: a smartphone, an MP3 player, a computer, or anything else you use regularly. Then conduct some research to learn what it takes to make your item. What is the story of your stuff? Where do the resources come from? Where is it manufactured? How did it get to you?

Effort to Trace "Conflict Minerals" in Electronics

Martin LaMonica

Martin LaMonica is a senior writer for CNET News, an online news site dedicated to stories about technology. LaMonica writes for and manages the Green Tech blog. He has been a journalist for more than 20 years and has covered innovation in energy and the environment since 2005. LaMonica's blog essay reprinted here addresses two ecological aspects of making electronic devices we don't often think about: where the minerals come from to make the devices and what happens to the money that pays for those minerals. As LaMonica reports, there is a human cost involved with the demand for electronic devices, one that must be accounted for in the larger understanding of sustainability and electronics.

Hewlett-Packard's efforts to be more socially and environmentally sustainable have taken it to an unexpected—and uncomfortable—place: the war-ravaged Democratic Republic of Congo.

Concerned that purchases of metals could be financing armed conflict in the West African country, HP and a handful of other companies are turning their attention to its suppliers of metals, including tin, gold, tantalum, and tungsten, which are used in everyday computing products and mobile phones.

At HP, it's an extension of an initiative that started over a decade ago to ensure that supply chain partners adhere to certain environmental and social standards. The near-term objective is to not purchase metals tied to armed conflict in the Democratic Republic of Congo, but there's a longer-term goal of certifying the source for minerals of all kinds, according to Zoe McMahon, HP's manager of supply chain social and environmental responsibility.

Proceeds from illegal mining operations, which are controlled by military factions, are helping fuel a complex conflict that crosses between the Democratic Republic of Congo and neighboring Rwanda.

HP felt pressure to act from outside groups, including enterprise customers, investors, and non-government groups pushing for more transparency of suppliers in the IT industry. In its investigation, HP decided to focus primarily on the source of tantalum because it is used far more than other metals, specifically in capacitors.

An initial review done a few years ago indicated that HP's metals purchases were not directly linked to the mines in question, and thus not directly contributing to the violence. But as the violence escalated, HP looked further and the picture became somewhat hazy.

"Because our suppliers are not using material from the DRC, that gave us some comfort. But to this day, there is still no certification mechanism that can assure us wholeheartedly that they are not sourced from the DRC," said McMahon. "Once metals are with smelters, it's difficult to know where the material comes from."

The push toward "traceability" in the metals extraction is an outgrowth of HP's practices of auditing its supply chain partners to make sure they do not contribute to human rights and environmental violations, said McMahon. By auditing its suppliers, HP reduces its chances of bad publicity or seeks to avoid other business risks. Other IT-related companies that have worked on the DRC conflict minerals issue include Intel, Motorola, Dell, and Philips, she added.

At this point, local groups don't advocate that metals purchasers stop buying from Africa or the DRC. On the contrary, the goal is to establish a "clean stream" of metals and promote environmentally and socially responsible mining practices there, said McMahon.

Rooting out the sources of tantalum

Within the overall IT industry, there have been a number of efforts to lighten the environmental footprint of computing, with the most visible being development of more energy-efficient computers.

Also, as awareness over the impact of exported electronic waste has grown, there have been efforts to certify recyclers. State regulations have also led to an increase in local electronics recycling options.

But the issue of metals traceabilty is very challenging, admits McMahon. Getting reliable information is not easy, particularly when you consider the complexity of the supply chain. A laptop computer, for example, could have 15 suppliers for its main components. Each one of those suppliers has multiple suppliers, which in turn can have suppliers. All told, a single product could be sourced from dozens of places.

Funding to create maps and audit different facilities relies in large part on U.S. government funding, which is uncertain even though there are conflict minerals bills under consideration and there has been diplomatic pressure on this issue in Africa.

There are, however, some efforts that could serve as a template for IT industry-specific certifications, said McMahon. The Electronics Industry Citizen Coalition is preparing a report, due to come out next month, that creates maps to trace the path of tin to market. Next month, representatives from the tantalum supply chain industry will meet with EICC members in an effort to create a sourcing certification to be applied in the DRC.

The hope is that the electronics industry can pressure other industries, such as aerospace, jewelry, and automotive, to pursue certification, said McMahon.

"We have some gaps in our understanding of our products and we want to continue filling gaps (from suppliers)," she said. "Who isn't in the room [discussing the issue] are the traders in the DRC, that's the hard part. In pulling together all parts of the tantalum supply chain, it's been evident that greater action is needed."

Analyzing the Situation

1. It would seem that part of Martin LaMonica's purpose in writing "Effort to Trace 'Conflict Minerals' in Electronics" is to create an awareness of a situation. In what ways is awareness of a situation like this important? How might one become more informed about a situation like this?

2. If you were to participate in this situation by learning more about the situation and sharing information with your peers, what media might you use to best inform your audience and why?

3. In what ways is kairos of particular importance in this situation? How is the importance of kairos tied to the players in this situation?

Analyzing the Rhetoric

1. Martin LaMonica's "Effort to Trace 'Conflict Minerals' in Electronics" is divided into two sections. What distinguishes the two sections and why do you suppose LaMonica opted to divide the essay rather than transition from one subject to the next?

2. Why do you suppose Martin LaMonica uses abbreviations throughout this essay: HP, DRC, IT, and EICC? What does he accomplish in using these abbreviations?

3. In what ways does Martin LaMonica use evidence to support his position?

Discussing

1. As a class, watch the following videos produced by the ENOUGH Project about conflict minerals and electronics; then discuss the videos in light of Martin LaMonica's "Effort to Trace 'Conflict Minerals' in Electronics."

"I'm a Mac ... and I've Got a Dirty Secret" found on YouTube

"Conflict Minerals: Stories from the Mouth of the Mine" found on YouTube

"Conflict Minerals 101" found on YouTube

2. Were you aware of the role of conflict minerals in the electronics you use? How do you respond to

what LaMonica tells us about our own complacency in the conflict mineral situation?

Writing

1. What minerals are used in making the electronics we commonly use? Learn a bit more about what minerals are needed to make electronics, where those minerals come from, and what purpose they serve in the design of electronics. Then write a report detailing what you have learned about those minerals, their use, and their sources.

2. In 2000, the United Nations published a report—known as the Fowler Report after Robert Fowler, Canada's UN ambassador who headed the commission to write the report—that identified the connection between illegal diamond trade and many third-world conflicts. These diamonds have popularly become known as "blood diamonds." Following the recommendations of the Fowler Report, in 2003 the UN adopted the Kimberley Process Certification Scheme to certify diamonds as non-conflict minerals before they can be traded. (Kimberley, by the way, is a city in South Africa where a meeting was held to draft the process certification scheme.) Conduct some research to learn more about how world governments have worked to end the trade of blood diamonds and then write about those efforts and how those efforts might be used to inform similar approaches for ending the trade in conflict minerals for use in electronic devices.

3. There are many websites and online sources through which information about conflict minerals and electronics is circulated. Create a blog or website of your own that serves as an aggregate site to pool various discussions together in a comprehensive and unified location.

Tuna's End

Paul Greenberg

Paul Greenberg is a regular contributor to *The New York Times Magazine*. His writing also appears in *The Times of London*, *GQ*, *Vogue*, *Cooking Light*, *Food and Wine*, *National Geographic*, and many other publications. Greenberg has also been a guest commentator on *All Things Considered*. In 2002, Greenberg's first novel, *Leaving Katya*, was selected by Barnes & Noble as a Discover New Writers selection. In 2005 his article about Chilean Sea Bass was awarded the International Association of Culinary Professionals' Bert Greene Award for Excellence in Food Writing. Greenberg has been honored as a W.K. Kellogg Foundation Food and Society Policy Fellow and as a National Endowment for the Arts Literature Fellow. In 2011, Greenberg's book *Four Fish: The Future of the Last Wild Food* was awarded the 2011 James Beard Award for Writing and Literature. *Four Fish* is a smart investigation of our relationship with the four fish that have

been primary food sources for people: salmon, tuna, cod, and bass. In the book, Greenberg takes a detailed look at the depletion of these wild food sources. Reprinted here is Greenberg's *New York Times Magazine* essay "Tuna's End," which is adapted from *Four Fish*.

In the international waters south of Malta, the Greenpeace vessels *Rainbow Warrior* and *Arctic Sunrise* deployed eight inflatable Zodiacs and skiffs into the azure surface of the Mediterranean. Protesters aboard donned helmets and took up DayGlo flags and plywood shields. With the organization's observation helicopter hovering above, the pilots of the tiny boats hit their throttles, hurtling the fleet forward to stop what they viewed as an egregious environmental crime. It was a high-octane updating of a familiar tableau, one that anyone who has followed Greenpeace's Save the Whales adventures of the last 35 years would have recognized. But in the waters off Malta there was not a whale to be seen.

What was in the water that day was a congregation of Atlantic bluefin tuna, a fish that when prepared as sushi is one of the most valuable forms of seafood in the world. It's also a fish that regularly journeys between

America and Europe and whose two populations, or "stocks," have both been catastrophically overexploited. The BP oil spill in the Gulf of Mexico, one of only two known Atlantic bluefin spawning grounds, has only intensified the crisis. By some estimates, there may be only 9,000 of the most ecologically vital megabreeders left in the fish's North American stock, enough for the entire population of New York to have a final bite (or two) of high-grade *otoro* sushi. The Mediterranean stock of bluefin, historically a larger population than the North American one, has declined drastically as well. Indeed, most Mediterranean bluefin fishing consists of netting or "seining" young wild fish for "outgrowing" on tuna "ranches." Which was why the Greenpeace craft had just deployed off Malta: a French fishing boat was about to legally catch an entire school of tuna, many of them undoubtedly juveniles.

Oliver Knowles, a 34-year-old Briton who was coordinating the intervention, had told me a few days earlier via telephone what the strategy was going to be. "These fishing operations consist of a huge purse-seining vessel and a small skiff that's quite fast," Knowles said. A "purse seine" is a type of net used by industrial fishing fleets, called this because of the way it draws closed around a school of fish in the manner of an old-fashioned purse cinching up around a pile of coins. "The skiff takes one end of the net around the tuna and sort of closes the circle on them," Knowles explained. "That's the key intervention point. That's where we have the strong moral mandate."

But as the Zodiacs approached the French tuna-fishing boat *Jean-Marie Christian VI*, confusion engulfed the scene. As anticipated, the French seiner launched its skiffs and started to draw a net closed around the tuna school. Upon seeing the Greenpeace Zodiacs zooming in, the captain of the *Jean-Marie Christian VI* issued a call. "Mayday!" he shouted over the radio. "Pirate attack!" Other tuna boats responded to the alert and arrived to help. The Greenpeace activists identified themselves over the VHF, announcing they were staging a "peaceful action."

Aboard one Zodiac, Frank Hewetson, a 20-year Greenpeace veteran who in his salad days as a protester scaled the first BP deepwater oil rigs off Scotland, tried to direct his pilot toward the net so that he could throw a daisy chain of sandbags over its floating edge and allow the bluefin to escape. But before Hewetson could deploy his gear, a French fishing skiff rammed his Zodiac. A moment later Hewetson was dragged by the leg toward the bow. "At first I thought I'd been lassoed," Hewetson later told me from his hospital bed in London. "But then I looked down. " A fisherman trying to puncture the Zodiac had swung a three-pronged grappling hook attached to a rope into the boat and snagged Hewetson clean through his leg between the bone and the calf muscle. (Using the old language of whale protests, Greenpeace would later report to Agence France-Presse that Hewetson had been "harpooned.")

"*Ma jambe! Ma jambe!*" Hewetson cried out in French, trying to signal to the fisherman to slack off on the rope. The fisherman, according to Hewetson, first loosened it and then reconsidered and pulled it tight again. Eventually Hewetson was able to get enough give in the rope to yank the hook free. Elsewhere, fishermen armed with gaffs and sticks sank another Zodiac and, according to Greenpeace's Knowles, fired a flare at the observation helicopter. At a certain point, the protesters made the decision to break off the engagement. "We have currently pulled back from the seining fleet," Knowles e-mailed me shortly afterward, "to regroup and develop next steps." Bertrand Wendling, the executive director of the tuna-fishing cooperative of which the *Jean-Marie Christian VI* was a part, called the Greenpeace protest "without doubt an act of provocation" in which "valuable work tools" were damaged.

But the main damage that took place that day was indisputably to the bluefin. After the encounter, the fishermen aboard the *Jean-Marie Christian VI* transferred the fish alive into a holding cage and slowly towed them away. Soon those tuna would be brought to feeding pens where they will spend at least several months putting on weight. Afterward, they will be slaughtered and sent to Japan, where 80 percent of the world's Atlantic bluefin tuna are eaten with oblivion.

•••

There are two reasons that a mere fish should have inspired such a high-strung confrontation reminiscent of Greenpeace's early days as a defender of whales. The first stems from fish enthusiasts who have for many years recognized the particular qualities of bluefin tuna—qualities that were they land-based creatures would establish them indisputably as "wildlife" and not just another "seafood" we eat without remorse. Not only is the bluefin's dense, distinctly beefy musculature supremely appropriate for traversing the ocean's breadth, but the animal also has attributes that make its evolutionary appearance seem almost deus ex machina, or rather machina ex deo—a machine from God. How else could a fish develop a sextantlike "pineal window" in the top of its head that scientists say enables it to navigate over thousands of miles? How else could a fish develop a propulsion system whereby a whip-thin crescent tail vibrates at fantastic speeds, shooting the bluefin forward at speeds that can reach 40 miles an hour? And how else would a fish appear within a mostly coldblooded phylum that can use its metabolic heat to raise its body temperature far above that of the surrounding water, allowing it to traverse the frigid seas of the subarctic?

Yes, bluefin tuna are warmblooded.

That bluefin can be huge—10 feet and more than a thousand pounds—is a side note. For those of us who have seen their football silhouettes arise and vanish in less than a blink of an eye or held them alive, their hardshell skins barely containing the surging muscle tissue within, they are something bigger than the space they occupy. All fish change color when they die. But with tuna the death shift feels more profound. Fresh from the water, their backs pulsing neon blue, their bellies gleaming silver-pink iridescence, they seem like the ocean itself.

And in a way they are, which explains the second reason bluefin have come to possess such totemic power. For bluefin tuna and all species of tuna are the living representation of the very limits of the ocean. Their global decline is a warning that we just might destroy our last wild food.

In prehistoric times, the hunting of fish began close by, in freshwater rivers and lakes and coastal ocean waters. But as human populations grew, easily accessed grounds fell short of demand. By the late Middle Ages, European stocks of freshwater fish and near-shore ocean

species proved insufficient. By then, Basque and Viking fisherman had already moved on to the continental shelves off Canada, ushering in the Age of Cod—an age that escalated until the late 20th century, when some of the largest fishing vessels ever built devastated the once-two-billion-strong stock of cod on the Canadian Grand Banks. But there were still new places to fish. In the 1980s and '90s, virgin fishing grounds were found in the Southern Hemisphere, and supplies of replacement fish like New Zealand hoki and Chilean sea bass helped seafood supplies keep pace with demand.

But appetites continued to outstrip supply. Global seafood consumption has increased consistently to the point where we now remove more wild fish and shellfish from the oceans every year than the weight of the human population of China. This latest surge has taken us past the Age of Cod and landed us squarely in the Age of Tuna. Fishing has expanded over the continental shelves into the international no-man's territory known as the high seas—the ocean territory that begins outside of national "exclusive economic zones," or E.E.Z.'s, usually 200 nautical miles out from a country's coast, and continues until it hits the E.E.Z. of another country. The high seas are owned by no one and governed by largely feeble multinational agreements. According to the Sea Around Us project of the University of British Columbia's Fisheries Center, catches from the high seas have risen by 700 percent in the last half-century, and much of that increase is tuna. Moreover, because tuna cross so many boundaries, even when tuna do leave the high seas and tarry in any one nation's territorial waters (as Atlantic bluefin usually do), they remain under the foggy international jurisdiction of poorly enforced tuna treaties.

The essentially ownerless nature of tuna has led to the last great wild-fish gold rush the world may ever see. The most noticeable result of this has been the decline of the giant Atlantic bluefin tuna. But the Atlantic bluefin is just a symptom of a metastasizing tuna disease. The United Nations' Food and Agriculture Organization reports that 7 of the 23 commercially fished tuna stocks are overfished or depleted. An additional nine stocks are also threatened. The Pew Environment Group's tuna campaign asserts that "the boats seeking these tuna are responsible for more hooks and nets in the water than any other fishery."

Tuna then are both a real thing and a metaphor. Literally they are one of the last big public supplies of wild fish left in the world. Metaphorically they are the terminus of an idea: that the ocean is an endless resource where new fish can always be found. In the years to come we can treat tuna as a mile marker to zoom past on our way toward annihilating the wild ocean or as a stop sign that compels us to turn back and radically reconsider.

•••

"We find ourselves in a precarious situation." So wrote Ritchie Notar, a co-owner of the internationally acclaimed Nobu restaurant chain, to Greenpeace U.K. back in 2008 after Greenpeace intensified its tuna-defense efforts and put forward the idea that bluefin should no longer be served at Nobu's establishments. "We are dealing with thousands of years of cultural customs," Notar continued in correspondence Greenpeace forwarded to me. "The Japanese have relied on tuna and the bounties of the sea as part of their culture and history for centuries. We are absolutely appreciative of your goals and efforts within your cause, but it goes far beyond just saying that we can just take what has now all of a sudden been declared an 'endangered' species off the menu. It has to do with custom, heritage and behavior."

Many nations have contributed to the Atlantic bluefin's destruction. Europeans and North Africans do most of the catching and ranching of the fish in the world today. The United States continues to allow bluefin fishing in its waters even though the Gulf of Mexico–spawned stock is considered by many scientists to have entered into full-scale collapse. But it is Japan, the world's largest bluefin importer, that has taken perhaps the most aggressive pro-tuna-fishing position, sometimes assisted by Westerners like Ritchie Notar, who declaim the country's long tuna-eating tradition. But history shows that Japan's stake in tuna fishing is recent and, more important, part of the same endgame that has dragged all of humanity into the Age of Tuna. Before 1800, Japanese tuna sushi didn't even exist.

Trevor Corson is an East Asia scholar turned popular nonfiction writer and author of the 2007 book *The Story of Sushi*, and for select groups he will act as a "sushi concierge," hosting dinners often at the Jewel Bako Japanese restaurant in Manhattan's East Village, one of which I attended this past winter. A Corson-guided meal aims to reveal the historical truth of tuna and to represent the very different fish that were the staples of sushi in earlier times. Plate by plate I watched as Corson walked a group of Manhattan professionals through a traditional Edo-period meal of snappers, jacks and other white-fleshed, smaller fish that most definitely did not include "red" tuna. Afterward, Corson sent me an excerpt from a 1999 Japanese anthology titled "Fish Experts Teach the Secrets of the Deliciousness of Fish" to further underline his point. "Originally, fish with red flesh were looked down on in Japan as a low-class food, and white fish were much preferred," one of the book's contributors, Michiyo Murata, writes. "Fish with red flesh tended to spoil quickly and develop a noticeable stench, so in the days before refrigeration the Japanese aristocracy despised them, and this attitude was adopted by the citizens of Edo [old Tokyo]." Other Japanese scholars like the sushi historian Masuo Yoshino confirm this. Murata, meanwhile, goes on to note that tuna were introduced into sushi only 170 years ago, when a large catch came into Edo one season. On that day a local sushi chef marinated a few pieces of tuna in soy sauce and served it as "nigiri sushi." The practice caught on. Occasionally a big bluefin became sushi, but Corson notes these fish were nicknamed *shibi*—"four days"—because chefs would bury them for four days to mellow their bloody taste.

By the 1930s, tuna sushi was commonplace in Japan, but demand could be met by local supplies of tuna, including the Pacific bluefin species, which dwells in Japan's coastal waters. It was World War II that took tuna fishing to the next level. "To recover from the devastation of the war," Ziro Suzuki, formerly of the Japanese Far Seas Research Laboratory, wrote me, "Japanese fishermen needed more tunas to secure food for domestic demand and also to earn more money by exporting tunas for canning industries in Europe and the U.S. Those needs urged the expansion of fishing grounds outside of the historic grounds of the western Pacific." But this next fishing expansion was technological as well as territorial. Throughout the postwar period, the Japanese perfected industrial long-lining, a practice that employs thousands of baited hooks. In the 1970s Japanese manufacturers developed lightweight, high-strength polymers that were in turn spun into extensive drift nets that could be many miles long. Though drift nets were banned in the high seas by the early '90s, in the 1970s hundreds of miles of them were often deployed in a single night. When drift nets and long lines were coupled with at-sea freezing technology invented around the same time, Japanese fishermen were able to fish the farthest reaches of the oceans while keeping their frozen tuna sushi-ready for as long as a year.

A major yield of all of this Japanese fishing effort was yellowfin tuna. Though they ate bluefin, Japanese did not hold them in high regard before the 1960s, and it took a confluence of socioeconomic factors in both Japan and the West to bring bluefin to the fore. By the late 1960s, sportfishing for giant bluefin tuna was starting in earnest off Nova Scotia, New England and Long Island. Like the Japanese at the time, North Americans had little regard for bluefin on the plate, usually discarding them after capture.

Bluefin sportfishing's rise, however, coincided with Japan's export boom. In the 1960s and '70s, Japanese planes stuffed with electronics unloaded in the U.S. and returned empty—a huge waste of fuel. But when a Japanese entrepreneur realized he could buy New England and Canadian bluefin for a song, he started filling up all those empty cargo holds with tuna. Exposure to beef and other fatty meats during the U.S. occupation had already drawn the Japanese to appreciate bluefin's fatty belly (*otoro*, in sushi terms). The Atlantic bluefin, the biggest bluefin, became the most favored of all. This appreciation boomeranged stateside when Americans started to develop their own raw-fish habit in the late 1970s.

Added to the already significant fishing pressure from the tuna canning industry, Japan's and now the West's sushi jones has come to stress populations of large tuna around the world, starting with the most environmentally sensitive Atlantic bluefin but with the risk of spreading to other species. In fact, one subpopulation of Atlantic bluefin has already vanished after heavy fishing by Japanese long-liners: The bluefin that used to congregate off Brazil disappeared in the early bluefin boom of the 1970s. The remaining Atlantic bluefin stocks are trending similarly, and the two other species of bluefin—the Pacific, which ranges between California and Japan, and the southern bluefin, which plies the waters around Australia—are not far behind. In the United States, the direct fishing pressure on bluefin continues—but perhaps a larger problem is that a large quantity of North American bluefin are caught accidentally as "bycatch" when industrial long-liners deploy their legions of hooks in search of yellowfin tuna over the bluefin's spawning grounds in the Gulf of Mexico. By law, nearly all bluefin caught as by-catch must be dumped back into the sea. Usually by that point they are already dead.

All of this has led the bluefin to become a cause célèbre among conservation groups and the target of several organized "save the bluefin" campaigns. None of them have influenced Japanese consumers. In the case of Nobu, after numerous exchanges with Greenpeace, the sushi restaurant's owners remained unpersuaded of the need to stop serving the fish. Their only concession was a haiku-esque warning on the menus of its London eateries:

"Bluefin tuna
Is an environmentally threatened species
Please ask your server for an alternative."

Willie Mackenzie of Greenpeace U.K. responded angrily in a note to Ritchie Notar: "Despite the assurances that you take these issues seriously and that you want Nobu to be a leader in this field, you have essentially tried to abdicate responsibility by suggesting that it is down to your customers to decide if they want to eat an endangered species."

•••

Away from restaurant menus and the entree preferences of individual consumers, more far-ranging choices are presenting themselves to humanity than picking a California roll or a sliver of *otoro*. These are choices that will shape the fate of not just Atlantic bluefin tuna, not just all tunas, but all the great sea creatures—sharks, swordfish, marlin, even whales. For every one of these animals is highly migratory and roams the high seas, the vast, ownerless seascape that makes up some 60 percent of the oceans.

Until the 1970s, fishing in the high seas tended to be based on the principles of Hugo Grotius's 1609 treatise "Mare Liberum"—a document that advocated free use of the oceans by all. But in the last 40 years, Grotius's "free sea" has grown progressively more circumscribed. Today, high-seas and highly migratory fish are overseen by 18 regional fisheries-management organizations. These "consensus-oriented" institutions, in which each member nation has equal status, can be guided more by political horse-trading than by sound science. A former chairman of the scientific committee of the International Commission for the Conservation of Atlantic Tunas (or Iccat), the body responsible for Atlantic bluefin, told me, "Even though scientific advice says you should stick to a specific catch number, in order to negotiate a deal they tend to nudge that number over a little bit." That little nudge can be enough to put a population of tuna in jeopardy.

In 2008 Iccat set Atlantic bluefin catch limits that were nearly double what its own scientists recommended. Conservationists howled, and the quotas were reduced sharply. But by the time Iccat met again, in November 2009, environmentalists had come to home in on the historic mismanagement of Atlantic bluefin, many of them arguing that a simple reduction in catch quotas for the coming fishing season was not enough—that in fact a zero-catch quota was the only thing that would stave off the fish's extinction. Iccat rejected the zero-quota idea. This in turn forced a much more high-pitched confrontation this spring between parties like Japan, which seems to feel that fishery-management problems can be resolved within the status quo, and those who are looking to take the high seas in a profoundly different direction.

The debate was joined when delegates gathered this past March in Doha, Qatar, for a meeting of the United Nations Convention on the International Trade in Endangered Species of Flora and Fauna, or Cites (pronounced SY-tees). It was a meeting that, for fish, could have been as important as the 1982 meeting of the International Whaling Commission that voted to establish a moratorium on commercial whaling worldwide. For if conservationists got their way, Atlantic bluefin would be included in the Cites treaty's Appendix One—a result that would ban the international trade of the tuna and put them under the jurisdiction of the same U.N. body that oversees tigers, white rhinos and giant pandas. It would be the beginning of a process that would transition Atlantic bluefin tuna from seafood to wildlife.

It is precisely this kind of recasting that happened with whales in the 1980s, and Japan was intent on avoiding a similar recategorization with Atlantic bluefin tuna. As Masanori Miyahara, the director of the Fisheries Agency of Japan, put it to me: "Cites Appendix One is too inflexible … once a species is listed in a Cites appendix, it will never be delisted or down-listed as the history of Cites clearly shows." In other words, once a fish becomes wildlife, it will stay wildlife. A Cites treaty would also allow those countries that happen to have bluefin in their territorial waters to continue to catch them for their own market while excluding all the other treaty member nations—a result that Masanori would surely find not only unfair but also capable of leading to further overfishing. (The European Union has indicated it will continue to catch its allowable quota even if a Cites resolution is passed.)

Japan's touchiness about fairness on the high seas is understandable given its dependence on seafood. Its per capita seafood consumption is among the highest of any industrialized country. And Japan has not been blind to the problems that come with overfishing and excessively large fishing fleets. Indeed, in the last few years it has tried to rein in its industrial fishing effort, decommissioning vessels, literally pulling hooks out of the water. But this has failed to resolve another problem of the Age of Tuna. Just as the industrialized countries are starting to realize the need for more sensible management of the high seas, developing countries are heading in the opposite direction. "Developing countries firmly believe they have a right to expand their fisheries and that developed countries should reduce their fishing effort to compensate," Ziro Suzuki wrote me. "In the process of trying to resolve the conflict of interest, the stocks become overfished, and overall fishing effort grows to an unacceptable level. ... It's really just another example of the North–South problem, just like CO_2 emissions."

The conflict between the developing and developed world plays an increasingly greater role in tuna negotiations, and at a certain point it is hard to figure out who is manipulating whom in an intrigue involving 175 countries, each trying to game the system. Representatives from both the WWF and the Pew Environment Group told me of a curious imbroglio as the Qatar Cites meeting neared its vote on bluefin. Japanese delegation members supposedly told African representatives that European bluefin fleets would relocate to the coast of Africa and catch African yellowfin tuna if the Cites bluefin motion passed. This despite the fact that European vessels are geared up specifically for bluefin fishing and lack the capacity to pursue yellowfin. Masanori Miyahara of the Fisheries Agency of Japan dismissed this claim as "completely wrong and unfounded. We never told such a thing to anybody. We even haven't thought such an idea, ever."

True or not, African nations lined up with Japan. After Libya and Sudan forced a vote, the Atlantic bluefin's Cites Appendix One listing was rejected by a large majority.

Delegates flew away from Qatar with the status quo in place. The monthlong bluefin purse-seining season set earlier by Iccat for the Mediterranean would stand as it was with quotas above what many scientists had recommended. A month after the Cites meeting, BP's Horizon Deepwater oil rig collapsed into the sea and spewed oil into the only bluefin spawning ground in the Americas just as the few remaining North American stock giant bluefin were preparing to mate in the Gulf of Mexico. Though the U.S. National Marine Fisheries Service has been deeply critical of the Mediterranean bluefin catch—in 2007, it went so far as to call for a moratorium—it has been noncommittal about the American fishery. When I asked the Fisheries Service if it would consider closing the bluefin season on the heels of the BP spill, I was offered a statement, part of which, recast in verse form, has an almost Nobu-type haiku quality:

> "N.O.A.A. Fisheries is carefully monitoring
> The spawning of bluefin tuna in the Gulf of Mexico
> By collecting larval samples and analyzing reports
> from scientific observers."

It seems then that no single nation is ready to commit to a sustainable future for the fish. Some would argue that extirpation might just have to be the bluefin's fate. Other, smaller tuna might be better suited to industrial exploitation. The bigeye and yellowfin tuna generally grow faster and spawn earlier. And indeed these lesser tuna are already starting to fill in for the bluefin's absence. In the United States most Americans usually end up eating bigeye when they order *otoro*—the fatty zebra-striped flesh that fetches the highest price on most sushi menus nowadays. But major populations of bigeye tuna are also declining. Should they go away, it's hard to say what would come next.

Can we get ourselves out of the Age of Tuna with our moral center and our food supply intact? Can we develop a civilized hunter–gatherer relationship with tuna and indeed with all other fish and reach a point of equilibrium with our last wild food? Can the management bodies that have overseen the collapse of the most magnificent food fish we've ever known be trusted to manage what is left in its wake?

The answer depends on where you fall on the fairly broad political spectrum of the world's different tuna watchers. The Fisheries Agency of Japan maintains that "Japan is committed to ensure the recovery" of the Atlantic bluefin and has stipulated it will support a complete shutdown of the bluefin fishery at next fall's Iccat meeting, should the scientific committee recommend it. Greenpeace meanwhile has punted on the bluefin political process. "Others have failed our oceans," Oliver Knowles told the press as he prepared his mini armada off Malta, "so Greenpeace will act." Greenpeace is calling for a radical realignment of the high seas, to take stewardship away from regional fisheries-management organizations and establish 40 percent of the world's ocean territory as a marine reserve, a kind of Antarctica-style agreement with shades of whale, where nations, instead of bargaining over quotas, would simply not be able to do any fishing at all in large areas of the oceans. Most other environmental organizations are behind the marine-reserve idea, but they vary in opinion on how big those reserves should be. The Blue Ocean Institute calls for a five-year moratorium on Atlantic bluefin fishing everywhere. The WWF further advocates that the industrial fishing methods that spread during the Age of Tuna—the drift nets, long lines, purse seines and spotter planes—be done away with. In their view, the "artisanal" single-hook-and-line fishing practices of old are the only way to sustainably hunt big and naturally scarce predators like bluefin.

But if we are to embark on a global project of ramping down tuna fishing, what are we to eat?

Until the modern era, the response to wild-game decline has been a primitive one: widespread destruction of the animals that can't stand up to our hunting followed by the selection of a handful of ones that we can tame. Out of the many mammals that our forebears ate before the last ice age, humans selected four—cows, pigs, sheep and goats—to be their principal meats. Out of all the many birds that darkened the primeval skies, humans chose four—chickens, turkeys, ducks and geese—to be their poultry.

And indeed, this is a process that is taking shape rapidly with fish. Atlantic salmon are now commercially extinct throughout almost the entirety of their range but have become one of the most widely farmed fish in the world.

But while leaps have been made in taming marine fish, tuna, particularly bluefin tuna, may not make very much sense for the farm. Bluefin ranching as it is practiced in the Mediterranean, and with the Pacific bluefin in Japan and the southern bluefin in Australia, rightly faces strong environmental criticisms since it relies on catching juveniles from the wild and denies those

baby bluefin a chance to reach adulthood and breed. Now, however, the final steps of fully taming or "closing the life cycle" of bluefin tuna are under way, which will make it possible for bluefin to be grown from an egg in a laboratory to a full-size adult. In such a system, an isolated "domestic" family of bluefin can be established that need not have any interaction with the wild at all. For several years Japan has been producing small amounts of closed-life-cycle Pacific bluefin (known as Kindai tuna in the market). In Europe and Australia, scientists have used light-manipulation technology as well as time-release hormone implants invented by the Israeli endocrinologist Yonathan Zohar to bring about the first large-scale captive spawning of Atlantic and southern bluefin.

But there are considerable complications ahead. As Richard Smullen, an Australia-based feed-company specialist working to come up with a suitable diet for farmed bluefin, explained: "The thing is the metabolic rate of these fish is very high compared to other fish; they swim fast, they heat their brains and vital organs and are warmer than the surrounding water, so this is energetically expensive. An analogy is like trying to feed an ultramarathon runner—they have the potential to eat a lot and not put on any weight." Though Smullen says that it is possible to bring feed-conversion ratios for bluefin down, currently it may take 15 pounds of feed to produce a single pound of tuna, roughly 10 times as much as is needed for farmed salmon.

As fisheries decline globally, more and more countries are trying to replace their wild fish with farmed ones. Today 30 million tons of small forage fish are removed from the oceans yearly, with the majority of it going to feed farmed fish. If we end up farming bluefin on the same scale as we now farm salmon, the tuna, with its poor feed-conversion rate, may end up taking the food of the remaining wild fish that we haven't yet got around to catching.

In addition there is little evidence to suggest that taming a species saves its wild forebear. Tiger farms in China have not halted tiger declines in the wild. Hundreds of millions of farmed Atlantic salmon have not stanched wild Atlantic salmon's continued decline. Just because we can tame something doesn't mean we should. The example of whales again rises. As the science historian D. Graham Burnett points out in a coming book on the Save the Whales movement, collaborations between American nuclear scientists and marine biologists were once proposed in the 1960s whereby tropical atolls, leveled by nuclear testing, could be used as giant corrals for the commercial farming of cetaceans. But fortunately for the whale—and I think for us too—we have come to see the whale not as something we fish for, not as something we farm, but as something we appreciate and maybe empathize with. Instead of expanding our stomachs or our wallets, whales have expanded our consciousness, our very humanity. So we have to ask ourselves, is there any rational argument for humans to eat bluefin tuna, wild, ranched or farmed? Is the fish really so special that no substitute will do? If the Japanese adapted to a higher-fat diet in half a century, could they and all sushi lovers not shift gears again and adapt to a sustainable diet?

It was in answer to these questions that I went looking for a farmed fish that could satisfy tuna-eaters at the sushi bar. A fish that had the dense "bite" of tuna but with a smaller ecological footprint—a Volkswagen instead of a Hummer.

My search led me to the coast of the Big Island of Hawaii, where I motored with a tall, optimistic Australian named Neil Anthony Sims. As we donned wetsuits, fins and scuba tanks, Sims rejoiced in telling me tales of his adopted land. Eventually we spat in our masks, adjusted our regulators and dived into the water above Sims's farm—a huge underwater ziggurat that is the center of his company, Kona Blue Water Farms.

Until recently, most of the fish we've chosen to domesticate have been accidents. Salmon, striped bass, trout—we have chosen those species because we knew them as wild game. We seldom considered their biological profiles or whether they jibed well with the ecological limitations of a crowded planet.

But Neil Sims was a fisheries biologist before he was a fish farmer. And it was his direct personal experience with the limitations of fisheries management that persuaded him that fish farming, done right, was a better choice than fish catching.

Sims began his career in the remote Cook Islands of the South Pacific. There he was responsible for managing a giant snail called a trochus that produces an attractive pearly shell, valuable to native jewelers. Over half a decade, he implemented numerous management strategies. Nothing worked—not even shortening the harvest season drastically. The day after one season ended, he came across a bare-chested Polynesian elder who had pulled his dugout canoe onto the beach. Sims looked inside the boat and saw it filled with trochus.

"I yelled at him," Sims remembers. "Then he yelled at me. He started to cry. Then I started to cry, and then the old bugger finally says: 'Why? Why did you close the season? There are still some left!'" This moment prompted him to look beyond fishing, to an entirely different approach.

Sims was drawn to Hawaii, with its deep near-shore waters and strong currents—attributes favorable to aquaculture that he believed could make ocean farming sustainable. But the fish farming he found on arrival in Hawaii didn't impress him. "People were trying milkfish and mullet," Sims recalled. "They start with the letter 'm' and they're all really kind of hmmmmm in the mouth, if you know what I mean." Sims found the fish too bony and small, with loose, mushy flesh. This was important. Sims's long-standing beat in the South Pacific had persuaded him that "there was an opportunity for a high-value, sushi-quality fish," a fish that could fit into the dense-flesh category that the Age of Tuna had cultivated in Japan and indeed throughout the developed world.

After parsing many species he came across *Seriola rivoliana*. Known in Hawaii as kahala, it is a speedy, firm-fleshed animal of the same family as yellowtail and amberjack. They are only very distantly related to tuna and do not have tuna's ruby red color, but they still have dense flesh and could easily pass for white albacore sushi. The fat content in Sims's farmed kahala is around 30 percent, and indeed it is the presence of fat that accounts for much of a sushi fish's tunalike flavor.

Sims was further intrigued when he found that ka-hala had barely been fished commercially. In their wild form kahala can carry ciguatera poison—a toxin some-times deadly to humans that kahala ingest when they feed around coral reefs. But when kahala are isolated away from reefs and fed a traditional aquaculture diet of soy and fishmeal, they are ciguatera-free. (Sims asserts that ciguatera has never been detected in the flesh of his fish.) Since they have not been fished commercially, wild kahala populations are large and unlikely to be severely damaged through interaction with farmed fish. Moreover, kahala are much more "feed efficient" than tuna. The amount of fish required to produce a pound of kahala ranges from 1.6 pounds to 2 pounds, an order of magnitude better than bluefin. And Sims recently began feed trials using diets that contain no directly harvested forage fish. Lastly, unlike tuna, which require a tremendous investment in spawning technology, kahala are naturally fecund: they breed frequently, at least weekly, throughout the year.

• • •

There are, of course, those who would disagree with Sims's approach. When I asked Casson Trenor, author of the 2009 book *Sustainable Sushi*, for his impression of the kahala as a farmed fish, he responded that the farming of any carnivore is "fighting the current." "You may have a farm that has a more efficient protein ratio," Trenor wrote me, "but produces more waste streams. Perhaps you have a feed pellet that knocks your feed conversion ratio down to 1 to 1, but you continue to host a rampant parasite infestation. ... We need to iden-tify fish that through their physiology and life history actually lend themselves to clean farming operations." Trenor's own compromise is to serve wild "small for-mat" tuna like skipjack or albacore, fish that he feels can embrace the "principles of seasonality, local awareness and sustainability" that sushi originally expressed before it was "transformed through cultural misinterpretation and overzealous globalization into exactly the opposite."

But as I plunged into the calm blue waters off Kona and inflated my diving vest to gain equilibrium in the water column, I couldn't help thinking that in a world of environmental evils prosecuted against fish, the farm-ing of a more efficient carnivore than a bluefin under the stewardship of a knowledgeable, environmentally conscious biologist was a good deal better than the rapacious industrial harvesting of "large format" tuna. Looking down at this "cathedral" of fish, as Sims called it, the possibility of a certain balance presented itself. Using technology developed over the last 10 years, Kona Blue has constructed diamond-shape cages that can be moored in the open ocean away from sensitive coastal areas. As I glided down, past the fish swimming in uni-son in their net pen, I felt a cautious optimism. The site of these pens had been carefully chosen; the swift cur-rents meant that nutrients did not accumulate below the pens. And regular monitoring has found the fish to have no internal parasites, unlike the wild kahala. Sims's commitment to transparency is also encouraging. He regularly posts water-quality reports on his Web site and presumably will do the same as the operation expands.

Sims waved me over to the side of the net pen. I floated above him, close enough to see that the fish ac-tually seemed to recognize him. In what he would later describe to me as the "rock-star effect," the fish crowded to be close to him. Sims spread his arms out wide and seemed to take in their adulation.

Sims has trademarked his kahala with the name Kona Kampachi—"Kona" for its point of origin, "Kam-pachi" for the similar animal in Japan. They retail for $18 to $20 a pound in fillet form and to date have a tenuous foot in the market. Production reached more than a mil-lion pounds in 2008, about a third of the amount of blue-fin caught in American waters that year. After a hiatus during most of 2009 and the first part of 2010 while Sims reconfigured his cages, the product will be reintroduced this July with even more capacity. Kona Kampachi may not have the rich ruby color of tuna (a color that is often enhanced artificially by "gassing" with carbon monox-ide), but it is an extremely pleasant sushi experience. It satisfies the sashimi yen that has been created over the last 30 years—the yen for the firm, energy-rich muscula-ture of a fast-swimming open-ocean fish.

Can we embrace a new set of species that we don't know intimately in their wild form? Can we come to an understanding of which fish work for us as "seafood" and which fish don't? I would hope so. The survival of the wild ocean could very well depend on it. I took one more look at Neil Sims floating with arms outstretched, his kahala finning in the current, each one mutely appraising this conductor of a silent concert. The only sound was the whir of bubbles rising by my ears.

•••

Seafood. How many species suffer those two mean English syllables? Other languages are no kinder. Romance European cultures use the expression "sea fruit," while Slavs say "sea gifts." So-called vegetarians rue the killing of farmed terrestrial animals but regularly eat wild fish. Kosher laws mandating merciful animal slaughter don't apply to fish.

These thoughts were in my head recently when I got perhaps my last look at a wild bluefin tuna, just a month before the Deepwater Horizon rig exploded and collapsed into the Gulf of Mexico. I was 20-odd miles off the coast of Cape Hatteras, N.C., aboard the *Sensation*, a vessel chartered by the Tag-a-Giant Foundation, a nonprofit organization trying to decode the complex migration patterns of the bluefin and help lay the scientific foundation for the fish's protection. Tag-a-Giant had been fishing for a couple days, and many people had sat in the fighting chair I now occupied, reeling in tuna after tuna. But for me this was a first. I had never caught a bluefin before.

In the past I would have wanted to savor the fight, to do battle with the fish with lighter, more "sporting" tackle. But considering everything I'd learned about tuna, humans and the chances of the great fish's survival, it suddenly seemed infinitely more appropriate to fight this tuna with the full expression of humanity's power. For in the end tuna are no match for us. We have in this final phase of exploitation achieved dominion over the entirety of the watery world, from inland lakes and rivers to the littoral zone to the continental shelf out to the abyss of the high seas. Sitting in the huge fighting chair with the huge rod and reel, in the well of the huge sportfishing vessel, it was inescapably apparent who had the edge.

As my bluefin breached, one of the scientists opened a door at the stern of the boat. A blue vinyl mat was laid down on the deck. The fish came through the door, still "hot," banging its tail excitedly. But in an instant a biologist named Andre Boustany placed a moist cover over the tuna's giant eye and a hydration hose in its mouth. The tuna motor mellowed, and at last the fish was beatifically still.

"Do you want to tag him?" Boustany asked me.

I took the sharp four-inch needle from his hand and positioned it just behind the fish's dorsal fin. Pricking the skin slightly I started to pull my hand away.

"No," Boustany said, "you gotta really stick it in there."

Applying more pressure, I felt the needle slide into the flank, felt the resistance of the dense sushi flesh, raw and red and most certainly delicious. But for the first time in my life I felt tuna flesh for what it was: a living, perfect expression of a miraculous adaptation. An adaptation that allows bluefin to cross oceans at the speed of a battleship. An adaptation that should be savored in its own right as the most miraculous engine of a most miraculous animal, not as food.

Perhaps people will never come to feel about a tuna the way they have come to feel about whales. Whales are, after all, mammals: they have large brains; they nurse their young and breed slowly. All of that ensconces them in a kind of empathic cocoon, the warmth of which even the warmest-blooded tuna may never occupy. But what we can perhaps be persuaded to feel, viscerally, is that industrial fishing as it is practiced today against the bluefin and indeed against all the world's great fish, the very tigers and lions of our era, is an act unbefitting our sentience. An act as pointless, small-minded and shortsighted as launching a harpoon into the flank of a whale.

Analyzing the Situation

1. Throughout *Writing Situations*, the idea of "players" in rhetorical situations has referred to people who may not be an audience of a text, but who may be affected by the text, nonetheless. In "Tuna's End," though, we can identify a nonhuman player: the tuna (or perhaps all fish or all wildlife). What are the implications for thinking about the situation in which "Tuna's End" participates and for the very idea of rhetorical situations if we consider nonhuman players in situations?

2. What kinds of constraints are most prevalent in the situation in which "Tuna's End" participates?

3. Given that "Tuna's End" was first published in *The New York Times Magazine*, what can you infer about the audience Paul Greenberg was attempting to reach? Why do you suppose this audience is of relevance in this situation?

Analyzing the Rhetoric

1. What role do questions play in "Tuna's End"?

2. What is the "hook" Paul Greenberg uses to catch readers' attention and draw them into "Tuna's End"? Is it an effective strategy? Why or why not?

3. In "Tuna's End," Paul Greenberg makes an important distinction in the rhetorical use of "seafood" as opposed to "wildlife." What role does his rhetorical analysis of these terms contribute to his overall position? How do you respond to the point Greenberg makes about the distinctions between seafood and wildlife?

Discussing

1. Do you eat tuna? Were you aware of the issues Paul Greenberg raises concerning tuna? Has "Tuna's End" influenced your thinking about the consumption of tuna? Discuss your reactions to "Tuna's End."

2. Paul Greenberg writes that "tuna then are both a real thing and a metaphor." What does he mean by this? As a class, discuss what we might learn from tuna-as-metaphor.

3. One of the interesting points Paul Greenberg makes in "Tuna's End" focuses on the conflict between sustainability and culture. Cultural customs—like eating tuna—are probably some of the most difficult constraints in a situation to overcome or change. As a class, discuss what happens when culture and sustainability conflict. Can you think of other examples in which cultural customs or traditions conflict with sustainable practices or ideas?

Writing

1. Tuna fishing is only one of many activities that contributes to overharvesting and depletion of marine resources. What other human activities contribute to the loss of marine life and the ecological destruction of the world's marine environments? Conduct research to learn more about ocean sustainability and write an essay documenting what you have learned.

2. There are many resources available online to help individuals improve their awareness of marine degradation and resource depletion and to provide resources and suggestions for leading a more marine-friendly life. Spend some time online locating and reading as many of these sources as you can find. Then create a web page that serves as a hub to direct others to the resources you have identified. Don't make your page a simple list of links; instead, to make the site useful, provide summaries of what each linked site offers.

3. The distinction Paul Greenberg makes between "seafood" and "wildlife" is an important indicator of language's reflecting our perceptions of a particular population of animal. But how realistic is that perception? Create a series of interview questions about how people respond to the distinctions between wildlife and seafood and interview at least ten people about the issue. Then, using the information you have gathered, write a document that explains how people talk about the differences between those two ideas. Would people eat wildlife? Is seafood something we might want to take pictures of? Would people patronize a wildlife restaurant? Would people visit a seafood preserve? Do people prefer their wildlife fried or broiled? Do they want tartar sauce with that?

How to Queer Ecology: One Goose at a Time, A Lesson Plan

Alex Johnson

Alex Johnson was a master's student at the University of Montana when he wrote "How to Queer Ecology: One Goose at a Time, A Lesson Plan" in 2011. An environmental studies student who lives and writes in Missoula, Montana, Johnson serves as the editor of *Camas: The Nature of the West*, a literary magazine that encourages a dialogue on environmental and cultural issues in the West. He is also the Director of Outreach for All Against the Haul, a grassroots effort to stop the construction of a "permanent industrial corridor for oversized loads to the Alberta Tar Sands through Oregon, Washington, Idaho, and Montana."[4] Johnson has led conservation crews across much of Alaska and the Western United States. His essay "How to Queer Ecology: One Goose at a Time, A Lesson Plan" was originally published in *Orion* magazine, a prestigious magazine that publishes writing about environment, nature, and culture. As Orion's web page explains, "*Orion*'s mission is to inform, inspire, and engage individuals and grassroots organizations in becoming a significant cultural force for healing nature and community."[5] Johnson's writing has also appeared in *Astrobiology*, *Camas*, and *Ugly Accent*.

I once thought I knew what nature writing was: the pretty, sublime stuff minus the parking lot. The mountain majesty and the soaring eagle and the ancient forest

---

[4]"Who We Are." *All Against the Haul.* Web. 14 Nov. 2013.
[5]"Mission and History." *Orion.* Orion, n.d. Web. 14 Nov. 2013.

without the human footprint, the humans themselves, the mess.

Slowly, fortunately, that definition has fallen flat. Where is the line between what is Nature and what is Human? Do I spend equal times in the parking lot and the forest? Can I really say the parking lot is separate from the forest? What if I end up staying in the parking lot the whole time? What if it has been a long drive and I really have to pee?

The problem is, the Nature/Human split is not a split. It is a dualism. It is false.

I propose messing it up. I propose queering Nature.

As it would happen, I'm queer. What I mean is this: A) I am a man attracted to men. B) Popular culture has told me that men who are attracted to men are unnatural, and so C) if my culture is right, then I am unnatural. But D) I don't feel unnatural at all. In fact, the love I share with another man is one of the most comfortable, honest, real feelings I have ever felt. And so E) I can't help but believe that Nature, and the corresponding definition of "natural," betray reality. From my end of the rainbow, this thing we call Nature is in need of a good queering.

Step #1: Let Go of Ecological Mandates.

Not so long ago, I read David Quammen's essay "The Miracle of the Geese." In the essay, Quammen says this: "wild geese, not angels, are the images of humanity's own highest self." By humanity, I can only assume that he means all humans, collectively, over all of time. "They show us the apogee of our own potential," Quammen says. "They live by the same principles that we, too often, only espouse. They embody liberty, grace, and devotion, combining those three contradictory virtues with a seamless elegance that leaves us shamed and inspired." Quammen seems to be on to something. Who could possibly be against liberty, grace, or devotion? But then he starts talking about sex. How geese are monogamous. How a male goose will in fact do better evolutionarily if he is loyal to his mate. "They need one another there, male and female, each its chosen mate, at all times," he says. "The evolutionary struggle, it turns out, is somewhat more complicated than a singles' bar." I'm a little concerned about the evolutionary struggle thing, but I'm still tracking. Life sure is complicated. And then he says this: "I was glad to find an ecological mandate for permanent partnership among animals so estimable as *Branta canadensis*."

Boom. There it is. Geese are wild. Geese are pure. They aren't all mixed up with the problems of civilization and humanity. What we really need is to behave more like geese. If you are a male, then you must find a female. You must partner with that female, provide for that female, fertilize that female, and love that female for the rest of your life. If you are a female, well, you'll know what to do.

When I first read about Quammen's geese, I'd been out as bisexual for a year. It was around the second Bush election, and I was writing very serious letters to my conservative grandparents about my sexuality and politics. Now I know why his essay, so considerate, so passionate, so genteel, hit me in the gut. I was not natural.

Step #2: Stop Generalizing.

My instinct is to give Quammen the benefit of the doubt; it was the late '80s after all. Regardless of his intentions though, Quammen's notion that Canada geese offer humans an ecological mandate not only reinforces a Nature-as-purity mythos (*against* which humans act), but at an even more basic level, his assumptions are simply inaccurate: plenty of geese aren't straight.

In 1999, Bruce Bagemihl published *Biological Exuberance*, an impressive compendium of thousands of observed nonheteronormative sexual behaviors and gender nonconformity among animals. Besides giraffes and warthogs and hummingbirds, there's a section on geese. Researchers have observed that up to 12 percent of pairs were homosexual in populations of *Branta canadensis*. And it's not because of a lack of potential mates of the

opposite gender. "In one case," says Bagemihl, "a male harassed a female who was part of a long-lasting lesbian pair and separated her from her companion, mating with her. However, the next year, she returned to her female partner and their pairbond resumed."

Red squirrels are seasonally bisexual, mounting same-sex partners and other-sex partners with equal fervor. Male boto dolphins penetrate each other's genital slits as well as blow holes. Primates exhibit all sorts of queer behavior between males and males and females and females. Observing queer behavior in nonhumans is as easy as a trip to the nearest primate house, or a careful observation of the street cats, or the deer nibbling on your shrubs, or the mites on your skin.

The world itself, it turns out, is *so queer*.

Quammen assumed that geese are straight because it was easy to do. It was easy to assume I was straight, too; I did so for the first eighteen years of my life. But generalizing about the habits of both humans and the more-than-human living world not only denies that certain behavior already exists, it limits the potential for that behavior to become more common, and more commonly accepted.

Step #3: Honk.

I don't mean to insist that there is an ecological mandate for being gay. My interest in queering ecology lies in enabling humans to imagine an infinite number of possible Natures. The living world exhibits monogamy. But it also exhibits orgies, gender transformation, and cloning. What, then, is natural? All of it. None of it. Instead of using the more-than-human world as justification for or against certain behavior and characteristics, let's use the more-than-human world as a humbling indication of the capacity and diversity of all life on Earth.

So many of us humans are queer. Across all social, political, and physical boundaries, 2 to 10 percent of people take part in nonheteronormative behavior. Beyond the scope of sexuality, humans are capable of any number of imaginable and unimaginable behaviors. That I do not eat bull testicles does not mean that that behavior is any less human than my eating of baby back ribs. Why then, if I cohabitate with another man, sharing the same bed, yes even having sex in that bed with that man, am I somehow less human?

A goose is a goose is a goose.

Step #4: Acknowledge the Irony.

In a review of Peter Matthiessen's book *The Birds of Heaven: Travels with Cranes*, Richard White indicts the "relentless and blinkered earnestness" of nature writing. White claims that because of its "reluctance to deal with paradox, irony, and history, much nature writing reinforces the worst tendencies of environmentalism." White points out that Matthiessen's unflinchingly sincere narrative baldly contradicts the circumstances: "The birds are immortal, timeless, and they transport us back into the deep evolutionary past," writes White. "But then Matthiessen gives us the details. He is sitting in a loud and clattering helicopter during this particular trip to the Eocene."

If you depict cranes as pure and ancient, with no place in this modern world, then you must ignore all those species that have done quite well in the rice paddies. Writing about nature means accepting that it will prove you wrong. And right. And render you generally confused. Nature is mysterious, and our part in the pageant is shrouded in mystery as well. This means contradiction and paradox and irony. It means that there will always be an exception. Nature has always humiliated the self-congratulatory scientist.

Let's stop congratulating ourselves. Instead, let's give a round of applause to the delicious complexity. Let us call this complexity *the queer*, and let us use it as a verb. Let us queer our ecology. Cranes can be ancient, but they can also be modern. Might their posterity extend past ours?

We've inherited a culture that takes its dualisms seriously. Nature, on the one hand, is the ideal, the pure, the holy. On the other hand, it is evil, dangerous, and dirty. The problem? There's no reconciliation. We accept both notions as separate but equal truths and then organize our world around them. Status quo hurrah! Irony be damned.

Take sexuality, for instance:

We have come to believe, over our Western cultural history, that heterosexual monogamy is the norm, the *natural*. People who call gays unnatural presume that Nature is pure, perfect, and predictable. *Nature intended for a man and a woman to love each other*, they say. *Gays act against Nature.* And yet: we rip open the Earth. We dominate the landscape, compromising the integrity of the living world. We act as though civilization were something better, higher, more valuable than the natural world.

Our culture sets Nature as the highest bar for decorum, while simultaneously giving Nature our lowest standard of respect. Nature is at our disposal, not only for our physical consumption, but also for our social construction. We call geese beautiful and elegant and faithful until they are shitting all over the lawn and terrorizing young children. Then we poison their eggs. Or shoot them.

What I'm getting at is this: those who traditionally hold more power in society—be they men over women, whites over any other race, wealthy over poor, straight over queer—have made their own qualities standard, "natural," constructing a vision of the world wherein such qualities are the norm. And in so doing, they've made everyone else's qualities *perverse, against Nature, against God*. Even Nature—defined impossibly as the nonhuman—becomes unnatural when it does not fit the desired norm: *the gay geese must be affected by hormone pollution*!

A man who has sex with a man must identify himself by his perversion, by his difference. If straight is the identity of *I am*, then gay becomes *I am not*. Women are not men. Native people are not white. Nature is not human.

Instead of talking about nonconformity, I want to talk about possibility and unnameably complex reality. What queer can offer is the identity of *I am also*. I am also human. I am also natural. I am also alive and dynamic and full of contradiction, paradox, irony. Queer knocks down the house of cards and throws them into the warm wind.

Step #5: Don't Fear the Queer.

If theses were still in vogue, I would tell you my thesis is queer ecology. But as Zapatista leader Subcommandante Marcos told Pierluigi Sullo from the forest of southeast Mexico (and probably from a table in a house in a village in that forest), "I sincerely believe that you are not searching for a solution, but rather for a discussion." He's right.

So what discussion am I looking for?

Well, first, one that is happening at all. I've met many kind people (aren't we all sometimes?) who are so afraid of being politically incorrect that they don't speak at all—well, at least not about race or gender or sex (this on top of the three taboos of religion, politics, and money). How do I know how I should refer to Indians? Or blacks? Or gays? Or bums, for that matter? It's just all so complicated now. Queer, then, remains a gesture of hands under the table. A wink.

In the recent past, conversationalists have at least had the weather to fall back on. But the record heat of late with its strange winds of change have whipped away that golden ticket of banality too. So people stop talking, at least about difference, or flux, or complication, altogether. And the floor is left to those who are the loudest and quickest, and who never had any intention of complicating their conversation with anyone or anything that doesn't conform to their tidy but limited worldview.

Step #6: Enjoy the Performance.

The problem with unnameably complex reality is that it's really hard to pin down and even harder to write about. Yet anyone who gives a damn about the ecological health of life on Earth knows that there's no time for dillydallying.

In the late nineteenth century, a Danish scientist named Eugen Warming first used the term *ecology* to describe the study of interrelationships between living things. Henry Chandler Cowles, a doctoral candidate at the University of Chicago, brought ecology across the Atlantic with the 1899 publication of his treatise on the succession of the plant life of the Indiana Dunes. Instead of static forests and static lakes and static prairies, Warming and Cowles recognized that these features of the physical world were in flux. As Cowles wrote in his introduction, "Ecology, therefore, is a study in dynamics."

Queer ecology, then, is the study of dynamics across all phenomena, all behavior, all possibility. It is the relation between past, present, and future.

Yes, we need to act. But we also must recognize that any action is also a performance, and possibly in drag. Any writer who chooses the more-than-human world as subject must acknowledge both the complexity and paradox contained within the subject of nature, as well as the contradictions wrapped up within the writer's very self. Such a writer will write about the parking lot and the invasive knapweed and the unseasonably warm weather and how he or she is undeniably mixed up in the complications. The poet James Broughton calls it "the mystery of the total self." Henry Chandler Cowles called it ecology.

It is the relation within the human and the natural and the god and the geese and the past, present, future, body-self-other. A queer ecology is a liberatory ecology. It is the acknowledgment of the numberless relations between all things alive, once alive, and alive once again. No man can categorize those relations without lying. Categories offer us a way of organizing our world. They are tools. They are power.

Acknowledge the power. Acknowledge the lie.

Step #7: I'm Done with Steps.

Not so long ago, my father and I drove out of the city of Chicago going east on the Skyway.

On a map, the eastern boundary of the city is clean. It curls southeast along the shore of Lake Michigan, then cuts south at Indiana as straight as a longitudinal line. On the other side of the state line are Whiting, East Chicago, and Gary, towns that only gamblers and family members visit. Everybody else just lives there.

In reality, the eastern boundary of the city has no boundary at all. It continues its concrete, steel, and electrical-line unfurling along the southern shore of the great lake of Michigan. We were two white men, hurtling on four rubber wheels down the concrete Skyway, a corridor of semis and freight trains and transistors and faceless industrial complexes blinking out toward the lake.

I don't recall what my father and I were talking about. I do recall looking out the window onto the gray April sweep of the old glacial lake bed.

Then I saw the geese. More of them than I had ever imagined could gather. V after V after W after I after V. One after another, each flock waved several hundred feet above the ground. It was spring, and they all flew east along the metal and concrete corridor. They flew along the shore of the lake.

Less than half an hour later, we reached the Indiana Dunes. There were trees: oaks mostly. We opened our car doors to the calls of sandhill cranes. They were calls neither ancient nor modern. They were calls from the deepest present. As we stood in the parking lot, the car engine still pinging, the half-dozen cranes swung across the opening above us and out of sight.

My father and I made eye contact, then looked up from the parking lot into the trees where the cranes had gone. Then we both went off to pee.

Analyzing the Situation

1. What do you suppose was Alex Johnson's exigency for writing this essay?

2. What role do cultural constraints play in "How to Queer Ecology: One Goose at a Time, A Lesson Plan"?

3. In what ways is "How to Queer Ecology: One Goose at a Time, A Lesson Plan" ecological?

Analyzing the Rhetoric

1. How would you describe the introductory section of "How to Queer Ecology: One Goose at a Time, A Lesson Plan"? How does this section work as an introduction?

2. Why do you suppose Alex Johnson divides "How to Queer Ecology: One Goose at a Time, A Lesson Plan" into "steps" as he does? Do you find this to be an effective strategy?

3. Is "How to Queer Ecology: One Goose at a Time, A Lesson Plan" argumentative? Is it persuasive?

4. What role does personal narrative play in Alex Johnson's essay? How does it contribute to his purpose?

Discussing

1. Alex Johnson's "How to Queer Ecology: One Goose at a Time, A Lesson Plan" is written to encourage response. How do you respond to the essay? As a class, discuss the essay, both in terms of its content and its construction.

2. The final "step" in "How to Queer Ecology: One Goose at a Time, A Lesson Plan" is "I'm Done with Steps." What do you suppose Alex Johnson means by this, and why does he use it as the subtitle for the concluding section of his essay?

Writing

1. One of the more important points that Alex Johnson makes in "How to Queer Ecology: One Goose at a Time, A Lesson Plan" is that the idea of calling something "natural" is often used as a powerful rhetorical device to validate particular phenomena.

Things that are identified as "unnatural," then, are seen as invalid or wrong. Take some time to learn more about what it means to identify something as natural or unnatural. What kinds of things do we commonly identify as natural? What kinds of things do we ostracize as unnatural? In what ways do our classifications of natural and unnatural affect how we relate to things in those categories?

2. In "How to Queer Ecology: One Goose at a Time, A Lesson Plan," Alex Johnson makes the statement,

"The world itself, it turns out, is *so queer*." How do you respond to this claim and to the reasons Johnson provides for making it? Write a response to Johnson addressing this claim specifically.

3. Early in "How to Queer Ecology: One Goose at a Time, A Lesson Plan," Alex Johnson asks, "Where is the line between what is Nature and what is Human?" In an essay, answer Johnson's question.

Manufactured Landscapes

Jennifer Baichwal

Manufactured Landscapes is a documentary about the work of photographer Edward Burtynsky as he travels the world taking photographs of what he calls "manufactured land-scapes," which are landscapes that have either been altered or created by humans. However, *Manufactured Landscapes* is about much more than the work of a photographer. The documentary reveals the often unfathomable size of ecological destruction wrought at the hands of human industry. Together director Jennifer Baichwal and Burtynsky reveal images of massive factories in the Fujian and Zhejiang provinces of China, ship building on the beaches of Bangladesh, immense quarries, colossal slag heaps, and vast piles of e-waste that are almost difficult to imagine. In doing so, they work to bring to light global ecological destruction in locations unfamiliar to most Westerners and in sizes that are often difficult to comprehend.

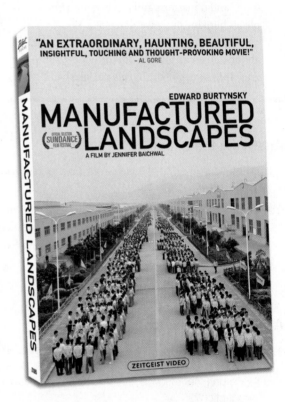

"AN EXTRAORDINARY, HAUNTING, BEAUTIFUL, INSIGHTFUL, TOUCHING AND THOUGHT-PROVOKING MOVIE!"
– AL GORE

EDWARD BURTYNSKY

MANUFACTURED LANDSCAPES

OFFICIAL SELECTION SUNDANCE FILM FESTIVAL

A FILM BY JENNIFER BAICHWAL

ZEITGEIST VIDEO

Analyzing the Situation

1. Chances are most of the people shown in *Manu-factured Landscapes* will likely not ever see the documentary. In this way they are (sometimes un-

willing) participants and also players in the situation. However, they are not the only players in the situation in which *Manufactured Landscapes* participates. Who else can you identify as players in this situation?

2. Is this a situation you were aware of? How might you explain to someone the situation in which *Manufactured Landscapes* participates?

3. What role does location play in the situation in which *Manufactured Landscapes* participates?

4. What role do relations play in the situation in which *Manufactured Landscapes* participates, particularly ecological relationships?

Analyzing the Rhetoric

1. *Manufactured Landscapes* is a documentary that is primarily carried out by way of visual depiction, both video and Burtynsky's photographs. There isn't very much talking in the film, though sound is always present. How would you describe the visual rhetoric of *Manufactured Landscapes*? How would you describe the role of sound in the film?

2. Why do you suppose Jennifer Baichwal opted to present parts of *Manufactured Landscapes* in black and white and other parts in color? Rhetorically, what are the different effects of black and white and of color?

3. What would you say is the rhetorical purpose of *Manufactured Landscapes*? Is it informative? Argumentative? Narrative? Descriptive? Analytical? Evaluative? How does it fulfill the rhetorical purpose(s) you identify?

Discussing

1. Which scenes in *Manufactured Landscapes* do you find most powerful or most compelling? Why? Discuss with your classmates which scenes you and they are most interested in.

2. At one point in *Manufactured Landscapes*, Edward Burtynsky talks about shooting photographs of a silver mine (41:30). He explains that he arrived at the mine in a car made of iron and filled with gas. He uses film that's "loaded with silver." As he explains, everything that he does "is connected to the thing I'm photographing." Discuss the implications of Burtynsky's recognition of this connectedness and to the situation. Do you ever find yourself in a similar kind of situation, one in which your own participation contributes to the very situation you are working to change?

3. Are Edward Burtynsky's photographs that appear in *Manufactured Landscapes* artistic? Are they enjoyable to view? How might you describe the photos? Discuss the photographs that are shown in the documentary and your reactions to them.

4. At one point in *Manufactured Landscapes*, Edward Burtynsky and his crew are told by what appear to be officials they may not take pictures of a particular site (the scene begins at about 49:23). The officials cite regulations and also claim it's not a good day to make beautiful pictures. Why do you suppose Jennifer Baichwal decided to include this confrontation in *Manufactured Landscapes*? What is its significance in the scope of the film? Given everything else you see in the documentary, how did you respond to this particular scene? Why? Discuss the scene and your response to it with your classmates.

Writing

1. Write an analysis of *Manufactured Landscapes*. Your analysis can take any analytical perspective, drawing from content analysis, rhetorical analysis, or visual rhetorical analysis.

2. At one point in *Manufactured Landscapes*, Edward Burtynsky comments about China's identity as a manufacturing society, its use of energy, and its ability to sustain levels of both (48:45). Burtynsky appears to question China's commitment to sustainability. But just how dedicated to sustainability is China, or any other country? Select a country you are not very familiar with. Take some time to learn about sustainability efforts in that country. Write an informative essay reporting what you have learned.

3. The places shown in *Manufactured Landscapes* are certainly not the only "manufactured landscapes" in the world. In fact, it is likely that there are manufactured landscapes in your community, though they may not be of the scale of those shown in the documentary. Write an image essay about an area in your community that you feel qualifies as manufactured landscape.

Thinking and Writing about the Chapter

Discussion Threads

1. Sustainability can be defined many ways, but the most commonly used definitions usually include three core parts: the social, the economic, and the ecological/environmental. These three categories are often portrayed as sites of crisis: social crises include issues of political power, global discrepancies in the distribution of wealth and resources, violence and corruption, and so on; economic crises include global economic pressures, economic growth at the expense of resource depletion, international debt, and so on; and ecological/environmental crises includes the degradation, contamination, and general destruction of the planet. Individually, each of these kinds of crisis can be daunting to think about, let alone feasible to find reasonable solutions to. Trying to develop ideas and solutions that bring all three issues together to find useful approaches to sustainability can be even more complicated. Discuss with your classmates how the very idea of sustainability can seem overwhelming and the kinds of strategies you might develop to not become overwhelmed in sustainable thinking.

2. Is the idea of sustainability a useful way of thinking about our future? If yes, in what ways? If not, why not? Discuss the value of sustainability as a concept. Be sure to address what you mean by "sustainability" as you consider its value.

3. Many colleges and universities participate in the green campus movement in order to institute green practices on campuses, including the reduction of waste and emissions. In conjunction with such efforts, many college and university presidents have signed the American College and University Presidents' Climate Commitment, which you can find online. The Presidents' Commitment is designed to address the physical and environmental sustainability of colleges and universities in the United States. In addition to such efforts, colleges and universities have also begun to develop curricula that focus on issues of sustainability. Some schools have sustainability curricula that extend across all courses and programs. Some schools have begun to add sustainability courses to the list of required courses students must take before graduating, along with math courses, writing courses, humanities courses, and other required general education categories. Should studying sustainability be required of students? Should it be required at all colleges and universities? Discuss the value of requiring students to take courses in issues of sustainability. What happens when something becomes "required"? Be sure to account for how your college or university does or does not address sustainability curricula.

Collaboration

1. As more people become alert to issues of sustainability, many have started making choices influenced by sustainable thinking in their professional and personal lives. Because there are so many aspects of our lives that can contribute to sustainable living, many people have begun developing personal sustainability plans to realistically think through the kinds of changes they can make and that they are willing to make. Personal sustainability plans can be complex, covering all aspects of one's life: transportation, diet and nutrition, health, work habits, recreation, and so on. Because personal sustainability plans can be so complex, a

small industry of consultants has begun to evolve to help individuals develop their plans. Likewise, you can now find many online resources for developing personal sustainability plans. Working in small groups and using resources you can locate online or through various organizations, develop a document to help college students build their own sustainability plan. Take into account the kinds of things that are often prevalent in students' lives: textbooks, technology, recreation, nutrition, transportation, and so on.

2. Sustainability is addressed differently in developing countries than it is in economically developed countries. Differences in resources, economies, and cultures all contribute to differences in sustainability needs, abilities, and approaches. The United Nations maintains a list of the world's Least Developed Countries (LDCs) based on three criteria: 1. low income; 2. human capital status based on percentage of population that is undernourished, mortality rate of children, health, education, and adult literacy rates; 3. economic vulnerability based on population size, remoteness, exporting, agriculture, forestry and fisheries, homelessness, and natural disasters. Based on these criteria, the UN identifies 48 countries as LDCs:

Africa (33)

- Angola
- Benin
- Burkina Faso
- Burundi
- Central African Republic
- Chad
- Comoros
- Democratic Republic of the Congo
- Djibouti
- Equatorial Guinea
- Eritrea

- Ethiopia
- Gambia
- Guinea
- Guinea-Bissau
- Lesotho
- Liberia
- Madagascar
- Malawi
- Mali
- Mauritania
- Mozambique
- Niger

- Rwanda
- São Tomé and Príncipe
- Senegal
- Sierra Leone
- Somalia
- Sudan
- Togo
- Uganda
- United Republic of Tanzania
- Zambia

Asia (14)

- Afghanistan
- Bangladesh
- Bhutan
- Cambodia
- Kiribati

- Lao People's Democratic Republic
- Myanmar
- Nepal
- Samoa

- Solomon Islands
- Timor-Leste
- Tuvalu
- Vanuatu
- Yemen

Latin America and the Caribbean (1)

- Haiti

Working in small groups, select one of the countries listed by the UN as an LDC and learn about how sustainability is addressed in that country. You may not find information about specific sustainability programs, but you are likely to find information about sustainability needs in that country. Be sure to learn about economy, resources/environment, and cultures of the country. Working together, develop and write a sustainability assessment report about that country. Consider establishing a wiki as a platform through which to consolidate and organize your research and to draft and distribute your report.

Writing

1. In his book *Earth in Mind: On Education, Environment, and the Human Prospect*, renowned environmental educator David W. Orr says that in order to understand sustainability, all college graduates should have a solid understanding of ten key concepts: (1) the laws of thermodynamics, (2) basic principles of ecology, (3) carrying capacity, (4) energetics, (5) least-cost and end-use analysis, (6) limits of technology, (7) appropriate scale, (8) sustainable agriculture and forestry, (9) steady-state economics, and (10) environmental ethics. Select one of these ten topics and learn what the concept means and how it ties to a larger concept of sustainability. Then write a document that explains in detail the term you have selected. When you have finished writing your document, remember that you have nine more concepts to learn about before you graduate.

    (Note: As a class, you may want to divide responsibilities so each student covers one of the ten items and all ten are covered. Then, when you and your classmates have completed your documents, edit them together to produce a volume of introductory materials to Orr's ten key concepts. You may also want to create an online resource, like a wiki or web page, to house and circulate information about the ten concepts.)

2. Sustainability can be a difficult concept to define, and many varying definitions are regularly circulated. There is a prompt at the beginning of this chapter that asked you to write about your thoughts and attitude toward sustainability before reading the materials in this chapter. Whether or not you took the opportunity to respond to that assignment, consider how the materials in this chapter affect how you think about sustainability. Write a reflective essay about whether the readings in this chapter have influenced you in any way and why they may or may not have. If you wrote in response to the chapter-opening prompt, compare your response to this assignment with what you wrote in response to that assignment.

3. Given the relationship between economy and sustainability, one way to learn more about your own sustainable practices is to consider where your money goes. Select a short time period: a day, three days, or a week. During that time period, keep a record where you spend your money. Make a list of everything you purchase, whether services or goods. At the end of the period analyze the kinds of things you exchanged your money for. Then select three categories of money exchanges (for example, food, books, transportation). For each of the three categories, trace the footprint of your money. For example, if you spent seven dollars on cheeseburgers this week, conduct some research into what your seven dollars pays for. Consider how much of that seven dollars is spent on cheese: where does that cheese come from? How was it transported from where it was made to your burger? What resources are needed by the dairy to raise the cows whose milk is made into cheese? What resources are needed to produce the cheese, wrap the cheese, and keep the cheese fresh, and so on? Trace backward the paths of all parts of your burger: the cheese, the burger, the bun, the lettuce, the pickles, the onions, the tomatoes, the bacon, the mustard, and the ketchup (don't bother tracing mayonnaise; it really doesn't belong on a burger). How much of what you traced is local? How much is transported great distances? What kind of ecological footprint does your money have over the allotted time you have selected? Write an essay explaining what you have learned.

4. What do you throw away? Keep a throw away journal (also called a waste journal) for one week. Every time you throw something away, describe in writing what you've thrown out. Record as much as you can about what you throw away: what is it made of? How much of it do you throw away? Is it biodegradable? Did it need to be thrown away? Where did you throw it away (home, school, work)? At the end of the week, count up what you have thrown away. What do you throw away most? Could any of what you throw away be recycled? How much food did you throw away? Did you buy replacements for anything you threw away? Why did you throw it away? How did you think about what you threw away? Were you glad to get rid of it—out of sight out of mind? Once you have a better sense of what you throw away, conduct some research to learn where your garbage goes. Learn what waste disposal companies are used by your college or university, your apartment complex or other housing development and by your work or other places you spend time this week. Where does that company take the waste it collects? Is it placed in landfills? Incinerated? Composted? Recycled? Is it trucked out of state or shipped overseas? Are the company's landfills near waterways? If so, to where do the waterways flow? Do its incinerators meet emissions quality standards? Learn everything you can about where your garbage goes, then document, analyze, and respond to what you learned about your garbage. (Note: You can find many waste journals online as blogs. You may even want to start blogging about what you throw away, why you throw it away, and where it goes.)

Local Situation

Water management plays a big role in sustainability. But water is something that people in the United States often don't think about simply because it is so readily available and seemingly unlimited in availability. After all, in the United States all we have to do is turn on a faucet and presumably clean, safe water flows—even in locations where water does not occur naturally in abundance. (Note: You may want to watch Annie Leonard's "The Story of Bottled Water"— available online—to learn more about water and sustainability.) In fact, many people think that because water falls from the sky and that our planet's surface is more than 70 percent water that water isn't really something we need to worry about. However, water plays a role in nearly every aspect of sustainability. Despite its importance, most people in the United States know very little about the water they rely on every day, both directly and indirectly. This assignment is designed to encourage you to learn more about the water you use by conducting a specific kind of guided research and writing about what you learn.

A. First, take some time to learn about how you use water at home. These questions are designed to help you do just that. Write down your answers for each as you track down information and perform calculations:

- How many people live in your household?
- How many faucets do you have in your household?
- How much water does your household use? You can calculate water use three different ways:

From your water bill—if your water comes from a community water system or utilities company, you probably receive a bill that reports how much water your household uses in a given period of time. Most bills only show usage for a given billing period, not for a single day, but you can easily figure your daily household use by dividing the total amount of water used by the number of days in the billing period.

Different billing systems may show water usage in various measurements: cubic meters (m^3), cubic feet (ft^3), gallons (gal), or liters (L). To convert these measurements to gallons, use these conversions:

$$m^3 \times 264 = gal$$
$$ft^3 \times 7.48 = gal$$
$$L \times 0.264 = gal$$

(Note: there are a number of conversion tools available online that you can use, as well.)

From your water meter—if you don't get a water bill or if your water bill doesn't report usage volume, you can read your water meter to see how much water you use. To see how much water you use in a 24-hour period, read your meter at the same time for two consecutive days. You may want to read the meter for several consecutive days and calculate your average usage. Some meters measure in gallons, some in liters, some in cubic meters, and some in cubic feet. Use the conversion chart above to calculate usage in gallons.

Without a meter or bill—if you do not have access to your water meter, if your water meter measures more than your household's use (as might be the case if you live in a dormitory or apartment complex), or if you do not receive a bill with a water measurement, you can still estimate your water usage. In order for these measurements to be accurate, be sure to measure all of your water usage inside and outside. You will need to measure the flow from every water fixture in your household.

To calculate flow for faucets (indoor and outdoor) and showerheads, turn on the faucet as you would when you use it. Hold a container under the faucet or showerhead for 10 seconds and measure the quantity of water in the container (a large measuring cup will make calculating easier). Multiply the measured quantity of water by 6 to figure the gallons per minutes (gpm).

The next time you take a shower, record how much time you spend in the shower. If there are other people living in the household, calculate their times in the shower, as well. What is the average time of showers taken in your household? How many showers per week are taken in your household? Calculate the amount of water per week the shower uses by multiplying the flow rate by the average time of each shower by the number of showers taken.

Baths usually use about 20 gallons. Which uses more water in your household: a bath or a shower?

Toilet flows are usually marked on the toilet as a certain number of gallons per flush (gpf) or liters per flush (lpf). How many toilets are there in your household? What is the average flush volume of all of the toilets in the household? How many times per day does your household flush toilets? How much water is used daily by flushing toilets?

If your appliances (like dishwashers and washing machines) are relatively new or contain energy rating information somewhere on the machine, you should be able to obtain flow rate from manufacturers manuals, on-product information, or even online sites that sell the same machines. If you can't locate this information in these ways, use these averages:

Washing machines: 41 gallons per use

Dishwasher: 9 gallons per use

Count how many times per day or how many minutes per day you use each appliance. Multiply the machine flow by the number of minutes per day you use the appliance. Multiply the flow average for each appliance by the number of times the appliance is used each week.

Do any of your faucets drip or leak? If so, measure how much water is leaked in an hour by placing a container under the drip for one hour. Multiply by 24 to calculate how much water is dripped in a day. If you don't have any leaks, you may want to simulate one by turning on a faucet just enough to create a drip and then measuring the water. How much water do drips and leaks waste in a day?

How much water does your household use in a day, and how did you determine that amount? In what ways does your household use water and how do those uses contribute to your household's total use? What uses the most water in your household?

B. Now that you have a better idea of how you use water, take some time to learn where your water comes from. Record your responses to these questions as you gather information:

- Where is your household located?
  Is your household serviced by a public water supply (like a water district), a private water system, or an individual water system (like a well)?
  If you are on a public system, who provides the water to your residence? What is the name of the agency, district, or company?

- Who owns and manages the system? If your water is owned by a company, is that company part of a larger company or is it independent and local? Is the water district managed by elected officials? Local commissioners? That is, who is responsible for your water?

  Access your water supplier's web resources or call the company or district office to find answers to the following:

- How many customers does your water provider serve?
- What is the source of your district's and your water?
- What percentage of your water is gathered from surface sources?
- What percentage of your water is gathered from groundwater?
- Where are the wells that provide ground water?
- Where are the surface sources (like lakes, rivers, or reservoirs)?
- From what watershed does your water come? (Note: The EPA provides numerous resources for identifying and locating watershed information, such as the resources found at http://water.epa.gov/type/watersheds/address.cfm.)
- How is the water delivered from its source to your home?
- Where are your district's water treatment facilities?
- What kind of treatment process does your water go through before arriving at your home?
- Every large water supplier is required to produce an annual "Consumer Confidence Report." Locate your water provider's report online or ask your provider to send you a copy. The United States Environmental Protection Agency provides links to many local Consumer Confidence Reports about drinking water (http://water.epa.gov/drink/local/).

Consumer Confidence reports generally provide information such as amount of contaminants in water, where water comes from, how water delivery mechanisms (like pipes) are maintained, and so on.

- What contaminants are found in your water in what amounts? Contaminants are generally measured and reported in parts per million (ppm) or parts per billion (ppb).
- Do these levels meet EPA requirements?
- If you get your water from your own well or a small private water system, when was the last time your water was tested? Were any threats detected in your water? How deep is your well? How much water does the well produce? Have you had water quality problems with your well?

C. Finally, where does your water go? Use these questions to assist you in learning about how your water is disposed of, recycled, or reclaimed.

- Is your household on a sewer or a septic system?
- Who is your sewer company?
- Does your sewer company treat wastewater or pass it along to a larger wastewater treatment company or other organization?
- Use the information provided on your sewer company's web page or call them to find this information. (Note: You may have to examine your sewer company's resources as well as a larger company's resources if your local company passes wastewater along.)
- Where does your sewage go?
- What treatment plant is it processed by?
- Where is that treatment plant located? How much sewage does the treatment plant treat?
- After it is treated, where is the water released?
- How is the sewage treated? What processes does the facility use?
- Consider the location of the treatment plant in relation to the location of your water's source. Consider the elevation of each. Does your sewage flow to the treatment plant, or does it have to be pumped? Where is the pump station located? What would happen if the pump station failed? Identify on a map the path of the sewer lines, the location of the pump station, and other relevant information like proximity to schools, neighborhoods, farms, water sources, and the like.
- If you are on a septic system, describe how your system works. Is it a one- or two-tank system? Where is your drain field? Do you have a reserve field in case your primary field fails? Locate a diagram online of how your system works. How would you know if your system failed?

Once you have gathered all of the information for all three parts of this inquiry, use the information to write a detailed account of your water. Once you complete a formal assessment of your water use, its origin, and its disposal, write about what you found most important or most interesting about the information you gathered.[6]

---

[6]This assignment is adapted from Mathematics Across the Community College Curriculum, MATYC.org.

Education

25

Before you read this chapter

What is education? What role do institutions like schools, governments, cultures, and families play in education? Has education changed recently? What is the relationship between digital technology and education? In your journal or blog, write about what you think education is, what it's for, and how it is conveyed.

Defining *education* can be tricky simply because education is a complicated concept. Education can be thought of as a process, but it is a process that is influenced by many factors. We might oversimplify and say that education is the process of how we learn things, but how we learn one thing may be entirely different from how we learn something else. We could also say that education is the process through which information, standards, practices, approaches, and even beliefs are passed from one group to another, from one group to its newer members, from one person to another, or one person to a group. No matter how we define it, though, education's complexity also makes it a problematic concept with many difficult questions: What should people learn? Who should decide what people should learn? Who should teach? Who should learn? Who should monitor learning? Who should pay for education? How much should people learn? and so on.

As college students, you have participated in educational systems and educational processes. You have also—to some degree or another—decided that education is valuable. This is why you are enrolled in college. It may be that you see education as a means to a better career, or you may see college as an opportunity for self-enhancement. Or you may be in college simply because that was what was expected of you or you really didn't have anything else to do. No matter the reason, though, as college students, you have a unique perspective on education (you may even be majoring in education with the plan of spending your career involved with education). That perspective is particularly important these days, as education is undergoing many exciting changes.

The readings in this chapter are brought together to consider some of the most important changes occurring in contemporary North American education. The selections in this chapter question traditions of U.S. educational systems; they ask about the relationship between current digital technologies and traditional educational processes; they question the purpose of education; and they rethink what education might be in a digital, global economy. As you read and view the selections in this chapter, think about your own education in relationship to what these pieces convey.

The Purpose of Higher Education

Richard Kahlenberg

Richard Kahlenberg is a senior fellow at The Century Foundation, a nonpartisan, progressive think tank and research institution founded in 1919 on the ideas that U.S. security and prosperity are dependent on an effective government, open democracy, and free markets. Kahlenberg is an expert in education and is known as "the intellectual father of the economic integration movement" in K–12 education. He is also an expert on teachers' unions, private school voucher programs, charter schools, and inequality in higher education.

The selection found here first appeared in *The Chronicle of Higher Education*, the primary newspaper and web news source for news and information for college and university faculty and administrators. In this essay, Kahlenberg recounts the five purposes he sees for higher education.

This past Tuesday morning, I gave the convocation address for new students at Flagler, a private four-year liberal-arts college in St. Augustine, Florida. Founded in 1968, Flagler College is a relatively new institution built around the grounds of a stunning 19th century hotel and set in America's oldest city. Perhaps because Flagler charges in tuition and fees about half of what the average private colleges does, it has attracted a fair degree of socioeconomic diversity.

I was asked in my remarks to reflect on the larger goals of higher education. Although speech givers are often advised to stick to three points, because studies find audiences don't remember more than that, I outlined five purposes. In addition to the standard rationales for taxpayer support of education—producing well-trained employees in a free-market economy and intelligent citizens in a self-governing democracy—I outlined several additional goals, and in each case evaluated how well higher education is doing.

1. To ensure that every student, no matter the wealth of her parents, has a chance to enjoy the American Dream.

It used to be that there were two major paths to economic security in the United States: Go to college or join a unionized occupation. But today, less than 7% of private sector workers are unionized, compared with 35% in the 1950s. So now, the most reliable avenue to economic security involves getting a four-year degree.

Overall, however, American higher education is not doing a very good job of promoting social mobility. According to recent data, 82% of those from higher-income families get a bachelor's degree by age 24, compared with just 8% from low-income families. A society in which children from wealthy families are about 10 times as likely to get college degrees as those from poor families is one marked by profound inequality.

2. To educate leaders in our democracy.

Thomas Jefferson famously wanted the United States to be led by a "natural aristocracy" of "virtue and talent" rather than an "artificial aristocracy" based on wealth and birth. And a system of free public education, coupled with accessible higher education, was critical, in his view, to producing America's leaders.

Yet, once again, in practice, many institutions of higher education fail to live up to this ideal today by admitting some students through so-called "legacy preferences." As Michael Lind noted in a book I edited entitled *Affirmative Action for the Rich*, "By reserving places on campus for members of the pseudo-aristocracy of wealth and birth, legacy preferences introduce an aristocratic snake into the democratic republican Garden of Eden."

3. To advance learning and knowledge through faculty research and by giving students the opportunity to broaden their minds even when learning does not seem immediately relevant to their careers.

As Louis Menand has written in *The New Yorker* magazine, college is a time for you to learn "things about the world and yourself that, if you do not learn them in college, you are unlikely to learn anywhere else." Later in life, they will be caught up in family and career, so at least some portion of their time in college should be spent becoming "a reflective and culturally literate human being."

Yet, here again, higher education falls short. Many colleges see themselves as vocational schools, and the study *Academically Adrift: Limited Learning on College Campuses* famously found than an astounding 45% of students learn little in the first two years of college, as measured by progress on the Collegiate Learning Assessment (CLA).

4. To teach students to interact with people different than themselves.

Our public schools are more segregated today than at any time in the last three decades. Even as our society is becoming more diverse, our student populations are being pulled apart into separate camps, divided by race and class. American colleges—because they draw upon students from a variety of neighborhoods and states, and countries—provide a unique environment in which students of different backgrounds can learn from one another.

Many colleges have done a fairly good job of promoting racial diversity through affirmative action programs, but most do a poor job of bringing students from different economic backgrounds together. As Walter Benn Michaels has noted, many colleges now have "rich kids of all colors."

5. To help students find a passion—and even a purpose in life.

When I was a senior in college, I wrote my thesis about Robert Kennedy's 1968 campaign for president, in which he built a powerful coalition of working-class white voters and black and Hispanic voters—who were, at the time, at war with one another—by making appeals to common economic interests. Kennedy thought that the economic divide in this country was even greater than the racial and ethnic divides, and that hypothesis—bolstered by lots of evidence—is something I've pursued in almost all my research and writing since college.

It's hard to know how well higher education is doing in helping students find a passion, helping them think through what they're really good at, what they're truly interested in, and what they believe are the most critical problems facing the country. But as students start a new academic year at Flagler—and at colleges across the country—I hope that officials in higher education think deeply about how best to spark in students a passionate interest that will help them lead truly meaningful lives.

Analyzing the Situation

1. Richard Kahlenberg begins this essay by providing some contextual details: where he gave the initial talk, who is audience was, and what part of his exigency was in providing his five points. Yet, when we read Kahlenberg's essay, we read it in print taken from an academic newspaper whose audience is not the same as Kahlenberg's original audience. How does the recirculation of this speech as an essay in an academic newspaper alter the parameters of the situation? What may have been Kahlenberg's reason for readapting his commencement address to the written article?

2. What kinds of institutional constraints might affect what Kahlenberg says in this essay?

3. Both audience and players appear to have a significant role in the situation Kahlenberg addresses. Who would you identify as the original audience for Kahlenberg's address? Who would you identify as the audience for the written article? Who are the players in this situation? How does Kahlenberg take these audiences and players into account in his writing?

4. How does Kahlenberg's role with The Century Foundation affect this article?

Analyzing the Rhetoric

1. From a reader's standpoint, is Kahlenberg's decision to subdivide the essay into five sections and the introduction effective? Why or why not?

2. In points 2, 3, and 4, Kahlenberg provides direct quotations from others in support of his position. What does he gain or lose in doing so?

3. In point number 1, Kahlenberg cites some "recent data" but does not provide a source for the data or qualify what "recent" might mean. How does the inclusion of these data affect Kahlenberg's argument and ethos?

Discussing

1. Before enrolling in college, you and your classmates probably had your own ideas about what the purpose of higher education is. You may also have refined or revised some of those ideas since you arrived at college. As a class, discuss your preconceptions about the purpose of higher education and your current ideas about why you and others seek college degrees.

2. Kahlenberg makes a distinction between racial diversity on college campuses and socioeconomic diversity. He is critical of American colleges' and universities' lack of attention to economic diversity. How do you respond to Kahlenberg's distinction and to the argument he makes? Discuss Kahlenberg's critique.

Writing

1. Do you feel that you have or will have the experiences in college that will provide the five points of preparation that Kahlenberg identifies as the

purpose of higher education? Write a response to Kahlenberg's claims based on your own ideas of what the purpose of higher education is and your own experiences in college thus far.

2. Select one of the five points that Kahlenberg makes that you most agree or disagree with. Write an argumentative essay that either supports or contests Kahlenberg's point.

3. Kahlenberg, of course, isn't the only one to write about the purposes of higher education. The subject is debated and discussed quite a bit.

A simple Google search or a Google Scholar search for "the purpose of higher education" reveals thousands of links to blogs, articles, books, and other online resources that address the subject. Conduct a bit of online research and identify other definitions and explanations as to what the purpose of higher education is. Write an essay that compares and/or contrasts Kahlenberg's five purposes of higher education with the purposes you have identified in your research. You should identify which approaches you find more accurate and why.

Envisioning a Post-Campus America

Megan McArdle

Megan McArdle is a senior editor for *The Atlantic*, and she is a Bernard L. Schwartz fellow at The New America Foundation, a nonprofit think tank and public policy institute that focuses on technology, education, health, energy, national security, and the economy. McArdle writes about government policy, business, and economics. Her writing has been published in the *New York Post, The New York Sun, The Guardian*, and Salon.com. She also writes for *The Economist*. In addition, she worked with three start-up organizations: a consulting firm, an investment bank, and a disaster recovery firm at Ground Zero. While working at Ground Zero, McArdle began a blog called *Live From the WTC*, which addressed economics, business, and cooking. Her blog, later renamed *Asymmetrical Information*, is considered to be one of the first major economics blogs. McArdle's article, "Envisioning a Post-Campus America," was originally published in *The Atlantic*.

MIT is going to offer certificates for completion of low-cost online coursework, an offering the university is calling MITx. Stephen Gordon ponders the implications:

Now, imagine a personnel manager at a mid-sized corporation who's looking for an employee with some particular knowledge. There are two candidates: one with an appropriate college degree from the local state school, a second with relevant MITx certificates. Let's say all other things between the candidates are equal. Which should the manager choose?

Given the caliber of professor at MIT, the online student may have learned just as much. The candidate who went to college probably enjoyed his experience more, but the potential employer is unlikely to care about that. Finally, there's the financial reality: To some extent, the student debt of the job candidate dictates his salary requirements. If the MITx candidate has the knowledge required and far less student debt, he probably can be hired more cheaply. Ultimately, the cheaper option will win.

I've seen a fair amount of speculation along these lines. I'm probably more skeptical than most of the boosters, however. When I was in business school, I saw opportunities for disruptive innovation everywhere—in autos, in groceries, in education. Since then, I've watched a lot of disruptive innovations get killed or co-opted by incumbents, or undermined by features of the market that weren't immediately obvious to an outside observer. (Why can't we just order perfectly customized cars online the way we do computers? Because dealers have a lot of political pull at the state and federal levels, and because the economics of auto plants make it hard to shut down or start up lines in order to follow demand.)

I can see all sorts of factors that might combine to preserve the status quo, from signaling and status and networking, to the desire of college students for a four-year debt-financed semi-vacation. On the other hand, disruption never looks inevitable until it suddenly is—if you'd told someone in 1955 that GM was going to have its lunch eaten by some Japanese upstart, they would have laughed until the tears came. So it's interesting and maybe even useful to contemplate what the college system would look like if this sort of distance learning becomes the norm.

1. *Education will end up being dominated by a few huge incumbents.* As we see with Facebook and Twitter and, well, almost everything, the internet offers huge returns to scale, and substantial network effects. There's a big benefit to having learned stuff the same way as the people around you—not least that they understand what a given certificate means. To offer a small example, during my time at the University of Chicago's business school, every class was curved to a 3.25. Most other business schools don't curve, and as a result, Northwestern, our nearest competitor, had an average GPA of something like 3.8.

Someone at Chicago who had a 3.4 GPA was slightly better than average. Someone at Northwestern who had a 3.4 average was kind of a screwup. This didn't matter unless your interviewer had gone to a different school—but if they had, you were apt to find yourself explaining that no, really, that 3.5 wasn't as bad as it looked. Which sounded like whining, even to us.

I would expect that economies of scale and network effects would compress the number of schools to a few—or at least, a few within each specialty. The winners might be the early-moving incumbents like MIT and Stanford, or they might be some dark horse who takes advantage of the disruption to rearrange the current status hierarchy. But either way, I'd expect

to see a few schools dominating, while many go out of business.

2. *Online education will kill the liberal arts degree.* Let's not have the same dismal discussion of whether liberal arts degrees are awesome or useless. The important aspect for this discussion is that what they teach is hard to test efficiently. There's enormous variation in grading of, say, English papers, and even if it were easier to standardize, that grading requires hours of expensive labor.

3. *Professors (course developers) will be selected for teaching instead of research brilliance.* The brilliant theorist who drones his way through two courses a year while his students fantasize about stabbing themselves in the eardrum with a plastic fork so they can't hear the boring anymore … that chap will have no place in the online future.

4. *95% of tenure-track professors will lose their jobs.* Or perhaps I should say, 95% of tenure-track jobs will be eliminated; I have no idea if things could change fast enough to knock current professors out of work. But if online education really becomes ubiquitous, very few professors will be needed to produce all the education. Oh, don't get me wrong—at the school level, the workforce will still be enormous. Probably bigger than it is now, for the schools that win. But that will be offset by all the schools that close.

5. The corollary of #4 is *the end of universities as research centers.* As I've noted before, tenured academics has worked a great scam. They've managed to monetize people's affection for regional football teams, and their desire for a work credential, and then somehow diverted that money into paying academics to work on whatever they want, for the rest of their lives, *without any oversight by the football fans or the employers.* While I'm sensitive to the complaints of conservative critics, I think that by and large, it's a very good thing. But it's not a viable business model in cyberspace.

We might see much of academia revert to an amateur pastime, as it was in the 18th and even the 19th century. Work with policy implications would likely move to think tanks or consultancies; and I assume that a lot of basic science would continue to be funded by the government, perhaps renting out the labs of defunct universities. On the other hand, I'd assume that folks like English professors will have a very difficult time getting funded to do much of anything. And before the English professors attack, this is not a commentary on your value to society, just my personal assessment of where the bulk of the funding dollars seem to be.

To get funding in the e-future, research will have to be relevant. More specifically, it will have to strike someone with a lot of money at their disposal as relevant.

6. *Young job-seekers will need new ways to signal diligence.* I'd expect to see a lot of free labor in the early years, something like what aspiring writers and visual artists already do with their blogs. There will be more freelancing, more try-out employment, and more unpaid internships.

7. *The economics of graduate school will change substantially.* I'm not sure what would happen to the master's and professional degrees—would there be a market for intense, focused instruction in small class groups? Medical school yes, law school probably, social work ... um, as long as the government requires it, I guess.

But the PhD would be radically upended. Right now, graduate students get miserly stipends in exchange for considerably easing the teaching and research loads of their professors. But in an online model, we won't need so many teachers. And the online schools will not necessarily be research centers any more. The implication is that most students, especially outside of STEM[1], will have to pay for their PhDs. Which should, at the very least, take care of the oversupply problem.

8. *Civil society will have to substitute for the intense friend networks that are built at college.* I'm not sure what form this would take—college-age students joining the Elks?—but something will have to substitute. Or perhaps people won't separate from their high school friends as much as they do now.

9. *The role of schooling in upward mobility will change.* This is kind of a cop-out, because I'm not sure which way

---

[1]STEM is Science, Technology, Engineering, and Mathematics

the change runs. I can tell a story where eUniversities make it radically easier for smart, poor kids to advance in their spare time. I can also tell a story where education is very complementary to the kind of personal networks and social capital that middle-class kids can tap through their parents. For poor kids who can get there (and stay there), college provides a lot of education on how to socialize with other college students, and of course, expert professionals who can help you find a job if you ask for help.

10. *The young will have a much lower financial burden in their 20s.* That's hopefully going to translate into more investment, and more risk-taking, which is great for everyone.

11. *The tutoring industry will boom.* While tenured professorships will go away, there will be lots of opportunity for those who can help an online student pull through a rough spot. (At least until computers learn to do this too).

12. *If the credentials become valuable, cheating will be a problem.* I'd expect online test-taking to eventually shift to test centers like the ones where the GMAT and various professional licensing exams are administered now.

Overall, I think it's very clear that people will have more opportunity to access education, but much less clear how that education will translate into opportunity, particularly for those who weren't born to successful, educated parents. And except for a few superstars, I think the shift would be unequivocally bad for tenured professors. The corollary, however, is that it would be unequivocally good for the legions who are lured into grad school by the chimera of a tenured professorship.

Would it be good for society as a whole? I tend to think that it almost always is when things get cheaper. But we will have to rethink how we fund important research, and quite possibly, about what the engines of mobility will be for strivers who start out in the bottom quintiles.

Analyzing the Situation

1. Megan McArdle's "Envisioning a Post-Campus America" was originally published in *The Atlantic*, a print and online magazine that has been recognized as a reputable, leading magazine of literary and cultural commentary as well as commentary about political issues including education since it was founded in 1857. Given that McArdle's article first appeared in *The Atlantic*, we can make many assumptions as to who the intended audience is. But the article also seems to implicate many kinds of players in this situation. Who might be players in this situation?

2. In what ways do relations play a role in what McArdle's article conveys?

3. How would you describe the situation in which McArdle's article participates?

Analyzing the Rhetoric

1. How would you characterize the tone of Megan McArdle's "Envisioning a Post-Campus America"?

2. How would you characterize McArdle's article? Is it argumentative, informative, analytical, evaluative, descriptive, or a combination of these?

3. As a reader, how do you respond to McArdle's providing a numbered list of the twelve facets she sees as pertinent to the situation? Does she explain each sufficiently?

Discussing

1. Given that you are likely using *Writing Situations* in a class taught by an English professor, a graduate student in English, or an instructor with a graduate degree in English and that Megan McArdle's article paints a less than positive picture of your teacher's future, discuss the article with your teacher, asking for your teacher's thoughts on the article and responding to them.

2. Would you like to earn your degree in the manner that McArdle describes? Why or why not? Is there a difference between "earning a degree" and "going to college"? Discuss the differences or lack of differences and what you understand each of those phrases to mean.

3. How do you respond to McArdle's prediction in point number 2 that "Online education will kill the liberal arts degree"? Discuss this claim.

Writing

1. McArdle's final point is that "If the credentials become valuable, cheating will be a problem," but she does not explain this with much detail. Do you agree with her claim about cheating and the value of degrees? Write an argumentative essay that either supports or contests McArdle's claim in point number 12.

2. What role did career objectives play in your decision to pursue a college degree? Are you in college to improve your chances of developing the career you want, or for another reason? Write a personal narrative describing what you see as your reason for being in college. Use McArdle's article to support your explanation, or refute her article to support your position.

3. Write a response to McArdle's prediction that "95% of tenure-track professors will lose their jobs."

Changing Education Paradigms

Sir Ken Robinson

Through his writing and speaking engagements around the world, Sir Ken Robinson has become known as one of the most influential educators of today. Two of his most famous talks are estimated to have been seen online by more than 200 million people in more than 150 countries. Robinson has worked with governments in the United States, Europe, and Asia, with Fortune 500 companies, and various cultural organizations around the world. For 12 years Robinson was a professor of education at the University of Warwick in the United Kingdom. He has been awarded numerous honorary degrees around the world and been given many awards for his work in education and the arts, including the prestigious LEGO Prize for international achievement in education. In 2003, Queen Elizabeth II knighted him for his service to the arts. Robinson has been called a "visionary cultural leader" and is known for his remarkable thought about human creativity and education.

In October 2010, the Royal Society of Arts (RSA) in London awarded Robinson the Benjamin Franklin Medal for outstanding contributions to cultural relations between the United Kingdom and the United States. On the occasion of that award, Robinson delivered a talk entitled "Changing Education Paradigms." In order to make the talk accessible to a larger audience, RSA Animate produced an animated version of the highlights of Robinson's talk, which can be accessed via Robinson's blog and the TED web pages.

You can find Sir Ken Robinson's "Changing Education Paradigms" through a simple online search or by searching either the YouTube pages or the RSA pages.

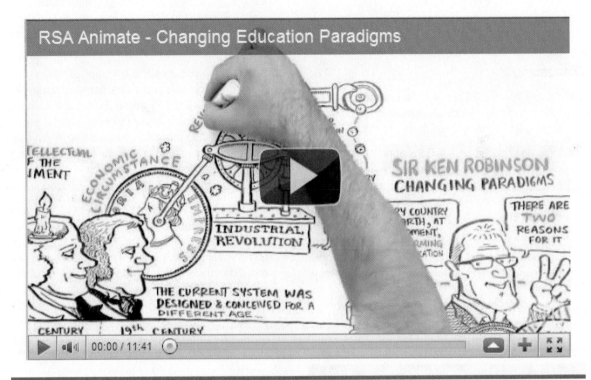

Analyzing the Situation

1. Ken Robinson initially delivered "Changing Education Paradigms" as a talk to an audience at the Royal Society of Arts in London. Since then, the RSA Animate video has been viewed more than seven million times on YouTube as well as viewed and shared on the RSA web page, the TED web pages, and Ken Robinson's web pages. In what ways does this degree of circulation change the situation in which Robinson's talk participates?

2. Ken Robinson's "Changing Education Paradigms" addresses education and education reform. Although the mass circulation of the RSA video creates some interesting situational considerations about audience, Robinson's argument seems also to implicate a large number of players. Who are the players in this situation? What role do they play in the situation?

3. What role do chronology and kairos play in the situation in which "Changing Education Paradigms" participates?

Analyzing the Rhetoric

1. In what ways does the RSA animation of Ken Robinson's talk change the talk by adding visuals to

it? Does it matter that the video is animated rather than made visual with photographs or another visual form? Does seeing the drawing hand affect how we read the text?

2. How do writing, sound, and visuals work together in this video? How do all three contribute to the text individually and synthetically?

3. What role does humor play in Robinson's argument? Can humor be argumentative?

Discussing

1. Discuss how Ken Robinson characterizes the intellectual and economic model of education. How does your thinking about education compare with Robinson's?

2. How do you respond to Robinson's characterization of the arts as part of an aesthetic experience and anesthetic approaches to shutting off the senses? Discuss Robinson's claims about education and anesthetics.

3. Robinson's "Changing Education Paradigms" addresses some rather complex ideas about education, yet the animated version does so in rather accessible ways. Discuss how the medium of this video affects the accessibility of the ideas Robinson wishes to convey.

Writing

1. At one point in his talk, Ken Robinson characterizes contemporary education as being based on a factory model. He stresses that this model emphasizes conformity and standardization. Robinson's tenor suggests that standardization is not necessarily a good thing. What do you think about this claim? Respond to Robinson in an essay that considers your view of education processes in light of Robinson's claim.

2. Robinson introduces the concept of "divergent thinking" in his talk and offers some rudimentary definitions. Divergent thinking has become an important part of contemporary conversations about education and innovation. Write a document that more fully defines divergent thinking, identifying how it is discussed, what seems to be useful in the concept, and what about it is being criticized.

3. The full, original version of Ken Robinson's talk was just under an hour long. The RSAnimate version is just over eleven minutes long. Watch the original talk and compare it with the shortened version. Write an analysis of the short, animated version in light of the full version. Is the short version a fair summary of the long version? What do audiences miss in the short version when they don't watch the full version?

Teachers without Technology Strike Back

Jeffrey R. Young

Jeffrey R. Young covers technology and its effect on teaching, research, and student life for *The Chronicle of Higher Education*. He also contributes to and oversees content for *The Chronicle of Higher Education's* Wired Campus Blog, which provides news about technology and education. In addition, Young cohosts the Tech Therapy monthly podcast. Young writes a regular news-analysis column in *The Chronicle of Higher Education* called College 2.0, from which the reading here is taken. His articles address topics like social media, changes in textbook publishing, and the effects of technology on lecture-model education. The article reprinted here addresses college teachers who do not use or allow technologies like laptops or smartphones in their classrooms. But the article is about much more; it is about the relationship between technology and teaching and learning. As you read "Teachers without Technology Strike Back," think about what Young's essay reveals about this larger conversation.

Mark James, a visiting lecturer at the University of West Florida, declared his summer course in English literature technology-free—he skipped the PowerPoint slides and YouTube videos he usually shows, and he asked students to silence their cellphones and close their laptops.

Banishing the gear improved the course, he argues. "The students seemed more involved in the discussion than when I allowed them to go online," he told me as the summer term wound down. "They were more attentive, and we were able to go into a little more depth."

Mr. James is not antitechnology—he said he had some success in his composition courses using an online system that's sold with textbooks. But he is frustrated by professors and administrators who believe that injecting the latest technology into the classroom naturally improves teaching. That belief was highlighted in my College 2.0 column last month, in which some professors likened colleagues who don't teach with tech to doctors who ignore improvements in medicine. Many low-tech professors were extremely distressed by that charge of educational malpractice. (They told me so in dozens of comments on the article and in e-mail messages.)

After interviewing a few of them this month, it seems to me the key debate between the tech enthusiasts and tech skeptics is really over broader changes in colleges, and anxieties about the academy being turned into just another business.

Teaching is not car assembly, the skeptics say, in that there's no objective checklist to follow. Nor is it brain surgery, because there is no agreed-upon group of vital signs to check.

"I see teaching as more of an art, and a relationship thing," said Mr. James. After we talked it out for a while, he settled on the metaphor of a carpenter's workshop to replace that of a doctor's clinic: "Let's say I want to get a really well-made table. I might go to someone who knows the old-style way of making a table, and I'm willing to pay a lot for that," is how he put it. By extension, tech-based learning feels more like IKEA—a lower-price, build-it-yourself option.

In that way, some professors see emphasizing the benefits of chalk-and-talk methods as defending their craft against pressures to cheapen it.

"This is where we have to ask, what kind of education do we offer?" said Mr. James. "We're preparing citizens that need to be able to communicate with each other. Knowledge isn't always something that's able to come out nicely packaged."

In Defense of Blue Books

When Barry Leeds explains why he makes his students write papers in blue books instead of on computers, he quickly recalls a favorite professor from graduate school. That was a long time ago—Mr. Leeds is 69, an emeritus professor of English at Central Connecticut State University, and he took that course when he was 22.

His professor made students write short papers and then gave extensive feedback, which forced them to hone their arguments and express themselves more clearly. And he made them write out the papers in longhand, in blue books, during class. "There's something about the immediacy or exigency of it," Mr. Leeds said. "When I took those written exams, I found that I made connections that I didn't know I knew—it shook up my brain cells like a supernova."

So today Mr. Leeds requires his students to write short, in-class papers. In blue books. By hand. Just like his favorite professor did.

How do today's students respond? "Once they're done kvetching about the blue books, they ultimately tell me for the most part that they found that it was a revealing experience," he told me. In other words, Mr. Leeds manages to get good teaching evaluations with an old-school method. And he feels that the students emerge with the same kinds of dramatic revelations that he experienced nearly 50 years ago.

His teaching has changed and evolved, though. For his favorite Hemingway course, he has dropped some books that didn't resonate, and he spends more time on ones that students connect with. At first he lectured for most of each class and left five minutes for questions.

Gradually, based on students' response, he turned classroom time into more of a discussion.

"There's the danger of becoming like the ancient mariner and telling the same tale again and again and again," he said, adding that he knows of professors who cling to their yellowed lecture notes. "I have to safeguard against getting too hidebound and giving the same presentation each time."

He's never felt pressure from administrators to try blogs, wikis, or any other technology, although he said he "resents" what he sees as a lack of recognition of the time teaching takes. "There's an overemphasis on scholarship and research and only lip-service paid to teaching," he said.

So even though his classroom is low-tech, he feels that his teaching skills are honed by the trial and error of years at the podium. "It's just like you wouldn't want to go to a dentist who just got out of dental school," he said. "You'd like them to practice on someone else for a few years."

Wariness of Fads

Jason B. Jones, an associate professor of English at Central Connecticut who helps run the ProfHacker blog, on *The Chronicle's* Web site (and thus enthusiastic about the promise of technology), said he understood why some longtime professors are wary of the latest gadgets in the classroom. After all, ed-tech fads have come and gone.

"There are still braces on the walls from where they had the last technology that was going to transform education—that was the TV's," he said. "Just about every semester I almost crack my head open on one of them." The television sets once supported by these metal brackets were long ago removed.

Some professors who are receptive to new technology attend the latest workshops and then decide it just doesn't work for them.

That was the case for Joanne Budzien, a postdoctoral lecturer in physics and engineering at Frostburg State University, who attended a session on using "clickers," devices that let professors instantly quiz students. The students click small remote controls, and professors can display the results on a screen.

"My classes are very small—I have at most 24 students, and it just seems impersonal to put up a question and use a clicker," she said. "I can just have a raise of hands, and I can call on them and say why do you think this and why do you think that."

Still, she remembers professors from her undergraduate days who put little effort into teaching—and she doesn't want to end up like that. "One would tell a joke that was way, way, way out of date," she said. Others' idea of a technological upgrade was taking their old transparencies and using them in the same way as PowerPoint slides.

So who's right? Fans of both old and new teaching approaches say they that have the students' interests at heart. Perhaps a better question is why there is a digital divide at all when it comes to teaching.

Some commenters have argued that tech enthusiasts lack research to prove that their methods work. In fact, reams of research have been produced, much of the results showing gains over those old-school methods. Some of the work is cited in a recent government report on the future of teaching, the "National Education Technology Plan 2010." Teaching experiments seem to deserve more attention than a flip dismissal.

Yet professors who worry about a move toward assembly-line education should be at the table as well, checking for oversteps. As one commenter on my last column put it: "Problem is, higher education in this country has rapidly taken on many of the qualities of business corporations, with instructors being expected to serve a student clientele in whatever way that is convenient for that clientele. Coming along as a student, I learnt a great deal from some 'boring' professors."

Both old and new approaches will probably have to live together on campus for many years to come. So why not get to know each other a bit better?

Analyzing the Situation

1. Why do you suppose that Jeffery R. Young uses mostly English professors as examples in "Teachers without Technology Strike Back"? In what ways does this emphasis on these examples help define how readers understand the situation in which the essay participates?

2. We know who Jeffery R. Young's intended audience is simply because the essay was written for *The Chronicle of Higher Education*, but who are the players in this situation?

3. Jeffery R. Young attributes the use of technology in classrooms to individual professors' choices, but is the situation actually more dynamic than that? Are certain subject areas and content areas more receptive to technology in the classroom than others? Likewise, Young's essay seems to suggest that the degree to which technology is used in a classroom is ultimately a choice of the professor. But what about students' needs and preferred learning methods? What role do students play in this situation?

4. Does the author's background affect how he represents this situation? In what ways, and how do you determine this?

Analyzing the Rhetoric

1. What is the rhetorical effect of Jeffery R. Young explaining that "Mr. James is not antitechnology—he said he had some success in his composition courses using an online system that's sold with textbooks"?

2. "Teachers without Technology Strike Back" was originally published in *The Chronicle of Higher Education*, the primary professional news source for college professors and administrators. Given his primary audience for this essay, how would you describe how "Teachers without Technology Strike Back" is written?

3. What is the rhetorical effect of the way in which Young concludes his essay? How do you respond to his ending as a reader?

Discussing

1. From the student perspective, how do you respond to this essay? How do you as a student feel about the quality of education you get when a teacher either uses or doesn't use current technologies? Discuss your perspectives on how students perceive professors' uses of technology in their teaching.

2. Young writes: "it seems to me the key debate between the tech enthusiasts and tech skeptics is really over broader changes in colleges and anxieties about the academy being turned into just another business." Discuss the implications and ramifications of this "debate" from the student perspective.

Writing

1. What have been your experiences in classrooms with teachers who use technology in their teaching and those who do not? Which classes do you value more? Which do you enjoy more? Write an essay in which you evaluate your experiences with teachers who do and do not use technologies in the classroom.

2. Write an analysis of teaching approaches that use technology in the classroom and those that do not.

How Khan Academy Is Changing the Rules of Education

Clive Thompson

Clive Thompson is a blogger and freelance writer who specializes in writing about technology and science. His writing regularly appears in *The New York Times* magazine, *Wired*, and *New York* magazine. He also writes a column about video games for *Slate*. He regularly appears on CNN and NPR to talk about intersections between science, technology, and culture. His blog *Collision Detection* also addresses science, technology, and culture and provides him the opportunity to write about more unusual kinds of research he encounters.

In 2006, MIT graduate Salman Khan started the nonprofit organization Khan Academy "with the goal of changing education for the better by providing a free world-class education to anyone anywhere." Khan Academy provides access to more than 3,000 video tutorials about math, biology, chemistry, physics, finance, and history. The Khan Academy website has delivered more than 125 million lessons to its users. Many commentators have begun to question whether the kind of educational approach Khan Academy provides might change how education is delivered. In the essay that follows, which was originally published in *Wired* magazine, Clive Thompson explores that very question, looking closely at Khan Academy.

"This," says Matthew Carpenter, "is my favorite exercise." I peer over his shoulder at his laptop screen to see the math problem the fifth grader is pondering. It's an inverse trigonometric function: $cos^{-1}(1) = ?$

Carpenter, a serious-faced 10-year-old wearing a gray T-shirt and an impressive black digital watch, pauses for a second, fidgets, then clicks on "0 degrees." Presto: The computer tells him that he's correct. The software then generates another problem, followed by another, and yet another, until he's nailed 10 in a row in just a few minutes. All told, he's done an insane 642 inverse trig problems. "It took a while for me to get it," he admits sheepishly.

Carpenter, who attends Santa Rita Elementary, a public school in Los Altos, California, shouldn't be doing work anywhere near this advanced. In fact, when I visited his class this spring—in a sun-drenched room festooned with a papercraft X-wing fighter and student paintings of trees—the kids were supposed to be learning basic fractions, decimals, and percentages. As his teacher, Kami Thordarson, explains, students don't normally tackle inverse trig until high school, and sometimes not even then.

But last November, Thordarson began using Khan Academy in her class. Khan Academy is an educational website that, as its tagline puts it, aims to let anyone "learn almost anything—for free." Students, or anyone interested enough to surf by, can watch some 2,400 videos in which the site's founder, Salman Khan, chattily discusses principles of math, science, and economics

Matthew Carpenter, age 10, has completed 642 inverse trigonometry problems at KhanAcademy.org.

(with a smattering of social science topics thrown in). The videos are decidedly lo-fi, even crude: Generally seven to 14 minutes long, they consist of a voice-over by Khan describing a mathematical concept or explaining how to solve a problem while his hand-scribbled formulas and diagrams appear onscreen. Like the Wizard of Oz, Khan never steps from behind the curtain to appear in a video himself; it's just Khan's voice and some scrawly equations. In addition to these videos, the website offers software that generates practice problems and rewards good performance with videogame-like badges—for answering a "streak" of questions correctly, say, or mastering a series of algebra levels. (Carpenter has acquired 52 Earth badges in math, which require hours of toil to attain and at which his classmates gaze with envy and awe.)

Initially, Thordarson thought Khan Academy would merely be a helpful supplement to her normal instruction. But it quickly became far more than that. She's now on her way to "flipping" the way her class works. This involves replacing some of her lectures with Khan's videos, which students can watch at home. Then, in class, they focus on working problem sets. The idea is to invert the normal rhythms of school, so that lectures are viewed on the kids' own time and homework is done at school. It sounds weird, Thordarson admits, but this flipping makes sense when you think about it. It's when they're doing homework that students are really grappling with a subject and are most likely to need someone to talk to. And now Thordarson can tell just when this grappling occurs: Khan Academy provides teachers with a dashboard application that lets her see the instant a student gets stuck.

"I'm able to give specific, pinpointed help when needed," she says.

The result is that Thordarson's students move at their own pace. Those who are struggling get surgically targeted guidance, while advanced kids like Carpenter rocket far ahead; once they're answering questions without making mistakes, Khan's site automatically recommends new topics to move on to. Over half the class is now tackling subjects like algebra and geometric

formulas. And even the less precocious kids are improving: Only 3 percent of her students were classified as average or lower in end-of-year tests, down from 13 percent at midyear.

For years, teachers like Thordarson have complained about the frustrations of teaching to the "middle" of the class. They stand at the whiteboard, trying to get 25 or more students to learn the same stuff at the same pace. And, of course, it never really works: Advanced kids get bored and tune out, lagging ones get lost and tune out, and pretty soon half the class isn't paying attention. Since the rise of personal computers in the early '80s, educators have hoped that technology could solve this problem by offering lessons tailored to each kid. Schools have blown millions, maybe billions, of dollars on sophisticated classroom technology, but the effort has been in vain.

Khan's videos are anything but sophisticated. He recorded many of them in a closet at home, his voice sounding muffled on his $25 Logitech headset. But some of his fans believe that Khan has stumbled onto the secret to solving education's middle-of-the-class mediocrity. Most notable among them is Bill Gates, whose foundation has invested $1.5 million in Khan's site. "I'd been looking for something like this—it's so important," Gates says. Khan's approach, he argues, shows that education can truly be customized, with each student getting individualized help when needed.

Not everyone agrees. Critics argue that Khan's videos and software encourage uncreative, repetitive drilling—and leave kids staring at screens instead of interacting with real live teachers. Even Khan will acknowledge that he's not an educational professional; he's just a nerd who improvised a cool way to teach people things. And for better or worse, this means that he doesn't have a consistent, comprehensive plan for overhauling school curricula.

Whatever Khan's limits, his site has become extremely popular. More than 2 million users watch his videos every month, and all told they answer about 15 questions per second. Khan is clearly helping students master difficult and vital subjects. And he's not alone: From TED talks to iTunes U to Bill Hammack the Engineer Guy, new online educational tools are bringing the ethos of Silicon Valley to education. The role these sites can (or should) play in our nation's schools is unclear. But classes like Thordarson's are starting to find out.

Teachers have long known that one-on-one tutoring is effective, but in 1984, the education scholar Benjamin Bloom figured out precisely *how* effective it is. He conducted a metastudy of research on students who'd been pulled out of class and given individual instruction. What Bloom found is that students given one-on-one attention reliably perform two standard deviations better than their peers who stay in a regular classroom. How much of an improvement is that? Enough that a student in the middle of the pack will vault into the 98th percentile. Bloom's findings caused a stir in education, but ultimately they didn't significantly change the basic structure of the classroom. One-on-one instruction, after all, is insanely expensive. What country can afford one teacher per student?

"We've always known that one-on-one is the best way to learn, but we've never been able to figure out how to do it," Khan explains when we first meet at his small, four-room office in downtown Mountain View, California. A hoodie-clad 34-year-old with big brown eyes and a mass of jet-black hair, Khan leans back in his chair as he talks, cracking a steady stream of jokes. He has a kinetic sort of wit; he's like a nerdy, South Asian–American Seinfeld, except for the occasional "y'all" that punctuates his speech, a vestige of a youth spent in New Orleans. His desk is made out of old telephone poles and is scattered with books on investing, physics, and heart disease—subjects for upcoming videos. Khan keeps up a breakneck pace of productivity: He has recorded every one of the videos on the site himself and produces up to eight new ones each workday. His offerings run from the straightforward—science and math topics like "Pythagorean Theorem 2," "Dirac Delta Function," and "Why Gravity Gets So Strong Near Dense Objects"—to the quirky, including a series of muckraking analyses of the Geithner bank bailouts. It helps that he has a ton of formal schooling, including three degrees from MIT (a BS in math and a BS and MS in computer science) as

well as a Harvard MBA. But he also frequently goes outside his areas of expertise, hitting Wikipedia, the web, his personal library, and his long list of brainy friends to bone up on new topics until he feels competent. His office contains several *Idiot's Guide to ...* books.

Khan never intended to become an education revolutionary. Talented at math in high school, he initially hoped to be a Richard Feynman–style theoretical physicist, before realizing he was far more likely to make his mark in computers. After finishing at MIT and working for a few Silicon Valley dotcoms, he headed to Harvard Business School in 2001, where he claims his main motivation was to get married. ("I'm dead serious," he says. "Silicon Valley in the late '90s was the absolute worst place to find a wife or a girlfriend." He found one and married her—a med student who's now a doctor in Mountain View.)

After business school, Khan went to work for Wohl Capital, a hedge fund, where he researched companies to find solid investments. At Wohl, he learned how to quickly orient himself in unfamiliar territory. (He also amassed an epic store of mental trivia. While we're having lunch, he casually mentions how many eggs the average chicken lays in a year: "It's 260!") Dan Wohl, his boss, discovered that Khan seemed unusually driven to teach. "I'd come back to the office," Wohl says, "and giant math equations were scrawled across the board." Khan was training the junior staff in the nuances of finance. "It's not the usual cutthroat Wall Street thing to do," Wohl adds. "But he had this natural gift and a really selfless approach."

Then, in 2004, Khan's 13-year-old cousin Nadia, who lived across the country, asked him for help in math. Khan agreed to tutor her on the phone. To illustrate the mathematical concepts he was describing, they'd log into Yahoo Messenger and Khan would use the program's drawing window to write equations while she watched remotely. When they couldn't meet, he'd just record a lesson as a video, talking through the material while writing in Microsoft Paint.

One day Nadia told him she didn't want to talk on the phone anymore; she wanted him to just record videos. Why? Because that way she could review the video as many times as she wanted, scrolling back several times over puzzling parts and fast-forwarding through the boring bits she already knew. "She basically said, 'I like you better on the video than in person,'" Khan says.

A lightbulb went off: Khan realized that remediation—going over and over something that you really ought to already know—is less embarrassing when you can do it privately, with no one watching. Nadia learned faster when she had control over the pace of the lecture. "The worst time to learn something," he says, "is when someone is standing over your shoulder going, 'Do you get it?'"

He also discovered that the state of math education in the country was pretty awful. He began tutoring several other cousins (word had gotten around the family: free lessons!), and he was disturbed to find that their grasp of the basics was shaky. Even on simple division questions, they answered tentatively and slowly. Khan wanted to get the kids to the point where they could confidently bark back these answers—they had to have this kind of automatic mental processing before they could handle more-advanced material.

What his cousins needed, he decided, was drilling. He programmed Java modules that would fire questions at them automatically. If they got 10 questions right in a row, the software would push them to the next level, which had harder problems. (As a bonus, he could peek at the database online to make sure they were actually doing the practice.) Though Khan didn't know the academic terminology at the time, he was implementing classic "mastery-based learning"—requiring students to prove they've conquered material before advancing.

Word soon spread to the rest of the world. Khan discovered that thousands of people were watching his videos on YouTube. Some were students mystified by physics, others were adults brushing up on basics before relaunching a stalled college degree. Khan gradually became more and more absorbed in his site, staying up past midnight crafting new videos and software lessons. Email messages poured in from fans, startling him with their intensity.

"You made me realize that anyone can learn the material when it is presented in the right way," wrote Tom Brannan, a 19-year-old about to enter a Pennsylvania college. After dropping to a C in math, Brannan learned enough from Khan to ace his last few high school tests and now plans to pursue a degree in computer science. "I

Teachers at all grade levels have begun using Khan Academy in their classrooms.

had been struggling with the unit circle, essentially trying to learn it out of the textbook," Brannan wrote. "I watched your videos and it all clicked."

In 2009, Khan decided to turn his hobby into a full-time job. He formed a nonprofit and got a small donation from Ann Doerr, wife of Silicon Valley investor John Doerr. Demand had taken off; now tens of thousands of people were watching his videos every month. Khan quickly got to work recording more clips in his closet.

Then, last summer, he received a text from Doerr, who was attending the Aspen Ideas Festival: "Bill Gates is talking about your stuff onstage." Khan dialed up the online video from Aspen and watched Gates, whom he'd never met, singing his praises; indeed, Gates revealed that his own kids were using Khan Academy as a study aid. ("I shit a brick when I saw that," Khan says.) He met with Gates soon after and received $1.5 million from the Bill & Melinda Gates Foundation. Google kicked in another $2 million.

"Math is the killer," Gates told me recently. His foundation had researched unemployment and found math to be a significant stumbling block. "If you ask people, 'Hey, there are these open nursing jobs, why don't you go and get one?' math is often the reason they give for not applying," Gates says. "'Why didn't you pass the police exam?' Math."

In the new era of popular, YouTube-friendly education videos, Khan's site is unique in that it's ruthlessly practical: It's aimed at helping people master the basics, the humble bread-and-butter equations they encounter in elementary and high school. Traditionally, these kinds of videos can be dry and difficult to slog through. But Khan manages to pull off his lessons with a casual air that keeps the viewer engaged. He says his relaxed approach isn't faked—it's a result of the way he prepares. He never writes a script. He simply researches a topic until he feels he can explain it off the cuff to "a motivated 7-year-old." (Preparation can take anywhere from 10 minutes with a familiar subject like algebra to nearly a week in the case of organic chemistry.) Khan also never edits. Either he nails the lecture in a single take or he redoes the entire thing until it satisfies him.

Khan suspects there is a hidden power in the fact that he never appears onscreen in his videos. The only visual is his handwriting, slowly filling the screen. "That way, it doesn't seem like I'm up on a stage lecturing down at you," he says. "It's intimate, like we're both sitting at a table and we're working through something together, writing on a piece of paper."

After you've listened to a lot of Khan's stuff, instructional videos by for-profit educational firms begin to sound gratingly phony. At his desk, he pulls up a YouTube video about how the sodium-potassium pump in a cell membrane works. As the video plays, a singsongy female voice-over fills his office with the cloying, condescending tone of a teacher who's convinced her students are idiots. "I mean, I can't pay attention for one minute to that," he says.

Several students I spoke to also pointed out that Khan is particularly good at explaining all the hidden, small steps in math problems—steps that teachers often gloss over. He has an uncanny ability to inhabit the mind of someone who doesn't already understand something.

"He explains things step by step, rather than assuming you already know how to get from A to B," Brannan says.

"It's just super-impressive that Sal explains stuff so well," Gates says. "The fact that one guy can do so many subjects is pretty amazing."

Last November, Khan Academy made the jump from hot new website to actual classroom tool. Khan had coffee with a member of the Los Altos school board who suggested that the district try using Khan's system. Three schools offered up classes as test subjects—two fifth-grade classes (including the one run by Kami Thordarson) and two seventh-grade classes.

Khan thought he could offer teachers crucial new insight into how students learn. He envisioned a dashboard system that would track students' individual statistics, showing them and their instructors how many videos they'd watched, how many questions they'd answered, and which ones they'd gotten wrong or right. Normally, of course, teachers fly blind. They use quizzes, homework, and their own observations to try to figure out how much their students understand, but it's a crude process. Day to day, it's hard to know what a student is and isn't learning. A dashboard, Khan says, can change all that.

In the fall of 2010, flush with the infusion of money from Google and Gates, Khan hired a programmer, Ben Kamens, and a designer, Jason Rosoff, and tasked

Students appreciate the portability and convenience of Khan Academy video learning.

them with, among other things, building the dashboard. These sorts of performance-measuring apps have become increasingly common in the business world, so the duo didn't think teachers would be terribly impressed by their software. Wrong: They were astounded. "We'd go collect some data and make a chart, and the teachers were blown away—every time," Kamens says. "This isn't taxing the edge of technology. But they were completely shocked, as if this had never existed before."

Among those impressed was Courtney Cadwell, a seventh-grade math teacher at Egan Junior High in Los Altos. When I visited her class, she pulled me over to her laptop and showed me her kids' statistics. She flicked through screenfuls of colorful charts illustrating what subjects the kids were working on and how many videos they'd watched and problem sets they'd done. The software even told Cadwell how many minutes the students had worked at home.

"Oh my gosh," she exclaims when she gets to one student's account. "Kristofer, he's working on systems of equations and subtracting fractions?" Clearly, even after working with the system for almost five months, it still has the ability to surprise her. A look at the data shows that the students seem to advance in spurts: A kid will grind away at a subject, seemingly stuck, until suddenly something clicks and he vaults forward, sometimes going on a tear and mastering several new subjects in a day or two.

Cadwell has already gotten so used to these metrics that she feels unmoored in her other classes, where they're not yet using the system. "In those, I get to a quiz or a test and I'm blindsided when they don't know something—or when they ace something."

Cadwell needs all the help she can get: She teaches remedial math to the school's struggling students, some of whom come from immigrant families with parents who don't speak English and can't easily help with homework. When her seventh-grade class arrived last fall, some barely had third-grade math skills. But by being able to target her students for special help exactly when they needed it, Cadwell saw stunning results: The class's test scores improved more than 106 percent in half a year. One girl I met in the classroom had advanced

an astonishing 366 percent. "I hated math," the girl tells me cheerfully. "But now it's actually fun." She began the year unable to do basic fractions; during my visit, I watched her plow through complicated long division, carefully working problems on the Khan software.

Borrowing another trend in software, Khan's team also added gamelike rewards to the interface. They came up with a welter of points, badges, and awards that kids can vie for. The Los Altos teachers were surprised—almost flabbergasted—by how powerfully the rewards motivated their students. When I visited the fifth-grade class of Kelly Rafferty at Santa Rita Elementary, the room teemed with kids milling around the school's laptops, checking out one another's latest achievements and trying to help each other on various modules. Rafferty pointed to a boy pecking away at division problems. "He's done something like 500 multiplication problems," she said. "Could I ever get him to do 500 of anything? No. So it's funny the things that motivate them." She noticed that one student had worked on problems at home from midnight to 2 am the night before.

Of course, kids who've grown up on computers are quick to spot the weaknesses in Khan's system. They discovered ways to cheat on the drills: In the logarithms unit, for example, they noticed that the third multiple-choice answer was always the right one.

Some students also told me they were unsettled by their teachers' ability to monitor precisely how much work they've done. "I just think that's kind of awkward," Maddy Zib, 12, said to Cadwell the day I visited. "It's like you're able to spy on our progress! I know you're the teacher and that's your job ... but it's just a bit weird."

Not all educators are enamored with Khan and his site. Gary Stager, a longtime educational consultant and advocate of laptops in classrooms, thinks Khan Academy isn't innovative at all. The videos and software modules, he contends, are just a high-tech version of that most hoary of teaching techniques—lecturing and drilling. Schools have become "joyless test-prep factories," he says, and Khan Academy caters to this dismal trend. Khan's approach "suffers from this sort of 'school über alles' philosophy: They're not going to question anything the schools do. They're not going to challenge any of the content." Stager admires the fact that Khan is trying to improve education, but he says research has shown that kids who are struggling at math won't be helped by a "filmstrip."

As Sylvia Martinez, president of Generation YES, a nonprofit focusing on technology in the classroom, puts it, "The things they're doing are really just rote." Flipping the classroom isn't an entirely new idea, Martinez says, and she doubts that it would work for most kids: If they can't understand the lecture in a classroom, they're not going to grasp it better when it's done through a video at home.

Khan's critics are mostly "constructionists." This school of thought holds that kids lose interest in math because it's so often taught as a bunch of mechanical routines you follow to solve problems disconnected from everyday life. Constructionists argue that it's better to give kids activities that let them discover the principles of math and physics on their own—for instance, having them play around with kid-friendly programming languages like Logo. "Students 'fumbling around' is actually where the learning happens—and there's no shortcut for this process," Martinez wrote in a blog post savaging Khan's system. Gates and Khan claim they're trying to shake up the classroom, but Khan's critics say he's not being radical *enough*.

Salman Khan approaches education with the mind-set of a Silicon Valley entrepreneur: Make something cool and people will use it.

As you might imagine, Khan heatedly rejects the notion that he's promoting a return to rote learning. "It's the exact opposite!" he says: The more that teachers flip their classrooms—with students watching his lectures at home—the more time is freed up for creative activities during the school day, like arts, games, or collectively brainstorming more abstract stuff. "You're actually liberating the classroom; you're making it more human," he says. He takes a dim view of the constructionist idea that students won't really understand math unless they discover each principle on their own. "Isaac Newton would not have invented calculus had he not had textbooks on algebra." Bill Gates is even more scathing: "It's bullshit," he says. "If you can't do multiplication, then tell me, what is your contribution to society going to be?"

Another limitation of Khan's site is that the drilling software can handle only subjects where the answers are unambiguously right or wrong, like math or chemistry. And Khan has relatively few videos on messier, gray-area subjects like history.

And Khan and Gates both admit there's no easy way to automate the teaching of writing—even though that subject is just as critical as math and students score equally poorly on it in national tests. Khan thinks one way to teach writing online is with peer review—have kids upload their writing so that the entire class can read and comment on it. (Many teachers, in fact, already do this.) In the next year or so, he wants to launch a community section of Khan Academy, where students can help each other with writing. He envisions students posting questions they can't solve and getting guidance from other students or teachers around the world, any time of day; those who offered the best help would get voted upward.

Even if Khan is truly liberating students to advance at their own pace, it's not clear that the schools will be able to cope. The very concept of grade levels implies groups of students moving along together at an even pace. So what happens when, using Khan Academy, you wind up with a kid in fifth grade who has mastered high school trigonometry and physics—but is still functioning like a regular 10-year-old when it comes to writing, history, and social studies? Khan's programmer, Ben Kamens, has heard from teachers who've seen Khan Academy presentations and loved the idea but wondered whether they could modify it "to stop students from becoming this advanced."

Khan's success—and tech-darling status—has injected him into the heated wars over school reform. Reformers today, by and large, believe student success should be carefully tested, with teachers and principals receiving better pay if their students advance more quickly and getting canned if they fall behind. They're generally in favor of privately run charter schools and hotly opposed to the seniority rules of the teachers' unions, if not the existence of unions altogether. Though the ranks of reformers include many Wall Streeters and Silicon Valley honchos, Khan himself winces when I apply the label to him. He says he has no particular animus toward the public school system; in fact, his experience with Los Altos has shown him that public school teachers can be as innovative as anyone else. "Don't call me an education reformer, all right?" he says. "We're not out to fight some political battle. We're out to build stuff that's useful."

Khan doesn't seem to care whether he changes the school system. Indeed, he's leery of working too closely with school districts, because it would require him to adhere to their rules and expectations. Until now, he has followed his own instincts in building his library of videos and software—recording the subjects his cousins needed, then gradually adding those that he found interesting or that he thought students would benefit from. But schools have a firm curriculum they have to march through, and the Los Altos teachers often find they're moving on to subjects that Khan hasn't covered in detail.

Khan is gamely attempting to fill those holes. But he's not breaking his back, because he doesn't want the school system and its Byzantine standards determining what he does with his site. Indeed, he argues, trying to serve taskmasters in different districts in 50 states is one of the reasons so many educational software companies produce such dull sludge: Much like teaching to the mythical "middle" of a class, the process strips teaching

materials of any eccentricity and playfulness. "I don't want to be a vendor," he says with a shrug.

In essence, Khan doesn't want to change the way institutions teach; he wants to change how people learn, whether they're in a private school or a public school—or for that matter, whether they're a student or an adult trying to self-educate in their kitchen in Ohio. Or Brazil or Russia or India: One member of Khan's staff—now up to 13 people—is spearheading a drive to translate the videos into 10 major languages. It's classic startup logic: Do something cool, do it quickly, and people who love it will find you.

In the spring, Cadwell's principal visited her classroom to see how Khan Academy was working out. The students were watching a video with their headsets on. Each was viewing it in a slightly different way, pausing and rewinding the parts that confused them and writing down notes—which is precisely what customized learning ought to look like. But Cadwell realized that, as she sat there watching, she—the teacher—appeared to be slacking. "It was just very weird when the kids had their headphones on, all watching the same video and listening to the same information, but I wasn't in control of it!" she says.

But the principal didn't object. As more high-quality lecture materials go online, teachers and administrators alike are beginning to realize that when it comes to simply explaining something, there's probably someone out there who's doing it better. So, they tell me, why compete? Focus instead on offering the sort of fine-grained, personalized help that only a live teacher can offer.

As it happens, even some teachers who've never heard of Khan Academy are already practicing some of Khan's ideas: They flip their classrooms and use free tools like Google Docs to make their students' learning as visible and trackable as possible. Many teachers are resourceful, and they'll use any tool at their disposal—sanctioned or not. It could be that the kind of fundamental changes promised by sites like Khan Academy are going to upend the classroom, no matter what happens at the district or state level.

For his part, Khan says he's now considering starting his own private school, as a way to see just how much you could wrap learning around Khan Academy. His ideas are intriguing: Among other things, his school wouldn't divide kids by age; teenagers would mix in with kindergartners. "I have no research to back this up," he says, "but younger kids act more mature around older kids, and older kids act more mature around younger kids." If the classrooms were fully flipped, students could spend more of the school day doing creative activities. He'd use board games to teach negotiation, and he'd teach history backward. ("Why are the Israelis and Palestinians pissed at each other? Let's go back a couple of years. Wait—they were pissed at each other even then! So you go back even further ...") He also thinks he'd teach kids subjects that have more real-world applicability—like "statistics, law, accounting, and finance. Why are you teaching people civics? Teach them law. That's more relevant, and you learn civics at the same time." He calculates that it would cost only $10,000 per child, "affordable for professional couples out here."

If Khan does start such a school, he'll have a powerful advantage. He's been posting videos online for five years and students have answered more than 50 million questions in his software: Khan and his team are now sitting on a massive pile of data about how people learn and where they get stuck. He plans to mine the information to discover previously invisible patterns. How many times do students need to view the statistics video before they can answer questions about the subject? If you examine all the kids who stumble on, say, fractional division and basic algebra, can you predict what other subjects they'll have trouble mastering? In the long run, Khan believes, such data mining could help him create customized lessons that are perfectly keyed to each kid's learning style.

But in the meantime, he's got videos to record. Back at his office, he slips on his headset. His next video will be about diabetes, and he'll use the subject to sneak in some tricky, Khan-style math—calculating how many teaspoons of sugar are floating around in your bloodstream. "It's almost 1 teaspoon per average-size human at any point in time!" he says somewhat gleefully. Then he turns around, hits the record button, and starts talking.

Analyzing the Situation

1. How would you describe the situation in which Clive Thompson participates with this essay? How would you describe the situation in which Salman Khan participates?

2. In many ways, what Clive Thompson describes about Khan Academy is a description of how situational constraints as well as institutions and power are being disrupted. With this in mind, how would you describe the role of Khan Academy in the situation in which it participates?

3. What do you see as some of the most significant ecological relationships in which this essay and Khan Academy participate?

Analyzing the Rhetoric

1. Why do you suppose Thompson focuses so much of his essay on examples of individuals and classes that use Khan Academy instead of just focusing on Salman Khan and his objectives? In what ways do the examples affect the essay?

2. When discussing Bill Gates's relationship with Khan Academy, Clive Thompson identifies that "'Math is the killer,' Gates told me recently." Why in this instance does Thompson specify that Gates was talking to him rather than Khan or someone else?

3. Why does Thompson address the critiques of Khan Academy? How does the inclusion of these criticisms affect the essay?

Discussing

1. What is your response not just to Clive Thompson's essay, but to the very idea that Khan Academy puts forward about education? Discuss your thoughts and the thoughts of others in your class.

2. Clive Thompson writes: "Khan's programmer, Ben Kamens, has heard from teachers who've seen Khan Academy presentations and loved the idea

but wondered whether they could modify it 'to stop students from becoming this advanced.'" How do you respond to a request like this? Discuss.

3. Have you used Khan Academy? What were your experiences?

Writing

1. Spend some time on the Khan Academy web pages and watch a few videos to get a feel for how the resource works. Then write an evaluation of the web resource and one or two of the videos you watched.

2. Clive Thompson's title tells us that the essay will address "How Khan Academy Is Changing the Rules of Education." But is Khan Academy really changing education? Write an argumentative essay that takes a stance as to whether Khan Academy really is changing things or not.

3. How would you describe Khan Academy and Salman Khan's educational philosophies to someone unfamiliar with the resource? Write a detailed description of Khan Academy and its objectives.

4. Clive Thompson explains that "Khan and Gates both admit there's no easy way to automate the teaching of writing—even though that subject is just as critical as math and students score equally poorly on it in national tests." Why can't writing be taught in the same ways that Khan teaches subjects like calculus or biology? Write an essay that considers why writing is a difficult subject to teach in the same ways as other Khan Academy videos teach other subjects.

Waiting for Superman

DAVIS GUGGENHEIM AND BILLY KIMBALL

Waiting for Superman is an award-winning documentary about the failure of public education in the United States. The film follows several students who are hoping to be selected by lottery for a new charter school. The new school is anticipated to provide students with more opportunities than traditional public schools, so demand for entrance is high and spaces are limited. The film earned a good deal of praise and criticism from both movie critics and education experts.

Waiting for Superman was directed by Davis Guggenheim, who cowrote the film with Billy Kimball. Guggenheim is a well-known director and producer, having made films like *Training Day* with Denzel Washington and Ethan Hawke and television shows like *The Shield*, *Melrose Place*, *24*, *NYPD Blue*, *ER*, *Deadwood*, and *Party of Five*. He is perhaps best known, though, for having directed Al Gore's

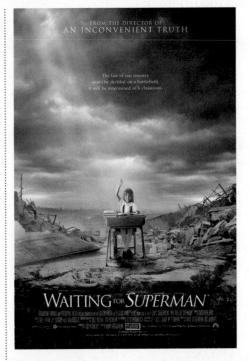

Academy Award–winning documentary *An Inconvenient Truth* about global warming. He also directed Barack Obama's biographical film and his campaign infomercial, both of which were used in Obama's successful 2008

presidential campaign. In 2012, Guggenheim directed a second campaign film for Barack Obama that features Tom Hanks narrating about the president's successes.

Davis Guggenheim cowrote *Waiting for Superman* with writer/producer Billy Kimball, who earned a reputation as writing for comedy networks that preceded Comedy Central. He has written for *Saturday Night Live* and *Cedric the Entertainer Presents*. He was the original executive producer for *The Late Show with Craig Kilborn*. Most impressive, though, Kimball has written scripts for five episodes of *The Simpsons*.

Analyzing the Situation

1. As college students, does this situation matter to you? Does it involve you?

2. If you wanted to respond to *Waiting for Superman* and participate directly in the same situation with your response, what might be the best genre, medium, and method for doing so?

3. What role does kairos play in the situation in which *Waiting for Superman* participates?

Analyzing the Rhetoric

1. Why do you suppose Davis Guggenheim opted to state his position in this situation through film? As a medium, what does film provide that other media cannot? What does film lack that other media could provide? Could Guggenheim have accomplished the same effect in a book?

2. What is the visual rhetorical effect of the animation Davis Guggenheim uses throughout *Waiting for Superman*, particularly at moments when the film delivers what might be understood as difficult information or complicated data?

3. From a rhetorical standpoint, what is the most powerful part of *Waiting for Superman*? What is the weakest part of the film?

4. How would you describe the organizational strategy Guggenheim uses in presenting *Waiting for Superman*?

Discussing

1. Many of the people interviewed in *Waiting for Superman* suggest that students' getting into college is one of the measures of a successful school or school system. By that measure, you and your classmates attended successful schools. As a class, discuss your school experiences and the relationships between those experiences and your college learning experiences. Be sure to be patient and let every student share his experiences. Once everyone has shared his experiences, discuss the similarities and differences of experiences in your class.

2. Certainly, *Waiting for Superman* is about education, but it is also about a number of other social issues. Discuss the other issues that this documentary addresses and the ecological relationships among those issues and education.

3. After watching *Waiting for Superman*, discuss the implications of the film.

Writing

1. In addition to the praise *Waiting for Superman* received, the film also garnered a substantial amount of criticism. The Grassroots Education Movement—a group of teachers and parents opposed to the kind of charter school approach described in *Waiting for Superman*—for example, produced its own film to critique Guggenheim's film. *The Inconvenient Truth Behind Waiting for Superman*, which plays on the title of Guggenheim's *An Inconvenient Truth,* argues against the privatization of schools forwarded in *Waiting for Superman*. The film critiques the idea that charter schools are what the country needs and also argues against the ways in which the charter school movement undermines teachers' unions and real education reform. You can watch a trailer for *The Inconvenient Truth Behind Waiting for Superman* on YouTube. Take some time to watch the trailer and to learn more about criticisms of *Waiting for Superman*. Then write a document that informs readers about the various critiques of *Waiting for Superman*.

2. Are there charter schools in your community? If so, what are the processes for attending those schools? If not, what options are there for students other than public schools? Write an informative document about those schools.

3. Like other controversial films, *Waiting for Superman* drew the attention of many writers in the blogosphere. Blogger szhamilton, for example, posted a well-researched commentary about the public and private funding used to develop the Harlem Children's Zone. Take some time to read the post, and then write a response to the post, directing it to the same audience as the original post.

A Vision of Students Today

Michael Wesch

Wired magazine has called Michael Wesch "The Explainer." He is an associate professor and Coffman Chair for Distinguished Teaching Scholars at Kansas State University. He is a cultural anthropologist who studies the effects of new media technologies on society and culture. His past research has included studying the effects of writing on a remote indigenous culture in Papua New Guinea's rain forest. He often uses video as the medium through which to convey his research. Some of his videos have been translated into more than 15 languages and are often featured at international film festivals. Wesch won one of *Wired* magazine's Rave Awards, which are given for "innovators, instigators, and inventors." He has also been named an Emerging Explorer by National Geographic. He also won the John Culkin Award for outstanding praxis in media ecology. In 2008, Wesch won the prestigious CASE/Carnegie U.S. Professor of the Year for Doctoral and Research Universities.

In 2007, Wesch posted the video "A Vision of Students Today" to YouTube. The video, which was made as a promotion for Wesch's Mediated Cultures program at Kansas State, was created by Wesch and the 200 students in his Introduction to Cultural Anthropology course. The video has been viewed more than four and a half million times and has received a tremendous amount of response. You can watch the video on YouTube.

Analyzing the Situation

1. In what ways are you part of this situation?

2. Given that this video was released in 2007, has the situation changed since it was posted?

3. Who do you see as the primary audience for this video: students, educators, or the general public? Why?

Analyzing the Rhetoric

1. What role does writing play in this video? Why do you suppose Michael Wesch chose to use writing instead of student voices in the video? What does he gain or lose in doing so?

2. Would you describe Wesch's video as persuasive? informative? narrative? Why?

3. How would you describe Wesch's rhetorical approach in this video? How would you describe his visual rhetorical approach? Do the visual and the rhetorical work well together in this video? Explain.

Discussing

1. Michael Wesch's video was posted on YouTube in 2007. As of this writing, it has been viewed in the original post nearly five million times. That doesn't account for reposts and shares. You are encountering the video through this textbook at least six years after it was posted. Given what the video conveys about students in 2007 and your experiences as students, have things changed since Wesch posted the video? As a class, discuss how you see the Wesch video in your current situation.

2. What do you see as the most striking features of Wesch's video? Discuss what is effective and ineffective about the video.

3. Wesch's video has garnered a lot of response on YouTube, both in the comments section for the video page and in response videos, including parodies, remixes, and copycat videos. Why do you suppose so many people have identified an exigency to respond to this video?

Writing

1. Wesch's video claims to provide a vision of students; it tells us something about the general characteristics of college students. Many other resources, both official and unofficial, also describe students using different kinds of criteria. The United States Department of Education and The United Nations Educational, Scientific, and Cultural Organization, for example, provide lots of statistical data about college students. Conduct some research to find information about how either one of these organizations characterizes college students today. Then, write a document that compares Wesch's representation of students with the information you locate from the Department of Education or United Nations.

2. In 2011, Michael Wesch posted submissions for a remix of the "A Vision of Students Today" video to be called "A Vision of Students Today 2011 Remix," which you can find on YouTube. Watch the remix video and write a comparison of the newer video and the older.

3. Make a video that presents a view of students today from your perspective that adds to the conversation in which Wesch's video participates.

Thinking and Writing about the Chapter

Discussion Threads

1. What is the purpose of education, particularly higher education? Why are you pursuing a college degree? How do others in your class view the purpose of higher education? As a class, discuss the differences in response.

2. One of the points that Megan McArdle makes in "Envisioning a Post-Campus America" is that "Online education will kill the liberal arts degree." How do you respond to such a claim? Discuss this claim and your response with others in your class.

3. Many of the readings in this chapter address issues like credentialing and content delivery, what count as official education and what doesn't, and what's right about educational systems and what's wrong. But few of these readings address the content of what's being

taught and learned. Do any of the changes discussed in these readings also change *what* is taught and learned, or do they just change *how* information is taught and learned?

Collaboration

Working in small groups, locate an education-based resource like Khan Academy and select one tutorial that is offered for free. Then, individually, work through the tutorial. Individually, analyze your experience with the tutorial and your feelings about whether such approaches could serve as a primary form of education. Next, in your group, discuss what each group member observed about the tutorial. Using what each of you found and how you each responded to the tutorial process, collaborate to write an evaluation of that tutorial and the resource from which it is taken.

Writing

1. Many of the readings in this chapter address the ways in which digital technologies have changed contemporary educational processes. But, of course, at any given historical moment, technology has changed education. Think, for example, about the technologies of the printing press, the chalkboard, the notebook, or the pencil, each of which changed education and also received a good deal of criticism about those changes. Conduct some research to learn about how a pre-digital-era technology that we now consider commonplace or obsolete affected education. Learn about whether that technology was resisted or embraced. Then write an informative document about the role of that technology in changing education.

2. What is education? What is the purpose of education? Write a document that explains the role and objective of education in contemporary U.S. culture. Use both your observations and research.

3. Given what you've read and seen in this chapter, as well as your own experiences and research, how might you convey to people your own age in other countries what education in the United States means culturally? What visual media might best help you convey such information? Would simply writing an academic type of essay work? What genre, medium, and method would you choose to use? Spend some time addressing the rhetorical and functional problems that you would face in addressing a transnational audience about such a subject. Then write, design, and circulate the text you build.

4. Is education political? Write an argumentative essay in which you take a position as to whether education is or is not political.

Local Situation

It is more likely than not that you are reading *Writing Situations* as part of an academic curriculum at an institution of higher education. This book, this assignment, your instructor, your school, your reason for being in college, and your professional and personal goals are all directly involved in the situations addressed in this chapter. In fact, without you and your classmates and other students around the country and world, this situation wouldn't exist. With that in mind, and with the readings you engaged in in this chapter in mind, write and design a document that details how your college or university, your community, and you and your peers actively participate in this situation.

26 | Food

Ask yourself how you think about food. How have you accounted for food throughout your life? Do you eat particular kinds of foods? Is food for you mostly about nutrition or pleasure? Is there a difference? Are there particular foods that you associate with particular events? In your journal or blog, write about how you think about food and the role food plays in your life.

One cannot think well, love well, sleep well, if one has not dined well.

—Virginia Woolf

Fundamentally, food is any substance that provides nutrition when ingested. Food sustains life, provides energy, and promotes growth. Traditionally, we have understood the immediate basic needs of any human being as being food, shelter, and clothing. Food is what sustains the human body; it keeps us alive. Humans digest food to extract nutrients: protein, carbohydrates, vitamins, fats, and minerals. Overconsumption of food can cause health problems; underconsumption—or hunger—can likewise cause health problems. According to the International Covenant on Economic, Social and Cultural Rights (ICESCR), a treaty adopted by the United Nations General Assembly in 1966, the right to food is a basic human right, as is the fundamental right to be free from hunger. Food is energy. It is measured in calories, and it participates in an economy of calorie exchanges. Starvation is the inability to taken in enough calories to sustain life.

Food is a complex subject. Traditionally, people obtained food through either hunting/gathering or through agriculture. Because food is a basic need, a basic requirement for life, obtaining it has always been a primary human activity. Historically, food was acquired from local sources, and so food preparation and customs were local. In this way, traditions surrounding food acquisition, preparation, and consumption contributed to and were affected by local cultural practices. Food, that is, is an inseparable part of culture. As such, food is also deeply enmeshed with economics, politics, and religions.

Food is a basic need, but for many, food is also central to celebration. In many cultures sharing food is symbolic of friendship. We associate certain foods with our celebrations, with our families, and with particular events. Holidays are punctuated with food: Thanksgiving turkey, Hanukkah latkes, Passover matzos, Christmas ham, New Year's Day black-eyed peas, and so on. We eat funnel cakes at the fair; we eat hot dogs at the ball park. Clam chowder in New England; pizza in New York; barbeque in North Carolina; grilled cheese in Wisconsin; mofongo in Puerto Rico; gumbo in Louisiana; cheesesteak in Philadelphia; and grits in the South. "You are what you eat," the old saying says. It's an accurate saying in that our foods reflect our cultures and our foods sustain our lives.

Though people have historically gathered calories through agriculture and hunting/gathering, more recently industrial efforts produce and distribute the majority of the world's food. The industry is a diverse and complex array of businesses around the world. The food industry regulates, educates, develops, manufactures, grows, processes, markets, distributes, and sells the majority of the world's calories. Food is big business.

Food is also no longer local in the way it once was. Crops that grow in one location can easily be shipped to be available in another location. South American–grown produce is sold all over the United States as is U.S.-grown corn. You can get Florida orange juice in London and Chinese takeout in Arkansas. This globalization also affects culture. For example, consider sushi, which is a traditional Japanese method for preparing rice with shari vinegar and then serving the rice with some form of sea-food, most often raw fish. As more people of Japanese descent immigrated to the United States and as global trade and travel exposed more people to Japanese foods, sushi began to be available in the United States. Now sushi is a ubiquitous food in the United States, readily available in restaurants, supermarkets, convenience stores, food courts, even gas stations. Sushi, that is, is now an ingrained part of U.S. food culture.

The readings in this chapter provide starting points for critical thinking and asking rigorous questions about food. These readings ask you to become more alert to the issues that surround food rather than just taking food for granted. They introduce questions about culture and food, how we think about food, where our food comes from, food safety, food preparation, hunger and waste, and food quality. The intent is to encourage you to think about the role food plays in your life and in the world. That is, this chapter is designed to encourage you to not take food for granted.

Talking to the Owls and Butterflies

John Fire Lame Deer

John Fire Lame Deer was a medicine man and Sioux chief; he lived from 1895 until 1976. He was renowned for his leadership and spiritual guidance to both the Sioux people and to Native Americans in general. His only book, *Lame Deer, Seeker of Visions*, from which the essay printed here, "Talking to the Owls and Butterflies," is taken, was translated into more than ten languages. The book, which addresses a variety of subjects concerning the lives of Native Americans, offers important commentary on the role white people have played in Native American lives and the relationships between Native Americans and nature. Lame Deer makes it clear that Whites and Indians see nature differently, and in "Talking to the Owls and Butterflies" he addresses the differences in how Whites have consumed nature as opposed to how Native Americans see food. As you read this piece, pay attention

to how Lame Deer establishes voice and uses the power of that voice to convey his message. Consider, too, what Lame Deer's argument suggests about the ways that different cultures think about food.

Let's sit down here, all of us, on the open prairie, where we can't see a highway or a fence. Let's have no blankets to sit on, but feel the ground with our bodies, the earth, the yielding shrubs. Let's have the grass for a mattress, experiencing its sharpness and its softness. Let us become like stones, plants, and trees. Let us be animals, think and feel like animals.

Listen to the air. You can hear it, feel it, smell it, taste it. Woniya waken—the holy air—which renews all by its breath. Woniya, woniya waken—spirit, life, breath, renewal—it means all that. Woniya—we sit together, don't touch, but something is there; we feel it between us, as a presence. A good way to start thinking about nature, talk about it. Rather talk to it, talk to the rivers, to the lakes, to the winds as to our relatives.

You have made it hard for us to experience nature in the good way by being part of it. Even here we are conscious that somewhere out in those hills there are missile silos and radar stations. White men always pick the few unspoiled, beautiful, awesome spots for the sites

of these abominations. You have raped and violated
these lands, always saying, "Gimme, gimme, gimme,"
and never giving anything back. You have taken 200,000
acres of our Pine Ridge reservation and made them into
a bombing range. This land is so beautiful and strange
that now some of you want to make it into a natural
park. The only use you have made of this land since you
took it from us was to blow it up.

You have not only despoiled the earth, the rocks,
the minerals, all of which you call "dead" but which
are very much alive; you have even changed the animals, which are part of us, part of the Great Spirit,
changed them in a horrible way, so no one can recognize them. There is power in a buffalo—spiritual,
magic power—but there is no power in an Angus, in a
Hereford.

There is power in an antelope, but not in a goat
or in a sheep, which holds still while you butcher
it, which will eat your newspaper if you let it. There
was great power in a wolf, even in a coyote. You have
made him into a freak—a toy poodle, a Pekingese, a
lap dog. You can't do much with a cat, which is like an
Indian, unchangeable. So you fix it, alter it, declaw it,
even cut its vocal cords so you can experiment on it
in a laboratory without being disturbed by its cries. A
partridge, a grouse, a quail, a pheasant, you have made
them into chickens, creatures that can't fly, that wear
a kind of sunglasses so they won't peck each other's
eyes out, "birds" with a "pecking order." There are farms
where they breed chickens for breast meat. Those birds
are kept in low cages, forced to be hunched over all the
time, which makes the breast muscles very big. Soothing
sounds, Muzak, are piped into these chickens' hutches.
One loud noise and the chickens go haywire, killing
themselves by flying against the mesh of their cages.
Having to spend all their lives stooped over makes an
unnatural, crazy, no-good bird. It also makes unnatural,
no-good human beings.

That's where you fooled yourselves. You have not
only altered, declawed and malformed your winged and
four-legged cousins; you have done it to yourselves. You
have changed men into chairmen of boards, into office
workers, into time-clock punchers. You have changed

women into housewives, truly fearful creatures. I was
once invited into the home of such a one.

"Watch the ashes, don't smoke, you stain the
curtains. Watch the goldfish bowl, don't breathe on the
parakeet, don't lean your head against the wallpaper;
your hair may be greasy. Don't spill liquor on that table:
it has a delicate finish. You should have wiped your
boots; the floor was just varnished. Don't, don't, don't …"
That is crazy. We weren't made to endure this. You live in
prisons which you have built for yourselves, calling them
"homes," offices, factories. We have a new joke on the
reservation:

"What is cultural deprivation?" Answer: "Being
an upper-middle-class white kid living in a split-level
suburban home with a color TV."

Sometimes I think that even our pitiful tar-paper
shacks are better than your luxury homes. Walking a
hundred feet to the outhouse on a clear wintry night,
through mud or snow. That's one small link with nature.
Or in the summer, in the back country, leaving the door
of the privy open, taking your time, listening to the
humming of the insects, the sun warming your bones
through the thin planks of wood; you don't even have
that pleasure anymore.

Americans want to have everything sanitized. No
smells! Not even the good, natural man and woman
smell. Take away the smell from under the armpits,
from your skin. Rub it out, and then spray or dab some
nonhuman odor on yourself, stuff you can spend a lot of
money on, ten dollars an ounce, so you know this has to
smell good. "B.O.," bad breath, "Intimate Female Odor
Spray"—I see it all on TV. Soon you'll breed without any
body openings.

I think white people are so afraid of the world
they created that they don't want to see, feel, smell
or hear it. The feeling of rain and snow on your face,
being numbed by an icy wind and thawing out before
a smoking fire, coming out of a hot sweat bath and
plunging into a cold stream, these things make you feel
alive, but you don't want them anymore. Living in boxes
which shut out the heat of the summer and the chill of
winter, living inside a body that no longer has a scent,
hearing the noise from the hi-fi instead of listening to

the sounds of nature, watching some actor on TV having a make-believe experience when you no longer experience anything for yourself, eating food without taste—that's your way. It's no good.

The food you eat, you treat it like your bodies, take out all the natural part, the taste, the smell, the roughness, then put the artificial color, the artificial in. Raw liver, raw kidney—that's what we old-fashioned full-bloods like to get our teeth into. In the old days we used to eat the guts out of the buffalo, making a contest of it, two fellows getting hold of a long piece of intestines from opposite ends, starting chewing toward the middle, seeing who can get there first; that's eating. Those buffalo guts, full of half-fermented, half digested grass and herbs, you didn't need any pills and vitamins when you swallowed those. Use the bitterness of gall for flavoring, not refined salt or sugar. Wasna—meat, kidney fat and berries all pounded together—a lump of that sweet wasna kept a man going for a whole day. That was food, that had the power. Not the stuff you give us today: powdered milk, dehydrated eggs, pasteurized butter, chickens that are all drumsticks or all breast; there's no bird left there.

You don't want the bird. You don't have the courage to kill honestly—cut off the chicken's head, pluck it and gut it—no, you don't want this anymore. So it all comes in a neat plastic bag, all cut up, ready to eat, with no taste and no guilt. Your mink and seal coats, you don't want to know about the blood and pain that went into making them. Your idea of war—sit in an airplane, way above the clouds, press a button, drop the bombs, and never look below the clouds—that's the odorless, guiltless, sanitized way.

When we killed a buffalo, we knew what we were doing. We apologized to his spirit, tried to make him understand why we did it, honoring with a prayer the bones of those who gave their flesh to keep us alive, praying for their return, praying for the life of our brothers, the buffalo nation, as well as for our own people. You wouldn't understand this and that's why we had the Washita Massacre, the Sand Creek Massacre, the dead women and babies at Wounded Knee. That's why we have Song My and My Lai now.

To us life, all life, is sacred. The state of South Dakota has pest-control officers. They go up in a plane and shoot coyotes from the air. They keep track of their kills, put them all down in their little books. The stockmen and sheep owners pay them. Coyotes eat mostly rodents, field mice and such. Only once in a while will they go after a stray lamb. They are our natural garbage men cleaning up the rotten and stinking things. They make good pets if you give them a chance. But their living could lose some man a few cents, and so the coyotes are killed from the air. They were here before the sheep, but they are in the way; you can't make a profit out of them, more and more animals are dying out. The animals which the Great Spirit put here, they must go. The man-made animals are allowed to stay—at least until they are shipped out to be butchered. That terrible arrogance of the white man, making himself something more than God, more than nature, saying, "I will let this animal live, because it makes money"; saying "This animal must go, it brings no income, the space it occupies can be used in a better way. The only good coyote is a dead coyote." They are treating coyotes almost as badly as they used to treat Indians.

You are spreading death, buying and selling death. With all you deodorants, you smell of it, but you are afraid of its reality; you don't want to face up to it. You have sanitized death, put it under the rug, robbed it of its honor. But we Indians think a lot about death. I do. Today would be a perfect day to die—not too hot, not too cool. A day to leave something of yourself behind, to let it linger. A day for a lucky man to come to the end of his rail. A happy man with many friends. Other days are not so good. They are for selfish, lonesome men, having a hard time leaving this earth. But for whites every day would be considered a bad one, I guess.

Eighty years ago our people danced the Ghost Dance, singing and dancing until they dropped from exhaustion, swooning, fainting, seeing visions. They danced in this way to bring back the dead, to bring back the buffalo. A prophet had told them that through the power of the Ghost Dance the earth would roll up like a carpet, with all the white man's works—the fences and the mining towns with their whorehouses, the factories and the farms with their stinking, unnatural animals, the railroads and the telegraph poles, the whole works. And underneath this rolled-up white man's world we would find again the flowering prairies, unspoiled, with its herds of buffalo and antelope, its clouds of birds, belonging to everyone, enjoyed by all.

I guess it was not time for this to happen, but it is coming back, I feel it warming my bones. Not the old Ghost Dance, not the rolling-up—but a new-old spirit, not only among Indians but among whites and blacks, too, especially among young people. It is like raindrops making a tiny brook, many brooks making a stream, many streams making one big river bursting all dams. Us making this book, talking like this—these are some of the raindrops.

Listen, I saw this in my mind not long ago: In my vision the electric light will stop sometime. It is used too much for TV and going to the moon. The day is coming when nature will stop the electricity. Police

without flashlights, beer getting hot in the refrigerators, planes dropping from the sky, even the President can't call up somebody on the phone. A young man will come, or men, who'll know how to shut off all electricity. It will be painful, like giving birth. Rapings in the dark, winos breaking into liquor stores, a lot of destruction. People are being too smart, too clever, the machine stops and they are helpless, because they have forgotten how to make do without the machine. There is a Light Man coming, bringing a new light. It will happen before the century is over. The man who has the power will do good things too—stop all atomic power, stop wars, just by shutting the white electro-power off. I hope to see this, but then I'm also afraid. What will be will be.

Analyzing the Situation

1. How would you describe the situation in which Lame Deer participates? Does this situation still exist?

2. What role does rhetorical ecology play in Lame Deer's argument about food?

3. To whom do you think Lame Deer intended his writing to be directed? Why do you think so?

Analyzing the Rhetoric

1. Why do you suppose that Lame Deer opted to write this essay in the second person, directing his words to "you"? Who is the "you" in this essay?

2. How do you interpret the last line of "Talking to the Owls and Butterflies"?

3. How would you describe the tone of "Talking to the Owls and Butterflies"? What specifically within the essay leads you to such a conclusion?

Discussing

1. In "Talking to the Owls and Butterflies," John Fire Lame Deer discusses a number of issues: food, consumption, culture, nature, spirituality, sustainability, and oppression, to name a few. Because

this essay covers so much territory, we can assume that for Lame Deer there is a connection between food and how we think ecologically. As a class, consider first how Lame Deer makes these connections. Then discuss how or if these connections are also evident in how your local community addresses food.

2. How do you respond to Lame Deer's description of what good food is? How do you respond to his characterization of the foods that "white people" eat?

3. Why does Lame Deer emphasize the relationship between "food" and "nature"? How would you describe the relationship between food and nature in terms of the foods that you most often eat?

Writing

1. Does "Talking to the Owls and Butterflies" affect how you think about food? Why or why not? Write an essay that addresses what "Talking to the Owls and Butterflies" leads you to think about regarding your own food.

2. Of course, there are many other positions about food that one could take in response to Lame Deer's claims about food. Write an essay that argues against Lame Deer's cultural concept of food,

offering both a critique of his claim and an alternative approach to thinking about eating and food acquisition.

3. For this assignment, obtain a local hunting license and learn your local hunting regulations. Then hunt and kill a buffalo, unless it's illegal in your region, in which case you should legally hunt and kill a different large mammal (a deer,

perhaps). As you dress the animal for butchering, eat some of the freshly killed animal; challenge a friend to an intestine-eating race like the one Lame Deer describes in "Talking to the Owls and Butterflies." Then write a narrative about your experiences. Or don't do any of this, and write a narrative explaining why you wouldn't hunt or eat the animal.

The Pleasure of Eating

Wendell Berry

Wendell Berry is a well-known contemporary American author. His writing often addresses the tradition of the American family farm, self-sustaining economic enterprises, family bonds, human obligation to natural environments, and critiques of what American culture has lost to modernization. Berry is particularly skeptical about the elevation of technology in the United States. In some of his writing he has argued against the use of computers. Berry doesn't own a television and often explains that he is suspicious of screen technology. Berry has written more than 15 novels, 30 books of nonfiction, and more than 25 books of poetry. In his famous essay "Why I'm Not Going to Buy a Computer," Berry explains that he writes by hand on legal pads, his wife later typing his manuscripts on a 1956 Royal standard typewriter.

In his 1989 essay "The Pleasure of Eating," Berry shows how eating is part of an agricultural process and that most urban eaters have little awareness of that process. He explains why knowing at least part of that process is important and provides seven specific guidelines for eating to help make the process more visible. As you read "The Pleasure of Eating," consider the language Berry uses to make his argument and your own response to how that language affects how you receive his argument.

Many times, after I have finished a lecture on the decline of American farming and rural life, someone in the audience has asked, "What can city people do?"

"Eat responsibly," I have usually answered. Of course, I have tried to explain what I mean by that, but afterwards I have invariably felt there was more to be said than I had been able to say. Now I would like to attempt a better explanation.

I begin with the proposition that eating is an agricultural act. Eating ends the annual drama of the food economy that begins with planting and birth. Most eaters, however, are no longer aware that this is true. They think of food as an agricultural product, perhaps, but they do not think of themselves as participants in agriculture. They think of themselves as "consumers." If they think beyond that, they recognize that they are passive consumers. They buy what they want—or what they have been persuaded to want—within the limits of what they can get. They pay, mostly without protest, what they are charged. And they mostly ignore certain critical questions about the quality and the cost of what they are sold: How fresh is it? How pure or clean is it, how free of dangerous chemicals? How far was it transported, and what did transportation add to the cost? How much did manufacturing or packaging or advertising add to the cost? When the food product has been manufactured or "processed" or "precooked," how has that affected its quality or price or nutritional value?

Most urban shoppers would tell you that food is produced on farms. But most of them do not know what farms, or what kinds of farms, or where the farms are, or what knowledge or skills are involved in farming. They apparently have little doubt that farms will continue to produce, but they do not know how or over what obstacles. For them, then, food is pretty much an abstract idea—something they do not know or imagine—until it appears on the grocery shelf or on the table.

The specialization of production induces specialization of consumption. Patrons of the entertainment industry, for example, entertain themselves less and less and have become more and more passively dependent on commercial suppliers. This is certainly true also of patrons of the food industry, who have tended more and more to be mere consumers—passive, uncritical, and dependent. Indeed, this sort of consumption may be said to be one of the chief goals of industrial production. The food industrialists have by now persuaded millions of consumers to prefer food that is already prepared. They will grow, deliver, and cook your food for you and (just like your mother) beg you to eat it. That they do not yet offer to insert it, prechewed, into our mouth is only because they have found no profitable way to do so. We may rest assured that they would be glad to find such a way. The ideal industrial food consumer would be strapped to a table with a tube running from the food factory directly into his or her stomach.

Perhaps I exaggerate, but not by much. The industrial eater is, in fact, one who does not know that eating is an agricultural act, who no longer knows or imagines the connections between eating and the land, and who is therefore necessarily passive and uncritical—in short, a victim. When food, in the minds of eaters, is no longer associated with farming and with the land, then the eaters are suffering a kind of cultural amnesia that is misleading and dangerous. The current version of the "dream home" of the future involves "effortless" shopping from a list of available goods on a television monitor and heating precooked food by remote control. Of course, this implies and depends on, a perfect ignorance of the history of the food that is consumed. It requires that the citizenry should give up their hereditary and sensible aversion to buying a pig in a poke. It wishes to make the selling of pigs in pokes an honorable and glamorous activity. The dreams in this dream home will perforce know nothing about the kind or quality of this food, or where it came from, or how it was produced and prepared, or what ingredients, additives, and residues it contains—unless, that is, the dreamer undertakes a close and constant study of the food industry, in which case he or she might as well wake up and play an active an responsible part in the economy of food.

There is, then, a politics of food that, like any politics, involves our freedom. We still (sometimes) remember that we cannot be free if our minds and voices are controlled by someone else. But we have neglected to understand that we cannot be free if our food and its sources are controlled by someone else. The condition of the passive consumer of food is not a democratic condition. One reason to eat responsibly is to live free.

But if there is a food politics, there are also a food esthetics and a food ethics, neither of which is dissociated from politics. Like industrial sex, industrial eating has become a degraded, poor, and paltry thing. Our kitchens and other eating places more and more resemble filling stations, as our homes more and more resemble motels. "Life is not very interesting," we seem to have decided. "Let its satisfactions be minimal, perfunctory, and fast." We hurry through our meals to go to work and hurry through our work in order to "recreate" ourselves in the evenings and on weekends and vacations. And then we hurry, with the greatest possible speed and noise and violence, through our recreation—for what? To eat the billionth hamburger at some fast-food joint hellbent on increasing the "quality" of our life? And all this is carried out in a remarkable obliviousness to the causes and effects, the possibilities and the purposes, of the life of the body in this world.

One will find this obliviousness represented in virgin purity in the advertisements of the food industry, in which food wears as much makeup as the actors. If one gained one's whole knowledge of food from these advertisements (as some presumably do), one would not know that the various edibles were ever living creatures, or that they all come from the soil, or that they were produced by work. The passive American consumer, sitting down to a meal of pre-prepared or fast food, confronts a platter covered with inert, anonymous substances that have been processed, dyed, breaded, sauced, gravied, ground, pulped, strained, blended, prettified, and sanitized beyond resemblance to any part of any creature that ever lived. The products of nature and agriculture have been made, to all appearances, the products of industry. Both eater and eaten are thus in exile from biological reality. And the result is a kind of solitude, unprecedented in human experience, in which the eater may think of eating as, first, a purely commercial transaction between him and a supplier and then as a purely appetitive transaction between him and his food.

And this peculiar specialization of the act of eating is, again, of obvious benefit to the food industry, which has good reasons to obscure the connection between food and farming. It would not do for the consumer to know that the hamburger she is eating came from a steer who spent much of his life standing deep in his own excrement in a feedlot, helping to pollute the local streams, or that the calf that yielded the veal cutlet on her plate spent its life in a box in which it did not have room to turn around. And, though her sympathy for the slaw might be less tender, she should not be encouraged to meditate on the hygienic and biological implications of mile-square fields of cabbage, for vegetables grown in huge monocultures are dependent on toxic chemicals—just as animals in close confinements are dependent on antibiotics and other drugs.

The consumer, that is to say, must be kept from discovering that, in the food industry—as in any other industry—the overriding concerns are not quality and health, but volume and price. For decades now the entire industrial food economy, from the large farms and feedlots to the chains of supermarkets and fast-food restaurants has been obsessed with volume. It has relentlessly increased scale in order to increase volume in order (probably) to reduce costs. But as scale increases, diversity declines; as diversity declines, so does health; as health declines, the dependence on drugs and chemicals necessarily increases. As capital replaces labor, it does so by substituting machines, drugs, and chemicals for human workers and for the natural health and fertility of the soil. The food is produced by any means or any shortcuts that will increase profits. And the business of the cosmeticians of advertising is to persuade the consumer that food so produced is good, tasty, healthful, and a guarantee of marital fidelity and long life.

It is possible, then, to be liberated from the husbandry and wifery of the old household food economy. But one can be thus liberated only by entering a trap (unless one sees ignorance and helplessness as the signs of privilege, as many people apparently do). The trap is the ideal of industrialism: a walled city surrounded by valves that let merchandise in but no consciousness out. How does one escape this trap? Only voluntarily, the same way that one went in: by restoring one's consciousness of what is involved in eating; by reclaiming responsibility for one's own part in the food economy. One might begin with the illuminating principle of Sir Albert Howard's that we should understand "the whole problem of health in soil, plant, animal, and man as one great subject." Eaters, that is, must understand that eating takes place inescapably in the world, that it is inescapably an agricultural act, and how we eat determines, to a considerable extent, how the world is used. This is a simple way of describing a relationship that is inexpressibly complex. To eat responsibly is to understand and enact, so far as we can, this complex relationship. What can one do? Here is a list, probably not definitive:

1. Participate in food production to the extent that you can. If you have a yard or even just a porch box or a pot in a sunny window, grow something to eat in it. Make a little compost of your kitchen scraps and use it for fertilizer. Only by growing some food for yourself can you become acquainted with the beautiful energy cycle that revolves from soil to seed to flower to fruit to food to offal to decay, and around again. You will be fully responsible for any

food that you grow for yourself, and you will know all about it. You will appreciate it fully, having known it all its life.

2. Prepare your own food. This means reviving in your own mind and life the arts of kitchen and household. This should enable you to eat more cheaply, and it will give you a measure of "quality control": you will have some reliable knowledge of what has been added to the food you eat.

3. Learn the origins of the food you buy, and buy the food that is produced closest to your home. The idea that every locality should be, as much as possible, the source of its own food makes several kinds of sense. The locally produced food supply is the most secure, freshest, and the easiest for local consumers to know about and to influence.

4. Whenever possible, deal directly with a local farmer, gardener, or orchardist. All the reasons listed for the previous suggestion apply here. In addition, by such dealing you eliminate the whole pack of merchants, transporters, processors, packagers, and advertisers who thrive at the expense of both producers and consumers.

5. Learn, in self-defense, as much as you can of the economy and technology of industrial food production. What is added to the food that is not food, and what do you pay for those additions?

6. Learn what is involved in the best farming and gardening.

7. Learn as much as you can, by direct observation and experience if possible, of the life histories of the food species.

The last suggestion seems particularly important to me. Many people are now as much estranged from the lives of domestic plants and animals (except for flowers and dogs and cats) as they are from the lives of the wild ones. This is regrettable, for these domestic creatures are in diverse ways attractive; there is such pleasure in knowing them. And farming, animal husbandry, horticulture, and gardening, at their best, are complex and comely arts; there is much pleasure in knowing them, too.

It follows that there is great displeasure in knowing about a food economy that degrades and abuses those arts and those plants and animals and the soil from which they come. For anyone who does know something of the modern history of food, eating away from home can be a chore. My own inclination is to eat seafood instead of red meat or poultry when I am traveling. Though I am by no means a vegetarian, I dislike the thought that some animal has been made miserable in order to feed me. If I am going to eat meat, I want it to be from an animal that has lived a pleasant, uncrowded life outdoors, on bountiful pasture, with good water nearby and trees for shade. And I am getting almost as fussy about food plants. I like to eat vegetables and fruits that I know have lived happily and healthily in good soil, not the products of the huge, bechemicaled factory-fields that I have seen, for example, in the Central Valley of California. The industrial farm is said to have been patterned on the factory production line. In practice, it looks more like a concentration camp.

The pleasure of eating should be an extensive pleasure, not that of the mere gourmet. People who know the garden in which their vegetables have grown and know that the garden is healthy and remember the beauty of the growing plants, perhaps in the dewy first light of morning when gardens are at their best. Such a memory involves itself with the food and is one of the pleasures of eating. The knowledge of the good health of the garden relieves and frees and comforts the eater. The same goes for eating meat. The thought of the good pasture and of the calf contentedly grazing flavors the steak. Some, I know, will think of it as bloodthirsty or worse to eat a fellow creature you have known all its life. On the contrary, I think it means that you eat with understanding and with gratitude. A significant part of the pleasure of eating is in one's accurate consciousness of the lives and the world from which food comes. The pleasure of eating, then, may be the best available standard of our health. And this pleasure, I think, is pretty fully available to the urban consumer who will make the necessary effort.

I mentioned earlier the politics, esthetics, and ethics of food. But to speak of the pleasure of eating is to go beyond those categories. Eating with the fullest pleasure—pleasure, that is, that does not depend on ignorance—is perhaps the profoundest enactment of our connection with the world. In this pleasure we experience and celebrate our dependence and our gratitude, for we are living from mystery, from creatures we did not make and powers we cannot comprehend. When I think of the meaning of food, I always remember these lines by the poet William Carlos Williams, which seem to me merely honest:

There is nothing to eat,
seek it where you will,
but the body of the Lord.
The blessed plants
and the sea, yield it
to the imagination intact.

Analyzing the Situation

1. How would you describe the situation in which "The Pleasure of Eating" participates? Is it an important situation, one you think many people are invested in?

2. What are the roles of institution and power in the situation in which "The Pleasure of Eating" participates?

3. One can fairly explicitly identify who the audience and who the speaker are in the situation in which "The Pleasure of Eating" participates, but what role do players have in this situation? Who might the players in this situation be?

Analyzing the Rhetoric

1. How would you characterize Berry's language in "The Pleasure of Eating"?

2. What rhetorical appeal does Berry rely mostly on to make his arguments?

3. Why do you suppose Berry decided to title his essay "The Pleasure of Eating" when the essay is primarily about how Americans have lost touch with their food? What does he accomplish through this title?

Discussing

1. Berry says that eating is an agricultural act and then explains what he means by that. But is eating, as Berry explains it, also an ecological act? Why or why not?

2. Berry describes knowing about one's food as a kind of ethical responsibility, and he suggests that not wanting to know about one's food is embracing ignorance. On a daily basis, do you really want to know about your food in the ways that Berry says we should know about our food? As a class, discuss whether you want to know your food, or if the convenience of ignorance has a particular kind of merit.

3. Do you think your eating habits would change if you had a more intimate knowledge of the food you eat?

Writing

1. Make a list of everything that you have eaten today. Then, next to each item in the list, identify the ingredients included in that item. Then, next to each of those ingredients, identify where that ingredient comes from. Then make a list of what it takes to bring all of those ingredients together to provide you with the food: the act of growing and what is needed for growing, transporting the food, processing the food, packaging the food, advertising the food, selling the food, transporting the food from the store to you, and so on. In writing these lists, think about what you know about the items in the lists, what you assume about the items, what you don't know about the items, and what you want to learn about the items.

2. What is your all-time favorite food? What is the thing that you love to eat most? In an essay, trace the steps it takes to put that item of food on your plate. Consider what goes into making the food item, where it comes from or where its ingredients come from, how it is prepared, how it is transported, and so on. You will probably have to conduct some research as many of the answers you'll need are not things that most of us would know off the tops of our heads. For example, have you considered the energy cost of producing the piece of parsley with which a restaurant garnishes your plate and that you probably leave on your plate when finished with your meal? Or do you know and understand the process for producing the cheese slice (or cheese-like slice) on your cheeseburger? You should find

that the research and writing of this essay will help you better understand not just what it is you like to eat but what it takes to provide you with that food.

3. Conduct some research to find out what foods are produced closest to your campus. "Production" can refer to farms or to processing plants. Once you discover what food is "made" closest to you, continue your research to discover where that food is distributed. Does most of it remain local or regional? Is it transported nationally or internationally?

Dive!

Jeremy Seifert

Jeremy Seifert is an activist concerned with the state of food. He has directed two documentaries about food. In 2013 he directed *GMO OMG* which examines genetically modified organisms in our food and what Seifert describes as the systematic corporate takeover of the world's seed banks. You can watch the trailer for *GMO OMG* on the *GMO* film home page. Seifert's first documentary, *Dive!*, which is addressed in this chapter, examines the extensive amount of food wasted in Los Angeles and the ramifications of such waste. In the film Seifert and his friends dumpster dive behind several grocery stores to show the enormous amount of food that is thrown away each day in the United States. *Dive!* premiered in 2009 at the Gig Harbor Film Festival, a film festival dedicated to independent films that promote understanding, tolerance, and global awareness. *Dive!* won the Audience Choice Award when it premiered at Gig Harbor. The film has won numerous other awards, including Best Documentary at the DC Independent Film Festival, the oldest independent film festival in Washington, D.C., which includes not only the screening of films from around the world but seminars, workshops, and discussions with members of the United States Congress. *Dive!* also won best film at the Dutch Environmental Film Festival. You can watch the premiere for *Dive!* on the divethe-film web page. The film itself is available through many rental services or for purchase through online vendors and stores

(it's also available streaming on Netflix). Take some time to watch the film and consider the questions below in relation to the film.

Analyzing the Situation

1. Do you believe that Jeremy Seifert accurately represents this situation?

2. Is the situation that Jeremy Seifert participates in a local or global situation? How does *Dive!* participate in that situation at either the local or global level?

3. Were you aware of this situation? What more would you like to know about this situation?

Analyzing the Rhetoric

1. What role does visual rhetoric play in *Dive!*?

2. What is Jeremy Seifert's purpose in including his son in the documentary?

3. Jeremy Seifert's documentary could have simply told the story of his dumpster diving in Los Angeles, but he decided to include research, statistics, and interviews along with his narrative. How does the inclusion of the research and his interviews with various people, like Dr. Jones, affect the documentary?

Discussing

1. Would you eat food taken from dumpsters like the food in *Dive!*? Why or why not?

2. Do you agree or disagree with the claims in *Dive!* that distinguish between what is just and what is legal when it comes to taking food from dumpsters located on private property?

3. After having watched *Dive!*, how do you respond to the documentary? In particular, how do you respond to the distinction the film makes between abundance, waste, and need?

Writing

1. Write an evaluation of *Dive!* as a documentary. Be sure to identify your criteria for how you evaluate the documentary.

2. In *Dive!* Jeremy Seifert writes a letter a day to the CEO of Trader Joe's asking about the amount of waste the grocery chain leaves in its dumpsters and encouraging the CEO to increase its donations of "waste" food to local food banks. However, as the documentary showed, Trader Joe's did not respond to Jeremy Seifert's letters, asking him, in fact, to stop sending the letters. Of course, this aspect of *Dive!* was noted by many movie reviewers, reporters, and activists as a significant issue in the film. In the press, Trader Joe's has responded to the allegations Seifert makes in *Dive!*. "Fighting hunger is central to what we do," Trader Joe's customer relations manager, Nicole High, responded to one newspaper. "We are a grocery store [and] providing food for people in need is one of our most important giving priorities." High explained that in 2010, Trader Joe's donated more than 25 million pounds of food and that "Trader Joe's long running policy is to donate products that are not fit for sale but are safe for consumption." Take some time to learn more about Trader Joe's company policies regarding food waste and then write a response to *Dive!* with your new information in mind.

3. In early 2013, Grist, an online environmental news source with a wry sense of humor (their motto is "Gloom and doom with a sense of humor"), reported that Doug Rauch, the former CEO of Trader Joe's wanted to open a supermarket in a poor neighborhood in Boston that sells Trader Joe's nearly expired foods at reduced prices. The report from Grist, which was published on February 28, 2013 and is titled "Former Trader Joe's CEO: Let them eat cake—as long as it's cake we weren't going to eat ourselves" is available on the Grist .com web pages. Take some time to read the article.

   Given what you saw in *Dive!* how do you respond to Doug Rauch's idea? Why is it relevant that the idea is forwarded by a former Trader Joe's CEO? Note that Rauch retired from Trader Joe's after 31 years in 2008—the year Seifert started filming *Dive!*.

My Mom Couldn't Cook

Tom Junod

Tom Junod is an award-winning journalist and magazine writer who has twice won the American Society of Magazine Editors' National Magazine Award, the most prestigious award for magazine writers. Junod's essays have appeared in *Esquire*, *Life*, *Sports Illustrated*, and *GQ*. Three of Junod's essays, in particular, are considered to be of the best in contemporary American magazine writing: "The Abortionist," "The Rapist Says He's Sorry," and "Richard Drew, The Falling Man," which is reprinted in this book. In 2011, he won the James Beard Award—an award often referred to as "the Oscars of Food"—for his *Esquire* essay "My Mom Couldn't Cook," which is reprinted here.

"My Mom Couldn't Cook" is a powerful essay about why Tom Junod cooks for his family and the relationship between food and family. The essay addresses how we learn about food and the emotions that food can evoke. As you read this essay, pay particular attention to how Junod uses pathos in his writing, but note, too, how his firm, authoritative voice works in conjunction with his appeal to emotion.

I cook for my family. To put it another way: I am my family's cook, and so I cook almost every night. I cook three hundred days a year, and have cooked three hundred days a year for *years*. I cook for the three of us—for my wife, my daughter, and myself—and before there were three of us, I cooked for the two of us. I am a husband who cooks for his wife, which makes me a man who

cooks for his woman and now his women, which in turns makes me a man who to some extent cooks *like* a woman: out of love and generosity, yes, but also out of service, out of duty. I cook because it's my job. I don't get many days off from cooking. I don't *take* many days off cooking, because I only like to eat at restaurants that serve food better than my own, or that serve Mexican food or sushi. Hell, I don't even take days off from cooking when I go out for days on the road, because before I leave I prepare my family food to be eaten in my absence. I cook so that there is no absence. I cook so that I am always there, even when I'm gone, even when I die, and my cooking translates in my daughter's memory as, simply, this: time.

This is not to say that my cooking is selfless. It is anything but, because in order to endure cooking like a woman I have to cook like a man—which is to say, for myself. The food I cook for my family is the food I like to eat. The food I like to eat is the food I cook for my family. I cook out of hunger, and so, to the degree that I am selfless as a cook, I am also despotic and fanatical. I do everything myself, make everything myself, from salad dressings to chili powder. I do not ask for help and I do not consider shortcuts. I want to take time, not save it, aware of the paradox born of my driven dedication, aware that if the time I spend at the stove is time given to my family, it is also time taken away.

This, however, is not a story of my cooking, or the odd combination of freedom and thralldom it confers. It's the story of what—or who—inspired my decision to be my family's cook, gave me the will to do it, and made it both a practical and, apparently, a psychological necessity. It is the story of my mother—of my mother's cooking.

My mother, Frances Junod, was not just a mother, not just a mom. She was a dame. She was a broad. She was a beauty from Brooklyn who wore fantastic hats, when they were in style, and furs, even when they were not. She went through her entire life as a Harlowesque platinum blonde, and I never knew the real color of her hair. She liked go to the track, and she liked to go out to restaurants. She did not like to cook. That she did it anyway—that she had no choice—owed itself to generational expectations, and to the fact that if my mother was a doll, in the Runyonesque sense of the word, my father was a guy, a pinky-ringed sharpie who spent many nights going to the New York City restaurants my mother longed to frequent, but who, on nights when he came home, loudly expected food on the table. So my mother put food on the table. She was my family's cook. She cooked three hundred nights a year.

She cooked for my father, and, when he was away, which was often, she cooked for me and my brother and my sister, and then, when they, both ten years older than me, left home, she cooked for me. She cooked me spaghetti with butter and cheese. She cooked me hamburgers, "pan-fried" without added fat on a hot, salted cast-iron skillet, until they formed a hard crust. She cooked me scrambled eggs, made idiosyncratic by the addition of a teaspoon of water. She cooked me shell steaks sprinkled with salt and Ac'cent—MSG—and she cooked chicken parts lathered in a sweet-sour sauce called Saucy Susan and she cooked me chicken or veal cutlets bought "scallopini" style at the supermarket and coated in Progresso Italian-Style breadcrumbs. For dessert she made Junket or Jell-O or My-T-Fine chocolate pudding. Except for Friday nights, when she served a cold meal—what she called a "platter" of cantaloupe slices, cottage cheese, and tuna fish salad—she never cooked for herself, to satisfy her own hunger.

It took me a while to figure out that she hated cooking, and a while—much—longer to figure out that she hated cooking because she couldn't cook. For one thing, she was my mother, and mothers were supposed to know how to cook. For another, I was her child, and so for most of my childhood she was the only cook in the world. I had to like her cooking, and I did, as long as she observed the Mashed Potato Rule. The Mashed Potato Rule, simply stated, is this: There is no such thing as bad mashed potatoes as long as they're actually potatoes, mashed. We had mashed potatoes a lot when I was a

kid—I can still see the blood and, better, the clear juices from the pan-fried hamburger running into them on my plate—and it didn't matter that they were lumpy and grainy and that my mother had no talent for making them; they were *Edenic* so long as she did. I loved them, as I loved her. That she was not the kind of mother who made everything from scratch, the way the mothers of my Italian friends did; that for her the words "homemade" and "gourmet" were virtually interchangeable, to be pronounced with the same dreamy covetousness she employed when she pronounced the word "Paris" or "Aruba" or some other exotic destination she knew she'd never visit; that the only vegetables I ever ate came not from a field but rather from a can (LeSeur) or a freezer pack (Jolly Green Giant); that she favored convenience foods to the extent that I came to fear them, and cringe at commercials for the Pillsbury Doughboy: all this was not forgiven but simply forgotten when the mashed potatoes were potatoes, mashed. But while on my plate they formed the barrier between the battleship-gray lamb chops and the olive-drab green beans, in my heart they formed the barrier between the discovery that my mother hated cooking and the altogether different discovery that my mother hated cooking so much that she even hated cooking for me.

See, I had figured that my mother hated cooking for the obvious reason that she hated cooking for my father. She could never satisfy him. Indeed, she hated cooking for him so much that he kept their marriage intact by absolving her of the responsibility—by taking her with him to Roosevelt Raceway, where they ate at the Cloud Casino, while I stayed home and panfried a shell steak in the salted pan and made spaghetti with butter-and-cheese. But I was absolved of responsibility as well. I was in high school, stoned and rapacious and suddenly free to be disloyal, by which I mean I was suddenly free to tell the truth. Like most human beings, I grew up making the connection between food and love; what I began to realize when I started cooking for myself was that the more necessary connection was between food and honesty. My parents were both charmingly dishonest people; my father's lies were such that he couldn't admit them except to urge me to develop, like him, "a little larceny in your soul," but my mother could, since most of her lies were about food. "Oh, I'm a terrible fibber," she'd say, and then blithely assert that the Mott's applesauce she'd doctored with lemon and cinnamon was "homemade" or that she'd spent "hours over a hot stove" cooking the package of frozen Banquette fried-chicken drumsticks on our plates. She'd say this with a knowing cackle that served simultaneously as an admission of guilt and as a warning that we must never say that she was guilty. Food was love, all right, and we had to tell my mom that we loved her by buying into her "fibs" about it. To do otherwise was not only to make her cry but also to risk the wrath of my dad, who was as fearsome in his defense of my mother as he was in his attacks upon her. And so dinnertime became an exercise in swallowing a fiction that everybody knew was untrue, and the story that was repeated over and over and over again in my family (the other enforced fiction in my family being the fiction that the story you were hearing for the hundredth time was a story you'd never heard before) was the time my mother made a huge vat of her "homemade" applesauce for my brother's wrestling-team dinner and my brother ate the whole thing in order to spare my mother the knowledge that nobody else did.

I was still in high school and living at home when my mother first broke the Mashed Potato Rule: when the mashed potatoes she served started tasting like the mashed potatoes that were served in my high school cafeteria; when it was clear that, in fact, they were neither mashed nor potatoes. From another perspective: I was in high school when I first broke the rule that if food was to be love then so was the obligation to accept my mother's untruths about it. Me: Ma (I always called her Ma), what's with the potatoes? My mother: What's wrong with the potatoes? Me: They're not potatoes. My father: Just eat the potatoes. Your mother slaved over a hot stove to make those potatoes. Me: They're not potatoes. They came from a box. My mother: So what if they come from a box? They're still potatoes. Me: They're not potatoes! My mother: *You can't tell the difference.*

And with that my mother uttered the signal words of my culinary existence, which happened to be the signal words of my familial existence as well. I could tell the difference, and I spent the rest of my life proving that I could. My mother, for her part, spent the rest of her life trying to prove that I couldn't. I refused to eat the potato flakes that she served me, or the potato buds, or the potato powder, and my mother refused to admit that they were potato flakes and potato buds and potato powder. I mean, she would hide the box. She would peel a potato and put the peelings on top of the garbage, and the box of French's at the bottom. I used to think that she should have used her ingenuity just to mash the damned potatoes, while using my own ingenuity to find the box and to produce it, with prosecutorial flourish. "Come on," my father said, "enough's enough. Just eat the potatoes. You're breaking your mother's heart." But enough was never enough, because just as my mother had come to the conclusion that *It's not worth it,* I was coming to the conclusion that *It is.* The only thing left to be decided was the matter of what that mysterious "it" might be, and the only thing we both understood was that a lot more was at stake than the authenticity of my mother's "mashies."

My mother was a good mother. I was a good son. My mother was a betrayed woman—I think I knew that, from an early age—and so I was careful never to betray her, as she, by instinct, never betrayed me. But now I felt betrayed, and I betrayed her in return, by learning to cook. No: by cooking. No: by marrying a girl who had no interest in cooking, and cooking for her. No: by cooking for my wife as I wished my mother had cooked for me. No: by cooking as my father would have cooked, had he taken up the toque—by cooking unyieldingly, despotically, ball-bustingly, hungrily, not just selflessly but also selfishly, as an assertion of prerogative. When my mother came to visit, I made her chop, according to specification. "How's this?" she'd ask, showing me the cutting board of haphazardly chopped broccoli, and when I'd say she had to chop it smaller, finer, more uniformly, she'd say, "You're some pain in the ass" or "What a pill." I was perversely proud of her exasperation, perversely proud to be addressed in terms heretofore reserved for my old man. A pill? I had never been a pill before. I had always been, in my mother's estimation, "a good egg," but now I'd become a pill by insisting that my eggs taste good. My mother wasn't college-educated, but she wasn't stupid, either. She knew what was going on. When, much later, I wrote a flattering profile of my father for a magazine, she dismissed it tersely: "Don't forget who raised you, kid." But my cooking—my decision to cook—was a rejection of the way I'd been raised, a rebuke of the way she'd raised me. I had been on my mother's side, but now, unforgivably, I was on my father's, by taking my mother's job.

And yet hunger won out, as it always does in human affairs. As I learned to cook, I eventually learned what to cook for my parents—what made them hungry and satisfied their hunger at the same time, without carrying an implicit *statement* meant to divide or offend them. It was pot roast. On Sunday nights after they moved near us, we'd have them over for Sunday supper—a term that seemed the province of a family not my own—and I'd serve the one meal that, as any novice cook knows, obeys its own variant of the Mashed Potato Rule: there's no such thing as a bad pot roast as long as you put enough stuff in the pot and you roast it long enough. But my mother didn't know. Because she'd become too old and uncertain to chop, she'd watch me do the work and laugh to herself, as was her habit: "What are you laughing at, Ma?" "Nothing. Just laughin'." But she was interested not just in what she still regarded as my folly but in what made my folly *worth it*—what made the food good. There was a word that my mother used in restaurants, used, indeed, almost any time she was eating food she didn't have to cook, and that was "de*licious*," as in, "Hey, Ma, how's that pork chop?" "De*licious*." She said it with a combination of relief, wonder, and her own kind of hunger, which was the hunger to be free—to be what she was when she first married my father: a pampered beauty, a spoiled child. Now she used it, admitted it, in regard to my pot roast, and she wanted to know why. "What kind of meat do you use?" she'd always ask, and

when I wondered why she wanted to know, she said, "Well, it's always so tender." And that's how I knew what I wasn't supposed to know all along: my mother didn't know how to cook. She didn't know the rule that can get you through just about any meal, the rule that's even more fundamental than the one governing the preparation of mashed potatoes: If it's tender, cook it fast over high heat; if it's tough, cook it slow over low. I used to wonder why my mother hated cooking so much. I used to wonder why she cooked salmon fillets for two hours and pot roast for one. I thought for a long time that it was because she was a bad cook, because she rejected cooking as a way of rejecting us, because she was, at heart, a liar. Now I understood that she hated cooking because she didn't know how to do it and so had no idea how a meal might turn out. I understood that she simply wasn't cut out for it, and yet, because she was part of the postwar suburban vanguard, she knew she was going to be judged on it—and so she *demanded* to be judged on it, meal after awful meal. Hence, the fibs; hence, the lies. She was as innocent of culinary knowledge as the housewives of her era were supposed to be innocent of sexual knowledge, and once I figured that out, I came to the same conclusion I came to when I figured out the extent of my father's infidelities: they were in over their heads. They were more unhappy than I ever allowed myself to know. They deserved the love they got, and the forgiveness they didn't.

Did she forgive me? Did she forgive me for being a pill and a pain in the ass—for taking my father's side? I know damned well she never thought of it that way. I was her son, after all, and I was a good egg. But that's how I thought of it, and I can tell you that the narrative arc of a life is more unforgiving than a mother could ever be. After my father died, my mother went into assisted living—or, to be more precise and unsparing, I put her there. She flourished, though food was an issue. "Ma, eat something." "I'm not hungry." "C'mon. The food's not bad"—and to prove it, I'd eat large platefuls of it, including the mashed potatoes that were neither mashed nor potato. "It stinks," she'd say, and that was that. One day, in her ninety-second year, she simply stopped eating, and when she went to the hospital for intravenous fluids, she suffered a stroke that deprived her of her ability to feed herself. I had a conversation with her gerontologist, in which he told me the way she would die, in which he told me that unless she was fed via feeding tube she would die of the complications of malnutrition—of hunger. He didn't want to give her a feeding tube. Neither did I, versed as I was in the letter and spirit of her living will and her medical directives. But I never asked her about it. I never told her that we planned for her to die.

I simply went every day, and tried to spoon-feed her cottage cheese that dribbled from her mouth like sand. I even cooked for her—the spaghetti with butter and cheese that was the first food I ever loved; the pot roast that was the last food she called delicious. I was the family cook, which meant that I was driven to preserve my family by making them care about something they had to do: eat. But my mother didn't have to care anymore. She didn't even have to eat. The family cook, I fed her tenderly to the last, and she starved to death.

Analyzing the Situation

1. Is this a personal situation which Tom Junod relates? If so, then why do you suspect that he shares it publically and how does it form an ecological relationship with a public audience?

2. Does institution play a role in this situation?

3. How would you describe the relations not just of the people Junod writes about but about the relations of food in this essay?

Analyzing the Rhetoric

1. What would you describe as the rhetorical strengths of Junod's essay?

2. What does Junod mean when he writes, "My mother, Frances Junod, was not just a mother, not just a mom. She was a dame. She was a broad"?

3. What role do direct quotations and vernacular language play in this essay?

Discussing

1. Does your family tell food lies to perpetuate a family custom or family dynamic?

2. Tom Junod uses the pronoun "I" 112 times in "My Mom Couldn't Cook." What does that fact reveal about the essay? How does it affect how you read the essay?

3. What is the one food custom in your family that you wish was not part of your family's custom? Why?

Writing

1. Have your eating habits changed since you were a child? Do you eat differently at home than away from home? Are there foods that remind you of home that you hope to have when you return home? Write a personal narrative that addresses the differences between your home eating and your away-from-home eating.

2. The invention of instant mashed potatoes has been attributed to Canadian food chemist Edward Anton Maria Asselbergs, who filed for a Canadian patent for instant mashed potato flakes in July 1966; he had begun selling them as early as 1962. However, the process of grinding and drying root vegetables has been used for hundreds of years in many cultures. Take some time to conduct some research about the use of dried foods and the history of dehydrated instant potatoes, in particular, and write an informative essay about your findings.

3. How would you describe the relationship between food and your family? What role does food play in your family's daily life? In its days of celebration? Write a narrative that speaks to "Food and My Family."

Ingredients: Top Ramen, Ramen Noodle Soup, Chicken Flavor

Nissin Foods

Nissin Foods is a Japanese company that produces instant ramen noodles, a food that many college students are familiar with because the noodles are affordable and convenient.

Nissin employee Momofuku Ando, in fact, invented the instant ramen noodle in 1958 (Chikin Ramen) and cup noodles in 1971. Nissin has factories in seven countries around the world and sells noodles globally—over three billion dollars' worth of noodles per year. But how often do consumers think about what goes into those popular noodle packs? Printed here is the ingredient list from a pack of chicken-flavored Top Ramen ramen noodle soup. As you read this list of ingredients, think about the rhetorical situation of an ingredient list and how that situation affects the writing of the list. Of course, you should also take note of what is included in the list, as the document's content reveals a catalog of the product's content.

Ingredients: Ramen Noodles: Enriched Flour (Wheat Flour, Niacin, Reduced Iron, Thiamin Mononitrate, Riboflavin, Folic Acid), Vegetable Oil (Contains One or More of the Following: Canola Oil, Cottonseed Oil, Palm Oil), Contains Less than 2% of Salt, Sodium Tripolyphosphate, Potassium Carbonate, Sodium Carbonate, Sodium Alginate, Tocopherols, TBHQ. Seasoning Mix: Salt, Monosodium Glutamate, Onion Powder, Hydrolyzed Soy Protein, Hydrolyzed Corn Protein and Hydrolyzed Wheat Protein, Chicken Powder, Soy Sauce Powder (Wheat, Soybeans, Maltodextrin, Salt), Garlic Powder, Spices, Chicken Fat, Calcium Silicate (Anticaking Agent), Celery Powder, Sugar, Dehydrated Leek, Turmeric (Color), Autolyzed Yeast Extract, Citric Acid, Disodium Guanylate, Disodium Inosinate, Natural Flavors, Artificial Flavors.

Analyzing the Situation

1. Who reads ingredient lists? Why are they included on food packages?

2. In what situation would you say an ingredient list participates? How would you describe the function of an ingredient list in that situation?

3. What role does institution play in this situation?

Analyzing the Rhetoric

1. This list includes 40 ingredients. Of these, how many are things that you don't know for sure what they are? How many of them don't sound like food?

2. What is the purpose of an ingredient list?

3. An ingredient list is a particular kind of technical writing, part of a technical document: the product package. From a rhetorical standpoint, then, how would you describe this ingredient list?

Discussing

1. Do you eat Top Ramen ramen noodles? If not, did you know what Top Ramen noodles are? Prior to seeing them in this list, had you ever read the ingredient list on a Top Ramen package? Discuss your experience with Top Ramen and your response to this ingredient list.

2. How often do you read ingredient lists? Under what circumstances do you most often find yourself reading them? What kinds of information do you specifically look for when reading ingredient lists? Discuss your ingredient list reading habits.

3. Are there food items for which you don't want to know the ingredients? When do you want to know what ingredients are included and when do you not want to know?

Writing

1. In the list of 40 different ingredients included in a package of Top Ramen chicken-flavored ramen noodle soup, there are several items that are likely to be unfamiliar to you. Make a list of these words, and then look up each word to learn what those items are and what their functions are in the noodle soup. Write a definition for each term in your list.

2. What is your favorite processed and packaged food? Read the ingredient list for that food item. If there are items in the list with which you are unfamiliar, look them up. Then write an essay that describes your feeling about the food before and after having read the ingredient list and learning about the content of the food.

3. In 1962 President John F. Kennedy signed the Consumer Bill of Rights granting consumers the right to safety, the right to be informed, the right to choose, and the right to be heard. In 1966 President Lyndon B. Johnson signed the Fair Packaging and Labeling Act, which requires that consumer products be honestly and informatively labeled, and that the U.S. food and Drug Administration (FDA) enforce provisions for food and drug labeling. These laws are the reason that companies like Nissin Foods include ingredient lists on their packages. Conduct some research to learn more about these laws, other food safety laws as they pertain to ingredient lists, and write a document that informs an audience of your peers about the history of ingredient lists.

Hamburger Grown in Laboratory

Voice of America News

Voice of America (VOA) is an official US Government news outlet that broadcasts a variety of kinds of programming via radio, television, and internet globally in 43 languages. Founded in 1942, VOA now reaches an audience of more than 123 million people worldwide. VOA's charter dictates that it must "serve as a consistently reliable and authoritative source of news" and that its news must always be reported objectively. However, that charge should be understood within the frame of VOA's mission "to promote freedom and democracy and to enhance understanding through multimedia communication of accurate, objective, and balanced news, information and other programming about America and the world to audiences overseas."

During the summer of 2013, many news agencies worldwide began reporting about the introduction of laboratory-grown meats—also known as cultured meat or in-vitro meat—and the possibility of mass-produced meat grown in laboratories rather than being taken from animals. On August 5, 2013, VOA posted the story reprinted here about laboratory-grown beef. The news report also includes an embedded video showing Austrian Nutritionist Hanni Ruetzler tsate testing the laboratory-grown meat, which you can view on the VOA web page where the report was originally published (voanews.com). VOA also included an embedded video from YouTube called "Cultured Beef (culturedbeef.net)" that you may want to watch in conjunction with reading the following news report. As you read this report, consider how what the report conveys might alter our cultural perceptions of meat as food.

Today, scientists unveiled what they are calling the first hamburger to be made from meat produced in a laboratory instead of a cow.

Professor Mark Post, whose laboratory at Maastricht University in the Netherlands developed the processes behind the new burger, which he and his team are calling cultured beef. On Monday, a professional chef cooked the test tube burger in a frying pan and then had two volunteers taste it in front of reporters in London.

The beef was grown in a lab using muscle stem cells taken from a cow. The cells were then placed in a nutrient rich solution in a ring-shaped form around a hub of gel. The muscle stem cells then grew into small strands of meat. It takes about 20,000 such strands to make a 140-gram burger.

Professor Post said the cultured beef production method could be developed into a solution to the growing global demand for meat. The method could also be more environmentally friendly than high-density livestock farming.

"What we are going to attempt is important because I hope it will show cultured beef has the answers to major problems that the world faces," said Post. "Our burger is made from muscle cells taken from a cow. We haven't altered them in any way. For it to succeed it has to look, feel and hopefully taste like the real thing."

In addition to the muscle cells, other ingredients such as salt, egg powder and breadcrumbs went into the burger and red beet juice and saffron were added for color.

Commercial production of cultured beef could begin within 10 to 20 years, the scientist said.

One of those to taste the burger was Austrian food researcher Hanni Rutzler.

"There is quite some intense flavor," Rutzler said. "The look was quite similar to meat. It has quite a bite. The surface of the meat was crunchy - surprisingly. The taste itself was as juicy as meat can be, but different. It tastes like meat, not a meat-substitute like soya or whatever."

Post's research, which began in 2008, was funded partially by a $330,000 donation from Sergey Brin, co-founder of Google.

Analyzing the Situation

1. The VOA report suggests that in-vitro meat is part of a long-term, global situation. The report suggests economic and ecological aspects of the situation, but only nods to the cultural aspects of this situation. How would you describe the cultural aspect of the situation in which this report participates?

2. Are you a player in this situation? In what ways are or aren't you?

3. In what ways do institution and power play a role in this situation?

Analyzing the Rhetoric

1. How does the VOA report establish the context for this information?

2. How might the fact that VOA broadcasts to audiences around the world affects how this news report was written?

3. In the headnote to this report, we learn that VOA strives to provide objective information. How does the writing in this report work toward that objective? Does it succeed in that objective?

Discussing

1. How do you respond to this report? Would you eat in vitro meat? Why or why not?

2. The VOA report cites Professor Mark Post as saying that "cultured beef has the answers to major problems that the world faces." To what problems to you think Professor Post refers? How do you respond to his claim that these problems might be answered by cultured beef?

3. Is meat made in a laboratory meat?

Writing

1. Recently, in vitro meat has received a good deal of attention in the news, popular media, and scientific publications. Take some time to locate sources from each of these kinds of sources and to learn more about in vitro meat. Then, write an informative essay that provides information about the possibility of in vitro meat becoming a substantial source of protein in global food systems. Remember: this essay should be informative, not speculative. It should convey information, not your opinion about the situation.

2. In what ways do ethics play a role in the situation in which this report participates? Write an essay about ethics and cultured meat.

3. As the issue of laboratory-grown meat becomes more public and more widely addressed, more individuals are and will be adding to the conversation about the possibility of lab-grown meat products. In many ways, the success or failure of in vitro meat as a viable protein source will depend upon its acceptance by individuals. For this writing assignment, conduct some primary research by way of a surveys and interviews to determine how at least 25 people feel about in vitro meat. Ask at least ten questions of each respondent; be sure you ask all respondents the same series of questions. Consider beginning by asking if each respondent is aware of in vitro meat. If the respondent is aware, provide one set of questions; if the respondent is not aware, then provide information about in vitro meat prior to the questions. Or, of course, you might want to base your study on surveys and interviews with only those already aware of the situation. Once you have gathered your information, write a document that reports and assesses what you learned.

4. During the same summer in which VOA reported about laboratory-grown meat, Professor Mark Post, whose laboratory at Maastricht University in the Netherlands developed one of the processes for growing meat, delivered a TEDxHaarlem talk called "Meet the New Meat." The talk is available on YouTube. Watch the video and write either a response to what Professor Post conveys in the talk or write an informative document reporting the information Professor Post conveys.

Food as Art: A Venerable Tradition

Gloria Bley Miller

Gloria Bley Miller was born in New York City in 1921. During the 1940s Miller worked as a comic book writer, writing for more than 17 series, including *Police Comics* (1941), *Blackhawk* (1944), *Marmaduke Mouse* (1946), and *Hollywood Diary* (1949). After her career in comics, Miller wrote what has come to be known as the most comprehensive Chinese cookbook written in English. Published in 1966, *The Thousand Recipe Chinese Cookbook* is still in print and still one of the best-selling cookbooks of all time. In the foreword, Miller explains that she spent more than 12 years conducting research in order to write the book. As she puts it, "I have eaten in elegant and humble Chinese restaurants, haunted Chinese grocery stores, tracked down every scrap of literature on the subject, compared notes with Chinese friends and, most important, I constantly cooked and experimented." The result of this rigorous (and delicious) research, *The Thousand Recipe Chinese Cookbook*, remains as a remarkable contribution to our understanding of food. Gloria Bley Miller died in 2008.

The essay reprinted here is a brief essay about Chinese attitudes toward food and the historical and cultural respect Chinese cultures display for food. The essay is one of many introductory essays included in *The Thousand Recipe Chinese Cookbook*; Miller wanted her readers not only to learn recipes for Chinese food but also to understand food's role in culture so they might respect it as well. As you read this essay, think about the role it might play in the larger text of the cookbook and about how it functions as a stand-alone essay.

Chinese culture is the oldest continuous civilization in the world. It goes back some four thousand years, and the art of Chinese cooking goes back with it. The Chinese people were early farmers who planted not only staple crops, but also such spices as anise and ginger, long before anyone else knew what these were. They were among the first discoverers of fire. Most likely, they cooked their food in a civilized way while the rest of mankind was still gulping it down raw.

Many forces shaped the character of Chinese cooking. There was always a leisure class: men with the wealth, curiosity and time to cultivate their palates and delight their senses. These men dreamed about and fussed over food. One thousand years before the birth of Christ, they were already experimenting with fancy cooking, recording their recipes on silk and bamboo. As early as 1115 B.C. the Imperial Court appointed a dietitian who held the rank of medical officer. His job was not only to supervise the cooking, but to study the effects (both psychic and physical) of the various dishes served. These men of leisure brought refinement to the Chinese cuisine and discovered its rarest and most exquisite delicacies.

Yet famine as well as feast was to influence Chinese cooking. Many times in the country's history flood and drought destroyed the crops and devastated the economy. The Chinese were forced by these disasters to become great domestic economists. Fuel, for example, was chronically scarce, but the Chinese soon discovered it took less wood or charcoal to steam rice than to bake bread. And to make their limited fuel supplies go even further, they evolved several techniques for cooking food very quickly.

In order to survive, the Chinese had to put their land to the best possible use. They found, for example, that raising cattle as work animals was more economical than raising them for food. (Draft animals need no special grazing areas. They can subsist on uncultivated grass and straw.) Thus the land was used for growing grain, which in turn directly fed larger numbers of people than the beef ever could. On the other hand, pigs and poultry could be raised without agricultural displacement and so became mainstays of the diet, but not for the very poorest Chinese; the mainstays of their diet were rice and vegetables.

Adversity forced the Chinese always to seek new sources of food. They were gastronomically courageous, setting no limits as to where they would look. They explored rivers and oceans and found shrimp, crab, sea cucumber, lobster and squid. They put everything edible to use, finding wonderful ways to utilize strange plants and roots: lily buds, fungi, chrysanthemum petals. By the end of the first century A.D., the Chinese had formulated a list of 365 varieties of edible plants along with similar lists of edible seafood, fowl and animals. In addition, they evolved various salting and drying techniques to preserve many ingredients indefinitely.

In their long history, the Chinese had limitless opportunities to experiment with all kinds of foods in all kinds of ways. Their most successful experiments have become part of our culinary heritage. They represent the imaginative spirit of countless men and women, often forced by circumstance to make something of very little.

The imaginativeness of the Chinese was coupled with a strong sense of artistry. Inevitably, this artistry (beautifully demonstrated in jade, ivory, porcelain, bronze and calligraphy) was to find expression in Chinese cooking. Every aspect of food was analyzed, from palatability and texture to fragrance and color. Every dish was given proportion and balance, delicacy and harmony. In the hands of the Chinese, cooking was elevated from a menial and repetitive task to a satisfying art form.

The art was not in the cooking alone. It was in the eating as well. Sharing the pleasures of good food became part of the Chinese social tradition. Friendship and food were inseparably linked. Friends on a visit were always urged to stay for a meal. A gathering without food was considered incomplete and improper. The meal hour became the symbol of the good life, a time for relaxation and pleasantry, when the harsher realities could be forgotten—a ceremonial of friendship and sociability.

Twenty-five hundred years ago Confucius described the enjoyment of food as one of the beautiful and gentle things which contribute to the peace and harmony of society. Similar references to cooking as an art appeared in China's earliest literature, and continued to appear as a traditional theme.

For thousands of years Chinese men of letters were gourmets. As a matter of fact, China is perhaps the only country in the world where scholars wrote learned treatises on food and poets wrote cookbooks.

Yet the primary way of passing Chinese cooking from one generation to the next was not by the written word but by demonstration and word of mouth—from mother to daughter, from master chef to youthful apprentice. Each in turn was to add his own ideas, to work out his own culinary variations on what had gone before.

Thus, over the centuries, out of a relatively small range of ingredients, the Chinese created vast numbers of dishes. They invented more than two hundred ways to cook pork and so many ways to cook chicken that one might eat it every day for a week, at every meal, without tiring of it. The Chinese cuisine, unsurpassed by any other in variety, is said to include some eighty thousand different dishes.

Analyzing the Situation

1. Why does Gloria Bley Miller want her audience to have this information about Chinese cooking? What role does such information play for a reader who wants to locate recipes in a cookbook?

2. What role does kairos play in this essay?

3. When Gloria Bley Miller began researching and writing *The Thousand Recipe Chinese Cookbook*, Chinese restaurants were much rarer than they are now, yet Miller's book remains a popular cookbook. In what ways has the availability of Chinese food altered the situation in which Miller writes, and what do the continued sales of the book suggest about the consistency of the situation?

Analyzing the Rhetoric

1. In what ways is Miller's research evident in her essay? How does she use her research in order to write the essay?

2. What is the purpose of Miller's essay?

3. What role do numbers play in Miller's essay?

Discussing

1. In many communities in the United States, Chinese food and Chinese restaurants are commonly understood as "take out" restaurants; they are often associated with "fast food." How does that understanding compare with Miller's claims in this essay?

2. Of course, in China, Chinese restaurants are simply restaurants and Chinese food is food, neither set apart from other food or restaurants. Nearly 20 percent of the world population is Chinese and almost 6 percent of the total U.S. population is Chinese or of Chinese descent. Why, in the United States, do we distinguish Chinese food from food? What is the cultural significance in doing so and what are the cultural ramifications of doing so?

3. Do you like Chinese food? What do you like or dislike about it?

Writing

1. Miller's essay can certainly be characterized as an informative essay that is part of an informative/instructional document. However, when read independent of the rest of the cookbook—as you have read it here—the essay can also be characterized as introductory in that it does not provide substantial information or detail. Using "Food as Art: A Venerable Tradition" as a starting point, write your own informative essay about one of the points Miller makes in the essay, extending her claim to provide substantial details about her point. That is, learn some more about one aspect of Chinese cultural approaches to food and write a more detailed account of that point.

2. Miller's essay is an overview of her assessment of the relationship between Chinese culture and food. Her assessment, of course, is an informed assessment, influenced by her substantial research. Her essay also generalizes "Chinese culture" as Chinese culture is incredibly more diverse than this essay suggests. Within the constraints of your class, including the time you have to complete this assignment and the research resources available to you, write an essay about the relationship between a culture (other than Chinese) and its food.

3. Write an informative essay that defines the terms *food* and *culture* and identifies the relationship between the two. Your essay should be informative, not speculative, narrative, or argumentative; rather, you should focus on informing your audience about the relationship between these concepts.

Food, Inc.

Robert Kenner

Robert Kenner is a director, writer, and producer whose award-winning documentaries have earned Kenner a reputation as one of the most accomplished documentary makers in the country. His documentaries have appeared on the National Geographic Channel, PBS, and HBO. His HBO documentary series *When Strangers Click* examines five stories of individuals looking for love through the Internet. Kenner's documentaries have earned many awards, including Peabodys, Emmys, Cable ACE Awards, a Strand Award for Best Documentary, and a Grierson. He has also made many

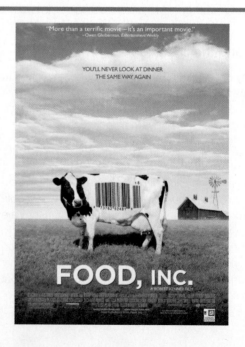

commercials and corporate videos. In 2008 Kenner released *Food, Inc.*, a detailed examination of the industrialization of the U.S. food systems. *Food, Inc.* is one of the top-grossing theatrical documentaries of all times and has sold more than 500,000 DVDs. The documentary won more than a dozen awards and received an Oscar nomination for best documentary.

It took Kenner six years to make *Food, Inc.* In an interview with *The Ecologist*, a global environmental affairs magazine founded in 1970, Kenner explains that he did not know much about where food comes from. He read Eric Schlosser's book *Fast Food Nation* and Michael Pollan's *Omnivore's Dilemma* and became intrigued with the industrialization of the food system in the United States. He tells *The Ecologist*, "The illusion is that food comes from a farm with a white picket fence and barns but it's not. It's from huge mega factories where tens of thousands of animals are confined in one space." *Food, Inc.* strives to disrupt this myth and reveal the truth about the food industry. As you watch *Food, Inc.*, consider what you had thought about where your food comes from and how the images and the data included in *Food, Inc.* affect your thinking. Also, keep in mind that *Food, Inc.* was inspired by two books; knowing this reveals a bit of the ecology in which *Food, Inc.* participates. Consider how the documentary functions within that ecology.

Analyzing the Situation

1. What role do institution and power play in the situation described in *Food, Inc.*?

2. The information in *Food, Inc.* is delivered through a medium of video and through a genre known as documentary. In what ways do this medium and genre serve the situation?

3. Taking into consideration the range of issues that *Food, Inc.* covers, who are the players in the situation in which the documentary participates?

Analyzing the Rhetoric

1. What do you suppose the film means by "the notion of a tomato"?

2. Why did Robert Kenner include the sequence with Barbara Kowalcyk, the food safety advocate whose 2½-year-old son Kevin died from an *E. coli* infection caused by tainted hamburger meat?

3. Why do you suppose Robert Kenner opted to divide his documentary into "chapters" and signify their distinction with subtitles, much as a writer would in a written document?

4. Traditionally, the genre of documentary implies an impartial delivery of information, but *Food, Inc.* steps beyond the informative into the argumentative. The text at the end of the documentary, for example, is a flagrant argument. In what other ways is *Food, Inc.* argumentative?

5. From a rhetorical standpoint, why do you suppose Robert Kenner chose to end the documentary with background music of Bruce Springsteen singing the Woody Guthrie song "This Land Is Your Land"? What is the rhetorical function of the song in the film?

Discussing

1. How would you describe the role of the "animal" in *Food, Inc.*? What is the role of the "person" in the documentary?

2. After having watched *Food, Inc.*, how do you respond to the film?

3. What role does writing play in *Food, Inc.*? Why does Robert Kenner opt to deliver some of the information in the film by text on the screen and some of it through the voices of the people interviewed?

Writing

1. What is the difference between calling a food "natural" and calling it "organic"? What are the regulations behind such labels in the U.S. food industry? Write an informative essay that defines and

describes these terms and provides details as to how the food industry is required to regulate the use of such words.

2. *Food, Inc.* introduces the role of genetically modified organisms (GMO). What are GMOs? What role do they play in U.S. food systems? Write a report detailing what you learn about GMOs.

3. After having watched *Food, Inc.*, what is the one thing you wish you knew more about regarding the food you eat? Take some time to research and learn about that issue and write an essay that explains the issue in which you are interested and what you learned.

Thinking and Writing about the Chapter

Reflection

The prompt at the beginning of this chapter asks you to write about how you think about food and the role food plays in your life. Now that you have read, discussed, and thought about some of the readings included in this chapter, write a follow-up entry in your blog or journal that addresses how those readings have changed how you think about food and the role food plays in your life. Be sure to include specific examples from the readings in order to support and explain what you identify as changes in your thinking.

Discussion Threads

1. Food is a basic need; it is, by some claims, a basic human right, as well. But, as the readings in this chapter show, there's really nothing "basic" about food. It is a complex subject to address. After having read selections from this chapter, what do you see as the most important aspect of food? Why is the issue important? In discussion groups or as a class, discuss what you and others think is important about food.

2. There are many cultural food customs that many people might find unusual. Some cultures eat foods that other cultures don't. Some cultures incorporate foods into their rituals; others do not. As a class or in smaller discussion groups, talk about food customs that might seem out of the ordinary to you.

3. Is there bad food? Is there good food? How would you define whether or not a food should be considered "good" or "bad"? Discuss the characteristics you would attribute to good or bad foods; keep a list of those attributes. As you discuss the attributes, consider whether the class reaches consensus as to whether an attribute should be considered good or bad. Once you have developed your list of attributes of good and bad food, begin listing examples of food that meet the criteria of each attribute. Identify what foods carry the greatest number of good attributes and what foods have the most negative attributes. When you have reached a close consensus about this last list, discuss whether you and your classmates eat those foods. Why or why not?

Collaboration

1. In addition to the two documentaries addressed in this chapter, there many other documentaries about food (including Morgan Spurlock's 2004 Academy Award–nominated documentary *Super Size Me*). Locate and watch two other documentaries

about food with a group from your class. Then discuss your responses to those two films in light of what you have read and seen in this chapter.

2. Working in teams, develop a list of genetically modified organisms (GMOs) that are used in food production. Then expand the list to identify specific products that include GMOs. Collect images of those products—as many as you can. Using the images, create a media project that shares the product images as a method for informing an audience about products that include GMOs.

3. There is an Internet adage in the "Rules of the Internet" known as Rule 34, which states that if something exists there is porn of it. Although Rule 34 can be taken to mean that there is literally pornography available, it is generally understood to refer to hyper-real visuals that elicit a kind of voyeuristic response from an audience. We want to watch. With this in mind, we can safely say that the Internet is home to a mind-boggling amount of "food porn," images of food items that glamorize food and depict food through spectacular visual appeal. Websites like foodporndaily.com emphasize the visual attraction of food. Working in groups of no more than four, locate ten visuals on the Internet that you would categorize as food porn. Then create a media presentation of these images along with a companion text that describes the images and helps pull them together into an image essay.

Writing

1. Listed below are 18 food items. Select one of the items and write a history of that item and how that item came to be part of U.S. culture and cuisine. Take into consideration the food's trade history: where it originated, when and how it came to the United States, and its value globally and locally. Consider its culinary history: how it has been and is used. Consider contemporary production and distribution. Consider cost. Consider cultural effect.

cabbage	oats	salt
chicken	peaches	sugar
cocoa	peanuts	tea
coffee	pork	watermelon
corn	potatoes	wheat
grapes	rice	yams

2. Food can be a deeply personal subject. We connect food with family, culture, and events. There is food we love and food we dislike. Some foods remind us of particular moments or people in our lives. Write a narrative telling the most important food story of your life thus far.

3. Select a single item of food that you regularly eat. Conduct some primary research and trace that food to its origins. If the food is processed, follow its path to the processing company and then identify from where the company gets the food or the ingredients to make the food. For this assignment, find, adapt, or make visuals to represent each part of the process. Using these images, create an image essay to depict and inform an audience as to where the food comes from.

4. Write a description of your perfect meal, the meal you would most want right now. Then expand your description to describe where the ingredients to make the meal would come from and how you would acquire them for your perfect meal.

Local Situation

What food is available on your campus? What choices do you have regarding availability? Where does the food on campus come from? Who are the suppliers and producers? Where do they get the food? Does your campus provide local farmed options? What policies must vendors on campus follow to sell food? Does your campus emphasize nutrition in the food it makes available? How might a first-time visitor to your campus judge the food options offered?

Millennials

CHAPTER 27

Before you read this chapter

It's a common thing to hear or read someone saying "your generation is…" or "my generation was …" When you hear someone use language that distinguishes one generation from another, how do you respond to the idea that you belong to a generation that is characterized as a singular group with similar characteristics? In your journal or blog, write about what it means to you to hear someone characterize "your generation."

The term *millennial* refers to the generation of people born, generally speaking, between the early 1980s and the early 2000s. Of course, there's no way to specifically identify dates when a generation begins or ends. Millennials are often called *Generation Y*, showing a relationship to Generation X, which was the generation born between the early 1960s and the early 1980s. Others have called millennials *Generation We, The Net Generation, The Global Generation, Generation Next, The Peter Pan Generation*, and *Echo Boomers*, because their population size is roughly equivalent to that of the Baby Boomers and they are, for the most part, the children of Baby Boomers. They have also been called *The Boomerang Generation* because many return to live with their parents after college because of difficult economic situations. In a 2012 *USA Today* article titled "After Gen X, Millennials, What Should Next Generation Be?" Bruce Horovitz credited William Strauss and Neil Howe with naming millennials in their book *Millennials Rising: The Next Great Generation*. Strauss and Howe identify the millennial generation as starting with those born after 1982 and before 2004. Interestingly, the Australian Bureau of Statistics uses 1983–2003 to identify millennials.

No matter the dates used to frame the millennial generation or any other generation, there is a general understanding that each of the generations has characteristics common to the generation that distinguish it from other generations. According to Strauss and Howe, every fourth generation shares some overlapping characteristics; thus, they predict that millennials will be more civic minded like the G.I. Generation born between the 1920s and 1940s (Tom Brokaw called the G.I. Generation "the Greatest Generation any society has ever produced"). One critic of this theory pointed out that the fact that voluntary military enrollment decreased when the War on Iraq began.

Other generational experts have characterized millennials as confident, narcissistic, and entitled. Since 1975, the University of Michigan has conducted a study called "Monitoring the Future," which surveys high school seniors about their attitudes toward life situations. Similarly, the University of California Los Angeles has conducted a survey since 1966 of first-year college students in the United States. The UCLA American Freshman survey has shown that being wealthy was important to 45 percent of surveyed Baby Boomers, 70 percent of Gen X, and 75 percent of millennials. Likewise, the study shows that 50 percent of Baby Boomers surveyed identified keeping up with political affairs as important, whereas 39 percent of surveyed Gen X did, and 35 percent of millennials.

Some experts have identified that millennials draw a good deal of their common characteristics from having grown up in a digital environment and being comfortable with media and communications technologies. Interestingly, though, despite this characterization, the consulting firm Millennial Branding and Internships.com conducted a survey in May 2013 in which they asked 1,345 college students about their views regarding the future of education. The survey showed that 53 percent of those surveyed identify online colleges as a "reputable form of education," but only 43 percent see online classes as being equivalent to or surpassing traditional brick-and-mortar classes. 78 percent of those surveyed said that it was more efficient (easier) to learn in a traditional classroom than in an online course.

In May 2013, *Mashable* blogger Stephanie Buck wrote "Millennials are a stubborn bunch. Likes: looking smart, being right. Dislikes: looking dumb, being wrong. That's why we turn to search engines to ask some of life's most pressing questions. Because when we need to learn how to boil an egg, we can't just call our moms." She then identifies the top ten things millennials ask the Internet:

1. What is a meme?
2. How do I use Pinterest?
3. How to boil an egg?
4. What is hummus?
5. What is twerking?
6. What is 401k?
7. What is *The Great Gatsby* about?
8. What is a hashtag?
9. What is a narcissist?
10. How to tie a tie.

Of course, Buck is poking fun at millennials and the influence of the Internet on millennials. And although millennials have grown up in the Internet age, a 2012 survey by "The Digital Life" indicates that more than half of the 7,213 millennials surveyed harbor significant worries that a family member or friend will post personal or inappropriate information about them. The survey also shows that two thirds of the surveyed millennials believe that their generation has no sense of personal privacy. Millennials are seen as "digital natives," and their attitudes about business, government, and global change are generally positive.

The readings in this chapter examine some of the kinds of problems millennials face, particularly economic. Millennials face the hard reality that the average students currently in college will work an average of 20 jobs over their lifetimes, changing the very idea of what a career is. These readings are not intended to be depressing; rather they have been gathered here to elicit response—and, yes, depression is a legitimate response, but there are other, more productive ways to engage these readings. As you read these selections, think about the situation in which these readings participate and where you fit in this situation.

Millennials: The Me Me Me Generation

Joel Stein

Joel Stein is a journalist who writes for *Time* magazine. When he graduated from Stanford University, where he majored in English, Stein worked as a writer and researcher for *Martha Stewart Living*. Stein often jokes that Stewart fired him twice in the same day. Stein then wrote for *Time Out New York*, a magazine that provides information about art, music, and culture in New York. In 1996, Stein was featured as a contestant on MTV's game show *Idiot Savants*. He started writing for *Time* in 1997. He also writes for *The Los Angeles Times*.

Born in 1971, Stein is part of what is known as "Generation X," the population born after the World War II baby boom in the years comprising the 1960s and 1970s. In May 2013, Stein published a *Time* cover story called "Millennials: The Me Me Me Generation," which is reprinted here. Stein's article is critical of the population often referred to as "Millennials" or "Generation Y," the population born after Generation X, between the 1980s and 2000s. Chances are you are a Millennial.

I am about to do what old people have done throughout history: call those younger than me lazy, entitled, selfish and shallow. But I have studies! I have statistics! I have quotes from respected academics! Unlike my parents, my grandparents and my great-grandparents, I have proof.

Here's the cold, hard data: The incidence of narcissistic personality disorder is nearly three times as high for people in their 20s as for the generation that's now 65 or older, according to the National Institutes of Health; 58% more college students scored higher on a narcissism scale in 2009 than in 1982. Millennials got so many participation trophies growing up that a recent study showed that 40% believe they should be promoted every two years, regardless of performance. They are fame-obsessed: three times as many middle school girls want to grow up to be a personal assistant to a famous person as want to be a Senator, according to a 2007 survey; four times as many would pick the assistant job over CEO of a major corporation. They're so convinced of their own greatness that the National Study of Youth and Religion found the guiding morality of 60% of millennials in any situation is that they'll just be able to feel what's right. Their development is stunted: more people ages 18 to 29 live with their parents than with a spouse, according to the 2012 Clark University Poll of Emerging Adults. And they are lazy. In 1992, the nonprofit Families and Work Institute reported that 80% of people under 23 wanted to one day have a job with greater responsibility; 10 years later, only 60% did.

Millennials consist, depending on whom you ask, of people born from 1980 to 2000. To put it more simply for them, since they grew up not having to do a lot of math in their heads, thanks to computers, the group is made up mostly of teens and 20-somethings. At 80 million strong, they are the biggest age grouping in American history. Each country's millennials are different, but because of globalization, social media, the exporting of Western culture and the speed of change, millennials worldwide are more similar to one another than to older generations within their nations. Even in China, where family history is more important than any individual, the Internet, urbanization and the one-child policy have created a generation as overconfident and self-involved as the Western one. And these aren't just rich-kid problems: poor millennials have even higher rates of narcissism, materialism and technology addiction in their ghetto-fabulous lives.

They are the most threatening and exciting generation since the baby boomers brought about social revolution, not because they're trying to take over the Establishment but because they're growing up without one. The Industrial Revolution made individuals far more powerful—they could move to a city, start a business, read and form organizations. The information revolution has further empowered individuals by handing them the technology to compete against huge organizations: hackers vs. corporations, bloggers vs. newspapers, terrorists vs. nation-states, YouTube directors vs. studios, app-makers vs. entire industries. Millennials don't need us. That's why we're scared of them.

In the U.S., millennials are the children of baby boomers, who are also known as the Me Generation, who then produced the Me Me Me Generation, whose selfishness technology has only exacerbated. Whereas in the 1950s families displayed a wedding photo, a school photo and maybe a military photo in their homes, the average middle-class American family today walks amid 85 pictures of themselves and their pets. Millennials have come of age in the era of the quantified self, record-ing their daily steps on FitBit, their whereabouts every hour of every day on PlaceMe and their genetic data on 23 and Me. They have less civic engagement and lower political participation than any previous group. This is a generation that would have made Walt Whitman wonder if maybe they should try singing a song of someone else.

They got this way partly because, in the 1970s, peo-ple wanted to improve kids' chances of success by in-stilling self-esteem. It turns out that self-esteem is great for getting a job or hooking up at a bar but not so great for keeping a job or a relationship. "It was an honest mistake," says Roy Baumeister, a psychology professor at Florida State University and the editor of *Self-Esteem: The Puzzle of Low Self-Regard.* "The early findings showed that, indeed, kids with high self-esteem did bet-ter in school and were less likely to be in various kinds of trouble. It's just that we've learned later that self-esteem is a result, not a cause." The problem is that when people try to boost self-esteem, they accidentally boost narcis-sism instead. "Just tell your kids you love them. It's a bet-ter message," says Jean Twenge, a psychology professor at the University of San Diego, who wrote *Generation Me and the Narcissism Epidemic.* "When they're little it seems cute to tell them they're special or a princess or a

rock star or whatever their T-shirt says. When they're 14 it's no longer cute." All that self-esteem leads them to be disappointed when the world refuses to affirm how great they know they are. "This generation has the highest likelihood of having unmet expectations with respect to their careers and the lowest levels of satisfaction with their careers at the stage that they're at," says Sean Lyons, co-editor of Managing the New Workforce: International Perspectives on the Millennial Generation. "It is sort of a crisis of unmet expectations."

What millennials are most famous for besides narcissism is its effect: entitlement. If you want to sell seminars to middle managers, make them about how to deal with young employees who e-mail the CEO directly and beg off projects they find boring. English teacher David McCullough Jr.'s address last year to Wellesley High School's graduating class, a 12-minute reality check titled "You Are Not Special," has nearly 2 million hits on YouTube. "Climb the mountain so you can see the world, not so the world can see you," McCullough told the graduates. He says nearly all the response to the video has been positive, especially from millennials themselves; the video has 57 likes for every dislike.

Though they're cocky about their place in the world, millennials are also stunted, having prolonged a life stage between teenager and adult that this maga-zine once called twixters and will now use once again in an attempt to get that term to catch on. The idea of the teenager started in the 1920s; in 1910, only a tiny percentage of kids went to high school, so most people's social interactions were with adults in their family or in the workplace. Now that cell phones allow kids to socialize at every hour—they send and receive an average of 88 texts a day, according to Pew—they're living under the constant influence of their friends. "Peer pressure is anti-intellectual. It is anti-historical. It is anti-eloquence," says Mark Bauerlein, an English professor at Emory, who wrote *The Dumbest Generation: How the Digital Age Stupefies Young Americans and Jeopardizes Our Future (Or, Don't Trust Anyone Under 30).* "Never before in history have people been able to grow up and reach age 23 so dominated by peers.

To develop intellectually you've got to relate to older people, older things: 17-year-olds never grow up if they're just hanging around other 17-year-olds." Of all the objections to Obamacare, not a lot of people argued against parents' need to cover their kids' health insurance until they're 26.

Millennials are interacting all day but almost entirely through a screen. You've seen them at bars, sitting next to one another and texting. They might look calm, but they're deeply anxious about missing out on something better. Seventy percent of them check their phones every hour, and many experience phantom pocket-vibration syndrome. "They're doing a behavior to reduce their anxiety," says Larry Rosen, a psychology professor at California State University at Dominguez Hills and the author of *iDisorder*. That constant search for a hit of dopamine ("Someone liked my status update!") reduces creativity. From 1966, when the Torrance Tests of Creative Thinking were first administered, through the mid-1980s, creativity scores in children increased. Then they dropped, falling sharply in 1998. Scores on tests of empathy similarly fell sharply, starting in 2000, likely because of both a lack of face-to-face time and higher degrees of narcissism. Not only do millennials lack the kind of empathy that allows them to feel concerned for others, but they also have trouble even intellectually understanding others' points of view.

What they do understand is how to turn themselves into brands, with "friend" and "follower" tallies that serve as sales figures. As with most sales, positivity and confidence work best. "People are inflating themselves like balloons on Facebook," says W. Keith Campbell, a psychology professor at the University of Georgia, who has written three books about generational increases in narcissism (including *When You Love a Man Who Loves Himself*). When everyone is telling you about their vacations, parties and promotions, you start to embellish your own life to keep up. If you do this well enough on Instagram, YouTube and Twitter, you can become a microcelebrity.

Millennials grew up watching reality-TV shows, most of which are basically documentaries about narcissists. Now they have trained themselves to be reality-TV-ready. "Most people never define who they are as a personality type until their 30s. So for people to be defining who they are at the age of 14 is almost a huge evolutionary jump," says casting director Doron Ofir, who auditioned participants for *Jersey Shore, Millionaire Matchmaker, A Shot at Love* and *RuPaul's Drag Race*, among other shows. "Do you follow me on Twitter?" he asks at the end of the interview. "Oh, you should. I'm fun. I hope that one day they provide an Emmy for casting of reality shows—because, you know, I'd assume I'm a shoo-in. I would like that gold statue. And then I will take a photo of it, and then I will Instagram it." Ofir is 41, but he has clearly spent a lot of time around millennials.

I have gone just about as far as I can in an article without talking about myself. So first, yes, I'm aware that I started this piece—in which I complain about millennials' narcissism—with the word I. I know that this magazine, which for decades did not print bylines, started putting authors' names on the cover regularly in 2004 and that one of the first names was mine. As I mocked reality shows in the previous paragraph, I kept thinking about the fact that I got to the final round for 1995's *Real World: London*. I know my number of Twitter followers far better than the tally on my car's odometer; although Facebook has a strictly enforced limit of 5,000 friends, I somehow have 5,079. It was impossible not to remember, the whole time I was accusing millennials of being lazy, that I was supposed to finish this article nearly a year ago.

I moved home for the first six months after college. When I got hired at *Time*, my co-workers hated me for cozying up to the editor of the magazine. I talk to one of my parents every other day and depend on my dad for financial advice. It's highly possible that I'm a particularly lame 41-year-old, but still, none of these traits are new to millennials; they've been around at least since the Reformation, when Martin Luther told Christians they didn't need the church to talk to God, and became more pronounced at the end of the 18th century in the Romantic period, when artists stopped using their work to celebrate God and started using it to express themselves. In 1979, Christopher Lasch wrote in *The Culture of Narcissism*, "The media give substance to, and thus intensify, narcissistic dreams of fame and glory, encourage common people to identify themselves with the stars and to hate the 'herd,' and make it more and more difficult for them to accept the banality of everyday existence." I checked my e-mail three times during that sentence.

So while the entire first half of this article is absolutely true (I had data!), millennials' self-involvement is more a continuation of a trend than a revolutionary break from previous generations. They're not a new species; they've just mutated to adapt to their environment.

For example, millennials' perceived entitlement isn't a result of overprotection but an adaptation to a world of abundance. "For almost all of human history, almost everyone was a small-scale farmer. And then people were farmers and factory workers. Nobody gets very much fulfillment from either of those things," says Jeffrey Arnett, a psychology professor at Clark University, who invented the phrase emerging adulthood, which people foolishly use instead of the catchy twixters. Twixters put off life choices because they can choose from a huge array of career options, some of which, like jobs in social media, didn't exist 10 years ago. What idiot would try to work her way up at a company when she's going to have an average of seven jobs before age 26? Because of online dating, Facebook circles and the ability to connect with people internationally, they no longer have to marry someone from their high school class or even their home country. Because life expectancy is increasing so rapidly and technology allows women to get pregnant in their 40s, they're more free to postpone big decisions. The median age for an American woman's first marriage went from 20.6 in 1967 to 26.9 in 2011.

And while all that choice might end in disappointment, it's a lottery worth playing. "I had one grandfather fight in the Pacific and one in the Atlantic theater. One became a pilot; one became a doctor. When you grow up during the Great Depression and fight off the Nazis, you want safety and stability," says Tucker Max, 37, who

set an example for millennials when instead of using his Duke law degree to practice law, he took his blog rants about his drunken, lecherous adventures and turned them into a mega-best-selling book, *I Hope They Serve Beer in Hell*, that he got an independent publisher to print. "Everyone told you that everyone above you had to s — on you before you got to s — on people below you. And millennials didn't want to do that."

In fact, a lot of what counts as typical millennial behavior is how rich kids have always behaved. The Internet has democratized opportunity for many young people, giving them access and information that once belonged mostly to the wealthy. When I was growing up in the 1980s, I thought I would be a lawyer, since that was the best option I knew about for people who sucked at math in my middle-class suburb, but I saw a lot more options once I got to Stanford. "Previously if you wanted to be a writer but didn't know anyone who is in publishing, it was just, Well, I won't write. But now it's, Wait, I know someone who knows someone," says Jane Buckingham, who studies workplace changes as founder of Trendera, a consumer-insights firm. "I hear story after story of people high up in an organization saying, 'Well, this person just e-mailed me and asked me for an hour of my time, and for whatever reason I gave it to them.' So the great thing is that they do feel entitled to all of this, so they'll be more innovative and more willing to try new things and they'll do all this cool stuff."

Because millennials don't respect authority, they also don't resent it. That's why they're the first teens who aren't rebelling. They're not even sullen. "I grew up watching Peanuts, where you didn't even see the parents. They were that 'Wah-wah' voice. And MTV was always a parent-free zone," says MTV president Stephen Friedman, 43, who now includes parents in nearly all the channel's reality shows. "One of our research studies early on said that a lot of this audience outsources their superego to their parents. The most simple decision of should I do this or should I do that—our audience will check in with their parents." A 2012 Google Chrome ad shows a college student video-chatting all the details of her life to her dad. "I am very used to seeing things where the cliché is the parent doesn't understand. Most of my friends, their parents are on social and they're following them or sharing stuff with them," says Jessica Brillhart, a filmmaker at Google's Creative Lab, who worked on the commercial. It's hard to hate your parents when they also listen to rap and watch Jon Stewart.

In fact, many parents of millennials would proudly call their child-rearing style peer-enting. "I negotiate daily with my son who is 13. Maybe all that coddling has paid off in these parent–child relationships," says Jon Murray, who created *The Real World* and other reality shows, including *Keeping Up With the Kardashians*. He says that seeing regular people celebrated on TV gives millennials confidence: "They're going after what they want. It can be a little irritating that they want to be on the next rung so quickly. Maybe I'm partly responsible for it. I like this generation, so I have no issues with that."

Kim Kardashian, who represents to nonmillennials all that is wrong with her generation, readily admits that she has no particular talent. But she also knows why she appeals to her peers. "They like that I share a lot of myself and that I've always been honest about the way I live my life," she says. "They want relationships with businesses and celebrities. Gen X was kept at arm's length from businesses and celebrity." When you're no longer cowed by power, you are going to like what a friend tells you about far more than what an ad campaign does, even if that friend is a celebrity trying to make money and that friendship is just a reply to one tweet.

While every millennial might seem like an oversharing Kardashian, posting vacation photos on Facebook is actually less obnoxious than 1960s couples' trapping friends in their houses to watch their terrible vacation slide shows. "Can you imagine if the boomers had YouTube, how narcissistic they would've seemed?" asks Scott Hess, senior vice president of human intelligence for SparkSMG, whose TedX speech, "Millennials: Who They Are and Why We Hate Them," advised companies on marketing to youth. "Can you imagine how many frickin' Instagrams of people playing in the mud during Woodstock we would've seen? I think in many ways you're blaming millennials for the technology that

happens to exist right now." Yes, they check their phones during class, but think about how long you can stand in line without looking at your phone. Now imagine being used to that technology your whole life and having to sit through algebra.

Companies are starting to adjust not just to millennials' habits but also to their atmospheric expectations. Nearly a quarter of DreamWorks' 2,200 employees are under 30, and the studio has a 96% retention rate. Dan Satterthwaite, who runs the studio's human-relations department and has been in the field for about 23 years, says Maslow's hierarchy of needs makes it clear that a company can't just provide money anymore but also has to deliver self-actualization. During work hours at DreamWorks, you can take classes in photography, sculpting, painting, cinematography and karate. When one employee explained that jujitsu is totally different from karate, Satterthwaite was shocked at his boldness, then added a jujitsu class.

Millennials are able to use their leverage to negotiate much better contracts with the traditional institutions they do still join. Although the armed forces had to lower the physical standards for recruits and make boot camp less intensive, Gary Stiteler, who has been an Army recruiter for about 15 years, is otherwise more impressed with millennials than any other group he's worked with. "The generation that we enlisted when I first started recruiting was sort of do, do, do. This generation is think, think about it before you do it," he says. "This generation is three to four steps ahead. They're coming in saying, 'I want to do this, then when I'm done with this, I want to do this.'"

Here's something even all the psychologists who fret over their narcissism studies agree about: millennials are nice. They have none of that David Letterman irony and Gen X ennui. "The positivism has surprised me. The Internet was always 50–50 positive and negative. And now it's 90–10," says Shane Smith, the 43-year-old CEO of Vice, which adjusted from being a Gen X company in print to a millennial company once it started posting videos online, which are viewed by a much younger audience. Millennials are more accepting of differences, not just among gays, women and minorities but in everyone. "There are many, many subcultures, and you can dip into them and search around. I prefer that to you're either supermainstream or a riot grrrl," says Tavi Gevinson, a 17-year-old who runs Rookie, an online fashion magazine, from her bedroom when she's not at school. It's hard, in other words, to join the counterculture when there's no culture. "There's not this us-vs.-them thing now. Maybe that's why millennials don't rebel," she says.

There may even be the beginning of a reaction against all the constant self-promotion. Evan Spiegel, 22, co-founder of Snapchat, an app that allows people to send photos, video and text that are permanently erased after 10 seconds or less, argues that it's become too exhausting for millennials to front a perfect life on social media. "We're trying to create a place where you can be in sweatpants, sitting eating cereal on a Friday night, and that's O.K.," he says.

But if you need the ultimate proof that millennials could be a great force for positive change, know this: Tom Brokaw, champion of the Greatest Generation, loves millennials. He calls them the Wary Generation, and he thinks their cautiousness in life decisions is a smart response to their world. "Their great mantra has been: Challenge convention. Find new and better ways of doing things. And so that ethos transcends the wonky people who are inventing new apps and embraces the whole economy," he says. The generation that experienced Monica Lewinsky's dress, 9/11, the longest wars in U.S. history, the Great Recession and an Arab Spring that looks at best like a late winter is nevertheless optimistic about its own personal chances of success. Sure, that might be delusional, but it's got to lead to better results than wearing flannel, complaining and making indie movies about it.

So here's a more rounded picture of millennials than the one I started with. All of which I also have data for. They're earnest and optimistic. They embrace the system. They are pragmatic idealists, tinkerers more than dreamers, life hackers. Their world is so flat that they have no leaders, which is why revolutions from Occupy Wall Street to Tahrir Square have even less chance than previous rebellions. They want constant approval—they post photos from the dressing room as they try on clothes. They have massive fear of missing out and have an acronym for everything (including FOMO). They're celebrity obsessed but don't respectfully idolize celebrities from a distance. (Thus *Us* magazine's "They're just like us!" which consists of paparazzi shots of famous people doing everyday things.) They're not into going to church, even though they believe in God, because they don't identify with big institutions; one-third of adults under 30, the highest percentage ever, are religiously unaffiliated. They want new experiences, which are more important to them than material goods. They are cool and reserved and not all that passionate. They are informed but inactive: they hate Joseph Kony but aren't going to do anything about Joseph Kony. They are probusiness. They're financially responsible; although student loans have hit record highs, they have less household and credit-card debt than any previous generation on record—which, admittedly, isn't that hard when you're living at home and using your parents' credit card. They love their phones but hate talking on them.

They are not only the biggest generation we've ever known but maybe the last large birth grouping that will be easy to generalize about. There are already microgenerations within the millennial group, launching as often as new iPhones, depending on whether you learned to type before Facebook, Twitter, iPads or Snapchat. Those rising microgenerations are all horrifying the ones right above them, who are their siblings. And the group after millennials is likely to be even more empowered. They're already so comfortable in front of the camera that the average American 1-year-old has more images of himself than a 17th century French king.

So, yes, we have all that data about narcissism and laziness and entitlement. But a generation's greatness isn't determined by data; it's determined by how they react to the challenges that befall them. And, just as important, by how we react to them. Whether you think millennials are the new greatest generation of optimistic entrepreneurs or a group of 80 million people about to implode in a dwarf star of tears when their expectations are unmet depends largely on how you view change. Me, I choose to believe in the children. God knows they do.

Analyzing the Situation

1. Joel Stein's "Millennials: The Me Me Me Generation" was originally published in *Time*, the world's largest-circulation news magazine. Thus, when Stein makes the claims he does about millennials, chances are that a rather large audience hears him. In what ways does Stein's ability to reach a large audience affect the larger cultural understanding of the millennial generation?

2. Are you a part of the situation in which Stein participates? In what ways are or aren't you? Why do you think your role in this situation is important? Why do you think everything is about you?

3. At the beginning of this essay, Stein makes the consolation that what he claims about millennials is really no different from what previous generations have always claimed about the next generation. In what ways, then, is this situation tied to a historically larger situation?

Analyzing the Rhetoric

1. Does Stein's essay seem to you to take a negative tone, a positive tone, or an indifferent tone in his discussion of millennials? What language in the essay leads you to such an evaluation?

2. What does Stein achieve in separating himself from millennials through a language of "us and them"?

3. What role do Stein's "cold, hard data" really play in this essay?

Discussing

1. Chances are that you and many of your classmates (if not everyone in your class, perhaps even your instructor) are millennials. That being the case, how do you and your classmates respond to Stein's essay? If you have classmates who fall outside of the millennial generation, be sure to include their take on the essay as well.

2. Given that Stein's observations take the perspective of an outsider looking in, how would you describe your generation? As a class, discuss what it means to be a millennial from your perspective. Keep in mind that *millennial* refers not just to you and your friends but to an entire generation, so don't limit your discussion to just what you experience in your immediate surroundings; think beyond the immediate.

Writing

1. Stein has provided one particular characterization of millennials, but his is not the only way to describe millennials. Write an essay in which you explain to the same audience to which Stein writes what millennials are what they/you stand for, and what characterizes them/you as millennials.

2. When *Time* magazine published Joel Stein's "Millennials: The Me Me Me Generation," the *Time* editors asked Stein to live like a millennial for a day and to let them record his experiences. The result is a short video called "Watch Joel Stein Live Like a Millennial for a Day," which you can find with a simple search on the *Time* pages. Locate and watch the video. Then record and edit a video responding to Stein's depiction of the millennial life from your perspective.

3. Interestingly, Stein discusses millennials from the perspective of an older generation examining a younger generation, an activity that Stein readily acknowledges as both traditional and not unique. But how do millennials see Gen Xers or Baby Boomers? Write an essay that characterizes an older generation; if you are older than millennials, write your essay about the generation that preceded yours.

Millennials Rising: The Next Great Generation

Judy Denny

In 2000 demographer, economist, and historian Neil Howe and historian and writer William Strauss published the book *Millennials Rising: The Next Great Generation*. Previously, Howe and Strauss published two books, *Generations* and *13th Gen*, which established the ways in which we talk about generational difference in the United States. *Millennials Rising* addresses the generational characteristics of the generation born after 1982 and before 2004 and is credited for coining the term *millennials* to identify this generation.

In October, 2004, the U.S. Department of the Interior's Federal Consulting Group published a review of *Millennials Rising* written by Judy Denny, which is reprinted here. The review originally appeared on the Federal Consulting Group's web pages. As you read the review, consider how it, by way of the book, establishes definitions of what it means to be a millennial.

Neil Howe and William Strauss have been interested in generational histories since the early 80's. They published Generations in 1990, publicly naming and describing Millennials before the generation that preceded the Millennials—Generation X—was even named. They wrote two other relevant books: *13th Gen* in 1993 and *The Fourth Turning* in 1997.

The Millennials are defined as those born in 1982 and approximately the 20 years thereafter. The book was written in the year 2000 when the oldest Millennials were graduating from high school. Part of the motivation for the book was the authors' enthusiasm for the generation and the disappointment with the poor news coverage it was getting.

A baby boomlet was noticed in the early 80's, and by the 90's, nursery schools, as well as elementary school classes, were overflowing. Now at the end of the generation, the Millennial is clearly the largest generation in history. It also ranks at the top in many other areas. Its members are the most affluent, the most educated, and the most diverse (36% non-white). They are self-described optimists and team-players. They follow rules more readily and accept authority easier than their parents did at their age. Not surprisingly, they surpass their parents in the use of technology.

The reason for the large size of the generation is the decision of many Boomers to delay childbirth (thus the much smaller Generation X). But as depicted in a 1982 Time cover story "a floodtide of thirtysomething Boomers [were] choosing at long last to become moms and dads." And, of course, many Gen Xers were also having children at a more traditional time.

Howe and Strauss set the stage this way:

"Wanted. Protected. Worthy. Thus did the heralded Class of 2000 arrive in America's nurseries and cribs. Soon a much longer glossary of (mainly) positive adjectives would describe them. From conception to graduation, this 1982 cohort has marked a watershed in adult attitudes toward, treatment of and expectations for children. Over that eighteen-year span, whatever age bracket those 1982-born children have inhabited has been the target of intense hope, worry, and wonder from parents, pollsters, pundits, and politicians" (p. 32).

As the focus of adults on the generation is different, so is the persona of the generation, which has seven distinguishing traits:

> *Special.* From "precious-baby movies" to effusive rhetoric.

Sheltered. Explosions of child safety rules and devices.

Confident. High levels of optimism. Often boasts of power and potential.

Team-oriented. New emphasis on group learning, tight peer bonds.

Achieving. Accountability rising. Best-educated and best-behaved.

Pressured. Pushed to study hard, take advantage of opportunities.

Conventional. Takes pride in behavior. Comfortable with parents' values.

The generation will be known for its reversal of most trends measuring poor behavior, including violent crimes, suicide, sex, and alcohol and illicit drug use. "Boomers started out as the objects of loosening child standards in an era of conformist adults. Millennials are starting out as the objects of tightening child standards in an era of non-conformists adults. By the time the last Millennials come of age, they could become...the cleanest-cut young adults in living memory" (p. 46).

This generation will also be known for its hard work "on a grassroots reconstruction of community, teamwork, and civic spirit. They're doing it in the realms of community service, race, gender relations, politics and faith" (p.214). They have a tremendous capacity to mobilize volunteers for worthwhile causes, largely by using the Internet.

The bulk of the book goes into more depth describing the Millennials and discussing issues such as health and safety, schools, employment, discipline, spending patterns, the environment, homework, pressure, sheltering, cyberspace, music, etc. There is a wealth of information from studies and history and numerous sidebar comments, with quotes from notables as well as many teens and younger Millennials.

The last few chapters are an interesting historical perspective of the "hero" generations in America since 1588.

According to Howe and Strauss, the Millennials are in line to be the next "hero" generation because they follow a pattern common to the last four "hero" generations in American history. The pattern early in life is as follows:

- A hero generation arrives just after an era of society-wide upheaval in values and culture that many historians call a "spiritual awakening" and passes through childhood during a time of decaying civic habits, ebbing institutional trust, and resurgent individualism.

- A hero generation directly follows a youth generation widely deemed to be disappointing, reacts against the older "postwar" generation that fomented the spiritual awakening as young adults—and fills a void left by the passing of an elder generation known for civic purpose and teamwork.

- A hero generation, early in life, becomes the target of passionate adult efforts to encircle and protect the childhood world, to promote child achievement, and to attach a new sense of destiny to youth—to which it responds by meeting and beating adult expectations. (p.326)

Later in life, the pattern is as follows:

- The special treatment and protections follow them into young adulthood and blossom into a sense of collective confidence and power.

- They and their elders declare a new determination to rid society of dangers that had ravaged the prior youth generation, but which only now are deemed intolerable.

- Entering young adulthood, they undergo a heroic trial, a climactic moment in history in which their courage and fortitude are tested.

- In midlife, as an honored generation of civic heroes, they create powerful land enduring institutions, build big new infrastructures, craft a new modern world, and dominate politics and economics deep into their old age.

- Entering elderhood, they reveal a hubris that sparks angry quarrels with their own children, who help foment a spiritual awakening to challenge their parents' social discipline and secularism. (p.345)

Howe and Strauss think we now have a "rendezvous with destiny." It is simply "a generational cycle." They believe that "a constellation of old Boomers, midlife Gen Xers and young-adult Millennials is a lineup of maximum power and civic risk." What is clearly missing from a book published in 2000 is the effect of 9/11 and the war in Iraq. Could they be the surprises that Howe and Strauss predict?

Because my daughter was born in 1982 and my son in 1985, I was fascinated by the book. We are having several 1982 birth year Millennials over next week to talk about the last four years and "update" the book.

The nugget for the Group is that birth year and place in history is a major factor in how a person is wired and therefore how he/she operates in the workplace. So for coaching, teamwork, leadership, etc., it is always helpful information.

Analyzing the Situation

1. Why do you suppose the U.S. Department of the Interior's Federal Consulting Group decided to publish a review of Howe and Strauss' book? In what ways are the book and Federal Consulting Group related in this situation?

2. How does the placement of Judy Denny's review on a US Government web page affect how we respond to the review?

Analyzing the Rhetoric

1. What role does summary play in this review?

2. How would you describe Judy Denny's method in this essay? What strategies does she employ to convey her position?

3. How do you respond to the final paragraphs of the review in relation to the remainder of the review?

Discussing

1. How do you feel about Howe and Strauss' definitions (as Judy Denny reports them)? As a class, discuss your response to the information in this review.

2. Discuss the seven traits that Howe and Strauss attribute to the millennial generation. Do you agree that these generalizations can be used to describe this generation?

Writing

1. Do you see what Judy Denny reports as Howe and Strauss' information as accurate? Write an evaluation in which you take into account information (research) other than Howe and Strauss' work and other readings in this chapter as support for your evaluative criteria and your evaluation of How and Strauss' position.

2. Judy Denny writes: "Howe and Strauss think we now have a 'rendezvous with destiny.' It is simply 'a generational cycle.' They believe that 'a constellation of old Boomers, midlife Gen Xers and young-adult Millennials is a lineup of maximum power and civic risk.'" Do you agree with this claim? Write a response to Howe and Strauss' prediction regarding civic risk.

3. Judy Denny writes: "What is clearly missing from a book published in 2000 is the effect of 9/11 and the war in Iraq. Could they be the surprises that Howe and Strauss predict?" Write a document that takes up Denny's question and analyzes the description of Millennials that Howe and Strauss propose in light of 9/11 and the war in Iraq.

Millennials Come of Age as America's Most Stressed Generation

Arianna Huffington

Arianna Huffington was born Ariánna Stasinopoúlou in Athens, Greece. When she was 16 she moved to England. She graduated from Cambridge University with a master's degree in economics, and at 21 she became president of the famous debating society, the Cambridge Union. In 1980 she moved to New York. Huffington has written a number of books, including *The Female Woman*, which attacked the Women's Liberation movement; she has also written a biography of Maria Callas, one of the most renowned opera singers of the twentieth century and a biography of Pablo Picasso. But, mostly, Huffington is known for her politics, aligning herself at times with the Republican Party and at others with the Democratic Party. In 1994, Huffington's husband, Michael Huffington, ran unsuccessfully as a Republican for a senate seat. Arianna Huffington became known as a supporter of conservative politics. In 2004, though, on *The Daily Show*, she announced that she would support Democratic presidential candidate John Kerry. In 2003, she ran against Arnold Schwarzenegger as an independent in the California gubernatorial recall election; she did not win.

In 2005, Huffington launched *The Huffington Post*, an online news aggregator and blog, which has become one of the most read news sources in the United States. *The Huffington Post* tends to be a liberal-minded site, which is interesting since Huffington's first foray into political blogging was through her website resignation.com, where she called for President Bill Clinton's resignation. The essay reprinted here is taken from her column in *The Huffington Post* and in it she weighs in on millennials in response to President Barack Obama's 2013 State of the Union address.

First came the "Baby Boomers," then came "Generation X." The branding of the subsequent generation, the one that came of age during the 2000s, was less definitive, ping-ponging between "Generation Y" and "The Millennials." I'd like to add a third name: "Generation Stress." According to *Stress in America*, a study commissioned by the American Psychological Association, Millennials are the most stressed demographic. And from what we heard out of Washington last week, the conditions creating that stress aren't going away anytime soon. But there's still cause for hope.

The study asked participants to rank their stress level on a scale of 1 ("little or no stress") to 10 ("a great deal of stress"). Millennials led the stress parade, with a 5.4 average. Boomers registered 4.7, and the group the study labeled the "Matures" gave themselves a 3.7.

The findings were consistent across almost every question. Nearly 40 percent of Millennials said their stress had increased last year, compared to 33 percent for Boomers and 29 percent for Matures. Over half of Millennials said that stress had kept them awake at night during the last month, compared to 37 percent for Boomers and 25 percent for Matures. And only 29 percent of Millennials say they're getting enough sleep, compared to 46 percent of Matures.

These levels of stress are taking their toll. Irritability and anger from stress were reported by 44 percent of Millennials, 36 percent of Boomers and 15 percent of Matures. And 19 percent of Millennials have been told they're suffering from depression, compared to 12 percent of Boomers and 11 percent of Matures. "Stress is a risk factor for both depression and anxiety," says Norman Anderson, psychologist and CEO of the APA. "We don't have data on the specific causes of depression and anxiety in this sample, but it does make sense scientifically that the Millennials who report higher levels of stress in their lives are also reporting higher levels of depression and anxiety."

In fact, it's reasonable to assume that higher levels of stress put the Millennials at higher risk for all sorts of destructive downstream consequences of stress. "Stress is a huge factor when we look at medical problems such as obesity, hypertension, diabetes, cardiac disease," says Dr. Nancy Snyderman, NBC's chief medical editor.

Over 25 million Americans already suffer from diabetes, and almost 70 million have high blood pressure, making them four times as likely to die from strokes and three times as likely to contract heart disease. And yet only 17 percent of Millennials believe their health care providers give them "a lot or a great deal" of support in managing their stress.

Not surprisingly, work is one of the biggest causes of stress, with 76 percent of Millennials reporting it as a significant stressor, compared to 62 percent of Boomers and 39 percent of Matures. "Many of these young people have come out of college or graduate school with horrendous student debt into a job market where there are not very many jobs," said Katherine Nordal of the APA. "This has put their life plans, probably, on hiatus."

The job numbers are indeed grim. According to Generation Opportunity, the unemployment rate for Millennials rose to 13.1 percent in January, up nearly 2 points from December. Among young African-Americans, it's a whopping 22.1 percent. And if you count those 18–29-year-olds who have given up and dropped out of the labor force, the overall youth unemployment rate stands at 16.2 percent.

And even for the lucky ones who are working, the picture remains bleak. According to the Economic Policy Institute, between 2000 and 2011 wages adjusted for inflation fell by over 11 percent for young high school grads and by 5.4 percent for young college grads. It doesn't help that, as a study by the Center for College Affordability found, 48 percent of working college grads are in jobs that don't require a college degree and 38 percent are in jobs that don't require a high school diploma. The report concluded that from 2010 to 2020, while 19 million college grads will be hitting the job market, the economy will add fewer than 7 million jobs requiring a college degree. That's a pretty serious—and stress-producing—gap.

Those numbers add context to President Obama's push for colleges and universities to increase enrollment and the number of degrees they grant. That's a great goal, but it highlights the fact that, to the extent that we even talk about jobs in our political conversation, we tend to talk about them without mentioning what kind of jobs. Nearly all the conversation on the first Friday of each month when the previous month's jobs numbers come out is about whether the number went up or down. But when there's an uptick—and don't get me wrong, an uptick is much better than a downtick—nobody talks about the context and conditions that have far more impact on people's actual lives, such as the fact that putting heavily indebted young adults to work at half the salary they had four years ago isn't exactly a way to win the future.

And any of those heavily indebted, heavily stressed-out Millennials listening to President Obama's State of the Union speech would not have gotten much stress relief. He did acknowledge the increasingly untenable cost of higher education—"Today, skyrocketing costs price too many young people out of a higher education, or saddle them with unsustainable debt"—and declared that he would "ask Congress to change the Higher Education Act so that affordability and value are included in determining which colleges receive certain types of federal aid." That sounds promising. If it ever happens. But it's hard to imagine Washington wielding that stick strongly enough to truly make quality higher education affordable. Even if college tuition stopped increasing right now and just stayed exactly where it is for the next decade—which we all know is not going to happen—it's still a huge problem.

A more promising approach would be to take strong action on student debt, which last year hit a record $1 trillion. The disastrous 2005 bankruptcy "reform" bill, which excluded student debt from being discharged in a bankruptcy, has created a new form of indentured servitude, in which tens of thousands of college grads live their entire lives with a crushing debt burden. Consumer Financial Protection Bureau head Richard Cordray seems open to reform, but actually doing it will take a sense of urgency. "It would be prudent to consider whether they [Congress] wish to modify the code," he told *The Huffington Post* in July.

Color me skeptical that, in the absence of being pushed, John Boehner is going to wake up one day with a burning urge to modify student debt regulations. It would be great to hear the president say something along the lines of: "If Congress won't act soon to protect future generations, I will." That's what he said about climate change during the State of the Union. That's certainly a vital issue, and so is "protecting future generations" from crushing student debt.

As for the perspective from the other side of the aisle? "Today, many graduates face massive student debt," acknowledged Senator Marco Rubio in his response to the State of the Union. So what's Rubio's solution to this massive student debt? "We must give students more information on the costs and benefits of the student loans they're taking out." Ah, yes, more information! Not exactly problem solved! All the more reason to include student debt in the president's "Things I Will Take Executive Action On" folder.

Even those lucky Millennials who land a decent job often face a workplace rife with destructive definitions of success. And, given how few jobs there are for them, it's the Millennials who have the least amount of leverage to push back. This is still a world in which, according to Tony Schwartz, author and CEO of The Energy Project, the prevailing work ethic is one in which "downtime is typically viewed as time wasted," and "rewards still accrue to those who push the hardest and most continuously over time." But, he adds, "that doesn't mean they're the most productive."

As Schwartz points out, more than one-third of American workers regularly eat lunch at their desks, and a recent study showed that an average of 9.2 vacation days were skipped last year. All this overwork inevitably leads to sleep deprivation, which costs American businesses over $63 billion a year—even though studies show that for each 10 hours of additional time off, productivity increased by 8 percent. "Strategic renewal," Schwartz writes, "including daytime workouts, short afternoon naps, longer sleep hours, more time away from the office and longer, more frequent vacations, boosts productivity, job performance and, of course, health."

But given the harsh job market they're entering, Millennials are incentivized to ignore the path to strategic renewal. Even so, we know they are looking for ways to lower their stress level. The APA study found that 62 percent of Millennials had tried to reduce their stress in the last five years. But only 29 percent of them, compared to 38 percent of Boomers and 50 percent of Matures, reported that they were doing a good or excellent job of it.

Amidst all this gloom, there is a sliver of sunshine: a recent Gallup poll that found that, even given the battered economy they're entering, 80 percent of Millennials were optimistic about their standard of living getting better.

Yes, as the cliché goes, the next generation is the future, etc. etc. etc. And, without fail, at some point, the future will be theirs. So here's hoping that as they advance through the ranks of the workplace, Millennials will channel that optimism to do themselves—and the generation after them (Generation Z?)—a favor by redefining success. Perhaps the mountain of stress they are currently scaling will give them the perspective to change what my generation has handed off to them.

Analyzing the Situation

1. Would you describe the situation in which Arianna Huffington writes as a medical situation or an economic situation? Why?

2. Who do you suppose Huffington sees as her audience for this piece? What leads you to such a conclusion?

3. What role do power and institution play in this situation?

Analyzing the Rhetoric

1. Given what Arianna Huffington argues in this essay, how do you respond to her introductory identification that calling millennials "millennials" is a form of branding? What does she mean by the term "branding"?

2. What is Arianna Huffington's strategy in beginning her essay discussing stress and health-related issues, but then shifting to address employment, economic, and political factors in the situation?

3. What does Arianna Huffington accomplish by maintaining a first-person position in her writing?

Discussing

1. Arianna Huffington's essay responds to a State of the Union address by a president of the United States and appears in one of the most-read news aggregators in the country. Huffington, that is, participates in a pretty high-level conversation. As college students, what do you think about this and similar high-level conversations about a situation in which you are players? How do President Obama's participation and Huffington's participation in this situation affect your participation in this situation?

2. Is Huffington talking about you? Do you see yourself and your peers accurately represented in Huffington's writing?

Writing

1. Huffington wrote her essay in response to President Barack Obama's 2013 State of the Union address, which you can easily locate online. Take some time to read Obama's speech and then write a response to the situation in which Obama's and Huffington's pieces participate and overlap.

2. Part of Huffington's position in her essay is to establish that there is a relationship between a college education and the expectation of the kind of job most college graduates expect on graduation. However, part of what she shows is that there won't be as many new jobs as there are college graduates. As a college student, how do you see the relationship between your academic work and your anticipation regarding employment after you graduate? What are your plans for using your degree to leverage employment opportunities? Write an essay that describes what your see as the relationship between your college experience and your employment expectations.

Student Loan Problems: One Third of Millennials Regret Going to College

Halah Touryalai

Halah Touryalai is a staff writer for *Forbes* magazine, where she reports about Wall Street, banking, and investment news. She explains that she has a "love–hate relationship with the world of finance. I am fascinated by the industry's power and influence around the globe, and the ingenuity of the people it employs. Not so much a fan of the lack of accountability when the system fails—which it often does."

Reprinted here is her May 2013 article about the effect of student loan debt on millennials.

Here's an indication of how burdensome student loans have become: About one-third of millennials say they would have been better off working, instead of going to college and paying tuition.

That's a according to a new Wells Fargo study which surveyed 1,414 millennials between the ages of 22 and 32. More than half of them financed their education through student loans, and many say if they had $10,000 the "first thing" they'd do is pay down their student loan or credit card debt.

That's no surprise when you consider student borrowing topped the $100 billion threshold for the first time in 2010, and total outstanding loans exceeded $1 trillion for the first time in 2011. Student loan debt now exceeds credit card debt in the U.S. which stands at about $798 billion.

Delinquencies are also on the rise. The number of borrowers who are at least 90 days late on student loan payments has jumped from 8.5% in 2011 to 11.7% today, according to a study by the New York Federal Reserve.

The problem sometimes is that not all college educations are worth their cost since they can't guarantee a high-paying job to help pay off that student debt. A report from the National Association of Consumer Bankruptcy Attorneys says the rising student debt problem can have a bad impact on the economy. Even in the best of economic times when jobs are plentiful, young people with considerable debt burdens end up delaying life-cycle events such as buying a car, purchasing a home, getting married and having children.

The other problem with student debt is a lack of financial education. The first major financial decision many students are making is with their college loans. It's a major decision and often times there's been little financial education, if any, that's been taught. The Wells Fargo survey found that 79% of millennials think personal finance should be taught in high school; basic investing, how to save for retirement and how loans work were the top three topics they "wished" they'd learned more about.

The Consumer Financial Protection Bureau found student debt has also affected home ownership in the country. Census data reveals that nearly 6 million Americans ages 25 to 34 lived with their parents in 2011, a sharp increase from 4.7 million in 2007.

The CFPB cited The National Association of Home Builders (NAHB) saying higher student debt burdens "impair the ability of recent college graduates to qualify for a loan." According to NAHB, high student loan debt has an impact on consumers' debt-to-income (DTI) ratio—an important metric for decisions about credit-worthiness in mortgage origination.

It's no wonder then that more than half (54%) of millennials from the Wells survey say debt is their biggest financial concern with 42% calling it "overwhelming."

Analyzing the Situation

1. How does reading Halah Touryalai's article affect how you see the situation in which she participates?

2. What role do institutional powers play in this situation? Which institutional structures appear to have more power, and which appear to have less?

3. Why do you suppose organizations like Wells Fargo conduct surveys like the one Halah Touryalai cites in her article?

Analyzing the Rhetoric

1. What role do Halah Touryalai's research and data play in her writing?

2. Relatively speaking, Touryalai's article is rather short compared to the complexity of the situation she addresses. As a reader, how do you respond to her brevity in terms of what you take away from her article and its position in the situation?

3. Throughout her article Touryalai refers to millennials with the third-person pronoun "they." What does she accomplish rhetorically by separating herself from "them"?

Discussing

1. So, if your teacher handed you $10,000 right now, what would you do with it after having read Touryalai's article? (And, no, your teacher is not going to actually hand you $10,000. This is a hypothetical situation. Your teacher probably has large student loans of her own and has opted to pursue a career of intellect instead of economic prosperity. Teaching writing is honorable and fulfilling, but rarely financially rewarding.)

2. Part of what we can take away from Touryalai's article is a better understanding of the relationship between the cost of a college education and the long-term effects of those costs. For the sake of discussion, though, let's add some other information to the situation:

> According to the United States Census Bureau, of the total U.S. population over the age of 18, just over 19 percent have some college experience with no degree earned, less than 4 percent earn occupational associate's degrees, just over 4½ percent of the population earn academic associate's degrees, and less than 18 percent of the

population earn bachelor's degrees. That's a total of just less than 46% of the U.S. population over the age of 18 having college interaction at some level. According to a May 2004 report by the Education Trust, in 2001, 58 percent of the U.S. population enrolled in college on graduation from high school, though 25 percent of those will never complete their degrees. Perhaps more telling, though, are enrollment rates of the world population. Worldwide, there has been tremendous growth in the numbers of students enrolling in tertiary educational programs—including colleges, universities, technical institutes, polytechnics, community colleges, distance education centers, nursing schools, teacher-training facilities, and many more. Despite such significant growth globally, we should acknowledge that given the United Nations Population Division's estimate for world population in 2005 of 6,514,751,000, just over 2 percent of the world population enters into tertiary educational programs.

With these numbers in mind, how do you respond to Halah Touryalai's article and to the situation in which she participates?

Writing

1. Part of Halah Touryalai's objective in this piece is to show that student loan debt has long-term effects on the economy. In showing this, she starts to establish a view of the situation and the rhetorical ecology of the student debt situation. Using the connections Touryalai introduces as a starting point, write a document that expands the view of the ecology of this situation and shows readers how this ecology might unfold from student debt loan.

2. Halah Touryalai's article is relatively short. Ask ten of your peers who are not enrolled in your class and who are not reading the piece for another class to read the article. Develop a ten-question survey about how your peers respond to Touryalai's article. Using the information you gather through your survey, write a document that explains how your respondents view Touryalai's position and information.

3. Given that data like that Halah Touryalai reports change over time, and given that Touryalai's article was published in May 2013, how has the situation changed since she wrote the article—or has it? Conduct some research to identify current information about the things Touryalai addresses, and then write a document that conveys what you have learned. Compare your newer data with Touryalai's and address what changes have occurred, if any, and what these changes or lack of changes suggest about the situation.

Are Millennials a "Lost Generation"?

Nicole Goodkind and Lauren Lyster

Nicole Goodkind is an associate producer at Yahoo!, where she also writes and reports for Yahoo! Finance. In the past she has worked as a production assistant and writer's assistant at Fuse TV, and as an intern with the *TODAY Show*. Lauren Lyster is a co-host of the "Daily Ticker" on Yahoo! Finance, where she interviews figures from the financial world.

She is also host of "Hot Stock Minute," a daily pre-market show live from the Nasdaq Market site. She has offered financial commentary on CNBC, ABC, Fox, and HuffPost Live.

The reading reprinted here was originally published by Nicole Goodkind on the Yahoo! Finance blog. Included in the post is a video interview that Lauren Lyster conducts with Gerald Celente, an American trend forecaster and publisher of *Trends Journal*, which analyzes and forecasts political, socioeconomic, and financial trends. You can find the video on the Yahoo! pages by searching for the title of the blog post reprinted here: "Are Millennials a "Lost Generation"?"

It's hard out there for a Millennial. While the national unemployment rate has kept firm at 7.9%, the jobless rate for Millennials (or the 80 million Americans born

LAUREN LYSTER
YAHOO! FINANCE

GERALD CELENTE
THE TRENDS JOURNAL

between 1980 and 2000) continues to increase, reaching the alarming rate of 13.1% in January. Millennials now have the highest generational unemployment in the United States.

The Pew Center calls Millennials the "boomerang generation," because nearly 40% of all Americans between the ages of 18 and 34 still live at home with their parents; numbers this high haven't been seen in over 70 years. And the boomerang trend is expected to continue or even worsen. The National Bureau of Economic Research reports that those who graduate during a recession will earn 10% less over a decade of work. Unfortunately for Millennials, research shows that 70% of overall wage growth occurs in the first 10 years of one's career.

But those who do manage to find jobs are also struggling. Young people with high school degrees have seen their inflation-adjusted wages decline by 11.1%; college graduates have seen a smaller, yet significant, decline of 5.4%, according to the Economic Policy Institute.

As a result, Millennials aren't taking on debt or making economy-boosting purchases. Young people aren't buying houses or cars and they're delaying marriage and children. According to The Pew Center, home ownership amongst young people has fallen from 40% in 2007 to only 34% in 2011. 73% of young households owned or leased a car in 2007 compared with only 66% in 2011.

Many have also begun to wonder if college is worth the cost—outstanding student loan debt now tops $1 trillion. In 2011, two-thirds of college seniors graduated with an average of $26,000 in student loan debt.

Gerald Celente, Editor and Publisher of the *Trends Journal*, believes the depressed livelihoods of today's younger generation—"generation eff'ed" as he refers to it in a recent edition of his magazine—will lead to a revolution of sorts.

"The new frontiers are going to be the burnt out urban centers, so it might be the Millennials who become the homesteaders, farmers, and gardeners of Detroit, or Camden," says Celente. "When people lose everything and have nothing left to lose, they lose it. And you're going to start seeing a lot of young people losing it in a lot of different ways."

These are startling statistics and advocates have run with them calling Millennials a "lost generation," attempting to parlay unrest amongst America's youth into some sort of rallying cry or at least attempting to appeal to them as a voting bloc.

Yes, the numbers are staggering but calling Millennials a lost generation and telling young people to stop attending college seems alarmist at best.

While the unemployment rate for young workers is nearly twice as high as the overall rate, it still pays to stay in school. Between 2011 and 2012 the unemployment rate for high school graduates was 31.1% while the unemployment rate for college graduates was 9.4%, a significant difference.

Of course young people have a harder time finding employment than their adult contemporaries; they have less experience and are new to searching for work. In both recessions and expansions young unemployment is historically nearly double the national rate.

Millennials aren't the new homesteaders, they're not moving in droves to abandoned urban centers like Detroit to farm and start art galleries. This view of young Americans applies largely to those with liberal arts educations and money to fall back on.

Analyzing the Situation

1. Why do you suppose Yahoo! Finance takes up this situation as something to write about?

2. In the video interview, Gerald Celente says that "this is the first generation of modern Americans where they're looking to the future and it being darker than the past." Given Celente's position as a speaker in this situation, how does his statement affect the overall situation?

3. In what ways does location come into play in this situation?

Analyzing the Rhetoric

1. What is the relationship between the written text and the video portion of the text? Does this relationship change when reading the written portion here in a textbook and watching the video online versus reading the written portion online in the same location as the video segment? If it changes, how does it change? What effect does reading/seeing these parts of the article together or separately have?

2. Which part of this selection is more informative, the written segment or the video segment? What makes each piece effective, and what distinguishes between them?

3. In watching the video segment of this article, how do you respond to Gerald Celente's attire? Does his attire affect his ethos? In what ways?

Discussing

1. According to the video segment of this report, the average student graduates with $27,000 of college debt. Given your position in this situation as college students, how do you respond to this figure?

2. Gerald Celente argues that millennials will need to become the "new homesteaders," reclaiming the decrepit and burnt-out urban centers in places like Detroit and Camden. Discuss how you respond to Celente's comments about this kind of resourcefulness.

Writing

1. "Are Millennials a 'Lost Generation'?" claims that "while the unemployment rate for young workers is nearly twice as high as the overall rate, it still pays to stay in school. Between 2011 and 2012 the unemployment rate for high school graduates was 31.1% while the unemployment rate for college graduates was 9.4%, a significant difference." Given this information and the information in the article that shows millennials as leaving college with $27,000 of college loan debt, is a college degree worth the investment of time and money? Write an essay in response to this question.

2. This article poses a question in its title: "Are Millennials a 'Lost Generation'?" Write an essay that answers this question. Conduct research to support your stance in response to the question.

Thinking and Writing about the Chapter

Reflection

Now that you've read some selections in which writers/speakers address the condition of being millennial, how do you feel about how these writers/speakers characterize the millennial generation? Look back to the journal entry or blog post you wrote in response to the prompt at the beginning of this chapter. Have these readings affected how you might respond now that you have read these selections? Write a new entry or post that addresses how these readings affect or don't affect how you feel about others talking about "your generation."

Discussion Threads

1. How would you describe the ecology of the readings found in this chapter? That is, other than addressing the topic of millennials, how are these pieces connected and where do their connections lead beyond just these documents?

2. Does when you are born matter? Do people born in relative chronological proximity share generational characteristics? Are there differences between generations?

3. There are a lot of bleak predictions for millennials in these readings. Discuss how you and your peers respond to these negative predictions.

Collaboration

1. In many ways, the representations of millennials in these readings limit the view of millennials to a specifically U.S. view. Working in small groups, learn about how millennials in another country are perceived and addressed. Then, collaboratively, write a document about millennials in the country you selected.

Writing

1. Several of the readings in this chapter indicate that millennials, or Generation Y, are a demographic distinct from Generation X and Baby Boomers. The readings in this chapter address various problems millennials face, but Generation X and Baby Boomers faced problems, too. Pick one of the pre–Generation Y generations and learn how those generations were talked about in the media and what problems they faced collectively. Write a document that explains the problems of one of these other two named generations.

2. In many ways, the readings in this chapter are limited. They are limited by, for the most part, their reliance on writing rather than visual media. They are limited in their focus. They are limited in their perspectives. Take some time to consider what these pieces, either individually or collectively, don't say about millennials. Then make an original video with the theme "Millennials: What the Media Isn't Talking About."

Local Situation

Many of the selections found in this chapter rely on some rather broad definitions of who make up the millennial generation, what characteristics they have in common, and what problems they face. Many of the details of the millennial situation vary based on an array of factors: geography, economic background, educational background, and so on. It may very well be that none of the descriptions of millennials in these readings accurately reflect what you observe in millennials. These readings may be understated or overstated. But they do provide some criteria on which to develop your own evaluation of millennials on your campus. Take some time to analyze and evaluate characteristics like student loan rates for students on your campus, job placement information, and student attitudes. Then write a document in which you provide an evaluation of your local view of millennials.

Editing Writing

28 | Correcting Errors

NO FISHING/NO ADMITTANCE TO NON — SYNDICAT MEMBERS TACKLE WILL BE SEIZED TRESSPASSERS PROSERCUTED ZERO TOLLERANCE

Learning Objectives

28.1 Identify what constitutes correctness in writing

28.2 Describe the relationship between good writing and correctness

28.3 Apply strategies to correct your writing

Before you read this chapter

As a reader, what kinds of writing errors get your attention? How do you respond when you notice an error in something you are reading? Why do you identify errors as errors? In your journal or blog, write about how you respond to errors in texts that you are reading.

From 1996 to 2000 Lynn Truss was a well-known sports writer for the *Times* newspaper in London. In 2002, she wrote a small number of radio spots for the BBC called "Cutting a Dash" that addressed how to correctly use punctuation. Her objective had been to provide an informative and entertaining program; what she ended up with was the foundation for a book she would publish in 2006: *Eats, Shoots & Leaves: The Zero Tolerance Approach to Punctuation*. The book professes a no-nonsense approach to punctuation and shows what can happen when punctuation is used incorrectly. The book became a *New York Times* best seller.

In the introduction to the book, Truss explains that when it comes to correct punctuation and correct grammar, "everywhere one looks, there are signs of ignorance and indifference." But, she laments, of course, the world doesn't care, and when any of us try to alert others to an incorrectly punctuated sign, advertisement, newspaper article, or other text, we are usually met with a reply of "get a life." But Truss reminds us that although we may dismiss daily sightings of signs that read "We dont accept bill's greater than $50," "We've made to much bread," "sorry are atm is not working," or "Computer Repair's," lack of correctness does have its ramifications. Truss's point is that even the minutest deviation from correctness affects meaning, and meaning is important.

Correctness

28.1 Identify what constitutes correctness in writing

Simply put, correctness refers to getting it right, to showing no mistakes. The reason correctness is important is fairly easy to understand: readers expect sentences to be error free; they expect writing to be "correct." Correctness, of course, isn't universal; it is situational. What might be considered correct in one situation might not be in another. What might be considered correct when writing a blog post, a user comment, or a text message might not be considered correct when writing an academic essay, a newspaper article, or an online product review. Correct writing, then, is not just about knowing rules—it's about understanding the situation.

As college writers, we have to acknowledge that "the rules" and correctness are, indeed, important, and that many readers will evaluate your writing based strictly on how correct your writing is because they understand correctness to be indicative of what is and is not "good writing." By no means does correctness alone imply superior writing; instead, we should understand correctness in writing to indicate that a writer understands the constraints of correctness within the situation. The only way to understand the constraints of correctness is to learn them; they are not innate, even to native speakers of a language. Native English speakers, for example, do not naturally know the rules of standard written academic English; they must learn them. As writers learn situational rules for correctness, they internalize them, making them part of how they write and what they value in their writing. Correctness does not indicate intellectual superiority; nor does it necessarily indicate superior writing. Correctness indicates a writer's effort to recognize a situation's constraints of correctness and generate writing that adheres to those constraints.

Nonetheless, in many rhetorical situations, readers expect writers to adhere to standards of correctness. Consider for example in your own experiences how often teachers have pointed out when your writing is "incorrect." Note, too, how teachers rarely point out when a sentence is "correct." This is because correctness is an expectation of the academic writing situation, not a noteworthy moment. Likewise, correctness is a kind of quantifiable feature that teachers can concretely point to and identify a need for improvement, unlike issues of clarity or style, which can often be more subjective and difficult to explain.

Correctness and Style

Many people believe that correctness facilitates clarity and that clear writing is good writing. Writing clearly is a matter of politeness, a matter of caring enough about readers to provide them with clear sentences so they do not have to struggle to figure out what the writer intends. But what makes writing clear? Certainly we can say that clear writing is good or easy to read, but as Joseph M. Williams points out, saying so doesn't actually describe the writing; it describes how the reader feels about the writing. Writing is clear when a reader thinks it is clear. Thus, writing clearly depends on careful consideration of audience and situation.

Ultimately, clarity amounts to a kind of situational style. Clarity in a lab report differs from clarity in a personal essay, which differs from clarity in a research paper. Simply put, a writing style is the choice a writer makes in how to write; style is how writers put together sentences and groups of sentences. The difficulty is that there are no rules for style; style is subjective. However, every rhetorical situation provides some clues as to what styles might or might not be effective. Academic writing situations, for example, generally require that writers adhere to a particular kind of grammatical, mechanical correctness. Yet, even within academic writing situations, styles may vary according to the specifics of the situation. In an argumentative research paper in a humanities class, using passive voice may be considered incorrect, whereas using passive verbs in scientific writing like a lab report would likely be deemed correct. Of course, correct writing doesn't guarantee a readable style; a correct sentence may still be unclear to a reader. Thus, the connection between correctness and style can be attributed to the situation and the audience. There are two maxims writers should be alert to in academic writing situations:

1. *Correctness counts.* Writers writing in academic situations need to adhere to the rules of standard academic written English, including grammar rules, punctuation rules, diction rules, and citation rules.
2. *Rules change.* Even though we can say that writers writing in college need to adhere to the rules of standard academic written English, those rules are not consistent across academic rhetorical situations. Thus, writers need to learn the

nuances of rules and acceptable styles for the various disciplines and academic situations in which they write.

What this means, then, is that readers—like teachers and peers—understand correctness to reflect a writer's understanding of the academic writing situation. Readers are likely to interpret a writer's failure to adhere to those expectations as signifying the writer as not an authentic part of the situation.

Correctness and Authority (Ethos)

28.2 Describe the relationship between good writing and correctness

Ethos is a writer's appeal to character and credibility. Writers establish credibility and authority through the tone of their language, the accuracy of their information, their reputations, the authenticity they convey, their trustworthiness, their appearance as well meaning, the presentation and medium of their writing, and the correctness of their writing. Often, readers believe that correctness reflects the writer's ability (or inability) or even the writer's attention and care. If correctness counts in academic writing, it counts because readers in academic situations use correctness to judge a writer's authority to contribute to the situation. Lack of correctness—poor grammar, misspelled words, misused words, and so on—often signals readers that the writer does not have the full authority to participate in the situation simply because the writer does not display full knowledge of the situation's constraints and expectations.

Academic readers generally interpret writing that does not meet correctness expectations to suggest one of two things about the writer (ethos): either the writer doesn't know any better (an attribution of ignorance) or the writer doesn't care enough about the writing to pay attention to the errors (an attribution of apathy). Neither of these are the characteristics any of us want readers to attribute to us as writers or as people—particularly when the reader is assigning your grades and responding to your ethos in ways that will affect your life in very real ways. To create and maintain an ethos of authority, adhere to the rules of correctness for the situation.

The Incorrectness of Plagiarism

Plagiarism—wrongfully appropriating someone else's words, ideas, thoughts, or expressions—is a form of academic dishonesty. That is, plagiarizing is not correct within academic writing situations. In college, plagiarism is considered a violation of academic standards; college-level research respects scholarly values and builds ethically on the work of others. Part of this ethic requires that writers and researchers always acknowledge when they rely on others' ideas, approaches, words, and methods. Failure to do so is incorrect in college writing.

In this regard, plagiarism contributes to a writer's ethos in three ways:

First, academic situations usually define *plagiarism* in relation to whether writers "intentionally" represent someone else's work or ideas as their own. In many situations, plagiarism is seen as akin to theft and the plagiarist as akin to a thief—an attribution that negatively affects the writer's ethos.

Second, in some instances of plagiarism, readers and writers may acknowledge that the writer plagiarized because the writer did not know standards for research and citation and that the plagiarism was "unintentional." In such instances, though, the plagiarism is still understood as a sign of incorrectness and the ethos of the writer interpreted to be one of ignorance and incompetence—also an attribution that negatively affects a writer's ethos.

Third, in other situations, readers consider plagiarism to indicate a writer's apathy. Readers interpret plagiarism to suggest that the writer did not care enough about the writing to invest an adequate amount of energy and time in the writing, opting instead to simply present others' words and work as her own in lieu of doing the work. In such situations, the plagiarism is understood as indicative of laziness and perhaps a lack of regard for or an attitude of disrespect for the situation, such as the assignment—also not the ethos a writer desires in college situations. Keep in mind, too, that how you cite your research is a matter of correctness, and in many college writing situations, readers expect writers to adhere to specific standards and styles for identifying source materials. Often, these standards are disciplinary, and you should always confirm what citation style readers expect in the situations in which you write (APA in many social sciences and MLA in the humanities).

Strategies for Adhering to Correctness

28.3 Apply strategies to correct your writing

Correctness is not innate. For every rhetorical situation you enter, you will need to be sure you understand what the rules of correctness are. Once you know the rules, you will need to ensure that you have applied them and that your writing exhibits correctness. The following strategies can help, and since checking for correctness takes time and focus, you will find that the more times you conscientiously employ them, the more you will internalize them as part of your writing process. Once you develop awareness of the errors you make consistently, you can focus on those parts of your writing.

Strategies for Ensuring Correctness

Strategy	Application
Look stuff up	Grammar handbooks, style guides, and online writing guides all provide explanations and examples of the rules of correctness. Use these resources.
Distance yourself	Our familiarity with our own writing usually results in our reading what we think the writing should say to an audience as opposed to what it actually says. Learn to defamiliarize yourself from your own writing. This can be a difficult task, particularly when the time we have in which to write is limited by situational constraints like due dates, relevance, and timeliness. Consider writing responses to assignments as soon as they are made so that you can take a day or two away from the writing before you read it for correctness. Write early; read often.

Strategy	Application
Break it up	Don't try to read your entire document for correctness at once. It is likely that your attention will waiver. Read for correctness in small chunks, a paragraph or two at a time.
Consider the situation	The only way writing can be correct is if it is correct for a specific situation. Make sure you know what the situation considers correct.
Consider audience	Be certain that you understand what your audience anticipates regarding correctness. Write for your audience.
Consider your sentences	Read each of your sentences independently. Ask yourself questions about the sentences: what punctuation marks do I use in this sentence? What are the rules for using those punctuation marks? Does my sentence adhere to those rules? What parts of speech do I use in this sentence? What are the rules for using those parts of speech? Do I use those parts of speech according to those rules?
Look for patterns	Do I repeat sentence patterns? Do I rely on passive voice? Do I use abstract or empty subjects? Is my tone consistent?
Consider words	Do I use words correctly? Have I used words whose meanings I am unclear about? Have I used words that I would not usually use? Do I use words that sound overly simple? Do I use words that sound overly complicated? Do I use specific terms consistently? Do I explain key terms efficiently?
Consider grammar	Check verbs, subjects, adjectives, and pronouns for agreement. Check adjectives and adverbs for modification. You may want to start by confirming that you know the basic grammar rules of correctness. For example, you may start by asking, "What are the rules of subject/verb agreement?" and then asking, "Do I adhere to one of those rules in each sentence?" Do the same for as many grammar rules as you can.
Consider punctuation	There are thirteen commonly-used punctuation marks in English: periods, question marks, exclamation points, commas, semicolons, colons, dashes, hyphens, parentheses, brackets, apostrophes, quotation marks, and ellipses (there are a few others, but these are the most commonly used). Start with one and check to be sure you have used it correctly each time you use it in your writing. Then do the same for each of the marks that appear in your writing.
Consider spelling	Read your document word by word, carefully pausing with each word to be sure you have spelled the word correctly. Remember: spell checkers don't always get it right, particularly when the situation in which you write calls for a specific or peculiar spelling.
Read out loud	Often we read what we want to read in our own writing rather than what they actually display. However, if you slow down and read your writing out loud, often hearing the sound of your writing can reveal instances in which you stumble in reading due to a point of incorrectness. Slowing down and reading out loud forces you to be more alert to what your writing actually says.
Involve readers	Ask someone to help you by reading your writing and identifying issues of correctness to which you should be alert.
Record your errors	As you read your writing for issues of correctness, keep a record of errors you make. Then, look for consistencies over time and multiple writing projects. Knowing that you make consistent errors will allow you to focus on those parts of your writing and work to be more alert to your writing's correctness.

Summary

Correctness refers to getting it right. Readers expect writing to be "correct." Correctness isn't universal; it is situational. Correctness is a way of identifying that the constraints of a situation include the grammatical and mechanical rules by which a writer must abide. Correct writing is about understanding the situation. Part of the reason teachers emphasize correctness in college writing is that many people believe that correctness facilitates clarity and that clear writing is good writing. Plagiarism can be thought of as a matter of correctness. Correctness is not innate. For every rhetorical situation you enter, you will need to be sure you understand what the rules of correctness are. Checking for correctness takes time and focus.

Chapter Review

1. What does it mean to say that a piece of writing is "correct"?

2. Why is correctness important?

3. Why do teachers emphasize correctness in college writing?

4. What is the role of correctness in establishing ethos?

5. How does plagiarism relate to ethos?

6. What are ten strategies for adhering to correctness?

Thinking and Writing about the Chapter

Reflection

Now that you have had a chance to learn more about correctness, how will you approach correctness in your own writing? How will you think about instances of incorrectness you identify in others' writing?

Discussion Threads

1. Thus far in your academic career, how have official readers—like teachers—addressed correctness? Do they assess your writing for correctness? Do they teach you grammar, mechanics, or other issues of correctness?

2. How do you respond to the idea that plagiarism can be seen as a matter of correctness in specific academic situations?

Collaboration

For the next writing assignment you have due, trade final papers with another student before submitting them. Then read each other's documents for correctness. Once you have identified grammatical errors in each other's documents, return the papers. Then discuss the errors each has made, making certain each participant understands how the reader is reading the writing in light of correctness.

Local Situation

How does your college or university generally address issues of correctness? Are there published, set parameters about expectations that identify how correctness should be approached? Where are they located? Does your institution or specific programs/departments within the college require adherence to a specific set of rules? Do they require using a specific handbook or style guide?

29

Writing Sentences

Learning Objectives

29.1 Understand the importance and ethics of clarity in sentences

29.2 Apply guidelines for writing clear sentences

29.3 Use correct grammar to write clear sentences

Clarity

Ludwig Wittgenstein, one of the world's most influential philosophers who studied and wrote about language, once said, "whatever can be thought can be thought clearly; whatever can be written can be written clearly." Similarly, writing specialist Joseph M. Williams has famously said "it is good to write clearly, and anyone can do it." *Clearly*, of course, can mean a lot of things. What may be clear to one reader may not be to another. Writing clearly requires coordination between writers and readers. Writing clearly requires that writers write for their audiences and write for specific situations. Clarity, like correctness, that is, is always situational.

Readers want to read writing that conveys information clearly. Readers do not want to be confused by or unsure of what writing tells them. Unclear writing can distract readers, can cause readers to lose interest, and can confuse readers. Unclear writing is unsuccessful writing.

In order to write clear texts, writers have to focus on the clarity of a text's parts, namely its sentences. Being able to write clear sentences has always been important to writing prose, and the move into the digital age has made doing so even more important. Because writing now works with and competes with visual elements to convey meaning, successful writers need to write clear, concise sentences to deliver information efficiently. As readers negotiate between words and visuals, they need sentences that clearly contribute to the flow of a text and to conveying needed information. This chapter focuses on writing sentences and on understanding how sentences work so you can better control how you write clear sentences. This chapter provides guidelines for writing clear sentences in academic writing situations, but the guidelines can also be used to craft sentences for other public and personal situations. Much of this chapter provides guidelines, strategies, and general rules, but like all guidelines, strategies, and rules, you will need to carefully adapt each one to the situations in which you write.

Clarity and Authority (Ethos)

Ethos is a writer's appeal to character and credibility. Writers establish credibility a number of ways, including through their tone, their accuracy, their reputations, their authenticity, their trustworthiness, their presentation, and their correct use of punctuation and grammar. But, perhaps more than any of these, the clarity of a writer's writing affects how readers interpret writers' credibility. Writing that is unclear reflects poorly on readers' perceptions of writers. Readers interpret unclear writing as indicative of a writer's lack of attention, lack of interest, or lack of ability. In college-level writing, clarity is particularly important because many readers—particularly teachers—read writing to assess the writer's comprehension of information. Teachers frequently interpret unclear writing to show unclear thinking or lack of understanding of a subject. Unclear writing, then, is read as displaying a writer's lack of knowing.

Academic readers generally interpret unclear writing to suggest one of three things about the writer (ethos): either the writer doesn't have a clear understanding of the material (an attribution of ignorance), the writer doesn't care enough about the writing to revise for clarity (an attribution of apathy), or the writer doesn't know how to write well enough to write clearly (an attribution of inexperience and ignorance). None of these are the characteristics any of us want readers to attribute to us as writers or as people—particularly when the reader is assigning your grades and responding to your ethos in ways that will affect your life in very real ways.

This being the case, all college writers should recognize that clarity conveys authority, but clarity is not automatic. Every writer must learn to write clearly in the given situation, and in college writing, you should anticipate that all readers—especially your teachers—always read clarity as reflective of your ethos. To create and maintain an ethos of authority, pay particular attention to clarity and revise specifically for clarity. Unfortunately, clarity is a truly subjective characteristic. What might be clear for one reader may not be for another. However, there are specific guidelines you can adapt to most writing situations that will help you produce clear writing.

29.1 Understand the importance and ethics of clarity in sentences

Clarity and Ethics

As noted, unclear writing can distract readers, can cause readers to lose interest, and can confuse readers. Although writers certainly don't want to distract, bore, or confuse their readers, unclear writing can also be thought of as unethical writing. Unclear writing can obfuscate, can make things obscure, can hide details, and can present information out of focus. Whether intentionally unclear or not, unclear writing can deceive readers. Unclear writing clouds meaning. Writing clearly, then, is not only a rhetorical choice but also an ethical choice. Ethical writers understand that readers not only need clear writing, but also deserve clear writing.

Writers should understand that the ethics of one's writing contributes directly to the writer's ethos. Unethical writing betrays the audience's trust, and, in turn, casts the writer as untrustworthy. Writers, of course, can choose to be deceptive and duplicitous as easily as they can choose to be honest and forthcoming. Writers can choose to write in overly complex language to confuse, just as they can choose to write in clear, direct language to explain. Understanding *how* to write clearly does not guarantee that a writer will write ethically, but it will provide better tools for choosing to. Writing clearly does not guarantee readers will clearly understand, but doing so improves the likelihood that they will.

29.2 Apply guidelines for writing clear sentences

Guidelines for Writing Clear Sentences

Recognize How Sentences Work

It's one thing to write a sentence; it's another to understand how that sentence works. In many ways, this is the distinction between a professional and an amateur: an amateur may know *how* to do something well, but a professional knows *why* she does it well. Part of becoming a better writer in any situation includes understanding how the parts of writing work together. Most successful writers understand that clear writing requires making choices about how each sentence works and understanding how the parts of a sentence work together to form clear writing. That is, writers should understand the parts of a sentence and how those parts work to form the sentence.

Interestingly, communications experts have traditionally referred to the parts of a sentence as the "parts of speech" a phrase reminiscent of oral culture. Traditionally, experts have identified eight parts of speech:

Part of Speech	Function
Verbs	Assert the actions or state of being of the subject
Nouns	Name the person, place, thing, or idea that the sentence is about
Pronouns	Replace nouns or other pronouns to provide stylistic options in a sentence
Adjectives	Modify nouns or pronouns by describing, identifying, or qualifying
Adverbs	Modify verbs or adjectives by indicating location, cause, time, or degree
Prepositions	Link nouns, pronouns, and phrases, usually by indicating a spatial relationship between the linked objects
Conjunctions	Connect words, phrases, and clauses
Interjections	Convey emotion or response and are generally not directly bound to any other word in the sentence

Sentences are made up of these parts of speech, but because sentences are written and we "see" sentences, we have to include a ninth part:

Part of Speech	Function
Punctuation	Written symbols used to indicate parts of a sentence and direct readers in how to read and understand that sentence

Knowing how to identify, use, and discuss each of these parts can help you become more adept at writing clear sentences.

Use Active Verbs

Action verbs move readers through a sentence. Readers are more likely to follow the meaning of a sentence when an active verb clearly reflects the action of a subject. Passive verbs can render the subject of a sentence unclear and can potentially obscure who or what was responsible for an action:

PASSIVE VERB: The lesson was not explained well.

ACTIVE VERB: The professor did not explain the lesson well.

Passive verbs are usually constructed by using a form of "to be" verbs. *To be* verbs express states of being, not action. Passive verb forms, though, can be useful and expected in many situations. Some forms of scientific writing, for example, commonly use passive constructions to emphasize results.

Use Agent-Action Patterns

Just as action verbs contribute to sentence clarity, so do strong, identifiable agents. The agent is the person or thing that performs the action in a sentence. In an agent-action sentence, an identifiable agent performs a strong action.

Avoid absent-agent sentences: readers need and want agents. They need to know what the sentence is about. Many passive verb forms eliminate agents from sentences, confusing readers and deferring responsibility for the action.

ABSENT AGENT: A decision was rendered about the case.

STRONG AGENT: The jury rendered a decision about the case.

STRONG AGENT: The dean rendered a decision about the case.

Notice that the absent agent in the first sentence can be replaced in a number of ways, each of which conveys different information.

Avoid abstractions as agents: often, beginning writers will use passive verb forms in conjunction with abstract nouns, what are often called "dummy subjects." Dummy subjects are vague references that do not provide a clear sense of who or what the agent of the sentence is:

ABSTRACT AGENT: There are a number of ways to begin the essay.

STRONG AGENT: You can begin the essay a number of ways.

ABSTRACT AGENT: It has been said that things can only get better.

STRONG AGENT: Dean Hardin says things can only get better.

Eliminate Wordy Verbs

Beginning writers often try to elevate the sound of their writing by making their verbs more complex than they need to be. Instead of complicating verb structures by adding words to your verbs, simplify them whenever possible.

WORDY VERB		SIMPLIFIED
are suggestive of	→	suggest
has knowledge of	→	knows
makes use of	→	uses
makes a decision	→	decides
takes into consideration	→	considers

Move from Familiar to New

Sentences tend to be clearer to readers when they flow from the familiar to the new. Readers are familiar with two aspects of sentences: information and words. Deliver familiar information before new information; present familiar words and concepts before new ones:

I often wonder if I should throw away my older video games and just keep the newer ones. I know I might want to play them **[familiar information]** again, but they take up storage space and memory **[new information, new concepts]**. I don't want to run out of memory **[repeated word, old information]** by storing games I don't play anymore **[new information]**.

Notice that the second sentence begins by reminding readers that it conveys information related to the previous sentence by using the pronoun "they" which refers to the previous sentence. Then the second sentence introduces new information about storage space and memory. The third sentence uses the familiarity of memory introduced in the preceding sentence, and then introduces new information about games I don't play.

Keep Sentences Concise

Sentences are clearer when they get right to the point. Concision certainly implies writing shorter sentences, but concision is really about choosing the most efficient words in a sentence. Readers tend to lose focus when extra words make a sentence difficult to follow. Readers are more likely to understand sentences when writers use just enough words to convey what they mean.

Delete Meaningless Words

Writers often use excessive words because we are used to hearing them in spoken communication. However, those words don't often convey pertinent information and can clutter a written sentence. Words like:

actually	basically	certain	generally
given	individual	kind of	particularly
practically	really	virtually	usually

> **EXAMPLE:** Innovation actually requires certain patterns that usually involve a kind of chain of particular events.
>
> **REVISE FOR CONCISION:** Innovation requires patterns of events.

Delete Repetitive Words

Writers often think they are clarifying their sentences by pairing words together. However, many of these pairs often duplicate meanings, rendering one word redundant and adding unnecessary words to a sentence. Some redundant pairs include:

full and complete	hope and trust	any and all
true and accurate	each and every	basic and fundamental
hope and desire	first and foremost	various and sundry
leaps and bounds	bits and pieces	tried and true

WORDY: First and foremost, we need to be sure that each and every one of the students has a full and complete set of lab materials.

CONCISE: First, we need to be sure that each student has a complete set of lab materials.

Replace a Phrase with a Word

Writers often make sentences wordy and unclear by using many words to convey what a single word might convey more clearly.

WORDY: My teacher has made available several kinds of things to help the class learn a lot.

CONCISE: My teacher provides many resources to make the class educational.

Change Negatives to Affirmatives

When writers express a concept in a negative form, readers must calculate what the writer really means. Negative forms often require more words than do affirmative forms:

NEGATIVE		AFFIRMATIVE
not different	→	same
not careful	→	careless
not allow	→	prevent
not many	→	few
not stop	→	continue
not the same	→	different
not notice	→	overlook
not often	→	rarely
not include	→	omit

NEGATIVE/WORDY: Do not write in the negative.

AFFIRMATIVE/CONCISE: Write in the affirmative.

NEGATIVE/WORDY: Not many of the students realized they should not include a second answer to question 2 and not stop before completing question 3.

AFFIRMATIVE/CONCISE: Few of the students realized they should omit a second answer to question 2 and should continue to question 3.

Delete Useless Adjectives and Adverbs

Writers often think they improve the sound of their writing by adding adjectives and adverbs as often as they can. They believe that doing so adds details. However, adverbs and adjectives often only provide unnecessary information that clutters a sentence. Writing expert William Zinsser, in fact, says that adverbs are unnecessary. Horror writer Stephen King has famously said "the road to hell is paved with adverbs."

WORDY: Our teacher adamantly insisted that we carefully conduct detailed research to move beyond our limited and unsophisticated understanding of the frustrating economic situation.

CONCISE: Our teacher insisted that we conduct research to move beyond our understanding of the economic situation.

Avoid Noun Strings

Sometimes writers string nouns together to modify other nouns. Some familiar phrases like *space shuttle*, *student center*, and *capitol building* need nouns to modify nouns, but generally speaking, it is best to avoid noun strings because they can be difficult to understand.

NOUN STRING: In our economics class, we had to outline the most recent government agriculture economic stimulus plan.

REVISED: In our economics class, we had to outline the government's most recent plan to stimulate agricultural economies.

Reduce Numbers of Prepositional Phrases

Prepositional phrases, especially when strung together, can disrupt a sentence's rhythm and can confuse readers. Reduce the numbers of prepositional phrases you use by converting the objects of prepositional phrases into subjects or adjectives.

EXAMPLE: My friend had to pay $600 for the cost of the lab materials at his school as part of his student fees.

REVISED: My friend had to pay his school's $600 student fee for the cost of lab materials.

Avoid Nominalizations

Nominalizations are nouns that are derived from verbs or adjectives. Nominalizations can contribute to wordy sentences and can change how readers understand the sequence of actions.

WITH NOMINALIZATION: The restaurant offers the combination of several Asian cuisines.

WITHOUT NOMINALIZATION: The restaurant combines several Asian cuisines.

Verb nominalizations:

NOUN		VERB
Nominalization	⟶	Nominalize
Movement	⟶	Move
Combination	⟶	Combine
Reaction	⟶	React

Adjective nominalizations:

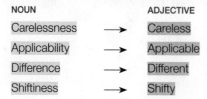

NOUN		ADJECTIVE
Carelessness	→	Careless
Applicability	→	Applicable
Difference	→	Different
Shiftiness	→	Shifty

WITH NOMINALIZATION: Sara blamed the delay on the disorganization of her filing system.

WITHOUT NOMINALIZATION: Sara blamed the delay on her disorganized filing system.

29.3 Use correct grammar to write clear sentences

Use Correct Grammar

College writers often hear about how important it is to use correct grammar. But there really is no such thing as correct grammar. *Grammar* and *correct* are terms that can only be applied to specific contexts. That is, "correct grammar" can only be situational. Academic writing, or Standard Written English, has its own frame of correctness and its own grammar. Correct grammar is an expectation within college writing situations; in fact, many college teachers identify grammatical correctness as the primary marker of being able to write. (Of course that's problematic, too. When many college teachers say "my students can't write," what they really mean is that "my students can't write grammatically correct sentences.") Just as you would be at a disadvantage to play a game without knowing and understanding the rules of that game, you can be at a disadvantage as a college writer by not knowing and understanding the rules of grammar in academic writing. How writers use grammar—whether correctly or incorrectly—affects their ethos and how readers respond to their writing. Although *Writing Situations* can't present every grammar rule there is, the following sections provide a substantial overview of some that contribute most directly to writing clear sentences.

Sentence Fragments

A sentence fragment is an incomplete sentence that is punctuated to look like a sentence. A complete sentence must contain at least a subject and a verb (i.e., an independent clause). Writers should avoid using sentence fragments because they can interrupt the flow of a document. They feel choppy, causing readers to stumble and alerting them to the fact that some element is missing.

Writers often produce sentence fragments by simply forgetting to include a key word, like a verb or a noun. Fragments are most easily corrected by inserting the missing word(s) or repunctuating the fragment as part of the sentence that appears before or after the fragment.

FRAGMENT: Played the piano.

CORRECTION: Amanda played the piano.

FRAGMENT: Because Amanda played the piano. The choir director asked her to accompany the choir during their rehearsals.

CORRECTION: Because Amanda played the piano, the choir director asked her to accompany the choir during their rehearsals.

Run-On Sentences

Run-on sentences occur when writers punctuate two or more independent clauses as though they are one sentence. Run-on sentences can confuse readers by forcing too much information into a single sentence.

RUN-ON SENTENCE: Wikipedia is a good resource for general knowledge it should not be cited as a source in academic essays.

CORRECTION: Wikipedia is a good resource for general knowledge. However, it should not be cited as a source in academic essays.

RUN-ON SENTENCE: Wikipedia is a good resource for general knowledge, it should not be cited as a source in academic essays.

CORRECTION: Wikipedia is a good resource for general knowledge, but it should not be cited as a source in academic essays.

Run-on sentences can be corrected in four ways:

1. Dividing the run-on into multiple, independent sentences

   RUN-ON: Legend states that you can kill a vampire with a stake through the heart you can also kill a vampire by dismembering it.

   CORRECTION: Legend states that you can kill a vampire with a stake through the heart. You can also kill a vampire by dismembering it.

2. Combining the two independent clauses with a comma and a coordinating conjunction

   RUN-ON: Left-handed people were once forced to learn to write with their right hands they were punished if they used their left hands.

   CORRECTION: Left-handed people were once forced to learn to write with their right hands, and they were punished if they used their left hands.

3. Combining the two independent clauses by making one subordinate to the other

   RUN-ON: I did not think I would enjoy Astronomy 101 it is now my favorite class.

   CORRECTION: I did not think I would enjoy Astronomy 101, but it is now my favorite class.

4. Combining the two independent clauses with a semicolon

   RUN-ON: MP3 is a compression format designed specifically for audio files it shrinks audio files by eliminating components less audible to human hearing.

   CORRECTION: MP3 is a compression format designed specifically for audio files; it shrinks audio files by eliminating components less audible to human hearing.

Modifiers

Modifiers explain and clarify the meaning of parts of a sentence. Modifiers can be single words, phrases, or clauses in adjective or adverb form.

ADJECTIVE MODIFIER: blue eyes

ADJECTIVE MODIFIER: twelve apples

ADVERBIAL MODIFIER: Chris submitted his project late.

ADVERBIAL MODIFIER: The results of the experiment significantly changed the researcher's hypothesis.

Dangling and Misplaced Modifiers

Modifiers must have clear referents to modify. To correct a dangling modifier, writers should provide a logical referent. A misplaced modifier should be placed in close proximity to the relevant word.

DANGLING MODIFIER: Although unclear, the agency accepted the proposal.

CORRECTION: Although the proposal was unclear, the agency accepted it.

DANGLING MODIFIER: On reading the report, a dangling modifier caught the CEO's attention.

CORRECTION: On reading the report, the CEO identified a dangling modifier.

MISPLACED MODIFIER: The owner's manual came with the car that John had read.

CORRECTION: The owner's manual, which John had read, came with the car.

MISPLACED MODIFIER: The contractor told the homeowner eventually the renovations would be complete.

CORRECTION: The contractor told the homeowner the renovations would be complete eventually.

Pronouns

Pronouns are words that can replace or stand in for nouns. Different kinds of pronouns serve different purposes.

INTERROGATIVE PRONOUN: To whom was the e-mail sent?

PERSONAL PRONOUN: The theater has released its schedule for this season.

RELATIVE PRONOUN: The design that the team chose was the most interactive.

INDEFINITE PRONOUN: Elena told everyone after she became engaged.

Agreement

In order for pronouns to be understood, they must clearly identify or reflect the nouns that they replace, that is, their antecedents. Pronouns must agree with their antecedents in both number and gender.

INCORRECT AGREEMENT: The school purchased these computers because it is the best on the market.

CORRECT AGREEMENT: The school purchased these computers because they are the best on the market.

Writers should confirm gender when names are not gender specific or are culturally unfamiliar.

Verbs

Verbs are words that denote action and states of being (often called "to be" verbs).

ACTION: The IT technician replaced the hard drive.

STATE OF BEING: The calendar is incorrect.

Infinitives

Infinitives are the basic form of verbs. Most often, they are presented with "to" and then the root of the verb; they can function as nouns, adjectives, or adverbs.

INFINITIVE AS NOUN: To write a novel would be fun.

INFINITIVE AS ADJECTIVE: Here are the plans to review.

INFINITIVE AS ADVERB: On weekends I drive to visit my grandmother.

Gerunds

Gerunds are *-ing* forms of verbs that function as nouns.

GERUND: Editing requires careful attention to detail.

GERUND: One of the most challenging things about playing Monopoly is keeping score.

Participles

Participles are verb forms that can work as adjectives.

PARTICIPLE: Many find the sound of running water to be peaceful.

PARTICIPLE: The executives were impressed when they read the approved budget.

Agreement in Number and Person

Verbs must agree with their subjects in number and in person.

INCORRECT NUMBER AGREEMENT: The cupcakes comes in ten different varieties.

CORRECT NUMBER AGREEMENT: The cupcakes come in ten different varieties.

INCORRECT PERSON AGREEMENT: You is the winner.

CORRECT PERSON AGREEMENT: You are the winner.

Voice

Verbs can appear in either the active voice, indicating that the subject acts through the verb, or in passive voice, indicating that the subject receives the action of the verb.

ACTIVE VOICE: Maria took the children to the swimming pool.

PASSIVE VOICE: The children were taken to the swimming pool by Maria.

Active-voice sentences add clarity because they show who or what is acting. Passive-voice sentences can obscure meaning by de-emphasizing the role of the subject, or they can emphasize results. Active-voice verbs are generally preferable.

30 | Punctuation and Mechanics

Learning Objectives

30.1 Apply guidelines to punctuate sentences correctly

30.2 Use conventions of capitalization, abbreviation, and spelling

Punctuation

Punctuation is a system of symbols writers use to indicate structure and organization. Punctuation guides readers in how to read a piece of writing; it shows readers how to understand sentences and their relationships with other sentences. We can think of punctuation as a set of conventions within a given situation. That is, punctuation varies from situation to situation. For example, how you punctuate an academic essay for your anthropology course is likely to be different from how you punctuate a text message you send your best friend. Deciding how to use punctuation is rhetorical; think of using punctuation as a way of solving rhetorical problems within specific rhetorical situations.

Punctuation helps readers interpret meaning in writing. Consider, for example, the famous distinction between the phrases "eats shoots and leaves" and "eats, shoots, and leaves." The addition of one simple punctuation mark alters the meaning of the phrase considerably. Or consider this famous example: "King Charles walked and talked; half an hour after, his head was cut off" as opposed to "King Charles walked and talked half an hour after his head was cut off."

Punctuation conventions change with time, location, genre, writer, purpose, and so on. Punctuation evolves as readers and writers need it to do different things. For example, before the advent of the personal computer and printer, punctuation conventions dictated that there should be two spaces after a colon and after a period at the end of a sentence. However, the personal computer and printer could maintain a consistent amount of space between letters, characters, and punctuation. Likewise, as the cost of paper increased, writers, organizations, and companies found it more economical to use only one space after periods and colons, because those extra spaces add up to whole sheets of paper and then add up to increased costs for purchasing materials.

Punctuate Correctly

30.1 Apply guidelines to punctuate sentences correctly

Periods

Periods end all complete sentences except for exclamations and direct questions.

    PERIOD TO END A SENTENCE: The medical examiner filed the report earlier this week.

See also the sections on sentence fragments and run-on sentences.

With Parentheses

When parenthetical information ends a sentence, the period belongs outside the closing parenthesis. However, when parentheses contain a complete sentence, the period precedes the final parenthesis.

    PERIOD OUTSIDE PARENTHESES: The graph shows how the global demand for quinoa has changed in the past five years (see figure 2).

    PERIOD WITHIN PARENTHESES: Please submit your research proposals by January 28. (This date may be pushed back if we lose days because of snow.)

With Quotations

When a quotation ends a sentence, the period belongs inside the quotation marks.

QUOTATION ENDING A SENTENCE: In his Gettysburg Address, Abraham Lincoln declared that "government of the people, by the people, for the people, shall not perish from the earth."

With Abbreviations

Periods are generally used in the following abbreviations, but writers should consult the style manual for their particular field.

PRENOMINAL TITLES: Mr. Mrs. Ms. Dr.

POST NOMINAL SUFFIX: Jr. Sr.

LATIN TERMS: etc. e.g. i.e.

Periods are not used in postal code abbreviations, such as AL, FL, ME, PA, WI.

Question Marks

Question marks indicate interrogatives.

Direct Questions

A question mark ends a sentence that is a direct question.

DIRECT QUESTION: When will the evaluation take place?

Indirect Questions

A question mark does not end a sentence containing an indirect question.

INDIRECT QUESTION: The customer asked who the supervisor is.

Shortened Questions

Question marks end questions that are not fully expressed.

SHORTENED QUESTIONS: Will the announcement be made in the newspaper? The company newsletter? The board meeting?

Questions within Sentences

Question marks are used with questions embedded in sentences.

QUESTION WITHIN A SENTENCE: The Baylor Group—or was it the Taylor Group?—conducted the initial survey.

Question Marks in Titles

If a title of a work contains a question mark, the question mark is always retained.

TITLE QUESTION MARK WITHIN A SENTENCE: The film *O Brother, Where Art Thou?* is loosely based on Homer's *Odyssey*.

Question Marks with Quotations

Question marks are placed outside quotation marks unless the quotation itself is a question.

QUESTION MARK OUTSIDE QUOTATION MARKS: Will we need to review "Ten Tips for Student Writers"**?**

QUESTION MARK INSIDE QUOTATION MARKS: The survey asked, "Do you own a smartphone**?**"

Exclamation Points

Exclamation points indicate excitement or urgency, but they do not strengthen the meaning of a sentence or boost the argument in a document.

EXCLAMATION POINT AT THE END OF A SENTENCE: What a lesson we learned**!**

With Quotations

An exclamation point is placed outside quotation marks unless the quotation itself is an exclamation.

EXCLAMATION POINT OUTSIDE QUOTATION MARKS: How useless to keep saying that "we're over budget"**!**

EXCLAMATION POINT INSIDE QUOTATION MARKS: The speaker ended the presentation by shouting, "Show me the money**!**"

Commas

Commas are misused and overused, often because writers insert a comma to indicate a pause even though written pauses and spoken pauses are different.

Compound Sentences

Commas are used before a coordinating conjunction—*and, but, or, nor, for,* and *yet*—to link two independent clauses in a single compound sentence.

COMMA USED IN A COMPOUND SENTENCE: I needed to save my draft**,** but the file was larger than my flash drive memory.

When compound sentences are made up of two short independent clauses and the meaning of those clauses is clear, the comma is not necessary.

COMPOUND SENTENCE WITHOUT A COMMA: The supervisor retired and the manager resigned.

Series

Use commas to separate three or more items in a list of words, phrases, or clauses.

COMMAS IN A LIST OF WORDS: The school's graduation requirements state that all students must take a writing course**,** a lab science**,** and at least one social science.

COMMAS IN A LIST OF PHRASES: The applicant submitted a résumé**,** talked with the director**,** and toured the facility.

In informal writing, such as e-mails and casual letters, writers may opt not to include the comma that precedes the conjunction in a list.

Introductory Words, Phrases, and Clauses

A comma usually follows introductory phrases and always follows introductory dependent clauses.

> COMMA AFTER INTRODUCTORY PHRASE: Having already been to Europe several times, Jeremy decided that his next vacation should be to South America.

> COMMA AFTER INTRODUCTORY CLAUSE: After she learned the process, the intern was more confident in her ability.

If an introductory word is a transitional word like *however* or *therefore*, a comma follows.

> TRANSITIONAL WORD: Therefore, we must redistribute the responsibilities for our group project.

Multiple Adjectives before a Noun

When a noun is preceded by two or more adjectives that could be joined by *and*, they are separated by commas.

> MULTIPLE ADJECTIVES WITH A COMMA: The old, damaged phone in the conference room was replaced.

If a noun and a preceding adjective are seen as a unit, another preceding adjective is not followed by a comma.

> MULTIPLE ADJECTIVES WITHOUT A COMMA: The lecturer was a talented corporate speaker.

Direct Quotations

A comma precedes a direct quotation. If a comma follows the quotation, it precedes the quotation marks.

> COMMA WITH A DIRECT QUOTATION: He said, "I don't understand how the Krebs Cycle works."

Restrictive and Nonrestrictive Modifiers

Restrictive modifiers supply necessary, or essential, information within a sentence and are not set off by commas. Restrictive clauses often begin with *that*.

> RESTRICTIVE CLAUSE: The e-mail that announced the meeting was posted last week.

> RESTRICTIVE PHRASE: The syllabi with revised due dates will be available next Monday.

Nonrestrictive modifiers supply extra, or nonessential, information within a sentence and should be set off with commas. Nonrestrictive clauses often begin with *which*.

> NONRESTRICTIVE CLAUSE: The presentation slides, which showed pictures from the event, enhanced the teacher's lecture.

> NONRESTRICTIVE PHRASE: Wendy's neighbor, who was a lawyer at the firm, put in a good word for her with the intern recruiter.

Determining whether a clause or phrase is restrictive or nonrestrictive is critical because the distinction can change the meaning of a sentence. Consider the following examples of driving directions:

RESTRICTIVE: Turn left at the fourth street that has a traffic light.

NONRESTRICTIVE: Turn left at the fourth street, which has a traffic light.

In the first case, the driver will count traffic lights and turn left at the fourth one. In the second case, the driver will turn left at the fourth street, which just happens to have a traffic light.

Parenthetical Words and Phrases

Parenthetical information is nonessential and interrupts the flow of the sentence. Parenthetical elements are set off by commas.

PARENTHETICAL WORD: The latest shipment, however, will not be delivered on time.

PARENTHETICAL PHRASE: Annual flowers, of course, only bloom for one season and must be replaced each year.

Direct Address

Proper nouns used in direct address should be set off by commas.

INTRODUCTORY DIRECT ADDRESS: Christopher, your argument is flawed.

DIRECT ADDRESS WITHIN A SENTENCE: Your argument, Christopher, is flawed.

Geographical Names

Commas are used to separate geographical elements and to set them off from the rest of the sentence.

GEOGRAPHICAL NAMES: The office opened in Muncie, Indiana, at the end of the year.

Dates

Dates written as month/day/year insert commas before and after the year.

MONTH/DAY/YEAR FORMAT: We signed the agreement on February 28, 2014, before beginning construction.

Dates written as day/month/year—a format commonly used in the U.S. military and other parts of the world—do not use commas.

DAY/MONTH/YEAR FORMAT: Please attend the opening reception on 15 June 2014.

Titles after Names

When a title follows a proper name, a comma separates the name from the title.

NAME AND TITLE SEPARATED BY A COMMA: Ms. Leslie Darnell, accounts manager

NAME AND TITLE SEPARATED BY A COMMA: Dante Hicks, PhD

Salutations in Personal Correspondence

Salutations in personal correspondence—letters or e-mails—are followed by a comma.

SALUTATION IN PERSONAL CORRESPONDENCE: Dear Teresa,

Semicolons

Semicolons are stronger than commas but weaker than periods.

With Independent Clauses

A semicolon can join two independent clauses to signal a close relationship between the information in the two clauses.

TWO RELATED INDEPENDENT CLAUSES: The picnic's hosts did not prepare a rain plan; the picnic will have to be rescheduled for a later date.

Connecting two independent clauses with just a comma would result in a run-on sentence.

In a Series

When a series of items contains internal punctuation, semicolons signal the division between items.

ITEMS IN A SERIES WITH INTERNAL PUNCTUATION: The home office has expressed interest in opening branch offices in Sydney, Australia; Rome, Italy; Rio de Janeiro, Brazil; and Allentown, Pennsylvania.

Colons

Colons are used primarily to introduce or to separate.

Lists, Quotations, Explanations, Appositives

Colons follow an independent clause to introduce lists, quotations, explanations, or appositives. What follows the colon explains or illustrates what precedes it.

INTRODUCING A LIST: All students will need to bring these items to class: the assigned textbook, a graphing calculator, and a notebook or laptop for taking notes.

INTRODUCING A QUOTATION: The director made his directions clear: "We have to flood the set, so we can only film this scene once."

A colon does not follow an introductory word or phrase like *such as, including,* and *like.*

A LIST FOLLOWING AN INTRODUCTORY WORD: The job posting asked applicants to submit standard information such as educational background, work experience, and salary requirements.

A colon that follows a quotation always appears outside the closing quotation marks.

Salutations in Professional Correspondence

Salutations in professional correspondence are followed by a colon.

SALUTATION IN PROFESSIONAL CORRESPONDENCE: Dear Ms. Marcum**:**

Quotation Marks

Quotation marks indicate exact words, either written or spoken.

Direct Quotations

Quotation marks identify exact spoken or written words.

Misquoting is unprofessional; intentionally changing a direct quotation is unethical. Writers should identify the source of a quotation—both speaker and context—and should offer citation information when quoting from a written document.

DIRECT QUOTATION: The safety inspector announced, **"**The plant will have to be closed**."**

DIRECT QUOTATION: Author Alice Yang Murray stresses in her introduction that she hopes readers **"**will have a greater understanding of why people view history in such different ways**"** (p. 7).

Titles

Quotation marks identify the titles of works like reports, articles, essays, chapters of books, and special sections within a periodical. The titles of longer works, like books or periodicals, are italicized.

TITLE IN QUOTATION MARKS: The summer camp's director gave each staff member a pamphlet titled **"**Preventing Swine Flu**"** before the campers arrived.

Special Terms

Quotation marks indicate that a word or phrase is used in an unusual or ironic way.

QUOTATION MARKS INDICATING SPECIAL USE: The **"**irreplaceable**"** assistant was let go.

Quotation marks should not be used to indicate emphasis.

Single Quotation Marks

Single quotation marks surround a quotation that appears within a quotation.

SINGLE QUOTATION MARKS: Early in his speech, the president stated, "I recognize that we are in the middle of a **'**budget crisis**.'"**

Punctuation with Quotation Marks

See individual marks of punctuation.

Parentheses

Parentheses are used for explanations, digressions, afterthoughts, and supplementary information. Parenthetical information is generally not essential to the meaning of a text but may be useful.

EXPLANATORY INFORMATION: The library's fourth-floor study room (the small one with the new chairs) will be closed this week because of maintenance work.

SUPPLEMENTARY INFORMATION: Luis Jorge will be retiring this week (he's moving to Miami).

Abbreviations

Parentheses may follow a word or phrase to introduce an abbreviation that will be used subsequently.

INTRODUCTION OF AN ABBREVIATION: The World Fact Book is maintained by the Central Intelligence Agency (CIA).

Numbers that are spelled out should not be followed by numerals in parentheses.

Run-In Lists

Parentheses enclose numbers or letters designating items in a list or series that is run into the text.

NUMBERS DESIGNATING A SERIES: A standard essay contains three main parts: (1) an introduction, (2) a body, and (3) a conclusion.

With Other Punctuation

Parentheses do not affect the punctuation of the rest of the sentence. All other punctuation should follow the closing parentheses.

Dashes

Em Dashes

Em dashes enclose, separate, and connect. Em dashes can indicate sudden changes in thought and can offset parenthetical information. In typing, two hyphens indicate an em dash (a dash the width of a capital M), and most word processors automatically convert them. There should be no spaces before or after the em dash.

SUDDEN SHIFT: I was late returning my book to the library—I will have to pay a fine.

PARENTHETICAL INFORMATION: External storage devices—for example, flash drives, portable hard drives, and zip drives—are useful for backing up files.

En Dashes

An en dash (a dash the width of a capital N) can be used in place of *to* (with a sense of *through*) with letters, numbers, and sometimes words.

WITH NUMBERS: The information you will need is on pages 127–138.

WITH LETTERS: The files are organized alphabetically: A–K, L–S, and T–Z.

Hyphens

Hyphens can link words or parts of words.

Compound Words

Hyphens link words together in compounds. A dictionary determines whether compounds are linked with a hyphen, written as a single word, or written as separate words. If a compound does not appear in the dictionary, it is written as separate words.

LINKED WITH A HYPHEN: As we learned later, the initial rumor was only a half-truth.

SINGLE WORD: The old post office serves as a landmark for passing tourists on their way into town.

SEPARATE WORDS: The problem seemed to be with the remote control.

Modifiers

Hyphens can link multiple-word adjectives that precede a noun; if they follow the noun they modify, the words are not hyphenated.

HYPHENATED MODIFIER: The investor had a reputation for collecting hand-carved artifacts.

MODIFIER WITHOUT HYPHENS: The investor had a reputation for collecting artifacts that were hand carved.

Sometimes a hyphen is necessary to avoid ambiguity.

AMBIGUOUS: We will have to use multiple degeneration techniques in order to collect accurate data.

CLEAR: We will have to use multiple-degeneration techniques in order to collect accurate data.

Modifiers using letters or numbers use hyphens.

LETTER MODIFIER: Although he became famous for playing Dracula, Béla Lugosi was largely a B-movie actor.

NUMBER MODIFIER: The plans called for a 10-meter line of PVC pipe.

Prefixes and Suffixes

All prefixes that begin with *cross-*, *ex-*, *self-*, and *great-* are hyphenated.

PREFIX BEGINNING WITH CROSS-: Cross-references are important to verify.

PREFIX BEGINNING WITH EX-: The ex-president of the student council offered her congratulations to the incoming new president.

PREFIX BEGINNING WITH SELF-: Recreational diving is a self-regulated industry.

PREFIX BEGINNING WITH GREAT-: Alex used to boast that his great-grandfather had been friends with Duke Ellington.

Suffixes ending with *-elect* are hyphenated.

SUFFIX ENDING WITH -ELECT: The president-elect will have a difficult time with the transition.

A dictionary or style manual can help with other prefixes and suffixes.

Apostrophes

Apostrophes indicate either possession or omitted letters.

Possessives

Possession is indicated by an apostrophe and an *s* added to singular nouns:

engineer**'s** office
essay**'s** length
Charles**'s** mother

Most singular nouns that end in *s* also add an apostrophe and an *s* to indicate possession. Exceptions vary according to style manuals. Plural nouns that end in *s* form the possessive by adding an apostrophe only. Irregular plural nouns add an apostrophe and an *s*.

Writers**'** organization
women**'s** movement

Joint possessives make the last noun in the list possessive.

Juan, Deidra, Shelley, and Anne**'s** presentation

Individual possessives make each noun possessive.

Sean**'s** and Clay**'s** computers

Compound nouns form possessives by adding an apostrophe and an *s* to the last word of the compound.

the officer of record**'s** decision
my brother-in-law**'s** promotion

Contractions

Apostrophes identify missing letters or numbers within contractions.

cannot = can**'**t
will not = won**'**t
it is = it**'**s
2006 = **'**06

Contractions should be avoided in most formal documents but can be appropriate in less formal documents like e-mails.

Plurals

Apostrophes are sometimes used to create plurals of letters and numerals.

PLURAL LETTERS: The misprint eliminated all of the *p***'s** and *r***'s**.

PLURAL NUMERALS: How many 3**'s** and 4**'s** are in the URL?

Some style manuals dictate forming these plurals with just an *s*.

Brackets

Brackets generally indicate an insertion into a direct quotation to explain or fill in missing information.

The report explained, "Ten percent of all profits [from last quarter] will be redirected to shareholders."

The speaker announced, "[After the environmental impact study] has been completed, we will begin excavation."

Brackets are also used to enclose parenthetical information inside parentheses.

The brochure touted the additions to the resort's amenities (including a newly renovated spa [with a new sauna and mineral pool]).

Ellipses

Ellipses identify omitted words in a direct quotation. Omissions are indicated by three periods separated by spaces (. . .).

WORDS OMITTED: The *Declaration of Independence* states "We, therefore, the Representatives of the United States of America . . . do, in the Name, and by Authority of the good People of these Colonies, solemnly publish and declare, That these United Colonies are, and of Right ought to be Free and Independent States."

If the omission is one or more complete sentences, a period precedes the ellipsis.

FULL SENTENCE OMITTED: In the weekly staff meeting, the project supervisor told us to "consider all members of the research team as independent authorities. . . . They will be reporting directly to the research commission without confirming their data with the team or the manager."

Ellipsis points are not used at the beginning of a quotation.

Capitalize Correctly

Capitals signal proper nouns, the first letter of the first word in a complete sentence, the first word in salutations and closings, and essential words in titles. Many dictionaries address capitalization conventions.

Proper Nouns

All proper nouns are capitalized, including names of people, places, and things.

Proper Nouns	Common Nouns
Atlantic Ocean	an ocean
University of Florida	a university
Britain/British history	history
Auntie Raul	my aunt
Chemistry 4351	chemistry
Supreme Court	the court

30.2 Use conventions of capitalization, abbreviation, and spelling

Days of the week, holidays, and months are considered proper nouns and are capitalized as such; the seasons are considered common nouns and are not capitalized.

DAYS OF THE WEEK, HOLIDAYS, AND MONTHS: In the United States, **T**hanksgiving is celebrated on the fourth **T**hursday of **N**ovember.

NAMES OF SEASONS: The first day of **w**inter occurs on the twenty-first day of December this year.

First Words

The first letter of the first word of a sentence is capitalized, as is the first letter of a quotation that is a complete sentence. Style manuals differ about capitalizing the first word of a complete sentence after a colon.

FIRST WORD OF A SENTENCE: **A**lways capitalize the first word of a sentence.

FIRST WORD OF A COMPLETE SENTENCE IN A QUOTATION: The quote "**W**hat is history but a fable agreed upon?" is often attributed to Napoleon Bonaparte.

The first word in salutations and closings is also capitalized.

FIRST WORD IN A SALUTATION: **D**ear Ms. Herrington:

FIRST WORD IN A CLOSING: **S**incerely,

Titles

Titles of Works

Capitalize the first and all important words in a title. Articles, conjunctions, and prepositions are not generally capitalized; however, style manuals differ.

REPORT TITLE: "**A R**eport to the **C**ommissioner"

BOOK TITLE: *Of Mice and Men*

Professional Titles

Titles that precede proper names are capitalized, as are titles that follow proper names in the addresses and signatures of letters.

TITLE BEFORE PROPER NAME: **D**ean **M**ontoya

TITLE AFTER PROPER NAME: E. **M**ontoya, **D**ean of **S**tudent **A**ffairs

In other cases position titles are generally not capitalized.

TITLE IN GENERAL USE: E. Montoya, the dean of student affairs, will attend the conference.

TITLE WITHOUT PROPER NOUN: The dean of student affairs will attend the conference.

Letters

Letters used to indicate shape or used in a name are capitalized.

LETTER INDICATING SHAPE: The road came to a dead end, so I made a **U**-turn.

LETTER IN NAME: vitamin **E**

Abbreviate Correctly

Abbreviations can increase efficiency and save space in documents. They are formed either by shortening a word or by using the first letter of each word in a string. Writers must make sure that readers understand what abbreviations represent.

Names and Titles

Abbreviations in personal names are followed by a period and a space.

> **J. P.** Morgan

Some titles should always be abbreviated, such as *Mr.*, *Mrs.*, and *Ms.* Other titles used with last names alone are spelled out.

> I asked Professor Kidd for a letter of recommendation.

Titles and degrees that follow a proper name are generally abbreviated.

> Charlene Garcia, **CEO**
> Hienrich Jansen **Jr.**
> Fadiya Birhanu, **PhD**

Style manuals differ on the use of periods in some abbreviations.

Dates and Time

Some time and date indicators are commonly abbreviated: a.m., p.m., AD, BC, BCE, and CE. (Only AD comes before the date—AD 1492.) Months and days are spelled out in formal documents, although they may be abbreviated in notes and charts. *May*, *June*, and *July* are not generally abbreviated.

> The class will begin on Thursday, September 13, 2014, at 9:00 a.m.

Geographical Names

In a formal document, place names and geographical names are spelled out. A few conventional abbreviations—USA and UK—are exceptions. Abbreviations are appropriate in informal documents and when text formatting demands brevity.

Organization Names

Organization names that may not be familiar to readers should be spelled out the first time they appear in a document, followed in parentheses by the abbreviation that will be used. Some abbreviations of organization names are formed without any punctuation. An appropriate style manual should be consulted.

PBS	AMA	DNC
NATO	NRC	SEC
IRS	APA	GOP
AFL-CIO	MLA	NCAA
IEEE	UCLA	FAA
STC	NSF	IDF
NAACP	CIA	NAFTA
FCC	FBI	ATF

Measures

Terms of measure are spelled out in formal documents.

kilograms	miles
ounces	kilobytes

A few exceptions may always be abbreviated: Hz (Hertz) and other International System of Units (SI) measurements (daHz, hHz, etc.), mph, rpm, and dpi, for instance.

Specialized Terminology

Within the text of formal documents, specialized terminology is spelled out, such as technical terms, Latin terms, or academic terms. Many of these terms are commonly abbreviated in parentheses, notes, documentation, and other instances that demand economic use of space, such as charts and tables.

IN TEXT: for example, all primary colors

IN PARENTHESES: (e.g., all primary colors)

Commonly Misspelled Words

A
acceptable
accidentally
accommodate
acquire
acquit
a lot
amateur
apparent
argument
atheist

B
believe
bellwether

C
calendar
category
cemetery
changeable
collectible
colonel (kernel)
column
committed
conscience
conscientious
conscious
consensus

D
daiquiri
definite(ly)
discipline
drunkenness

dumbbell

E
embarrass(ment)
equipment
exceed
exhilarate
existence
experience

F
fiery
foreign

G
gauge
grateful
guarantee

H
harass
height
hierarchy
humorous

I
ignorance
immediate
independent
indispensable
inoculate
intelligence
its/it's

J
jewelry
judgment

K
kernel (colonel)

L
leisure
liaison
library
license
lightning

M
maintenance
maneuver
medieval
millennium
miniature
minuscule
mischievous
misspell
momentum

N
neighbor
noticeable

O
occasionally
occurrence

P
pastime
perseverance
personnel
possession
proceed
principle/principal

privilege
pronunciation
publicly

Q
questionnaire

R
receive/receipt
recommend
reference
referred
relevant
restaurant
rhyme
rhythm

S
schedule
separate
sergeant
supersede

T
their/there/they're
threshold
twelfth
tyranny

U
until

V
vacuum

W
weather
weird

Contents by Rhetorical Purpose

Contents by Rhetorical Strategy

Contents by Genre

Credits

Text Credits

Chapter 1

p. 13: "Judge assigns essays to some Red Sox fans arrested after Game 7" by Staff Writer from Associated Press. Copyright © 2007. Used by permission of the YGS group.

Chapter 2

p. 29: "Top 10 Languages in the Internet (millions of users)" from Internet World Stats, © 2000-2013. Used by permission of Miniwatts Marketing Group.

Chapter 3

p. 32: Movie Dialogue, "We gotta find a way to make this fit into a hole for this using nothing but *that*" from *Apollo 13*. Published by Imagine Entertainment, © 1995.

p. 41: Kenneth Burke's Pentad by Kenneth Burke from *A Grammar of Motives*. Published by The Permissions Company, Inc., © 1969.

Chapter 8

p. 115: Excerpt from the Blog Post, Men in Black by Buzzell from *My War: Killing Time in Iraq*. Published by Penguin USA, © 2006.

p. 166: "Lives; Not Close Enough for Comfort" by David P. Bardeen from *New York Times Magazine*, Copyright © February 29, 2004. Used by permission of David P Bardeen.

p. 121: Woods, Summer, "A Southern State of Mind."

p. 123: "The Manipulation Game: Doing Life in Pennsylvania" by Diane Hamill Metzger from *Crime and Punishment: Inside Views,* edited by Robert Johnson and Hans Toch. Used by permissions of Oxford University Press (UK) - Academic.

p. 137: "3 Pages from a Graphic Novel" by Gloeckner, Phoebe from *The Diary of a Teenage Girl: An Account in Words and Pictures*. Copyright © 2002. Used by permission of North Atlantic Books.

Chapter 9

p. 146: "Excerpt from Description of Earth from Apollo 8" by James Lowell, William Anders and Frank Borman from Our Moon Journey, *Life* Magazine. Copyrights © January 17, 1969. Used by permission of William Morris Agency.

p. 148: Excerpt from "Describing Environment" by Rachel Carson from *The Edge of the Sea*. Published by Houghton Mifflin Harcourt Publishing Company.

p. 150: Madu, Ndidi, "Student Essay, NCAA Tournament Experience."

Chapter 10

p. 176: "Biography of Celia Cruz" from *Contemporary Hispanic Biography*, Copyright © 2002. Used by permission of Cengage Learning/Nelson Education.

p. 177: Albert, Bertrhude, "Student Essay, The Stand against Social Injustice: Projects For Haiti, Inc."

p. 182: "The Inside Scoop on The Fake Barf Industry" by Lisa Hix from *Collectors Weekly*, Copyright © 2011. Used by permission of Collectors Weekly.

p. 193: "The Water Cycle" by United States Geological Survey.

p. 194: Eat Your World, LLC (eatyourworld.com)

Chapter 11

p. 201: "Men in Love: Is Brokeback Mountain a Gay Film?" by David Leavitt from Slate.com. Used by permission of The Wylie Agency.

p. 205: Bargoot, Alexandra, "Student Essay, Argument in Response to Importance of education lost in the mix".

p. 214: "Nothing Is So Necessary for a Young Man" by Ta-Nehisi Coates from *The Atlantic*, Copyright 2010. Used by permission of Tribune Media on behalf of The Atlantic Monthly.

Chapter 12

p. 232: Excerpt from "Raby's Report" by Mark Raby from *Analysis: The YouTube Effect - Changing the Face of Elections.* Published by T.G. Daily, © 2007.

p. 234: "Straight from the Heart" by Tim Collins from *The Guardian*, Copyright © 2005. Used by the permission of The Guardian.

p. 239: Cadiz, Nicky, "Student Essay, *The Jersey Shore* and *Harper's Bazaar*."

p. 244: "When Will White People Stop Making Movies Like *Avatar*?" by Annalee Newitz from io9, Copyright © 2009. Used by permission of Gawker Media.

Chapter 13

p. 267: Ly, Quang, "Student Essay, Have You Been Bitten? Evaluating the Success of the Twilight Craze."

Chapter 10 (continued)

p. 154: Excerpt from "Perspective on Travel Writing" by Rolf Potts from *Vagabonding*. Used by permission of Rolf Potts.

p. 154: "The Sacred Grove of Oshogbo" by Jeffrey Tayler from *The Atlantic* Online, Copyright © 1999. Used by permission of Jeffrey Tayler.

p. 274: "Square Water Bottle Raises $126K on Kickstarter. We Test It Out" by Sean McCoy from *Gear Junkie*, Copyright © 2012. Used by permission of Gear Junkie LLC.

p. 262: "Rate My Professors Screen grab" from ratemyprofessors.com. Used by permission of Viacom.

Chapter 14

p. 293: "Animal Rights" by Peter Singer from Slate.com, Copyright © 2001. Used by permission of Peter Singer.

p. 296: Horn, Brooke, Lauren, "Student Essay, The First-Year Dilemma: To Write or Not to Write?"

p. 301: "Whites Swim In Racial Preference" by Tim Wise, from Znet, Copyright © 2003. Used by permission from Tim J Wise.

p. 314: Rowe, Ian, "Student Example: Comic Strip, A Day in the Life of Your Child on Adderall."

Chapter 15

p. 324: "In Bed" by Joan Didion from *The White Album*. Copyright © 1979. Used by permission of Farrar, Straus and Giroux.

p. 324: "Essay, In Bed" by Joan Didion from *The White Album*. Copyright © 1979. Used by permission of Janklow & Nesbit Associates, Inc.

p. 328: Trotta, Eric, "Student Essay, Handling the Snakehead Invasion."

p. 335: "Essay, A Proposal to Abolish Grading" by Paul Goodman from *Compulsory Miseducation*. Copyrights © 1964. Used by permission of Random House, Inc.

Chapter 16

p. 354: "Screenshots, Mariah O'Toole adapted images she found online to fit her needs" from Shutterstock. Used by permission of Shutterstock.

p. 363: O'Toole, Mariah, "Student Example: Mariah O'Toole's Wireframe Used to Design Her Image Essay."

Chapter 17

p. 379: Reproduced by the permission of United Nations Human Settlements Programme, 2003.

p. 398: Excerpt from "Literary Map of the USA" by Geoff Sawers from The Literary Gift Company Blog, Copyright © 2011. Used by permission of The Literary Gift Company.

p. 399: US Literary Map by Geoff Sawers and Bridget Hannigan from theliterarygiftcompany.com. Used by permission of The Literary Gift Company.

Chapter 18

p. 411: "Screenshot, Library Web Page. You Can Use Many of Your Library's Resources Just by Learning What the Library has Available On-line" from George A Smathers Libraries. Used by permission of University of Florida Library.

p. 412: "Screenshot, Search Results Using Online Library Catalog" from University of Florida Libraries Catalog. Used by permission of University of Florida Library.

p. 413: "Screenshot, Detailed Search Results Using Online Library Catalog" from University of Florida Libraries Catalog. Used by permission of University of Florida Library.

p. 415: "Screenshot, Using the Online Catalog to Locate a Journal" from University of Florida Libraries Catalog. Used by permission of University of Florida Library.

p. 417: "Screenshot, Using the Online Catalog to Locate Reference Materials" from University of Florida Libraries Catalog. Used by permission of University of Florida Library.

p. 418 : "Screenshot, Using the Online Catalog to Locate Bibliographies" from Screenshot, Using the Online Catalog to Locate Bibliographies. Used by permissions of University of Florida Library.

p. 418: "Screenshot, An online bibliography" from Animal Studies Bibliography, Michigan State University. Used by permission of Michigan State University Press-Journals Division.

p. 419: "Screenshot, Link to Materials Available Through Interlibrary Loan" from University of Florida Libraries Catalog. Used by the permission of University of Florida Library.

p. 421: Screenshot from the website, www.gpo.gov.

p. 424: Different Search Engines Return Different Search results from Google. Used by permission of Google.

p. 425: Screenshot, Different Search Engines Return Different Search Results from Bing.com. Used by permission of Microsoft Corporation.

p. 426: Screenshot, Google Scholar Provides More Academically Relevant Links from the website Google Scholar. Used by permission of Google.

Chapter 19

p. 445: Excerpt from "Source" by Rebecca Moore Howard from Plagiarism, Authorship, and the Academic Death Penalty *College English*. Vol. 57. No. 7. Published by National Council of Teachers of English, © 1995.

p. 450: Otaku culture, as exemplified through comics and anime, still often maintains an image of youth culture by Hiroki Azuma from Dobutsuka suru posutomodan: otaku kara mita nihon shakai. Copyright © 2009. Used by permission of Regents of the University of Minnesota.

p. 450: "Roth v. United States - 354 U.S. 476 (1957): Justia US Supreme Court Center." US Law, Case Law, Codes, Statutes & Regulations: Justia US Supreme Court Center. Web. 29 Jan. 2012. http://supreme.justia.com/cases/federal/us/354/476/case.html.

p. 451: Quote by Steven Jenkins from *Cheese Primer*. Published by Workman Publishing Company, © 1996.

p. 453 : "Article, World's Longest Bullet Train Line Opens in China" by Damon Lavrinc from Magazine, *Wired*. Used by permission of Wired.com.

Chapter 20

p. 461: Woods, Summer, "Student Essay, From Protest to Resistance: Evaluating the Evolution and Ultimate Success of the Non-Violent 1968 May Protests and the Violent Red Army Faction."

Photo Credits

WPA Outcomes for First-Year Composition	How *Writing Situations* Can Help You Meet These Outcomes
RHETORICAL KNOWLEDGE By the end of first year composition, students should • Focus on a purpose • Respond to the needs of different audiences • Respond appropriately to different kinds of rhetorical situations • Use conventions of format and structure appropriate to the rhetorical situation • Adopt appropriate voice, tone, and level of formality • Understand how genres shape reading and writing • Write in several genres	Ch. 1 Understanding Rhetorical Situations Ch. 2 Purpose and Audience Part Three: Writing Projects Mapping Your Situation helps students navigate any writing situation by suggesting questions to ask ranging from purpose, audience, medium, context, and networks, providing a starting point for planning and invention. Ch. 17 Designing Documents Alternate Contents by Rhetorical Purpose Alternate Contents by Genre
CRITICAL THINKING, READING, AND WRITING By the end of first year composition, students should • Use writing and reading for inquiry, learning, thinking, and communicating • Understand a writing assignment as a series of tasks, including finding, evaluating, analyzing, and synthesizing appropriate primary and secondary sources • Integrate their own ideas with those of others • Understand the relationships among language, knowledge, and power	Part Six: Readings Ch. 3 Generating Ideas Ch. 6 Thinking Ch. 7 Reading and Viewing Ch. 16 Finding, Adapting, and Making Visuals Road to a Strong Thesis fosters analytical thinking by making visible a writer's interior monologue about purpose, audience, and rhetorical situations when developing a strong thesis. Side by Side develops analytic reading skills by comparing three readings in each chapter and spotlighting decisions each writer made when solving rhetorical problems in similar situations. Mapping Your Situation helps students navigate any writing situation by suggesting questions to ask ranging from purpose, audience, medium, context, and networks, providing a starting point for planning and invention. Ch. 18 Planning and Conducting Research Ch. 19 Evaluating and Synthesizing Information Ch. 1 Understanding Rhetorical Situations
PROCESSES By the end of first year composition, students should • Be aware that it usually takes multiple drafts to create and complete a successful text • Develop flexible strategies for generating, revising, editing, and proof-reading • Understand writing as an open process that permits writers to use later invention and re-thinking to revise their work	Ch. 3 Generating Ideas Ch. 4 Drafting and Organizing Ch. 5 Revising Writing Process Guidelines ensures students respond effectively to their writing situation: concrete action steps guide writers through their writing process from invention and research to drafting, revision, evaluation, and distribution. Prepare and Respond identifies characteristics of different kinds of writing and walks writers through steps for developing content of their own.